Nazi Films in America,
1933–1942

ALSO BY HARRY WALDMAN
AND FROM McFARLAND

*Scenes Unseen: Unreleased and Uncompleted Films
from the World's Master Filmmakers, 1912–1990* (2014; paperback 1991)

Maurice Tourneur: The Life and Films (2001; paperback 2008)

*Missing Reels: Lost Films of American
and European Cinema* (2000; paperback 2008)

Nazi Films in America, 1933–1942

Harry Waldman

McFarland & Company, Inc., Publishers
Jefferson, North Carolina

The present work is a reprint of the illustrated case bound edition of Nazi Films in America, 1933–1942, *first published in 2008 by McFarland.*

LIBRARY OF CONGRESS CATALOGUING-IN-PUBLICATION DATA

Waldman, Harry.
Nazi films in America, 1933–1942 / Harry Waldman.
p.   cm.
Includes bibliographical references and index.

ISBN 978-1-4766-8079-8
paperback : acid free paper ∞

1. Motion pictures, German—United States—History.   I. Title.
PN1993.5.G3W35   2020   2008029415

British Library cataloguing data are available

© 2008 Harry Waldman. All rights reserved

No part of this book may be reproduced or transmitted in any form or by any means, electronic or mechanical, including photocopying or recording, or by any information storage and retrieval system, without permission in writing from the publisher.

Cover photograph: *Pour le Mérite,*
the first air show in Nazi Germany

Printed in the United States of America

*McFarland & Company, Inc., Publishers
Box 611, Jefferson, North Carolina 28640
www.mcfarlandpub.com*

To my father,
Carl

TABLE OF CONTENTS

Preface	1
Introduction	3
1933: Deutsche Universal	19
1934: "You Are Jewish, Right?"	43
1935: Casino Film Exchange and Its Imports from Germany and "Vienna"	67
1936: "A Relief to Those Who Feared the Worst"	95
1937: From Traitors to Patriots	123
1938: The Circle of German Stars	159
Prewar 1939: *Hans Westmar* Signals German-Soviet Cordiality	193
September 1939–April 1940: "Where's the Enemy Hiding?"	218
May 1940–1942: *Feldzug in Polen, Der Sieg im Westen*, and More	248
Epilogue: Bedeviled Gold	279
Selected Bibliography	285
Index	287

Preface

It's impossible to imagine any Nazi film circulating in the U.S. today. There was a time, however, when the opposite was true. From 1933 until the U.S. entered World War II, nearly 500 Nazi films were shown in America theatres. That represents nearly half the number of films the Nazi regime produced from 1933 to 1945. The films are described as Nazi for many reasons. Joseph Goebbels commissioned them; they were produced by Germany's top studios; they featured prominent German, pro–German, and Nazi-party actors, directors, and technicians; or they had been quietly, if not secretly, co-produced with non–German studios. Most importantly, the films were Nazi films because nearly all featured no Jews yet had anti–Semitic plot lines. The films masqueraded as cinema, the filmmakers as artists.

The critical reaction by the *New York Times*, *Variety*, the *Chicago Tribune*, the *New Yorker*, *Time*, *Motion Picture Herald* and other outlets inside the U.S. and abroad was often indifference and ignorance. While it's true that, to assuage concerns, Nazi Germany also made apparently entertaining films and released pre–Hitler productions, it was, nonetheless, all quiet on the home front regarding clearly racist German films, which made the regime money and heartened its supporters.

The films and their filmmakers were only pieces of the picture puzzle that was Nazi Germany. Yet from their most musically "entertaining" to their most vile productions, just about all their films implied one thing: a world without Jews. The filmmakers and their films were signaling the future of Europe's Jews.

Nazi Films in America, 1933–1942 is the first book to detail the regime's anti–Semitic feature films, documentaries, and shorts released in the U.S.; to examine the careers of major directors, stars, and technicians; to emphasize the centrality of music in German films of the era; and to investigate the central role played by the American distributor Casino Film Exchange, especially in New York, even after World War II began.

I thank David and Lorraine Swerdloff for reading the manuscript and copying stills; Richard Hamilton for his computer wizardry; Henry Okun for translations of German material from the Library of Congress; Madeleine Matz of the Library of Congress for guidance to German collections and stills; Ellis Fabian and Steve Shirey for their spirited interest; Michael Lavin and Carol Givner for their belief in the project; and my dear friend Michael Zamm, my daughter Laura, and son Jonathan for their unalloyed encouragement. I thank my wife Susan for her editing, and for her fortitude in the face of my apparently endless research (at the National Archives, Library of Congress, and Georgetown University) and chatter on this subject.

Introduction

"The function of propaganda is ... not to weigh and ponder the rights of different people, but exclusively to emphasize the one right which it has set out to argue for. Its task is not to make an objective study of truth, in so far as it favors the enemy, and then set it before the masses with academic fairness; its task is to serve our own right, always and unflinchingly."

In 1933, eight years after Adolf Hitler wrote these words, *Mein Kampf* sold 1.5 million copies—and German filmmakers were among those taking its words to heart. They put new energy into idealizing "pure-bred" institutions and traditions—and demonizing non–Germans. But one group received special attention—Jews. The Nazis' cinematic attack on Jews was breathtaking. Although many German films of the Nazi era have been characterized as merely entertaining—and have been described this way ever since—a closer look reveals that a *majority* of the films produced in Nazi Germany were anti–Semitic. And many of these German films were screened in the United States before the Third Reich was destroyed.

In the film-going world, it was no longer news that a movie could reveal much—sometimes even more than its filmmaker intended—about the society in which it was made. D.W. Griffith's *Birth of a Nation* (1916) depicted the sinister underside of patriotism by glamorizing the Klan. Sergei Eisenstein's *Potemkin* (1925) pilloried Czarist rule while romanticizing the Communist Revolution. But somehow, with German films, the world missed the overt and covert messages they contained. That was at least the case in the United States.

A few months after Hitler assumed power, the first German-language films extolling the new German state and supporting an increasingly vocal racism were released in the U.S. The pace of these Third Reich imports increased as the Nazis consolidated their rule. The outbreak of the war in Europe did not impede the distribution and release in the United States of films from Hitler's Germany. Only the U.S. entry into World War II put a stop to that.

Between 1933 and 1942, nearly five hundred German-language films were shown in the States. That number represented nearly *half* of all foreign-language film imports to America during these years. The bare essentials of these Nazi films were to manipulate and steer emotions along guided paths; to impress and frighten; and to predict the future. German filmmakers stood with the leaders of the regime in these efforts. At the time and later they pleaded that they had no choice—they would lose their jobs, suffer violence, be shipped off to concentration camps, or be executed.

American film critics and others may have noticed the open anti–Semitism in a few German productions, but they missed the subtle anti–Semitism and racist content in nearly all of them. When they did sense racist content, they dismissed it as mere propaganda, inept and ineffective. In the 1930s, in fact, the U.S. was no friend to Jewish immigrants. It closed its doors to Jews seeking escape from Hitler's Germany. Its anti-Jewish stance did not contradict the Nazi worldview regarding "non–Aryans."

Besides, importing German films was good business, serving the interests of American distributors and motion picture producers afraid of alienating one of the biggest German-speaking audiences outside the Third Reich.

At the same time, a seemingly innocent breed of German film also made its appearance. The German films that screened in the U.S. between 1933 and the end of World War II included scores of pre–Hitler—that is, Weimar—productions. By marking these films for distribution in America, the Nazis ameliorated their image abroad, hiding the growing terror within the Third Reich and obscuring Nazi threats to Germany's neighbors and to the world.

These German films, which had been made before Hitler came to power, included productions from Universal's German affiliate, Deutsche Universal, which was Jewish-dominated. These films had been directed by Jews and starred German-Jewish actors who had made their names in the Weimar era and fled Germany after January 30, 1933.

Showing these films in America when German film studios were systematically purging Jewish directors, actors, and technicians from cinema screens and removing their credits was a masterly act of deception. Only rarely in the U.S. was a German film boycotted, let alone withdrawn, on grounds of offensive content.

Why didn't the American public object to the flood of racist propaganda in its theaters? How is it possible that so few Americans appear to have even noticed that most Nazi films were anti–Semitic, subtle, state-manufactured terror productions?

Aside from the obvious reason that producers and distributors made money, the reasons were politics and aesthetics. America's isolationists deflected attention from the Nazis by arguing that the real problem was *British* propaganda. Harold Levine and James Weschler, in their book *War Propaganda and the United States* (1940), called British propaganda a dark force, sinister and pervasive. Having dragged the U.S. into the First World War, British propaganda could embroil the U.S. in another European conflict.

In the 1930s, Germany's films often reflected changes in national policy. German films would, for instance, work up a self-righteous fury over the alleged mistreatment of Germans in Poland or by Bolsheviks. Then they would beat a retreat if political events demanded it. Most notably, German films of 1936, the year of the Berlin Olympics, signaled an uncharacteristic and hypocritical German friendliness towards the outside world. Most of the world wanted to buy into this lie.

Equally important was the fact that Nazi films contained glorious music, especially the strings of Vienna, the rich orchestral sounds of greats such as Strauss, Beethoven, and Mozart. The music drove home a point or lifted the mood. A prime example was director Detlef Sierck's *Schlussakkord* (*Final Chord*, 1936). In the drama, a German woman in America regains her health and returns to the fatherland after hearing a live radio broadcast of Beethoven from Berlin.

Dozens of German composers and musicians lent their talents to making German films palatable, even enjoyable. But they offered no music the Nazis thought inconsistent with their worldview. American filmgoers could catch, week after week, a Third Reich operetta, "comedy," country, or society film containing plenty of engaging music. But behind the soothing sounds lay a harsher reality: a new German music industry purged of Jewish composers, performers and conductors.

Alongside these entertaining films, however, appeared special kinds of Third Reich cinematic productions. These were the ones that Joseph Goebbels, head of the *Reichministerium für Volksaufkärung und Propaganda* (Ministry for the Enlightenment of the People and Propaganda), approved, financed, and sent over Germany's borders and across the Atlantic.

As the political leader, or *Gauleiter*, of Berlin, Goebbels did his job at the epicenter of German filmmaking. Goebbels nationalized Germany's film studios, most notably Tobis in 1936, eight years after it was founded; and Ufa in early 1937. Sometimes the German studios

Ufa's studio in Babelsberg.

received instructions from Goebbels' ministry regarding who to hire, what films to make, and how to film them. Goebbels preferred to remain in the background rather than openly dominate the film studios in the name of Germany. But the propaganda minister supervised productions through final stages in the editing room and sanctioned their release.

Goebbels controlled a medium that could reach a global audience. But he made America a particular target. One of his ministry's goals was to "win our country fellowmen in the United States to the ideology" of the Nazis and to "create understanding and recognition for the Third Reich" among Americans.

Goebbels' target audience was the 23 million Americans of German ancestry. His ministry declared that not a single German in America "will ever forget he is a German!" "Once a German, always a German" was the message. America, said Germany, would recognize "in time the direction of destiny."

"German film," Goebbels declared, "has reached the point where it must fulfill its duty to the State, nation, and culture. It must exercise international influence. It must become a spiritual world power. The German film particularly has a world mission." Its mission included being a source of income for the German state.

During the war years, Goebbels claimed, "Film production is flourishing almost unbelievably." "What a good idea of mine it was to take possession of the films on behalf of the Reich," he said. "It would be terrible if the high profits now being earned by the motion picture industry were to flow into private hands."

Goebbels and his ministry funded more than one hundred films in the twelve years of the Third Reich. These films became the *Staatsauftragsfilme*—state-produced films—that accounted for ten percent of the Third Reich features released in Germany during the Nazi years. These

Top: Ufa's sound studio, Babelsberg. *Bottom:* Typical work table of Ufa sound engineer.

were *the* official Nazi films. Some were shown commercially in mainstream American theatres, not just in American movies houses catering to German speakers. By the time World War II began, films produced in Hitler's Germany were filled with Nazi ideology.

Those films that weren't available in America were viewable by westerners in Germany. Yet American observers in Germany failed to give them serious analysis and interpretation. Nazi productions in 1941, for instance, included *Carl Peters*, which depicts the racist nineteenth-century administrator of German East Africa who relished his reputation as "Hanging Peters." The film was openly anti–Semitic.

The 1941 Nazi production *Heimkehr* (*Homecoming*) predicted a Germany—if not a world—that would be racially pure and rid of Jews. Germany, said the film, would be entirely "German." American critics residing in Germany could have reviewed these Nazi productions, at least until December 1941. It was even possible for foreigners to see Nazi films in Germany *after* Pearl Harbor.

Critics and foreign correspondents, working in Germany for the *New York Times*, *Variety*, the *New Yorker*, the *Washington Post*, the *Chicago Tribune*, and other media outlets, overlooked Nazi productions. When, on rare occasion, a writer mentioned one of them in print, as was the case with the anti–British *Ohm Krüger* (*Uncle Krüger*, 1941), he invariably failed to present them as a real threat.

In the U.S., New York's little known German-Jewish publication *Aufbau* (November 1940) noted the existence of a particularly odious Nazi film: *Jud Süss*. The Nazis depict an eighteenth-century Jewish financier as a power-hungry, money-grubbing sexual predator who schemes against Germany's Protestant population. All Jews were held accountable for his crimes and swept out of the region.

None of America's major newspapers had anything to say about this film, which is now regarded as the vilest of Nazi productions. While many German films contained racist stereotypes, *Jud Süss* demanded the mistreatment and killing of Jews. It strains credulity to believe that major Western critics were unaware of this film and others like it. Critical reporting about films shown in Europe was possible throughout the 1930s and into the 1940s. But American critics rarely offered analysis or interpretation of German films—except if the films had some bearing on the United States. Examples abound.

When *Variety* (March 9, 1938), for instance, reviewed *Rätsel um Beate* (*Conjectures About Beate*, 1937/38), in Berlin, it simply called the tale about Beate Kaiserling (Lil Dagover), who becomes the target of small-town gossipers, a "neat product and a great relief from the ponderous dramatic spouting characteristic of so many German pictures." But the film was more than that. While the protagonist was born Beate Rödern, German to the core, her husband is depicted as a philandering Jew.

When Beate Kaiserling's husband suddenly dies, gossip connects her to his death. Matters come to a head when her husband's friend Dr. Normann (Albrecht Schönhals) invites her to his club. There they meet the aristocratic Ursula von Pöttkamp (Sabine Peters) who, although engaged to Heinz Hübner (Wilhelm H. König), had been having an affair with Kaiserling. It turns out Kaiserling died during an argument. Ursula, realizing that Beate and Dr. Normann are in love, admits the truth.

Perhaps there was no point in telling Americans about the film, since it never screened in the U.S. commercially. In April of 1940, the *Chicago Tribune*'s Sigurd Shultz in Berlin did report to Americans about Hans Bertram's *Feuertaufe* (*Baptism of Fire*, 1939/1940). "Germany tonight showed how it conquered Poland last September," wrote Schultz. The film blamed Britain for war. "What do you say now, Mr. Chamberlain?" asks the narrator. "All this is your work," he says. "You betrayed Poland and the curses of this country will be upon you… Just as our air force hit here [Warsaw] it will know where to find the guiltiest of the guilty." The film included a brief appearance by Göring in which he suggests that what Germany had "accomplished against Poland, it could, and would, accomplish against France and Britain." Schultz offered no commentary.

A month later, the *Chicago Tribune* ran a lengthy piece by E.R. Noderer called "Berlin Newsmen View Movies of Nazi Blitzkrieg." "The smashing power of the German war machine," wrote Noderer, "was demonstrated to foreign newspapermen here tonight in a film showing the burning and surrender of Rotterdam, the fall of Sedan, the cracking of the Maginot line, and of the blitzkrieg in the West." Noderer offered no personal commentary about Germany's invasion of the West. In July 1941, *New York Times* correspondent C. Brooks Peters reported from Berlin, "propaganda is still a mighty weapon of the Nazis," without so much as mentioning any anti–Semitic Nazi production. On December 7, 1941, the *Chicago Tribune*'s Alex Small reported from Berlin that "Drama and Opera" were thriving in "most of Europe." "Legitimate stages, three opera houses, and a half a dozen 'shows,' all going full tilt, are not enough to satisfy the demands of a theatre crazy, wartime Berlin audience," he wrote. But "problem plays," he noted, "are relegated to the movies if the problems are not too close to the political issues."

In late 1942, the *Washington Post* wrote that in Belgium, American and British films were being "muzzled." In December 1943, also in the *Post*, William L. Shirer wrote—in a column titled "Propaganda Front"—that the German films and newsreels were portraying America's soldiers as "brutal, vicious." Shirer was silent about German films' portrayals of Jews. Ironically, that was in line with the standard practice of U.S. film review publications since late 1940. Nearly every media outlet, including the *New York Times* (Theodore Strauss was the paper's main reviewer of German films in the 1930s), *Variety*, *Motion Picture Herald*, and *Film Daily* averted their attention from nearly all Nazi films released in the States or abroad for more than year before December 1941.

German films that screened in America between 1933 and 1942 addressed four primary audiences: the millions of Americans of German ancestry; the 350,000 German nationals residing in the States; avowed Nazis in America, such as the German-American Bund; and other groups, individuals, anti–Semites, and isolationists who were susceptible to Nazi thinking and influence.

In America, pro–Nazi groups like the Silver Shirts and German-American Bund, which was the successor to the first Nazi party in America, were not shy about promoting and screening the new breed of German films to their members. The Bund and the German-American Business League, which promoted economic ties between America and Hitler's Germany, published the weekly *Deutscher Weckruf und Beobachter* (*German Wake-up and Observer*).

Separate editions of the *Deutscher Weckruf* were printed in New York, Philadelphia, Chicago, and Los Angeles. Almost every edition announced new affiliates from among German-American societies. The publication's task was to flood German- and English-speaking groups with Nazi ideology. Representing the Nazis as an aggrieved and undeservedly belittled group, as victims of a hostile world, the *Deutscher Weckruf* attacked opponents with the kind of hypocrisy that characterized Nazi publications in the fatherland.

Writing in the *Nation* (April 1, 1939), George Britt said *Deutscher Weckruf* tarred Americans, for instance, for their "nativistic spirit, the arrogant assumption that an unwritten clause of the Constitution grants them a patent on superiority ... that unless you can trace your ancestry to some shoemaker or weaver in Britain, then you are a citizen only by tolerance." To bolster the Nazis' arguments, exploit racist sentiment, support Germany's aggression and pro-war stance, and promote their ideology, the *Deutscher Weckruf und Beobachter* listed theaters that screened the new German films in New York and across the country. It also ran ads from German theatres in America. New York's 79th Street Theater (also called the Yorkville Theatre), for example, was a heavy advertiser. Subsidized by Berlin, the theatre only screened Nazi productions.

Nazi films were also released to German-American societies across America for a nominal fee. Had the U.S. not entered the war in late 1941, it's conceivable that all of Goebbels' productions might have been shown in America. Through these films, the Nazis told the world a few simple things: who they were, what the "New Order" was all about, and what they planned to do. Their films predicted war and the elimination of the Jews of Europe.

One of Goebbels' first orders had been to rescind pre–January 30, 1933, approval of German releases. From this date on, to be screened in Germany and elsewhere, German films had to reflect the ideology of the new regime. Thus, from Hans Steinhoff's *Robert Koch: The Battler Against Death* (1939), which screened in the U.S. after the start of World War II, you could get a hint about Nazi attitudes towards "medicine." The film depicts a famous nineteenth-century German microbe hunter calling for the destruction of Germany's "enemies"—Jews, that is—wherever they might be hiding.

Goebbels decided which of the ministry's films were to be shown abroad, scheduled release dates, and awarded prizes to Germany's top films. He called the earliest Nazi productions the "heroic, military and world-war stamina" films. Later Nazi films lauded the leadership principle, as exemplified by Frederick the Great; zeroed in on the crimes of Bolshevism; vilified Russia and Britain as Germany's great adversaries; and advocated the annihilation of Jews (*Die Rothschilds*, *Der Ewige Jude*, and *Jud Süss*).

But they all had one commonality. Jews were the cause of any and all trouble. Nazi films demonized Jews; questioned Jews' right to live; and depicted non–Germans—they invariably had Jewish surnames—as cheats, crooks, thieves, and scoundrels. They portrayed bankers, accountants, and businessmen as gougers and foreign-looking characters as shady and untrustworthy. Their names were invariably Jewish-sounding. Contemporary American reviews had nothing to say about these depictions.

This book uses quotes around the names of certain characters in Nazi films to emphasize that those names are Jewish or Jewish-sounding. In Nazi films, the names of characters were significant and a signal to audiences and supporters of the regime. This is something that was overlooked in the 1930s and not mentioned by film critics or historians then or now. But it has a great bearing because of its relevance to anti–Semitism. The Jews or those who carried Jewish names were almost always the culprits or evildoers in the films.

Some German productions hid their messages from Americans, especially when they lacked subtitles. These productions were often set in the repressive nineteenth century or during the First World War. Many German films used code words. "Profiteers," "exploiters," "usurers," "big capitalists," "international money power," "plutocrats," "November criminals," "aliens," "foreigners," and "traitors" were all synonyms for Jews. "The press" was understood to mean "the Jewish-controlled press."

Yet not every Nazi film dealt with traitors to the fatherland, featured open political propaganda, praised Aryan patriots, or used Nazi salutes and swastikas. Germany's leading studios, Ufa (Universum Film Aktien), Tobis, Terra, and Bavaria, also turned out detective films and adventure stories. But while criminal plots remained popular and were often set outside Germany, murderers, thieves, bandits, and villains were never depicted as German, Italian, or Japanese.

The racist message was in nearly all German films, whether entertainment or propaganda. The absence of Jews from the German silver screen was the first sign. Hans Hinkel, the regime's director of non–Aryan art, called Aryanization (*Arisierung*) "purely an internal affair which in no case should be connected with the international film business," reported the *New York Times* (August 7, 1935). As thousands of German-Jewish artists, directors, producers, actors, screenwriters, and technicians fled Germany, non–Jews from around the world rushed to fill the vacancies. In April 1935 in Berlin, when Goebbels held an international film congress to emphasize the "cultural and political importance" of German films, the German press reported that 2,000 attendees from 40 nations had streamed into Hitler's Germany.

Italian, Swiss, Spanish, Russian, Dutch, Danish, Swedish, and Austrian film workers helped keep the Nazi film industry alive. They too were Hitler's willing entertainers. Co-productions—German-Italian, German-Austrian, and German-French—made German films palatable. Every now and then, a German-British or German-U.S. production came along. After Austria joined the Reich, reports circulated that in the new Austria, Nazi leaders had "doubles." This was also the case for Nazi films. They too had their "doubles": co-productions that masked Nazi involvement in "foreign" films.

In addition, Czech-German films also reflected the anti–Semitic nature of the film industries in Nazi-threatened Europe as Jews were removed from the screen. Two examples were Hugo Haas's *Bílá nemoc* (*The White Disease*, 1937) and Otakar Vavra's *The Merry Wives* (1938), both produced in Czechoslovakia and released in the U.S. in 1940, after Czechoslovakia had been dismembered.

While Germany expelled its Jewish film artists, it demanded allegiance from its non–Jewish artists. Well-known German filmmakers working abroad—Emil Jannings, Lilian Harvey, and Marlene Dietrich especially—were ordered to the fatherland.

"It is considered unpatriotic—yes, even treason to the country—if now, in the midst of the great work of upbuilding in the German film world, German artists combine abroad with

Marlene Dietrich (center) attracting a London crowd, 1930.

Left: Ufa star Lilian Harvey, 1929. *Above:* Ufa star Emil Jannings in the late 1930s.

film companies or film workers who either emigrated from Germany or participate in agitation against Germany," wrote the German film publication *Film-Kurier* in early 1934. "The new Germany will turn with all the means at its disposal against such economic and ideological traitors." This was really a message for all Germans—not just film artists.

After Goebbels initiated his Jew elimination—*Beseitigung*—campaign from the movies, he went a step farther: he forced out Jewish employees of Tobis and Ufa in offices outside of Germany. This was the end of what Goebbels labeled the "Jewish-American domination of the German cinema." Yet the Nazis rejected the suggestion that German cinema was changing. When, in May 1934, the German newspaper *Deutsche Allgemeine Zeitung* argued that an overly optimistic and romantic representation of German life imperiled the artistic and ethical value of film, the propaganda ministry denounced the article. Calling the piece "sabotage," the ministry barred the writer from publishing his opinions on movies in any German newspaper.

American films were subject to German censorship, too. The Nazis warned American actors against accepting roles in Hollywood anti–Nazi films. Otherwise, Nazi Germany would ban films by their production companies. Also, if American films had Jewish actors, authors, directors, or producers, the relevant facts had to be "openly and honorably stated," insisted Goebbels' ministry.

Accordingly, one Hollywood film suppressed after a two-week run in Berlin in March 1934 was W.S. van Dyke's *The Prizefighter and the Lady* (1933), starring the Jewish boxer Max Baer. The reason German officials gave for ending the run was the film's "slight regard for womanhood." This was incompatible, they said, with the "high morality" of the Third Reich.

Soon after Hitler came to power the Nazis issued a warning to American studios operating within the country. They were ordered to "give notice of the dismissal of your representatives, rental agents, and branch managers of Jewish extraction and to give them leave of absence immediately." Contracts with Jews were to be cancelled. "It is not religion," said the Nazis, "but race that is decisive," reported the *New York Times* (April 2, 1933). Warner Bros. closed its German operations, rather than adhere to the policy. Universal's German affiliate, Deutsche Universal, shifted its operations to Vienna and Budapest, where it survived until 1935. Other American studios complied with the order. But still more restrictive orders followed, and by 1936, all American studios ceased operations in Germany.

In Hollywood, studio head Samuel Goldwyn reacted by offering work to "all able film figures" barred by the Reich.

German producers even tried erasing Jewish involvement from pre–Nazi German films. When Weimar films were released in the States after 1932, German producers credited them to non–Jews. Sometimes they renamed films, removed the credits, or released them unsubtitled.

The German film industry's campaign of hatred took a political break in 1936, the year of the Berlin Olympics. That year, the Nazis hid behind the cloak of civilization. They produced films meant to present a moderate, civilized Germany. Most Americans fell for the bait. German exports were marketed as "light entertainment" with "gripping plots, music, costumes, and design," said Goebbels. "Light" films from Germany would camouflage the regime's murderous rages.

The year of the Berlin Olympics offered Germans a golden opportunity at image enhancement. German studios opened offices in New York, they said, to "break down anti–Hitler feeling in the U.S." and "re-establish the German film to its place of eminence in the American art film market."

As the Olympics came to a close, the Nazis, through their films, resumed their glorification of war and campaign against Jews. When Karl Ritter's spy film *Verräter* (*Traitor*, 1936) premiered at the 86th Street Garden Theatre, *Variety* (January 27, 1937) was full of praise for the production, which had received a "special recommendation" at the 1936 Venice Film Festival. "If Ufa," it said, "expended as much ingenuity on its average product as 'The Traitor' gets, there would probably be fewer stories about distributors guaranteeing the exhibitors a weekly minimum to simply keep their houses open to German fare. 'Traitor' is in every aspect a class A piece of celluloid, if the matter of political viewpoints is left aside."

This is the kind of film, said the trade publication, that the "more nostalgic elements in German-American sectors will relish." That was asking a lot—for anyone watching developments in Germany. The finale is nothing but a review of Germany's military might: modern tanks, Stuka bombers, and ships. Don't dare to fight this giant, says the picture, neither by treason nor any other aggression. You would never succeed.

Some American critics had, however, urged the "cultural politicians" of the Third Reich to come to their senses. "The public," said the *New York Times* (January 26, 1937), "pays money at the box office to be entertained, not to have party publicity crammed down its throats."

In the 1930s, Hollywood decided to keep politics out of films. In 1933 Hollywood producer Al Rosen had tried to go beyond entertainment. He announced he was filming *The Mad Dog of Europe*, whose central character was named Rudolph Hitler.

"They tell me I am dealing with a controversial subject," said Rosen. "There have been plays and pictures before based on the crime of oppression and social bigotry, so why not again?" (*Washington Post*, October 15, 1933). The consensus in Hollywood was that the film, scripted by Herman Mankiewicz and slated for direction by Phil Rosen, was a nonstarter.

The film was never produced because Hollywood's studios were frightened about opening themselves to accusations of trying to influence American foreign policy toward Hitler's regime. Hollywood might also lose its share of the German film market if it antagonized Hitler.

Jews in Hollywood and elsewhere also worried that any efforts to limit, censure, or ban German imports could raise the cry of Jewish meddling in foreign affairs. Jews were liable to be accused of being in league with Britain—the Nazis referred to Britons as the "Jews of the Aryan nations"—and of hoping to plunge the U.S. into a European war.

In the face of such self-censuring, U.S. documentary filmmaker Julien Bryan had the temerity to make one of America's first anti–Nazi films. Bryan shot 25,000 feet of film in two months in Germany, and managed to get the footage out. The film is a no-holds-barred account of the regime, included ordinary shots of German signs warning Jews not to congregate or sit in towns, parks, and benches. His 100-minute film was called *Inside Nazi Germany* (1938).

The German consul general in San Francisco characterized Bryan's revelations as "unfair." The Chicago Board of Censors—the city had a large and influential German-American population—banned Bryan's film on the grounds that it was "unfriendly to the German government." (Chicago Police Commissioner James P. Allman overruled the board.) At New York showings of Bryan's film, Nazi supporters screamed "Heil Hitler!" while opponents yelled "Send 'em back to Germany!" and "Down with Hitler!" Cowed, Warner Bros.—the same studio that had refused to accede to Nazi hiring restrictions inside Germany—would not screen Bryan's film in any of its 425 U.S. theaters.

When, in late 1939, U.S. filmmakers finally concluded that "neutrality" towards Germany was a sham, they were caught in a storm of controversy. The minute they started to shoot the anti–Nazi film *Confessions of a Nazi Spy* and admit that the "swastika is not a device used exclusively in Navajo rugs," as a Hollywood film executive put it, "alarmists began hollering that Hollywood is leading the country into war."

Pressure by pro–Nazi German voting blocs in Chicago, including voters of the German-American Alliance, the German-American Bund, and the Patriotic Research Bureau, forced some city theatres to stop showing the film. The city's police said they feared incitement to riot. The police, however, did not see fit to lift a finger to halt the screening in Chicago in early 1941 of the Nazi documentary glorifying war, *Feldzug in Polen* (*Campaign in Poland*, 1940).

The U.S. Congress, which had taken a hands-off approach towards Nazi films appearing on U.S. screens, attacked Hollywood filmmakers for *their* anti–Nazi films. More than a year after World War II had started, isolationist and pro–Axis Sen. Gerald Nye (R, N.D.), who served on a congressional subcommittee investigating "war propaganda" charges against the film Mecca, said Hollywood "swarms with refugees ... directors from Russia, Hungary, Germany and the Balkan countries" who are "susceptible to ... national and racial emotions." Nye, Senator Burton Wheeler, and their ilk concluded that the film capital was controlled by five or six men "dominated by hatred and determined to wreak vengeance on Adolf Hitler." Isolationists and representatives of the America First Committee accused Hollywood of employing Nazi propaganda techniques to turn the American public into "an infuriated mob" and force the U.S. into war. Jewish emigrants stirred up hatred, said Nazi supporters within the United States. A "war oligarchy rules movies," isolationists told the Senate, according to the *Chicago Tribune* (April 25, 1941).

Charles Lindbergh was the inspiration behind the Senate's investigation of Hollywood. In mid–1941, in a Des Moines speech, Lindbergh said, "[Jews'] greatest danger to this country lies in their large ownership and influence in our motion pictures, our press, our radio and our government." Yet Hollywood had tried to keep a low profile. Its prewar newsreels, purportedly made by Hollywood's Jews, averted attention from the anti–Semitism endemic to Nazi Germany. It was safer to avoid controversy. For instance, commentary that "Hitler had brought more evil on the Jews than any man in a generation" was the kind of distressful statement that studio executives excised before releasing the *March of Time* series of films.

From 1939 to 1941, Ufa Film, headquartered at 729 Seventh Ave., New York, was one of the major importers and distributors of German films and newsreels in the States. Its advertising motto was "The Insignia of Quality—Pictures of International Merit." The organization's president, George Nitze, claimed his firm was an American corporation, unbeholden to the giant German studio. After the start of World War II, Ufa Film, however, paid for bimonthly shipments of films to America via Clipper plane and vessels from Mediterranean ports. The films went from Germany to Italy and then were put aboard liners from, say, Naples to the U.S. Sometimes the films went to South America first—and then were rerouted to the States. A few had English subtitles but most were exhibited only in the original German. Their language was pro–Nazi, their content full of lies, and the political intent was anti-democratic, with camouflaged criticism of people of other nationalities.

By late 1941, Ufa Film had a long list of productions ready for U.S. release, several starring the well-known Nazi actor Willy Fritsch.

Several organizations had a hand in screening Nazi films for their supporters in the States. They included Ufa Film, the League of the Friends of New Germany (Die Freunde des Neuen Deutschland) on East 83rd Street, in New York—it claimed a city membership of 25,000—German consulates in New York and Chicago, and the German Railway Industrial Organization.

The British blockade of Germany at the outbreak of the war had only slowed the flow of German products, including Nazi films, into the States. When the U.S. entered World War

Falstaff in Wien, with Paul Hörbiger and Lizzi Hotzschuh.

Top: Karen Horney, in *Die Keusche Geliebte*. *Bottom: Der Laufende Berg*, with Hansi Knoteck.

II, federal authorities moved to confiscate Axis films in circulation and storage in America. In a broad sweep, they seized more than a thousand features and shorts that had been produced in Germany, Austria, Italy, France, Hungary, and Japan. Many of Ufa's productions would have had their initial American screening in New York's 86th Street Casino Theatre or at its East Side neighbor, the 86th Street Garden Theatre. The unseen German films included Fritz

Kirchhoff's *Anschlag auf Baku* (*Attack on Baku*); Leopold Hainisch's *Falstaff in Wien;* Carl Boese's *Hochzeitsnacht* (*Wedding Night*); Hans Bertram's *Kamfgeschwader Lützow*; Viktor Tourjansky's *Die Keusche Geliebte* (*The Chaste Beloved*), a tale of blackmail instigated by one "Edgar Simon" (Paul Dahlke) against a wayward banker's wife, "Renée Lemonier" (Camilla Horn); Hans Deppe's *Der Laufende Berg* (*The Current Mountain*); Paul May's *Links in der Isar—Rechts der Spree* (*Left in the Isar—Right of the Spree*); Johannes Meyer's *Männerwirtschaft* (*Male Economics*); Max W. Kimmich's *Mein Leben für Irland*; E.W. Emo's *Meine Tochter lebt in Wien*; Willy Forst's *Operette*; Arthur Maria Rabenalt's *...reitet für Deutschland* (*Riding for Germany*); Herbert Maisch's *Friedrich Schiller*; Karl Ritter's *Stukas*; Géza von Bolváry's *Traummusik* (*Dream Music*); Erich Waschneck's *Die Unvollkommene Liebe* (*Imperfect Love*); Eduard von Borsody's *Das Wunschkonzert*; and Erich Waschneck's *Die Rothschilds.*

Ufa's Kulturfilme (culture films) from 1939

Above: **Links der Isar—Rechts der Spree**, with **Fritz Kampers.**

Scenes from Ufa's short *Alpenkorps im Angriff* (1939).

to 1940 slated for American release included *Schnelle Truppen*; *Radium*; and Gösta Nordhaus' 20-minute *Alpenkorps im Angriff*. These shorts, particularly those the regime deemed of political value, often accompanied Ufa's newsreels "in order," according to Geobbels, "to give all racial comrades an opportunity to participate in the happenings of the present."

These films were representative of the range of Nazi productions that were shown here between 1933 and the U.S. entry into the Second World War: comedies, dramas, detective stories, romances in Vienna, musicals, biographies, colonial dramas, war stories, newsreels, documentaries, and propaganda.

But there was one unexpected Nazi feature in the group, which signaled how brazen the Nazis had become before Pearl Harbor. The film was Erich Waschneck's *Die Rothschilds* (1940), a justification of the Nazis' attack on Britain. To the Nazis, the Rothschilds represented Jew power. They were part of a British-Jewish plutocracy which ruled Britain and which had to be destroyed. This cinematic attack on one of the world's foremost Jewish families was another statement of the rightness of the Nazi goal to eliminate the Jews of Europe.

Yet its production was not a surprise. Since 1933, the Germans had been making films denigrating and stereotyping Jewish bankers and financiers. *Die Rothschilds* was merely the culmination of nearly a decade of prejudice on the screen.

Opposite: Traummusik, with Lizzi Waldmüller.

The expected release in America of these Nazi films was little short of appeasement of Hitler's Germany and its backers. America said it feared communism and the Soviet Union. It did little to fight the anti–Semitism that fed the sense that Nazi brutality against Jews was an exaggeration—by its victims. With its anti–Semitic banner, Germany's cinema influenced the world's opinion of Jews and Germany, and propounded the idea of a master race. The only lives that mattered in German films of the era were German lives.

But in the end, Germany in the 1930s had little to fear from America no matter how, when, or which German films were shown on American screens. Americans were, apparently, indifferent to the fate of Europe's nations and its Jews. If Americans didn't stand up for Jews in America, who were often under assault in the 1930s, why would they do so for Jews under threat across the ocean?

Perhaps the extent and number of German films released in America in the Hitler years is not that surprising. German films from the years 1933 to 1942 were transparent in message and offensive in content. Sometimes the obvious is the most revealing. All you had to do was acknowledge whom the Nazis were depicting as the villains in their films.

1933

Deutsche Universal

In late July 1932, Berlin's *Illustrierter Film-Kurier* reported dramatic news. The 37-year-old German director Arnold Fanck and the cast and crew of an American-backed production—Deutsche Universal's latest film—had survived danger and drowning. They had been stranded for more than a week in Greenland.

The wholly German filmmaker Fanck had cabled his boss, Jewish Hollywood studio head Carl Laemmle, with the news.

"A true miracle saved the lives of Fanck and associates ... among the icebergs of west Greenland. Ernst Udet, the pilot, making a low flight over huge icebergs ... lost power ... and crashed ... Udet was rescued by Eskimos.... Within a few minutes ... the iceberg ... broke up. Half of the gigantic ice mass crumbled to bits, carrying men and equipment into the water.... Eskimos in their kayaks rescued ten men and two women ... but considerable sound equipment was destroyed."

A geologist by training, "Dr. Fanck," as he was known in the German film world, became as famous as Austrian performer Luis Trenker through a series of mountain films that attempted to demonstrate the living reality of man triumphing against the forces of nature. Fanck's work, documentary-like, contrasted with expressionistic and German musical films of the Weimar era. Elemental, mythic, pantheistic in tone, glorifying the German wilderness and its people, Fanck's mountain films spoke to a new generation. If nature could be overcome, little could stand in the way of a new Germany. Fanck's films impressed Hitler and the Nazis. Strength and vigor and supreme dedication to a cause, they read in his films, can best the most hostile forces, whether of nature or world opinion.

For this venture, called *S.O.S. Eisberg*, Fanck had assembled scientists, technicians, artists, and outdoor lovers, including the Danish explorer Knud Rasmussen and German scientific advisor Ernst Sorge. The making of *S.O.S. Eisberg* had garnered publicity both in the U.S. and in Germany, especially since the highly touted Leni Riefenstahl was in the cast.

Fanck hired talented cameramen (Schneeberger, Angst, and Allgeier) who had an eye for the savage grandeur of mountains, changing weather, cloud formations, and the glitter of the snow. They would all cast their lot with Hitler.

Richard Angst (1905–84), for instance, was a skier and mountain climber who began working with Allgeier and Schneeberger on Fanck's early mountain films: *Der Grosse Sprung* (1927), *Die Weisse Hölle vom Piz Palü* (1929), *Stürme über dem Montblanc* (1930), *Der Weisse Rausch* (1931), and the Hitler-era *Der Ewige Traum/Der König des Montblanc* (1934).

Known for putting the romance of the great outdoors into film, Fanck—about to heartily embrace the new Germany—anticipated a masterpiece about man vs. mountain. However,

Fanck could be plodding, pedantic, and pedestrian, exhibiting outworn concepts of morality and Germanic predestination—elements of which were evident in the enormously wasteful footage he shot in Greenland. But it wasn't *his* money he was spending.

Ironically, *S.O.S. Eisberg* turned out to be a film in which art imitated life. It was based on German scientist Alfred Wegener's ill-fated expedition to Greenland in 1930 to set up the first weather station on the center of the ice cap. Wegener—he is most well known for theorizing continental drift in 1912—and a native sled driver made a bold attempt to resupply the cap before the onset of winter, but both perished.

Scientists from Wegener's expedition had joined Fanck's production crew to add verisimilitude to the filming. But having lost nearly everything in the process of trying to bring the tale of a true-life expedition to the screen, Fanck's unit had spent $350,000 to shoot 350,000 feet of film and had come up with 60 hours of little more than background scenery.

In Hollywood, at the start of 1933, Universal's studio head Carl Laemmle had to decide what to do. He opted on a rescue mission. By salvaging Deutsche Universal's film, Laemmle hoped to limit the damage to Fanck's outsize reputation and earn the gratitude of the new German regime. Deutsche Universal's future in Germany was on the line.

Laemmle sent U.S. director Tay Garnett to Germany. The 40-year-old Garnett sailed on the *Bremen*. In 1933, the "average American," he speculated, "shared my own preconceived image of Berlin. I expected," he said breezily in his autobiography, "to see a hearty, well-dressed people filled with schnapps, sausage, and song." On arrival on German soil, Garnett was "almost overwhelmed by beggars; not the professional panhandlers, but tattered, starving citizens, the flotsam left by the backwash of World War I and the Great Depression."

In the cultivated atmosphere of an opulent Berlin hotel, Garnett met the two people in charge of the production: Deutsche Universal's Jewish producer, Paul Kohner, and the well-known "Dr. Fanck."

Garnett decided on a film of seven reels, the standard length for a production in the early 1930s—but he needed a story. Though he had begun his career in Hollywood as a writer (he had co-scripted, for instance, William K. Howard's *White Gold*, produced in 1927), Garnett hired actor-turned-writer Edwin Knopf, who, although Jewish, was still in Germany. Knopf (who later became a producer at MGM) tailored a "semi-documentary" around the footage Garnett found salvageable, about thirty minutes' worth.

Director Arnold Fanck.

Knopf concocted a tale about a Danish expedition to Greenland, which is following the same route taken by famed explorer Alfred Wegener. However, it, too, is plagued by misfortune and catastrophe. When the group's support ship is ground to pieces by icebergs, the survivors take refuge on a huge polar ice floe.

Udet (Ernst Udet), the expedition's chief flyer, departs from base camp to save Hella Lorenz (Riefenstahl), and her husband, the expedition's leader, Karl Lorenz (Gustav Diessl). But the other male, the insignificant cook, Fritz Kümmel (Walter Riml) drowns as the floe—in true, dramatic ice floe fashion—rolls over him. The three then fly to safety.

Garnett and Fanck completed the narrative scenes for *S.O.S. Iceberg* and the German-language rendition *S.O.S. Eisberg* in Switzerland. Garnett took a few days to shoot a sequence, after which he turned the cameras over to Fanck. Garnett filmed his portions of *S.O.S Iceberg* without sound. The voices of Ernst Udet and Riefenstahl were dubbed into English. Garnett worked on the film until mid–May 1933 before returning to Hollywood. Garnett might have thought the Germans would be pleased. But German insiders and film critics chose to view the Americans' part not as an act of support or generosity but as attempt to denigrate the glory of the German version.

Deutsche Universal released Fanck's *S.O.S. Eisberg* at 103 minutes, with not much dialogue but with a great deal of gorgeous scenery in Berlin, on August 8, 1933. Nazi critics hailed Fanck's longer German-language version. His film was "not to be compared with the commonplace output of the studios, which disappear as quickly as they are made. It is the diary of a serious expedition; the self avowal of an artist. It is ... a consecrated thing." Germans were experienced with the harsh conditions of Greenland "which, a thousand years ago," wrote Sorge in 1936, "was already the bourne of German seafarers." Nazi thinking was solidly in place.

Germany's press gave another

Top: Leni Riefenstahl in *S.O.S. Iceberg* (1933). *Left:* Tay Garnett, director of *S.O.S. Iceberg*.

example of Nazi thinking. It attacked the Jewish-led Deutsche Universal, which had financed both versions, for its desire "to see and experience something in return for their money." The German-language rendition listed the studio and names of the Jewish producers, and the Berlin Symphony Orchestra had recorded Jewish composer Paul Dessau's score. But these would be some of the last Jewish names to appear on screens in Germany until after World War II.

Garnett's *S.O.S. Iceberg*, at 70 minutes, opened in New York in September 1933. Film critic Mordaunt Hall of the *New York Times* (September 25, 1933) called Garnett's film a "lusty drama of the frozen wilds.... There is a good deal of realism about the picture. One almost senses the cold, with the characters sleeping in great fur coats within ice walls." Leni Riefenstahl's appeal, meanwhile, was not as strong as she had hoped. Hall called her merely "a German actress."

Laemmle's rescue mission turned out to be for naught. Within a year, Deutsche Universal, faced with German pressure to fire its Jewish staff, moved its film production operations from Berlin to Budapest and Vienna.

In six years in Germany, Universal's German branch had produced more than 20 silent and sound films and distributed a hundred others by German producers. Despite Laemmle's efforts to retain businesslike relations with the new Germany—he had been born in the old Germany—Universal's days in Germany were over. Scores of non–Jewish German actors, directors, photographers, writers, and technicians had freely collaborated with German Jews within the subsidiary. The Jewish filmmakers fled Hitler's Germany; most of the studio's non–Jews stayed.

One non–Jew was Luis Trenker, the star of one of Deutsche Universal's biggest hits, *Der Rebell* (1932). Directed by Luis Trenker and Kurt Bernhardt, it's the tale of Severin Anderlan (Trenker), who spearheads an uprising against Napoleon's occupation forces in the Austrian Tyrol. The tale's concluding episode has the rebel arising from the dead, picking up a blood-splattered flag and marching at the head of a column of men, women, and children to a glorious future.

Trenker, an Austrian, was one of the creators of the mountain, or "berg," film. American producer Paul Kohner, who was Jewish, had gotten Trenker to make an English-language rendition, co-starring Jewish actors Vilma Bánky and Victor Varkoni. *The Rebel*, by Trenker and Edwin Knopf, was shown in the United States in July 1933. The photography came from the cameras of Sepp Allgeier, Hans Schneeberger, Albert Benitz, and Richard Angst, who would all serve Nazi cinema.

Angst was the photographer of Fanck's nationalistic *Die Tochter des Samurai* (*Daughter of the Samurai*, 1936), which would commemorate the world's first film agreement between two nations: Germany and Japan. Angst also directed the one-reel *In einer Chinesischen Stadt* (1937), an Ufa production depicting the Japanese occupation of Shanghai.

The Germans proudly referred to Trenker's anti-occupation production *Der Rebell* as a "liberation film." It became a favorite of Hitler's. Hitler asked in *Mein Kampf*, "Why could I not have been born a hundred years ago? Somewhere about the time of the Wars of Liberation, when a man was still of some value even though he had no 'business.'" And, "Why did not Austria take part in the war against the French in 1870? Why did not my father and all the others fight in that struggle? Are we not the same as the other Germans? Do we not all belong together?"

Trenker's film depicted one Austrian doing the right thing by Hitler. Trenker (1892–1990) had made his name in the 1920s in the mountain films of Arnold Fanck, several times opposite Leni Riefenstahl (1901–2003). His silent *Kampf ums Matterhorn* (*Struggle for the Matterhorn*, 1928), co-directed by Nunzio Malasomma, was about a heroic mountain guide, played by Trenker himself.

Producer Paul Kohner in 1930s Hollywood.

It was released in the States in 1938, when the word "Kampf" had become one of Nazism's favorite terms, alongside Sturm (assault), Rasse (race), Glaube (faith), Volk (people), Opfer (sacrifice), and Schicksal (destiny). These were ideal terms for German film titles and subject matter.

Athletic, handsome, and versatile, Trenker had a brief relationship with Hollywood. He had starred in Universal's drama about Austrian and Italian enemies at Verdun, *The Doomed Battalion* (1932), opposite the Jewish actor Victor Varconi. Trenker wrote the story, which was reminiscent of *All Quiet on the Western Front* (1930), *the* production that had outraged the up-and-coming Nazis who forced the Weimar government to ban it within Germany. Trenker also wrote, directed, and starred in Deutsche Universal's *Der Verlorene Sohn* (*The Prodigal Son*, 1933/34), a *Heimat* (or homeland) film about young Austrian Tonio Feuersinger (Trenker) who emigrates to New York, leaving behind his sweetheart Bärbl (Maria Andergast). In the Depression-ravaged New World he encounters frustration and disappointment. Life is unpredictable, work is unfulfilling, and starvation is a threat. What can he do? He flees from the ills of the

city to his place of birth and to a better life. His country village greets him with open arms. The film's depiction of the character's devotion to the earth and the fatherland had *Variety* (November 20, 1934) surmising that Trenker's "Nazi leanings may have had a good deal to do with the story." Although Bill Henry of the *Los Angeles Times* saw the film in Berlin and praised it, Trenker's American-financed production was not released commercially in the U.S.

Deutsche Universal produced one more film before closing operations within Germany. It was a comedy called *Nordpol Ahoi!* (*North Pole, Ahoy!*, 1934) about a motion picture company shooting a film in the Arctic. Unlike Fanck's *S.O.S. Eisberg*, this film (also shot in Greenland and Switzerland), directed by Hungarian Jew Andrew Marton, satirized the magnitude and magnificence of nature via a lighthearted attitude towards the great outdoors that Fanck and the Nazis took so seriously.

Nordpol Ahoi! vanished from German theaters after its premiere in April 1934, and was never shown in the States. In the cast was Guzzi Lantschner, who became a key cameraman in Nazi cinema. He was one of the photographers of Leni Riefenstahl's *Olympia* (1938).

In addition to Deutsche Universal's drama *S.O.S Eisberg*, Fanck directed two short works for the Jewish-owned studio: *Die Seehunde* (1933) and *Der Walfisch ll/Verarbeitung* (*The Whale/Processing*, 1933), each of which depicts a bit of science gleaned in the Arctic. Fanck (1889–1974) remained in the new Germany. He joined the Nazi Party—he later claimed he did it to keep on working—and directed his final "documentaries" during the war years. Two of his short films, which he never repudiated, idealize highly admired, Nazi-approved sculptors and supported Nazi ideology.

Fanck's one-reel *Joseph Thorak, Werkstatt und Werk* (1943), photographed by Walter Riml, Otto Cürlis, and Fanck, details Thorak's environment and work on classical figures. This includes busts of Copernicus, Johann Fischer von Erlach (Austria's greatest baroque architect), Frederick the Great (as a young and an old man), groups of lovers, horses, and other symbolic Nazi subjects whose monumental sizes overshadow the individual.

Fanck's one-reel *Arnold Breker* (1944), which Riefenstahl-Film produced and Riml and Fanck photographed, is set inside Brecker's studio, where it focuses on a bust of the Nazis' favorite composer, Richard Wagner. Breker, who became known for sculpting the ideal Nazi, is shown doing a charcoal sketch of "Kameradschaft," then outlining it in clay, forming a relief. He then enlarges it and copies it in plaster. The final, huge statue is then cast and finished.

Fanck, Trenker, Riefenstahl, Ernst Udet, and most of the German cast and crew of Deutsche Universal's final German-language films had plenty of work and a chance for greater glory in the thousand-year Reich. Knopf, Kohner, Marton, and other Jews associated with Deutsche Universal departed Germany.

American filmgoers soon had the chance to see what Nazi films were about: the removal of Jews, especially, from the world of German cinema; the collaboration between real "German" and European filmmakers, likewise.

Removal

In the late nineteenth century, the German Conservative Party pledged "to the fight against the aggressive and demoralizing Jewish influence on the life of our nation."

Nationalist Heinrich von Treitschke (1834–96) had caught the mood of the Wilhelmine period (1890–1914) when he said, "There is a cry that resounds today as with a single voice, even in the most highly educated circles, amongst men who would reject with horror the least notion

Opposite: S.O.S. Iceberg **playing New York (1933).**

of religious intolerance or national pride: 'The Jews are our misfortune!'"—Die Juden sind unser Unglück!

Hate speech and reprisals against German Jews increased after the First World War; Jews were called carriers of baser personal and "racial" qualities. Democrats, representatives of progressivism, and leftists in the newly founded Weimar Republic were defamed. Germans referred to Weimar as the "Jewish Republic," its modern, cosmopolitan capital as "Marxified, Jewified Berlin."

In its 1920 party platform, the German National People's Party (DNVP) pledged to fight the "hegemony of Jews in government and public life." In the same year the "German National Protective and Defensive League"—Deutschvölkische Schutz-und Trutzbund—distributed seven million leaflets expressing racism and anti–Semitism.

The answer to this came from Hitler. Hitler loved the idea of "removal"—Entfernung—when referring to his favorite subject. In 1920 he had said, "Removal of the Jews from our nation, not because we begrudge them their existence—we congratulate the rest of the world on their company, but because the existence of our own nation is a thousand times more important to us than that of an alien race."

In *Mein Kampf,* Hitler's attitude toward war, politics, history, foreigners, and anything else revolved around the "removal" of Jews from all areas of life.

He had written, "Only the elimination of the causes of our collapse, as well as the destruction of its beneficiaries, can create the premise for our outward fight for freedom.... It's the inexorable Jew who struggles for his domination over nations. No nation can remove this hand from its throat except by the sword."

The removal of Jews from German life was quick and relentless. In April 1933 the Nazis barred Jews from serving in the legal profession and in public service; in June all political parties—other than the Nazi—were banned; in July, the regime decreed that married women should not work; and in September, the Nazis introduced the "Hereditary Farm Law," which held that Jews could not inherit land in the new Germany. By year's end, 37,000 Jews left Germany, which proved to be the largest Jewish exodus from Germany in any single year thereafter.

Concurrently, while the new Nazi regime banned the screening of films from the Weimar era, it sent them abroad for consumption and profit.

Three days after Hitler came to power, the Weimar-era musical comedy *Zapfenstreich am Rhein* (*Retreat on the Rhine*, 1930) opened in New York. Distributed by J. R. Whitney and directed by Jaap Speyer, its story was an excuse to show dashing German officers and enlisted men chasing fair-haired young girls, cultured women, and the kitchen help. There were also fine views of the Rhine country.

The film was typical of the comedies, musicals, and melodramas that the Nazis hated. The question of why it came to America years after it was made was "one of those things," wrote *Variety*. It had been billed as one of the best of its day in a bygone, pre–Hitler Germany, when Jewish directors and performers had their names in lights. This one starred two Jews: Siegfried Arno and Ernö Verebes.

A second Speyer film starring Arno, called *Moritz Macht sein Glück* (*Moritz Makes His Fortune*, 1930/31), was released a few days later in the city—but this film lacked screen credits or any hint of its origins. The news of Hitler's rise to power made for bad press for this German-language film in the States.

The bad press didn't last. German films came pouring in. The new Germany distributed Fritz Friedmann-Friederich's musical drama *Friederike* (1932) in America. The title is the name of Goethe's first love and was based on Franz Lehar's operetta. It starred Mady Christians in her final German film alongside an upcoming giant in Nazi cinema Veit Harlan, as the Duke of Weimar.

Theodor Körner (1932), directed by Carl Boese and released by the General Film Corp. in mid-1933, is a nationalistic tale about the mythical Prussian poet-playwright-songwriter (Willi Domgraf-Fassbände) who achieves immortality when he loses his life heroically opposing Napoleon. Körner's patriotic ditties were said to have "kindled the masses." In the cast was Heinz Klingenberg (1905–1959), who subsequently starred in the vitriolic *SA-Mann Brand* (1933).

Two pre–Hitler German films whose depiction of strong leadership meshed with the Nazis' worldview had their American screenings in Hitler's early years. They were Heinz Paul's Prussian history films. *Tannenberg*'s hero is General Hindenburg. The drama was of his glorious German victory over Russia in 1914. *Trenck*, also made in 1932, was set during the reign of Frederick the Great.

Biographies of inspirational Germans would figure prominently in Nazi cinema, as would unsympathetic portrayals of an anti–German Napoleon and caricatures of Jews.

Gefahren der Liebe (*Driven Love*) opened in New York in April 1933. Its story put a spotlight on German films. Quickly, it was pulled from the theatre, but not because it was a Nazi production. Rather, the tale of a rape victim who contracts syphilis, kills the rapist, is charged with murder, and has the medical facts revealed at her trial, was banned by New York's censors.

Directed by Eugen Thiele, a Jew, it starred Hans Stüwe and the anti–Nazi actors Else and Albert Bassermann. The censors had done Germany a favor. This film was not the kind that represented the new Germany. It had been made in 1931.

American censors did give their stamp of approval to films along the lines of Viktor Janson's Aafa Film AG comedy *Die Frau von der man Spricht* (*A Woman They Talk About*, 1931), which centers on a couple (Mady Christians and Szöke Szakall) who are the "toast of Paris." Even though this wasn't a Nazi-era production, the chances of the film making money were "certainly hopeless in view of the current skeptical German feeling" in the U.S., wrote *Variety* in April 1933, when Hitler celebrated his 44th birthday.

If pre–Hitler comedies and dramas with or without Jews faced rejection in America, what could the fatherland do? War films would arouse interest.

The Nazis' first blockbuster in the States—*Morgenrot* (*Red Dawn*, 1933)—had taken its cue from *Mein Kampf*. The state did its part to get it into every German's hands. One way was to present Hitler's memoirs as a wedding gift. In the film industry, adhering to its themes became an advantage in getting a script filmed. The pro-war and hate-filled *Mein Kampf* offered inspiration and ready material for aspiring, opportunistic scriptwriters.

Morgenrot is a tale of German U-boats and Germany's sink-without-mercy policy of the First World War. Hitler, in *Mein Kampf*, had admitted to admiring King William II of Prussia. "I looked upon him," Hitler wrote, "not only as the German Emperor but, above all, as the creator of the German Navy."

As the first film to screen in Germany after Hitler became chancellor, *Morgenrot* was produced by Ufa, which had sensed the rising power of the Nazis. The fact that *Morgenrot* presaged a new day in German filmmaking was not surprising. At its Berlin premiere—Hitler was in rare attendance—the film received a standing ovation. Goebbels considered it "very good within limits."

Less than four months after Hitler came to power, *Morgenrot* was in U.S. theatres. The film was the antithesis of *All Quiet on the Western Front* (1930). Nazi filmmakers would turn to the subject of the First World War often, sending a message that in a Second World War, *they* would be the victors.

Morgenrot starred one-time Hollywood actor Rudolf Forster (1884–1968) and the established Adele Sandrock (1863–1937) in a tale of desperation and chaos on the seas during the

First World War. U-boat 21 is led by Lt. Commander Liers (Forster), a knight of the Ordre Pour le Mérite (Order of Merit), which was Germany's highest decoration for battlefield valor. (We shall hear much more of "Pour le Mérite" later.)

He's from Meerskirchen, in the North German flatlands. On submarine patrol, Liers is a determined leader, sinking a British cruiser on its way to Russia with provisions for the Czar's army. Liers's submarine eludes the depth charges of three escorting British destroyers. However, a camouflaged sailing ship coming towards the sub turns out to be armed—and British. It strikes, setting his submarine ablaze. Smoke keeps the U-boat crew from spotting a second British destroyer bearing down. The destroyer rams the U-boat.

Ten German crewmembers face a life-and-death situation as their sub starts to go under. They have only eight life vests. Rather than drawing lots for the vests, two Germans put duty first. They shoot themselves, leaving life vests for the others.

Rescued by a steamer, commander and crew return home to a joyous welcome. Despite the pacifist pleas of a grieving mother (Sandrock) who had lost two sons to the war, captain and crew return to the sea to fight again for the fatherland.

The ideas for the film came from up-and-coming scriptwriter Gerhardt Menzel (1894–1966), a Nazi Party member who would script more than 20 films in the next 12 years. He penned Liers's line, "Perhaps we Germans do not know how to live, but how to die, we know incredibly well." This glorification of death was a way of recasting the huge losses that the German navy had suffered in the First World War. Because of its themes, characters, and plot, *Morgenrot* foreshadowed the new German cinema. This first and most infamous Nazi-released film of the year was directed by the Czech-born Gustav Ucicky (1899–1961), photographed by the silent-screen master Carl Hoffmann (1885–1945), and scored by Herbert Windt. Paul Heinreid, who later left Germany for America, was in the cast, along with veteran Jewish actress Rosa Valetti, who in 1933 fled to Vienna, and died in Palestine in 1937.

Holland, Poland, and others countries banned *Morgenrot*. British officials, said the *Chicago Tribune* (February 11, 1933), objected to its depiction of the Royal Navy as "un-chivalrous and treacherous." However, *New York Times* critic Mordaunt, writing from Berlin on March 19, 1933, had liked *Morgenrot's* "tragic glamour," which wasn't far from the Nazi ideal. *Variety* (May 28, 1933) wrote, "Considerable interest revolves around this film because it was the last big picture made by Ufa before the Hitler thing broke.... It might have been the better part of wisdom for the distributor [Leo Brecher] to shelve it for six months or so, when it could go out and get what it deserves." It got that. The National Board of Review (December 29, 1933) called it one of the year's "best foreign films."

(One German film that *was* shelved in 1933 was Fritz Lang's *Testament of Dr. Mabuse*, released in 1933. Suppressed within Germany—the Nazis believed its director was Jewish—it wasn't released commercially in America until after World War II.)

Early in the year, Goebbels outlined Germany's filmmaking viewpoint. "German films can become a force in the world," he said. "The more closely a film reflects national contours, the greater are its chances of conquering the world.... Art is only possible if it has its roots firmly embedded in National Socialist soil. I must strongly warn films against taking as low a view of the German people as the other branches of the arts unfortunately did before the advent of films.... We have no intention of allowing those ideas that are being destroyed lock, stock, and barrel in the new Germany to reappear in films, whether in camouflaged or open form.... In any case, public taste is not as it is conceived in the mind of a Jewish director."

Goebbels had specific productions in mind. One had come from Jewish director Lewis Milestone and the Jewish-owned studio Universal. The film was *Im Westen nichts Neüs* (*All Quiet on the Western Front*) which had opened in Berlin's Mozart Theatre in December, 1930. The theatre's Jewish manager Hanns Brodnitz had been the first one to show American sound films in Berlin.

A success in the United States, the film had outraged the Nazis. Adapted from Erich Maria Remarque's novel, *All Quiet on the Western Front* follows a group of German schoolboys whose pro-war teacher convinces them to enlist in the German army at the start of World War I. The Weimar film highlights the futility of war. As the boys witness death and mutilation, their preconceptions about the enemy and the rights and wrongs of the conflict evaporate. They are left angry and bewildered. In a key scene, one of the young Germans wounds a French soldier and then cries trying to save his life while trapped in a foxhole. The French soldier dies.

The Nazis decried the film's depiction of sensitive, emotional young Germans afraid of war. After Nazi-led riots, the so-called conscientious civil servant-lawyer Ernst Seeger (who later worked for Goebbels) banned the film on the grounds that it was a "threat to German esteem." Further, he declared, "it would not be reconcilable with the dignity of a people if they would allow a performance of their own defeat, filmed by a foreign producer."

German leftists, however, also rejected the film, the reason being its "surface reality of the imperialistic war." However, Otto Braun, the prime minister of Prussia, was "deeply affected and totally impressed," he said, "convinced that I have seen nothing which a German who loves his native land and who wants to defend and to augment its reputation in the world has to refute." It remained suppressed in the last years of the Weimar Republic and, of course, under Hitler.

A second Weimar-era film that had angered Goebbels and the Nazis was Victor Trivas's *Niemandsland* (*No Man's Land*, 1931). Produced in English, French, German, and Yiddish, and released in America in April 1933, the war film stresses universal humanity through stories of ordinary men who meet under fire. A German, a Frenchman, an Englishman, a black American, and a Russian Jew are in a ditch, a dead man's zone, between the fronts during the First World War.

Trivas's film is not a realistic rendition of battle. Rather, symbolic scenes convey the idea that humans can understand each other despite differences, and that borders and barriers have to vanish. Dialogue is minimal; Hanns Eisler's music is emotional.

Near the end, each character speaks and the others comprehend. In the culminating scenes, the soldiers leave the foxhole and march on the battlefield, beating down barbed wire. Together, they head "to peace, to a new life."

Niemandsland reflected Leonhard Frank's 1918 novel *Der Mensch ist gut*/*Man Is Good*. Frank, who was Weimar's best-known novelist, collaborated with Trivas on the script—with a bit of cinematic influence from G.W. Pabst.

Their sympathetic portrayal of the injured Jewish soldier (Vladimir Sokoloff), the German fighter (Ernst Busch) who helps him, and the cosmopolitan and resourceful black American (Louis Douglas) infuriated the Nazis. Busch was later forced to leave Germany.

When the film premiered at Berlin's Mozartsaal, the "reactionaries," wrote the *New York Times* (January 1932), were "looming threateningly in the background." The Resco Film Company, its producer, "has done something very closely verging on the heroic," wrote American critic C. Hooper Trask from Germany. "The judges who award the Nobel Prize for peace could do worse than consider the parents of this film for their next award."

Instantly, Jewish-born Trivas was in the news. When Hitler came to power, Trivas left Germany. Ufa and its right-wing industrial backer Alfred Hugenberg, an early supporter of Hitler and head of the German Nationalist Party, were among those who castigated anti-war films from the likes of Trivas. They favored such pro-war films as *Das Flötenkonzert von Sanssouci* (*The Flute Concert at Sanssouci*, 1930), directed by the then up-and-coming Austrian Gustav Ucicky. A glorification of the march to battle and bloodshed of an earlier era, it hinted at things to come. Diminutive and idiosyncratic Frederick the Great (Otto Gebühr) leads Prussia into the Seven Years' War against Germany's archenemies: France, Russia, and Austria.

During the Hitler era, Ucicky's film was released in America, Germany's largest foreign market. (After World War II, Germany banned *Das Flötenkonzert von Sanssouci*). Releasing Weimar-era films abroad was a financial boost to Hitler's regime. German studios began dumping films made by Jews and starring Jews, to maximize receipts. Productions from the old era that were shown in America in 1933 included Joe May's *Ihre Majestät die Liebe* (*Her Majesty Love*, 1930). Critics called it the best German sound film after *The Blue Angel*, starring Franz Lederer, Szöke Szakall, Otto Wallburg, Kurt Gerron—all Jews—alongside the "Aryan" actress Käthe von Nagy.

Another of May's films was a mystery-comedy of marital infidelity set at a masquerade ball, shown under the titillating title *Eine Liebesnacht* (*A Night of Love*). The film was actually ...*Und das is die Hauptsache* (...*and That's the Main Thing*, 1931), with Otto Wallburg, Julius Falkenstein, and the one-time matinee idol Harry Liedke, a former favorite of Ernst Lubitsch's. In the tale there's a handsome young swindler—*Hochstapler*—posing as a prince.

Two of the biggest Weimar hits had been Géza von Bolváry's musical *Zwei Herzen im dreiviertel Takt* (*Two Hearts in Three-Quarter Time*, 1930)—re-released in the U.S. as late as spring 1939—and *Ich will nicht wissen wer Du bist* (*I Do Not Want to Know Who You Are*, 1932), starring the ubiquitous Hungarian Jew Szöke Szakall, with music by Bolváry's collaborator, Robert Stolz.

Carl Lamac's musical comedy *Eine Nacht im Paradies* (1931/32), a Cinderella tale, had been a Weimar hit. Photographed by Czech-born Otto Heller and starring the popular Anny Ondra as well as Oscar Sabo, it showed up in New York in early 1933.

Jewish actor Fritz Kortner had directed his earliest films in Weimar Germany. His tale *Der Brave Sünder* (*The Upright Sinner*, 1931), which Alfred Polgar scripted, screened in New York's Europa Theatre in early 1933. Built around the misadventures of a bank official in a small German town, it starred Vienna-born Jew Max Pallenberg, one of Germany's foremost stage comedians, in his only German sound film as "Leopold Pichler." Entrusted with taking 8,000 shillings to Vienna, Pichler spends a bit of the money. When he goes back home to admit his guilt, he discovers that his bank director, "Max von Härtl" (Ekkehard Arendt), had run off with a whole lot more cash. The amount Pichler took wasn't even missed. Better yet, Pichler then got his boss's job.

Plots about bankers, money, theft, and Jews would become standard in Nazi productions. Kortner's *So ein Mädel vergisst man nicht* (*A Girl You Don't Forget*, 1932), a Projectograph production, starred the Jewish actress Dolly Haas opposite Willi Forst. Haas had to flee Germany; Forst was free to stay. Destined to make his mark in German film, Willi Forst (1903–1980), born Wilhelm Anton Frohs in Vienna, was an actor first. In Géza von Bolváry's comedy *Der Liebling von Wien* (*The Darling of Vienna*), which was released in the States in early 1933, Forst played a professional toastmaster and stand-in for officials and VIPs too busy to attend all the affairs to which they were invited. On one such occasion he "dubs" a stutterer (Paul Hörbiger) from behind a curtain.

American critics failed to reveal that Bolváry's film had been produced in Weimar Germany in 1930 as *Der Herr auf bestellung* (*The Gentleman for Hire*), noting only that identifying it as strictly German would likely hamper its appeal.

Dolly Haas was in Nazi-to-be Hans Steinhoff's romantic story of a Berlin waif, called *Ein Mädel der Strasse* (*A Girl of the Street*, 1932), who finds love and a better life with the bank director Maximilian (Carl Ludwig Diehl). The film, which screened at New York's Tobis Theatre in spring 1933, was based on Billy Wilder and Max Kolpe's story.

Fred Sauer's comedy *Der Tanzhusar* (1930/31) starred Jewish actor Oscar Karlweis as a prewar opera singer obliged to serve six weeks' military service alongside the funny and adroit Jewish actor Ernö Verebes. The film stressed the idea of compulsory service to the nation, a theme that would dominate numerous Nazi films.

The film career of Austrian-born Conrad Wiene—his brother Robert was the famous director of *The Cabinet of Dr. Caligari* (1919)—came to a close in the last years of Weimar Germany. Conrad Wiene directed *Madame Blaubart* (*Madame Bluebeard*, 1930/31), starring future Nazi golden girl Lil Dagover, which ran in New York in summer 1933; *Wiener Blut* (*Viennese Blood*, 1931), a Strauss extravaganza with Michael Bohnen, Gretl Thiemer, and Lee Parry that was filmed in French as *Sang Viennois* with Gustav Fröhlich and Maria Paudler; and *Walzer vom Strauss* (*A Waltz by Strauss*, 1931), starring Fröhlich and Paudler, which was a huge hit when shown in New York.

Under Nazi filmmakers, the Strauss family came to represent idealized Germans: the perfect family of tradition and unity.

Conrad Wiene died in 1934; Robert died in Paris four years later.

A colleague of the Wiene brothers, Vienna-born Richard Oswald, one of Germany's great directors and a Jew, had several late Weimar successes that were released in America, including *Viktoria und Ihr Husar, Der Hauptmann von Köpenick,* and *Ein Lied geht um die Welt* (*My Song Goes Round the World*), the latter of which featured the hugely popular tenor Joseph Schmidt in his screen debut. Schmidt's film was shown in the U.S. in late 1936, the year when the Nazis were apparently on their best behavior. American radio networks thought of hiring Schmidt before Hitler came to power. Afterwards, *Variety* (June 6, 1933) from Berlin called his first film "good b.o. [box office] in spite of the fact" that Schmidt "is a Jew."

Fleeing the Nazis after the start of the war, Schmidt found refuge in Vichy France. In 1942 he entered Switzerland illegally and was interned in a labor camp where he died of heart failure at age 38. His complaints of chest pains had been ignored. "They take me for a malingerer," he said. An hour before his death he was said to be singing.

Jewish director Max Reichmann's *Das Lockende Ziel* (*The Enticing Goal*, 1930), which was produced by Bavaria, starred Weimar's "favorite tenor" and one of the "best voices of his generation," Richard Tauber. The Jewish-born tenor played a country choirboy discovered by a smart Berlin manager and turned into an opera singer of the first rank. "Tauber's voice and singing flatter the film," wrote *Variety* (June 17, 1933) when it ran at New York's Vanderbilt Theatre.

The Emelka studio produced Reichmann's last films, and they featured Tauber. In the comedy *Die Grosse Attraktion* (1931), shown in the U.S. in July 1933, Tauber played Ricardo, the head of a variety troupe, who is being pursued by determined American dancer Kitty (Marianne Winkelstern). The music was by Bruno Kaper and M. Brodsky, after Franz Lehar. Siegfried Arno was in the troupe, playing the dancer Felipe. By the time of the film's release in America, in mid–1933, Arno was in Portugal. In 1937, Arno directed a film in Belgium and then sailed to safety in America. He moved to Hollywood.

Max Reichmann's *Ich glaub' nie mehr an eine Frau* (*I'll Never Believe in Women Again*, 1929/1930), co-scripted by Walter Reisch, came to America three years after its completion. Its theme of a German returning home struck the right chord with the Nazi regime.

After a dozen years at sea, a sailor (Werner Fütterer) falls for a music hall performer (Maria Solveg). He tries to help her resolve her marital problems. Then he makes the startling discovery that she is his sister. She ends up happily but he heads back to sea emotionally distraught. Tauber, singing five numbers, played an older and wiser navy man, and up-and-coming actor named Gustav Gründgens had a small role as the villain. The music was by Paul Dessau.

Coincidently, a few weeks after that film's release in New York, Synchro Art Pictures released *La Voce del Sangue* (*Voice of the Blood*) in the city's newly renamed Caruso Theatre. Dubbed into Italian, the film was credited not to Max Reichmann, its actual director, but to Gustav Ucicky. The *New York Times* (April 17, 1933) surmised that perhaps, "due to the shortage of Italian-made talking pictures in the New York market," distributors were forced to seek musicals from Germany!

Georg Asagaroff (born Georij Azagarov in Moscow) made his last film in Germany in 1932, a comedy called *Der Tolle Bomberg* (*The Mad Bomberg*), about a nobleman forced by relatives to marry against his will, who then falls in love with his new wife. This was one of the first films that a new distributor, called Casino Film Exchange (CFE) based in New York, distributed in the U.S.

This was the start of something big for Casino Film Exchange.

In the period 1933–1942, CFE released scores of German and Austrian films. Its numerical impact in the U.S. was second only to that of Ufa. CFE, like Ufa, fed America a terrible lies: the illusion that within German cinema little had changed and that there was no connection between German politics and its film entertainment.

In late 1934, CFE opened up its own theatre, the Casino Theatre, on East 86th Street, in the pro–German Yorkville section New York. This area, extending from 79th Street to 96th Street, between Third Avenue and the East River, had a German population of nearly 75,000. Visiting Germans described Yorkville as a miniature Munich. Its beer halls, which never closed during Prohibition, were Bavarian.

America in the 1930s was home to millions of citizens of German descent. The market for German films in New York and other cities was extensive. In addition to the Casino Theatre, New York outlets for German-language films included the 1,100-seat Ufa Cosmopolitan, the Criterion, the Europa Theatre, the Fifth Avenue Playhouse, the 55th Street Theatre, the 72nd Street Playhouse, the 78th Street Tobis Kino, the 79th Street Theater (also known as the Yorkville Theatre), the Little Carnegie Playhouse, the 86th Street Garden, the 96th Street Theatre, Das Deutsche Sprechtfilm Theatre, the Rivoli, the Roxy, and the Hindenburg.

Renamed the Caruso Theatre after Hitler came to power, the Hindenburg Theatre screened comedies such as Franz Seitz's *Der Schützen König* (*The Champion Shot*, 1932), starring the plump Bavarian Weiss Ferdl and Polish-born Max Adalbert as rivals in business and on the rifle range. "The Nazi regime," wrote the *New York Times* (May 3, 1933), "may have wiped out officially the differences among the various States of the Reich, but the age-long aversion of true Bavarians for the Prussians will probably continue to furnish German film producers with material for fun-making for a long time to come."

Germany's "fun-making" films also screened in Manhattan's Bijou Theatre. Other outlets for German films were the Wagner and Mozart theatres in Brooklyn.

The Casino Theatre showed new films produced in Prague, Vienna, Budapest, Bavaria, and elsewhere German was spoken, in addition to revivals. The 86th Street Garden Theater often screened the bigger hits from Germany. The Casino and the Garden had staying power. They showed German-language films until the U.S. entered the war. Even after Pearl Harbor, when U.S. authorities seized all Axis films in circulation or storage in America, the owners of the Casino Theatre requested permission to screen German-language films.

According to officials of the Theatre Owners Board of Trade, Germany was eager to export its films to America because they cost little to exhibit and made money. One enthusiastic supporter of German imports was Louis Geller, owner of the 86th Street Garden Theatre. Another well-known purchaser of German films was the owner of the German outlet down the street, the 79th Street Theater.

The 79th Street Theater showed second runs on double bills. The Roxy showed English-language renditions like Ufa's *Bomben auf Monte Carlo/Monte Carlo Madness*, by Hanns

Schwarz). The Criterion showed *Mädchen in Uniform* (1931) in late 1932. The Little Carnegie screened Gustav Ucicky's *Mensch ohne Namen* (*Man without a Name*, 1932), which was Balzac's *Colonel Chabert* transposed to the early twentieth century (the film's protagonist is named Heinrich Martin) and *Yorck* (1931), both starring Werner Krauss. The Europa screened Pabst's *Kameradschaft* (1931) in late 1932.

In April 1933, after the "Jewish War Veterans' Protest March against Nazi Germany," New York's Europa Theatre faced a surprise: an anti–Nazi boycott. Having shown too many German films—the final straw was, ironically, Richard Oswald's operetta *Viktoria und ihr Husar* (1931)—the theatre's management made amends. It screened—on Hitler's birthday, April 20—a pro–Soviet film called *The Return of Nathan Becker*, starring famed Jewish performer Solomon Mikhoels. He played the father of a bricklayer (David Gutman) who returns to his native Russian village after a quarter century in America, eager to put himself and his skilled hands at the service of Stalin.

The directors, wrote the *New York Times* (April 15, 1933), "have presented many highly entertaining incidents of Jewish life in Russia." Especially noteworthy, wrote the paper, was the "humming and singing of Jewish folk songs."

Elsewhere in America, the largest cities with the most diverse populations hosted German-language films. By peddling films made by Jewish directors and starring Jewish or anti–Nazi entertainers, the distributors contributed to the illusion of normality in Germany. But they unloaded the late Weimar and early 1933 films as fast as possible, perhaps sensing an uncertain future.

North Bergen, N.J., was home to the Transfer Theatre. Chicago, with its powerful German-American voting bloc, hosted two German-language theatres—the Sonotone and the World Playhouse. Buffalo, Cleveland, Milwaukee, Los Angeles (The Continental Theatre), San Francisco, Seattle, St. Paul, Detroit, Baltimore, St. Louis, Philadelphia, Harrisburg, and Cincinnati had theatres devoted to German-language films. They were all going full tilt until September 1939, after which theatres in St. Louis, Philadelphia, and Cincinnati stopped screening German and Austrian films.

The Austrian duo of the Jewish-born Jacob Fleck and his non–Jewish wife, Luise Fleck, directed several Austrian-German comedies, including *Ein Auto und kein Geld* (*An Auto and No Money*, 1931) and *Unser Kaiser* (*Our King*, 1933), which were later released in the U.S.

Leftist filmmaker Slatan Dudow's *Kühle Wampe* (1931), as well as his *Seifenblasen* (*Soap Bubbles*, 1933/34), a short down-and-out skit, were shown in the U.S., the latter in November 1937. Phil Jutzi's *Berlin-Alexanderplatz*, which had been suppressed in Nazi Germany, made a profit in the U.S. for the German producer, while Hans Behrendt's *Ich geh' aus und Du bleibst du* (*I Go Out and You Stay Here*, 1931) and *Grün ist die Heide* (*The Heath Is Green*, 1932) starred Nazi favorite Camilla Horn.

Of the two films by Behrendt, the latter film, which reached the States in 1935, was a Berlin hit produced by Robert Neppach and scored by Grete Walter, daughter of conductor Bruno Walter. The story centers upon a romance between a handsome young forest ranger and his lady friend. After spending years trying to track down a poacher, the hero is taken aback to discover that the man he's looking for is his girlfriend's father. Rather than run off, the poacher elects to make amends. After the old man is wounded in a fight against other poachers, his daughter persuades him to move to the city.

Under Nazi filmmakers, poachers became prime, easy-to-hate symbols of immorality and evil. They were of little consequence. Anything could be said about them; no one, of course, would defend their right to be poachers, especially if they were Jews.

In early 1933, Jewish director Robert Siodmak directed a final film in prewar Germany. Deutsche Universal was the distributor. Based on a story by the Jewish writer Stephan Zweig,

Brennende Geheimnis (*The Burning Secret*) was filmed as a silent in the Weimar Republic, then remade in sound by Siodmak and released in Berlin on March 29, two months after Hitler was named chancellor. Siodmak's film, photographed by Richard Angst, is a psychological investigation of infidelity.

A mother (Hilde Wagener) and son are on a trip. Along the way the woman welcomes the advances of a man who has struck up a friendship with her son. But the boy soon becomes uneasy, and then realizes that the man has used him to get to his mother. Shocked that his mother could be unfaithful, he runs home to his father (Willi Forst). His mother quickly follows. At home, the father is kept in the dark about the "burning secret" that wife and son share.

A month after the film's premiere in Berlin—at which no credits appeared for director, composer, lyricist, and original author—Siodmak faced trouble: the Nazis zeroed in on him. In a piece in the party's organ *Volkischer Beobachter*, Goebbels labeled Siodmak a "corrupter of the German family." When Siodmak's film was yanked from theaters as *fremdstämming*—of alien origin—Siodmak and his brother bolted Germany. They resurfaced in Paris and then fled to Hollywood.

Siodmak's 1932 film *Quick,* with music by the German-Jewish expatriate Werner Richard Heymann, screened in the U.S. in December 1933. It teamed performers Lilian Harvey and Hans Albers in a farce filled with mistaken identities and lover's quarrels. Harvey played Eva, a young woman visiting a health spa and spending her evenings in the town's vaudeville theatre. Eva attracts the amorous attention of a heavily made-up clown called Quick. The clown, having failed to win her heart as Quick, tries to woo her by masquerading as the theatre's manager. She's conflicted until she learns her admirers are one and the same.

While the stars apparently lacked the chemistry Ufa attained in the Harvey/Fritsch films—Harvey comes across as domineering, Albers as insecure—the tension between them worked to advantage in Siodmak's film.

Jewish director Hermann Kosterlitz's film *Der Storch hat uns Getraut* (*Married by the Stork*), which reached New York's Yorkville Theatre, had merely been retitled. In Germany it had been called *Das Abenteurer der Thea Roland* (*The Adventure of Thea Roland*, 1932), and was about a modern sculptor (Lil Dagover) seeking a healthy model for a statue she's sculpting to be placed in front of a Berlin hospital. She finds it in the form of a London policeman-boxer (Hans Rehmann) visiting the capital. She's also interested in having a

Top: Director Robert Siodmak in the 1940s. *Above:* Lilian Harvey, 1932.

German-Jewish emigrés included (from left) Henry Koster and his wife Kato Kiraly, Ernst Lubitsch and wife Vivian Gaye, and producer Joe Pasternak.

baby, but can do without a husband. "The curious part about the film," said *Variety* (December 6, 1933), "is that it might be farce, straight comedy or romantic drama—one is never sure."

Many Weimar-era films were similarly re-titled for American release. In 1933, Herman Kosterlitz (Henry Koster in Hollywood) directed a final film in Germany, *The Ugly Girls*. It showed up in the States in 1936 as *Die Privatsekretärin Heiratet* (*The Private Secretary Gets Married*), starring Dolly Haas, a ballet-trained actress who began her film career with Deutsche Universal in 1930.

The film co-starred the Danish-German comedian Max Hansen, and the Jewish actors Julius Falkenstein and Otto Wallburg. The Nazi actor Hasso Preis entered film lore when the Nazis, rather than credit a Jew, listed Preis as "director" of *Das Hässliche Mädchen*.

The cinematic flood to America from Jewish filmmakers who became anonymous in Nazi Germany included Friedrich Zelnik's comedy *Spione im Savoy-Hotel* (1932), with Alfred Abel and the Comedian Harmonists, also known as *Die Galavorstellung* (*The Gala Performance*); Reinhold Schünzel's *Wie sag' ich's Meinen Mann?* (*How Shall I Tell My Husband?*, 1932) an Ufa comedy starring Renate Müller; and *Saison in Kairo*, from a story by Walter Reisch and libretto by Robert Winterfeld (later Robert Gilbert), starring Müller and the anti–Nazi actor Leopoldine Konstantin.

The latter production was completed just after Hitler came to power. It was praised for its shots of the pyramids, a camel race, a native wedding procession, Arab dances, and depictions the grand foreign hotels, justifying the "belief that they were made right there in Egypt. If not," wrote the *New York Times* (December 25, 1933), "they constitute a triumph for the

Left: Actress Dolly Haas. *Right:* Actress Leopoldine Konstantin in Hollywood.

German Hollywood in Neubabelsburg." Jewish composer Werner Richard Heymann's music, wrote the *New York Times*, "adds materially to the entertainment." *Saison in Kairo* had a French version called *Idylle au Cairo*, co-directed by Claude Heymann and co-produced by Ufa's French affiliate, L' Alliance Cinématographique Européenne (A.C.E.)

German filmmakers would soon lead the world's filmmakers in the use of music as manipulation and co-productions as a means to hide their films' origins.

Other films from the late Weimar years that reached the U.S. in Hitler's first year included Paul Czinner's French-German tragedy of doomed love, *Der Träumende Mund* (*Dream World*, 1932), with Elisabeth Bergner; E.A. Dupont's first German-language sound film called *Trapeze* (1932), with Anna Sten; Rudolf Walther-Fein's last films, *Korvettenkapitän* (1930), about a heroic navy man (Harry Liedke), and *Das Schicksal der Renate Langen* (*The Fate of Renate Langen*, 1931), with Mady Christians and Franz Lederer in *his* last German film; and Richard Oswald's drama *Alraune* (1930), with the anti–Nazi actor Albert Bassermann.

Bassermann's last film from Germany was Ufa's *Ein Gewisser Herr Gran* (*A Certain Mr. Grant*, 1933), a message-filled drama about espionage, which was directed by Gerhard Lamprecht (1897–1974), who served Nazi filmmaking handily. The film screened in New York in winter 1933–34. The evildoer's name is what gives the film away. Its opening depicts a big touring car, driven by an Italian engineer, climbing an alpine road. Suddenly a shot rings out. The car skids, leaps over the side, rolls down a cliff, overturns, and bursts into flames. A man appears. The smoking gun is still his hand. He runs to the wreck from which he snatches a suitcase. Another car suddenly appears. Its driver, who is beautiful, picks up the gunman.

The gunman is wily, older, rich, and sinister. He deals in antiquities, but he also deals in other not-so-harmless merchandise, including stolen drawings of secret weapons. The man's name is "Tschernikoff" (Bassermann). But Tschernikoff will meet his match against—and find his fate is sealed by—the dynamic personality going by the name of "Mr. Grant," actually daredevil Capt. Bergall (Hans Albers), of the German Secret Service. The tale, set in luxurious Venice, with its fancy hotels, outsize yachts, ancient strongholds, fast cars, and soaring planes, was one of the first Nazi fictional films to depict a Jew this way.

The Russian-German actress Olga Tschechowa—she may have been a Soviet spy in real life—played the fast-driving British spy named Mrs. Mervin. Longtime supporting actor Fritz Odemar (1890–1955) appeared as a gentlemanly detective. In the French version, co-directed by Roger Le Bon and produced by A.C.E., Roger Karl (1882–1984) played Tschernikoff.

Bassermann left Germany for Hollywood because, wrote the *New York Times* (February 24, 1934), "the Nazi rules of art refused to allow his non–Aryan wife to appear on the stage with him." The paper couldn't bring itself to say "Jewish." An actor for 40 years, Bassermann died on a plane in 1952 en route from New York to Switzerland.

One of Lamprecht's earliest films had gained more than an ordinary amount of attention in early 1933. New York censors had banned his *Was wissen den Männer* (*What Men Know*, 1932), an Ufa production that distributor Leo Brecher attempted to release under the title *Herthas Erwachen* (*Hertha's Awakening*).

Brecher protested the ban through ads in New York newspapers and through word of mouth. He argued that Hollywood had filmed similar tales. He gave press screenings and free showings to groups that were apt to find the film objectionable: the clergy and social workers. He even shut down the Little Carnegie Theatre, where the film was slated to run, and went to Albany to appeal his case. Public and newspaper support led to the film's release and a rush of business.

So, what was the fuss about? The trouble had nothing to do with Nazism. Rather, the story about illegitimacy had caused a backlash in the U.S. In this Weimar-era film, Karl Christians (Hans Brausewetter), a representative of a confectionary firm, becomes acquainted with the daughter of a country bookseller, Hertha Barthel (Toni van Eyck). They fall in love and promise to remain faithful. As soon as he gets a raise, he says, they will marry. When fate intervenes and he's fired, he tells Hertha nothing, leaves town in shame, and accepts a job as a driving instructor in Berlin. He's unaware of her anguish. Her letters come back unopened and people begin to gossip. When her father discovers she's pregnant, he banishes her. Finding refuge with a sympathetic old friend of his, she gives birth. When Karl finally finds out what has happened, he heads back to Hertha. She's overjoyed and forgives him.

Nazi filmmakers produced numerous films about the subject of illegitimacy, about which they would always make a show of support.

Another of Lamprecht's German films later faced censure in Germany. His late Weimar drama *Spione am Werk* (*Spies at Work*, 1932/1933), which was based on a story by Max W. Kimmich, is a World War I tale in which Austrian officer Michael von Hombergk (Carl Ludwig Diehl) is suspected of being an Italian spy. To clear his name, he volunteers for a dangerous mission. Parachuting into Italy, which at the time was Austria's enemy, he encounters a real spy, Marchesa Marcella Galdi (Brigitte Helm), with whom he falls in love.

The film "is having a long and successful run at the Gloriapalast," reported *Variety* (April 29, 1933) from Berlin, because "it fits in nicely with the present trend of public opinion ... and should appeal to American audiences, except those fed up with war atmosphere and spy stories." That assessment killed its chances in America.

In late 1935, the Nazis shelved the film because of embarrassing Jewish involvement in the production: prominent cast member Oskar Homolka and the film's producers, Arnold Pressburger and Gregor Rabinovitch.

Spione am Werk was one of Julius Falkenstein's last films. A prolific actor since 1914, he preferred to play good tragic-comical roles under good directors—roles where the audience had to laugh and to cry at the same time. He died in Berlin in 1933, at 54.

Ufa's Gloria-Palast Theatre, Berlin.

Franz Wenzler was the director of Ufa's comedy *Wenn die Liebe mode Macht* (*When Love Sets the Fashion*, 1932), scripted by Fritz Zeckendorff, which was shown in the U.S. in fall 1933. Here a seamstress (Renate Müller) becomes a rich dressmaker. At the Paris "International Style Conference" she convinces attendees (Max Ehrlich played one of them) to buy into a peculiar fashion idea, thus saving the day for a particular investor (Otto Wallburg).

Jewish actors Ehrlich and Wallburg would soon become but faint memories in German films.

Coincidentally, the first of what came to be called the "anti–Hitler pictures" from America opened at New York's Cameo Theatre in October 1933.

George Roland's *Der Vanderer Yid* (*The Wandering Jew*, 1933), a JAFA production in Yiddish starring Jacob Ben-Ami, Ben Adler, Abraham Teitelbaum, Natalie Browning, and M.B. Samuylow, incorporated documentary footage of Nazi outrages against Jews in the story of a fictitious director of the Berlin Art Academy and his painting "The Wandering Jew." Fired from his post, the Jewish professor loses his friends and sweetheart when the Nazis physically attack him. Then the painting comes alive. It recounts the persecution of Jews throughout history, but prophesies a better ending in contemporary times because of anti–Nazi protests worldwide.

Jewish director Max Ophüls's Weimar–era *Lachende Erben* (*Laughing Heirs*, 1932), which was produced by Ufa, presented wine, women, and song to a troubled Germany. Protagonist Peter Franck (Heinz Rühmann) has to stay sober if wants to inherit the fortune of deceased champagne manufacturer Bockelmann. However, Bockelmann's greedy relatives set Peter up with Gina (Lien Deyers), the daughter of business rival Stumm. Under the stress of trying to convince Gina of his feelings for her, Peter starts drinking again. Despite this, Peter manages to keep his inheritance, thanks to a hidden clause in Bockelmann's will.

Arnold Pressburger and Fritz Lang, director of *Hangmen also Die,* were also German exiles.

In Europe, Szöke Szakall, a Jewish actor from Hungary, was often one step ahead of the Nazis, although you wouldn't have known it from the late Weimar films in which he starred and which were released in the U.S. after Hitler came to power. He was in Carl Boese's *Eine Frau wie du* (*A Woman Like You*, 1933), playing a parvenu razor-blade maker seeking the hand of Liane Haid; and in E.W. Emo's comedy *Der Unbekannte Gast* (*The Unknown Guest*, 1931), which was produced by the Jewish-born Max Glass and designed by Erno Metzner and shown in the States in 1935.

Szakall was also in Friedrich Zelnik's Vienna–based musical comedies *Walzerparadies* (*Waltz Paradise*, 1930/31), opposite Gretl Theomer and Charlotte Susa, and in Zelnik's *Kaiserwalzer* (*Emperor's Waltz*, 1933). In the latter film, an aristocrat and his son (Willi Eichberger) fall for the same young woman (Martha Eggerth). That production included three performers who would serve Nazi films for 12 years: Paul Hörbiger, Fritz Kampers, and Otto Gebühr. Moviegoers, wrote the *New York Times* (December 29, 1934) about *Kaiserwalzer*, are "sure to enjoy the lovely views of life in the 'good old days'" of Emperor Franz Josef, and the catchy music.

Zelnik began his career in film as an actor in 1910. His visit to Hollywood in the early 1930s helped him make the transition to sound. He and his wife fled Germany in 1933 and settled in London.

Kurt Siodmak, who left Germany in 1933, was the scriptwriter of E.W. Emo's pre–Hitler *Marion, das gehört sich nicht* (*Marion, That's Not Nice*, 1932/33) produced by Itala Film, which was based on Charles Röllinghoff and Jacobi's play. The music was by Otto Stransky. Magda Schneider played the subject of the scandalous painting "Susanne and the Elders" by a member (Hermann Thimig) of the Academy of Arts. Also in the film were Julius Falkenstein and Otto Wallburg (born Otto Maximilian Wasserzug). Wallburg, known in Germany as the "celluloid cherub," after fleeing to apparent safety in the Netherlands, was murdered at the age of 55 in Auschwitz, in 1944.

Supporting actor Erich Fiedler (1901–1981) appeared in this and scores of German films during the Nazi years and afterwards.

Der Sohn der weissen Berge (*Son of the White Mountain*) was a Weimar production that was released in the States in late October 1933. An Alpine adventure-romance directed by Mario Bonnard and Luis Trenker, it starred Trenker, Renate Müller, and Maria Solveg (who made no other film in Nazi Germany). The production company was Itala Film, whose chief producer was Alberto Giacalone (1891–?). From 1930 to 1941, Itala Film, headquartered in Berlin, came out with 30 films, many of which were screened in the States as "Italian" films.

Weimar productions also had their uses *after* Hitler came to power. They could be re-edited to conform to the new reality within Germany. One such example was Rolf Randolf's *Tod über Schanghai* (*Death Over Shanghai*, 1932), which was shown in Germany four weeks before Hitler's rise to power. At that time, it was merely a drama about the American secret agent Baxter (Peter Voss) who is sent to Shanghai to free a captive American official, John Harris (Max Ralf-Ostermann) To do that, Baxter must outwit the shady international businessman James Biggers (Theodor Loos) on land, water, and in the air. Baxter succeeds, and falls in love with Harris's daughter, Maud (Else Elster).

When the film was released in the States, at New York's 79th Street Theater in late 1933, the film had been refashioned to become pro–Japanese. German produces had inserted documentary footage of the Japanese capture of the Chinese city.

In January 1932, Japanese naval infantry units had attacked Chinese-controlled areas of Shanghai to "protect" Japanese industrial property and the Japanese living in that part of Shanghai. The local Chinese garrison troops, called the Cantonese 19th Route Army, had to defend the populace. Over the next six weeks, however, the Japanese advanced. By the time a ceasefire was agreed upon, the Japanese had pushed the Chinese forces to a defensive position to the north and west of the city.

In 1941, the Nazis distributed in the States another pro–Japanese drama. *Port Arthur* (1936) concerned the Japanese defeat of Russia in 1904.

Yet another German military tale opened up in New York at the Yorkville Theatre in late

Peter Lorre and wife Celia Lovsky attending premier of *The Life of Emile Zola* (1937).

December 1933. George Jacoby's *Kadetten* (*Cadets*, 1931)—not to be confused with Karl Ritter's later film of the same title—was about a Prussian cadet (Franz Fiedler, 1902–1965) reluctantly serving in a military academy. His father (Albert Bassermann) is a general and his stepmother (Trude von Molo) is young and all too attractive. The sensitive, music-loving cadet warns a fellow officer (Johannes Riemann) about forcing his attentions on the Frau General—and winds up charged with his murder.

At the end of 1933, one of the first U.S.-German productions opened at New York's Seventh Avenue Roxy. It was the Fox-Gaumont-British-Ufa English-language drama *F. P. 1* (1932), based on a story by Walter Reisch and Kurt Siodmak. *Floating Platform No. 1* was about the fantastic super-construction of a 1,500-by-400-foot landing strip (basically an aircraft carrier) in the mid–Atlantic.

In the drama, commercial interests favor the development of a sea-based landing strip and hotel while others, particularly steamship companies, oppose the scheme. Intrigue, sabotage by the chief engineer "Lubin" (George Merritt), disaster, and supernatural events—favorite Nazi themes—follow the construction of this engineering marvel. The plot, rather than the human element, carried the tale, which was a smash hit in the U.S. Directed by Karl Hartl, it starred a dashing Conrad Veidt, Leslie Fenton, and Jill Esmond. The German-language version, called *F. P. 1 antewortet nicht* (*F. P. 1 Doesn't Answer*), didn't screen in the States. It had starred Hans Albers (1891–1960) as the pilot, Peter Lorre as his sidekick, Hermann Speelmans as the Jewish-named saboteur "Damsky," and Sybille Schmitz (1909–55), who had been discovered by Jewish producer Erich Pommer.

An anti-American film from Goebbels' ministry, Max Obal's war comedy *Zwei gute Kameraden* (*Two Good Comrades*, 1933), photographed by Guido Seeber, screened in the U.S. as the year was coming to its end. It's set in a German-occupied French village near the western front in the latter stages of the First World War. Two German soldiers, Paul Hanke and Fritz Lehmann (Fritz Kampers and Paul Hörbiger) are in love with a French girl, Jeanette (Jessie Vihrog). They become rivals for her affection—until the Americans show up and re-take the village. Duty and a common enemy bring the two German soldiers together. To outfox the Americans, they disguise themselves as American infantrymen, re-enter the village, and convince their new "comrades" that the Germans are about to return in force. The gullible, cowardly American soldiers flee; the two heroic German soldiers renew their friendship. To top it off, each gets a girl.

A subplot involves the financial machinations of a theatrical director named "Emanuel Nagel" (Hans Hermann Schlaufuss) and his wife, Emma (Senta Söneland).

"At last," wrote the *New York Times* (December 4, 1933), "German motion picture producers have turned out a military comedy timed during the World War and not harking back to the 'good old days.'"

But why would the Nazis do that, since it was a new day in Germany and the Nazis loathed the repressive "good old days"? The critic was blind to what the new Germany was all about.

1934
"You Are Jewish, Right?"

The second year of Hitler's rule brought worrisome developments. In January, Marinus van der Lubbe, 24, was guillotined for being a communist. That same month, Germany signed a 10-year non-aggression pact with Poland. In July, SS-Reichsführer Himmler assumed control of German concentration camps. In October, in violation of the Treaty of Versailles, the peace treaty Germany had been forced to sign in 1919 as the price for losing World War I, Germany expanded its army and navy, and created the Luftwaffe.

On screen, the portents of sweeping political and social change became more ominous, too. In 1934 two hardcore Nazi films, *SA-Mann Brand* and *Hitlerjunge Quex*, and a little-remembered Swedish production, *Pettersson & Bendel*, made their screen debuts in the U.S. These imported productions signaled that Jews in Germany faced trouble.

Inside Germany, the movie screens conveyed other troubling messages. One year into Hitler's rule, western film critics overlooked an innocuous 90-minute tale that had the financial backing of Goebbels. The film was called *Das Alte Recht* (*The Old Right*, 1934), featuring Bernhard Goetzke (1887–1964), Fritz Hoopts (1875–1945), and Edith Linn. Scored by Wolfgang Zeller, this peasant love story summed up one of Nazism's central Aryan tenets: "Blut und Boden"—blood and soil.

Produced and directed by Igo Martin Andersen and scripted by Andersen and Armin Petersen (1888–1952), *Das Alte Recht* supported the policy of *Erbhofgesetz*—the hereditary farm law—to decide who could inherit farmland. Eligible farmers had to be able to prove that their ancestors had no Jewish blood as far back as 1800.

The Nazis had put the law into effect September 1933, drawing the idea from the Anti–Semites' Petition of 1880, which had railed against the fact that rural land, "the most significant preservative basis of our [German] political structure," was falling into Jewish hands. Under the 1933 law, only Aryans retained the right to the soil. German peasantry would forever be the "blood source" of German society.

In January 1934, Universal's German subsidiary Deutsche Universal, trying to stay afloat within Germany, distributed *Das Alte Recht* in Oldenburg, where the film takes place and where the Nazis, in 1932, had come to power. The anti–Semitic film screened in Berlin on Hitler's birthday.

Anti–Semitism was also at the core of a more widely viewed film that impressed the Nazis. The film was Svensk Filmindustri's *Pettersson & Bendel* (1933), directed by Per-Axel Branner and distributed in Europe and in the U.S. by Warner Bros. It made its American premiere at New York's 55th Street Theatre in February 1934.

Hitler would refer to *Pettersson & Bendel* when he introduced the sweeping anti–Jewish

Nuremberg Laws in mid–1935. Nazi filmmakers would use it as a model for *Robert und Bertram* (1939), a production that stereotypes Jews.

The Swedish "comedy" begins when the destitute "Josef Bendel" (Semmy Friedmann) sneaks into the Aryan nation of Sweden as a stowaway from eastern Europe. Klezmer music is playing prominently on the soundtrack. On a rainy night in Stockholm the short and dark Bendel meets the tall, handsome, easygoing Karl-Johan Pettersson (Adolf Jahr) who, like Bendel, has no job or source of income. At loose ends, they team up in moneymaking schemes: buying and selling antiques and furniture to adults and pawning off noisemakers to children.

Based on the 1931 bestseller by Waldemar Hammenhög, the film, a study in contrast, depicts the Jew Bendel as greedy and deceitful. Property is all that matters to him. Pettersson is honest, guileless, and romantic. When things go awry, Bendel is heard to mutter "Oy vey, oy vey." When the two compete for the attentions of a girl and Bendel is rejected, his reaction is to retaliate against his partner.

The *New York Times* (February 22, 1934) found nothing objectionable in the depiction of the "crooked" businessman's identity. When Pettersson first meets Bendel, he asks, "You are Jewish, right?" To which Bendel responds, "No, no, of course not, of course not." But Bendel's manner of speech, exaggerated make-up, and outsize gestures indicate he is lying. In addition to Bendel's unflattering portrait and denial of his heritage, the film features a Swede giving the Nazi salute and making a throat-cutting movement in reference to Bendel's betrayal of Pettersson. At the film's end, Bendel tries to sneak out of Sweden. Klezmer music again is played in the background.

Waldemar Hammenhög, the author of the story, also got into the act. Referring to the actor playing Bendel (Semmy Friedmann), Hammenhög denied the existence of Jewish stereotyping, claiming rather that viewers would feel pity for the character.

That a Swedish studio could make such a film in the 1930s is not surprising. In the late nineteenth and early twentieth centuries, Swedish scientists were involved in their own brand of anti–Semitism: "racial biology," the investigation and measurement of skeletal remains, especially skulls of Jews, to validate the superiority of northern Europeans. Humanity was divided according to skull shape. Swedish universities, including Uppsala, had anatomical institutes devoted to such study, amassing hundreds of items. These were catalogued and tagged, for instance, as "No. 88a, Cranium of Jew." The leap from pseudo-science to pseudo-drama was easy. Sweden's attitude towards Jews swerved along the same paths as the Nazis' attitudes.

In July 1935, when the Nazis introduced the Nuremberg Laws, *Pettersson & Bendel* screened in Berlin. It was a big hit, especially since Goebbels singled out the film for its depiction of "unscrupled Jewish 'business prowess,' which is repugnant to every Aryan graced with healthy common sense." Goebbels designated it *Staatspolitisch wertvoll*—"politically worthwhile to the State." It was the first foreign film so named by the Nazis. After Kristallnacht, in November 1938, the Nazi regime dubbed *Pettersson & Bendel* into German and re-released it.

In an address to the Reichstag in which he introduced the Nuremberg Laws, which defined "them," Hitler referred to *Pettersson & Bendel*, noting that "Serious complaints have been launched from numerous sides about the provoking behavior of individual members of this [Jewish] race" and that "a certain course of action became apparent. This conduct climaxed [in] demonstrations which occurred in a Berlin movie house against a foreign film through which, however, Jewish circles believed themselves hurt." Hitler then issued a warning. Unless there was an "amicable relation between the German people and the Jews," he said he would be forced to turn over the "problem" to the Nazi party for "final solution" (Associated Press, December 16, 1935).

In the U.S., audiences in 1934 were seeing the last works of German Jewish filmmakers who had tried to maintain amicable relations with the German people. Early in the year, the Weimar comedy *Es wird schon wieder besser* (1932), which translates as *Things Are Getting Better Already*, was shown at New York's Yorkville Theatre. Its director, Kurt Gerron, would later have his name and face associated with the "final solution." The Nazis would stereotype Gerron in *Der Ewige Jude* (*The Eternal Jew*, 1940).

Gerron's comedy, produced by Ufa, starred the Jewish actors Dolly Haas and Fritz Grünbaum in a tale of a fast-driving daughter of an auto manufacturer. Her scrapes with the law keep busy the "most expensive lawyer in Berlin." In the end she falls in love and all ends well.

U.S. critics pointed out that by 1934, Fritz Grünbaum was no longer making films in Germany. Unmentioned was the fact that Kurt Gerron's services were also no longer needed in Germany. He had been an actor Ufa shorts. The first full-length feature he directed had been Ufa's *Mein Frau, die Hochstaplerin* (*My Wife, the Adventures*, 1931), about a timid bank clerk (Heinz Rühmann) married to an ambitious woman (Käthe von Nagy). *Variety* (February 1932) forecast that Gerron "will go far in Germany because he has a good sense of pace, an almost astounding thing in German films." The assessment of his talent was accurate. The prediction was not.

In late 1932 German censors had suppressed his film about drug traffickers, called *Rauschgift* (*Dope*), starring German screen idol Hans Albers. When in early 1934 New York theatres were showing Gerron's comedy of mix-ups involving girls, guests, and hotel rooms, *Ein Toller Einfall* (*A Crazy Idea*, 1932), produced by Ufa and starring Rose Barsony and Willy Fritsch, Gerron was anxiously seeking safety outside Deutschland.

The Nazis had forced him off the set in early 1933 during the making of Ufa's comedy *Kind, ich freu' mich auf Dein Kommen* (*Child, I'm Happy on Your Coming*, 1933). The feature performers, including husband-and-wife team Magda Schneider and Wolf Albach-Retty, stood in silence while Gerron, humiliated and trembling with fear, was thrown out of the studio. The Aryan directors Erich von Neusser (1902–1957) and Hans Steinhoff were called in to complete his film.

Elsewhere in Germany, similar scenes took place, while non–Jews stood by. Victimization was none of their business.

In the U.S., in late February 1934, who could think of victimization off the screen when viewing the tale of a young blonde in love with a violinmaker from the small, peaceful German town of Mittenwald? That was the plot of *Die Blonde Christl* (1932–33), directed by Franz Seitz (1888–1952). It was based on a novel by one of the Nazis' favorites, Ludwig Ganghofer. Germans were familiar with his stories of an idealized, law-abiding, and secure Germany as the home, or *Heimat*, for true Germans.

Ganghofer, born in 1855, became one of the nation's chief Heimat writers. Three dozen of his novels were turned into films, including two popular Nazi-era productions: *Das Schweigen im Walde* (*The Silence of the Forest*, 1937) and *Waldrausch* (*Forest Fever*, 1939).

Produced by Bavaria Film, Seitz's *Die Blonde Christl* (*Blonde Christl*) presented pleasingly entertaining scenes of skiing and hunting in the Alps, along with Bavarian love songs to transport viewers away from the harsh realities of the Depression.

Seitz and Bavaria Film subsequently exported to America *Der Meisterdetektiv* (The Master Detective, 1933), starring Bavarian comedian Weiss Ferdl, who imagines himself a great investigator. In the film, which screened at New York's Yorkville Theatre, Ferdl played a character named "Jakob Hase," a clerk who is called the "Schnauzer," because of his nose, prying behavior, and dog.

"Hase" is an Ashkenazi surname from the German *Hase*, or hare.

The pseudo-detective Hase is always on the lookout for suspicious activity or crimes. When his niece Betty (Ria Waldau) gets a boyfriend, "Fritz Körner" (Rolf von Goth), Hase investigates his background. Annoyed, the two lovers plant a story to get him out of the way.

It concerns a reward for locating "kidnapped" Chicago heiress Alice Radley (Ery Bos). In search of the victim, Hase blunders into an actual crime being committed by "Max Müller" (Hans Stüwe) and "Paul Krause" (Fritz Kampers).

The *New York Times* (February 13, 1934) called the film a "happy mixture of interesting scenes in a Bavarian city, along the countryside and in a noted winter sport resort [Garmisch], with a little light music and dancing and some slapstick work."

Other light Seitz-Bavaria releases in the U.S. included *Mit dir durch dick und dünn* (*With You Through Thick and Thin*, 1934) and *Bei der blonden Kathrein* (*At Blond Katherine's*, 1934), the latter a poor attempt at a parody of pre–Hitler college life.

Carl Boese's and Heinz Hille's light-hearted *Der Frechdachs* (The Cheeky Devil, 1932), an Ufa production based on the work by Louis Verneuil, featured Maria Forescu. Born Maria Fullenbaum, she would die at age 67 in a concentration camp in 1942. She played alongside Camilla Horn, Else Elster, and a dashing Willy Fritsch. Boese's *Wie man Männer fesselt* (*How to Catch Men*), which was shown at the 79th Street Theater (also known as the Yorkville Theatre) in early 1934, starred the lively Hungarian Jewish actress Franziska Gaál as a bubbly Budapest girl in search of her lover in the heart of the German capital. In fact, this production was really Deutsche Universal's Weimar comedy *Paprika* (1932), photographed by Franz Wachsmann, and had been Gaál's screen debut. An American critic noted that Gaál "has humor and personality and is different, a type not found among German actresses."

By 1934, Gaál was also no longer welcome in Germany.

Universal Studio brought Gaál to Hollywood in the mid–1930s. Ever watchful of the unfolding events in Europe, Gaál returned to her family in Hungary when the nation's Jews came under assault in 1944. She survived the onslaught.

Boese's pre–Hitler *Annemarie, die Braut der Kompanie* (*Annemarie, the Bride of the Company*, 1932) featured Lucie Englisch as the center of attention in a comedy about the good "old" German army. Who could say with certainty that the Nazis, by releasing such a film in the U.S. in 1934, had forsaken all connections to the old world Second Reich?

Heinz Hille, born in Düsseldorf, directed Ufa's $100,000 German–Hungarian production *... Und es Leuchtet die Puszta* (*...And the Puszta Gleams*, 1932–33), a drama that Hungarian-born Jew Emeric Pressburger scripted. The film, which screened in the U.S. in early 1934, is set in the great Hungarian plains and the Budapest of song and romance, starring the Budapest-born Jewish dancer Rose Barsony opposite up-and-coming Nazi star Wolf Albach-Retty. Filmmaker Hille was a noteworthy exception in the Third Reich: he made no films in Germany during the war years.

The Nazis would soon enough show their contempt for films that romanticized Germany's or Europe's past.

Jewish director Alfred Zeisler, born in Chicago, was responsible for pre–Hitler productions that Ufa released in the States after January 1933. Zeisler's *Der Hochtourist* (1931) is about romantic exploits in the White Mountains, starring Jewish actors Trude Berliner, Otto Wallburg, and Max Ehrlich. Zeisler's *Strich durch die Rechnung* (*Spoiling the Game*, 1932), a comedy about bike racing, has Willy Streblow (played by the popular German actor Heinz Rühmann) crossing the finish line first, winning the golden bicycle, getting the girl, and upsetting the devious plans of the would-be briber Gottfried Paradies (Otto Wallburg).

In Zeisler's *Eine Tür geht auf* (*A Door Opens*, 1932–33), a Ufa production which screened at New York's Little Carnegie Playhouse in early 1934, the detective Hans Braumueller (Herman Speelmans) tracks down 300,000 marks stolen in a bank job. There were five thieves with interesting names: "Franz Zengler" (Oskar Sima), from Vienna; "Julius Kloth" (Peter Erkelenz), from Cologne; "Acki" (Hans Deppe), from Berlin; the good-looking "Jonny Schlichting" (Fritz Odemar); and "Vera Bessel" (Lily Rodien), the gang's leader.

Zeisler's crime drama *Schuss im Morgengrauen* (*A Shot at Dawn*, 1932), a critic wrote, had "enough powder exploded to make the producers of American gangster films seem to have been playing with toy pistols." Photographed by Konstantin Irmet-Tschet and Werner Bohne, both of whom would serve Nazi filmmaking, the production featured Peter Lorre in his next-to-last film from Germany.

Zeisler's and Ufa's French-language version *Coup de feu a l'aube* (1932) was an A.C.E. co-production that was co-directed by Serge de Poligny and that starred Antonin Artaud. Although it was apparently French, it contained "pure Teutonic atmosphere," said *Variety*.

The drama *Der Stern von Valencia* (*The Star of Valencia*, 1933), produced by Ufa, which mingles German and Spanish, was director Zeisler's last from Germany. In the film, which Friedrich Zeckendorf and Axel Rudolf wrote, white slave traders, led by Patesco (Oskar Sima), kidnap the cabaret singer Marion (Liane Haid) aboard the *Estrella de Valencia*. The ship is heading for South America, a locale that Nazi filmmakers would use to signify an aimless exoticism and an arena for adventure. Her husband, Sergeant Savedra (Paul Westermeier), a petty officer aboard a coast guard cutter, foils the gang's plans.

In the cast playing another kidnap victim was Ossi Oswalda, one of Ernst Lubisch's silent-screen stars. She had been called the "German Mary Pickford." *Der Stern von Valencia* was *her* last German film. "It seems probable that Ufa made this film in Spanish," wrote the *New York Times* (April 21, 1934) when the film screened at New York's 79th Street Theater. Critics were apparently ignorant of the fact that Ufa had been producing French-language renditions of its films since the late 1920s. The production company was called A.C.E. In this case, A.C.E. produced *L'Etoile de Valencia* (1933), which Serge de Poligny directed, and which starred Jean Gabin and Brigitte Helm.

Coincidentally, the aptly titled *Adieu les Beaux Jours* (*Goodbye, Beautiful Days*, 1933) came to New York's 55th Street Playhouse. It starred Brigitte Helm as Olga, the pawn of a gang of non–German, high-class jewel thieves hopping from one European country to another. Pierre Laverney (Jean Gabin), an engineer, saves her from the culprits' clutches. The cast was French—except for Brigitte Helm (1906–96). Scenes of the French and Spanish countryside, as well as from Biarritz, San Sebastian, and other lavish locales furnished the ideal way to sidestep political realities taking shape on the continent. Although A.C.E. was listed as producer, *Adieu les Beaux Jours* "has that excellent production value for which Ufa was once famous," observed *Variety* (May 1934). "Possibly realizing that its appeal is limited, distributors have not bothered with superimposed titles," said the trade paper. Or were there no titles so as to hide the story? Johannes Meyer and André Beucler (1898–1985), whose novel was the basis for A.C.E's *Gueule d'amour* (*Loverboy*, 1937), were its directors.

Karl Lamac's un-subtitled *Die Tochter des Regiments* (*The Regiment's Daughter* (1932–33), a German-Austrian production scripted by Hans H. Zerlett (1892–1962), screened in the States in early 1934. Its A.C.E version was *La Fille du regiment* (1933). The tale begins in France during World War I when Sergeant Bully (Otto Wallburg) finds an abandoned blonde baby. Eighteen years later she's the adopted daughter Mary Dreizehn (Anny Ondra) of a regiment of Scottish Highlanders. Apparently stressing the idea that "it takes one to know one," the film depicts the Highlanders on a special mission in the Bavarian mountains: to suppress a band of whisky smugglers.

Suppression of foreign smugglers became another popular Nazi theme.

North Americans were satirized in Nazi supporter Viktor Janson's AAFA production *Lügen auf Rügen* (*The Isle of Lies*, 1931), in which country girl Vanda Bilt (Maria Solveg) is mistakenly taken for the niece of an American millionaire. Having won first prize in a toothpaste contest, she earns a trip to the Baltic seashore where confusing complications ensue—yet another favorite German/Nazi plot development.

Janson's romantic comedy *Es war einmal ein Walzer* (*Once There Was a Waltz*, 1932), an AAFA production with music by Franz Lehar, featured blonde star Martha Eggerth opposite Rolf von Goth in a bus ride through contemporary Vienna and an ending in Berlin, where the principals set up a Vienna-type café and make a modest but happy living thereafter. The script was by Billy Wilder.

When this German film reached New York, in 1934, Wilder was in Hollywood struggling to make ends meet. He had left Germany after scripting Géza von Bolváry's *Was Frauen träumen* (*What Women Dream*, 1933), a comedy-drama co-starring Peter Lorre as a "comic songster," which had premiered in Germany on Hitler's birthday in 1933. Although *Variety* reviewed it in Berlin, it didn't screen in the U.S.

In Wilder's story, an attractive woman who favors fine jewelry, Rina Korff (Nora Gregor), is unable to resist temptation. What's strange, however, is that every time she steals something, the same mystery man comes forth to pay for it. A bumbling detective comes across an important clue: a strongly scented woman's glove. Walter König (Gustav Fröhlich), his friend, realizes where he's come across that scent. It radiates from a popular nightclub performer. There he becomes enamored of the woman, but then so does her mystery man, who turns out to be a notorious international criminal, named Levassor, alias John Constaninescu (Kurt Horwitz). Eventually he's arrested, leaving Walter with the field to himself.

A copy of the film is purportedly locked away in Switzerland.

In early 1934, Ufa's comedy *Tausend für eine Nacht* (*A Thousand for One Night*, 1932) quietly slipped into New York's 79th Street Theater. The film was by German-born Jewish director Max Mack, who by the time of the film's release in the States was in exile in Hollywood. Max Mack had made his reputation as a producer in Germany, where he introduced Albert Bassermann to the screen and made the first German sound film with Hans Albers.

Shot around the famous Czech resort of Marienbad, *Tausend für eine Nacht* concerns a German mother anxious to see her daughter (Trude Berliner) married to a nobleman rather than to a jazz musician (Harald Paulsen).

German-Jewish actress Berliner also found refuge in Hollywood, where she appeared in *Casablanca* (1942), *The Strange Death of Adolf Hitler* (1942), and *Hotel Berlin* (1945).

Jewish director Erich Schönfelder, a prolific filmmaker in the Weimar era, had no chance to make films in the new Germany. His *In Wien hab' ich einmal ein Mädel geliebt* (*Once I loved a Girl in Vienna*, 1931), shown in America in mid–1934, was a musical romance of pre- and postwar love starring Gretl Theimer. His comedy *Zu Befehl, Herr Unteroffizer* (*At Your Orders, Sergeant*, 1932) also screened in the U.S. in 1934. Produced by Erich Engels, scripted by Arnold Lippschitz, and starring Ralph Arthur Roberts and Henry Bender, it poked fun at prewar Germans and their military exercises.

Schönfelder had died in Berlin in early 1933 after a brief illness. Jewish film colleague and fellow director Walther-Fein died the same year in Berlin of a heart attack.

New German Cinema

The meaning of apparently harmless German films became clear on March 1, 1934, when the Nazis officially mandated a new norm in German film.

A "Reich Cinema Law" required that feature film scripts would have to be evaluated by a Reich film advisor whose job was to prevent the filming of "contents that run counter to the spirit of the times." No German film would be allowed to endanger "essential interests of the state," or "jeopardize German prestige or German foreign relations." German film would be National Socialist film.

While new films were to be strictly regulated, however, old ones still had value. Those were the harmless tales from the last years of the Weimar Republic, which the new Germany had no trouble taking credit for. They continued to be sent to the States years after completion, as long as there was a chance to make money from them.

But the new German cinema showed its ugly face quickly enough in America. It came in Paul Wegener's first sound film to reach the U.S., playing at New York's Yorkville Theatre. The film was *Inge und die Millionen* (*Inge and the Millions*, 1933), directed by the purported liberal German director Erich Engel. No critic made note of its insidious message.

Wegener played a hard-hearted Berlin banker named "Seemann" who, with his partners "Conrady"(Otto Wallburg) and "Kutzer" (Ernst Behmer), uses his guileless, pure German secretary Inge Hensel (Brigitte Horney) to smuggle money to Switzerland. Seemann, through his greed, drives the honest German debtor Böttcher (Ernst Karchow) to suicide. But because of Böttcher's death, Inge realizes the harm she's done working for the corrupt banker. As he's about to flee from Germany with his stolen millions, she turns Seeman in to the authorities.

The *New York Times* (April 13, 1934) took no notice of the bankers' names, but did say that Inge's love affair with the scrupulous Walter Brink (Willy Eichberger) "runs like a thread of silver in a gloomy pattern" through Ufa's crime drama. This pattern—the stereotyping of Jewish bankers and money—became a trademark in Nazi productions. The stereotyping could take many forms: by profession, physical appearance, accent, body language, and gestures.

In May 1934, there was no hiding the fact that a film called *A Romance of Our Day* was anti–Semitic. It had the dubious distinction of being called the first outspoken Nazi propaganda film to get a commercial showing in the States. Directed by Franz Seitz, produced by Bavaria Film, scripted by Joe Stöckel and scored by Toni Thoms (1880–1941), this film was actually *SA-Mann Brand* (1933). It introduced the brown-shirted SA, or Storm Battalion, to American filmgoers. These thugs represented the anti-communist fighting spirit of millions of young Germans who destroyed Weimar Germany and helped bring Hitler to power.

The film's protagonist is Hans Brand (Heinz Klingenberg), a young truck driver who joins the Storm Battalion because he can't make a living in postwar Germany. When he is murdered by Marxists and becomes a martyr to the cause, frenzied Nazis carry the day at the polls. Germany's enemies are singled out by the names they carry. They are the Soviet agent "Turrow" (Max Weydner), a Communist named "Spitzer" (Theo Kaspar), and the factory owner "Neuberg" (Rudolf Franck).

Notable also were scenes of Nazi mobs shouting *Juda Verrecke*!—"Let the Jews Croak!" The Nazis' victory at the polls causes Neuberg, the man who had fired the about-to-be martyred Brand, to flee to Switzerland. The depiction of him as greedy and unsympathetic is a caricature of a Jewish industrialist.

The production was elaborate, with 1,600 extras and complex street sets, but the Nazi press was unsatisfied, attacking Seitz and the authors of the screenplay for their inability to produce a stupefying success. The German filmmakers were faulted not for the film's message and ideas but for its execution. But the *New York Times* (May 28, 1934) came to the startling conclusion that the film has "no anti–Semitic bias."

A month later, on June 30, 1934, Hitler instigated a "blood purge" of party rivals. Among those killed in the Night of the Long Knives were *Sturmabteilungen* (SA) leaders Ernst Roehm and Karl Ernst. By destroying the SA, Hitler brought to power Himmler's black-shirted SS. The massacre, however, was misinterpreted within Germany and abroad. Instead of concluding that a gang of criminals was heading the Third Reich, Germans and foreigners surmised that Hitler wanted to restore legality to the country.

Simultaneously there appeared in America a second German film about Hitler thugs in action. This production was titled *Unsere Fahne flattert Uns voran* (*Our Flags Lead Us Forward*).

"There was no indication in front of the theatre screening the film of the subject matter or intent," wrote *Variety* (July 17, 1934). But since this film too was showing in the New York's heavily German Yorkville area, there was little chance this was an anti–Nazi production. Pro–Hitler sentiment was strong in Yorkville, an area likened to Munich, with innumerable beer halls. The German–American Bund was active there. By the late 1930s, Nazi admirers liked to goose-step through these streets to advertise their leanings.

The German American Bund comprised German expatriates living in the United States. Bund members were anti–Semitic and opposed to U.S. intervention in European affairs. By the time the Second World War began, there were hundreds of branches across the country, totaling 25,000 dues-paying members. That number included 8,000 members who liked to dress and march as German storm troopers.

The German American Bund propagandized for its causes, published magazines and brochures, organized demonstrations, and maintained groups along the lines of Hitler Youth camps. Bund activities and rallies often led to clashes and street battles with their main adversaries: Jewish American veterans of World War I.

Bund members attended theatrical releases of imported German productions and watched privately screened German films. But even on the pro–German Upper East Side of New York in mid–1934, Ufa, the producer and distributor of the euphemistically titled *Our Flag Leads Us Forward,* didn't hint at the actual title of the newest German film to come to the United States.

The film was really called *Hitlerjunge Quex* (*Hitler Youth Quicksilver*, 1933). Directed by Hans Steinhoff, it was scored by Hans-Otto Borgmann (1901–1977), with marching tunes by Hitler Youth leader Baldur von Schirach. Russian-born Konstantin Irmen Tschet, a rising cameraman within Germany, was the photographer.

The story takes place in the years leading up to 1933, when young Heini Völker (Jürgen Ohlsen) is living in a poor section of town, and the Nazis are vying for power. Völker's father (Heinrich George) is unemployed—and a communist, to boot—who drags the young man to dreary party functions. But young Völker is in thrall to someone else: Hitler. Learning of a planned communist assault on a new Hitler Youth hostel, Völker warns the intended targets, thereby saving the day. Fearing reprisals, his mother (Franziska Kinz) attempts to end her life along with that of her son. However, only she perishes. At that point, the boy knows his duty. He volunteers to spread the Nazi word in a dangerous part of town. What does his life matter? The Nazi Party is all. He dies at the hands of communists. His martyrdom, however, is a glorious thing. As a rallying cry for the Nazis, his death helps them attain power. The principal songs in the movie were "Our Flag Leads Us Forward" and "The Internationale."

Jürgen Ohlsen was 16 when he made this film. He made one other film in Nazi Germany. He died in Germany in 1994.

That this film wasn't run out of New York still startles today.

Goebbels loved it. He wrote in his diaries that those associated with the film "had distinguished themselves in the artistic presentation of National Socialist ideals." He liked the ending, recalling, "There in the bleak, gray twilight, yellowed, tortured eyes stare into emptiness. His tender head has been trampled into a bloody pulp.... Yet it is as if life stirs anew out of pale death.... Look now, the slender, elegant body begins to move ... a frail child's voice is heard as if speaking from all eternity.... What is mortal in me will perish. But my spirit is immortal, will remain with you. And it ... will show you the way."

Variety proclaimed the production an "interesting example of how good German technique is; it's a fine job for what it is; it accomplishes its purpose admirably. Film, in fact, is cleverly done."

Shamefully, the Museum of Modern Art accepted a copy of *Hitlerjunge Quex* from the

German production company in September 1936. The Nazis and collaborators made use of Steinhoff's film well into the war years. *Hitlerjunge Quex* premiered in Paris in March 1942 as *Le Jeune hitlérien*, when the French were rounding up Jews. Germany banned the film after the war.

Nazi supporter Steinhoff was also a director of comedies, as evidenced by his *Liebe muss verstanden sein* (*Love Must Be Understood*, 1933), an Ufa production starring the Hungarian-Jewish actress Rose Barsony in her last film from Germany. It screened at New York's 79th Street Theater in early 1934. In this musical comedy, scored by Willi Kollo, Margit Raday (Barsony) is the stenographer to "Bruno Plaumann" (Max Gülsdorff), a presumed Jew and tight-fisted industrialist who wants to buy the patent to a remote-control device. After he rejects Margit's request for a raise, Plaumann asks her to make a bank deposit of 3,000 marks as a pre-payment on the patent. Plaumann then heads to Dresden to pick up the device from its inventor, Peter Lambach (Georg Alexander).

Margit, however, fails to get to the bank on time to close the deal. Frantic, she heads to Plaumann's hotel in Dresden. Arriving there exhausted, all she wants to do is sleep. But then she's caught in a compromising position in her room with Lambach. That's because Lambach's cold-blooded, non–German fiancée, Ellen Parker (Hilde Hildebarand), was out to discredit him.

Steinhoff also directed Ufa's *Freut Euch des Lebens* (*Enjoy Yourselves*, 1933), which was shown at New York's 79th Street Theater, and the Henny Porten vehicle about mother love, *Mutter und Kind* (*Mother and Child*, 1933).

In the former, the Munich waitress Gusti Melzer (Dorit Kreysler) is beloved by all the diners, including the penniless music teacher "Gottlieb Bumm" (Leo Slezak). When Bumm wins money in a contest, he invites blonde-haired Gusti on a trip into the country. There she has a run-in with handsome Carl Maria (Wolfgang Liebeneiner) and his mother, Camilla Raveck (Ida Wüst), who imagines Gusti is Bumm's girlfriend. The *New York Times* (November 3, 1934) wrote that "There are plenty of amusing complications, temperamental outbursts, alluring scenes in the frosty hills before the scrappy lovers finally emerge, smiling and reconciled, from a huge snowball."

Steinhoff's *Mutter und Kind* contains scenes of "simple folk living along the seashore," wrote the *New York Times* (November 30, 1934). American viewers apparently enjoyed the slapstick and the singing and dancing in Steinhoff's lighter films while ignoring racial innuendos.

One American expatriate worked within Nazi Germany. Arthur Robison, employed at Ufa, directed *Eines Prinzen junge Liebe* (*A Prince's Young Love*), which starred the Aryan-qualified Willy Fritsch. While the film, which was shown in the U.S. in spring 1934, harkened back to the "good old days" of the Second Empire, it presented the iron-fisted era of Bismarck that Hitler much admired.

In a small German city of the nineteenth century, Prince Leopold von Anhalt-Dessau (Fritsch) wants to marry his childhood sweetheart, Anneliese (Trude Marlen), who is the daughter of a lowly pharmacist. Overcoming obstacles and intrigue by the nobility, they manage to wed. In addition to proclaiming the need for a classless society, the film had another message that was in line with attitudes in the Third Reich. The prince declared that every Anhalt-Dessau woman must have lots of children.

This film by Chicago-born Robison (1888–1935) had been released in Germany as *Des Jungen Dessauers grosse Liebe* (*Young Dessau's Great Love*, 1933). Ufa called Marlen (1912–2005) the Jean Harlow of the new Germany. The French version by Robison and André Beucler was called *Tambour Battant* (*Beating Drum*, 1933), produced by Ufa and its lackey subsidiary, A.C.E.

Robison's *Fürst Woronzeff* (*Prince Woronzeff*, 1934), starring Brigitte Helm and new discovery Hansi Knoteck, concerns a former Russian prince (Albert Schönhals). That makes him pro–German. He's living in exile on the Riviera thanks to the fortune he managed to hold

Jürgen Ohlsen in *Hitlerjunge Quex* (1933).

onto after the Russian Revolution. Prince Woronzeff has a close friend and double, the goodhearted German Franz von Naydeck. When the prince becomes mortally ill, he asks his dear German friend to pose as the father of Woronzeff's daughter, Nadia (Knoteck), because his anti-German family covets his inheritance. Diane (Helm), who loves the real prince, does not betray this secret.

The German film screened here in late 1934. Robison and André Beucler collaborated on a French-language version, *Le Secret des Woronzeff*, which was an Ufa production from its lookalike collaborator, A.C.E. Ufa had other partners in the 1930s as well. It joined forces with Fox and Gaumont-British to present a pictorial musical hit set in the background of France's Third Empire. That film was the English-language *Heart Song* (1932–1933), which opened at the 55th Street Playhouse in New York in June 1934. Jews had been central to its creation. London-born Friedrich Holländer was the director, Vienna-born Walter Reisch and Berlin-born Robert Liebmann were the scriptwriters, Franz Wachsmann wrote the music, and Erich Pommer produced it.

Their musical romance concerns a garter that falls into the hands of a duke who falls for an empress. It featured Lilian Harvey, Charles Boyer, Ernest Thesiger, and the German–American actress Mady Christians.

In the German-language version, called *Ich und die Kaiserin* (*The Empress and I*, 1932–1933), which was well received in Berlin in early 1933, Conrad Veidt starred as the handsome aristocrat. Veidt, a Jew, would be forced to leave Germany.

A few films released in America in spring 1934 argued against the string of entertainment from Nazi Germany. Among them were the Jewish epic *Chalutzim* (*Pioneers of Palestine*, 1932), by Aleksander Ford; Alfred Werker's *House of Rothschild* (1934), starring George Arliss and his wife Helen Westley, who earned admiration for her portrayal of the glowing old Jewish mother; Jewish director Max Nosseck's comedy *Der Schlemihl*, a Weimar-era film starring Curt Bois who, reviewers noted, was barred from working in Germany because he was Jewish; and *Hitler's Reign of Terror* (1934), advertised as a one-hour "pictorial record of Nazi activities," directed by Michael Mindlin.

Hitler's Reign of Terror begins at an American Legion rally at Madison Square Garden, where a number of prominent liberals—including Rabbi Stephen Wise, the entertainer Fannie Hurst, and Helen Keller—denounce Hitler. The journalist Edwin C. Hill addresses the rally and then phones his friend Cornelius Vanderbilt, who is on a fact-finding mission in Germany and Austria. The film then becomes a discussion with Vanderbilt about his trip abroad, along with an interspersed series of newsreel sequences, stills, and shots of German newspaper headlines. These included scenes of Jews being tortured, books being burned, and the Nazis confiscating footage that Vanderbilt shot.

In the production, actors pose as high-ranking Nazis and Germans whom Vanderbilt interviews, including "Hitler" and Germany's former ruler, "Kaiser Wilhelm." Even though American critics considered *Hitler's Reign of Terror* wishy-washy and characterized American filmgoers as already cool towards Hitler, New York State censors twice refused to countenance its release. In Chicago's Loop district, German consul Rolfe L. Jaeger got the Windy City to halt its showing, calling it an inauthentic record of conditions in Germany since Hitler's rise to power. Goebbels, recognizing its power and fearing the film could rouse anti–Hitler sentiment, banned it from the Third Reich.

Jewish director Nosseck, who was born in Poland and became persona non grata in Germany, made a final film there in 1932: the musical comedy *Einmal Möch' Ich keine Sorgen haben* (*For Once I'd Like to Have No Troubles*). A Biographfilm production, it screened at the Tobis Theatre in New York in early 1934, starring the Danish singer Max Hansen as a jobless barber posing as a rich auto magnate (since he drives the right kind of car). Hansen sang the title number along with Josef Danegger (born Deutsch), who was making a rare film appearance. This film was Fritz Grünbaum's final film. He died in Dachau in 1941.

One of Max Neufeld's last German films, a Tobis production called *Rund um ein Million* (*Approximately Around a Million*, 1933), had been re-titled and released as *Geld regiert die Welt* (*Money Governs the World*) by Europa Film in New York's Yorkville Theatre, in May 1934. It's about 5 million francs that change hands one weekend between the "Russian countess" Lilly (Camilla Horn) and the French "millionaire" Léon Saval (Gustav Fröhlich).

Erich Engels (1889–1971) directed *Wenn Herzen sich finden* (*When Hearts Meet*), another tale about the lure of money. Charlotte Ander, an ugly duckling, turns the head of a distant cousin (Johannes Riemann) during a search for missing documents. Along the way she becomes a graceful swan. He then rejects a $2 million legacy and marries her for love. This comedy, which screened at the Casino Theatre in late 1934, was actually the 1932 Weimar production *Das Millionentestament* (*Million-Dollar Will*). The Nazis made use of its theme and the opportunity to cash in on its release while Arnold Lippschitz, its scriptwriter, had to find refuge in Hollywood.

In 1934, German actor Ralph Arthur Roberts (1884–1940), born Ralph Arthur Schönherr, adapted to the new German cinema without Jews. He had, for instance, starred alongside Jewish star Siegfried Arno in Carl Boese's Weimar comedy *Keine Feier ohne Meyer* (*No Celebration without Meyer*, 1931), which concerns the joys and tribulations of a Jew who runs a combination matrimonial agency and divorce bureau.

With that film behind him, Roberts became a star in Third Reich films and directed one film in the Hitler era, for Ufa. His *Spiel mit dem Feuer* (*Playing with Fire*, 1934) screened in America in late 1934. A charming, intelligent, and guileless young blonde wife, Annette (Trude Marlen) cures her busy architect-husband, Alfred Kramer (Paul Hörbiger), of his infatuation with the beautiful-but-scheming brunette singer named "Sylvia Bernhardt" (Elga Brink). Annette gives him plenty of rope with which to hang himself, and she then exposes Sylvia's duplicity to the press. Bustling scenes of Berlin and a pleasant depiction of an inviting seashore resort implied all was well within the nation.

Contrasting the merits of country folk with the faults of urban dwellers was the theme of *HeideschulmeisterUwe Karsten* (*Uwe Karsten, Schoolmaster of the Heath*, 1933), produced by Ufa and shown at the New York's 79th Street Theater in mid-1934. The film was directed by the once highly-regarded Weimar filmmaker Carl Heinz Wolff.

Uwe Karsten Alslew (Hans Schlenck) goes to Hamburg to give a lecture on his beloved heath, Lüneburg. There he is offered an appointment to the university. But Uwe turns it down because he believes it's more important to "shape" the minds of the young people of his German heath. He would often speak to them of the importance of "Heimat und Boden" (home and earth). In Hamburg, Uwe calls upon his childhood friend, Ursula Diewen (Marianne Hoppe), whom he loves. Her feelings for him are reciprocated even though she is practically engaged to Heinrich Heinsius (Heinrich Heilinger), a shipbuilding magnate. But when she learns that Uwe doesn't want to live in Hamburg, Ursula permits her father to announce her engagement to the purported rich man.

Heinsius, however, is on the verge of bankruptcy. He's also a womanizer. One of his affairs was with his secretary, Marthe Detlefsen (Brigitte Horney), who is pregnant. Heinsius wishes to marry Ursula for one reason only: her money. Marthe is determined to reveal the truth about Heinsius to Ursula but Urusla's brother stops her because he wants to avoid a scandal. Just after Ursula marries, Marthe has a talk with Ursula. Ursula immediately returns to the heath country and to Uwe. Gossip ensues. Frantic, Heinsius, whose credit is gone, heads to the heath, seeking to reconcile with his wife. On the way, he learns that another of his sweethearts is on her way to see Ursula. His wild journey across the heath involves a ride in an ox-cart, which overturns. Heinsius breaks his neck. Thus the way is cleared for the reunion of Uwe and Ursula. In addition, Marthe falls in love with Uwe's assistant. The picture ends with a double wedding.

However, the film's real message is revealed in the songs of Herman Löns, a nationalist and sentimental poet, and the depictions of simple country life: the "back to the soil" movement of Alfred Rosenberg, the Nazis' chief ideologue and later Reich minister for the occupied eastern territories as well as Goebbels' rival in the arena of German propaganda.

Wolff (1883–1942) had directed the pre–Hitler farce *Husarenliebe* (*Hussar Love*, 1932), which was released in the States as *Tant Gusti Kommandiert* (*Aunt Gusti Commands*). Here three daughters of a tax official (Max Adalbert), who were raised by a maiden aunt (Hansi Niese), become engaged to three troopers assigned to their small city.

By the time this film screened at New York's Yorkville Theatre in mid–1934, Adalbert and Niese were dead.

Two years after its German debut, Leni Riefenstahl's mystical, back to the soil *Das Blau Licht* (*The Blue Light*, 1932) premiered in the States. Although a pre–Hitler film, it meshed with Nazi beliefs in the powers of the occult and the supernatural, and in its call for Germans to return to the land as well as to the mountains. The film deceptively listed Riefenstahl as the screenwriter because the real writer, *Béla Balázs, was Jewish and hadn't been paid for his work.*

Junta (Riefenstahl) is athletic, daring, and alluring. Only she is able to ascend the nearby mountains to a cave that emits a mysterious, soothing blue light when the moon is full. The light has a mysterious, curative power. Many young men of the village have lost their lives trying to find the elusive source of the blue light. The ignorant, older women of her village, however, suspect Junta of being a witch, forcing her to take refuge in the mountains. Eventually Junta reveals the location of the blue light to one man. He betrays her to the villagers; she takes her life.

Erich Waschneck's *Abel mit der Mundharmonika* (1934), produced by Ufa and shown in the U.S. in September 1934, further hammered home the message of harmony within nature—and away from man—in scenes of the north German lowland with its vast stretches of meadow and heath. Waschneck (1887–1970) had worked as the cameraman in Ernst Lubitsch's *Anna Boleyn* (1920) and launched his career in sound films with Deutsche Universal, directing the psychological tragedy *Zwei Menschen* (*Two Humans*, 1931), which was photographed by Richard Angst. The National Board of Review called *Zwei Menschen* the best foreign film of 1931.

In the 1930s, Richard Angst was also the photographer of *Die Wasserteufel von Hieflau*, *Brennendes Geheimnis*, and *Nordpol—Ahoi!*, all films which Deutsche Universal produced or distributed in Germany.

Angst later worked in Borneo, the Himalayas, and Japan, but when war began he returned to Nazi Germany, to continue what he called his "objective" career. It lasted until the early '70s.

Austrian-born director Fred Sauer's *Heimat am Rhein* (*Home on the Rhine*, 1933), when it screened at New York's 79th Street Theater in late 1934, offered the irresistible charms of the Rhine region, and the wholesomeness of a German male (Werner Fuetterer), and his beautiful Viennese companion Mizzi (Lucie Englisch). It also presented a

Leni Riefenstahl, October 1934.

Advertisement for *Heimat am Rhein* (1933).

wicked city slicker named "Mecklinger" (Walter Steinbeck), who attempts to seize control of the ancestral inn and vineyard of young, good-hearted Hannes Lorenz (Fuetterer).

After Mizzi foils Mecklinger's scheme, she abandons the blue Danube for life with Hannes in the countryside.

Sauer's *Die Beiden Seehunde* (*The Two Seals*, 1934) had a pseudo-subversive premise: a mustached ruler of a fictitious principality, discovering that the people resent his spending so much time hunting, allows his more generous twin to rule.

Again the theme of illusion versus reality comes into play. Hitler did not worry about what his people thought of him. Germans worried what he thought of them.

Max Obal's comedy *Die Lustigen Musikanten* (*The Merry Musicians*) offered a look at the workaday world of ordinary German shopkeepers (played by Camilla Spira, Hermann Picha, and Fritz Kampers) as well as how "more fortunate" Berliners (Julius Falkenstein, for one)—the kind of people the Nazis loathed—spent their weekends: in garden colonies in the suburbs. A German-Dutch production from 1930, it reached New York in mid–1934.

Austrian-born Friedrich Feher, who had costarred in *The Cabinet of Dr. Caligari* (1919), was responsible for a Weimar drama about escaped convicts living under assumed names, *Gehetzte Menschen* (*Hunted Men*, 1932). It was a Czech-German production released by Deutsches Lichtbild starring the Jewish performers Joseph Schmidt, Vladimir Sokoloff, and Camilla Spira. The action is set in the south of France where, it turns out, director Feher found refuge after Hitler came to power. His film was shown in the States in June 1934.

Carl Boese's *Roman einer Nacht* (*Story of a Night*, 1933), which ran in New York's Yorkville Theatre in mid–1934, has a French setting. Here Helga (Liane Haid), the daughter of the chief of the Copenhagen police, Petersen (Paul Otto), returns from Paris by train and meets a fascinating "stranger" (Gustav Diessl). He's after a criminal with the Russian-Jewish name Professor "Kolski." Max Schreck, in one of his last films, played the professor.

The prolific, Austrian-born Georg Jacoby directed the comedy *Liebe in Uniform* (1932), a Reichs-Liga Weimar-era production that was shown in the U.S. in October 1934. The pre–World War I tale of a "woman-hating" cavalry captain (Harry Liedke) who falls for the rich girl (Ery Bos) contains another hint of the new Germany: the surprising element of modern passenger planes.

That month, there was an even bigger surprise in store for American filmgoers. A heart-stopping film from the new, modern Germany, it should have brought Americans back to the reality of the Third Reich. This film was called one of the most successful German features of 1933–34, opening at the 79th Street Theater in New York. It was titled *Flüchtlinge* (*Fugitives*).

Here was a costly, no-holds-barred Nazi production because the story concerned "real" people. In 1928, in war-torn Manchuria, the town of Harbin is crawling with undesirables: Japanese, Manchurian, and Russian solders. A group of frightened Volga Germans, led by the engineer Laudy, is on the Soviets' wanted list. These Germans on foreign soil are one step ahead of gangsterish Soviet agents, seeking sanctuary in the International Settlement. But the high commissioner of the League of Nations dithers while their fate hangs in the balance. It seems that a Russian commissar is taking advantage of the chaos by rounding up Germans. But there is one German who sees things clearly. He's Arneth Hans (Albers), a one-time officer who had fled Weimar Germany to make his life here. Joining their fight, he will lead the desperate Germans in their quest for safety and a return home. They see themselves as refugees. Their enemies call them fugitives. His efforts—they can be compared to Hitler's—unite the fractured group.

Arneth accomplishes this by ridding the group of "miserable human material" while the rest of the Germans, he says, must follow orders because "it's not your business to think."

Ufa's Babelsberg studio showing sets from *Flüchtlinge* (1933).

When a young zealot perishes, Arneth notes, "To die for something, that's the best thing there is. I wish I could die like that." The Germans repair an abandoned train and board it towards safety—and the fatherland. Ironic is the fact that this anti–Soviet, nationalist tale depicts Russian soldiers as heartless and the (German) refugees/fugitives as frail and human. The Germans sing the tune "Pack up Your Troubles" as they depart.

The rabble-rousing Austrian-born Gustav Ucicky directed Ufa's carefully paced production, which was released when Germany announced its withdrawal from the League of Nations. With music by Herbert Windt (1894–1965) and Ernst Erich Buder (1896–1962), it co-starred Kathe von Nagy, Ida Wüst, Franziska Kinz, and Veit Harlan, among a huge cast, none of them Jews. Fritz Arno Wagner served as photographer. Robert Herlth (1893–1962) and Walter Röhrig (1893–1945) were the designers. The linchpin of the tale was the infamous Gerhard Menzel. His script on the pre–Hitler production *Morgenrot* (1933) had made his reputation with the Nazis. Menzel scripted *Flüchtlinge*, based on his novel *Germans Want to Go Home*. Goebbels named the film winner of a National Film Prize.

Its message to Germans and the outside world resonated until 1939, when Germany signed the Nazi-Soviet pact. Politics suddenly demanded that the anti–Russian production vanish—and Goebbels shelved the film for the time being. Ucicky and Henry Chomette (René Clair's brother) directed a version for the French market called *Au bout du monde* (*At the End of the World*, 1933–34), which was produced by Ufa-A.C.E.

From this film and others, the Nazis were learning they had nothing to lose with co-productions. Hungarian-born Géza von Cziffra (1900–1989) and Géza von Bolváry directed the musical *Mindent a Nöért* (*Everything for the Woman*, 1933), which was produced by the Hun-

Desperate Germans, in *Flüchtlinge*.

garian company Hunnia with German financing and was shown at the Tobis Theatre in New York in late 1934. Szöke Szakall, who had worked in pre–Hitler Germany, and other Magyar actors take part in a bit of mischief about winning a horse race at the Derby Club in Budapest.

Cziffra's career took an upswing when he began working for German studios. He scripted and directed films in Nazi Germany throughout the war. One film that Cziffra scripted, called *Der Grüne Kaiser* (*The Green Emperor*, 1938–39), is an example of the venomous nature of Nazi filmmaking. Reviewed by American critics abroad, it never screened in the U.S. Produced by Ufa, directed by Paul Mundorf, and shown in Vienna six months before the start of World War II, its central character was named Jan Karsten (René Deltgen), a pilot sentenced to three years in prison for murdering his employer. Flying to London, the pilot had made an emergency landing—but his passenger had vanished. Circumstantial evidence—two bullets were missing from Karsten's gun—implicated Karsten in the disappearance/killing.

After his release from prison, Karsten does a bit of investigating. He discovers that man who had set him up was his boss, the banker Hendryk Mylius (Gustav Diessl). He's actually a British thief named "Henry Miller," and he not only stole funds from his bank but he married Karsten's girlfriend, Joana (Carola Höhn).

The Nazis were inspired to make this film, which Ufa produced, by a news item. In the late 1930s, a Belgian-Jewish banker named Loewenstein had mysteriously vanished from his plane while it was crossing the English Channel.

Hans Albers jumps on board in *Flüchtlinge*.

After the war, Cziffra paid a small price for working in Nazi Germany. He served a two-month prison term in Prague for collaboration.

German-born Jew Ludwig Berger (Ludwig Gottfried Heinrich Bamberger) got out of Germany just in time. When his *Walzerkrieg* (*Battle of the Waltzes*, 1933) was shown at the 55th Street Playhouse in November 1934 as *Waltz Time in Vienna*, costarring Renate Müller, Karl Stepanek, and Rose Barsony, it had the distinction of being the first Ufa production on Broadway since Hitler took over. Because the production company's name had been omitted from the credits, Berger's film appeared to be a musical from the land of the Strauss family, Austria. It was a case of "don't ask, don't tell."

It's a delicate and captivating operetta of 1840s Vienna and London, when Johann Strauss (Adolf Wohlbrück) and Joseph Lanner (Paul Hörbiger) compete in composing their rapturous music for the greater glory of the Austrian capital. "This film impresses this delighted column," wrote Andre Sennwald of the *New York Times* (November 19, 1934), "as the equal" of Bolváry's 1930 worldwide musical hit, *Zwei Herzen im dreiviertal Takt*. That film, which Robert Stolz scored, was the first subtitled film released in America.

The *Chicago Tribune* (May 14, 1935) called Berger's film a "rest cure for jaded nerves and a joy to ears that crave music" when it ran at the Sonotone Theatre.

In Germany, however, the reception had been different. Berger's name had been scratched from the credits, as were the names of Jewish scriptwriters Robert Liebmann and Hans Müller. Ufa-A.C.E had made a French-language version, *La Guerre des Valses* (1933), starring Fernand Gravey and Jeanine Crispin.

Director Ludwig Berger, in the late 1920s.

Variety noted that when the musical premiered in the U.S., Berger was "one of the Jewish refugees in London." Berger's name had last appeared on German screens in December 1932, with the hit Weimar comedy *Ich bei Tag, Du bei Nacht* (*I by Day, You by Night*), which was made in Hollywood in 1933 as *Rafter Romance*.

In *Ich bei Tag, Du bei Nacht*, a nightclub waiter (Willy Fritsch) and a manicurist (Käthe von Nagy) share a room: he sleeps there by night and she by day. They've never met, but based on how each lives in the room, they can't stand each other. Then they run into each other, not knowing who's who, and fall in love. The film co-starred the six-member German singing group known as the Comedian Harmonists. Three members of the group were Jewish.

In Budapest, Hungarian-born Bolváry directed one of Deutsche Universal's last comedies from Europe, *Früharsparade* (*Spring Parade*, 1934), produced by Joe Pasternak and starring the Jewish actress Franziska Gaál. Bolváry, whose film screened abroad late in the year but not in the U.S., had begun his career in Hungary in the early 1920s directing the Jewish actors Vilma Bánky and Paul Lukas.

In November 1934, the Nazis lobbed over another film bombshell: Paul Wegener's nationalistic *Ein Mann will nacht Deutschland* (*A Man Wants to Get to Germany*). The film, about a German stuck in Latin America, buttressed the message that had come from *Flüchtlinge*. *Film-Kurier* had written in July 1934, "With the first film in its new program, Ufa has shown that it is determined to sustain the great ideological line of its production." Starring Karl Ludwig Diehl and Brigitte Horney, the drama depicts Cubans as exotic and sensual, the English as oafish, and West Indians as subhuman—but Germans as noble and homebound. Its music was by the prolific Hans-Otto Borgmann.

The film by Wegener (1874–1948) and Horney was direct testimony about the precarious position of Jews in Nazi Germany.

On the eve of the First World War, three engineers—a German named Hagen (Diehl), an Englishman, and a Frenchman—are working in a factory in Venezuela. When the news of the outbreak of the war in Europe arrives, Hagen's duty becomes clear: the fatherland needs him. He must return home. The three friends are now enemies. They are under direct orders to return home to join the ranks of their own fighting men.

Producer Joseph Pasternak in Hollywood.

But Hagen's way back is thick with obstacles as well as pleasure, ranging from the allure of the beautiful Manuela (played by Horney) to imprisonment in a British "concentration camp" in Jamaica, escape by sea to Cuba and a clandestine voyage on a Danish steamer to the British Isles, before he safely arrives home. There the Ibero-American Manuela is more than eager to become his frau.

Ein Mann will nacht Deutschland (1934).

The speedy release in the United States of Wegener's film, which was co-scripted by Fred Andreas, can be attributed to several factors. For one, it had been released in Germany barely weeks before the twentieth anniversary of the start of the First World War in August 1914, earning a place as one of the most popular films of the year in Nazi Germany. Why not reveal what the new German admired on the screen? Second, the news that Germany's army pledged its loyalty to Hitler signaled a new kind of Germany military force. Third, the ninth day of November also marked the anniversary of Hitler's 1923 Beer Hall Putsch in Munich.

Ein Mann will nacht Deutschland was the second of eight films that the once-celebrated Paul Wegener directed in Nazi Germany. Four were shown in the U.S, including his first, *Die Freundin eines grossen Mannes* (*The Girlfriend of a Big Man*, 1934), which was produced by Ufa and starred Hungarian Käthe von Nagy as a famous actress who saves a small theater from going bankrupt. Its anti–Semitic message came via its denigration of a conservative banker named "Rieder" (Hans Leibelt) and a snoopy, obnoxious Jewish reporter named "Banz" (Werner Finck), described as "not a regular newspaper man."

The anti–Semitism was along the lines Hitler admired. "What soon gave me cause for very serious consideration were the activities of the Jews in certain branches of life, into the mystery of which I penetrated little by little," wrote Hitler in *Mein Kampf*. "Was there any shady undertaking, any form of foulness, especially in cultural life, in which at least one Jew did not participate? On putting the probing knife carefully to that kind of abscess one immediately discovered, like a maggot in a putrescent body, a little Jew who was often blinded by the sudden light."

On the other hand, the Gaumont-British drama, *Power* (1934), directed by Lothar Mendes, was a call for toleration in the light of contemporary events in Germany.

Released in the U.S. in October 1934, *Power* is a faithful and honorable adaptation of Lion Feuchtwanger's novel called *Jud Süss*. Its central character is the controversial early eighteenth-century German Jew Süss Oppenheimer, who seeks political influence in order to ameliorate the anti–Semitism of his day. It starred the German expatriate Conrad Veidt, who had starred in Kurt Bernhardt's *Die Letzte Kompanie* (*The Last Company*, 1930), which had been one of Germany's first sound films.

Veidt was pilloried by the Nazi press for his work in the British production. "Veidt," wrote the *Völkischer Beobachter*, "was paid for this betrayal of his native country by the praise of the Jewish public."

Other genres served the needs of Hitler. Films of the supernatural and the occult were another form of distraction from political and social goings-on in Germany. Some of the films were made in multiple languages to insure that somewhere, someone would watch them. They too were used to attack Germany's enemies, especially Jews.

In Karl Hartl's *Gold* (1934), produced by Ufa, Hans Albers plays engineer Werner Holk, determined to prove that his mentor, Prof. Achenbach (Friedrich Keyssler), knew what he was talking about when he set out to manufacture "artificial" gold. The real metal, reasons the professor, is "both the happiness and the curse of our world." To get it, "kinsmen, tribes, nations go to war" and "men cheat, persecute, slaughter each other." A manufactured version of gold could avoid all this. The professor's interest is portrayed as noble and scientific and completely absent of greed.

On the verge of discovering the philosopher's stone—a nuclear-powered "Frankenstein electric machine" able to make the synthetic metal—the professor dies in an explosion. The press dismisses his death as carelessness, But Holk believes it was something sinister: sabotage.

His investigation leads him to the offices of British industrialist John Wills (Michael Bohnen), a man obsessed with acquiring wealth and power. At the conclusion of the tale, Holk proves that it was Wills who had sent an individual named "Vesitsch" (Heinz Wemper) to kill Achenbach and to steal his ideas.

Wills himself dies in an explosion. Holk, fearing that the news of artificial gold would set off pandemonium, vows to abandon the dream of turning lead into gold.

"Fabulous from the technical point of view," Goebbels called it in his diaries. A.C.E. also filmed the production in French, as *L'Or* (co-directed by Serge de Poligny), starring Pierre Blanchar and Brigitte Helm, to cash in on the French market and perhaps release French renditions of its film in America. But there was nothing to worry about. Hartl's German rendition was well received in New York.

So was Harry Piel's over-the-top, science fiction action film *Der Herr der Welt* (*The Master of the World*, 1934). It's the story of single-minded, half-crazed, supernatural "Professor Wolf" (Walter Franck), inventor of death rays and complex robotic machines he uses to try to gain power. Dr. Heller (Walter Janssen), his assistant, and Vilma (Sybille Schmitz) are on to the mad professor, but he's nearly unstoppable. When the mad scientist is slain, it is by his own devices. Absent any explanation of events or morality—was it real, a dream, or a fantasy?—the uncertainty suggested that the film had been edited for its American release in late 1934.

Harry Piel (1892–1963) had joined the Nazi Party in 1933. After the war the British sentenced him to six months in prison and banned him from film until 1949. Thereafter, Piel directed five forgotten films and then retired.

In Berlin in late 1934, Tobis released the fast-paced military drama *Heldentum und Todeskampf unserer Emden* (*Heroism and the End of Our Emden*, 1934), directed by and starring the Austrian-born Louis Ralph (1884–1952). It depicts the inspirational exploits of the German cruiser *Emden* during the First World War and of its heroic captain, von Müller, who died in 1923. For Germans, the ship's proud history of combat and victories had become nearly mythical. The tale couldn't be recounted often enough. Commissioned by Goebbels, this film never reached U.S. shores. Perhaps that was because in late 1932, the Weimar-era *Kreuzer Emden* (*Cruiser Emden*, 1932) had screened in the U.S. Directed by and staring Louis Ralph, it had featured the debut of actor—later turned director—Helmut Käutner.

In late 1934, American critics abroad missed the more powerful Nazi upgrade *Heldentum und Todeskampf unserer Emden* and its message of heroism in service of Germany. In 1914, the Emden was at Tsingtau, China, and from there joined the cruiser squadron led by the German battleship *Graf Spee*. She then receives orders to set out towards the Indian Ocean. There she sinks Britain's 3,400-ton *Indus*, the passenger ship *Diplomat*, and the 4,050-ton coal freighter *Trabork*. Also recounted is the attack and destruction of the oil storage tanks in Madras, and the sinking of Britain's 4,000-ton *Tymeric*.

At Penang, the Russian cruiser *Schemtschung* meets its end at the hands of the *Emden* while most of the Russian officers are ashore. Then off the coast of Australia's Cocos Islands, the British cruiser *Sidney* captures the *Emden*. But King George allows von Müller and his crew to retain their weapons in recognition of their bravery in action.

Goebbels' last commissioned effort for 1934 was *Um das Menschenrecht* (*For the Rights of Man*), which was also not shown in America. American critics abroad missed its anti–Semitic message as well. The production was a Nazi film rarity in that it needed no music to back up its hysteria. Directed by and adapted from the work of the writer Hans Zöberlein, it is set in Germany in November 1918 when the corps of volunteers known as the Freikorps (free corps) battle Jews and communists in the streets. The members of the free corps, which became the nucleus of Hitler's storm troopers, form secret organizations, one of which was the German Workers' (later the Nazi) Party that Hitler joined.

The First World War is over; Germany has lost, but (says Nazi ideology), there is no peace in Germany, only revolution. Four ex-soldiers (Hans, Girgl, Fritz, and Max) return to a Germany beset by anarchy. Two join the communist party, one joins the Freikorps, and the last retires to his farm. The streets are barricaded and communists are everywhere, plundering, looting, murdering. Three of them meet when it becomes clear none of Germany's political parties is worth supporting. At the farm, they join their other comrade. There's only one thing to do: emigrate—and wait until moral authority returns to Germany.

The theme of a cleansed Germany would be picked up again in later Nazi films, which *were* released in America as World War II drew near.

When Nazi films failed to be released to the States, the subject matter was often too alien for Americans. In one such production, German women were included in the call to serve the fatherland. Carl Froelich's *Ich für Dich—Du für Mich* (*I'm for You—You're for Me*, 1934) centers on the Bund deutscher Mädel (League of German Girls), a social organization and labor camp wrapped into one somewhere in Germany. It's the female version of the Hitler Youth. We see more than a score of girls from all walks of life brought together in friendship and work. The young women lend a hand harvesting crops of the local peasants, helping in the house, doing handicrafts, singing, acting as midwives. Although love stories are interwoven in the events of the day, duty to the group is always uppermost in their minds.

Meanwhile, Carl Froelich had something more pleasing for Americans. His Weimar musical comedy *Die—oder Keine* (*She, or Nobody*, 1932), a Metropol release in late 1934 in New York, featured Hungarian singing beauty Regina (Gitta) Alpa—who was once married to Gustav Fröhlich. Her opposite was Max Hansen as the ruler of a typical operetta kingdom who is in love with her.

This was Alpar's second and last German film. She was Jewish, and headed to Hollywood to stay out of the reach of the Nazis.

Hans Behrendt's operetta *Hochzeit am Wolfgangsee* (*Wedding at Lake Wolfgang*, 1933), with music by Robert Stolz, was made during Hitler's first year in power. Scenes of the Austrian Tyrol furnish the background to the tale of a big-city actress (Else Elster) who urges a resort innkeeper (Hugo Schrader) to try his luck on the Berlin stage.

This was one of the director's last films, shown in late 1934 in New York, when Behrendt was working in Spain. Behrendt, who began directing in 1920s Weimar, died in Auschwitz.

In late 1934, one of Germany's most famous filmmakers worked in Hollywood. Great things were expected from G.W. Pabst. But his listless effort on Warner Bros.' *A Modern Hero*, a tale about a young man's meteoric rise in industry and equally fast fall, based on the novel by Louis Bromfield, sank his prospects in Hollywood. Pabst had failed to meet Hollywood's expectations, especially since his *L'Opéra de quat' sous* (*The Beggar's Opera*, 1930–31), a Tobis-Warner Bros. production shot in Europe, had been well received when it was shown to select American filmgoers in late 1932 and at its premiere in the U.S. in December 1933.

Pabst's episodic *Don Quixote* (1933), filmed simultaneously in German and French and shown in the U.S. in December 1934, did garner acclaim. Most notable was the ending, which doesn't jibe with the novel. In Pabst's more somber version, the protagonist's books are *burned* and the broken old man dies.

The next time Pabst's name was seen on U.S. screens was January 1945, when his *Le Drame de Shanghai* (1938), starring Chrystl Mardayn, premiered in New York. By then Pabst's reputation was in shambles. An avowed leftist, he had stung the film world and his admirers when he returned *to* Germany in late 1939 and made films in Hitler's Third Reich. Not many German filmmakers who worked in the Third Reich would suffer opprobrium: especially not leftist filmmakers Erich Engel, Werner Hochbaum, Hans Schweikart, Willi Forst, and Detlef Sierck.

But that was in the future. At present, Europe was at peace. Few places better represented an imagined peace than Vienna.

1935

Casino Film Exchange and Its Imports from Germany and "Vienna"

In 1935, the year Alfred Dreyfus died, the social atmosphere in Germany was worsening for "non–Germans." In April Hitler's regime prohibited the publishing of "non–Aryan" writers. In September, the Nuremberg Laws stripped Jews of their citizenship and created gradations of Jewishness, legalized anti–Semitism, and turned the purity of German blood into the formal standard for Aryanism. The swastika was made the official symbol of the Third Reich. In November, non-belief in Nazism became a basis for divorce.

In the U.S., a small organization called Casino Film Exchange had geared up for big business. Not yet a year old, it was already the main American distributor of German-language films. These films came from Germany's biggest studios: Ufa, Tobis, and Bavaria. In 1938 Wien Film joined the group.

The films obscured the true face of the new Germany. From its East 86th Street headquarters in New York, Casino Film Exchange imported apparently innocuous German and Austrian films—most of them musicals and comedies—and showed them first at the Casino Theatre on East 86th. The Casino Theatre had opened in October 1934 with Karl Hartl's anti–British *Gold* (1934). The theater had 600 seats, having been converted from a meeting hall once owned by a musicians' union.

The man behind the operation was Joseph Scheinmann, president of CFE. Scheinmann's assistants were Mendel Grünberg and Munio Podhorzer. Scheinmann's Casino Theatre, like other theaters across the country that screened German films, lived up to the requirements of Goebbels' Nazi propaganda office. CFE had signed a contract whose clauses implied collaboration with Germany. The agreement stipulated that the films CFE distributed in the U.S. would "not be edited, arranged, published, exploited, or advertised in a manner that will tend to injure or reflect adversely upon the picture in whole or in part, or upon the country of origin of said picture ... or upon any nations friendly toward the country of origin of such picture."

In its own advertising, CFE went out of its way to praise the films. That praise was often repeated in local reviews. Munio Podhorzer arranged bookings. The programs were repeated from noon to midnight each day of a run. Most of the films played for a week. The Casino Theatre offered double features, including Ufa shorts. During its most popular years, in the mid–1930s, the theater attracted about 2,000 patrons a week and had a mailing list of 5,000 interested filmgoers. Most patrons understood German. They had to, because often the films shown lacked subtitles. One notable attendee was Marlene Dietrich, who had an apartment in Manhattan.

New York's papers, particularly the *Daily News*, rarely if ever ran a totally negative review of a film from Germany. Instead, the city's papers repeated CFE's publicity, suggesting filmgoers would be delighted with these imported productions. Ufa then made use of their reviews in *its* promotional material.

After the films ended their run at the Casino Theatre, CFE would distribute them beyond New York. It would send them to the Wagner Theater, in Ridgewood, N.J. and to the Irvington Theatre, in Irvington, N.J. When those runs ended, CFE distributed the German-language productions to American cities that had sizeable German-speaking populations: Chicago, Milwaukee, Harrisburg, Cincinnati, Cleveland, etc. In Milwaukee, the German influence was so strong, in fact, that German was a second language for schoolchildren.

CFE imported German-language films for as long as possible. Even after the U.S. entered the war and had seized German films in the U.S., CFE, undaunted, attempted to screen German films at the Casino Theatre. This necessitated the laborious process of getting a license for each film from the Office of Alien Property Custodian (APC), which confiscated German films in circulation or storage in America after the U.S. entered World War II. The German films that CFE managed to show after the U.S. entered the war were re-releases of so-called light operettas from Austria, Weimar-era productions, and other German and Austrian fare that APC deemed free of Nazi propaganda. While it appears that no profits were sent to Hitler's Germany after the U.S. entered the war, the insidious nature of Nazi films as a group went unrecognized by U.S. authorities.

Through it all, these imported films traded especially on Austria's reputation for neutrality and on the popularity of Viennese comedies and musicals. The Nazis did nothing to disabuse filmgoers of those illusions. Instead, they assigned to them a lighter tone. No thematic propaganda, clash of systems, or obvious attacks against Hitler's enemies would be launched from the blue Danube. Rather, harmless and soothing messages would flow from "Vienna," especially through its glorious music.

In 1935, in fact, the Nazis paid German music a special tribute. The aim was to bind Germans and German speakers—excepting German Jews—to Hitler's regime. This year the regime promoted the "German Bach-Handel-Schutz Festival," marking Bach's two-hundred-and-fiftieth, Handel's two-hundred-and-fiftieth, and Heinrich Schutz's three-hundred-and-fiftieth birthdays. Mozart wasn't eligible to join this pantheon: he had been born a mere 179 years earlier.

At the celebration of the Drei Altmeister ("Three Old Masters"), President of the Reichskulturkammer Goebbels spoke to an audience that included the Berlin Philharmonic. Flanked by swastikas, Goebbels stressed that it was the "duty of every generation of Germans" to "ensure the immortality" of the "Volk," as had the Drei Altmeister. Goebbels declared that the German-born trio was "German" because they "shared the blood of the German Volk" and because "their whole lives were a struggle to master the best forces of their Germanness."

Although the "forms" of their classical mastery were outmoded, he said, "their spirit lives." More importantly, because external conditions changed, Goebbels noted, "the essence of Germanness (*Deutschtum*) remains constant—as long as the German Volk survives."

A typical operetta that CFE imported and distributed in New York (and later in Chicago) was a tale about life in Austria called *Rosen aus dem Süden* (*Roses from the South*, 1934), directed by Walter Janssen. Its protagonist is Viennese composer and conductor Johann Strauss (Paul Hörbiger). When the roguish, doggy-eyed Strauss shows up at a party in Vienna and conducts the orchestra, he makes such a hit that he saves the business of a wine merchant (Oscar Sabo) and his daughter (Gretl Theimer).

Filmgoers might have imagined that since the theme was Austrian, this film was Austrian too, and shot in or around Vienna. American critics certainly thought so. This depiction of prewar Vienna is "bound to please Yorkville audiences," wrote the *New York Times* (May 25, 1935), "or any other listeners familiar with the German tongue and its variations."

German producers had filmed *Rosen aus dem Süden* in Berlin. In fact, most of the so-called Viennese films of the era were shot in Berlin. Hitler despised the Austrian capital. In *Mein Kampf*, he had written about life in Vienna: "This conglomerate spectacle of heterogeneous races which the capital of the Dual Monarchy presented, this motley of Czechs, Poles, Hungarians, Ruthenians, Serbs and Croats, etc., and always that bacillus which is the solvent of human society, the Jew, here and there and everywhere."

Yet gaiety and a pseudo-sense of calm were the norm in German films distributed in America early in 1935, including the CFE-distributed relic from Weimar: Jewish director Richard Oswald's *Gräfin Mariza* (*Countess Mariza*, 1932), starring Dorothea Wieck opposite the Jewish actors Szöke Zsakall and Ernö Verebes. The film was based on Jewish composer Emmerich Kalman's catchy operetta of the same name.

While director Oswald (born Richard W. Ornstein) left Germany in 1933, Reinhold Schünzel managed, after Hitler came to power, to hang on at Ufa for half dozen films. His gender-bender *Viktor und Viktoria* (1933) was an Ufa production that Deutsche Universal released in America, starring Renate Müller and Hermann Thimig. Schünzel was also responsible for *Amphitryon, Donogoo Tonka, Das Mädchen Irene*, and *Land der Liebe* (1937).

In his diaries, Goebbels characterized the last film, which starred Valerie von Martens, as "typical Jewish sham." When Schünzel could bear Germany no more, he accepted Louis B. Mayer's offer to relocate to Hollywood. Schünzel's first American film was *New Wine* (1941), a musical about Schubert's life that co-starred expatriate actors Albert Bassermann (as Beethoven), Sig Arno, and Ernö Verebes.

Working along Schünzel's side in 1930s Germany was assistant director Kurt Hoffmann (1910–2001). He remained in Nazi Germany throughout the war, directing a half-dozen films between 1938 and 1945, including *Kohlhiesels Töchter* (1943), a story about two sisters that had been previously filmed by two former German-Jewish directors: Ernst Lubitsch in 1920 and Hans Behrendt in 1930. Hoffmann, who was the son of photographer Carl Hoffmann, entered the Germany military in 1945, in the last months of the war, and was taken prisoner by the Allies. Resuming his film career in 1948, Hoffmann directed a score of films until 1971, and picked up countless awards from West Germany.

New German discovery Karen Horney—daughter of famed British therapist Karen Horney and wife of Russian-born photographer Konstantin Irmen-Tschet—had been touted as a possible "find" for Hollywood. The vehicle of hers that attracted the Americans was Ufa's suspenseful *Liebe, Tod und Teufel* (*Love, Death and the Devil*, 1934)—a drama of the occult and supernatural inspired by Robert Louis Stevenson's 1893 story "The Bottle Imp." Directed by Heinz Hilpert (1890–1967) and Reinhart Steinbicker, and scripted by Kurt Heuser and Lieselotte von Gravenstein, the un-subtitled film reached American screens in mid–1935. On the island of Hawaii—far enough from German soil to imply exoticism—the schooner *Tropic Bird* with its motley crew is anchored after an absence of three years. One of its sailors named Kiwe (Albin Skoda) wanders into a novelty shop and pays $50 for a strange, unbreakable, supernatural bottle. Legend has it that the bottle fulfills its owner's wishes. But there's a price to pay: the devil gets to keep the owner's soul until he can sell the bottle for less than he paid for it.

Kiwe's dreams come true when he meets Kokua (Käthe von Nagy) and inherits a fortune. But the sailor then sells the bottle just as Kokua becomes deathly ill. Only the bottle can save her, but reacquiring it is complicated by the jealousy of an unscrupulous rival, the sultry singer Rubby (Horney), and the fact that the bottle has passed through many hands. When Kiwe finds it—he pays but a penny for it—he prays for Kokua's recovery. Then Kiwe must sell it for less than he paid. His girlfriend Kokua does the impossible. She sells it to the drunken, non–German sailor "Mounier" (Albrecht Wäscher) for a centime.

Hilpert, Steinbricker, and Raoul Ploquin (1900–1992) directed a French version, *Le Diable en Bouteille* (*Devil in a Bottle*, 1934), which A.C.E. produced.

Rising German star Käthe von Nagy was also the prime attraction in Gerhardt Lamprecht's exotic *Prinzessin Turandot* (1934), which was produced by Ufa and scripted by Thea von Harbou. It takes place a thousand years before the Third Reich, recounting the legend of the Chinese princess whose aversion to marriage led her to a simple expedient. She would marry the first man who could answer a riddle she posed to him; if he failed, he would be beheaded. Many a would-be husband had his head put on public display. In the end, when one suitor succeeds, the princess faces a quandary. She still doesn't want marriage, but she's given her word. In Nazi ideology, as opposed to Weimar culture, no matter how exalted the woman, a good, ordinary German can win her heart, and besides, her place is beside a man. She marries the commoner.

Ufa's collaborator, A.C.E., produced a French rendition, *Turandot, princesse de Chine*, co-directed by Serge Véber (1897–1976).

Gerhard Lamprecht's *Einmal eine grosse Dame sein* (*Once a Great Lady*, 1934) was a contemporary drama about a young German (Käthe von Nagy) who longs to achieve great status. Working as the secretary at an important Berlin auto company, she tries to impress a wealthy Australian. Desperately she impersonates a countess from abroad. Before she is exposed, her dream comes true: she becomes engaged—but to a German, who then accepts her for herself.

Lamprecht and Serge Véber again collaborated on a French version, *Un Jour viendra*, again produced by A.C.E.

The Casino Theatre, however, was not averse to showing non-musicals, including anti–Semitic and hard-core Nazi productions. Franz Seitz's *Zwischen Himmel und Erde* (*Between Heaven and Earth*, 1934), produced by Bavaria Film, centers on Fritz (Atilla Hörbiger), who is a Jekyll and Hyde type. Unfortunately, it's his selfish, drunken, and abusive side that often prevails. At the end of this drama set in the years 1870–71, Fritz dies in a fall. Everybody in his village believes he committed suicide in order to make amends. But there is an overlooked subplot involving the village's dealer in building materials, named "Motz" (Otto Wernecke), and his daughter, Lily (Vera Liessem), who schemes to marry Karl (Heinz Klingenberg), Fritz's honorable younger brother. The little music teacher, Christine (Karin Hardt), foils their plans when *she* marries Karl.

The "scenes in the mountain village are delightful," wrote the *New York Times* (January 21, 1935).

In Viktor Janson's operetta *Die Grosse Chance* (*The Big Chance*, 1934), which CFE distributed in spring 1935, there were numerous gibes at social standards based on wealth and family connections that were anathema in the new Germany. So when a struggling young German inventor (Hans Soehnker) crosses social barriers to capture the heart of rich heiress and aviatrix Helga, played by the star Camilla Horn, it is all to the good.

Max Obal's *Die vom Niederrhein* (*Lower Rhine Folks*, 1933), which Casino Film Exchange imported in early 1935, joined the parade with its views of the Rhine and its palaces and castles and scenes of Heidelberg. There were also hints of a new Germany being born in scenes of efficient German steel production in Düsseldorf.

Outdoor settings played an important visual part in German films of the era. They served to distract viewers from the less attractive daily realities of Nazi life. "What camps?" one might have asked. The mountains were gorgeous in these movies.

The chance encounter between Irmgard Faber (Karin Hardt), an aristocrat's daughter with a heart of gold who plans to take part in a small-town's passion play, and Erich Büchner

(Walter Ladengast), a near-starving artist from Munich, was at the heart of the Nazi writer-director Richard Schneider-Edenkoben's drama *Die Törichte Jungfrau* (*The Foolish Virgin*, 1934–35), produced by Ufa. The aimless lives of Bohemians—their salvation, according to Nazi ideology, lies in real work—was the subject of a production by Latvian-born Johannes Guter (1881–1967), called *Fräulein Liselott* (1934), starring Magda Schneider (1909–96) and imported to America in 1935 by CFE.

In February 1935, CFE showed the war film *Stosstrupp 1917* (*Shock Troop 1917*), which had been completed in Germany a year earlier. The music-less film reflected Hitler's views from *Mein Kampf* about the causes of Germany's economic and social decline during and after the Great War. It was also the Nazis' response to G.W. Pabst's 1930 anti-war, Weimar classic, *Kameradschaft 1918* (*Comradeship 1918*).

Episodes cover the activities of a troop of German soldiers and the various battles from the German side in the Great War: against the French, in Flanders, August 15–16, 1917; at the breakthrough at Cambrai by the English with hundreds of tanks; and finally during Christmas 1917 when a British prisoner of war dies in the German trenches.

The film makes a point of noting the anti–German treachery of German civilians in contrast to the heroism and devotion to duty of the ordinary German fighting man.

Hans Zöberlein (1895–1964) and costar Ludwig Schmid–Wildy (1896–1982) had directed the film with the blessing of the Nazis and the active assistance of the Reichwehr (army) and Hitler's storm troopers, based on Zoberlein's super-nationalist book, *Germany's Faith*. Zöberlein was a World War I veteran and an early member of the Nazi party. From 1933 to 1934 he was member of the Munich city council. In April 1945 as the war was coming to a close,

The fighting men of the German army in *Stosstrupp 1917*.

Zöberlein spearheaded a raid against striking miners in Hausham. Several workers were murdered. After the war, Zöberlein was sentenced to death. The German government's cynical abolition of the death penalty in 1948, however, saved his life and the lives of convicted Nazis and collaborators. Zöberlein received a 20-year prison term.

CFE followed with another German militarist production, an apparently harmless little picture with, wrote the *New York Times* (March 16, 1935), "excellent views of the Austrian Tyrol." It was called *Drei Kaiserjäger* (*Three Imperial Light Infantrymen*, 1933), and was directed by Robert Land and Franz Hofer (1882–1945). Land (1887–1939), born Robert Liebman, had directed Marlene Dietrich in the late 1920s Weimar hit *Ich küsse Ihre Hand, Madame* (*I Kiss Your Hand, Madame*, 1929), which had reached the States in August 1932.

Drei Kaiserjäger is a tale whose themes of duty to country and hatred of the Habsburg Empire were much admired by Hitler. The story begins three years before the First World War. The nobleman Hans von Roth (Paul Richter)—an officer in the infantry—is about to be married. At his bachelor party he drinks too much, starts betting, and loses a fortune to "Lt. Glaser" (Michael von Newlinski), a presumed Jew. His family pays his debt, but in disgrace he resigns his commission and departs for America. In August 1914, the archduke is assassinated, and the young von Roth, having failed to make anything of himself in the New World, returns to Innsbruck via Trieste, penniless. His father, the commanding officer of the light infantrymen, refuses to see him; only his onetime fiancée Liesl (Else Elster) stays true to him. But the outbreak of the war opens up new opportunities for everybody. Since his country needs every man now, von Roth knows his duty: he rejoins his old regiment. Amid much fanfare and flag waving, the young German, along with soldierly comrades Rixner (Heinrich Heilinger) and Sonnleitner (Fritz Kampers), marches off to war.

Produced by Sirius/ABC, this was the seventh of nine films that Goebbels' ministry financed in the first year of Hitler's rule. What American critics had said about *Morgenrot* could be said of *Drei Kaiserjäger*. It was both a demonstration of Germany's military commitment to the spirit of World War I and a recognition of film's ability to serve as a valuable form of national historiography. Hitler had said in *Mein Kampf*, "It was the hand of the goddess of eternal justice and an inexorable retribution that caused the most deadly enemy of Germanism in Austria, the Archduke Franz Ferdinand, to fall by the very bullets which he himself had helped to cast. Working from above downwards, he was the chief patron of the movement to make Austria a Slav State.... The burdens laid on the shoulders of the German people were enormous and the sacrifices of money and blood which they had to make were incredibly heavy."

The struggle to keep Austria out of enemy hands is at the heart of the CFE release called *Der Judas von Tirol* (*Judas from the Tyrol*, 1933). Starring Hanns Beck-Gaden (1891–1950) and Camilla Spira and scored by Gottfried Huppertz, it was promoted in Germany as a film "of the people" and "for the people." Directed by Franz Osten, it recalls the early nineteenth-century nationalistic Austrian rebel Andreas Hofer, who resisted French rule during the Napoleonic Wars. The film implies that money led to Hofer's downfall.

In 1810, Hofer (who's played anonymously) is a fugitive in the Tirol, yet he refuses to yield to the French. However, the dull-witted Austrian farmhand Franz Raffel (Fritz Rasp) seals Hofer's fate. For 200 gold pieces, Raffel leads the French to him. The money will allow Raffel to become a landowner, with its attendant privileges. Before he surrenders, Hofer forbids his few followers from wasting their lives in resistance. Executed, Andreas Hofer becomes a martyr. Raffel comes to symbolize eternal betrayal and treachery.

After taking part in this film, Jewish actress Spira was interned in a concentration camp. When Spira was set free, she left Germany. CFE re-released *Der Judas von Tirol* in the U.S. in June 1941.

On April Fools' Day, 1935, CFE released a pseudohistorical drama that well represents the Nazis' goal of distributing German films that were artistic, that offered international appeal, and that were ideological: Johannes Meyer's *Schwarzer Jäger Johanna* (*Johanna the Black Corps Volunteer*, 1934), produced by Terra-Film with music by Winfried Zillig. Recalling one of the myths of the Napoleonic wars, the "resistance" in 1809 of the duke of Brunswick against invading French forces, the film depicts Austria as Hitler presented it in *Mein Kampf*—as un–German. The film also demonstrates the Nazis' belief in supernatural symbols. The heroine is a proto-Nazi type. In this tale, Major Korfes (Paul Hartmann) is organizing underground resistance to Napoleon. Johanna (Marianne Hoppe), innocently involved in his plans, falls in love with him and helps him evade the French. To join him on the battlefield she cuts her hair and dons black armor, which symbolizes near invincibility. She fights with the detachment of soldiers led by Prince Sulkowski: the Black Corps of the Duke of Brunswick (Paul Bildt, 1885–1957). However, the Austrians stab the Germans in the back when they sign an armistice with the French, which the duke—a real German—opposes.

He aims to reach the North Sea with his Black Corps in order to join his allies, the British. However, double agent "Dr. Frost" (Gustav Gründgens) betrays them to the French. The French try to make Johanna confess. Incredibly, her resistance and heroism, bordering on the supernatural, so impresses the Westphalian Germans allied to the French that they lay down their arms. The French retreat and release Johanna, who rides to join Korfes.

A familiar refrain ran through these German war films from the early years of Nazi rule: Germans know their duty, Germans belong at home, the nation is rearming and ready for the fight, and this time, victory! Further, Austrians shorn of their Habsburg history have strong ties to Germany. Hitler was the prime example: although born in Austria, he had enlisted in the German army. But there was one arena of entertainment that was uncritically accepted by just about everyone: so-called comedies.

One of Dolly Haas's last comedies from Germany, *Der Page vom Dalmasse-Hotel* (*The Page of the Hotel Dalmasse*, 1933), directed by Viktor Janson and produced by Terra, centered on deception. The Casino Theatre screened it in New York in late March 1935. Dressed as a male, Friedl Bornemann (Haas) earns a living as the page Friedrich Petersen in a big Berlin hotel. She helps a German detective on a special case. They save the handsome middle-aged Baron Arthur von Dahlen (Harry Liedke) from losing his money to a band of high-class crooks: two self-styled American women named Mrs. Wellington (Trude Hesterberg) and her daughter Mabel (Gina Falckenberg); and their accomplice, a foreign confidence man called "Count Tarvagna" (Hans Adalbert Schlettow). Friedl and the baron, of course, fall in love after her identity is revealed.

Numerous comedies, for instance by the prolific Berlin-born Carl Boese (1887–1958), often featuring the hard-working folk actress Lucie Englisch (1906–65), looked at the surface reality of the complications of ordinary (and apparently un-political) German life. However, there was almost always a catch in these films. The bankers, crooks, and scoundrels were invariably Jewish or foreign. American critics didn't seem to care and didn't often mention this stereotyping. Boese had made his name in 1920 when he and Paul Wegener directed the well-received, if subtly anti–Semitic, *Der Golem*, a sixteenth-century tale about a mythical clay figure protecting the Jews of Prague. Boese worked briefly for Deutsche Universal and directed nearly 50 films during the Nazi era.

In the 1930s, Boese's German and Austrian films constituted a blizzard of distraction for filmgoers. Many of his films were screened at the Casino Theatre. Although his films concerned themselves with the trivial events of daily life, they were not free of Nazi ideology. As the horrors of German life grew, less and less of what was taking place found its way into contemporary German films. Instead, movie fare revolved around quotidian affairs. For example, Boese's *Meine Frau, die Schützenkönig* (*My Wife the Champion Shot*, 1934) concerns itself with a small-town crack shot trying out for the big time in Berlin; and in *Die Kalte Mamsell* (*The Sandwich Girl*, 1933), distributed by CFE, a pretty waitress makes a mess of an upcoming wedding. The joys of peacetime army life were at the heart of Boese's Weimar-era *Drei von der Kavallerie* (*Three Cavalrymen*, 1932), distributed by CFE, in which an entire outfit is confined to quarters for three weeks because officers and enlisted men have been chasing women. The punishment pleases the city fathers—until business in the town begins to suffer.

Boese's musical comedy *Gretel zieht das grosse Los* (*Gretel Wins First Prize*, 1933), also distributed by CFE, reflects ideas of the new German regime. The protagonist is Gretel Schmidt (Lucie Englisch), who, although she forges a winning lottery ticket—she changes 22883 into 22888—comes across as modest and full of domesticity. Her big dream is to work in radio. By contrast, her opposite is the brunette Gerda (Hilde Hildebrand), an emancipated woman of the roaring twenties who drinks too much. Since it's often said that you know people by the company they keep, Gerda's good friend is the banker "Herklotz" (Walter Steinbeck).

In Boese's *Liebe dumme Mama* (*Dear, Stupid Mama*, 1934), a young, good-hearted German takes over the running of a high-class hotel from her inept mother (Leopoldine Konstantin). The subject of a young German successfully turning a rundown business into an enterprising success couldn't be repeated often enough in Nazi films. It was at the center of *Jungfrau gegen Mönch* (*Maiden vs. Monk*, 1934), directed by E.W. Emo, about longtime rival hotels—idealized Germans—in the Bavarian mountains. The lively young schoolteacher Mutz Hagedorn (Dorit Kreysler) inherits The Maiden, while the honorable young German Konrad Leitner (Paul Richter) runs The Monk.

Boese's musical comedy *Die Unschuld vom Lande* (*The Innocent Country Girl*, 1932–33), which CFE distributed in May 1935, featured Lucie Englisch as the village maiden Annerl Lechleitner, who gets a chance at becoming a big star on the Berlin stage.

Boese's *Der Schüchterne Felix* (*Bashful Felix*, 1934), produced by Terra and distributed by CFE, was an early Nazi rarity: a satire about Jewish business control and how easy it was to become a success. There were Jews galore in this production. It concerns traveling salesman "Felix Kaminski" (Rudolf Platte) who works at the firm of Zehnschock & Son. Other Jewish businessmen in town were named "Meyerhoff" (Hans Hemes), "Mahlke" (Friedrich Ettel), "Strich" (Gaston Briese), "Jacubeit" (Karl Harbacher), and "Scherzinger" (Hans Hermann).

Kaminski has a simple job: to sell a new line of bathing suits. A total failure, he writes his resignation and is about to mail it in when he encounters a postmaster's niece, the lively "Lilli Passerow" (Ursula Grabley). This girl with the Jewish surname is willing to be his model—and expose herself. Of course, when Lilli is at her most exposed, she encounters "Amelie Scherzinger" (Leonie Duval), the wife of a local merchant. Lilli avoids humiliation by claiming to be Mrs. Kaminski. As Felix's sales boom, the pseudo-couple then set up their "marriage" as purely a matter of business. Felix, however, is too intimidated to tell Lilli he really loves her until his firm's boss, "Julius Zenschock" (Paul Heidemann), notices her. A bit of liquor and bravado on the rifle range make it easier for Felix to ask Lilli for her hand.

Boese's comedy *Das Lied vom Glück* (*The Song of Happiness*, 1933), which screened at the Casino Theatre, was one of the last films by German Jewish producers Jacob and Max Brodsky. Here American heiress Thea Warner (Ery Bos) finds herself engaged—in the newspapers—to rising young German composer Carl Roland (Ernst Groh). That's because Roland's friend, Bernhard Probst (Paul Kemp), had made it all up, hoping to stave off Roland's creditors. However, the unintended consequence is that Roland's fiancée, Erna Vogel (Ilse Stobrawa), flees the country.

The film's theme song, "Es gibt nur eine Melodie" ("There Is Only One Melody"), the *New York Times* (November 30, 1935) wrote, would "likely to stick in the memories of the spectators for some time." In German films, music would drown out reality.

CFE imported the screen debut of American tenor Charles Kullman: the AAFA operetta *Die Sonne geht Auf* (*The Sun Rises*, 1934). He played an opera star settling down with a beautiful stenographer in Berlin—so long as he's assured his widowed mother is taken care of in her home in the country. Mother love in German films would reach its peak with Gustav Ucicky's *Mutterliebe* (1939). In *Johannesnacht* (1933) the great actress Lisa Lers (Lil Dagover) is attracted to life in the German mountains thanks to the honest love of a real man. Giving up her city life and her empty stage triumphs, she settles down as the wife of a respected country playwright, Heinrich Radegast (Hans Stüwe).

Willy Reiber (1898–1980), who had been the art director of Hitchcock's *The Mountain Eagle* (1926), directed both AAFA productions. In 1943 Willy Reiber produced the anti–Semitic *Titanic*.

The Ufa comedy *Frischer Wind aus Kanada* (*Fresh Breeze from Canada*, 1934–35), by Heinz Kenter and Erich Holder (1901–1974), featured a wholesome youth returning to the fatherland in order to save his family's business from two men portrayed as Jewish: a crooked accountant named "Meinkel" (Paul Hörbiger) and a scheming lawyer named "Bernetzki" (Oskar Sima). Harald Paulsen played the "fresh breeze" from Canada who puts his father's money to wise use.

Financial woes of struggling young Germans are at the heart of *Pechmarie* (*Hard Luck Mary*, 1934), produced by Klagemann-Film and by the German subsidiary of the American studio Fox. Its director was Erich Engel (1891–1966), a proclaimed Marxist and friend of Bertolt Brecht's who managed to collaborate with the Nazis for 12 years. In Weimar Germany, Engel had directed Deutsche Universal's *Fünf von der Jazzband* (*Five from the Jazzband*, 1932), which had made Jenny Jugo a star. Hermann Kosterlitz scripted it. In *Pechmarie*, which Engel and Eva Leidmann scripted, Jenny Jugo played poor Mary, a young woman who lives in a furnished room in a depressed section of Berlin. She's had a run of bad luck, and her boyfriend Peter (Friedrich Benfer), a house painter, becomes jealous when she makes friends of "the vagabond" Bonse (Willy Schur). Mary's fortunes change thanks to a winning lottery ticket. She then reconciles with her boyfriend—and they move into a new suburban home in the new Germany. The *New York Times* (April 22, 1935) was impressed by the "realistic" depiction of Berlin residents.

Posing as someone else was often a plot element in Nazi productions. Czech-born Martin Fric directed a comedy with just that idea: *Der Doppelbräutigam* (*The Double Fiancé*, 1934), produced by Itala-Moldavia Film and shown at the 79th Street Theater in New York in March 1935. Husky Nazi star Fritz Kampers was the whole show as the young composer Viktor Lange who lands a job at a publishing house by representing himself as his own uncle, that is, "Prof. Alfred Ritter." He wins the hand of the boss's daughter (Lien Deyers) and escapes marriage to a future sister-in-law (Carsta Löck) because of his pose as the "uncle."

Fritz Kampers was the director of one of the earliest openly anti–Semitic Nazi films: *Konjunkturritter* (*Financial Opportunists*, 1933). When it screened at New York's 79th Street Theater in April 1935, little was said about its theme. The film's title was a well-known Nazi term of opprobrium about Jews. Set in the early 1920s, when speculative fever was everywhere, two real estate agents—Jews named "Untermeier" and "Glaser" (Otto Wallberg and Theo Lingen)—set up honest German law-firm employee Ferdinand Mühbauer (Weiss Ferdl). Ferdinand is charged with stealing a fortune. However, the firm's self-effacing young attorney, Günther (Curt Vespermann), comes to the rescue, turning the tables on Untermeier and Glaser and saving the young German from a jail sentence.

Money is also a key element in another anti–Semitic film that Fritz Kampers directed in the Third Reich: *Ich sing' mich in dein Herz hinein* (*I Sing Myself into Thy Heart*, 1934), based on Max W. Kimmich's novel, which CFE distributed in June 1935. Here Hans Weiringen (Hans

Söhnker)—who loves to listen to the title number—discovers that his father Gustav (Hans von Zeditz) has borrowed money to invest in a boxers' training camp. However, the whole thing's a fraud. The con artists are "Countess Alexa Tschernoff" (Lotte Loring) and her "chauffeur," James (Fritz Odemar). Critics merely noted that the film comprised a series of mix-ups and developments divided between the big city and the beautiful countryside.

More memorable German musicals came to America through the more forceful and engaging films of Austrian-born director Willi Forst. His musicals helped dampen concerns about the nature of the German-speaking Nazi regime. The American starting point for his films was New York's 79th Theatre. Forst's first directorial effort was a rare British-Austrian-German production about Franz Schubert called *The Unfinished Symphony* (1934), which garnered acclaim in America, ironically, because of the performance by Jewish actor Hans Járay as the gentle, sad-faced composer struggling to achieve fame and find love. He fails to complete the B Minor Symphony because he loses the woman he wants, Countess Caroline Esterhazy (Marta Eggerth). Her rich father had opposed their marriage. The strings of the symphony rise and swell as the plot develops and as Schubert, crestfallen, composes "Ave Maria."

Variety (September 1, 1934), when it reviewed the film in London prior to its U.S. debut in early 1935, called Forst's film "one of the most artistic pictures ever made anywhere." But it is the "romantic atmosphere that gets to you." In addition to the local shots of a serene Austria, the film featured the Vienna Philharmonic Orchestra, the Wiener Sängerknaben, the chorus of the Vienna State Opera, and the Gyula Howarth band.

Forst's Austro-Hungarian colleague, director Georg Jacoby (1882–1965), also had a passion for music. Many of his musicals, starring his wife Marta Eggerth, entertained Americans as well. Jacoby's Ufa-produced *Die Czardasfürstin* (*Dance Princess*, 1934) takes viewers to the all's-well-with-the-world upper crust, theatrical-life society in Budapest and Vienna, where a vaudeville performer (Eggerth) wins the heart of a handsome officer-prince (Hans Söhnker). The tale was based on Jewish composer Emmerich Kálmán's operetta. In Germany, Ufa deleted Kálmán's name from the credits. At one stroke, the Nazis were depicting an era that was vanishing and erasing the Jews' connection to Germany.

In New York, however, composer Kálmán received top billing for his operetta about the young Viennese Hussar Edwin Weylersheim, who falls in love with the Budapest singer Sylva Varescu. His commanding officer is not pleased about this state of affairs because he knows that in Vienna a prospective bride awaits the officer. Edwin's father tries to save Edwin from what one of the characters calls the singer's "clutches." The efforts are all in vain until Count Feri (Paul Hörbiger) convinces Edwin to do his duty and accept an assignment in America. This was sure to separate the pair, he imagined. But Edwin's friend, Count Boni (Paul Kemp) intervenes: he "kidnaps" Sylva before Edwin's departure and releases her into Edwin's arms at the station.

The *Herald Tribune* (April 25, 1935) praised the film's "touches of gaiety, humor, and lilting music." Its critic added, however, that it "leaves a kind of nostalgia in its wake" for Ufa's great films of the "pre–Nazi years." To retain its market of non–German speakers after Hitler's rise to power, the studio incorporated the "czardas," the non–German Hungarian national dance, into a number of its musicals in the mid-1930s. In conjunction with A.C. E., Ufa also produced French versions of its musicals. The French version of *Die Czardasfürstin* was *Princesse Czardas* (1934), co-directed by André Beucler.

George Jacoby made one film with a Hollywood studio. The timing was fortunate. His operetta *Madonna, wo bist du?* (*Madonna, Who Art Thou?*, 1933) was produced by Paramount's German affiliate just as the Nazis came to power. It reached the States via CFE several years after its completion. It co-starred Jewish actors Fritz Schulz and Otto Wallburg. In the film, Liane Haid plays the star of an operetta engaged to its elderly director (Paul Otto) but in love with a dashing Bavarian (Viktor de Kowa) she met at a masked ball. When their love becomes evident—a musical number (by Franz Grothe) "Madonna, Where Are You?" continually plays on the radio—the old man does the honorable German thing: he steps aside for the young lovers.

Other Jacoby films released in the States included *Ehestreik* (*Matrimonial Strike*, 1935) produced by Ufa and scripted by Alois Johannes Lippl (1903–1957), which had a theme derived from *Lysistrata*. The locale is contemporary Bavaria where wives and sweethearts band together to keep their men from spending most of their time (and money) in the village inn, recently made more inviting by an attractive waitress (Trude Marlen) from the city. In Jacoby's short comedy *Der Störenfried* (*The Troublemaker*, 1933), produced by Ufa, Dutch-born Adele Sandrock played an impressive 1890s battleaxe of a mother-in-law.

Ufa's musical *Zigeunerbaron* (*Gypsy Baron*, 1935), directed by Karl Hartl (1899–1978), is set in the Vienna of the nineteenth century. Based on Johann Strauss's operetta of the same name, it has stirring czardas and preaches harmony among Austrians, Hungarians, and gypsies. In the film, which screened at New York's 79th Street Theater, Sandor Barinkay (Adolf Wohlbrück), the exiled and long-lost scion of a wealthy family, returns to Vienna in the guise of a gypsy, His mission is to reclaim his family's great estate, which the Austro-Hungarian government had seized because of his father's ties to the former Turkish rulers. The farmer Zaupan (Fritz Kampers) now owns it. In the end, Sandor wins back the family manor and marries the gypsy maiden, Saffi (Hansi Knoteck), rather than the farmer's daughter (Gina Falckenberg).

Variety (September 17, 1935) noted that the gypsy was a "distinctly non–Aryan type." It also wrote that the film would "probably be seen by more people in America than the average German film of today for two reasons. First, the Johann Strauss music; second, the story is laid in Austria without semblance of Nazi propaganda." A French-language rendition was produced by Ufa-A.C.E., called *Le Baron Tzigane* (1935). It was co-directed by Henri Chomette (1896–1941), René Clair's brother, who made several films for A.C.E.

Music fills the air in two films by E.W. Emo (Emerich Josef Wojtek), a Polish-born director who earned a fine livelihood in Nazi Germany while Jews vanished around him. Emo directed the Bavarian actress Magda Schneider as the girl whose "voice with a smile" attracts the interest of a philandering opera star in *Fräulein—falsch Verbunden* (*Wrong Number, Miss*, 1932), by Itala Film. Emo's ... *Und wer küsst mich?* (*...And Who Is Kissing Me?*), also by Itala Film, screened at New York's 79th Street Theater. The *New York Times* (January 28, 1935) called the latter film "one of the gayest romantic musical comedies that ever reached the Yorkville German-language cinemas." That's because the stars were effervescent ballet dancer Marian Taal and the lanky Jewish comic with floppy hair, soulful eyes and a big nose, Felix Bressart. This film was their last from Germany, made in 1932!

Bressart's earliest German sound films had their U.S. premieres after Hitler came to power, including *Der Glückszylinder* (*The Lucky Top Hat*, 1932), directed by Vienna-born Rudolf Bernauer (a colleague of Joe May's) who found safety in Britain. U.S. filmgoers had a chance to see Bressart in one of his best roles, that of an impecunious clerk. He falls for an unemployed blonde (Charlotte Anders), who then lands a fat film contract, which saves them both from the poor house.

Old-era military comedies were popular in the 1930s, at least for German-speaking audiences in the States, even if the films had been made years earlier, in the era of Weimar. One of these was Carl Boese's *Drei Tage Mittelarrest* (*Three Days in the Guardhouse*, 1930), a Weimar production which New York censors considered risqué. They banned it repeatedly. After several scenes were excised, the censors relented in May 1933, allowing the film to be screened at New York's Vanderbilt Theatre. Bressart and Fritz Schulz played soldiers garrisoned in the town of Flowinkel, chasing an attractive maid (Lucie Englisch). She becomes pregnant. She reveals only that the father is one of the soldiers. At the same time the regiment's officers (including Paul Otto) are up to no good themselves, their eyes on the mayor's daughter (Gretl Theimer).

Bressart had also been the star attraction in Viktor Janson's comedy-drama caper *Holzapfel weiss Alles* (*Holzapfel Knows All*, 1931–32). Bressart's Jewish colleague Fritz Schulz had starred in E.W. Emo's *Heute Nacht—eventüll* (*Tonight—Eventually*, 1930), which screened in the States after Hitler's rise to power. The comedian played a composer and head of a jazz band. Schulz also starred in George Jacoby's *Ja, treu ist die Soldatenliebe* (*Indeed, A Soldier's Love Is True*, 1932), a prewar military farce that was one of Schulz's last films from Germany. It screened in New York in April 1934.

Finding safety in Vienna, Schulz directed *Letzte Liebe* (*Last Love*, 1935), a musical by Richard Tauber featuring Hans Járay, Albert and Elsa Bassermann, and Oscar Karlweis. In Budapest, Schulz directed Hunnia studio's comedy *Helyet az Oregeknek* (*Room for the Aged*, 1934), with music by Nicholas Brodsky, starring Jewish colleagues Szöke Szakall, Rose Barsony, and Ernö Verebes. "Those who play the leads," noted *Variety* (December 18, 1934) "are Hungarian actors of non–Aryan extraction who have been exiled from Berlin." Schulz survived the Nazi assault on Europe's Jews and continued his film career after the war.

In 1933, British director Maurice Elvy turned E. Temple Thurston's play *The Wandering Jew* into a film. Shown in the U.S. in early 1935, it centers on the travails of a Jew who purportedly urged the Romans to crucify Jesus. For this act, Matathias (Conrad Veidt) is doomed to live forever. The film depicts his suffering through the ages: as a survivor of the Crusades; a persecuted thirteenth-century merchant in Sicily; and as a physician in Seville during the Inquisition. The clear implication was that in the 1930s, Europe's Jews were in just as much trouble. One American organization that agreed was New York's Non-Sectarian Anti-Nazi League. The League had its beginnings in May 1933, when Yiddish journalist Abraham Coralnik founded the American League for the Defense of Jewish Rights. Samuel Untermyer, his successor, renamed the organization the Non-Sectarian Anti-Nazi League to Champion Human Rights. The league's main goal was to highlight the plight of Germany's Jews; its weapon was a call to boycott German goods, including films from Nazi Germany and any of its collaborators. If the league couldn't stop the showing of German films, it could at least expose their origins, which it hoped would dampen filmgoers' interest in German films.

Vice-presidents of the Non-Sectarian Anti-Communist League included New York's Mayor Fiorello H. LaGuardia; Col. Theodore Roosevelt, Jr.; and the Zionist leader Abba Hillel Silver. The organization published the *Anti-Nazi Bulletin*, which exposed America's economic ties to Germany, including Germany's revenues from the screening of Nazi films in America. For the period of January-March 1934, the league reported a measure of success. Compared to 232,000 Reichmarks that Germany had earned in the pre–Hitler period of January-March, 1932, Germany earned only 110,00 Reichmarks from films exported to the U.S in the three months of 1934. By 1936, Germany's economic situation deteriorated further. It made only a third of the foreign films sales made in the year before Hitler came to power.

Yet the league hoped to do more. One way was to stress the fact that the chief distributor of German-language films in America was Casino Film Exchange. Exposure of CFE's role might cause filmgoers to boycott its releases and skip the Casino Theatre entirely. The league also pointed out that Ufa Film was affiliated with Hitler's regime and that films made by Tobis, Terra, Bavaria, Itala, and Wien Film were similarly tainted.

The American Jewish Congress, led by Rabbi Stephen S. Wise, had issued its own boycott declaration against German products in August 1933. Its Joint Boycott Council became a boycott proponent in the United States. The council, which was headed by Joseph Tennenbaum, lasted until the U.S. entered the war. However, the boycott activities of Untermyer's league and Tennenbaum's council were rarely in harmony and support for a nationwide anti–Nazi boycott never received the full backing of important U.S. organizations and leaders, the American public, or the American Jewish community. The American Jewish Committee and B'nai B'rith, in fact, opposed a boycott of Germany and its products, fearing a rise in American anti–Semitism. There is evidence that leading figures within the Nazi regime, however, were concerned about the impact of a widespread American boycott.

Concern of a different sort came from the FBI, which kept a close watch on the league's activities as well the activities of an unrelated, pro-Soviet organization: the Hollywood Anti-Nazi League. In Hollywood, producers and distributors had agreed only to boycott unidentified German/Nazi films. In the long run, that wasn't nearly enough.

One of the earliest productions that Goebbels had commissioned, *Der Choral von Leuthen* (*The Hymn of Leuthen*, 1933) screened in early 1935 at New York's 79th Street Theater—and was not identified as a Nazi film. It was the first Nazi rendition of the life of Frederick the Great. Directed by the Nazi supporter Carl Froelich and produced by Ufa, it recounts the military campaigns and leadership qualities of Prussia's greatest ruler. Frederick (Otto Gebühr) is the tough soldier of popular imagination and legend, according to the director and supporting cast, which included Veit Harlan, Paul Otto, and Olga Tschechowa. Frederick is depicted as single-minded and full of conviction. He permits no one to stand in his way. His powerful personality carries the day against his defeatist staff, officers, and generals. Frederick, wily and quick thinking, having escaped from a trap, then takes the biggest risk of his life: he stakes his fate and the fate of Prussia on the Battle of Leuthen, in December 1757. His army, outnumbered 34,000 to 90,000, overwhelms opposing Austrian forces. The following year, Frederick defeats his Austrian enemies in Silesia. Victorious, Frederick, the undisputed leader of his people, is able to reshape Prussia in his image.

The parallel to Hitler was obvious. Goebbels named the film a National Film Prize winner. The most elaborate German historical spectacle of them all—one that really glorified Hitler—was Veit Harlan's (and Goebbels') *Der Grosse König* (*The Great King*), produced by Tobis in 1942 and starring Otto Gebühr, Gustav Fröhlich, and Paul Wegener. In Austria, where Hitler was born, its title was *Der Führer seines Volkes* (*The Leader of His People*). In this film, Frederick the Great is near the end of his life, but he refuses to give up even after Austrian forces defeat his Prussian army at Kunersdorf in 1759, and his generals sink into despair. Only a miracle can save the House of Brandenburg. It materializes when Russia's Peter the Great comes to the rescue. Revived, Frederick scores victories at Schweidnitz and Freiberg, winning the Seven Years' War in 1763 in Europe.

Goebbels awarded Harlan's film the rare Nazi honor, Film of the Nation.

In early 1935 Hans Steinhoff's *Lockvogel* (*Bait*, 1934) was shown in America, and it also hinted at how Jews were doing in the 1930s. One member of the cast was Jewish and still living in Berlin. Produced by Ufa, Steinhoff's film mixed mystery, jewel smugglers, romance and racism in relating events surrounding the theft of an emerald necklace aboard a ship sailing between exotic Istanbul and Marseilles. The film's language is coarse, vapid, and pro-Nazi. The hero (Viktor de Kowa) and his father (Jakob Tiedke) are German, while the villains, crooks, and thieves and other assorted characters have non–German names like De Groot (Fritz Rasp), Makarian (Oskar Sima), and Delia Donovan (Hilde Weissner).

There's an explosion, thrilling incidents featuring attractive Jessie Vihrog, and scenes of Lower Saxony, the region where Steinhoff was born. Steinhoff and Roger Le Bon directed a French version of *Lockvogel*, called *Le Miroir aux Alouettes* (*The Mirror with the Larks*, 1934), produced by Ufa and its French lackey, A.C.E.

Lockvogel featured Jewish actress Sonja Sonnenfeld (born Krenzisky), playing the part of the foreign-looking dancer "Bumbawa." The part became hers after a talent scout for Steinhoff's production turned up during one of Sonnenfeld's cabaret performances, looking for someone who resembled a mulatto. Her parents on her father's side came from Filipov on the Russian-Polish border. In the 1870s, Sonnenfeld's father had fled the pogroms and settled in Sweden. Her mother was from Brazil. Sonnenfeld was born in 1912 but by 1914 the family was living in Berlin. Since Sonnenfeld was half Brazilian, she could get "very dark in the summer," she said—and got the role of the non–Aryan.

Sonnenfeld made two other films in Nazi Germany, the second being Ibsen's *Peer Gynt* (1934) with the film idol Hans Albers. Because she was Jewish, the Nazis omitted her name from any credits. Blacklisted from German productions, Sonnenfeld remained in Germany until 1938. By then, she recalled in the 1970s, things had "really gotten rough." She rejoined family members in Sweden. In 1979, Sonnenfeld became secretary of the Swedish Raoul Wallenberg Committee, which seeks the truth about the fate of the diplomat who helped save thousands of Hungarian Jews in 1944–45, and who was taken into custody by the Russians and vanished.

Country life, hunting, and mountains—blood and soil, in other words—comprised the milieu in films directed by Hans Deppe (1897–1969). Deppe, like Carl Boese, Georg Jacoby, E.W. Emo, and Max Obal, was a prolific director whose many German films made it to the U.S.

Deppe's first film in the U.S., *Schlöss Hubertus* (*Castle Hubertus*, 1934), is an allegory based on Ludwig Ganghofer's nineteenth-century novel. Its protagonist is rich and powerful Baron Egge (Friedrich Ulmer), who is at odds with his adult children. Each, he is sure, is in love with the wrong kind of person. Seeking respite from the emotional turmoil in his household, the baron heads for his mountain retreat. But while hunting, he is blinded by an eagle. Nazis, their supporters, and anyone familiar with Hitler's regime knew well that the eagle was a symbol of the Third Reich. The eagle's attack alters the old baron. Without sight to distract him, he undergoes a change of heart. Comforted by his family, he gives his daughter Kitty (Hansi Knoteck) his blessing to marry ordinary painter Hans Forbeck (Hans Schlenk); and he does likewise for his son.

Produced by Ufa, the film featured a cast of novice performers representing the cinema world of the new Germany. Deppe and Curt Oertel, one of the leading documentary filmmakers of the Weimar era, collaborated on *Der Schimmelreiter* (*Phantom Rider*, 1934). Its protagonist is Hauke Haien (Mathias Wieman), a horseman who lives along the coast of Friesland. When the North Sea breaks through an old dike, it wreaks havoc on the land and its superstitious people. However, the rider of the white horse—"the dreamer"—makes it known that the dike *he* built has saved parts of the area from destruction. He will help others recover from the disaster.

Scored by Winfried Zillig (1901–1963), the film, a favorite of Hitler's, was described by American critics as a "remarkable film devoted to man's struggle with the forces of nature and his own weaknesses." Goebbels named the film a cultural work of the "highest order," a designation the *New York Times* (February 25, 1935) called "no mistake."

Deppe's *Ferien vom Ich* (*Vacationing from Oneself*, 1934), an Ufa production, concerns a rich American businessman, George B. Steffenson (Hermann Speelmans), who is seeking relief from the demands of business. Traveling incognito, he finds it—and love with the noblewoman Eva von Dornberg (Carola Höhn)—at a rural sanitarium within Nazi Germany! The idiosyncrasies of the establishment's so-called patients were said to be a laugh.

Deppe's *Die Heilige und ihr Narr* (*The Saint and Her Fool*, 1935), which was shown at New York's 79th Street Theater in late 1935, is based on a popular, contemporary novel for those who, said the *New York Times* (November 29, 1935), "liked to suffer vicariously with exalted personages and thus partly forget their own troubles." Produced by Peter Ostermayr, it is set in the early nineteenth century, notable for its views of castles and countryside in Würtemberg—an area we will hear more of later—where a motherless princess (Hansi Knoteck) grows to womanhood and obtains the love of a worthy nobleman (Hans Stuewe) despite the machinations of her wicked stepmother (Lola Chlud). Retribution is dealt out to the latter when a runaway horse—a symbol of righteousness—kills her.

The name Ostermayr has a long history in German cinema. Peter was the head of Peter Ostermayr-Filmproduktion. He and his brothers, Franz Osten (real name, Franz Ostermayr) and Ottmar, had founded the German studio Emelka in Geiselgasteig after the First World War. *Der Reichfilmblatt* (*Imperial Film Gazette*) took particular note of the location of their film operations, which admirers called "Los Angeles in the Isar Valley." One of Emelka's earliest employees was photographer Franz Planer. Their first film was *Der Ochsenkrieg* (*The Ox War*, 1920), based on a novel by Ludwig Ganghofer. Soon thereafter Emelka began producing newsreels (Wochenschau), going head to head against American newsreels. Difficulties converting to sound, however, caused Emelka to fold by the time the Nazis came to power. A nephew, Paul May (1909–1976), also became a German filmmaker. The family remained in the Third Reich.

Hans Deppe's *Herr Kobin geht auf Abenteuer* (*Kobin Seeks Adventure*, 1934), another Ufa production that screened at New York's 79th Street Theater in late 1935, is about bored bank attorney Lutz Kobin (Hermann Speelmans) who inherits a bit of money. His bank director is named "Werder" (Hans von Zedlitz). Kobin's sudden good fortune spurs him to leave his wife Monika (Dorit Kreysler) and his home to seek excitement abroad. In Prague, Kobin finds more than he bargained for. The ensuing complications include the suicide of desperate art patron Baron von Dingenberg (Werner Schott) and a run-in with a con man calling himself the "Comte de Bary" (Walter Steinbeck) and his accomplice "Vilma" (Maria Meissner). To get at Kobin's money, Bary switches Kobin's identity with that of the dead baron. In the end Kobin is glad to make it back to Germany. Throughout all of this, Kobin's wife remains true to him.

Director Hasso Preis (1901–1983) also made a film that links Jews and money. His Ufa-produced *Die Liebe und die erste Eisenbahn* (*Love and the First Railroad*, 1934) revolves around the effects of the introduction of a railroad. Jakob Tiedtke plays a provincial postmaster in 1838 who earns his livelihood as a stagecoach operator. His daughter (Karin Hardt) meets a handsome construction foreman (Hans Schlenck) of the *Eisenbahn* ("iron-road") that will link Berlin with Potsdam and the villages between. While Karin's father is sure that steam engines can never replace horse-drawn wagons, she and her mother Helene (Ida Wüst) support the transportation breakthrough because it will bring business and development to their village. But if the rail system succeeds, the family's stagecoach operation is doomed. Therefore, to secure their future, Helene secretly buys shares in the new enterprise. The one thing holding it all up is the Berlin financier named "B.C. Fechner" (Max Gülstorff) who has been pocketing the railway workers' money, jeopardizing the whole enterprise. After he's exposed, things end well. The German trains begin to run on time and it's the dawn of a new day in the nation.

By the 1920s, in fact, German railroads had become a source of national pride. Their popularity spurred Germany to open the German Railroads Information Office (GRIO) in the U.S. With offices in New York, Chicago, and San Francisco, the GRIO promoted tourism through travelogues, highlighting Germany's beauty, mystery, and history. The best way to see the country, the GRIO said, was by train. Under Hitler, thousands of foreigners rode through the German countryside.

In one of the GRIO's 1930s films called *Germany: The Land of Hospitality*, Hitler's Deutschland was called "the heart of the old world" which "holds many a charm for the traveler." But, said the film, it was not enough "to learn something of the landscape, the history, and the amusements of the country. One must learn something of its people," says the narrator. Wherever he rides the German rails, the "stranger will find friends and a hearty welcome," concludes the film.

After the U.S. entered World War II, the U.S. Treasury Department shut the American offices of the GRIO, which, as part of its unofficial duties, had imported German feature films for screenings at meetings of the German–American Bund. One of the films that Bund members had a chance to see had especially impressed Hitler's admirers. Writing in the *Washington Post* (June 18, 1935), William Lyon Phelps also had been impressed by the film, and advised "all Americans who expect to be in Germany this summer" to see a documentary about the Nazi Party rally held in Nuremberg in September 1934, called *Triumph of the Will* (1934–35). "It helps to explain the success of Hitler," wrote Phelps. "It's really better than if one had been there actually, for in the picture we have a perfect view, can hear him plainly, and can see every detail of that historic day." Bill Henry of the *Los Angeles Times* was also in Berlin in mid-1935. He, too, found Leni Riefenstahl's Nazi pageant impressive. But he admitted to "some slight difficulty in reporting on the German film industry for the good and sufficient reason that he finds himself unfitted for the task of observing in one language and listening in another."

Riefenstahl, who was a "special representative of the National Socialist Party administration" when she was filming *Triumph of the Will*, claimed after the war that she had been coerced to take on the assignment. The truth was that this arrangement was a dream job. She had at her disposal sixteen of Germany's finest cameramen, as well as sixteen assistants with thirty cameras, sixteen newsreel cameramen, four sets of sound equipment, twenty-two chauffeurs, SS guards, and police. Riefenstahl, in fact, called the film a "triumphant progress of the knowledge, the courage, the strength to fight and win for our German people." Goebbels in 1935 said her film showed "the present ... the exhilarating events of our political life." Filmed to stirring music by the prolific Nazi-era composer Herbert Windt, it received Goebbels' National Film Prize. After the war, the Allies sentenced Riefenstahl to three years' house arrest for the crime of collaboration. In Germany she was labeled a *mitläfer* (fellow traveler). That barred her from something she never sought: public office.

In 1960, Britain's National Film Theatre invited her to give a lecture. Its controller, Stanley Reed, declared: "Satan himself is welcome at the NFT if he makes a good picture." But the invitation was withdrawn after this rare public reprimand. Although *Triumph of the Will* was never commercially released in the United States, its director was often in the news, wherever she was. One place that struck a chord for her and other German filmmakers was Africa — and its links to Germany.

In June 1935, German national cinema offered Americans a look back for inspiration, for solace, for who knows what. The German adventure film *Die Reiter von Deutsch-Ostafrika* (*The Horseman of German East Africa*, 1934) came to the States, thanks to CFE, six months after its release in Berlin. Its director was one of the most openly vitriolic supporters of the Nazi regime: Herbert Selpin (1902–1942).

The Great War serves as the backdrop to his film, set in Germany's former African colony called Deutsch-Ostafrika (German East Africa). Its borders had been established in 1886 in treaties with Britain (which controlled Kenya, Uganda, and Northern Rhodesia), Belgium (which ruled Belgian Congo), and Portugal (which claimed Mozambique). From the Indian coast, Germans penetrated Africa and established their rule. When Germany lost World War I, it also lost German East Africa. The colony was renamed Tanganyika, and was ruled by the British under the Treaty of Versailles.

In Selpin's film, the existence of the German colony is threatened because the fatherland is in danger of losing the Great War. German colonialists face a difficult choice: remain in Africa or return to Germany. They respond to the call for help, but not before burning down their African farms. The British are glad to see them go: there will be no war, at least, on

German colonials in *Die Reiter von Deutsch Ostafrika* (1934). Sepp Rist is in the center; the other actors are unidentified.

African soil. This theme of service and loyalty to the German nation, especially by Aryans and particularly in Germany's darkest hour, would become pro forma in Nazi films.

Selpin's first film under the Nazis had been *Der Traum vom Rhein* (*Dream of the Rhine*, 1933), a "glorification of the beautiful Rhineland," wrote the *New York Times* (December 9, 1935) when it screened at the 79th Street Theater. It depicts the sickly-sweet scenic trip of the rich, German-born American Jupp Steinweg (Schroeder-Schromm) who returns home to the fatherland after three decades abroad. In America he was called Stoneway. Accompanied by his daughter Mary (Gay Christie) and her American boyfriend Conny (Hubert von Myerink), Steinweg arrives at Bremen. The three then drive to the Rhine and sail to Steinweg's native village, Neidernheim, where Mary is won over by the unemployed German teacher Hein Fries (Eduard Wesener). The one "complication" in the film in which, wrote the *New York Times*, "everybody is happy," are the identities of the culprits who steal Steinweg's gold piece. They turn out to be Steinweg's driver "Karl Baumann" (Hugo-Fischer-Köppe), a presumed Jew, and the rich landlord Dellhausen (Paul Henckels).

Selpin and Terra's *Zwischen zwei Herzen* (*Between Two Hearts*, 1933–1934), which was shown in the U.S. a few months later, depicts a wealthy man's support for his putative, illegitimately born daughter, Ulla Georgius (Luise Ullrich). When she turns out not to be a relation, the middle-aged gentleman Detlev Sonnekamp (played by matinee idol Harry Liedke) marries her.

Two other Selpin Nazi hallmarks were the Canada-based tale of sabotage *Wasser für Canitoga* (*Water for Canitoga*, 1939), and *Trenck, der Pandur* (*Trenck, Officer of the Pandurs*, 1940), a tale about a rebellious Austrian—that is, a hero in the eyes of the Nazis—who served Empress Maria Theresa against Napoleon. The Nazis looked kindly on the empress of Austria for another reason. In 1778 she had issued a decree that threatened Bohemian Jews with punishment—flogging or deportation from Austro-Hungary—if they married without official approval. Goebbels named *Trenck, der Pandur* winner of a National Film Prize.

Herbert Selpin's Goebbels-Bavaria production *Geheimakte WB 1* (*Secret Document 1*, 1942), his next-to-last film, is the story of yet another glorious German: Wilhelm Bauer. He was the single-minded warrant officer in the Bavarian Corps who is credited with inventing the U-boat. NCO Bauer (Alexander Golling) is court-martialed for undertaking a bit of daring: undersea action to break Denmark's blockade of Germany in the 1850s. His superiors, however, soon enough become interested in his U-boat, which can be used to attach explosives to enemy ships. Bauer, by his insubordination and duty to the nation, becomes an authentic German hero.

The team of Zerlett-Olfenius and Selpin also collaborated on the infamous anti–Semitic production *Titanic* (1942–43), with music by Nazi-era composer Werner Eisbrenner (1908–1981) and photography by Friedl Behn-Grund. In Nazi lore especially, Jews are responsible for sinking of the British-owned ocean liner in April 1912. The disaster is blamed on upper class, Anglo-American Jews for skimping on lifeboats and building materials. That the toll wasn't worse the filmmakers attribute to the actions of second officer Lightholder (Herbert Tiede), who coincidentally did have a German grandparent. Of course, it is entirely due to Lightholder that any non–Jews survive the disaster. The last scene shows him holding two children in one arm as the ship slips under the sea; he then swims to the nearest lifeboat. However, the ship's destruction was considered allegorically damaging to German morale at the time—the Jews sink Germany, in effect. So during the war, the Nazis only distributed the film abroad. Scenes from *Titanic* were used in *A Night to Remember* (1958).

Selpin directed a score of films in Nazi Germany—only three of which were shown in the States—and he came to a well-deserved end in 1942. Jailed for "utterances undermining military strength," he was found dead in his cell.

Gustaf Heinrich Arnold Gründgens (1899–1963), a well-known German actor for most of his career, died by his own hands. He often played the heavy. He was the chief gangster in Fritz Lang's first sound film; a shady financier in Kurt Bernhardt's *Der Tunnel* (1932), which co-starred Ferdinand Marian in his first film; and played a Berlin safecracker in the Weimar crime drama *Teilnehmer Antwortet nicht* (*Party Doesn't Answer*, 1932), directed by Rudolf Katscher and Marc Sorkin, which was shown at the Hindenberg Theatre in New York.

One Weimar film that Gründgens directed—he directed six films under Nazi rule—reached the States. *Eine Stadt steht Kopf* (*A Town Stands on its Head*, 1932), which was released in Berlin the week Hitler took over and in New York a year later, is a Russo-German comedy after Gogol's *The Inspector General*. Scripted by Kurt Alexander, it starred Jewish performers Szöke Szakall, Lore Mosheim, Lotte Löbinger, and Lotte Stein, as well as Vienna-born Hermann Thimig (1890–1982), Fritz Kampers, Aribert Wäscher, Paul Henckels, Hans Deppe, and Jenny Jugo.

Gründgens' first film under Nazi rule, *Die Finanzen der Grossherzogs* (*The Grand Duke's Finances*, 1933), which screened at New York's 79th Street Theater in 1935, was anti–Jewish. When former Russian princess Diana von Russland (Hilde Weissner) falls in love with Duke Ramon Gomez von Sillorca (Viktor de Kowa), she saves his Mediterranean island during his absence from a revolt led by a creditor named "Mircovich" (Ernst Rotmund).

The final film Gründgens directed in the Third Reich was *Zwei Welten* (*Two Worlds*, 1940), a Terra production with music by composer Michael Jary (1906–1988). It's a far-fetched tale about a member of the Hitler Youth who falls for a girl outside his social class. Here again, the Nazis were pretending to be enemies of class distinction. The Allies banned that film after the war.

The need for leadership to battle oppression, to rise up, and to achieve mystical victory reached its peak this year with Ufa's Nazi-themed *Das Mädchen Johanna* (*Young Joan of Arc*, 1935). In this version of the story of the French heroine, France's Charles VII is depicted as the "cool, deliberate sovereign gifted with unusual political insight—a lonely genius," according to a contemporary film program. Thus the film's emphasis is on Charles, especially at the end. The king's desertion of Joan after she has served his purposes is presented as far-sighted and high-minded.

Directed by Gustav Ucicky and scripted by the infamous Gerhard Menzel, the tale is set in early fifteenth-century France, where a young woman leads her people to national rebirth. The country has been drawn into conflict with England. France's King Charles VII (Gustav Gründgens), who refers to his own people as a "breed of lice," is helpless in the face of internal power struggles, intrigue, and collaborators. Then a simple young woman named Johanna (Angela Salloker) emerges. Dressed in male clothing, she believes in victory. Humble and self-possessed, Johanna follows her instincts and intuition. She draws strength from the earth and heaven, from her homeland's soil, and from boundless faith. The people, moreover, have faith in this "assistant of God." With the battle cry, "God and the virgin," the French overcome the British-Burgundy alliance. In Reims, however, after plague breaks out, the people fear God's punishment. If Johanna were really holy, the people believe, she could contain the outbreak. Internal division weakens France while England again advances. Johanna is captured by the English and sentenced to death. On the night before the end, she cries, "Never to see the blue sky again, never to hear the birds sing again, never to see the golden sun, the silver moon—dead—dead—DEAD!" She is burnt as a heretic, an apostate, and layer of spirits. But she becomes a martyr. The French rally once more against their enemies, whose evil nature is given concrete expression. Standing against the background of a large banquet hall, the duke of Burgundy (Heinrich George) suddenly takes on a monstrous appearance. France, however, will survive because France has faith. Johanna is ultimately hailed as a saint—25 years after her death.

Before the film was allowed to open at New York's 79th Street Theater, the state's Board of Censors, chiefly concerned about inappropriate depictions of religion and sex, had the following phrases removed from the subtitles: "venereal disease," "bastard," "Holy Virgin Mary," "stallion," "by God," and "cursed." The *New York Times* (October 9, 1935) noted that the German director "has been somewhat free in his treatment of the sequences of the historical events.... He has also made a comparatively wise and patriotic king out of the supposedly weak and cowardly Charles VII.... Be that as it may, the picture is filled with excitement from start to finish." The *Chicago Tribune* (September 15, 1936) reported that the Sonotone Theatre advertised the film as "the most stupendous picture ever produced." What the critics didn't say was that Nazi ideology was being presented in a subtle fashion. The picture buttressed Hitler's leadership. Hitler had been presented as the "right man at the right time," as Germany's savior in her darkest hour. Wasn't Der Führer a man who follows his instincts and intuition? And didn't Hitler oppose the political power of the church, which had condemned Joan to death by fire? Lastly, the film implied something else: a British-French alliance is unnatural, according to historical events.

Nazi filmmakers often turned to history, and especially to World War I, to justify their actions. Erich Waschneck's *Mein Leben für Maria Isabell* (*My Life for Maria Isabell*, 1934–35) is set in Belgrade in the closing days of the conflict. The few remaining Austrian regiments are now made up of motley contingents of Russians, Poles, and Croatians—and they are plotting mutiny. This is the kind of thing Hitler had said about Austria in *Mein Kampf*: he loathed Austria-Hungary because it was pro-Slav.

A young Austrian lieutenant, Menis (Viktor de Kowa), is trying to save the regimental standards but it is too late: the war ends with the collapse of his army. Only then, having tried to do his duty for his regiment (called Maria Isabell), does he turn his interest to a young blonde of high rank, Resa Lang (Maria Andergast). The film, which co-starred Veit Harlan, concludes with the couple's arrival in Vienna, as the flags of the Austrian regiments are burned in the Imperial Palace rather than allowed to fall into enemy hands. Snipped from the American release by CFE in early November 1935 were scenes of German troops shooting the mutinous, traitorous, anti–German regiments.

The actress Maria Andergast (1912–95) had made her film debut opposite Luis Trenker in Deutsche Universal's *Der Verlorene Sohn* (1934). In 1936 she married Austrian-born director Heinz Helbig (b. 1902) and they moved to Berlin. She was in a dozen German films until the end of the war and was later married to the actor Siegfried Breuer (1906–54), who became most well known for his role as Popescu, one of Harry's three alleged colleagues in *The Third Man* (1948).

In November 1935, CFE distributed the anti–Weimar production *Die Vier Musketiere* (*The Four Musketeers*, 1934). The film, which Heinz Paul (1893–1983) directed, featured Fritz Kampers (1891–1950) as one of four frontline soldiers in the Great War. The film begins by depicting episodes from their wartime experiences along the western front, then leaps fourteen years to the final days of the Weimar era when a regimental reunion brings them together. When their discussion turns to politics, differences threaten their soldierly camaraderie. An older German veteran—another prodigal son who has returned from America—intervenes. He describes the living conditions abroad awful, naturally, most especially the factory conditions in the U.S. He tells the others they're lucky to be alive and to witness to the rise of the Nazis. He stresses the need to support the fatherland at this critical juncture. The story ends as Hitler comes to power, a signal that life will only improve in the new Germany.

The *New York Times* (November 9, 1935) had one objection to the film. It concluded that since the reunion "is dated 1932," it had to be an "oversight on the part of the 'coordinated' German filmmakers." Nonetheless, the film reflected Hitler's memories of the war in *Mein Kampf*, in which he wrote:

> Whenever Fate dealt cruelly with me in my young days the spirit of determination within me grew stronger and stronger. During all those long years of war, when Death claimed many a true friend and comrade from our ranks, to me it would have appeared sinful to have uttered a word of complaint. Did they not die for Germany? And, finally, almost in the last few days of that titanic struggle, when the waves of poison gas enveloped me and began to penetrate my eyes, the thought of becoming permanently blind unnerved me; but the voice of conscience cried out immediately: Poor miserable fellow, will you start howling when there are thousands of others whose lot is a hundred times worse than yours? And so I accepted my misfortune in silence, realizing that this was the only thing to be done and that personal suffering was nothing when compared with the misfortune of one's country.

Heinz Paul's most infamous film, which was financed by Goebbels' ministry, dealt with one of Germany's World War I heroes: Ernst Udet (1896–1941). Winner of the Blue Max in the First World War, Udet starred in *Wunder des Fliegens* (*Miracle of Flight*, 1935). Costarring Käthe Haack, with music by Guiseppe Becce and photography by Hans Schneeberger, it has a cameo by the head of the Luftwaffe, Hermann Göring—who famously had said, "Soldiers are there to die." The tale of hero worship and regret about German losses in the Great War focuses on Udet as an inspiration and role model to Heinz (Jürgen Ohlsen) who wants to become a pilot himself. The boy's mother opposes the idea because his father—Udet's onetime war comrade—had died in the war. Udet convinces the woman that flying is a noble work that serves the nation. Her son, inspired, joins a glider club, flies over the Zugspitze in the

Bavarian Alps in bad weather—and crashes. Udet takes to the air to rescue him. Udet's heroism is depicted as a glorious success and further proof of the worthiness of German aircraft and their pilots.

The film was not released in the U.S. but *Variety* reviewed it in Berlin, where it was produced under the working title *Wolkenrausch* (*Cloud Intoxication*). The change in title resulted from the success of the 1935 Berlin photo exhibit "Das Wunder des Lebens" which highlighted Hitler's family tree, healthy Aryans, and famous Germans who came from large families. The exhibit also included a series of anti-Jewish photos.

There was another period in German history that inspired the Third Reich, and that was when iron-fisted Frederick the Great ruled, in the mid-eighteenth century. Thus came the chance to experience the glories of the German past—repeated in the 1930s—through Deka's extravaganza, *Der Alte und der junge König* (*The Old and Young King*, 1935), which the General Foreign Sales Corp distributed in the States. New York's Bijou Theatre had the dubious honor of hosting the film under the title *The Making of a King*. Hans Steinhoff (1882–1945) directed the still-significant Emil Jannings in a subtitled German historical drama that preaches the necessity to suppress personal impulses for the general good.

Frederick Wilhelm, king of Prussia, is anxious about the development of his son (the future Frederick the Great): young Frederick is a court dandy, a hedonist, and a dreamer. The king's efforts at change have failed to improve the young man. After his father burns his books,

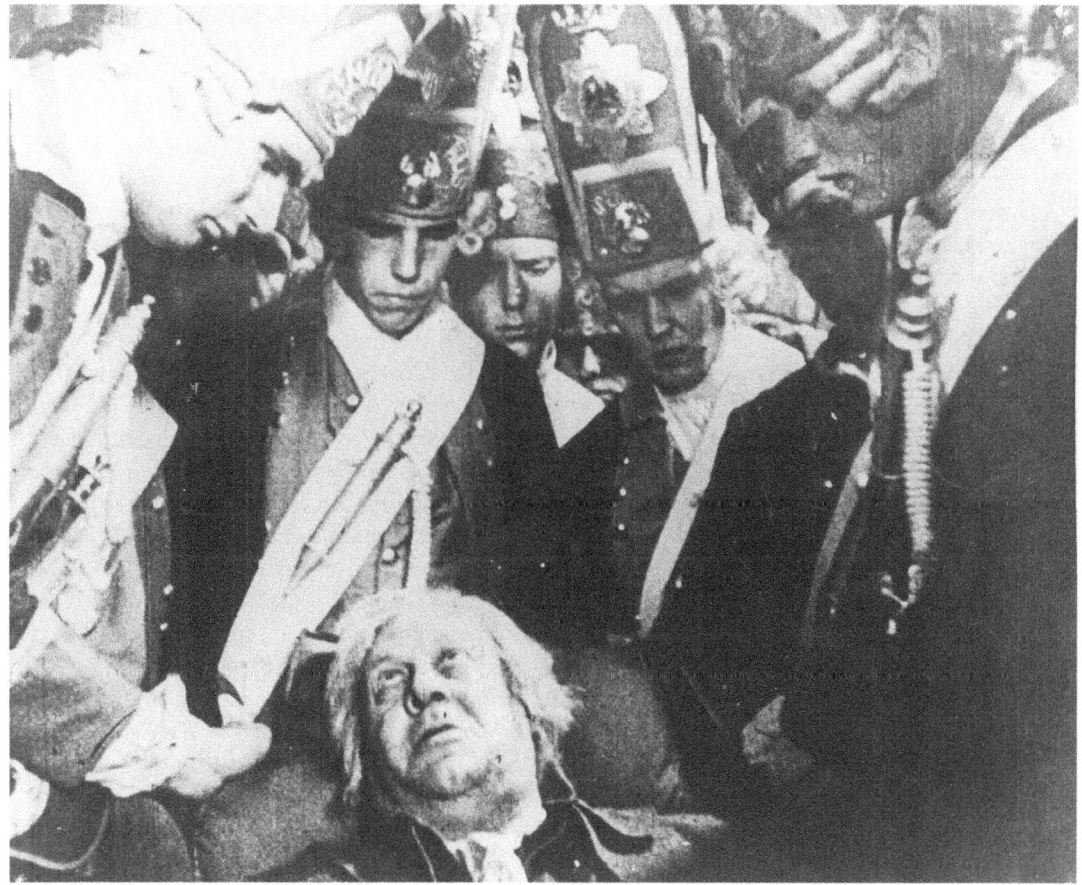

Der Alter und der junge König (1935), starring Emil Jannings.

destroys his music, and orders him into the military, crown prince Frederick (Werner Hinz), aided by Lt. von Katte (Claus Clausen)—a presumed Jew—attempts to flee to his mother's native England. The plot being discovered, von Katte is arrested, tried by court martial, and sentenced to life imprisonment.

The old king (Jannings), acting as the "supreme judicial authority," rejects the judgment of the court martial. He orders his son's accomplice beheaded. The prince, a witness to the execution, absorbs a key lesson: disloyalty to the nation's leader means death. The prince mends his ways. When he reconciles with his father near the end of Wilhelm's rule, Frederick is on sure ground, well aware of the sacrifices that must be made for the glory of Prussia and the necessary steps to rule a great nation!

That the ruler's will is law and the ends justify the means were the film's not-so-subtle messages. Goebbels named this one a "national film," in effect justifying the "blood purge," or Night of the Long Knives of June 1934. The Nazis also emulated the idea of execution via beheading as a powerful method of stifling dissent, a prime example being the fate they meted out to members of the anti–Nazi White Rose group in early 1943.

The critical reaction in America was mixed. On the one hand Goebbels' film was characterized as "an emotional orgy on behalf of the mailed fist, the militarist glory of the German State, and the stern principles of mass discipline" by Andre Seenwald of the *New York Times* (December 10, 1935). "The German cinema, with Dr. Goebbels' whip crackling merrily around its flanks, gives three rousing and obedient cheers for Nazi book-burning culture." But "judged strictly on its dramatic merits, it emerges as quite simply the best film to come out of Nazi Germany," concluded Seenwald. *New Theatre* (January 1936) said the film "furnishes a complete category of fascist tenets—hatred of other nations, male superiority, destruction of culture, suppression of individual rights, a total minimization of human life, and an insane glorification of the military." On the other hand, *Life* (February 1936) said that Jannings "is as good as we thought he was. He is still ... the greatest of all screen actors." The *New Yorker* (December 21, 1935) said the film "is a Jannings picture and not just Nazi propaganda, as some insist." When the film screened at Chicago's Sonotone Theatre in August 1936, *Chicago Tribune* reviewer Anna Nangle called it "one of the best of its kind," with Jannings's performance "masterful," "human," and "kindly."

What were the excesses of nationalism, assault on the individual, and a few book burnings when compared to Jannings's talent and the film's merits as dramatic entertainment? Jannings was a study in contradictions as an actor and as a man. Was he apolitical in his personal as well as his professional life, or was he a part of the Nazi machine cloaked as an actor? Ever since his return to Germany from Hollywood, critics expected Jannings to fail. He continued to surprise them, but his service on one of Goebbels' "arts committees" tied him to the regime. Of his role, for example, as the powerful father figure, Cesar, in *Schwarze Walfisch* (*Black Whale*), the German adaptation of Marcel Pagnol's *Fanny* directed by Fritz Wendhausen (1891–1962), *Variety* (March 20, 1934) in Berlin wrote, "A remarkable character study imbued with real life, the climaxes without obtrusive preparations are free of inappropriate sentimentality. Those who feared for Jannings' future may be sure he still has his place in the front row."

Only a few years earlier, in the Weimar period, German filmmakers had produced the story of another outsized king: *Ludwig der Zweite, König von Bayern* (*Lugwig II, King of Bavaria*, 1929). At 10 reels, it became one of the significant and ambitious German films of the era, directed by Wilhelm Dieterle and starring Max Schreck. It started Dieterle down the road of the biographical film—and to Hollywood. Carl Laemmle's Deutsche Universal was the production and distribution company behind it, releasing it in Berlin in March 1930. As the second film about the infamous and mad King Ludwig II (1845–87)—the first was made in 1920—Dieterle's film begins in 1883, the year of Richard Wagner's death. With a prologue, flashbacks, and rapid imagery, Dieterle's film brought to life the reign of a Prussian monarch who felt compelled to do his duty. His reign began when he was eighteen—without education or training. During his rule he faced war in 1866 and 1870 (which he won), but also delusion and then dissolution. Ludwig's soul, Dieterle's film made clear, was a soul scarcely moved by feeling and concern for human welfare. Under the Nazis, that became *the* basis for leadership.

Director Carl Froelich (1875–1953), who served on one of Goebbels' "arts committees," was another filmmaker who helped push Nazi ideology. His *Frühlingsmärchen* (*Spring Fairy Tale*, 1934) hinted at a new German-Italian relationship. In the tale, starring screen newcomers Maris Wetra and Claire Fuchs, a leading Berlin light opera singer apparently discovers in far-off Sicily a future Caruso!

Froelich also directed what Goebbels called a "very funny peasant comedy," *Krach um Jolanthe* (*The Trouble with Jolanthe*, 1934), based on a hit Berlin stage play, about the excitement among country people when the sheriff tries to collect a tax on a prize sow (named Jolanthe). This was one of those so-called German country films, which extended from comedies in south German dialect to rural melodramas featuring boys in lederhosen climbing through girls' windows. They were popular with audiences within Germany, and were regularly released to German-American audiences until 1942.

December 1935 saw the release in the States of *Was bin ich ohne Dich?* (*What am I to You?*, 1934), an apparently harmless little tale scripted by Nazi collaborator Thea von Harbou (1888–1954), about a struggling composer, Erwin Schwarz (Wolfgang Liebeneiner). He hits it big when he gets one of his pieces into a film program played by a Bavarian orchestra. His big objection was that his wife, Paula (Betty Bird), was too good for films. However, Paula captures the lead part in the film called *Fata Morgana*, besting Lilly Petrowa (Olga Tschechowa, 1896–1980).

Shown also in Austria and Switzerland, the musical contained cameo performances by rising stars of the German screen: Lissy Arna, Viktor de Kowa, Erna Morena, and Paul Richter. This film was one of the first of many films that Arthur M. Rabenalt (1905–1993) directed in Nazi Germany, a number of which were released in the U.S. Although he specialized in dance and circus films, and boasted about them, Rabenalt was also responsible for several notorious Nazi productions that western reviewers overlooked at the time of their release in Germany. Rabenalt did not boast about these.

His *Flucht ins Dunkel* (*Escape in the Dark*, 1939) is a World War I drama of intrigue and sabotage now banned in Germany. A second was *Achtung! Feind hört mit!* (*Beware! The Enemy Is Listening!*, 1940), with music by Franz Grothe (1908–1982). A third was the anti–Semitic production ... *reitet für Deutschland* (...*Riding for Germany*, 1941). The latter was named a winner of the National Film Prize. None of the films were screened in the States nor reviewed by American critics at the time of their release in Germany, before the U.S. entered the war.

The phrase "Achtung! Feind hört mit!" is representative of Nazi slogans that became part of daily life. The clipped syllables of "Feind hört mit!" and their ramifications are discernable. A child's appearance in a room of adults could be greeted with the phrase, and its meaning would range from "Do not talk about this in front of a child" to "The child can be an enemy." *Achtung! Feind hört mit!*, produced by Terra, warns against British efforts to uncover the secrets of Germany military production in the critical days of September 1938. There were fifth columnists at work everywhere, and a slip of the tongue could be disastrous. Everyone is watching everyone else, and the courage of a factory secretary combined with the "patriotism" of a young man can reveal the identities of British agents.

In Rabenalt's ... *reitet für Deutschland*, produced by Ufa, a German officer (Willy Birgel) is crippled in the eastern front in 1918. He regains his ability to ride horses (for the new Ger-

Willy Birgel on his horse, in ...*reitet fur Deutschland* (1941).

many) after the Nazis rise to power and "corruption of business life" as well as efforts by Jews to retain ownership of his stud farm become things of the past.

Rabenalt denied that these films were disreputable, and his career continued well into the 1970s, including directing *Alraune* (1952), starring Erich von Stroheim.

On the other hand, Alfred Abel, one of Germany's most esteemed silent-screen performers, who played the master builder in *Metropolis* and was often relegated to secondary roles in sound films, directed one of the more surprising tales of the year in Nazi Germany: the pro-British *Alles um eine Frau* (*Everything for a Woman*, 1935). It screened in the U.S. towards the end of 1935. It was a Delta production starring Charlotte Susa—a blonde with a regal Prussian accent—who plays Blanche Keyne, the wife of the English industrialist Frederick (Gustav Diessl) who was an aviator in the British Expeditionary Force during the Great War. After the armistice the former aviator made a fortune manufacturing airplanes. By chance, he crosses paths with an old war acquaintance—the German air ace Heinrich Droop (Paul Hartmann) who shot down his plane and then risked his life to pull him from the burning wreckage. The former German pilot has seen hard times: he's been reduced to running a gas station in Germany.

The sympathetic British industrialist offers him a job managing the largest aircraft factory in England. When the industrialist's wife meets the German, it's love at first sight. Unbeknownst to her husband, she is a woman with a past: she was once a dancehall girl. Out of that past emerges a former dancing partner (Hubert von Meyerinck) who discovers her affair with the handsome German. He tries to blackmail her.

Comradeship, however, wins out. The German heads off to his new British job, which implied harmony between two former enemies of the First World War.

Justice of a different sort was the subject of the Bavarian adaptation of Dickens, called *Klein Dorrit* (*Little Dorrit*, 1934), directed by the Austrian-born Karl Lamac (1897–1952).

Here, the Nazis indict the old British legal system regarding debtors. They side with the poor and the dispossessed while excising the tearful and gloomy parts of Dickens's Marshalsea tale, although the villainous Flintwich (Fritz Rasp) stays in the picture. Under British law, debtors were threatened with incarceration, the theory being this might force them to reveal hidden assets. Or their families might take pity and pay their ransom.

Set in London, the film, which screened at New York's 79th Street Theater in late 1935, revolves around a rich woman's refusal to let her son Arthur Clennam (Mathias Wieman) marry Amy Dorrit (Anny Ondra). That's because her father is William Dorrit (Gustav Waldau, 1871–1958), jailed for 19 years for falling behind in his payments. He's the oldest guest at Marshalsea. At the end, it's revealed that William has won a lawsuit, making him—and Amy—rich.

Debt is the central theme as well in a film by Karl Lamac that came to the Casino Theatre: *Karneval und Liebe* (*Carnival and Love*, 1934). Here popular, big-spending matinee idol Henry Rolland (Hermann Thimig), with a Hollywood contract, chases an apparently penniless blonde (Lien Deyers), while eluding a creditor. The girl is far from who she appears to be. But the creditor, named "Türkheim" (Herbert Hübner), is the stereotypical, heartless Jewish man of wealth.

Anny Ondra (1903–1987) often appeared in films by Karl Lamac. She was born Anna Sophia Ondrakova in Poland and raised in Prague. She got her start in films in the early 1920s thanks to Gustav Machaty. She was in Hitchcock's *The Manxman* and *Blackmail*. After Germany invaded Poland and Lamac left Germany, Ondra made two more films in Germany and then quit. One Lamac-Ondra production that came to New York's 79th Street Theater in late 1935 was *Polenblut* (*Polish Blood*, 1934), a Czech-German musical based on the operetta of the same name, scripted by Herman Kosterlitz and photographed by Otto Heller. It starred the effervescent Ondra as Helena Zaremba, the daughter of a Polish landowner (Hans Moser). She saves aristocratic neighbor Count Bolko Baransky (Ivan Petrovitch) from ruin by pretending to be an estate manager and applying her expertise. That mostly involves appropriating her father's castle. In the end they marry and join lands!

In the homeland film *Schwarzwaldmädel* (*Black Forest Girl*, 1933), by George Zoch, an operetta that was distributed by CFE, old choirmaster Blasius Römer (Walter Janssen) stands aside, allowing his young housekeeper Bärbele (Maria Beling) to marry a young student, Hans Fichtner (Hans Söhker). By now it had become the norm in Nazi productions to expect the older generation to shape up or to get out of the way for the next in the new Germany. But the best parts of the film, wrote the *New York Times* (October 12, 1935), were its "lovely views of the old village in the Black Forest and of the festival of St. Cecilia."

Young director Frank Wysbar was a representative of new German filmmakers, having made his first film at the end of the Weimar-era: the formula crime drama *Im Banne des Eulenspiegels* (*Spell of the Mirror*, 1932). Wysbar made his name in German films with the acclaimed spiritual tale *Anna und Elizabeth* (1933), about a young woman who heals the sick and raises the dead, starring Dorothea Wieck and Hertha Thiele, and produced and released by Terra in the first months of Hitler's reign. His film was shown in New York, thanks to CFE, and in Chicago in early 1937, which reinforced the impression that filmmaking was alive and well within the Third Reich.

Wysbar's *Hermine und die seiben Aufrechten* (*Hermine and the Seven Upright Men*, 1934), a Terra production that CFE distributed un-subtitled, is the story of seven upstanding men from the Swiss city of Aarau. They vow lifelong friendship and peace while Europe faces strife. But even they face conflict when Hermine Frymann (Karin Hardt), the daughter of one of them, a rich and powerful Zurich tradesman (Heinrich George), falls in love with Karl Hediger (Albert Lieven), the son of another of the seven, a lowly *North German* tailor. This intermarriage feels unnatural to them. However, after much soul searching and conflict, the lovers wed. The North German tailor is as worthy as any of them. The seven men attend a national shooting match under a banner that proclaims, "Friendship in Freedom." "From the technical side," wrote the *New York Times* (September 21, 1935), "the costumes and customs date back many years, but the rifles used are decidedly modern." The tale co-starred Karl Stepanek as one of the seven.

Swiss officials objected to the depiction of Swiss men and their adherence to a rigid code of honor: conservative and old-fashioned. This objection didn't stop Goebbels from entering Wysbar's film as a candidate for best film of the year at the 1935 Venice Film Festival. Venice awarded it a "special mention," making it the first Nazi feature to garner a foreign prize. Wysbar fled to Hollywood in 1938 after divorcing his Jewish wife and leaving her in peril.

Peril is at the center of a film the Swiss favored and which was set in Switzerland: Terra's *Wilhelm Tell: das Freiheitsdrama eines Volkes* (*William Tell: The Drama of Liberty of a People*, 1933). The movie was adapted from Schiller's play—Göring's favorite—and directed by Heinz Paul. In *Mein Kampf*, Hitler recalled seeing a dramatization of the story when he was 12. The Austrians, whom Hitler loathed, do not come off well in this film. A berg-film shot in the Alps, it recounts the Swiss revolt against Austrian tyranny in the fourteenth century, when freedom-loving peasants set aside regional differences to pour over the hillsides and defeat their oppressor.

The story focuses on the cruelty of the Austrian Landvogt Gessler (Conrad Veidt), the tyrannical bailiff who rules the Swiss. But the blinding of a man for refusing to betray his son and Gessler's ordering William Tell (Hans Marr) to shoot the apple on his son's head spark revolution. At Gessler's death at the hands of Tell, a liberated Swiss confederacy is born. The climax, however, is not Tell's mythical shot but rather something grander: his escape from a prison ship and a great assault against the Austrian oppressors. Stunning landscape and mountain photography by Sepp Allgeier highlighted the people's fight for freedom—a message at odds with the Nazis' oppression of German-Jews and others within the Third Reich. The General Foreign Sales Corp. released the film at New York's 55th Street Playhouse in late 1935.

Emmy Sonnemann (1893–1973)—the future Mrs. Hermann Göring—played the noble Frau Hedwig Tell. Sonnemann had been an actress at the National Theatre in Weimar. In 1948, a German denazification court sentenced her to a year in jail. When she was released, a third of her property was confiscated and she was banned from the stage for five years.

Fred Sauer's later *Pantoffhelden* (*Hen-Pecked Husbands*, 1935), which screened in the U.S. in late 1935, presents two country spouses who, by turning the tables on their wives, become real men while the wives are remade as real German women, according to the Hitler model. Films by the prolific Géza von Bolváry filled the screens in German theaters in New York and elsewhere this year. His *Stradivar* (*Stradivarius*, 1935) was the best received. Released by Boston Films (Berlin), it's the story of a Hungarian officer, an Italian girl who gooes to Budapest to study music, and a cursed violin. Josef von Baky was assistant director and Ernst Marischka wrote the script. The film depicts the First World War in a series of documentary shots, "combined with the right music," wrote *Variety* (November 6, 1935), "which puts across the idea of terror."

At the start, First Lieutenant Sandor Teleki (Gustav Fröhlich) takes top prize in the musical competition Concours Hippique of 1914. Awarded a violin, he resigns from the army to earn a living playing music, and becomes interest in the history of the violin. This leads him to Maria Belloni (Sybille Schmitz), with whom he falls in love, and to a purported Stradivarius that brings bad luck to any owner. Long ago, its maker had no luck in love and put a spell on the musical instrument. Sandor takes it. He also asks for Maria's hand in marriage, the ceremony to take place in Milan. But then war breaks out, duty calls, and he rejoins his old regiment. Sandor is badly wounded in the war. When his violin is found in the trenches, she assumes the worst and, blaming the curse, burns the instrument. But the actions of the self-sacrificing Dr. Pietro Rossi (Albrecht Schönhals) reunite the couple.

Co-starring Veit Harlan as Antonio Stradivari in the German version, Bolváry's film was also produced by Tobis in French, starring Edwige Feuillere and Pierre Richard Willm. Bolváry's *Ich kenn' Dicht nicht und liebe Dich* (*I Don't Know You, but I Love You*, 1933–34), by Boston Films and distributed by CFE, featured the charming and popular Willi Forst as the lead, playing Robert Ottmar, a composer of popular music who's inspired by the picture of a beautiful young woman, Gloria Claassen (Magda Schneider). He's determined to meet her and find out if her personality matches her looks. He heads for the Riviera and lands a job as a butler in her parents' villa. Then, as a mere servant, he has the audacity to kiss her, and she turns out to be his boss's daughter! Only when his identity is revealed does his social status permit the two to consider marriage.

Winternachtstraum (*Winter Night's Dream*, 1934–35), another film by Géza von Bolváry (1897–1961), was one of the last German films to be shown in the States this year. This was one of a dozen productions by Boston Films (Berlin) shown in the U.S. in the years 1933–36. Distributed by faithful CFE, it was another in the long line of productions that stirred Germans who longed for *Heimat*. A timely musical holiday, it featured beautiful young Hilde Müller (Magda Schneider) who is invited by her boss (Richard Romanowsky, 1883–1968) on a New Year's trip to the famous winter resort of Garmisch-Partenkirchen (site of the 1936 Winter Olympics). There she finds romance with the ski instructor Peter Kreutzberg (Wolf Albach-Retty) in the midst of Bavarian snow, skiing, and bulkily dressed mountaineers galore. Catchy tunes—"Mir Geht's immer; Danke Schön" and "Was ist das Leben, wenn du mich nicht Hebst?"—help to emphasize the romance. Yet at her posh hotel, Hilde comes across the "suspicious businessman" and high roller "Degenfels" (Hubert von Myerinck) and his high-class accomplice Vera (Hedda Björnson), "a moll" who, they said, "specializes in pocket picking."

Rudolf van der Noss was responsible for a musical story about a real German opera composer, called *Aufforderung zum Tanz* (*Invitation to the Dance*, 1934), a Cicero production shown in the U.S. in late 1935. Noss's film was an expansion of a 1931–32 Weimar short of the same name directed by Heinz Hille that starred the would-be Nazi party member Eugen Rex. Noss's feature film is a period piece about the heroic founder of the German opera, "rebellious" composer-conductor Carl Maria van Weber (played by Berlin opera singer Willy Domgraf-Fassbänder). Von Weber, born in 1786, became a choir director in Prague in 1813. Three years later he was music director of the Deutsche Oper—German Opera Company—in Dresden. There he took a stand in the name of Germanism: he supported the production of then little regarded German opera instead of the more popular Italian opera. He died in London in 1826. In Noss's film Weber, who marries the German opera singer Caroline Brandt (Margot Köchlin), has run-ins with the powerful music guilds that opposed recognition of German opera composition in the first decades of the nineteenth century. Weber's struggle to gain recognition for German opera put him in the pantheon of German intellectuals, in the eyes of the Nazis. Weber's masterpieces "Aufforderung zum Tanz" and "Der Freischütz" were, in fact, played for the first time in Berlin, a city that was open to change—until the Nazis took charge.

A different version of homeland is expressed Juda Leman's documentary *The Land of Promise* (1935). Narrated by David Ross, the film is a record of Palestine before Jews settled there in large numbers and then setting in motion the "rebuilding of the Jewish homeland." The picture, wrote the *New York Times* (November 21, 1935), "merits an audience beyond the generic limits of its theme…. Rarely has the camera presented such magnificent portraiture, nor used it with more telling effect." The lens is "opened wide upon a dancing, singing group of men and women on the foredeck of a liner, coming to give new life to a century-old city, coming to water its fields, run its factories, build its homes. The effect upon any audience is electric."

German films shown in the U.S. next year tried to put the lie to Juda Leman's film. They fed a dangerous deception: that a promised land for the Jews, who were under assault in Germany, was not necessary.

1936

"A Relief to Those Who Feared the Worst"

In 1936, Germans made an effort to appear more normal, extending camaraderie to the outside world. The reason is that it was the year of the Berlin Olympics. But there was one exception. Try as they might, their anti–Semitism still crept into in their films. The 1936 games, dubbed the "Nazi Olympics," were hailed in Berlin, the world's fourth largest city, as a spectacle of peace and an internationalist gesture that would encourage acceptance of the Nazi regime around the world. During the summer festivities, attended by people from across the globe, the German press published the news for visitors. German film programs included international features and shorts. The Nazis, however, banned non–Germans from taking photos and films of the Olympic Games as well as scenes of Berlin, even after the Nazis had removed signs that read, "Jews Are Our Misfortune—Whoever Buys From Jews Is a Traitor." New slogans proclaimed "Our Desire Is Peace."

The pattern had been set in February 1936 when Hitler had opened the fourth Winter Olympics, in Garmisch-Partenkirchen, twin villages 60 miles southwest of Munich. The *New York Times* (February 1936), in a report from Germany, noted that while the games propounded the Nazis' creed of "Strength through Joy," the "anti–Jewish signs have been removed from villages. The Stürmer, anti–Semitic newspaper, is being kept out of sight. A Jewish hockey player has even been drafted for the German team. In short, politics is being kept out of a sphere in which it has no place."

So why were officials from Goebbels' ministry there? They were there because they had financed the filming of these games, called *Jugend der Welt* (*Youth of the World*). The director was Carl Junghans (1897–1984). He had been one of the leading documentary filmmakers of the Weimar era and had assisted Arnold Fanck on *Fliegende Schatten* (*Flying Shadows*, 1932), a record of Ernst Udet's flying exploits over central Africa. The cameramen were Sepp Allgeier, Hans Ertl, Heinz von Jaworsky, Bernhard Juppe, Kurt Neubert, Heinz Kluth, Hugo Otto Schulze, Erich Stoll, Paul Tesch, Carl Heinrich Wenng, and Hans Winterfeld. Junghans' film, at 37 minutes, contains no dialogue, only German titles, a soundtrack of orchestral music and the cheers of spectators, and swastikas galore. It shows Hitler opening the games, followed by scenes of the Alpine and Nordic ski runs, ski jumping and bobsled runs, speed and figure skating, and ice curling competition. At the conclusion of the games, Hitler boards a train.

Jugend der Welt became available in the States in fall 1936 when Ufa gave New York's Museum of Modern Art a copy. The film was scheduled to open at the Capital Theatre in New York as part of Pete Smith's series of short subject films. However at the last minute, MGM, the distributor, pulled the film. The reason was that the Non–Sectarian Anti–Nazi

League had threatened to denounce MGM and boycott the theater. This was a rare victory for the league.

In March 1936, the Nazis returned to form. They warned Jews against voting in upcoming, one-party elections. The Jewish novelist Arnold Zweig was deprived of his German citizenship in April because he had "belittled the spiritual and ethical values of German culture." That same month, Hitler said that Germany's only judges were God and himself.

Another film true to Nazi form was Leni Riefenstahl's 39-minute *Tag der Freiheit—Unsere Wehrmacht* (*The Day of Freedom—Our Armed Forces*). American critics happened to be at its Berlin premiere. Demonstrating German air power, the film, observed *Variety* (January 1936), contains a "shimmer of romanticism hardly in keeping with the grimness of modern warfare" and "beautiful shots of cavalry and swooping airplanes."

Hitler called German soldiers "bearers of a great tradition," linking them to the great Prussian soldiers of earlier eras. In Riefenstahl's film, Germany's infantry, cavalry, aircraft, flak guns, and the first public appearance of its "forbidden" tank, bring viewers up to speed on Germany's military capabilities. These depictions implied that Germany was capable of swift attack and destruction. Hitler's presence at the Berlin release only enhanced the meaning of Riefenstahl's short, which had been shot by a half-dozen cameramen. Designed to show "patriotic" Germans what Hitler had accomplished in a mere three years and what he would achieve— Germany's military is depicted in mock action—the documentary was recommended for all members of the Hitler Youth, who were exhorted to carry on Prussian traditions. The film was not, however, commercially available in the States.

Reifenstahl was not the only woman directing films in Nazi Germany, but few Americans could name any other female German director. Like Riefenstahl, Edith Hart (who often worked with her husband Wolf), Clarissa Patrix (b. 1908), and Ursula Löwenstein shot propaganda films; Lola Kreutzberg (b. 1878) and Gertrud David (1872–1936) made documentaries; and Charlotte Reiniger (1899–1981) made animated shorts.

The Nazis' claims to be bearers of a great tradition were also revealed in German-Austrian efforts at scaling Nanga Parbat, the so-called German *Schicksalsberg* (mountain of destiny). Located in what is now Pakistan, the 8,000-meter mountain took the lives of four Germans and six bearers from Darjeeling in 1934. Fritz Bechtdold recorded the group's ordeal from the time it left Bombay until the snowstorm that drove its members, 400 meters from the peak and success, back down the mountain. Survivors included Peter Müllritter and a guide named Pasang. Premiering in Munich, *Nanga Parbat*, said *Variety* (March 11, 1936), is a "grandiose document full of moving heroism."

Carl Froelich's *Reifende Jugend* (*Maturing Youth*) was one of the first German films to screen in the U.S. in the new year. It was about molding Germany's future generation of heroic men. CFE and the Film Society Corp. released it in New York, where filmgoers may have sniffed its resemblance to the early 1930s Weimar boarding-school drama *Mädchen in Uniform*. (Even better, Hertha Thiele costarred again). Because it stressed youthful comradeship, the film had received the "highest approbation from the German censor," wrote the *New York Times* (January 4, 1936).

The film, which R.A. Stemmle co-scripted, centers on the emotional upheavals that transpire when three blonde girls enter a boys' school to study for an important exam. When master teacher Kerner (Peter Voss) and student Knud Sengebusch (Albert Lieven) both fall in love with Elfriede (Thiele), Knud threatens to expose the teacher—unless he is given a passing grade. The teacher refuses, yet Knud doesn't follow through with his threat. Informed of the young man's behavior, Headmaster Brodersen (Heinrich George) is impressed when Knud resists pressure to write a confession. Brodersen, delivering a rousing speech to the board of examiners, convinces them to give Knud a passing grade because of his manly character. Kerner marries Elfriede. Everyone then joins in singing "We Boys of the Sea." There's also a role for the "new woman" in German educational and professional spheres, says the film, until, however, she weds—and then it's hearth and home for her in the Third Reich.

The *New York Times* noted that *Reifende Jugend* is a "relief to those who feared the worst for the present tendency of German production; it is beyond all political strife and makes no concessions whatever." This production, however, had been made in the first year of Hitler's rule when Hitler's filmmakers were getting their feet wet. The year 1936 was an opportune time to release harmless entertainment like this in the U.S.

Froelich's subsequent production, *Oberwachtmeister Schwenke* (*Top-Sergeant Schwenke*, 1934), also scripted by Stemmle and scored by Emil Schünemann, depicts an upright official in Hitler's second year of rule. This film, which screened at the Casino Theatre, is more solidly grounded in Nazi ideology: the free use of swastikas helps define a model, disciplined German official. Berlin officer Schwenke (Gustav Fröhlich) is well liked by everybody. School children know him. He happily guides them through busy city streets. When Schwenke is assigned a serious case, a pretty fraulein (Marianne Hoppe) aids him in the investigation. The case involves the murder of two people: Erna (Sybille Schmitz), a woman Schwenke knew, and the crooked banker she worked for. His name is "Wenkstern" (Walter Steinbeck), a presumed Jew.

The story, said the *New York Times* (May 5, 1936), "turns into a tribute to the discipline which exacts the discharge of an officer for having kicked a notorious criminal." The film, which also ran at the Henka German Theatre in Passaic, N.J., was one of a series of Nazi propaganda films that admonished Germany's new generation to always seek the "cooperation of your police."

On February 29, *Knock-Out* (1935), directed by the busy Carl Lamac and Hans H. Zerlett and produced by Bavaria, screened at New York's 79th Street Theater. Those who did fear the worst from Nazi Germany zeroed in on this film because it starred German heavyweight champion Max Schmeling. The Non–Sectarian Anti–Nazi League called Schmeling a "German commodity" from which the Nazi regime profited. The league asked Americans to boycott not only Schmeling's upcoming summer match against Joe Louis but also Schmeling's films. Whenever Schmeling's films screened in America, a spotlight focused on Nazi films. Then Schmeling's films were gone, and things slipped back to normal. Frau Schmeling—Anny Ondra—was often Schmeling's co-star.

Knock-Out, which was also known as *Ein junges Mädchen—Ein junger Mann* (in Austria, *Liebe und Knock out*), is about husky stage electrician Max who is in love with a pretty blonde. When he breaks into show business, another admirer of hers—a professional boxer (Samson Körner)—challenges him to a match. Max wins the fight, loses his job—and *then* becomes a boxer. In Berlin, Max defeats a British champion (Hans Schonrath) in a well-staged bout; his girlfriend is in the audience, and wedding bells are heard through the roar of the crowd.

Another romance, Alfred Abel's *Glückliche Reise* (*Bon Voyage*, 1933), screened at the 79th Street Theater in early 1936. But it was a rarity of a different sort: a German film depicting young German Jews. Based on the operetta by Eduard Künneke, the story is of two men in Brazil who return to Hamburg, where the young, true German Robert Hartenau (Ekkehard Arend) falls into the arms of blonde Lola Vonderhoff (Carla Carlsen). His friend "Stefan Schwarzenberg" (Max Hansen), a Jew, has come back to dark-haired "Monika Brink" (Magda Schneider), not for love, but because she claims to be an heiress.

For real Germans, money proves no allure. In *Der Vetter aus Dingsda* (*The Cousin from Dingsda*, 1934), directed by George Zoch (1902–1944) and based on an operetta by Eduard Künneke, young Julia (Lien Deyers) waits for Roderich to return from India. Her impatient uncle, Emil (Jakob Tiedke), wants to marry her off to the rich merchant Mr. Wildenhagen

(Paul Heidemann). Julia, however, falls for handsome Hans (Walter von Lennep), a musician, whom she imagines is her cousin-lover from Dingsda.

Produced by Ufa, Zoch's film, which screened at the 79th Street Theater in early 1936, was one of the last films that Deutsche Universal distributed in Germany. Deutsche Universal and its Jewish filmmakers, forced to flee Germany, moved operations to Vienna and Budapest. Carl Boese's comedy *Greetings and Kisses, Veronika!* (1933), which "was produced by non–Nazi Germans," wrote the *New York Times* (February 24, 1936), was a Deutsche Universal film starring Franciska Gaál as a diminutive flower girl who falls in love with her boss (Paul Hörbiger), which leads merely to misunderstandings.

Similarly, Hermann Kosterlitz's comedy hit *Peter* (1934) was a product of Deutsche Universal's newly relocated operations in Budapest. Karl Lamac had been slated to direct it but he backed out under blackmail: the Nazis threatened to ban him from working in Germany if he associated with "non–Aryans."

Jewish actress Gaál starred as the 17-year-old Eva. When her grandfather can't afford the rent, they are evicted from their home. When Eva tries to earn money as a street musician, a thief, seeking a disguise, forces her to swap clothes with him.

Dressed as a male, Eva calls herself "Peter," but then runs into trouble with Dr. Robert Bandler (Hans Jaray) and is charged with a crime. The doctor, however, takes pity on the "boy," and unknown to Peter/Eva, he convinces a friend to hire "him." Eva is attracted to Bandler but her double identity continues to cause confusion.

Deutsche Universal, in a sense, had a sort of double identity of its own. It produced German-language films outside Germany. Its harmless post–1933 films that were released in the U.S. contradicted "those who feared the worst" from Hitler's Germany. An even better example of a film directed by a non–Nazi German that soothed anti–German feelings in America was Max Ophuls's film *Liebelei* (*Light o' Love*). A tragedy about lost love set in 1910, it opens and closes at the Vienna State Opera House. The hero, who at the end dies in a duel, tells his lover, "I will love you forever and forever." "You fumble for your handkerchief," wrote *Chicago Tribune* critic Mae Tinée. By the time the film screened at New York's 55th Street Playhouse and Chicago's Sonotone Theatre in early 1936, Ophuls was safely in France. No one said so, but Ophuls's film had been made in 1932–33. Ophuls's cast—Magda Schneider, Luise Ullrich, Wolfgang Liebeneiner, Gustav Gründgens, Olga Tschechowa, Willi Eichberger, and Paul Hörbiger—remained in Germany (or Austria). So did Paul Otto, but he managed to keep secret his Jewish background.

Nineteen thirty-six was the year outsiders (excepting Jews) were invited into Germany. The Nazis told the League of Nations that the treatment of German Jews was none of its business. On the German screen, there was only one way to treat Jews. Take Gerhard Lamprecht's aptly-named Ufa mystery *Einer zuviel an Bord* (*One Too Many on Board*, 1935), co-scripted by Fred Andreas (1898-?) from his own novel, which screened in the U.S. in early 1936. It starred Czech-born Lida Baarová, who was Goebbels' mistress. The film starts with the disappearance during a storm of a freighter's skipper, Captain Moltmann (Albrecht Schoenhals). The captain represents the born leader—who is not easily disposed of. When his ship docks in Hamburg, prosecutor Burger (Willy Birgel) and Commissioner Sörensen (Alexander Golling) investigate. Was it murder, an accident, or something else? They discover that two men wanted the captain dead. First Officer Rohlfs (René Deltgen) believed the captain was having an affair with his fiancée Gerda (Baárova); the engineer "Sparkuhl" (Alexander Engel) blamed the captain for his niece's suicide. At the end of the tale, when the captain turns up alive, "Sparkuhl," a presumed Jew, commits suicide.

The French version *Un homme de trop a bord* was co-directed by Roger Le Bon and produced by Alliance Cinématographique Européenne (A.C.E.). Director Lamprecht was also responsible for a true Nazi gem: the "patriotic rebel film," set during the Prussian Wars of Liberation, called *Der Höhere Befehl* (*The Higher Command*). Scored by composer Werner Eisbrenner, it was released in Berlin at the end of 1935 and came to the U.S. three months later. The theme is the call to duty, a rallying cry of Hitler's in *Mein Kampf*. Its title might as well have served as the collective title of all German patriotic films of the era. The "higher command"—courage, quick-mindedness, responsibility, and judgment—encapsulated the "leader qualities" that enable a man in doubtful or difficult situations to make decisions on his own, even if they run up against official policy. In Nazi terms, the leader decided for the "revolutionary right" against the legal and reactionary past.

In the film, Nazis recall the historic ties between England and Prussia that vanquished Napoleon as a "higher command" to duty and country. Lil Dagover (1887–1980) and Karl Ludwig Diehl (1896–1958) starred in a combination of fact and fancy set in 1806. In occupied Germany, Lord Beckhurst (Hans Mierendorf), acting as a special envoy of Britain's king, stops at Perleberg on the way to London from Vienna. He is to negotiate a pact among England, Austria, and Prussia—in effect trying to induce Prussia to break with its ally, France—which would then seal Napoleon's fate. On his way through Perleberg, however, Beckhurst is kidnapped.

Major von Droste (Diehl), the Prussian commander of Perleberg, disobeys orders and sets out to find him. The major risks everything, even the love of his life, Käthe (Heli Finkenzeller), to help the envoy complete his mission. A French spy, Madame Martin (Lil Dagover), involved in the disappearance, is exposed and shot. Although Droste succeeds in his mission, the army dismisses him for failing to "keep your hands off politics." Yet Droste is sure that after Prussia's liberation his actions will be especially honored. There's also a hint that he may reunite with his sweetheart.

A theme such as this one emphasized the gathering storm, as more and more lives were lost off screen. On screen, the sacrificial action of the "leader" served the collective regime. Goebbels called the film "national and engrossing"; *Variety* (April 1936) noted the "hand of the new German 'culture' lies heavily" on the film.

Werner Paul Adolph Hochbaum's *Leichte Kavalerie* (*Light Cavalry*, 1935) is also about duty and honor. But this takes place off the battlefield. It is a circus film in which the popular clown Rux (Karl Hellmer) *doesn't* love the popular dancer Rosika (Marika Rökk) and the owner of the show, Cherubini (Fritz Kampers), *doesn't* plot vengeance when his offer of marriage is refused. The man of honor does his duty by getting out of the way for the two lovers from Hungary, Geza von Rakos (Heinz von Cleve) and Rosika. Critics disliked the film, deducing, according to *Variety* (February 19, 1936) that "German producers today are so harried by governmental and propaganda problems that ... they've lost their cunning." They imagined that Ufa under Hitler was the same studio that had produced, for instance, E.A. Dupont's hugely successful circus drama *Variety* ten years earlier. *Leichte Kavallerie*, which screened at the 79th Street Theater, was the first film by Werner Hochbaum (1899–1946) to be shown in the States, based on the novel *Umwege zur Heimat/Detours to the Homeland* by Heinz Lorenz-Lambrecht. Ufa produced a French version, *Cavalerie légère* (*Light Cavalry*, 1935), co-directed by Roger Vitrac.

Hochbaum had directed the neo-realist *Razzia in St. Pauli* (*Raid in St. Pauli*, 1932), a tale about a doomed love affair between a sailor and a prostitute, starring Jewish actor Wolfgang Zilzer and Gina Falckenberg. This film garnered attention but it was *Der Ewige Maske* (1935) that made Hochbaum famous. Called the most original German-language filmmaker of the thirties—if you ignored the German-Jewish directors working in America—Hochbaum did not direct, or was barred from directing, in Germany after the war started.

Weimar actor Wolfgang Zilzer was the son of the comedian Max Zilzer. On Hitler's rise to power, Wolfgang Zilzer fled to Paris; and when he realized that his birth (in 1901) in the U.S. had made him an American citizen, he moved to Hollywood. Fellow Jew and countryman Ernst Lubitsch put Zilzer to work in *Bluebeard's Eighth Wife* (1938) and *Ninotchka* (1939). Zilzer was also in Sam Newfeld's anti–Nazi *Beasts of Berlin* (1939).

Arthur M. Rabenalt's first film under the Nazis, called *Pappi* (1934), also a circus drama, came to the U.S. upholding the virtues of yet another good German. The orphan Lilly (Petra Unkel) has winning ways and a large (but unknown to her) inheritance from her circus-performing parents. Much of the film takes place during circus acts, to establish the fact that Lilly's mother, an aerialist, is doomed. The girl's scheming relatives are aware of the loot-in-waiting. The hero is her compassionate uncle, Hans Werner (Viktor de Kowa), a liquor-store clerk. His responsibility—and duty to the next generation—manifests itself when he saves his niece from the clutches of those relatives.

In early 1936, CFE released a German film about "real humans of flesh and blood," according to the *New York Times* (February 10, 1936). Terra's comedy *Wer nimmt die Liebe ernst?* (*Who Takes Love Seriously?*), was directed by Erich Engel and starred Max Hansen. Erich Engel, who had been called Weimar Germany's finest stage director, showed that "his stage methods are equally adaptable to the screen," said the *New York Times* critic. Hansen plays a small-time crook with a big heart. On the run from the law, he hides in the bedroom of unsuspecting Ilse (Jenny Jugo), who, when the police arrive, tells them that Max is her boyfriend. Nevertheless, Max is sentenced to three days in jail. While in custody, he meets Bruno (Otto Wallburg), who keeps following him after their release from prison. Meanwhile Ilse, who was evicted by her landlady because of the incident with Max, wins a beauty pageant. Max, meanwhile, tries to reunite with her, but each time his new "life-time friend" Bruno prevents him from getting near Ilse. Finally, miserable Max returns home, where, surprisingly, Ilse is waiting for him.

The film, which was Engel's first, had been produced in Germany in 1931! Future Jewish exiles Hermann Kosterlitz and Curt Alexander scripted Engel's hit and Curt Courant photographed it. The Nazis were the ones who made money on this export to America. Engel would put his film talent to work for the Nazis for 12 years. Hansen (born Max Haller) became know for his Chaplin imitations. After Hansen took a daring, anti–Nazi step—he mocked Hitler as a lovelorn homosexual—he worked beyond the Reich, in Austria, starring in the hit *Csardas, ihre toolset Nacht* (*Csardas, Her Wildest Night*, 1935). He left for Denmark before Austria became part of the greater Reich.

A series of films by the now forgotten Max Obal (1881–1949) that were screened in the U.S. in early 1936 didn't quite exhibit the spirit of 1936. Obal's romance *Der Klosterjäger* (*The Monastery's Hunter*, 1935), an Ufa production, depicts Bavarian Germans in the era of the crossbow. It was based the popular 1892 novel by Heimat writer Ludwig Ganghofer, whom Goebbels admired for his allegiance to the Germany of blood and soil. In the tale, the hunter Haymo (Paul Richter), a good German widower and father, has difficulty providing a Berchtesgaden monastery with game and preventing poaching. His love for the simple, beautiful, but lowly peasant Gittli (Charlotte Radspieler), who is blonde, leads to the revelation that she is of noble birth—and, better yet, she is related to the region's German ruler. Haymo's position in life is secured.

Obal's German-Czech comedy *Annette im Paradies* (1933–34) offered an insider's view of middle-class life via a ruse. Wealthy young Annette Karstens (Ursula Grabley) inherits an entire industrial city. Immediately, one of the firm's directors, a villain with the Jewish-sounding name "Bertuch" (Max Gülstorff), seeks her hand in marriage. But Annette wants to learn about the business through practical experience. Going incognito, she pretends to be of modest means and takes a job in her own department store. This allows her to see and understand how the other half lives. She also falls in love with poor shipping clerk Hans Siebert (Hans

Söhnker). American critics were suspicious not of the implied racism but of the film's setting when it screened untitled at the Casino Theatre. "Just how realistic the scenes in the big store are must be judged by persons familiar with such Berlin establishments," concluded a *Times* critic (March 7, 1936).

As for the setting in Obal's murder-mystery *Schloss Vogelöd* (*Castle Vogeloed*, 1936), Ufa's "book into a film," the *New York Times* had no suspicions. The "winter scenes around the castle," it said, were "highly realistic." Based on a novel by Rudolf Stratz, the tale begins with the unexpected return of handsome young Andreas from exotic South America. He discovers to his shock that his sweetheart has married his older brother Leopold (Walter Steinbeck). She had forsaken Andreas because she believed he no longer loved her, according to Andreas's brother. Leopold is later found dead. The murderer turns out to be the unscrupulous major domo of the castle, Johann von Safferstätt (Hans Zesch-Ballot, 1896–1972).

In 1921, Uco–Film had produced F.W. Murnau's silent version of the story (which was being serialized at the same time in the *Berlin Illustrieter*) as a psychological drama containing an "oppressive, anguish-ridden milieu," as Lotte Eisner described it.

A fourth film by Obal, called *Die Fahrt ins Grüne* (*A Trip to the Country*), which is set at a quaint lake resort, is, on the surface, a riches-to-rags story of wealthy playboy "Robert Fink" (Hermann Thimig) who loses his yacht, his sweetheart, "Lotte Krause" (Lien Deyers), and his fair-weather friends when his banker (Leopold von Ledebur), identified only as the "general director," absconds with his money.

But did what happened between rich Jews in the new Germany really matter? The film, which screened at the 79th Street Theater in spring 1936, had been one of the earliest Nazi productions to stress the back-to-the-soil movement, depicted via a German farm run under ideal conditions by peasant Germans. It had been produced in 1933.

Hans Deppe's *Der Mutige Seefahrer* (*The Valiant Navigator*, 1935), which Bobby Lüthge (1891–1964) scripted and CFE distributed, is also set in a quaint locale. Deppe's comedy is mostly in pantomime, which, apparently, made it a natural for non–German-speaking American filmgoers. It's about "male Cinderella" Berthold Jebe (Paul Kemp, 1896–1953), one of three brothers, who finally musters the courage to pop the question (to Lucie Englisch). Jebe is spurred to action by a rich American relative offering 10,000 marks to any of the brothers willing to leave Germany for America. However, the pull of the fatherland and of his hometown are just too great. Jebe's call to stay at home is aided by a bit of superstition that alerts him to the dangers of an ocean voyage west. Sans the fortune, but thanks to his superstitious nature, the young man still gets the girl.

In the fatherland, the young protagonists in Hans Steinhoff's *Keine Angst vor Liebe* (*Don't Be Afraid of Love*), Liane Haid, Jessie Vihrog, Adolf Wohlbrück, and Theo Lingen, know their place and find their soul mates in a welcoming boarding house, which is symbolic of Hitler's Germany. (The title comes from the theme song and love-shy nature of one of the males.) CFE imported this film, which had been made in 1933.

The prolific Géza von Bolváry directed budding actress Haid in *Das Schloss im Süden* (*The Castle in the South*), a 1933 Boston Films production that CFE released in early 1936. Haid plays Maria Foreni, an actress who falls for an extra on the set. He turns out to be Prince Mirano (Viktor de Kowa). For one time only—since this is a film about a film people—she fails to get her man. Set in the Adriatic, the film was also shot by A.C.E. Called *Château de rêve* (1933), it was co-directed by Henri-Georges Clouzot.

Carl Froelich and Rolf Hansen were behind the rural comedy *Wenn der Hahn kräht* (*When the Cock Crows*, 1935–36), yet another CFE release, which is built around the early-morning romantic excursions of two honorable lovers in a North German village that is under the thumb of a crusty old mayor (Heinrich George).

The theme of salvaging German honor is the core of Carl Froelich's *The Private Life of Louis XIV*. In Germany the film's title was *Liselotte von der Pfalz* (*Liselotte of the Palatinate*, 1935). The heroine is young Heidelberg princess Liselotte (Renate Müller), who is lured by the Sun King (played by one-time Met Opera singer Michael Bohnen, 1887–1965), into marriage with the king's brother, Philippe d'Orleans (Hans Stüwe), called Ludwig. Although France said it would extend its rule into the domain of her father (Eugen Klöpfer) under Louis's "benevolence," the French attack the Palatinate. Unable to help her people from France, Liselotte returns home, her French husband by her side.

When the film ran at New York's Bijou Theatre, the (*N.Y.*) *Sun* (January 9, 1936) said it "proves the German studios have not lost their old knack," while the *Herald Tribune* (January 10, 1936) indicated that the "faintly Teutonic quality of the story ... gives it a heavy rather than sparkling surface" but the "logical and thorough characteristics of the German mind lend to the representation of the dazzling French court a steady factual interpretation." The *Chicago Tribune* (August 11, 1936) was alert enough to point out that the "entire dialogue is in German, with English titles—and non–German viewers probably lose a good deal in the translation." Goebbels named *Liselotte von der Pfalz* winner of a National Film Prize. Cast member Maly Delschaft (1898–1995) in 1930 had *almost* captured the role of Lola Lola in the classic *The Blue Angel*. After the war Delschaft starred in Erich Engel's philo–Semitic *Affaire Blum* (1948), with Paul Bildt. Actor and theater director Klöpfer was a Nazi party member.

A few days after *Liselotte von der Pfalz* screened in New York, *Die Marquise von Pompadour*, directed by Willi Wolff (1883–1947), opened at the Casino Theatre. Of the story of the Sun King's predecessor, Louis XV, and his infatuation with Madame Pompadour (Anny Ahiers), the *New York Times* (February 3, 1936) noted only that the production had "been remade and strengthened by the substitution of a number of excellent Teuton actors for some of the original cast." The incongruity could have been explained—but wasn't. The film had been produced in Germany during the Weimar era, in 1930. The original cast had included German-Jewish actor Kurt Gerron, who played the king. In 1936, however, Gerron was persona non grata in Germany. In addition, the film had co-starred two other Jewish performers long gone from German films: Max Ehrlich and Ernö Verebes.

Another sign of change had occurred when German-Jewish director Max Neufeld had completed *Das Lied der Sonne* (*Song of the Sun*, 1933). While his romantic musical about mistaken identity didn't reach the U.S., Itala's rendition, called *La Canzone del Sole*, starring a young Vittorio de Sica, had slipped quietly into New York. The Italian version, made in 1933, helped establish the pattern for other "Italian" films that would be unobtrusively released in America. They featured Italian and German members of the "circle of stars."

The music of *La Canzone del Sole* begins in Berlin with arias from "Puritani" and concludes in an open-air theatre in Verona with excerpts from "Ugonoti" and "Il Trovatore." "Spectators," wrote the *New York Times* (May 6, 1936), "are taken to some of the loveliest places in the peninsula, to the accompaniment of laughter and song." In the German-language version, an impresario named "Max Adler" (Erhard Siedel) is jailed. The film was a rare example of depicting a Jew behind bars in Germany.

Anti-German sentiment in America was most likely the reason behind the quiet release of Carl Lamac's subtitled *Frasquita* (1934), at New York's World Theatre. An "Atlantic-Vienna production," it had German backing, German cast members, and a German distributor, called Neues Deutsches Lichtspiel-Syndikat (N.D.L.S.). However, you wouldn't have known much else because "no other credits" were available, said *Variety* (January 22, 1936). But details didn't matter to the *N.Y. World-Telegram* (January 22, 1936). "Who cares," it asked, "if the music is light and gay and tuneful?" And *Motion Picture Daily* (January 21, 1936) raved: "Throughout the film the music is highly attractive." Inspired by Franz Lehár's 1910 operetta *Zigeunerliebe*

(*Gypsy Love*), the tale is about architect Harald (Hans Heinz Bollman) and his best friend Hippolit (Heinz Rühmann) and how they exchange romantic partners. The former falls for the gypsy singer Frasquita Benavente (Jarmila Novotna) while Hippolit marries his best friend's girl, Dolly Elemer (Charlotte Daudert). In this harmonious year, Austrian productions started to come to America. In fact most of them were German co-productions featuring German performers.

Between 1935 and 1938, Austrian productions were semi–Nazi productions. Austria, emulating Germany, had barred Jews from its films in April 1935. After March 1938, Austrian films were little more than Nazi films made in Austria. The Austrian-German production *Tanzmusik* (*Dance Music*, 1935), which CFE distributed in early 1936 sans subtitles, calls the shots in favor of Beethoven over African Americans' musical creation, jazz. Directed by the Austrian Johann Alexander Hübler-Kahla (1902–65), the film starred Liane Haid as the young American Gina Harding, who marries jazz composer-conductor Mario D'Almeida (Hermann Thimig), who has made it big in the States. In fact, the film's opening shot is of Times Square with the conductor, known as Max in America, giving a farewell performance. Their marriage falls apart, however, when it becomes clear that her man of music really craves old world, German culture: Beethoven rather than music from, as it is referred to in the film, "nasty jazzy America." After Max and Gina divorce, Max marries the German girl waiting in the wings, Hedi Baumann (Gusti Huber). Big-hearted Max also takes the time to give a helping hand to the young, struggling musician Franz Hegner (Hans Thimig).

Gina marries her kind of man, "Bob Crawler" (Georg Alexander). And in a bit of diversion, Leo Slezak plays the presumed Jew "Koppler," a formerly celebrated tenor reduced to concert agent. In his room Koppler has an oil painting of himself as "Raoul." He would tell all who ask that he really once was "that young sapling pine."

There was no glorious music in Ufa's *Savoy-Hotel 217*, which premiered in Berlin in early 1936 with Americans in the audience. Scripted by Gerhard Menzel and directed by Gustav Ucicky, this openly anti–Semitic film has *every* unscrupulous character carrying a Jewish name. Set in prewar Moscow, the central figure is the attractive, devil-may-care, non–Jewish hotel waiter Andrej Wolodkin (Hans Albers) who is wanted for murder. Found at the scene of the crime, he escapes from police custody in order to exonerate himself by locating the real killer. The victim in question was from room 217, Natasja Daschenko (Brigitte Horney). The real suspects are her husband, the merchant Fedor Fedorowitsch Daschenko (Alexander Engel), and the man in the room next door, Sergei Gawrilowitsch Schuwalow (René Deltgen), who had served time in Siberia for murdering *his* wife. The actual killer—Daschenko—is discovered hiding in a flophouse, amid scenes of brutality. He had killed his wife because she wanted a divorce after she had fallen in love with Andrej. Other characters in the film, which was not commercially distributed in the U.S., included a shady attorney named "Schapkin" (Jakob Tiedke); the magician "Pawlowitsch" (Aribert Wäscher); and the jealous hotel maid Anna Feorowna Orlowa (Käthe Dorsch).

In May 1936, as the Summer Olympic Games approached, Nazi storm troopers in Berlin were chanting, "Once the Olympics belongs to the past, we'll kill the Jews pretty darn fast." On August 1, the Eleventh Olympic Summer Games, dubbed the "Nazi Games," opened. Yet even in 1936, German film exporters—and their American importers—tested the film market to see what they could get away with. They screened, for instance, Johannes Meyer's anti–Semitic *Der Flüchling aus Chicago* (*The Fugitive from Chicago*, 1933–34). In this story a German heads towards Germany as if in the direction of a promised land. But since the film was shown in the U.S. in the year of the Olympics, heading towards Germany must have seemed to some like a sensible idea.

Meyer (1884–1972) had gotten his start at Deutsche Universal in the Weimar era. His early sound films had focused on personal problems. His film *Aschermittwoch* (*Ash Wednesday*, 1930) was a tale of a woman who dies to save her lover. It was distributed by CFE. Meyer directed Marta Eggerth in *Traum von Schönbrunn* (*Dream of Schönbrunn*), about a princess finding her prince charming during the reign of Emperor Franz Josef when he lived in his famous Vienna palace in summer. "With German pictures not doing so well" in America, said *Variety* (June 1933), *Traum von Schönbrunn* could lead to "improved chances" of success for "this Austrian picture." The film was actually a Weimar-financed production shot in Austria's capital in 1932.

Working for Atalanta-Film, Meyer directed *Der Flüchtling aus Chicago* (*The Fugitive from Chicago*, 1934) from a script by soon-to-be-infamous Max W. Kimmich. Although one of its settings is America, the film wasn't shot there. Protagonist Werner Dux (Hubert von Meyerink), heir to a German auto plant, is unable to assume his familial duties. That's because the Chicago police are holding Dux on a murder charge. So "Michael Nissen" (Gustav Fröhlich)—a presumed Jew—assumes the role of heir and crosses the Atlantic into the fatherland. The Jewish/German-American rejuvenates the factory in the new Germany. Years later, as a fugitive from justice, Dux makes his way back to Germany. In Hitler's Germany he proves that the charges made against him in America had been false. The Jew Nissen was the real killer. Nissen wanted to get his hands on all that German money and, if all went well, to marry a blonde!

The film portrays the real German as a scapegoat when it starts in the Windy City, which has a large German-American population, and as a hero in Munich, which has an even bigger German-speaking population—and which was a key city in Nazi lore.

American critics were oblivious of the film's message. Rather, *Variety* (March 25, 1936) noted that a German "peps things up in American style" back in the fatherland. However, the "director, author, and Bavaria Film [the distributor] display an extremely vague conception of Chicago, its hotels, cops, cabarets, streets, and people therein," said the trade daily. The film's star, Gustav Heinrich Fröhlich (1902–1987), was handsome, elegant, and charming, and served Nazi filmmaking until Hitler's end.

Fröhlich had gotten his start in motion pictures when Fritz Lang saw him on the German stage and signed him up for the part of the hero in *Metropolis* (1927). His performances in the psychological dramas *Heimkehr* (*Homecoming*, 1928) and *Asphalt* (1929), both directed by Joe May (Julius Otto Mandl), had *Variety* (June 1930) calling Fröhlich one of Germany's "most superior leading men ... who does not care a hoot for his appearance, but who can rise to a dramatic climax with magnificent power and sincerity."

Warner Bros. brought Fröhlich to America for its German-language productions *Kismet* (1931), directed by the German-Jew William Dieterle, and *Die Heilige Flamme* (1931), directed by another Jew, Berthold Viertel. Fröhlich directed his first film in Germany in 1934 and his seventh and last in 1955. His final role was in the German film *... and Nobody Was Ashamed* (1960).

Fröhlich's first directorial effort under Hitler, *Abenteuer eines jungen Herrn in Polen* (1934), had been produced by the up-and-coming Alberto Giacalone, for Itala Film, and was shown in New York in April 1936. Although re-titled to fit the year—*Liebe und Trometenklang* (*Love and Alarms and Excursions*)—the film carried a theme in line with the attitudes in the new Germany. An Austrian army officer falls in love with an attractive Polish girl (Olga Tschechowa) in St. Petersburg, at a New Year's party, in 1914. War soon breaks out. Then love vies with duty. It's not hard to guess which emotion always wins out in service to the homeland.

Emotion is at the heart of Fred Sauer's *Alles weg'n dem Hund* (*All for the Dog's Sake*, 1935), a tale about man's best friend, and it, too, carried a message from the fatherland. The protagonist, a dog, has a huge legacy attached to it. The upshot is that the animal receives much better treatment than any human. There would be more films from Germany that would also depict animals receiving better treatment than non–Aryans.

Sauer's *Alte Kameraden* (*Old Comrades*, 1934), which screened at the Casino Theatre in 1936, was billed as a comedy about a crude country girl named Maruschka (Charlotte Daudert), who is brought to Germany and turned into a fine lady by a none-too-scrupulous jeweler. Not only does the film patronize the young Polish girl, it contains a whiff of anti–Semitism, which was ignored by the critics. The jeweler carried a Jewish surname: "Röttgen" (Paul Henckels).

Sauer (1886–1952) was also responsible for two films starring the sad-faced, silent-era comedians called Doublepatte and Patachon. The actors, Danes in fact, were, respectively, Karl Schenstrom (1881–1942) and Harold Madsen (1890–1949). In *Mädchenräuber* (*Girl Kidnappers*, 1936), a Majestic comedy released by American Tobis in mid–1936, the pantomime duo kidnap a young American woman so that she can capture the heart of a young man. In *Blinde Passagiere* (*Stowaways*, 1936), also distributed by American Tobis, the duo played stowaway, down-and-out circus clowns on the *Cap Branco*, which is heading to South America. They find their fortunes are radically altered when they unexpectedly get their hands on a 300,000-mark lottery ticket. They also help uncover the identity of jewel thief Herbert Wendler (Rudolf Platte). A stowaway operating under the alias "Shah of Persia," Wendler had stolen pearls from Olivia Hawkins (Margarete Kupfer), an Australian.

The film co-starred Russian-born Genia Nickolajewa (1904–2001)—in her final German production—playing a secretary. After making two films in Austria she immigrated to the U.S. in 1938, and became one of Jack Warner's secretaries.

Herbert Maisch (1890–1974) was introduced to American audiences via his first film under the Nazis, Ufa's *Königswalzer* (*The Royal Waltz*, 1935). (Maisch's *Königswalzer* should not to be confused with Manfred Noa's Weimar-era *Der Walzerkönig*, 1930, also about the "waltz king." Noa's film had screened in New York in late 1932, depicting Strauss returning from Russia to Austria in 1848 to pour oil, that is, music, so to speak, on troubled waters.) With gossip aplenty, Maisch's operetta of easy-going court life contains the requisite number of waltzes as well as excerpts from Mozart's *Don Juan*. Munich of 1852 and the marriage of Elizabeth of Bavaria (Carola Höhn) and Franz Joseph of Austria (Kurt Jürgens) are the background for the romantic entanglements of lesser nobles. Count Tettenbach, the Elder (Anton Pointner), falls for a confectioner's youngest daughter while visiting popular King Max II of Bavaria (Paul Hörbiger). The count's nephew, Ferdl (Willi Forst), then falls in love with a commoner's daughter, Theres (Heli Finkenzeller). The final scenes are of German brass bands, flags waving, and the Emperor Franz Josef, then in his youth, arriving behind plumed horses.

This musical was released twice in New York. When it ran at New York's 55th St. Playhouse, its "few slight historical slips may be overlooked," wrote the *New York Times* (April 10, 1936), "as they are harmless." Characters said things like "she's hot stuff" and "I just got the bird." Six months later, re-subtitled, it ran at the Casino Theatre. In the cast was Ellen Schwanneke (1916–1972), who had also starred in S. Innemann's German-language Czech production *Sextanerin* (*Sweet Sixteen*, 1936). In an event of limited historical significance, Schwanneke fled Europe for America in 1938 despite the pleas of her godfather, Emil Jannings, because she said she hated Hitler.

At the advent of sound, Prague-born Carl Lamac (who died in Hamburg) had been praised for his ability to develop scripts and work with actors. Then he employed his talents in the service of the Third Reich. Herbert Grünewald assisted Lamac through the mid–1930s. In Lamac's *Die Schüchterne Casanova* (*The Bashful Casanova*, 1936), a Rota production released by American Tobis, a presentable German blonde getting along in years seeks almost any man as a matrimonial prospect. The *New York Times* (August 22, 1936) noted that the Casino Theatre was "filling in the summer 1936 season with a highly unimportant comedy" from Germany. One Lamac-Ondra film not to make it to the States, although American critics reviewed it in Berlin, was *Flitterwochen* (*Honeymoon*, 1936), a "comedy" about a woman who marries and then flees from her abusive husband (Hans Söhnker). As a more important Lamac film, it did not mesh with the image Germany was presenting to outsiders in 1936.

The films that Gustav Gründgens directed or starred in, however, did serve Germany. Gründgens married popular German actress Marianne Hoppe after divorcing Thomas Mann's daughter and was a Prussian state counselor.

In Johannes Meyer's *Das Erbe in Pretoria* (*Inheritance in Pretoria*, 1934), produced by Bavaria and released in the U.S. in mid-1936, he played the gentleman bad man "Eugen Schliebach," secretary to a British millionaire, who causes trouble for a woman in financial trouble. In the tale, Hamburg merchant Bernhard Fredersen (Paul Hartmann) tries to make a go of it in South Africa. However, when his business falters and then collapses, he goes blind. Friends, business associates, and clients desert him. The only one by side is his wife, Agnes (Charlotte Susa), the daughter of Admiral Wiethaus (Philipp Manning). She appeals to wealthy financier William Spenser (Max Weydner) for help. When Spenser suddenly dies, his secretary, "Eugen Schliebach" (Gründgens), then sees *his* chance to go after Agnes. However, Spenser's death is a blessing in disguise because Spencer had bequeathed her a fortune and an estate in Pretoria. Agnes is able to reject the vile Schliebach. Her husband then regains his sight.

The right man falls into the right woman's arms in *Alle Tage ist kein Sonntag* (*Every Day Isn't Sunday*, 1935), a comedy about a young draftsman (Wolfgang Liebeneiner) who hates to get up in the morning—but it's not because he's in Nazi Germany. His big winnings in a lottery don't stop him from becoming a dutiful workingman and husband in the new Germany. Walter Janssen (1887–1976) directed the Delta production.

Casino Film Exchange distributed Viktor Janson's operetta *Die Stimme der Liebe* (*The Voice of Love*, 1933) in May 1936. Ekhardt (played by Belgian-born tenor Marcel Wittrisch) is the prominent singer women just adore. The wealthy society woman Clare von Romberg (played by the soprano Maria Beling) bets she can meet him disguised as a simple maid.

Eine Frau, die weiss, was sie will (*A Woman Who Knows What She Wants*, 1934), also was directed by the Latvian-born Viktor Janson (1884–1960) from the Oscar Strauss operetta. Karin (Maria Beling), daughter of the hard-headed, South American businessman Erik Mattisson (Anton Edhofer), feels the call of the blood of her mother Manon Cavallini (Lil Dagover), who had forsaken husband and child for her stage career (in Weimar Germany). At the end of the film, which was shown at the Casino Theatre in July 1936, Karin—a stand-in for the younger generation of true Germans—gives up her career to do her duty. She will marry Axel Basse (Adolf Wohlbrück), her father's associate, and raise a family for the Reich—in accordance with her father's wishes.

In Ufa's *Königin der Liebe* (*Queen of Love*, 1935), also known as *Liebeslied* (*Love Song*), directed by Fritz Peter Buch, a great opera tenor (played by Alessandro Ziliani of the Milan Opera, making his German film debut) replaces a humble performer in a honky-tonk show and wins the heart of the leading soprano, Jeanette (Carola Höhn). The grand finale—*Madame Butterfly*—takes place at the Paris Opera. That was as it should be in Nazi films shown in the U.S. A fine German woman always attracts the right kind of man. This film was seen at New York's 79th Street Theater in mid-1936.

Views of a region that would soon fall into German hands—the Sudetenland—and action in Prague provided the backgrounds to the drama *Jana, das Mädchen aus dem Böhmerwald* (*Jana, the Girl from the Bohemian Forest*, 1935), a Czech-German production shown at the Casino Theatre. With music by Karl Hasler (1879–1941), the story is of an orphaned peasant maid, the blonde Jana (Leny Marenbach), who lands a job on a farm run by brothers. She marries the older brother Peter (Ewald Balser). Matters take a turn for the worse when Peter imagines his wife is unfaithful with his brother Michael (Fred Liewehr); but there's also the questionable hired man "Gottfried" (Wilhelm Tauchen). "Not the least of the picture's good points," wrote the *New York Times* (June 20, 1936), were "its realistic representation of country life and customs in a charming section of the Czechoslovak Republic." This included depictions of farming operations near the Bohemian Forest, whose "magnitude" was emphasized, along with spirited singing by field workers and, ominously, still shots of a nearby German city.

Leny Marenbach (1916–1984) and Ewald Balser (1898–1978) were established stage performers of the Vienna stage. Although Emil Synek was listed as director, there was no mention of the co-director, Robert Land, who by this time had left Germany. He died in 1942.

Franz Osten (1876–1956), a party member, was one of the older directors still working in Nazi Germany. His *Zu Strassburg auf der Schanz* (*At the Strassburg*, 1934), an early 1936 release in New York, also belied the worst from Germany, if you didn't look too closely. Set in Switzerland when the Confederation of German speakers was under French domination, Osten's film, his first under the Nazis, concerns brothers who love the same young woman, but the bigger issue in the film is about letting Germans live freely. So long as these people of long ago strived for liberty and the right to do as they wished, the Nazis were their supporters. The film co-starred Ursula Grabley (1908–1977).

Grabley also headed the cast in Franz Seitz's *Die Frauen vom Tannhof* (*The Tannhof Women*, 1934), with music by Seitz's collaborator Toni Thoms. This was a tale of the occult and a longstanding curse. The curse that has befallen generations of German Tanhoff women is that they die giving birth, supposedly because of the hard-heartedness of a Tanhoff woman of long ago. Grabley played the fearless mountain-climbing city girl Hertha—not unlike Leni Riefenstahl's character in *Blue Light*—who has to overcome her and her lover's fears about the ancient curse. She marries the heir to the Tanhoff estate with, wrote the *New York Times* (February 18, 1936), "all the picturesque ceremony native to the place."

Franz Seitz's films that screened in America misdirected filmgoers from the nature of Hitler's regime. His *Der Kampf mit dem Drachen* (*The Struggle with the Dragon*, 1935) concentrates on the time-honored German tradition of brewing, while his Bavarian comedy *1A in Oberbayern* (*1A in Upper Bavaria*, 1936) rejects odious city existence for glorious country living. Seitz's *Es Waren zwei Junggesellen* (released as *The Plain-Spoken Adele*, 1936), with the ubiquitous Adele Sandrock, puts the accent on healthy rural living in Germany.

Edmund Heuberger's Terra production *Das Verlorene Tal* (*The Lost Valley*, 1934) was yet another a rural drama, climaxing in a mystical, hidden valley near the villages of Puschlay and San Carlo in the Alps. The plot of this Heimat film has an occult ring as well. After many years, young René von Eisten (Mathias Wieman) returns to his ancestral estate. He finds that his childhood sweetheart, Verana (Marie-Luise Claudius), is betrothed to a rather disagreeable civil engineer named Hans Alteggen (Harry Hardt). In addition, the engineer has discovered a valuable source of water in the nearby forest. But any disturbance to the sacred forest, claim the villagers, would bring terrible consequences, including avalanches. Circumstances and the help of an old "forest guardian" named Josi (Olaf Bach) help him win back his girl and get rid of the engineer.

After making this German-Swiss film, which CFE released un-subtitled in the States in mid–1936, director Heuberger (1881–1944), who in the early 1930s had worked for Deutsche Universal, relocated to his native Switzerland.

The wrong man is the chief suspect of a crime in the countryside in Carl Heinz Wolff's *Der Wackere Schustermeister* (*The Honest Master Shoemaker*), which screened untitled at the Casino Theatre in mid–1936. In Germany, Albeo Film had produced it as *In Sachen Timpe* (*In*

Things Timpe, 1933). Its protagonist is an elderly, misjudged cobbler named Carl Timpe (Paul Beckers, 1878–1965), accused of stealing some of his boss's gold spoons. Acquitted in a trial at which his boss Gustav Fiedler (Paul Henckels) testified, Timpe seeks out the real culprit, making use of his particular skills: puns, word juggling, pantomime, and clowning. After the (Jewish) apprentice Otto (Rudolf Klicks) is revealed as the thief, Timpe's young assistant (Paul Richter) marries the boss's daughter (Else Ester). The *New York Times* (July 7, 1936) said the film offers "nothing especially new in complications."

On September 10, 1936, a new name from Germany appeared on American screens: Detlef Sierck. A producer, director, actor, and writer, Hans Detlef Sierck (1897–1987), born in Hamburg, became one of Nazi Germany's most important filmmakers.

Following their elimination of nearly all Jews from German cinema, the Nazis opened the arena to real Germans. Sierck was one of them. He began his film career in 1934 by making shorts for Ufa: *Zwei Genies, Der Eingebildete,* and *Dreimal Ehe*. His first feature came a year later: *April, April!* (The Dutch version, *'Twas 1 April*, was co-directed with Jacques van Tol.) There followed *Das Mädchen vom Moorhof* (*The Girl from Stormy Croft*, 1935), a rural folk drama based on a work by Nobel Prize-winning author Selma Lagerlöf that centers on one of the pillars of Nazi films: support for illegitimate children and their mothers. The young, single, marsh girl Helga, who is rejected by her conservative farming community because she bears a child out of wedlock, goes to court to save her reputation. During the paternity suit, however, Helga withdraws her case rather than see the child's father, a strapping farm lad, swear falsely under oath. Her display of moral courage impresses her detractors.

Sierck's first film to reach the States was the subtitled *Schlussakkord* (*Final Chord*, 1936), which he scripted and which Bruno Duday (1880–1946) produced for Ufa. Its themes are startling, even today. Hungarian Maria Tasnady (1911–2001) starred as the young German Hanna, newly married, who flees to New York with her husband because he had committed insurance fraud in the fatherland. A fugitive from his homeland, he kills himself in Central Park. Hanna falls into a deep depression. However, a "kind doctor" and sympathetic neighbors with "unselfish goodness" remain close at hand. The turning point comes when Hanna listens to a live radio broadcast of Beethoven's Ninth Symphony from Berlin's Philharmonic Concert Hall. Her spirits lift and her will to live is restored.

The magic music is like water to a thirsty plant, penetrating her dulled consciousness, bringing hope to her homesick soul. She regains her health and with the aid of close, kindly American friends she returns to the fatherland and to the son she had given up for adoption. Her son Peter (Peter Bosse), it turns out, lives in the household of the conductor she had heard in New York. Erich Garvenberg (Willy Birgel) had adopted the boy in order to save his marriage. Incognito, Hanna becomes his family's nanny. The musician's wife Charlotte (Lil Dagover), however, discovers Hanna's identity, and fires her. But the wife's excursions into adultery get too hot to handle, and she becomes ill. The family's doctor prescribes medicine, but warns Charlotte to take exactly ten drops; "an overdose could be fatal." Not much later, she is found dead. Garvenberg and Hanna are charged with her murder. But, it turns out, a blackmailing, séance-holding astrologer named Gregor Carl-Otto (Albert Lippert) had driven the conductor's wife to take her own life. One of the astrologer's best friends was the imperious "Baron Salviany" (Kurt Meisel). Later, Garvenberg conducts glorious music in the cathedral. Its immense space is lit by innumerable candles and flooded with the never-ending tones of Handel's great oratorio. In the mysterious dusk of the loft sits Hanna, with Peter beside her, near the organ bench. Three people have found each other; they know themselves to be one; and they have been granted a new life in the new Germany. Hanna's eyes meet Garvenberg's and their hearts quiver with the joy of the final chord. Out of the darkness of greed, fraud, murder, and suicide has come saving grace—the endurance of true Germans.

Willy Birgel conducts in *Schlussakkord* (1936).

Photographed by Robert Baberske (1900–1958), the outlandish melodrama contains Sierck's trademark emotional music (including Tchaikovsky's *The Nutcracker Suite* and Handel's *Judas Maccabaeus* by the Berlin State Opera and the Berlin Soloist Choir), fadeouts, dream sequences, and mirror shots—and a storyline that would soon mirror Sierck's own troubled ties to Nazi Germany and *his* abandonment of a son in Hitler's Reich. Sierck's film, said the critics, had been produced for one reason: to impress tourists in Berlin. "Having been filmed for the Olympic trade," wrote *Variety* (September 16, 1936), the film "shows its washing-behind-the ears." The appearance of the Berliner Staatsoper (national opera) enhanced the importance of the production to the regime.

Sierck's film was the premiere feature at New York's newest East Side outlet for German films: the 86th Street Garden Theatre, the "latest Yorkville cinema house to make a bid for the patronage of German-speaking"—or at least German-understanding-"audiences," wrote the *New York Times* (September 10, 1936). The paper commended the management for its good taste in picking *Schlussakkord*, which had been awarded a prize as the "world's best musical picture" at that summer's Venice Film Festival. The *Chicago Tribune* (February 21, 1937) wrote, "As for the music—beautiful!"

In early November 1936, Sierck's *Stützen der Gesellschaft* (*Pillars of Society*, 1935) reached the 86th Street Garden Theatre. Another Ufa production, starring the Nordic blonde Suse Graf, *Stützen der Gesellschaft* sets its sights on hard-boiled, selfish Norwegian shipbuilder

Karsten Bernick (Heinrich George), whose prosperity has been constructed upon a foundation of deceit. Although he is reputed to be honorable and has funded the town's hospital, the local fishermen loathe him. "Nothing but your greed for money," they say, "and your lies and nothing but your lies has brought you to the top; it is that time that a *new society* has to come; you are finished." Twenty years earlier, Bernick had gotten rid of his main rival Johann (Albrecht Schönhals), who had been forced to flee to America on suspicion of rape. Bernick had then married the man's sister. The innocent wanderer's return to put things right exposes the shipbuilder's involvement in municipal corruption, leads to Bernick's death, and almost results in the death of his nephew Olaf. At the end, an illegitimate girl cries out, "If only I would know a place to go where I would not find this so-called society." She baptizes a new ship because Bernick's rotten vessel has become stranded, exclaiming, "Happy future." Incongruously, the film includes a German rendition of "My Old Kentucky Home."

Stützen der Gesellschaft screened in America *without* subtitles. In addition, in the press materials, its German producer asked American theater managers *not* to cooperate with booksellers who often advertised the original sources of films being shown. Claiming that they didn't want this German film to "look too literary," the producers were deceitful. Hiding behind the name and fame of the story's Norwegian author in order to legitimize an attack on capitalism, the producers were confident that the average American filmgoer couldn't, without Ibsen's 1877 play in hand, discover that the Nazis were serving old wine in a new bottle, or that the film's liberalism wasn't Nazi born. Sierck was not taking aim at life in the new Germany, but rather at an easy target: the world of the pre–Hitler era.

American critics liked *Stützen der Gesellschaft* for its thrills, which was not surprising since it fit the genre called *Volksfilme* ("popular films"). The film does, however, proclaim the Nazis' disdain of middle-class morality, especially its intolerance of illegitimate children—especially if they're German children—combined with an apparent liberalism, so long as the story takes place in the past. Closer to the present, perhaps the Nazis' support for those deemed illegitimate signified the sense that the Nazis themselves felt illegitimate.

Another new German filmmaker who vilified the pre–Hitler era was Karl Ritter (1888–1977). Here was someone who would soon make Americans who hadn't "feared the worst" about the Nazis eat their words. Ritter began his vile career in Germany innocently enough, as production manager on Georg Jacoby's *Melodie der Liebe* (1932), starring Jewish tenor Richard Tauber. Ritter's first directorial effort, for Ufa, was the comedy *Weiberregiment* (*Women's Regiment*, 1936). The battleground in that film—the first of his films to reach the States, in September 1936—is the "war between the sexes" at a brewery in the snow-covered mountains of Bavaria. Camaraderie and intimacy pervade the Rosl brewery and household until a conniving aunt induces the female inheritor of the business to replace male workers with women. After the brief interlude of female domination, during which a brewer sabotages the beer and throws in a laxative for good measure, the combat is called a draw, or better, still, a victory by both sides.

Ritter imbued the film with eroticism for the glory of Hitler's master race. Containing overt depictions of lovemaking, the film declared: "Mind, we are no hypocrites." Candid in presenting a Biblical truth since Adam and Eve, it says "neither male nor female alone—only both together are good enough to do the job."

Ritter, who was good at creating the right atmosphere, directed a number of hardcore Nazi productions, but in *Weiberregiment* he didn't bare all his teeth, though the emphasis on Bavarian peasant customs and support of their attitudes towards the benefits of country life are in line with Nazi ideology.

Another heavy dose of Nazi ideology came from a performer familiar to American filmgoers, in the atmospheric *Traumulus* (*Little Dreamer*, 1936). The Nazi film world had desig-

Traumulus, starring Harald Paulson and Emil Jannings.

nated *Traumulus* its artistic film of the year, winner of its National Film Prize. That meant the film carried Nazi undertones. It supported the new, well-run, and soon-to-be–Jewish-free Third Reich via an attack on the old, bureaucratic, and Jewish-influenced old order. Goebbels, in his diaries, characterized it as a "brilliant caricature of prewar Germany." He screened the film for Hitler, who, Goebbels wrote, was "spellbound."

The star of the film was Hollywood's once-great Emil Jannings. He played the ingenuous Prof. "Gotthold Niemeyer," the Jewish head of the Royal High School in a small Prussian town at the close of the nineteenth century, in the era of Kaiser Wilhelm II, or *Kaiserzeit*. Niemeyer's acceptance of surface reality, order, and bureaucracy, and his confidence in what he calls the goodness of people get him in trouble. His values are depicted as old-fashioned if not dangerous. His unsophisticated and undisciplined students call their teacher "little dreamer." But they're all cut from the same cloth. Nearly all the school's students carry Jewish or Jewish-sounding surnames. The professor's favorite pupil is "Kurt von Zedlitz" (Hannes Stelzer). Other students go by the names "Franz von Mettke" (Hans Richter), "Emmerich Frommelt" (Rolf Müller), "Hans Klausing" (Hans Joachim Schaulfuss), "Erwin Putzke" (Alexander von Kraft-Hohenlohe), "Breitsprecher" (Walter Bienenstein), and "Pöhlmann" (Peer Baedecker). Zedlitz creates the crisis that causes Niemeyer's life to crash. Disregarding regulations, Zedlitz leaves the school grounds one evening. At a café, he meets a young actress, the Jewish-named "Lydia Link" (Hilde von Stolz). They spend a night together, but the word

> UFA FILMS, Inc.   -   RKO BUILDING   -   NEW YORK   -   CIrcle 6-2194
>
> INFORMATION MEMO
> ON
> T R A U M U L U S
> ************************
>
> Syndikat Film presents the Carl Froelich Film
> "TRAUMULUS", with Emil Jannings, a film based
> on the tragic comedy by Arno Holz and Oskar Jerschke.
>
> This film tells the story of a professor and the
> fate of his favorite student during the latter part
> of the last century. Through bad influence of an
> older student the boy Zedlitz spends evenings at a
> notorious nightclub where he becomes arrested
> during a raid. Professor Niemeyer is deeply shocked
> when he hears of it. With insulting words of horrifying
> anger he expels the boy from the school. During a
> sleepless night the Professor realizes that he has
> lived in a dream world. He begins to understand his
> paedagogical errors and decides to begin a new life
> when the boy Zedlitz who is believed to have run away,
> returns. However, the Professor no longer has an
> opportunity to express his thoughts to the young student,
> who committed suicide in youthful despair. But because of
> his death new hope for a new youth and better times grows
> within the "dreaming" professor.

Ufa's "Information memo" on *Traumulus*.

gets out. When Zedlitz denies it ever happened, Niemeyer backs him. When the facts are revealed, Niemeyer, disappointed and hurt, rejects Zedlitz as well as all his explanations. In despair before the final examinations, Zedlitz commits suicide. On top of that, the professor discovers that his young wife, the Polish-named Jadwiga (Hilde Weissner), whom he has neglected, has been unfaithful—with Fritz (Harald Paulsen), Niemeyer's son from his first marriage! Making matters even worse, Jadwiga has informed Niemeyer that if he loses his job, she will leave him. Shocked and disconsolate, the old professor asks himself, "Why was I so blind?" He then gets out of the way: he resigns his post.

The American Tobis release, which CFE distributed unsubtitled, was directed by Nazi supporter Carl Froelich, scripted by R.A. Stemmle and Erich Ebermayer, and scored by prolific Hansom Milde-Meissner (1899–1983). American reviewers failed to wake up to the film's shocking characterizations and meaning. "American cinema patrons," wrote the *New York Times* (September 19, 1936), were "likely to think that the German authorities were short on high-class films when they pinned their blue-ribbon" on it. The paper called it "pretty much of a letdown." In January 1940, distributor Frank Ferenz of Continental Films didn't see it that way. He brought *Traumulus* west for a screening at Los Angeles' Criterion Theatre.

Concurrently with these Nazi releases, and with the Berlin Olympics over, *Zot Hi Ha'aretz* (*This Is the Land*, 1935), which screened in New York, evoked a different, disciplined world: a Jewish land striving to be born. This message of hope came from the first Hebrew-language sound film. *Zot Hi Ha'aretz* is a 50-minute historical account of the half-century Jewish effort to create the state of Israel by literally making the desert bloom. Filmed in Palestine by Baruch Agadati and containing stirring songs by H. Kupnis and J. Goland, the production was financed by the Jewish National Fund.

Daring of another sort was on display when *La Kermesse Heroïque* (1935), known as *Carnival in Flanders*, opened at Manhattan's Filmarte Theatre, the city's fifth movie house dedicated to showing outstanding foreign films. *La Kermesse Heroïque* starred Françoise Rosay, Louis Jouvet, Jean Murat, André Alerme, and a score more performers in a satire of how, in 1610, the Belgian city of Boom "heroically" defends itself against Spanish invaders. Its menfolk, recalling the past cruelties of the Spanish invaders, panic and flee. They play dead. The burgomaster literally lies in state. Their women, however, led by the mayor's robust wife, take a different tack: they subdue the invaders by welcoming the regiment of foreign soldiers with true Flemish hospitality—and then cheerfully send them on their way. The village even wins a cancellation of a year's taxes.

La Kermesse Heroïque had been awarded the Grand Prix du Cinema Française and Feyder had captured the best director award at the 1936 Venice Film Festival. No mention was made of its German connection. Instead, "like all great comedies," wrote Frank S. Nugent of

The "French" film *La Kermesse Heroïque* (1935).

the *New York Times* (September 23, 1936), Feyder's film "speaks a universal language." In November 1936, *La Kermesse Heroïque* screened at the Belasco Theater in Washington, D.C. The *Washington Post* hailed it as a "Gallic comedy" and touted it as "one of the most useful exhibits of the Parisian sense of farcical humor that have come to these shores in years." The comedy was built on the struggle, in the seventeenth century, between Spain and the Netherlands. But 1936 fit the bill for this kind of film, especially since the enemy in the film is Spanish. Its "universal language" came with backing from the German production company Tobis. *La Kermesse Heroïque* was also produced in German, as *Die Klügen Frauen* (*The Heroic Village Fair*, 1935), directed by Feyder and Arthur Maria Rabenalt. The American Harry Stradling was the photographer.

Belgian-born Feyder was also the director of two other Tobis productions. One was *Pension Mimosas* (1935), a tale of overarching sacrifice, which had been released in New York in early 1936 by the Franco-American Film Corp. The title refers to a hotel on the French Riviera; the story depicts a headstrong young gambler and the godmother who fails to save him from his vices. The stars were Rosay, Arletty, and Alerme. Feyder's plot-filled tale of circus nomads, called *Les Gens du voyage/Fahrendes Volk* (*People Who Travel*, 1937–38), had been filmed in Nazi Germany. This production, which American critics reviewed in Berlin, did not screen in the States.

In France, Baron Philippe de Rothschild, of all people, had backed the making of the French-German production called *Lac aux Dames* (*Ladies Lake*, 1934), which was a Tobis production that screened at the Cinema de Paris in New York in early 1936. Beautiful views of the Tyrol, a little music, and a bit of acting, dancing, and swimming by newcomer Simone Simone, as well as by Illa Meery, Rosine Derean, and Jean-Pierre Aumont, made up Marc Allegret's romance. The film reportedly earned Baron Rothschild a profit.

Another well-known foreigner with ties to German films was another Belgian, the tenor Louis Graveure. He, too, had his name in lights and a short stretch of popularity in America. Johannes Riemann (1887–1959) directed Graveure in *Ich sehne mich nach Dir* (*I'm Longing for You*), an operetta from 1934 which CFE imported. Graveure played Fritz Brockmann, a boxing instructor for the Berlin police who sings on the side. Camilla Horn played Yvonne, his neglected wife. *Variety* (September 16, 1936) surmised, "Maybe the up-to-date German productions can't match the more venerable celluloid, or maybe the boys on this side of the Atlantic are trying to pare the rental costs ... the stuff that's dead and forgotten in Europe is now being refurbished for here," which "should satisfy patrons from the Vaterland."

Graveure starred in Georg Zoch's "refurbished" *Ein Walzer für Dich* (*A Waltz for You*) that CFE imported. The film, which was the last of eight films that Deutsch Fox had distributed in Germany in 1933–34, has Graveure playing Antonin Torelli, a prince turned singer in the mythical kingdom of Palamo, more attached to his art (via a concert tour in the U.S.) than his royal duty. In the end, however, he takes his rightful place as heir to the throne—ending the petticoat rule of the old-fashioned duchess von Palamo (Adele Sandrock). Camilla Horn, Theo Lingen, and Heinz Rühmann co-starred in the musical, which contains the catchy tune "A Waltz for You." "Dr. V. Badal" was identified as producer, the name apparently lending the production a certain air of legitimacy in this year of the Berlin Olympics.

Graveure also played opposite Jenny Jugo in an even older CFE refurbishment in 1936, Johannes Meyer's *Es gibt nur eine Liebe* (*There Is Only One Love*). Set in a Balkan retreat, the operetta, which co-starred Heinz Rühmann and Ralph A. Roberts, had been Graveure's first German film as well as the first film Deutsch Fox-Film A.G. had distributed in German—just as Hitler came to power.

International train travel and a grand hotel furnished the background for music, romance, and action in Erich Waschneck's *Die Ganze Welt dreht sich um Liebe/Abenteur im Sudexpress* (*The*

Whole World Revolves Around Love/Adventure on the Southern Express, 1934), which was shown at the Garden Theatre. Charlotte Susa played the blonde Lisa, a wealthy young widow on her way to the Italian Alps. Aboard the train she meets Hans (Karl Diehl), a German veteran working as a waiter. When her jewelry vanishes, Hans comes under suspicion. But the crook turns out to be someone else with whom Lisa had dined: the putative aristocrat "Tarnoff" (Ralph A. Roberts), a presumed Jew. The *New York Times* (November 27, 1936) noted that there were "numerous humorous incidents, a little pleasing music and plenty of fine bits of scenery before love and justice triumph in the last reel."

Waschneck's Europa production, called *Liebesleute* (*Lovely People*, 1935)—released at the Casino Theatre in fall 1936 as *A Pair of Lovers*—was inspired by the epic 1797 domestic poem *Hermann und Dorothea* by Germany's greatest man of letters, Johann Wolfgang von Goethe. Goethe's work was set amid the convulsions of the French Revolution, but Heinrich Oberländer revamped it to serve the new Germany. It became a back-to-the soil drama set in the 1890s, with sweeping views of lanes and wheatfields and quaint pastorals. Here, too, love and justice triumph.

Dorothea Rainer (Renate Müller), an orphan who grew up in drought-stricken Canada, returns to Germany and to its simple life in the farm country. Hermann von Goren (Gustav Frölich) is an aristocratic landowner who's fallen in love with her. But he's betrothed to Helga (Gina Falckenberg), the daughter of the banker von Barnstorff (Harry Liefdke), who holds the mortgage to his family's farm. Hermann's father, Freih von Goren (Heinrich Schroth), finds

Back to the soil, in *Liebesleute*, starring Gustav-Frölich.

Dorothea unworthy for two reasons. One, she's of a different social class; and two, Hermann's marriage to Helga would save the von Goren property. Hermann and Dorothea flee to the city where their tribulations only mount. They nearly starve to death. In the end, in Nazi fashion, Dorothea is willing to give up Hermann for the greater good of his family. This convinces the old baron that she is a worthy daughter-in-law. The drama co-starred Paul Klinger (1907–1971).

Gerhard Lamprecht's *Barcarole* (1935) was another adaptation of a classic piece of culture: Jewish composer Jacques Offenbach's opera *Tales of Hoffmann*. An Ufa production, it ran at the Garden Theatre, un-subtitled, in late October 1936. To the strains of the barcarole and the carnival atmosphere in Venice, Austrian producer Erich von Neusser and infamous Nazi scriptwriter Gerhard Menzel appended a hypocritical German version of honor. Set in a decadent Venice in 1911, where money is everything, the story takes place in a single night. The gambling, bon vivant Count Eugen Colloredo (Gustav Fröhlich) bets his life that he can "win"—that is, seduce—the fiery Giacinta (Lida Baarová), the wife of jealous Mexican Alfredo Zubaran (Willy Birgel). If he loses he must meet Zubaran in a duel. Eugen succeeds—it is love at first sight—but in good conscience he claims to have failed rather than humiliate the young woman and her jealous husband. When Eugen and Zubaran face each other with drawn pistols, Eugen shoots wide of his target. The hot-blooded Zubaran has no qualms about shooting straight and killing his opponent. The film's sets were called the most intriguing seen in months: the canal system with palaces and gondolas and a display of a Venetian carnival night built within Ufa's studios. The German-French connection was not overlooked. *Barcarolle* (1935), which A.C.E. co-produced and Roger le Bon co-directed, starred Edwige Feuillere and Pierre Richard-Willm.

The theme of honor and a tragic ending were also central to the operetta *La Paloma* (1934), directed by Karl Heinz Martin (1886–1948), produced by Robert Neppach and distributed by CFE. The production's exotic milieu, like that in *Barcarole*, lent the film an air of excitement. This production, wrote *Variety* (October 28, 1936), "contains more action, virile performances, and vivid scenes than any German feature to hit the American market in weeks." *La Paloma*, or *Song of Friendship*, starred Charles Kullman of the Metropolitan Opera as the young sailor, Fernando. He returns home after three years at sea to find his boyhood sweetheart, Manuela (Jesse Vihrog) engaged to his old friend, Alfredo (Fritz Kampers), who had assumed Fernando was dead. The film's ending supported the new thinking in the new Germany. When Alfredo dies saving Fernando's life, Fernando realizes he had misunderstood his old friend. Alfredo's sacrifice was so great that Fernando does *not* deserve Manuela. Instead, he packs his bags and leaves his homeland. The one bright spot, said the critics, was that the famous number "La Paloma" sounded as good in German as it did in Spanish. Other bright spots of a sort were the apparently innocent, lulling German films that slipped into the States in the fall of 1936.

One was Jewish director Richard Oswald's last German film, *Ein Lied geht um die Welt* (*A Song Goes Round the World*), produced by Terra in Hitler's first year in power. It starred Joseph Schmid—a diminutive Jewish artist with a big voice—as the opera singer longing to be loved for himself rather than for his abilities. Set in Venice, the romance featured the opera selections "Santa Lucia" and "O Paradiso."

Another such film was *Der Müde Theodor* (*Tired Theodor*, 1936), which was directed by the rising filmmaker Veit Harlan. Its complications involve money and possessions. "Using less slapstick than usual and talking comparatively straight German, instead of his favorite Bavarian dialect," wrote the *New York Times* (October 24, 1936), Weiss Ferdl (1883–1949) headed the cast as Theodor Hagemann. Ferdl, always a big draw in New York, plays a "retired" hotel proprietor who secretly takes a job to earn enough to buy back his wife's necklace, which he had pawned for 500 marks. Since his wife Rosa (Erika Glässner) holds the family the purse strings, Theodor has only one course open to him: he has to pawn a piece of her jewelry if he wants to help his niece, Helma René (Gretl Theimer), pay for singing lessons with the musician Wolfgang Kaiser (Rudolf Koch-Riehl). But because Theodor's job involves waiting tables at night, he naps during the day. He shrugs it off as sleeping sickness. When he's within 20 marks of his goal, his wife discovers the necklace is missing. She suspects their maid, Marie (Hilly Wildenhein), who asks her boyfriend Emil (Clemens Hasse) to find out what's going on. Meanwhile Theodor makes matters worse when he asks Wolfgang Kaiser to get involved in the cover-up.

Harlan's use of straight, modern German would become a hallmark of his films—and of his support for the anti-old-world Nazi regime. Unlike most of Harlan's later films, this one, which was shown at the Garden Theatre, ends on a happy note: Theodor is forgiven.

Numerous German films of the era had such complicated plots. Complication was the name of the game. Was that intentional, to train the audience to accept propaganda hidden in complicated themes? If an audience had to think about the convoluted nature of the plot, perhaps that same audience would be less aware of the poison injected into the mind-numbing details.

Carl Lamac directed Ondra in Ufa's *Der Junge Graf* (*The Young Count*, 1935), photographer Otto Heller's last film from Germany. In this one, which was shown in New York's Garden Theatre in late 1936, Ondra disguises herself as a young aristocrat: as the brown-haired Billy. The pose enables her to ingratiate herself with her stern, aristocratic, and wealthy grandfather, Count Priessnitz (Hans Junkermann). The old count and his son (Paul Heidemann) have been estranged ever since the younger man fell in love with a circus performer. But Billy, when revealed as a *blonde* (and illegitimately born) beauty, not only breaks down the enmity between father and grandfather, she gets the count to accept the ways of the world's younger people, including her love for the young teacher named Flint (Hans Söhnker).

Georg Jacoby's film *Ist mein Mann nicht fabelhaft?* (*Isn't My Husband Wonderful?*), another German comedy of complications, involves a newlywed (Lien Deyers) who informs her neighbors that her husband (Georg Alexander) is the owner of a Victrola factory, when in fact he merely works there. *Variety* (December 9, 1936) concluded that the film stood "alone among any dozen other films of similar origin." German filmmakers, it said, "seem to have a fetish for wasted talk and superfluous detail even in comedies," but not in this one. That's because it featured the excellent Belgian-born opera star Marcel Wittrisch. Having made a dozen German films since 1930, this was his last film. Because Terra produced the film in 1933, its pleasantness meshed with the Olympic spirit of 1936.

The same could have been said for *Glückspilze* (*Lucky Ones*, 1934), distributed by CFE in fall 1936. The director was Robert A. Stemmle (1903–1973) who scripted the well-received comedy *Glückskinder* (*Lucky Kids*, 1936). At the start of *Glückspilze*, a sensitive German youth is driven to desperation by the thought that his high school classmates believe him selfish and egotistical. Their having "cut him dead," he strives to get back into the good graces of the group.

In 1936, as the Nazis toned down their image, there was money still to be made on old Weimar productions such as Gaza von Bolváry's merry *Ein Lied, ein Kuss, ein Mädel* (*A Song, a Kiss, a Girl*), starring Marta Eggerth and Gustav Fröhlich. Written by Frederick Kohner, and with music by Robert Stolz, it had been produced in 1932. The same was true for Max Obal's romantic *Abenteuer im Engadine* (*Slalom*, 1932), a look at Europe's best skiers, skaters, and bobsledders in action at St. Moritz in Switzerland, which screened un-subtitled in ski-mad New York. Arnold Fanck wrote it; Hans Schneeberger, Guzzi Lantschner, and Richard Angst photographed it. "Landscape is our one solace," wrote the *New Yorker* (December 1936), referring to the film. "The nature-lovers may be right after all."

George Jacoby's operetta, *Der Bettelstudent* (*The Beggar Student*, 1936), featured Marika

Rökk, who represented one of Goebbels' favorite ideas of diversion: "dance must be lively and show beautiful women's bodies." It co-starred a newcomer to the Casino Theatre, Johannes Heesters, as the Polish student who is actually a pro–German duke. The subtext of the un-subtitled story is German control of Poland during the era of Augustus the Strong, the Saxon elector who was King of Poland from 1697 to 1706 and 1709 to 1733. In 1706, his cousin Charles XII of Sweden ousted him from the Polish throne. A big hit in New York and in Los Angeles (in 1939), the film is not to be confused with Viktor Janson's nineteenth-century Viennese operetta *Der Bettelstudent* (1930), co-starring Jewish actor Fritz Schulz, which had been shown in the U.S. in late 1933.

CFE also released the similarly themed *August der Starke* (*August the Strong*, 1936), Paul Wegener's Nazi-backed rendition of the Saxon monarch (played by opera singer Michael Bohnen) reclaiming the Polish throne from Karl XII (Günther Handack) in 1709—with the aid of the Russians. Throughout the story, which was shown un-subtitled, August is everywhere, in court scenes, at festivities—one scene borders on a bacchanal—and he does everything, including displaying feats of strength and manliness in the boudoir of two countesses (played by Marie Louise Claudius and Lil Dagover). His ego takes him to extremes in his pursuits, political or not, and it almost leaves him a broken man. But, unlike his cousin, he seeks the Polish crown by peaceful means. In the end, the throne is his—thanks to the help of Russia, which defeats Sweden.

The drama *Waldwinter* (*Winter in the Woods*, 1936), shown at the Garden Theatre in late 1936 advocated the Nazi ideal of relegating old-fashioned law to the ash heap and replacing it with instinctive justice. The film deals with the foresters, people, and customs in the mysterious, almost mythical, Silesian forests. The film was another example of the nature and back-to-the-soil ethos of the regime. Fritz Peter Buch (1894–1964) directed and Ufa produced this tale of the wife in name only who leaves her husband, Dr. Fritz Heidecke (Hans Zesch-Ballot), on the day of her marriage, having recognized his true nature just a little too late. She seeks refuge and finds it in an old castle in the Silesian Mountains. Austrian-born Hansi Knoteck (b. 1914) played the unhappy German woman Marianne von Soden, who meets the supportive young German writer Walter Peters (Viktor Staal). He too has run away, but from the city. During a snowstorm, the writer tracks her down and rescues her at the last moment. Her cowardly husband, promising a divorce, vanishes.

For Americans, however, the drama merely reinforced the notion that the thing dearest to the Teutonic heart around Christmas time is snow. The film offered it in abundance. There was plenty of it in Hanns Beck-Gaden's *Grenzfeuer* (*Frontier Fire*, 1934), set in the great outdoors of the Alps, where customs guards battle smugglers.

Smugglers and poachers were common outsiders in Nazi productions. They were small nuisances easily tamed. Few people objected to portrayals of poachers or smugglers, especially if they were non–Aryans. *Grenzfeuer* concerns the arrival at a lonely post of the energetic officer Behlke (Beck-Gaden) who soon has the other guards in tip-top, ready-for-duty, efficient shape to serve the fatherland. He captures a band of smugglers led by "Nothaas" (Fritz Rasp), the owner of an inn located near the patrol station. Behlke also grabs Nothaas' enticing girlfriend Afra (Elsa Krüger), the widow of a smuggler he had secretly killed years earlier. The *New York Times* (December 19, 1936) pointed out that the film contained "exciting ski runs" and "lots of shooting," and gave special credit to Rasp "who seems born for such parts."

The last weeks of 1936 might as well have been set aside for Carl Boese's films. Boese was one of the steadiest working directors in Nazi Germany. His Bavaria comedy *Ein Ganzer Kerl* (*A Real Guy*, 1935) is about the enterprising Karl Grosse (Hermann Speelmans), who convinces wealthy sausage maker August Bolle (Joe Stoeckel) to name him production manager of the faltering business. It seems the customers are complaining about the quality of the meat.

Grosse discovers the source of the problem: crooked dealings by the company's attorney, "Steinicke" (Walter Steinbeck). By putting the business back on its feet, Grosse wins the boss's daughter, Grete, played by the Dutch-born Lien Deyers (1909–1965).

American filmgoers then had a chance to catch Boese's comedy *Ein Falscher Füffziger* (*A Counterfeit Bill*, 1935), a Charles Unger release shown at the Casino Theatre, which had a taint of anti–Semitism. It starred Lucie Englisch as the honest German cashier who gets stung with a bad note, which, despite her best efforts, finds its way back into circulation. A presumed Jew named "Mrs. Strachwitz" (Hilde Hildebrandt) had passed the note. She and "Mr. Wallner" (Hubert von Meyerinck) are in the business of passing bad money. In the end, German law catches up with them.

Boese's name was also associated with a film he had made in the first year of Hitler's rule. That was *Drei blau Jungs—ein blondes Mädel,* which CFE distributed in America three years after it premiered in Berlin. But this apparently lighthearted musical tale of three young blue jackets from the "Hessen" on shore leave at Warnemunde and the fair Ilse that they're all chasing was no late Weimar production—even though it starred two Weimar era stars, Heinz Rühmann and the ubiquitous Fritz Kampers. The Nazis derisively referred to light films from the Weimar era as "Kintopp," especially the comedies from Jewish directors and performers. Filmgoers with a long memory might have imagined that Boese's film was along the lines of *Die Drei von der Tankstelle* (*Three from the Gas Station*, 1930), the classic Ufa operetta directed by Wilhelm Thiele and edited by Viktor Gertler. It was about three penniless men (Willy, Kurt, and Hans) in love with a rich and beautiful woman (Lilian Harvey) that featured Rühmann and Kamper as well as Kurt Gerron, Felix Bressart, and Oscar Karlweis. But, alas, Boese's film was true to its origins and Nazi ideology.

It featured concerted naval maneuvers, an impressive presentation of the workings of a modern German warship, and an ending that supports the philosophy that what matters is camaraderie among the new, young German sailors. The idea that duty comes first—no woman can tear that apart—fit into the worldview of the Nazis.

The title of Georg Jacoby's *Heisses Blut* (*Hot Blood*, 1936), starring Egyptian-born Marika Rökk (1913–2004) in her second feature, implied passion on the screen, but the film's star is a horse. In this one, Rökk played a member of a once-wealthy Magyar family, the von Körössys. There is hope, however, that the family might regain a racehorse called Satan, whose owners are "Bela von Peredy" (Max Gulsdorff), a presumed Jew, and his daughter Ilonka (Ursula Garbley). The former owners get the horse back, but only after Peredy sells it to them at a small fortune. The *New York Times* (September 26, 1936) noted only that this "simple film is embellished with many humorous incidents, considerable music, naturally including the 'Czardas,' and some fine rural scenes." Jacoby and Andre Hornez directed a French version called *Les Deux favoris* (1935–36), produced by Ufa-A.C.E.

Then something hot-blooded showed up on U.S. screens. It was the biggest shocker that Germany released in America in 1936. Late that year Goebbels had announced a new approach to film. Coverage of the arts, he said, "should confine itself to description. Such coverage should give the public a chance to draw its own conclusions." Thus, film criticism was no longer needed in Germany. But it had vanished in the Third Reich more than three years earlier. And as for criticism of Nazi films in America, there really wasn't that much for Goebbels to worry about. Few Americans had objected to Nazi films distributed in the States, especially in the Olympic year of 1936, and especially when German films contained engaging music and were mostly about entertainment, mistaken identity, or complications. Others films were acceptable because they apparently were of non–German origin, or were free of blatant politics, ideology, and overt racism. Those German films that were disturbing were either unsubtitled—a severe handicap if you didn't comprehend German—or ignored.

So was there much to fear when one of Nazi Germany's most satanic films came to the U.S.? This one was the real thing: the virulent, thundering, blood-and-soil *Friesennot* (*Frisians in Peril*, 1935). Subtitled *German Destiny on Russian Soil*, *Friesennot* was the Nazis' first openly anti–Soviet—and by implication, anti–Jewish—production. It screened at New York's Tobis Theatre in late October. The Olympic spirit was over. As the Olympic pause ended, attacks on Jews resumed in Germany. Hitler soon accused Jews of Bolshevism, unleashing violence. Distributed by American Tobis, *Friesennot* purports to catalogue the longstanding persecution of Germans who had migrated to Russia centuries ago, and argues for vengeance. The story begins when Frisian Germans first settle on the lower reaches of the Volga. They are loyal subjects of the czar, but their attitude is reflected in the slogan, "our blood weighs more than foreign blood." During the Russian Revolution, their descendants, led by Jurgen Wagner (Friedrich Kayssler) and the young blonde Mette (Jesse Vihrog), suffer at the hands of the Red Army. A "red" inspector, accompanied by a contingent of overbearing troops, arrives to impose heavy taxes and more severe penalties. His name is "Tschernoff" (V. Inkizhinoff). Violence breaks out between the blond-haired Frisians and local, Asiatic Russians. First the Russians rape a girl and massacre Germans. Then the Germans bring out their weapons and retaliate. It's a bloodbath. The Germans then pack up, burn down their homes, and start the long trek across the Russian steppes to safety in the homeland.

Friesennot was directed by "Peter Hagen." His real name was Willi Krause, a journalist on the Nazi Party paper *Der Angriff* who had joined the Propaganda Ministry in 1934. Walter Grosonstay (1906–1938) scored the diatribe. The film's cast included anti–Soviet émigrés such as V. Inkizhinof, the hero of V.I. Pudovkin's *Storm Over Asia* (1928) who played the Russian troop leader. American critics did note one thing: the plethora of blondes in the tale. Nazi politics later forced the film from German screens—and from showings at meetings of the German-America Bund—when Hitler signed the Nazi-Soviet pact, in August 1939. The Germans lifted the ban in June, 1941, when they attacked the Soviet Union, and re-released the film with a more powerful title: *Dorf im rotten Sturm—Village in the Red Storm*.

In late 1936, *Soldaten—Kameraden* (*Soldiers—Comrades*, 1936) directed by Toni Huppertz, hinted at a dark days ahead. Backgrounds came from the 48th regiment of Neustrelitz and the Ministry of War. Hosted by New York's 86th Street Garden Theatre, the film depicts life in the new German Army, rapidly filling up with bright, young men marching in goose-step and addressing officers as "Herr Unteroffizier." Its intent was to lend credence to the idea that this generation of German soldiers would be far superior to the one that had done battle for the kaiser. The superficial story is of two young men called up for military service. Willi Winkler (Ralph Arthur Roberts) is rich and spoiled; Gustav Menke (Franz Nicklisch) is hard-working, has character and quickly accepts the value of army discipline. Willi fails to adjust to the regimen until a fire breaks out in a nearby village. Called out to help, Willi rushes in to save to a child trapped in the flames while Gustav climbs up a ladder to get them out in time. The two young soldiers then bond—and receive medals for heroism. *Variety* (October 7, 1936) said *Soldaten—Kameraden* "is probably the brashest piece of propaganda for the Teutonic military machine as yet imported to the U.S. for public showing as entertainment.... The big boys in Berlin morally underwrote the thing.... If the patrons can close an eye to the propaganda aura ... it's got something on the ball for flag wavers."

Flags, patriotism, music, and the desirability of returning to the land all found a voice in a made-in–Germany motion picture of British life in the first decade of the eighteenth century. Karl Anton's *Letzte Rose* (*Last Rose*, 1935–36) consisted of so-called improvements on the original source: Friedrich von Flotow's 1847 opera, *Martha*. Titled *Letzte Rose* because of the frequent singing of the "Last Rose of Summer," the film screened at the Casino Theatre. The Nazis carried the idea of blood and soil across the English Channel, where Lady Harriet

Desperate Germans, in *Friesennot*.

Durham (Carla Spletter, of the Berlin State Opera Company), lady-in-waiting to Queen Anne (Hanna Ralph), has fallen in love with handsome young peasant Lyonel (Helge Rosenwange, of the Berlin State Opera), although she is promised to Lord Tristan (George Alexander). Queen Anne—inspired by her German-born lady-in-waiting—becomes a defender of Britain's farmers and peasants. The queen emancipates them, making them landowners, which puts Lyonel on the same economic and social footing as Lord Tristan. "On the whole," wrote the *New York Times* (October 10, 1936), the film "strikes one as being as accurate as most efforts of that kind and much more entertaining than the average."

In a simultaneous tale about aristocracy, Paul Otto had given a memorable performance as Emperor Franz Josef I in Willy Wolff's *Ein Liebesroman in Hause Habsburg* (*Romance in the House of Habsburg*), shown in New York's Tobis Theatre in late 1936. This film was actually *Das Geheimnis um Johann Orth* (*The Secret of Johann Orth*). CFE imported the blend of fiction and fact based on the book by Paul Merzbach, who fled Nazi Germany, which hinted at peaceful political change. The name change hid the film's Weimar origins. It had been made in 1932. The film was based on the fact that in the 1880s Archduke Johann Salvator had given up his Habsburg titles and birthright, changed his name, and married Viennese actress Milly Stübel (Gretl Theimer). In 1890, he and his wife vanished on an ocean voyage around South America. Legend had it that the couple disappeared so as to live in peace. There was also a bit of intrigue thrown into the tale: a plot is afoot to place Crown Prince Rudolph of Austria-Hungary on the throne of Bulgaria. Russia also has designs on the seat. Rudolf, however, suffers a tragic love affair and dies. It was a great loss for Austria and true German patriots.

Concurrently, *Campo di Maggio* (*The May Campaign*, 1934–35) screened at New York's Teatro Cine-Roma. This was a subtitled production directed by the playwright Giovacchino Forzano about a particular military hero. Released under the title *One Hundred Days of Napoleon*, it depicts the French leader in his last desperate days: from the instant he escapes from Elba and lands on French soil on March 1, 1815, until his abdication in Paris on June 22, four days after Waterloo. Napoleon hopes to continue on the road "which destiny has allotted me," he says at the start. "If I had been victorious at Moscow, my dream would have been fulfilled—a united Europe, an eternal peace after so many wars ... I must take up the fight again. If I succeed in uniting Europe, my name will live as long as the immortals." Napoleon has no use for the ineffectual and out-of-touch French Parliament, which he denounces. Rather it's the workers, artisans, soldiers and the "woman I took to be a petitioner and who then offered me her savings—they are the country," he tells the double-crossing politician Fouché, "and not your five hundred speechifiers in Parliament." But after losing his brilliantly planned battle at Waterloo in Belgium because of the incompetence of one of his generals, Napoleon is forced to turn to the French Parliament for salvation. He asks it to give him "extraordinary powers of absolute rule for a fixed period for the purpose of saving the nation." The hastily elected Chamber of Deputies, however, fails to do the right thing: to name him France's constitutional monarch. Abdicating, Napoleon concludes, "I have allowed a whole generation to be killed, and I will not shirk my responsibility for this. I saw it as a sacred mission to break up these ludicrous little states of Europe ... and to bring all nations together in one great community. Every nation as an active member of one great, unified country, no more war in Europe—that was my dream and that is my political testament."

Starring Corrado Racca as Napoleon and, in one of her last European films, Austrian-Jewish actress Rose Stradner as Marie Louise, the drama—purportedly Mussolini's idea—had American critics on their feet. "From every standpoint," wrote the *New York Times* (September 13, 1936), the film was "impressive; so much so that at times even hardened cinema patrons and despisers of militarism and all its works are likely to be carried away with the enthusiasm of Napoleon's followers and to feel a certain sympathy in his hour of distress with the man who perhaps thought of himself as destined to bring centuries of peace to Europe on the point of the sword." In Pennsylvania, censors had one objection to this tale of antiparliamentarianism. They eliminated scenes of Napoleon's incompetent general being killed and blood running down his forehead.

Campo di Maggio was the Italian rendition of Franz Wenzler's German-language *Hundert Tage* (*Hundred Days*, 1935), starring Werner Krauss, which was never released in the U.S. The Italian version sufficed in the U.S. But numerous Nazi militaristic and antidemocratic features would be released in the U.S. before Pearl Harbor closed the doors.

1937

From Traitors to Patriots

If most American filmgoers had doubts about Nazi ideology and Hitler's rationale for ruling Germany, those doubts ought to have been dispelled by a film from the *Vaterland* that opened in the U.S. in early 1937: *Verräter* (*The Traitor*, 1936). Of course, pro–German Americans were heartened by this film, which Ufa produced and released after the close of the Olympics. *Verräter* was a warning to, and a threat against, foreign spies, as well as a message for Germans. Attempts to outsmart German Intelligence Services would, said the film, lead to disaster. *Verräter* had premiered at the Reich's Party Day in Nuremburg, during which *New York Times* critic Claire Trask, on November 22, 1936, had noted, "The Bavarian panegyrics shook Berlin into eager expectancy and the equally overwhelming public success of the picture here proves them justified." The film was "super-educational," defining for Germans the meaning of "traitor" and, by implication, "patriot."

Nazi Party member Karl Ritter was its director. The SS referred to Ritter as "our dear friend, a political soldier, a political artist." Hans Weidemann, a Nazi party propagandist, served as the film's artistic director and Harold M. Kirchstein supplied the music. *Der Deutsche Film* hailed *Verräter* as one of Ritter's "cinematic tanks"; Ritter himself called it one of his heroic films. Goebbels rendered the credit to Ritter's cohort Weidemann, calling the production "brilliantly made."

The action takes place just before the First World War. Enemy agents, having infiltrated Germany, seek information about the nation's tanks, planes, and infrastructure (water works, especially). The documents they're after include important blueprints of Germany's newest weapons. These "foreign" spies, however, are hard to spot: they're blond and have a sporty build—that is, they're German in appearance. However, they betray a slight British accent and go by the names "Morris" (Willy Birgel), "Schultz" (Herbert Böhm), and "Geyer" (Payl Dahlke). Although the film doesn't say so, there's a strong chance they're all Jewish. One of them, carrying forged papers, gets a job at an airplane plant. Another manages to acquire classified information by bribing a debt-ridden designer named "Fritz Brockau" (Rudolf Furnau) who belittles the spy scare; while a third agent ingratiates himself with the German veteran Hans Klemm (Heinz Welzel), now a bank teller. Brockau, a presumed Jew, has sold out but Klemm informs German authorities about what is happening. The *Sicherheitsdienst*—Germany's counter-espionage service—goes into action. One spy dies in a crash as the service closes in. A second spy is quickly captured and executed on the spot. The lead spy escapes after being caught, is tracked by dogs, and drowns in a bog—an ending Nazi filmmakers liked to reserve for the lowest creatures. His sinking in the mire signals his depravity. Brockau, who had betrayed his country, commits suicide. The German veteran is given an award. The film's message that treachery against Germany was the worst form of criminal activity came from the last spy to die. When asked to name names, he says, "I do not know where the traitors are. Catch your own pigs yourself."

Verräter won its own rewards: a "special recommendation" at the 1936 Venice Film Festival and a National Film Prize from Goebbels. In New York, where *Verräter* was shown, the *New York Times* (January 23, 1937) noted that with the help of the German army, navy, air force, firemen, and police dogs, Ufa had "turned out one of the best-made spy pictures to reach the screen ... in a long time.... The audience is treated to a remarkable display of up-to-date military machinery and activities" that, *Variety* (January 27, 1937) noted, "can tear down forests. [The] bombing planes ... can turn barrel-rolls on a dime." For the American release, the Germans added titles "just in case the arty route," said *Variety*, "can be tackled." The trade daily noted that there would probably be a "squawk from anti–Nazi elements" if this were attempted. "It's still propaganda in a very major way, although the Teutons have tried their best to call their rose by another name." *Variety* liked Ritter's direction, which, it said, "has kept a needle sharp balance between sheer Nazi hokum and entertainment sugar-coating the [Nazi] doctrine," implying that Ritter might have been making a subversive film within Nazi Germany. What went unmentioned was that the enemy in the film was England and the agents were Jews in the British Secret Service.

In *Mein Kampf*, Hitler had roared about the reasons for the collapse of the Second Reich: "In comparison with traitors who betrayed the nation's trust every other kind of twister may be looked upon as an honorable man." After Hitler revealed his plans for war to the German army in 1937, Ritter directed the pro-war films *Patrioten* (1937), *Unternehmen Michael* (1937) and *Pour le Mérite* (*For Merit*, 1938). The three films were shown in the U.S. before the outbreak of the Second World War.

Ritter minced no words in *Filmwelt* (May 1938): "Pure film entertainment is only one aspect of our world view. The modern film is about tanks, aircraft, and troops at the front. It must bear the characteristics of contemporary Germany; it must be as heroic as our fate at this time demands. At the same time, it must show humor and a positive approach to life in accordance with our newfound beliefs." Nazi beliefs had included creating the powerful *Sicherheitsdeinst* (SD), the security service of the SS. Its head was Reinhard Heydrich. During the Second World War, the SD and the Gestapo formed the essence of the mobile killing squads, the *Einsatzgruppen*.

The Sicherheitsdeinst reappeared in the Goebbels-financed film *Falschmünzer* (*Counterfeiters*, 1940), by Hermann Pfeiffer (1902–1966). It was produced by Terra with music by Michael Jary, about international forgers operating out of Switzerland. They're led by Gaston de Frossard (Rudolf Furnau) and "Karl Bergmann," alias Harry Gernreich (Hermann Speelmans), who's Jewish. Their accomplices are also foreigners: Juliette Balouet (Kirsten Heiberg) and Nico (Hans Steibner). The Sicherheitsdeinst puts a stop to their operations before they can weaken Germany's financial system. This film was not released in America but viewable by American critics in Germany in 1940. Germany banned this film after the war.

Hardcore Nazism in film, especially anti–Semitism, was getting harder to miss even if critics abroad ignored a film like *Falschmünzer*. That was evident, for anyone paying attention, in several German films that were reviewed by American sources abroad before the start of the war. One of these films was the anti–Semitic *Togger* (1937), Jürgen von Alten's newspaper film that features Nazi slogans, SA parades, and a dyed-in-the-wool Nazi journalist. The music was by Harold M. Kirchstein. *Togger*, which Goebbels called "quite effective," has a true Nazi plot at its core. It seems that an international organization called the Reuler Company is secretly buying German businesses, including Berlin's daily *Der Neue Tag* (*The New Day*), edited by Togger (Paul Hartmann). Togger is one of the few people trying to expose this group.

His efforts backfire, resulting in a loss of readers, a drop in advertising revenue, and a strike threat from his paper's typesetters. Togger is forced to resign. Matters within Germany remain in a state of near anarchy until a critical date—January 30, 1933—and the ensuing cleanup by the Nazis. The real goals of the Reuler Company are revealed thanks to some undercover work by Hanna Breitenbach (Renate Müller), the daughter of the paper's owner; by journalist Peter Geis (Mathias Wieman); and by a Nazi party journalist (Just Scheu). The internationalists operating within Germany suffer a very mild fate: they are expelled from Germany. Their members include Reuler's leader, Dublanc (Fritz Rasp), and his rogue agents Mariano (Fritz Odemar) and "Rakovicz" (Ernst Waldow). The hero, Togger, is reinstated as the editor of the daily.

Goebbels' ministry financed the making of the film, which was not shown in the U.S. *New York Times* critic Claire Trask, in Berlin, noted (on March 14, 1937) that like Ufa's *Verräter*, "which ... is congenial in Nazi doctrinaire persuasions," *Togger* "proves in part a tense bit of entertainment." *Togger* was banned in Germany after the war.

Co-star Wieman was a member of one of Goebbels' arts committees. The Tobis production was Renate Müller's last film. The popular Müller was, in real life, the daughter of a newspaper editor. One of Müller's first films had been Constantin J. David's *Das Leibeslied* (*Dear Song*, 1930–31), which had been shown under the title *Herzblut* (*Heart's Blood*) in late 1932 in New York. It was an adaptation by Itala Film (Berlin) of a story by Pirandello about a young woman who cares for *her* mother's illegitimate child! That film was Turkish-born David's last from Germany.

Togger's director, Jürgen von Alten (1903–1994), was one of Goebbels' handpicked directors. He began his career by paying for his own acting lessons, and landed theatrical roles in Hanover and Berlin in the 1920s. He made his film debut in 1931, in the nationalistic production *Yorck*. Two more films Alten directed for Goebbels stressed Nazi ideology through the lens of the First World War. *Das Gewehr Über* (*Shoulder Arms*), which was released in Berlin a few months after the start of World War II, is an anti-democratic tale that starts in Australia. A German settler, having fled Weimar, believes his son is becoming decadent living in a democracy. When the Nazis come to power in Germany, he sends his son and his friend to the fatherland for military service. Neither young man is happy about this, but in the end they grasp the value of discipline, dedication, and the dogma of the new Germany. Produced by Germania Film and photographed by Phil Jutzi (1896–1946), it co-starred the rising performer Wolfgang Staudte (1906–1984).

Alten also directed *Sechs Tage Heimaturlaug* (*Six-Day Furlough*), another of Goebbels' war education films, which were paeans to soldiers, military equipment and technology, and the superiority of German forces. Produced by Cine Allianz and starring Gustav Fröhlich, Maria Andergast, and Käthe Haack, *Sechs Tage Heimaturlaug* centers on a World War I warrant officer on leave who receives and answers a letter addressed to an unknown soldier. A long correspondence ensues, and the soldier falls in love with the writer, a young woman. Then they meet and spend six days together in Berlin. They become engaged just before he has to return to do his duty at the front. This film was released in Berlin in October, 1941, when Nazi films were nearly all but gone from U.S. screens. A release in the States might have been a rough sell. Then again it might not have. "National Socialism is laid on so thick here," admitted Goebbels in his diaries, "that it becomes positively embarrassing."

Karl Ritter's *Patrioten* (*Patriots*, 1937), which screened at the Garden Theatre, laid it on thick and should have shattered the spell of complacency that had lingered regarding German productions released in the U.S. after 1936. But Americans weren't keeping tabs on which films or how many German films were being shown in America; when the Nazis had produced them; or how often the same messages were repeated.

Ritter's *Patrioten* redefines the term "patriot." The film's protagonist looks like an SS officer: he's black-uniformed, slim, nervous, and cynical. The film's guiding hand was that of Goebbels, who set what he called its "nationalistically slanted" tone and selected the lead actors: Mathias Weimann and Lida Baarová (Goebbels' mistress). Ufa, which was Germany's leading studio, produced it. Walter Rohrig designed the production, which is set in the war years of 1914–18. Peter Thomann (Wieman), a German pilot on a reconnaissance mission (another of Goebbels' ideas), is shot down 100 miles inside enemy lines. Trying to return to Germany, he is discovered by Therese (Baarovà), who nurses him back to health. Although they fall in love, he says to her, "There is something more important than love between man and woman—heroism." Trying to help German prisoners of war escape, he himself is taken prisoner. Brought up on charges of espionage because he's dressed as a civilian, he convinces a French military court that he's an honorable German officer. Therese vouches for him. The court shows leniency, jailing both of them for the remainder of the war. Therese is not depicted as a traitor to France. Rather, she has become a convert to his point of view: "Heroism" above all. Of course, if the tables had been turned, the fate of foreign officers and traitorous Germans in Nazi hands is easy to imagine.

Ritter's film presented the "rarely seen German side of the war," said *Variety* (September 23, 1937), "while the *New York Times* (September 18, 1937) merely made note of a "newer crop" of German screen players in the film: Karin Hardt (from *Abel mit der Mundharmonika, Schön ist es verliebt zu sein*), Dorit Kreysler (from *Frischer wind aus Kanada, Herr Kobin geht auf Abenteuer*), and Hilde Körber, who sings "O my Baby" and "Paris, Du bist die schönste Stadt in der Welt." The "singing and dancing in the picture," continued *Variety*, "do not retard any of the action and fit in nicely during narration. German music and dancing girls add to total of nearly everything else that can be put into a film without it having the appearance of a goulash which so many of the importations seem to be." Czechoslovakia was the one nation that banned the importation of *Patrioten*. It was also the only European nation that refused to "Nazify" its film industry so as to increase its motion picture revenues within Germany.

An unexpected American release this year was James Whale's *The Road Back* (1937), by Universal Studios. It's based on Erich Maria Remarque's novel of the same name, which the Nazis had termed "defeatist." The Nazis had nothing to fear from this cinematic follow-up to *All Quiet on the Western Front*, which is set in postwar Germany. Thanks to Hollywood's cowardice, there's no mention of Hitler in the film. In early 1941, Remarque's novel *Flotsam* fared a bit better. It became the source for the mildly anti–Nazi feature *So Ends Our Night*, a chronicle of a group of people one step ahead of Hitler's juggernaut.

Then came another powerful Nazi production that received a welcome reception in the U.S.: Veit Harlan's *Der Herrscher* (*The Master*). It was released subtitled by American Tobis. The film's protagonist, a steel-master played by Emil Jannings, exemplifies heroism and service to the state. He was as far from a traitor as could be. He could be considered the symbolic father of a state. His state is his steelworks, whose noises and rhythms create the impression of titanic force and violence. The action takes place in the industrial Ruhr region of Germany, and the shots of the steelworks were actually taken at the Hermann Göring Werke. The tale starts with a burial scene that Graham Greene called a "pleasantly savage opening, a funeral frieze of dripping umbrellas and heartless faces" as a minister drones on. The rich widower Klausen (Jannings), alone after the death of his wife, makes a decision that brings him into conflict with his children. He wishes to remarry. The woman he wants is his understanding young secretary, Inken Peters (Marianne Hoppe). His grown-up children, Wolfgang (Paul Wagner) and Egert (Hannes Seelzer), and their spouses know they stand to lose a huge inheritance. They decide to take him to court to have him declared incompetent or insane. When Klausen hears of that, he lashes out at those parasites. He slashes his wife's picture, denounces

Universal Studios, 1930s.

his family, and alters his will. The tale climaxes when the iron-willed industrialist, whom his workers call "Führer," disinherits his children and bequeaths his munitions factory and property to Germany! He defends spending millions on research. "It is duty to sacrifice everything for the good of the state ... even if it should mean bankruptcy," he tells his co-directors at a board meeting. He rejects the advice of those (enemies of Nazism) who like to say, "You can't turn the clock back."

Goebbels raved about *Der Herrscher* when it was shown in Berlin, in early 1937. He especially liked the line, "The genius of a born leader needs no teachers." Goebbels wrote that the film was the first successful National Socialist production, "a wonderful achievement." Full of Nazi terminology—allegiance, community of people, self-sufficiency—the film closes with the leader saying, "Work is everything ... man is nothing." *Der Herrscher* was awarded Nazi Germany's National Film Prize. Jannings took the best actor award at the 1937 Venice Film Festival and his film made the rounds in Europe—in Spain, France, Italy, Sweden, Switzerland, and the Netherlands. Thea von Harbou had scripted the tale from Gerhart Hauptmann's play *Vor Sonnenaufgang* (*Before Sunset*). After the war, Germany banned the film.

Gerhart Hauptmann was the dean of German literature and a former idol of the radical left but he, like millions of non–Nazis, voted "yes" in Hitler's first plebiscite. Hauptmann called his meeting with Hitler in 1933 the greatest moment of his life. It consisted of a handshake with the dictator. Harlan and Jannings, however, had longer, stronger ties with the Third

Universal's *The Road Back.*

Inside a U.S. theatre, late 1930s.

Reich. Harlan's ties to Goebbels, for instance, included serving on one of his arts committees. The first film Harlan had directed under the Nazis starred Henny Porten, in *Krach im Hinterhaus* (*Trouble Backstairs*, 1935), a tale of people in a Berlin tenement mingled with an all's-right-with-the-world ending in a (Nazi) courtroom. This film reached the States after *Der Herrscher*, having been one of the most successful of the year in Germany. The plot revolves around the fact that coal is disappearing from one of the coal cellars. Suspicion falls on the poor-but-honest Witwe Bock (Porten) living with her daughter (Else Elster). Witwe sets a trap to find the cold-hearted thief. After an explosion in the oven of the building's caretaker—because of booby-trapped coal—the culprit is revealed.

In *Mein Kampf,* Hitler *had* commented on the living conditions of the poor in a big city (Vienna):

> In order not to despair completely of the people among whom I then lived I had to set on one side the outward appearances of their lives and on the other the reasons why they had developed in that way. Then I could hear everything without discouragement; for those who emerged from all this misfortune and misery, from this filth and outward degradation, were not human beings as such but rather lamentable results of lamentable laws. In my own life similar hardships prevented me from giving way to a pitying sentimentality at the sight of these degraded products which had finally resulted from the pressure of circumstances. No, the sentimental attitude would be the wrong one to adopt.

Porten's silent-film colleague Hanni Weisse (1892–1967), who had opted out of sound films,

Der Herrscher, with Emil Jannings.

had a small part in *Krach im Hinterhaus*. After making a film for Nunzio Malasomma in Italy in 1942, Weisse retired. Also in the film was the veteran actor Eduard von Winterstein (1871–1961). His reaction to the Nazis' takeover was to make propaganda films, including *Bismarck* (1940) and *Stukas* (1941). After the war, Winterstein worked mostly in the theatre. Porten (1890–1960) had been one-half of the production company Henny-Porten-Froelich, which lasted from 1924 until the coming of sound in 1929. Porten, a blonde, had been one of Weimar's most popular actresses. She had starred opposite Gustav Gründgens in Froelich's historical nonsense *Luise, Königin von Preussen* (*Luise, Queen of Prussia*, 1931), shown in the U.S. in November 1932. As it turned out, the film contained a message from pre–Hitler Germany to the outside world.

Set in 1806—a favorite Nazi era—this is the story of Prussia's best-loved queen, as played by Henny Porten, one of Germany's best-loved actresses. Queen Luise's destiny—and, by extension, that of her homeland—is sealed by the weaklings and prevaricators around her, especially the vacillating, ineffectual King Friedrich Wilhelm III (Gründgens). The Weimar-era film, wrote *Variety* (October 1932), is "well calculated to make German audiences envision a fate for the Treaty of Versailles similar to what happened to the Peace of Tilset," which Napoleon forced upon a defeated Prussia in 1807. At the end of the story, Queen Luise predicts that when Prussia (that is, Germany) triumphs over France, it will be just as merciless. Hitler was said to be a Porten fan. Porten, however, made few films in Hitler's Germany.

When the Nazis came to power, the other half of the duo, Carl Froelich, joined the party. Adjusting to changing circumstances, Froelich remained in the front ranks of the German film industry as opportunities expanded. Froelich's first film as director in the new regime had been *Der Choral von Leuthen* (*The Hymn of Leuthen*, 1933). Its music came from composer Marc Roland (1894–1975) and it was distributed by the Jewish-owned Deutsche Universal. After the war Froelich was arrested. He was "denazified" in 1948, but, surprisingly, his film days were over.

Tobis was pressured in 1936 to join the parade of representing Germany as a forgiving neighbor. The studio produced *Die Nacht mit dem Kaiser* (*The Night with the Emperor*), which depicts a kindly Napoleon and—for one time only—a Jewish heroine. Directed by Erich Engel, the film screened at the 86th Street Garden Theatre in 1937. The story takes place in 1808, when Napoleon (Paul Henckels) convenes a peace conference at Erfurt with Czar Alexander of Russia (Otto Wögerer) and several German princes. The young German artist Heinz Heckmann (Friedrich Benfer) has the effrontery to caricature the French leader. The French arrest him. His girlfriend "Lisa Grossinger" (Jenny Jugo), a presumed Jew who is a dancer, succeeds in getting a part at a state performance in honor of the emperor. Noticing her, Napoleon invites her to his palace. During the evening, Lisa asks Napoleon to support German nationalism while deflecting his amorous intentions. This impresses the great general, and he pardons her lover.

The film avoids "showing the Emperor of the French in an unpleasant light," wrote the *New York Times* (August 14, 1937), perhaps because the Berlin Olympics had offered an arena in which to appear magnanimous. In 1937, productions like this one still served as useful propaganda. "History has not been twisted," concluded the *New York Times*.

Engel had directed a second historical production in 1936: Tobis's *Mädchenjahre einer Königin* (*Girlhood of a Queen*), which has been called a classy film about Queen Victoria (Jenny Jugo) and her historical connection to Germany. The film ranges from Victoria's days as the not very studious young girl to the young woman who becomes the assured ruler of the British Empire. After the death of her father, Victoria is about to take the throne. Marriage candidates emerge from the various European aristocratic houses. Victoria, however, rebels against any such union, and secretly heads abroad. Bad weather forces a stay in Dover where fate intercedes. She meets a young man who says he's a German student. In reality, he's Prince Albert von Saxonia Coburg Sachsen-Coburg-Gotha (Friedrich Benfer), who was sent against his will by relatives to Britain on a matter of great importance: to wed Victoria. Keeping their secrets to themselves, the young aristocrats fall in love. Victoria then discovers Albert's identity, however, and returns home. When she meets Albert again at court she's at first embarrassed, but their love prevails. They wed and Britain's tie to Germany is sealed! This film, which was reviewed by American critics in Berlin, failed to reach American theatres. *Mädchenjahre einer Königin* was really for British sympathizers of Hitler.

Engel's comedy, *Ein Hochzeitstraum* (*A Wedding Dream*, 1936), a Tobis-Europa release, also fit the spirit of 1936. It was a tale about Poles and Russians in friendly competition. Officers and royalty (real and fake) come to a well-liked tavern on the Polish-Russian border where its owner (Ida Wuest) is on the lookout for the right man for her unwed daughter (Inge List). *Ein Hochzeitstraum* never made it to the States. But Martin Fric's Czech-German co-production *Das Gässchen zum Paradies* (*Paradise Road*, 1936), did screen in the U.S. 1937, and it also melded with the spirit of the Olympics. Supporting the right kind of orphans and protecting innocent, harmless dogs were favorite Nazi subjects. The film was a vehicle for Austrian comedian Hans Moser, who played Tobias Haslinger, a dogcatcher in a poor section of town called Paradise Road. Alone and unhappy, he sees his life change for the better when he befriends young, abandoned Peter (Peter Bosse) and his stray dog. Haslinger gives up his much-despised work when he refuses to hand over the dog to authorities.

In 1933, Martin Fric, whose name was Martin Fritsch in Germany, had directed the German-language, Czech-produced military farce *Der Adjutant seiner Hoheit* (*His Majesty's Adjutant*), starring the Jewish actor Vlasta Burian. The surprising element of the film, wrote the *New York Times* (October 22, 1934), was that German actresses Gretl Theimer and Anny Markart had been relegated to secondary roles. The Third Reich relegated *Der Adjutant seiner Hoheit* to the dustbin because of Burian's starring role. Martin Fric had also directed *Revizor* (*Inspector*, 1933), starring Burian, which was the Czech version of Gustaf Gründgens' comedy *Eine Stadt steht Kopf* (1932). When *Revizor* was shown at New York's Squire Theatre under the title *The Inspector General*, the *New York Times* (November 25, 1937) pointed out that Burian "used to be seen in German comedies," but not that he was Jewish. Czech director Fric, to his credit, made one of the few European anti–Nazi films of the era, *Svet Patrí Nám* (*The World Is Ours*, 1937), based on the 1936 play *Heads or Tails* by Jewish actor George Voskovec and his long-time colleague Jan Werich.

The film is about Nazi efforts to stir up trouble in the Sudetenland. Voskovec and Werich star in their film adaptation. Brown Shirts are turned into gray hats, the Nazis are depicted as gangsters, and the Sudetenland has become an "un–European" country. The changes from play to film fooled no one, but satisfied Czech censors in 1937. In November 1938, the Nazis seized most prints of the film, but one copy was released in the States before the start of World War II. The American trade paper *Boxoffice* (April 26, 1939) said *Svet Patrí Nám* was "handled in the Chaplinesque tradition and makes for droll entertainment." Voskovec and Werich found refuge in America, where they made the anti-nazi *Crisis* (1939).

In the winter of 1936–37, Ufa's militaristic drama *Standschütze Bruggler* (*Home Guardsman Bruggler*) had an easy sell in the States. Having been released in Berlin the previous November, it arrived in the U.S. to acclaim. "There are crowds again at the 86th Street Garden Theatre," wrote the *New York Sun* (March 13, 1937). The film's attraction was the kind of patriotism and German resistance to outside forces about which Hitler had expressed admiration in *Mein Kampf*. Its smattering of English subtitles didn't hurt its appeal. "Yorkville eats it up," wrote the *New York American*.

Directed by Werner Klingler (1903–1972) and photographed in the Tyrolean countryside by Sepp Allgeier, *Standschütze Bruggler* focuses on the defense by the last reserves of Austro-

Tyrolean peasants against Italian forces in spring 1915. Most Austrians are fighting on other fronts when Italy changes sides in the Great War and declares war on Austria. The defensive situation is critical, so Austrian males barely 16 are allowed to sign up in the Standschützen, or Austrian home guard. The mountain range dividing Austria and Italy becomes their fighting front. Italian soldiers capture Toni Bruggler (Ludwig Kerscher), a one-time theological student who had disappointed his mother (Franziska Kinz) by joining the fight. Learning of planned attacks against his people, Bruggler arrives too late to warn the inhabitants of an Austrian village. He joins his comrades elsewhere, and just as the Italians are about to overwhelm them, German machine guns are heard from the flank—relief has arrived thanks to Bruggler's earlier warnings. The tale ends with a parade and the awarding of a medal to the young Austrian hero and patriot. His mother is proud of his warrior status. At the film's Berlin premiere, *Variety* (December 2, 1936) noted a certain truth in the tale, whose musical score added to its realism. Its "undercurrent of militarism is understandable when it is remembered that the pic is a product of present-day Germany." "Zealously pro-German," wrote the *Brooklyn Daily Eagle* (March 1937), the film was more than mere propaganda. Its anti–Italian slant suggested another truth about future German-Italian relations: the next time Germany goes to war, Italy had better remain its steadfast ally.

In the 1930s, Italian filmmakers had no qualms about allying themselves with the Third Reich. The list included directors who had worked in Weimar Germany: Carmine Gallone, Gennaro Righelli, Mario Bonnard, Nunzio Malasomma, Guido Brignone, and Luciano Albertini. Gallone (1885–1973) was the most prolific of them all. In the late 1920s Gallone had directed the German silents *Das land ohne Frauen* and *S.O.S. Schiff in Not*. In Weimar, Gallone had directed Polish-Jewish tenor Jan Kiepura and Brigitte Helm in *Die Singende Stadt* (*City of Song*, 1930), which was shown at the Hindenburg Theatre in the New York area in May 1932. The British co-produced, English-language version was called *Farewell to Love* (1930). This tale of an English woman (Betty Stockfeld) who falls for a guide (Kiepura) in Naples was one of the most expensive films of its time. Gallone's British-backed *Going Gay* (1933), ironically, had brought out the Nazis in Munich when it was shown there under the title *The Girl from Vienna* in late 1934. The tale's love scene between Jack (British actor Arthur Riscoe) and Grete (Magda Schneider) had the Brown Shirts jumping out of their seats shouting, "Shame! Scandal! He's a Jew and she's a German! Loyal Germans must leave!," according to the *New York Times* (December 16, 1934). Managers of the Luitpold Cinema canceled further showings. The film was released in the U.S. in early 1936 as *Kiss Me Goodbye*.

In 1934 Gallone had directed the British-German *Mein Herz ruft nacht Dir* (*My Heart Calls You*), starring the newly married couple Jan Kiepura and Martha Eggerth (b. 1912), which screened at New York's Roxy Theatre in April 1935. It's an operetta in which the adventures of a barnstorming grand opera troupe leads to romance between Mario (Kiepura) and Carla (Eggerth), and stowing away on the troupe's ship heading for Monte Carlo. When the Monte Carlo opera house director Arvelle (Hugh Wakefield) cancels their contract, the troupe gets even with him. It stages an outdoor performance of *Tosca*—and lures away the indoor patrons. One of Gallone's biggest hits was the musical *Opernring* (1936), which American Tobis distributed in America under the title *Thank You, Madame*. It had received a "special recommendation" at the 1936 Venice Film Festival. The Italian version, with English titles, screened at the Esquire Theatre in New York because an English-language version had been panned in Paris two years earlier. Better to release a subtitled film than nothing at all. Besides, the music of Rossini, Paganini, and Bellini was glorious, even if adapted by Nazi sympathizer Willy Schmidt-Gentner. Polish tenor Jan Kiepura played a singing taxi driver who becomes the unwitting protégé of a Vienna tenor's estranged wife. "Here is a film which may not be exceptional," wrote the *N.Y. World-Telegram* (April 27, 1937), "but which at least is diverting."

....a remarkably well-made World War picture...N.Y.Times.

....a pip of a picture....N.Y.American.

....Pictorial Splendor...N.Y.Herald Tribune.

....well photographed....N.Y.Sun.

Standschütze Bruggler

with

Friedrich Ulmer
Lola Chlud   Franziska Kinz
Ludwig Kerscher   Gustl Stark-Gstettenbauer

N.Y.American

Action and Acting Stand Out In German War-Theme Film

SOLE DISTRIBUTORS

UFA FILMS
729 SEVENTH AVE.   NEW YORK

A few months earlier, Gallone's *Casta Diva* (*Divine Spark*, 1935), which Alleanza Cinematografica Italiana distributed, had a run at New York's Broadway Cine-Roma. This Italian-German musical about the woman who inspired the nineteenth-century Sicilian composer Vincenzo Bellini (Philippe Holmes) starred the Hungarian-German actress Eggerth. The *Catholic News* (November 16, 1936) called the film "class A approved for adult audiences" and the National Legion of Decency (March 12, 1936) concurred, finding it "unobjectionable for adults." Gallone's *Wenn die Musik nicht wär* (*If It Were Not for Music*, 1935), an un-subtitled CFE release of a Tobis production, was just as acceptable. When it screened in early 1937, it had a more captivating title: *Liszt's Rhapsody*. Its diversions center on the way that honest and unworldly musician Florian Mayr (Paul Hörbiger) is able to attract the attention of the great Franz Liszt (Luis Rainer) and also find a charming, non-musical wife. All that stands in the way of his becoming *Hofkappellmeister* in Munich and marrying Thekla (Karin Hardt), the girl of his dreams, is a foreign musical charlatan named "Kusmitsch von Prschitschkin" (Hubert von Meyerinck), who also wants Thekla—but only for her money. One more Gallone film screened in the U.S. at about the same time: American Tobis's *Stimme des Blutes* (*Blood Bond*, 1937). This was a tale of rivalry between the Arlen brothers, Thomas and Robert (Attila Hörbiger and Albert Matterstock), trapeze performers in a circus in love with the same woman, daredevil performer Maria Morell (Anneliese Uhlig). Not to worry. German blood and camaraderie are thicker than love in the Nazi production, and things work out well.

More beautiful music and a different kind of story are at the heart of Georg Jacoby's *G'schichten aus dem Wienerwald* (*Tales from the Vienna Woods*, 1934), which screened at New York's 79th Street Theater. It afforded filmgoers peeks through streets, wine cellars, and concert halls, with music (under the direction of Willy Schmid–Gentner), dancing, and general high spirits, twists, and turns. Complications involve two women in postwar Vienna: a wealthy American, Mary Limford (Truus van Alten), who wants to live independently of her inherited money; and a local journalist, Millie Sheffers (Magda Schneider), who wants to live well. They switch identities. Meanwhile, Count Rudi Waldheim (Wolf Albach-Retty), working as a mechanic, inherits a heavily mortgaged castle. The holder of the deed, Alois Schlopf (Leo Slezak), in order to get his money, tries to engineer a match between the count and the (supposed) heiress. But there's one catch: wily Russian ex-prince "Kiriloff" (Georg Alexander), a presumed Jew who learns the real heiress's secret and tries to inveigle his way into marriage. The Vienna Philharmonic performs the music of Johann Strauss II at a benefit concert sponsored by the supposed rich American while the real American (Truus van Aalten, 1910–99) tries to keep her identity under wraps. The story of mistaken identity was as diverting as possible. "This is one of the best musicals that have come out of Austria," commented the trade journal *Hollywood Reporter* (April 16, 1937). "The picture is a strong card for the foreign houses and would be an acceptable novelty on many American double bills."

In Jacoby's *Ein Mädel wirbelt durch die Welt* (*A Girl Whirls By the World*, 1933) German womanhood eventually embraces traditional roles. The tale starts off by complaining that popular music is supplanting classical fare, and it depicts the heroine, named Lenox, sneaking off overnight with two composers, Paul Martens (Harald Paulsen) and Peter Barke (Hugo Schrader). Then it gets to the main point: Which one will she marry? CFE distributed the comedy un-subtitled in the U.S. in early 1937 under the more titillating title *Ein Stelldichein im Schwartzwald* (*Rendezvous in the Black Forest*). The film featured Bavarian beauty Magda Schneider (1909–1996), who starred in more than 20 films under the Nazis.

Austrian-born George Jacoby's *Der Letzte Walzer* (*The Last Waltz*, 1934), which Germania released in the U.S. three years after its European showing, was based on Oscar Strauss's

Opposite: Ufa promotional for *Standschütze Bruggler*.

operetta set in nineteenth-century St. Petersburg. It told viewers of those wicked Russians who threaten the true love of a heartfelt couple (Camilla Horn and Ivan Petrovich). Jacoby's Ufa-produced *Spiel auf der Tenne* (*Play on the Tenne*, 1937), ostensibly about the theatre, screened un-subtitled at the Garden Theatre later in 1937 as *Drama on the Threshing Floor*. A Bavarian village innkeeper hopes to establish a rural theater supported by a native cast as a way to attract the tourist trade, since business at his inn is falling. Two enthusiastic players emerge: Lena Feldhofer (Heli Finkenzeller) and Martin Jöchler (Richard Häussler). Local opposition comes in the form of the Chastity League, which looks upon theatre and acting as the work of the devil. This theatrical mix of German/Austrian music, dancing, and racy lines apparently worked—if filmgoers ignored the ideological ending, when the rich man's daughter Lena goes against her parents' advice and marries the poor but honest woodsman Martin. Jacoby's *Zwei im Sonnenschein* (*Two in the Sunshine*), an idyllic, sunny little romp set in Bavaria about young landscape painters named Annie (Charlotte Ander) and Olly (Wera Liessem) was a CFE release in 1937. In Jacoby's *Besuch am Abend* (*An Evening Visit*), another film released in the States three years after its German premiere, Liane Haid turns the head and heart of a finicky old bachelor (Paul Hörbiger).

When Austria emerged as a viable producer of films in the early 1930s, Liane Haid (1895–2000) was its first star. Trained as a dancer, she often appeared alongside Willi Forst, Heinz Rühmann, Theo Lingen (1903–1978), and Georg Alexander. Having rejected offers from Hollywood, Haid instead made a film in Britain about Mozart called *Whom the Gods Love* (1936), directed by Basil Dean and designed by Ernst Stern, which was shown in New York in October 1940. She fled Nazi Germany for Switzerland in 1942, because, she said, "Everything was bombed and because all the good directors had left." She married and retired from film.

Willi Forst, Jacoby's Austrian colleague, was one of those good directors who didn't leave. He had made a splash with his first German-Austrian directorial effort, the musical *Maskerade* (1934). He was immediately compared to Ernst Lubitsch. American critics reacted favorably when the prewar tale, a bit reminiscent of Max Ophul's *Liebelei* (*Light o' love*, 1932–1933), opened at the 55th Street Playhouse in New York under the title *Masquerade in Vienna*. Ophuls's atmospheric tragedy *Liebelei*, with music from Brahms, Mozart, and Beethoven, was credited with having started the "Vienna vogue" in America, although it didn't screen in America until 1936. (Cashing in on the screen success in Europe of Ophuls's film and Forst's *Maskerade*, MGM produced its own rendition of Forst's musical, called *Escapade* in 1935, starring Luise Rainer and William Powell.)

Maskerade was named best film at the 1935 Venice Film Festival. The title change in America deflected attention from *Maskerade*'s German connection. It was a Tobis production. *Variety* (January 27, 1937) had noted *Maskerade*'s "purely Aryan angle"—the Nazi regime's attitude towards women—but that the star Paula Wessely, "is worth watching for America." Her film "is a cinch for the few U.S. houses showing German talkers." A George Kraska release, the subtitled *Masquerade in Vienna* was acclaimed for being a frothy, sotto voce romantic comedy about an ingénue (Wessely) drawn into a scandal (about a nude painting) that originates at a prewar masked ball. In Vienna in 1905, after a carnival, the famous painter Heideneck (Adolf Wohlbrück) draws a picture of a jaded girlfriend wearing very little, blurring only her face. The image makes it into the newspapers the next day. The artist, embarrassed, identifies her as "Leopoldine Dur." In fact, a plain, wholesome, but poor woman named Leopoldine Dur (Wessely) does surface—and Heideneck falls in love with her. "The whole film is a delightful example of Viennese comedy," wrote Eileen Creelman in the *New York Sun* (January 26, 1937). William Boehnel, of the *New York World-Telegram* (January 26, 1937), considered the film "far superior to the usual run of films, foreign and domestic."

One of the biggest hits of 1936 in Germany had been Forst's *Allotria* (*Hokum*). In the musical, Java plantation owner Philipp (Adolf Wohlbrück) and race-car driver David (Heinz Rühmann) are best friends bound by a singular promise: never to court the same woman. But this seems to be the case when Philipp—neglecting his girlfriend Aimée (Hilde Hildebrand)—falls in love with lovely Viola (Renate Müller) during one of his journeys. Failing to declare his true feelings, Philipp returns home only to mistake Viola for David's fiancée. In fact, David wants to marry spunky Gaby (Jenny Jugo). The confusion of hearts continues to the end of the little drama, when the two completely mixed up honeymooning couples play blind man's bluff and sing "Der schönste Tonfilmschluss ist doch der Verlobungskuss ... Allotria ("The Most Beautiful Conclusion in Film Is Nevertheless the Engagement Kiss—Hokum"). But Germany's number one critic was not pleased. Goebbels attacked Forst's "exaggerated effects," finding his film "not entirely satisfying." *Variety* (June 1936), at its Berlin premiere, killed its chances in America by labeling it "too sophisticated for the wide open spaces" even though Forst "belongs in either Hollywood or London."

Instead, Films Corp. released Forst's Austrian-German musical *Vienna Burgtheater* (1936). The cherished illusion of prewar Vienna as a place of laughter and song, of charming naughtiness to a tune in three-quarter time, is betrayed in Forst's chest-heaving Nazi production. The protagonist is a noted Viennese actor (Werner Krauss), a favorite of his day (1898), who happens to find himself in love in the afternoon of his life with a beautiful young woman (Hortense Raky). But he is unaware that she has a lover (Willy Eichberger). Eventually the old actor's unselfish action, getting out of the younger generation's way, saves their relationship. His personal sacrifice ends his dreams of happiness. The critics missed the Nazis' real message, which was that the old German generation *had* to make way for the new. The *New York Herald Tribune* (September 28, 1937) praised the film's "true human motivation, while the film "will probably depress local Teutons," wrote the *New Yorker* (November 6, 1937). It became a "melancholy tale of heartbreak and depressing frustration," wrote the *New York Times*' Bosley Crowther (September 27, 1937). "The finger should be pointed at Krauss," said Crowther, "who opened the picture with a scene from 'Faust,' and maintained the Faustian mood from that point on." This was Werner Krauss's first Nazi-era film to be shown in America. (That was also the case for Austrian-born O.W. Fischer, 1915–2004.) Goebbels called it a "good film."

In fact, Krauss the actor had made a Faustian bargain with the Nazi regime. The next film to be shown in the U.S. with Krauss's name on it was the anti–Semitic *Robert Koch* (1939). Then Krauss starred in Veit Harlan's *Jud Süss* (1940). Willi Forst, to his credit, refused to have anything to do with the production. After Austria's union with Germany, Forst said, he made "pro–Austrian films." That is, he deliberately depicted hokum: an Austria and its capital that had vanished after presumably coming under the thumb of Hitler, rather than a nation that collaborated with the Third Reich. Forst's attitude explains the popularity of his musical *Operette* (1940). The music was by the Vienna Philharmonic. A German-Austrian production co-directed by Karl Hartl and starring Trude Marlen and Siegfried Breuer, *Operette* was slated to open in America in late 1941. Pearl Harbor ended its chances. Instead, *Operette* was one of the first Nazi-era films shown in the U.S. after the war, in June 1949.

Willi Forst also directed the silent-screen star Pola Negri in first of her six Nazi films. The Polish-born Hollywood screen performer Pola Negri had gone to Europe in the mid–1930s to resurrect her career, which had begun in the silent era in Germany. In Nazi Germany she declared she wasn't, as was rumored, Jewish. "The whole world knows that I am a Catholic," she said. "Der Führer must be a brilliant man. I haven't met him, but I would like to." Forst's *Mazurka* (1935) is a murder-trial melodrama of a mother's sacrifice for a daughter that, while reminiscent of *Madame X*, was keenly in line with the Nazi ideology of a German mother's giving her all for her offspring. In the tale, Vera Kowalska (Negri) is carrying a dark secret.

Scenes from *Operette*, with Hörbiger, Hardt, and Forst.

Actress Pola Negri, 1920s.

She is on trial for having killed a man-about-town named "Grigorij Michailow" (Albrecht Schoenhals). A pianist and composer, Michailow had raped her 18 years earlier, in Warsaw. She shot him dead before he could seduce her daughter—who was also *his* daughter. Costarring 17-year-old Ingeborg Theek and released by Tobis, the drama was the last German production by the team of Kiev-born Gregor Rabinowitsch and Bratislava-born Arnold Pressburger.

Paul Wegener was the next German to direct Negri. Their collaboration resulted in *Moskau-Shanghai* (1936). Max W. Kimmich was the scriptwriter and was the assistant director. In this melodrama, which begins in 1917, the widowed Russian noblewoman Olga Petrowna (Negri) meets the handsome young Russian officer Alexander Repin (Wolfgang Keppler) at a grand ball. Following the dance, she drops off her 7-year-old with the maid and leaves in the company of Sergei Smirnow (Gustav

Diessl), a confidant who has secretly loved her for years. They are halfway home when Bolsheviks attack their train. The two are separated. Olga loses track of her daughter as well as Alexander. She witnesses Bolshevik atrocities. The lives of all hang in the balance as the revolution takes it toll. Time jumps ahead to 1930. Now Olga works as a nightclub singer in Shanghai. There she runs into Sergei. Again he proposes, and again she rejects him since she still pines for the dashing Alexander. Later, at an Easter gala for expatriate Russians, Olga discovers that Alexander has also become a singer. She is surprised and then shocked to learn that he has become engaged her to her long-lost daughter! She then gives herself to Sergei.

Negri's only Nazi film to make it to the States was *Madame Bovary* (1937), a Deutsche Film Export directed by Gerhard Lamprecht. As the ambitions and pleasure-loving wife of a naïve country doctor in nineteenth-century France, Negri "still has plenty of charm and acting ability and she seems to be staging a 'come-back' in Europe ever since her 'Aryanization' was established to the satisfaction of Adolf Hitler in January, 1935," observed *Variety* (June 2, 1937). *Film Daily* (November 1, 1937) noted that the subtitled adaptation of Flaubert's novel, which was scripted by Erich Ebermayer (1900–1970), "has been toned down to a more sympathetic portrayal, but the story loses none of its essence." But the *New Yorker* (October 30, 1937) found the film "very German throughout ... [with] that somber, somewhat relentless gloom the German studios endorse these days." Ferdinand Marian played the dyed-in-the-wool lover. Giuseppe Becce scored *Madame Bovary*.

In *Tango Notturno* (1937) Negri played a character named Mado Doucet. Its director was Fritz Kirchhoff. Nunzio Malasomma (1894–1974) directed Negri in *Die Fromme Lüge* (*The Secret Lie*, 1938) and *Die Nacht der Entscheidung* (*The Night of Decision*, 1938). In both, which Philip Lothar Mayring scripted, Negri is the self-sacrificing married woman. Mayring was the director of the odious *Blutsbrüderschaft* (1941) that contains the music of Michael Jary. Pola Negri left Hitler's Germany for the United States before the start of the war. She had bet on the wrong horse. In Hollywood, Nazi sympathizer Walt Disney had a part for her in *Hi Diddle Diddle* (1943). But there were other filmmakers in Germany hoping to launch their careers.

The tragedy *Madame Bovary* was supplanted at the 86th Street Casino Theatre by the more lighthearted *Donner, Blitz und Sonnenschein* (*Thunder, Lightning and Sunshine*, 1936), starring Karl Valentin (1882–1948), Munich's famous comedian, and directed by Erich Engels (not to be confused with Erich Engel). Here, Andreas (Volker von Collande, 1913–90), who is the son of the disreputable landowner named Greizinger (Hans Liebelt), seeks the hand of the sprightly young blonde Evi (Ilse Petri), daughter of the upright village tailor Huckebein (Valentin). The problem is that the fathers hate each other. The young German with the heart of gold gets the girl, while her boyfriend's father gets his comeuppance. Pennsylvania censors excised the scenes in a nightclub where a man lifts a woman's dress.

That film was supplanted at New York's Casino Theatre by a film from a new, up-and-coming Third Reich director, the former actor Wolfgang Liebeneiner (1905–1987), who would direct 12 films for the regime. Goebbels called him "ambitious, industrious, and fanatical," and awarded him the honorary titles "state actor" and "professor." Liebeneiner's first directorial effort for the Nazis, Terra's *Versprich mir nichts!* (*Promise Me Nothing*, 1937) was scripted by Thea von Harbou and scored by Georg Häntzschel (1907–1992). It became an acclaimed "Volksfilm," promoting the idea that "art is art," that is, it's of little consequence who holds the brush—except if they're Jewish hands. It had a ready audience in New York's East Side. The story is less about Martin Pratt (Viktor de Kowa), a Bohemian artist who prefers starvation to selling what he calls "unworthy works" than it is about his wife Monika (Luise Ullrich), who thinks his work has merit, and, to prove it, sells his work under *her* name. "Her" pictures find a ready market. When Monika receives an offer to paint a large fresco, however, the deception is in danger of collapse. At that point, her husband paints the work while *she* washes the brushes! Their collaboration also saves their marriage, which is another theme of the film. Although she has been tempted to leave her eccentric mate for the art dealer named "Felder" (Heinrich George), in the end she remains faithful to their union. By coming clean about Martin/Monika Pratt's artwork, she is a voice for the Nazis, who cynically stress that honesty is the best policy. (Liebeneiner remade the film in 1950 as *Wenn eine Frau liebt*).

The summer of 1937 brought forth more musical productions, not necessarily German-language, to New York and Chicago. One was the rare British-German *Forever Yours* (1935–36), directed by Stanley Irving and starring the Italian opera singer Benjamin Gigli. Jewish-born producer-director Alexander Korda had financed the film in Britain, but then backed out when it came time to release it. He turned it over to Grand National rather than his regular distributor, United Artists. Korda didn't want his name associated with the film in advertising or billing. The story is of a sensitive shipboard romance, disappointed love, overcoming unrequited love, and finding solace in learning to care again for others. Gigli plays the great singer Enzo Curti who has been left with a young son after the death of his wife. At one of his concerts he notices Helen (Joan Gardner) who is in tears listening to his number, "Non ti scordar de me" ("Say You Will Not Forget Me"). He is attracted to her but his poor English holds him back. But great change often comes from happenstance. Helen must decide if she's gotten over a recent affair. Eventually the two lovers unite when Gigli brings along a huge English-language dictionary. "It's really a photoplay you'll remember with pleasure," said the *Chicago Tribune* (October 10, 1937), "for its appealing acting, its lovely music, its effective settings, some fine photography, and a certain quaint cunning on the part of the director, that keeps your interest animate and your sympathy alert."

The story is also known as *Forget Me Not*, which Augusto Genina directed in Germany as *Vergiss mein nicht* (1935), co-starring Erik Ode (1910–1983) and produced by Itala's Alberto Giacalone. Giacalone served as associate producer on the British-German production and Hans Schneeberger handled the camera work.

In the turn-of-the-century tale *Die Göttliche Jette* (*The Divine Jetta*, 1937), directed by Erich Waschneck and with music by Georg Häntzschel, a Berlin songwriter and showman wins the heart of music-hall star Jette (Grete Weiser)—"the toast of Berlin"—from a rural and undeserving aristocrat. The high point of the film, which ran in New York in summer 1937, occurs when the plain-speaking Jette tells the stiff-necked society people in the audience just how little she thinks of them! Here was yet another example of the Nazis attacking the morality of an earlier era.

In 1937, Ufa's *Das Hofkonzert* (*The Command Concert*), another production from the gentle year of the Berlin Olympics which was directed by Detlef Sierck, opened at the Garden Theatre. It too looks back. Set in an imaginary nineteenth-century German principality, it centers on an illegitimately born singer, Christine Holm (Marta Eggerth), who finds out that her country's benevolent ruler is actually her father. That fact enables her to marry within the appropriate social class. Her man is the young officer Walter von Arnegg (Johannes Heesters). At that point, when all's well with the world, the annual request concert can take place. In the cast was longtime actor Rudolf Klein-Rogge (1885–1955) who was then married to Thea von Harbou. The film "might have been a good musical in the ante-Hitler days because then it would (probably) have had delicacy and a light touch," wrote *Variety* (March 31, 1937). "Ufa evidently thought this one might have a chance to get out of the regular limited channels for German films in the U.S., so it decorated it with English titles (too many of them)." When Sierck's film screened in America, Sierck, a favorite of Goebbels, was no longer in Germany. Here too A.C.E. had made a French version, called *Le Chanson du souvenir*, co-directed by Serge de Poligny, but no matter: it was the German version that was seen in America.

Music near the Bay of Naples was the thing in Johannes Riemann's *Ave Maria*, a Berlin-

Ufa Berlin advises Ufa N.Y. to add more titles to *Hofkonzert*.

Rome (Ufa-Itala) production by Alberto Giacalone that had been shown in Germany to coincide with the Berlin Olympics. Here too Gigli, who had broken his contract with the Metropolitan Opera Company in 1932 for more money in Europe, was the feature performer. Singing from *La Traviata* and other classics, Gigli played Italian tenor Tino Dossi opposite Hungarian-German actress Käthe von Nagy, portraying the Montmartre cabaret gold-digger Claudette. While he pines for his first lover, Claudette falls in love with him, becoming his second Maria. To set things right, Claudette has get out of the clutches of her money-grubbing manager, "Michel" (Harald Paulsen), who blackmailed her because she let Tino believe that she's a plain country girl.

Ave Maria garnered a "special recommendation" at the 1936 Venice Film Festival thanks in no small measure to Alois Melichar's score, the Berlin State Opera Company, the Cathedral Boys Choir, and the rotund Benjamino Gigli. "The plot is unobjectionable, wrote the *New York Sun* (October 2, 1937). The Garden Theatre "should be proud" of the film, wrote the *New York Herald Tribune* (October 4, 1937). "It's the finest film seen in the theatre in many a long week." *Chicago Tribune* critic Mae Tinée told her readers, "I think you'll like it."

Carl Boese's *Die Herren vom Maxim* (*The Gentleman From Maxim's*) also contained plenty of music, romance, and a former Metropolitan Opera performer (and the father of Walter Slezak), the Austro-Hungarian "whale-weight comic" Leo Slezak. Predating Hitler, this Weimar-era film proved unpopular with U.S. viewers when CFE released it in 1937.

Austrian Jew Walter Reisch, who did not like the Nazis or their supporters, had fled Vienna for Hollywood in spite of the fact that his popular postwar Viennese musical *Episode* (1935) featured the newest star in the German film firmament: Austrian-born Paula Wessely. She had been named best actor for her performance in Reisch's film at the 1935 Venice Film Festival. Tobis distributed the film in the U.S. in mid–1937. When Reisch's film premiered in Germany, its credits had been read aloud while music played in the background. As Reisch's name was about to be announced, the music suddenly swelled, drowning it out. Wessely played Valerie Gärtner, a young woman who speculates and then loses her mother's money because her bank fails. Her salvation and protection comes from an honorable source: the married, middle-aged benefactor, Torresani (Otto Tressler). Valerie winds up falling in love with his sons' tutor Kinz (Karl Ludwig Diehl), an ex-officer. It is the stately, motherly Frau Torressani (Erika von Wagner), however, who is the key to clearing up complications involving forged checks made out to Valerie by "Torresani." The film then concludes with a waltz.

Jewish-born director Max Neufeld was blacklisted in Austria even though his Austrian/Dutch *Singende Jugend* (*An Orphan Boy of Vienna*) was a film from the year of the Olympics. In his tale, an orphan becomes a member of the celebrated Vienna Boys Choir and shoulders the blame for a theft. With excerpts from Handel, Brahms, Mozart, Schubert, and Strauss, "this is a distinguished importation from Austria which deserves to find a wide audience among discerning moviegoers," wrote T.J. Fitzmorris in the publication *America* (September 11, 1937). "The picture should prove of special interest to Catholics, to whom its atmosphere and its direct and reverent treatment of things sacred will be a refreshing contrast to Hollywood's occasional religiosity. It is recommended as a splendid entertainment for all." "Only the most cynical old meanies will be able to resist it," predicted *Cue* (September 18, 1937). Forced to flee to Catholic Italy, Neufeld worked under the name Massimiliano Neufeld, directing such works as the fantasy-comedy *Ballo al Castello* (*Ball at the Castle*, 1939), starring Alida Valli. Valli later starred opposite Benjamino Gigli and Paul Hörbiger in *I Pagliaci* (1942–43), which was an Itala-Tobis production that Leopold Hainish directed.

The illusionary, carefree and coach-and-four transportation era of a placid, long-ago Austria formed the backdrop in Carl Hoffmann's *Das Einmaleins der Liebe* (*Lessons in Love*, 1935), which CFE imported in 1937. It starred Luise Ullrich, who specialized in Cinderella and Ugly Duckling roles, as a simple country woman who changes character three times in order to test the affections of the local store manager, Weinberl (Paul Hörbiger). He, too, changes character (twice) before they wed. Nearly everyone else, including Theo Lingen, gets a whack at changing their identities before they embrace the joys of country living. A more serious note was at the heart of a film based on the ill-luck in the life of Austrian composer Franz Schubert and his romance with three sisters: Hederl, Heiderl, and Hannerl. It became the basis for a fanciful account of the composer's love life: E.W. Emo's *Drei Mäderl im Schubert* (*Three Girls Around Schubert*, 1936). It starred Paul Hörbiger, Gretl Theimer (of the early 1930s hit, *Two Hearts in Waltz Time*), Maria Andergast, and Else Elster. This film also reflected the spirit of the new Germany in 1936, and was "turned out with the care for detail for which Teuton period pictures are noted," noted the *New York Times* (June 5, 1937) when it screened at the 86th St. Casino Theatre.

Taken from the stage success *Lilac Time*, the film reaches a high point in the scene of Schubert's famous concert, which he conducts a few months before his death, in 1828. This reference to one famous Austrian could not have been lost on another well-known Austrian—Hitler—who wasn't married, nor on German viewers, especially women.

Another adaptation of a classic was *Die Ganze Welt dreht sich um Liebe* (*The World's in Love*, 1935), Victor Tourjansky's first film for the new Germany, which the Viennese Song Corp. released. An adaptation of Franz Lehar's operetta, *Clo-Clo*, *Die Ganze Welt dreht sich um Liebe*, called *Liebesmelodie* (*Dear Melody*) in Austria, starred Marta Eggerth as Ilona Ratkay, the popular and attractive Vienna musical comedy queen who has trouble with her press agent, "W.G. Miller" (Alfred Neugebauer), because he persists in planting off-color stories about her, which naturally affects her marriage prospects. Two well-to-do Germans, Adalbert von Waldenau (Leo Slezak), and his son, Peter (Rolf Wanka), fall for her, but publicity causes Adalbert to imagine that she is his illegitimate daughter from a long-ago affair. He tries to break off his son's affair with her. All ends well when the papers retract the story—and Peter gets the girl. When the film screened at New York's Filmarte Theatre, *Cue* (May 29, 1937) said it "wins over the most hardened spectator" and *Film Daily* (June 11, 1937) didn't hesitate to say that the musical "ranks well up among the top-notch screenplays to come out of foreign studios in recent months." Its screenwriter—uncredited—was the German Jew Felix Joachimson, who had been blacklisted in Germany in 1934.

Luis Trenker's *Der Kaiser von Kalifornien* (*The Emperor of California*, 1936), which American Tobis released in the States in 1937, helped break this nearly continuous spell of German musicals in America. Its intent was to show Germans what happens to any German when he strays from the fatherland. It's also an anti–American production. The protagonist is John Augustus Sutter (Trenker), who comes to America in 1834, fleeing debtors and leaving his family behind. In California, Sutter reclaims vast stretches of desert, eventually making himself the richest man in the territory. He becomes known as the "Emperor of California." His wife (Viktoria von Ballasko) and children join him. But then Sutter's luck runs out when gold is discovered on his land in 1848 and riff-raff sweep in. His fields are laid waste, his herds vanish, his possessions are despoiled, his sons are murdered, and his wife dies of grief. Countless graves testify to the crazed stampede for gold. But Sutter refuses to give up. He brings a lawsuit against the invaders, demanding justice. Although he wins in court in the nation's capital, mobs in California runs wild, burning down the new township of San Francisco. Sutter is eventually destroyed by his enemies, who are named Harper, Brown and Smith. His only true friend is named "Ermattinger."

In August 1936, Trenker's film had been named Best Foreign Film at the Venice Film Festival. The Nazis named the film winner of a National Film Prize. Although Trenker actually shot

Jewish scriptwriter Felix Jacobson (b. Joachimson).

his film in the West, its songs are more reminiscent of German marches than of cowboy country. The *New York Times* (May 8, 1937) noted that the "few historical slips and anachronisms are of slight importance." They include Lincoln in 1847 admitting California into the Union; the city of San Francisco apparently located in the Sacramento Valley; and Death Valley and the Grand Canyon lying just east of San Francisco. Trenker's film, which also screened in Washington, D.C., thanks to a copy from the Museum of Modern Art, ends with Sutter dying on the steps of the Capitol. As a study in American violence and as an unsubtle Nazi justification for retribution against non–Aryans, the film upset few in the nation's capital.

Karl Hartl's *Ritt in die Freiheit* (*Ride into Freedom*, 1936), which was released in the U.S. in 1937, is also set in the early nineteenth century. As an anti–Russian production, it was the kind of the film that Goebbels liked because of its "conviction." He noted, "I am pleased to have supported it." Produced by Ufa and photographed by Günther Rittau, it is the story of Polish resistance against Russian rule in Warsaw in 1830, wherein a Germanic sense of duty again triumphs over the pull of love. Willy Birgel (1891–1973) plays the Polish captain in the army of Alexander I of Russia who is torn between patriotism to his (lost) country and his love for the sister (Ursula Grabley) of the Russian governor of Grodno. When Polish compatriots rise up in revolt, he hesitates—and then forsakes his lover in order to lead the Polish cavalry in the charge to liberate Warsaw. He dies fighting, and becomes a glorious hero.

As was the case with Luis Trenker's film, German director Werner Hochbaum's *Der Ewige Maske* (*The Eternal Mask*, 1935) garnered attention when Arthur Mayer and Joe Burstyn distributed it un-subtitled in the U.S. An Austrian-Swiss production by Tobis-Europa, *Der Ewige Maske* seems to be a serious depiction of a doctor's reaction to a botched treatment. An idealistic doctor named Dumartin (Mathias Wieman), working in a Basel clinic, believes he's developed a serum against meningitis. Although hospital rules forbid experimentation on the sick, the doctor inoculates a patient suffering from meningitis. When he dies, the doctor concludes that the serum was the cause of death. Excoriated by the dead man's widow (Olga Tschechowa), the doctor attempts to take his own life. He's unsuccessful at this too, suffering instead a breakdown. The film then becomes a record of his descent into schizophrenia. Half of his personality comes across as his old self, half is described as being "in search of himself." The hospital staff works feverishly to save the doctor. Success is achieved when his boss, Professor Tscherko (Peter Petersen), concludes that the patient died of something else. The young doctor recovers his health—and is allowed to continue his experiments.

To insure verisimilitude, the American distributors enlisted the help of one Dr. Maurice Kornberg to vouch for the film's "medical phraseology." American critics concentrated on the doctor's dream-world meanderings, which had them on their feet—and which helped enhance Hochbaum's reputation in Nazi Germany, where Hitler himself had approved the film for release. The Vienna Philharmonic Society provided the music to emphasize the "aberrations of a distorted mind," wrote *Newsweek* (January 23, 1937), lending a patina of credence to the drama. *Literary Digest* (January 16, 1937) called Hochbaum's film "one of the best hospital pictures yet made in Europe and definitely an improvement over the Hollywood clinical cinema." "This will make swell fare for German art houses," concluded the trade paper *Philadelphia Exhibitor* (January 15, 1937). Mark Forrest of the *Saturday Evening Review* (May 30, 1937) praised *Der Ewige Maske* because "anything that makes one think in the cinema should be encouraged." The *New Yorker* (January 9, 1937) dissented, saying that the film was for the "serious, those not quite well, people who can't sleep nights, people who have a charge account at Bellevue, clinic loafers and analyst disciples. The schizophrenic will love it."

Hochbaum's film was one of nine films up for the top prize at the 1935 Venice Film Festival. The National Board of Review named it the Best Foreign Film of 1937. Tobis's un-subtitled *Kinderarzt Dr. Engel* (*Dr. Engel, Child Specialist*) portrays a kindly bachelor-pediatrician

(Paul Hörbiger) and the many juveniles and children under his care, one of them being the illegitimate son of a female violinist (Viktoria von Belasko). She's the unwed mother who waits for the doctor to say the words that will make her a truly fulfilled, and married, German woman. He utters them. Directed by Johannes Riemann in the year of the Berlin Olympics and distributed by CFE, the film, wrote *Variety* (September 17, 1937), "has more balance between comedy, pathos, and action than numerous recent Teutonic efforts." "The scenes in the specialist's office were realistic enough to give the viewers a sense of medical authenticity. There would be more Nazi medical films in the next few years claiming authenticity, but they would be far from kind.

In Germany in 1937, Herta Jülich (b. 1897) co-directed the little-known, two-reel medical documentary *Mysterium des Lebens* (*Mystery of Life*), which was one of the more eye-opening medically-based shorts that Ufa screened in the States before the U.S. entered the war. It deals with the biological development of cells and embryos, demonstrated with hedgehogs and rabbits. According to the Reichstelle für den Unterrichtsfilm—the Government Agency for Educational Films—"Impregnation and partition of the rabbit's egg are created under the supervision and scientific direction" of an esteemed German scientist, who, with unintended irony, shows great care and skill in the face of new life!

The new lives of animals might have been cherished, but the lives of certain humans in Germany needed to be ended, according to the docu-drama *Opfer der Vergangenheit* (*Victims of the Past*, 1936–37), which was shown throughout Germany in 1937. Made on Hitler's orders and produced by Goebbels' ministry, *Opfer der Vergangenheit* advocates sterilization of "useless eaters" living in "palaces with beautiful gardens." The care of those Jewish patients, says a narrator, means "healthy German citizens must work." The Nazis' ideology that "life is a fight for existence" meant that the reproduction of unworthy life should be prevented by law, that is, through medical experimentation and killing. This film, which Gernot Bock-Steiber scripted, was apparently unnoticed by American critics in Germany. Was *Opfer der Vergangenheit* overlooked because of the news that the concentration camp called Ettersberg was operational? Located near the city of Weimar, where Germany's Shakespeare Society and the Goethe-Schiller Archives are located, the campsite was named for the spot where Goethe wrote and sketched. The people of Weimar, however, objected to calling it Ettersberg. The Nazis renamed the camp Buchenwald (Beech Forest).

The Nazi fatherland was the target of protests when a certain foreign-language film came to New York in winter 1936–37. Members of the American Jewish Congress and the Non-Sectarian Anti-Nazi League took to the streets because tickets for *Les Dieux s'amusent* (*The Gods Have Fun*, 1935) were on sale. Why? Because the film in question was the French version of the German-language *Amphitryon* (1935), an adaptation of a play by Germany's nineteenth-century romantic playwright, Bernd Heinrich Wilhelm von Kleist. *Les Dieux s'amusent* caused a stir because a dirty little secret was coming to light. The film's production company, L'Alliance Cinématographique Européenne (A.C.E.), was Ufa's French lackey. A.C.E. had an honorable beginning. It began producing French versions of Ufa films in the Weimar era. Its first was Alexander Volkoff's *Geheimnosse des Orients* (*Secrets of the Orient*, 1927), an Arabian Nights tale that was shown in the U.S. in January 1932. During the Nazi era, however, German-French co-productions took on a new meaning and urgency. Until they ceased joint productions in 1940, Ufa and A.C.E made nearly 50 films in more than 10 years. Most of the films were produced in Berlin. Louis Untermeyer's Anti-Nazi League fought the release in America of any films with Nazi connections. *Les Dieux s'amusent* had been co-directed by Reinhold Schünzel (Richard Scheer), a German Jew.

Containing rhythmic dialogue and shifts to prose and song, *Les Dieux s'amusent*, co-directed by Albert Valentin, is about old Jupiter (Henri Garat) falling for the most virtuous

Amphitryon ad for a "French" film.

beauty in Thebes, young Alcmene (Jeanne Boitel). The beginning finds the women of Thebes pleading for their long-absent husbands and lovers who have gone to war. Alcmene, the wife of Amphitryon, the patriotic general of the Theban army, directs a plea to Jupiter to bring victory to the Theban army and to send her husband safely home. Jupiter decrees success for the Thebans. However, the hen-pecked god also goes to the earth in order to seduce her—in the guise of her husband Amphitryon. But Jupiter's resolute wife Juno (Marguerite Moreno) becomes aware of his scheme. She works to re-establish family unity, happiness, harmony, and honor in Olympus and on earth.

Martin Lewis, a German-born Jew, and Herman Weinberg, who also was Jewish, managed the 55th Street Playhouse in New York where *Les Dieux s'amusent* was set to open. At the behest of the Anti-Nazi League, they cancelled all showings after concluding that the film had indeed been shot in Berlin. Releasing the film as French-made had been the Nazis' attempt to sneak a film of theirs onto American screens. Not everyone, however, agreed with a boycott of German films. "Those bad Nazis," said *Stage* magazine (December 1936), "had a hand in financing this film the picketers ... would have us know. Which emblazoned news, it seems, is enough to stop (only temporarily, we hope) the showing of one of the most engaging comedies about town."

The boycott against *Les Dieux s'amusent* was short-lived. The film, subtitled, resurfaced at New York's Belmont Theatre in spring 1937. The Globe Film Distributing Company, headed by David Brill, then distributed it beyond New York. The *Hollywood Reporter* (October 29, 1936) had rated *Les Dieux s'amusent* "one of the finest pictures yet brought from France." Jon Mosher, writing in the *New Yorker* (April 3, 1937), had a change of heart regarding *Les Dieux s'amusent*. "For some reason or other, involving international relationships, the light little French item" had been withdrawn from "general observation. I must now confess that on seeing it again I found it more agreeable than I had at first.... The music seemed more attractive ... I rather suspect that the sound machinery has been oiled up a bit in this long period of waiting."

No protesters were out in the streets when several new releases came to the 86th Street Garden Theatre. One was E.W. Emo's *Fiakerlied* (*Cabbie's Song*, 1936), a Bavaria Film production from Austria, which is set in the Vienna of 1910 when Hitler's favorite mayor, the anti–Semitic Karl Lüger, and his "Reform Union," were running the city. It suggests that a historic break with the past had occurred during his rule. In this film, Ferdinand Strödl (Paul Hörbiger) is the driver of a two-horse carriage who sleeps in a shed with his beloved black horses. Although he seeks a decent life he also believes in luck. When he falls in love with "Ludmilla Berndt" (Gusti Huber), he can envision a future. But then he discovers that she's a vaudeville actress, and he breaks up with her. The wealthy, Jewish man-about-town "Max Jolander" (Franz Schaftheitlin), to whom Ferdinand is in debt, often offers him words of encouragement. Later, Ferdinand spots Jolander with Ludmilla. Ferdinand then breaks with Jolander, and rejects Ludmilla once more. Ferdinand now realizes that he must his way through life alone, without the help of non–Aryans.

Nazi director Richard Schneider-Edenkoben (b. 1899) had pleased Goebbels with his comedy *Inkognito* (1936), an Ufa production that also screened at the 86th Street Garden Theatre in 1937. Severin Matthias (Gustav Fröhlich) is the heir to a fortune, but he's tired of luxury and not very good at running his soap factory. The firm's director, named "Weiner" (Otto Stöckel), makes all the big decisions. So Severin decides to see the other side of life by getting a job incognito in a branch of his family's business. Along the way he meets Friedelchen (Hansi Knoteck) whose parents reject him because they think he's a fraud. Severin, however, uncovers real (Jewish) fraud and machinations on the part of the board of directors. Once he has the goods, he fires them all, assumes full control of the business operations, and marries Friedlechen.

Mistaken identity as a story idea had by now become a staple in German films. Herbert Maisch's *Liebesgeschichten von Boccaccio* (1936), an Ufa production that made its U.S. debut at the Garden Theatre under the simpler title *Boccaccio*, takes place in the medieval village of Ferrara, where everyone is absorbed by the spicy tales of a writer calling himself Boccaccio. Count Cesare (Albrecht Schönhals) takes advantage of the mystery to masquerade as the author so as to pursue the many damsels. The real Boccaccio turns out to be a court clerk (Willy Fritsch) who finds his material in divorce records. He grows rich and achieves popularity incognito, but then becomes concerned because his wife (Heli Finkenzeller), an apparently ideal spouse, shows an interest in the other Boccaccio. "The film is light and giddy and English captions make it easily understandable to those who don't speak German," wrote Anna Nangle of the *Chicago Tribune* (August 11, 1937), when it played at the city's World Playhouse.

The early twentieth-century drama *Die Sporck'schen Jäger* (*The Sporck Battalion*), which is set in the Masuren Lakes area of East Prussia, takes the idea of mistaken identity to a higher level. The film makes clear that the ideal woman is a blonde forester's daughter who catches the attention of several soldiers. Trouble often revolves around the actions of a dark-haired fisherman's daughter (Rotraut Richter). Yet it is she who willingly assumes blame in order to save Lieutenant von Naugaard (Fritz Genschow) from arrest, which preserves his battalion's honor. Since he is an officer obsessed with poaching, von Naugaard does the honorable thing to make amends: he kills himself. Rolf Randolf (1878–1941) directed this 1934 Bavaria production, which the Garden Theatre screened in 1937.

Hans Deppe's *Der Jäger von Fall* (*The Hunter of Fall*, 1936), which Ufa produced from a novel by one of the Nazis' favorite authors, Ludwig Ganghofer, is the nineteenth-century tale of a forest hunter's mountain sweetheart, named Burgl (Georgia Höll). She tries to live down the shame of a one-night stand with the poacher Hulsen Blasi (Hans A. Schlettow), which resulted in a birth of an illegitimate child. In the end, the forest hunter Friedl (Paul Richter), who turns out actually to be a forest ranger, apprehends game robbers and eliminates Blasi. The film's action through forests and streams takes viewers away from the twentieth-century world of the Nazis. The film screened at the Casino Theatre in 1937.

In Erich Engels' *Kirschen in nachbars Garten* (*Fruit in the Neighbor's Garden*, 1935), a city girl (Iris Arlan) falls for a nice young country lad (Theo Shall) whose aunt (Adele Sandrock) has other plans for him. It is in her rural garden, however, that their German love blooms.

Veit Harlan's *Maria, die Magd* (*Maria, the Maid*, 1936), a drama produced by Tobis-Minerva, centers on Maria Klimank (Hilde Körber), the servant of a self-absorbed actress, Alice Winter (Hilde Hildebrandt), and her busy attorney-husband (Alfred Abel). Maria has practically become mother to the star's neglected 6-year-old son, Gerd, even postponing her own marriage to German officer Franz (Hans Schlenk). Matters clear up when Alice returns from a tour and recognizes her motherly duties. But that's not before Maria takes the boy to her home village, which causes Alice to believe her son has disappeared. Pennsylvania censors opted to eliminate scenes of the naked boy in bed.

Karl Heinz Martin's *Der Abenteurer von Paris* (*The Paris Adventure*), which Tobis produced in the year of the Berlin Olympics and which the Casino Theatre screened, is a pro–British tale about Mabel (Karin Hardt) and her lover, émigré Russian prince Mitja Artamanof (Peter Voss). She's the daughter of British colonial official Sir Henry Vinston (Theodor Loos). The former prince dances midnights at the Russian House in Paris in order to pay for the Oxford University education of his younger brother, Igor (Hannes Stelzer). While the hardworking, self-sacrificing, educated Russians are depicted as Germany's friends, there's no mistaking who the culprit in the tale is: "Col. Fedor Lossew" (Andrews Engelman), a presumed Jew.

Herbert Selpin's *Ein Idealer Gatte* (*An Ideal Husband*, 1935), which Thea von Harbou adapted from Oscar Wilde's 1895 play, is set in contemporary London. The ideal person in the story is the wife. She represents the real brains of an upper-class British family, exhibiting loyalty, support, and courage while willing to risk scandal to save her family. The plot hinges on a British steel magnate's wife (Brigitte Helm) crossing swords with her husband's former lover-turned-blackmailer (Sybille Schmitz) to keep her marriage intact. Casino Film Exchange distributed Terra's production, which did only "so-so ... in Yorkville and equivalents," according to *Variety* (January 13, 1937), because it was "unlike average German dramatic fare." Selpin had directed the incongruously titled *Romanze* (1936), also known as *Die Frau des Anderen* (*The Other One's Woman*), a German-Austrian production that takes place in Africa, a favorite exotic locale of German films of the era. The theme is that Nazi favorite—industrial espionage of German facilities—built around the tale of an unhappily married woman who remains faithful to her marriage despite near tragedy. Walter Zerlett-Olfenius, who scripted 10 films between 1936 and 1945 and who was sentenced to a serve time in a labor camp from 1947 to 1952, must have had Oscar Wilde's "Lady Windermere's Fan" in mind when he scripted *Romanze* because there is a key scene involving a fan. Reviewed abroad, *Romanze* was not shown commercially in the States.

Then again, there's Martin's *Punks kommt aus Amerika* (*Punks Arrives from America*, 1935), an Ufa production shown at the 86th Street Garden Theatre. It's about a young German who, having made it in New World, returns to the fatherland, only to lose his money on the way from Hamburg to Berlin. Punks (Attila Hörbiger), the nicknamed German immigrant, who is mistaken for an American after so many years, must use his brains to prove himself to his fellow Germans. He establishes his credentials by foiling an attempted robbery of an uncle by the cheat (*Betrüger*) named "Sigorski" (Oskar Sima), presumably a Jew. Punks is then accepted back into the fold, his marriage to his sweetheart (Lien Deyers) a foregone conclusion.

Fritz Wendhausen satirized Swedes of noble birth in Tobis's *Familienparade* (1936), an un-subtitled CFE release in 1937. There's shock when, at a family gathering, it's announced that the (presumed) young count, Erik Sternenhoe (Curt Jürgens), whose 21st birthday they are celebrating, is really someone else: the son of servant girl. He was switched at birth with the real count—who is returning to the homeland after growing up abroad (in Canada). Erik's engagement to Alice Barrenkrona (Ellen Franck), the daughter of an aristocrat, is in doubt—until Alice overrides her father's objections. Other nobles in the film were called Thornberg, Wennergreen, and Appelquist.

Viktor Janson directed the Nordic beauty Suse Graf in Ufa's comedy about an attractive letter carrier, *Hilde Peterssen, Postlagernd* (*Hilde Petersen, General Delivery*, 1935–1936) opposite Rolf Wanka (1901–1982). Based on the novel by the German writer Dinah Nelken (1900–1989), the film screened in June 1937 at the Garden Theatre. Hilde has lost her job, but can't bear to break the news to her mother. That's the reason she asks would-be employers to answer her applications "general delivery." When she answers the ad for a writer seeking a secretary, she meets others who use ruses to avoid dealing with painful truths. It's not until she meets the right man, rather than getting the right job, that she finds happiness. Graf made a dozen films in Nazi Germany, and continued her career after the war.

Max Ohal's *Jede Frau hat ein Geheimnis* (*Every Woman Has a Secret*) was yet another a mistaken-identity story but with just a "trace of the Cinderella formula," wrote *Variety* (March 31, 1937). The 1934 comedy, which CFE distributed, has blonde Anne (Karin Hardt, 1910–92) finding the right way to happiness by finding a train ticket to Baden-Baden. Then, by pretending to be a socialite, she manages to introduce samples of her father's new perfume to the wealthy and the powerful at a posh hotel. There she also finds love.

The non-musical side of Austrian life was also behind several films by E.W. Emo that were shown at the Casino and Garden theatres in 1937. The hoax in Emo's *Schabernack* (*A Hoax*, 1936) is that American critics ignored its stereotypical anti–Semitism. Instead the film was characterized as a comedy about a headwaiter (starring the prolific Paul Hörbiger) saving a hotel from foreclosure through luck and $10,000 from "Mr. Vanderbilt" (Heinz Salfner). The luck involves the accidental burning-down of a nearby sanitarium owned by a wealthy man named "Manz" (Paul Richter). His wealthy patients, referred to by the villages as lunatics, are then, fortuitously, transferred to the German-owned hotel—which charges room rates. Emo's

Endstation (*Last Stop*, 1936), a German-Austrian production, offered a contemporary feel for Austria's capital (without any reference to Jewish life) via the life of a trolley car worker (Paul Hörbiger), who advances to the post of motorman and meets a hatmaker (Maria Andergast), whose fate runs along the same trolley lines.

In Harry Piel's *Sein bester Freund* (*His Best Friend*, 1937), released by American Tobis, the protagonist is a faithful German shepherd. Detective Harry Peters (Harry Piel) is training the animal, called Greif ("seize"), to be a police dog, but the results are mixed. That's because the dog once belonged to the notorious crook "Emil Kruppack" (Paul Westermeier), a presumed Jew whose alias (or other identity) is "William Hopkins." When Kruppack was the dog's owner, he called it Rolf. At the climax, when the dog's loyalty is still in doubt, it plays a key role in capturing Kruppack and his brother Max (Willy Schur). In a shootout between Harry and the gang, the dog takes a bullet meant for Harry. Greif then dies. The dog, like all good Germans, has done real duty! By its actions, this German shepherd—a fallen comrade—was no traitor to the fatherland. Heroic action laced with comedy in an exotic setting was what mattered to Nazi party member Harry Piel before World War II began. He was a director who used real game and an imaginary Asian locale in the Ariel-Film production *Der Dschungel ruft* (*The Call of the Jungle*, 1935), which American Tobis distributed, starring the alluring Austrian Gerda Maurus (1903–68).

The high water mark of so-called German comedies was Ufa's production of Paul Martin's lively *Glückskinder* (*Lucky Folks*, 1936). This film, shown in America in mid-1937, was deemed the best German screwball comedy of the era and an example of how the Nazi film industry tried to fill the gap it created after it expelled its best film comedians from the industry. Its locale is New York. Scripted by Curt Götz, *Glückskinder* appears to be about sacrifice. Aspiring poet Gil Taylor (Willy Fritsch), a struggling songwriter making a living as a cub reporter on one of New York's finest dailies, gallantly claims that an unlucky and pathetic-looking woman, Ann Garden (Lilian Harvey), is his fiancée. He says that to save her from being jailed for vagrancy. Pressing the matter, the skeptical judge (Paul Bildt) marries them on the spot. The bride's identity is something of a secret, and the film turns out to be about something more conventional—the purported kidnapping of an oil millionaire's niece, who resembles Ann!

U.S. critics noted that former Hollywood director Paul Martin had rounded up a fine cast that worked well together. Goebbels, writing in his diaries, objected to one aspect of the film: the "song texts celebrating idleness."

Taking action and accepting something new were themes in Nazi films, but the films were almost always set in the past. Or they were Weimar-era films that the Nazis were reselling abroad. In Fred Sauer's *Gordian, der Tyrann* (*Gordian, the Tyrant*, 1937), a CFE import, a hard-boiled but good-hearted district judge (Weiss Ferdl) in a small town in pre–Weimar Germany is opposed to progress, especially the construction of an electric light plant in the region. However, he changes his mind after an apparent double, a theater director named "Silbernagel," nearly ruins his hard-won reputation. Gordian also gives his blessing to his niece's marriage to his assistant and abandons bachelorhood himself.

In Carl Boese's comedy *Fraulein Frau* (*Miss Madame*), which Deutsch Fox-Film distributed in Germany and CFE distributed in the States three years after its production, the husband in a May–December marriage is driven to the point of desperation and drastic action through a misunderstanding during his honeymoon because he imagines his young wife is attracted to an actor. Carl Boese's musical comedy *Der Ungetreue Eckehart* (*The Unfaithful Husband*), starring Lucie Englisch, Fritz Schulz, and Ralph Arthur Roberts and produced by Tobis, was released in New York twice. The film's title tells it all. Made in 1931, it first showed up in the U.S. in early 1932. Schulz, a critic said, was a rising star in Germany. Surprisingly, when his comedy was re-released five years later in New York, Schulz, a Jew who was by then persona non grata in Germany, still was listed in the credits.

Franz Wenzler had his name in lights when his 1933 film, *Der Gipfelstürmer* (*The Peak Scaler*), produced by Peter Ostermayr, reached the U.S. Olympic champion-mountain climber Franz Schmid (of 1932 and 1936 fame) starred. Alpine scenery remained fair game in German films easily screenable in the States, particularly when the films combined love and action in the wonderful outdoors, slyly affirming the back-to-the-soil ethos within Nazi Germany.

Franz Osten's 1932 *Fürst Sepp'l* (*Prince Sepp'l*) was released in the U.S. four years after Hitler came to power. It starred the burly Beck-Gaden as the factotum of a mountain inn turned into a sort of grand hotel. In Johannes Meyer's *Eine von Uns* (*One of Us*), Brigitte Helm played the young woman nicknamed Gilgi, illegitimately born, who decides that marriage is not so threatening after all. This film was a late Weimar production that CFE distributed in the States five years after its completion.

The effort to stress an ordinary German to the movie-going public was behind the release of numerous films from Nazi Germany, including Robert A. Stemmle's *Ein Mädel mit Tempo* (*A Girl with Pep*). Like other films from the Weimar era that the Nazis released, this one also earned the Third Reich a bit of cash. Initially titled *Es tut sich was um Mitternacht* (*So This Is Midnight*), it starred Dolly Haas as a treasure seeker. In 1937, CFE released it as well as Johannes Meyer's un-subtitled comedy *Die Kleine Schwindlerin* (*The Little Crook*, 1933), which Paramount had produced in Germany just as Hitler was coming to power. Set on the French Riviera, *Die Kleine Schwindlerin* recounts the story of the debonair, rich young victim—Lord Bob E. Denver (Harald Paulsen)—of a gang of classy crooks. The thieves, all non–Germans, go by the names Viscount de Latour (Alfred Abel), Gwendolyn (Betty Amann), Annette (Dolly Haas), and "The Marquis" (Hans Deppe), who is a pickpocket. In the end, Annette falls for Bob, who foils the culprits' efforts to rook him. *Variety* had written that if the film had been good enough it would have been released in the U.S. years before. Whether or not it was meritorious production, the film carried a message for Germany's supporters and made a bit of money for Germany as well.

Georg Jacoby's comedy of errors involving film performers, a jewel robbery, and policemen, *Der Grosse Bluff* (*The Big Bluff*), also distributed by CFE in 1937, starred the Jewish actor Otto Wallburg. That was because this film was produced a few months before Hitler's rise to power, when Jews were still part of Germany's film industry. Walter Schlee wrote this script, whose working title was *All Is Comedy*. Going back further still, *Die Schwebende Jungfrau* (*The Soaring Maiden*), directed by Carl Boese, featured the Jewish performer Szöke Szakall as a well-meaning eccentric who attempts to patch up a row between his niece and her fiancé. The film, which had been made in Weimar Germany in 1931, co-starred Fritz Schulz and Max Ehrlich. It might have reminded viewers of the time before nearly all non–Aryans had been driven from the German and Austrian film industries. Max Ehrlich was a celebrated actor and director of German comedy and cabaret in the '20s and '30s. He had starred with Siegfried Arno in the gag-filled comedy *Der Storch Streikt* (*The Stork Goes on Strike*, 1931), produced by Joe Pasternak for Itala Film, which Deutsche Universal distributed in Germany. E.W. Emo directed, Franz Planer photographed, and Paul Ostermayr edited the nine-reel sound film. Ehrlich, who had fled Nazi Germany for the Netherlands, was arrested and sent to Westerbrook concentration camp in 1942. Undaunted, and making the best of the situation, Ehrlich formed a theater group of well-known Jewish show people. He was murdered in Auschwitz in 1944.

Gerhard Lamprecht's murder drama, *Ein Seltsamer Gast* (*A Strange Guest*, 1936), another Ufa production from the year of the Olympics, starred Alfred Abel, one of the last Jews allowed to act in Nazi films, as Bruneaux, a wealthy art dealer. On the day his daughter Yvette (Ilse Petri) becomes engaged to the attorney Henri de Valencours (Kurt Fischer-Fehling), she is blackmailed. She's asked to come up with 20,000 francs. Bruneaux's ex-wife Lou (Elisabeth Wendt) is then found dead—all in an offbeat, supernatural setting: a tiny Paris hotel where anything can happen. Suspicion falls on several people: the eccentric photographer Rompon (Aribert Wäscher), the scoundrel Morone (Werner Scharf), "Uncle" Théophole (Fritz Odemar), and the sulky waiter Gaston (Herman Speelmans). When released at the Garden Theatre in July 1937, the film, which Giuseppe Becce scored, contained several unidentified performers in order to lend mystery to the identity of the killer. But the killer turned out to be Gaston. Rompon, who turns out to be a police inspector on the trail of petty crook Morone, nabs Gaston. Gaston's name was the clue: in German it can mean "stranger."

One of Germany's biggest hits of the year was *Truxa* (1937), which ran at the Garden Theatre. Directed by Hans H. Zerlett, and distributed by American Tobis, it offered Americans a chance to catch a rising German star: the lithesome La Jana (1905–1940). American critics were blunt. They liked her figure. Born Henriette Margarethe Hiebel in Vienna, La Jana had made silent films in the waning days of Weimar Germany, including *Therese Raquin* (1928), by Jacques Feyder. Scored by Leo Leux (1893–1951), born Gottlieb Wilhelm Leuchs, *Truxa*, with English subtitles, is a drama about exposing the dangers posed by the *stranger*. Heinrich Seiler's novel *December with Truxa* formed the basis for the story, which begins in New York. In Zerlett's film, world-famous tightrope walker Truxa (Peter Elsholz) is in love with Yester (La Jana). But so is the mad non–German magician "Garvin" (Ernst Fritz Fürbringer). Truxa quits in the middle of a big New York performance because he says his nerves are shot. Meeting an aspiring look-alike aerialist named Husen (Hannes Stelzer), Truxa exchanges places with him—and then vanishes. At Berlin's Wintergarten, Husen rises to fame as the new Truxa. When Husen falls in love with Truxa's sweetheart Yester, Garvin makes plans to do away with this "Truxa" when he does his difficult somersault, the climax of his act. Only a last-second catch of the rope, however, saves Husen's life. At that point, Yester admits she loves him, and Husen tries the somersault again. The real Truxa shows up just in time to send Garvin to his death in a fall. *Film Daily* (August 11, 1937) called *Truxa* a "well-rounded attraction, strong in all departments." In 1938, Albert de Courville directed a British version of Zerlett's film, called *Star of the Circus*. Leo Leux provided the music.

A product of German films, Zerlett directed *Die Selige Exzellenz* (*His Late Excellency*, 1935), a tale of intrigue and espionage—led by a Jew—that follow in wake of the death of the popular leader of a German principality in the 1890s. It was shown in New York's 86th Street Casino Theatre in summer 1937. After the premiere's death, Lord Chamberlain "Buxbaum" (Eugen Rex) begins to clean house, which threatens those who had been closest to the premiere. But Madame Windegg (Hilde Hildebrand), a confidante of the former ruler, has a trick up her sleeve. She spreads a rumor that the premiere had kept a diary. Its publication would implicate most of the courtiers and the new ruler for treason.

Zerlett's *Liebe geht seltsame Wege* (*Ways of Love Are Strange*, 1937), which was not released in the States but reviewed in Europe, is set at the close of political upheaval in a South American country, where Captain Costali (Carl Ludwig Diehl) is condemned to death for taking up arms against the new regime. After a sensational escape, he shows up at the country home of his girlfriend, Antonia (Olga Tschechowa), and her niece, Delia Vigo (Karin Hardt). But it's all a ruse. Costali has been working incognito to uncover the real traitor (or stranger) within the new government, the police chief Montefranca (Edwin Jürgensen). Hans H. Zerlett directed other Nazi films not released in America. His hagiographic documentary about Max Schmeling's defeat of Joe Louis, called *Max Schmelings Sieg—ein deutcher Sieg* (*Max Schmeling's Victory—A German Victory*, 1936), was screened throughout Germany.

Zerlett's *Diener lassen bitten* (*Dinner Is Served*, 1936) was a Bavaria production satirizing British aristocrats named Wimple (Herbert Hübner), Spiller (Josef Eichheim), and Birry-

Birry (Helmuth Weiss), as well as the newly rich whisky tradesman James Potter (Joe Stöckel) and his wife Henrietta (Fita Benkhoff). Zerlett's *Moral* (*Morality*, 1936) is a hypocritical adaptation of Ludwig Thoma's 1909 drama of small-town Bavarian small-mindedness. Hiding behind the author's liberalism, the German filmmakers set the film in the late nineteenth century in a German grand duchy whose citizens are so shocked at the non–German, leg-kicking dancing then in vogue that they form the Society for Raising the Standard of Morality. Ernina Lapomme (Benkhoff), the French dancer responsible for the hysterical reaction, turns out really to be somebody else: Fräulein Appel of Cologne. That simple disclosure leads to embarrassment and a scandal for Princess Ottilie (Roma Bahn), who supported the society. Professor "Wasner" (Walter Steinbeck) and the local businessman named "Beermann" (Joe Stöckel), who were part of the opposition, come in for ridicule. In summer 1936, American critics abroad referred to the latter two productions as light, entertaining comedies, but they were not released in the States. If the anti–Semitism had anything to do with it, no one said so.

Zerlett, however, is also closely linked to two much more notorious anti–Semitic productions of the Nazi era: *Robert und Bertram* (1939) and *Venus vor Gericht* (1941). Shown in Berlin and Hamburg, Zerlett's Tobis-produced film *Robert und Bertram*, which he scripted and based on the 1859 burlesque work by Gustav Raeder, is about the vagabonds Robert and Bertram (Rudi Godden and Kurt Seifert). Breaking out of jail, they meet the beautiful Lenchen (Carla Rust) who is the daughter of poor restaurant owner Lips (Alfred Maack). He urges her to marry his Jewish creditor "Biedermeier" (Arthur Schröder), instead of the man she loves, Michel (Heinz Schorlemmer), who is the nephew of Strambach (Fritz Mampers). Robert and Bertram—going incognito as the Count of Monte Cristo and his music teacher—get themselves invited to the Jewish wedding. In attendance are a number of rich Jews ripe for the picking: "Nathan Ipelmeyer" (Herbert Huebner), "Forchheimer" (Erwin Biegel), "Samuel Bendheim" (Armin Muench), and "Dr. Cordvan" (Walter Lieck). Stealing their jewelry, Robert and Bertram give the loot to the innkeeper so that he can pay off his debts. Lenchen and Michel are able to marry while Robert and Bertram jump into a balloon that takes them directly to heaven—a supernatural ending in line with Nazi ideology that leaders and Germans who take decisive action are connected to the gods.

While this production went unmentioned in the Western press, *Film-Kurier* (July 1939) wrote that the film, photographed by Friedl Behn-Grund (1906–1989), "lent form" to the "attitude of the people" towards Jews. Goebbels' reaction to Zerlett's film, however, was less enthusiastic. He wrote in his diaries, "The Jewish question is touched upon very superficially, without any real sense of empathy." *Robert und Bertram* is banned from commercial screening in Germany.

Zerlett's *Venus vor Gericht* (*Venus on Trial*, 1941), a Bavaria production, was more to Goebbels' liking because it pillories Jews by setting up "German-Jewish art experts." Scripted by Zerlett and scored by Leo Leux, it's set in Weimar Germany in 1930, where the sculptor Peter Brake (Hannes Stelzer), actually depicted as a member of the Nazi Party, creates and then buries a statue of Venus. He's done this to prove a point about what he calls the "polluting product of Jewish decadence" within Germany. When the statue is discovered, art dealer "Benjamin Hecht" (Siegfried Breuer) buys the Venus of the Field for a pittance from the Aryan farmer who found it. Hecht then unloads the statue, which (Jewish) experts have declared is from antiquity, and makes a fortune. Peter then decides to expose this swindle in court. Not only does no one believe him because he's a party member, he's put on trial for perjury. His case seems hopeless, especially after "Dr. Knarre" (Hubert von Meyerinck) declares that Peter could never have sculpted the Venus. However, when a bailiff arrives at Peter's studio to requisition his art as evidence against him, the bailiff uncovers a swastika flag. Impressed, the bailiff leaves empty-handed, giving the Nazi salute and smiling! And then Charlotte Boller (Hansi Knoteck), the model for the statue, comes forward.

No Western critic denounced this film when it premiered in Berlin in June 1941. Ironically, like victims of the Holocaust, Zerlett died in a concentration camp: in Buchenwald, under detention by the victorious Russians in 1949. His *Venus vor Gericht* is banned in Germany.

Weisse Sklaven (*White Slaves*) stresses the necessity of a Nazi onslaught against the Bolsheviki. This film ought to have shocked Americans when it screened at the Garden Theatre, six months after its premiere in Berlin in early 1937. At the start of this Tobis feature directed by Austro-Hungarian Karl Anton (1898–1979), the cruiser *Sevastopol* is lying at its home port in late 1917. Officers and townspeople are celebrating on deck when catastrophic news arrives: a revolution has broken out. Just as suddenly, the ship's sailors, with surnames like "Kurloff," "Turbin," "Nikitin," and "Panin," massacre the officers. Murder become the order of the day and servants become masters. The former governor (Theodor Loos) of Sevastopol, who has become a broken old man, is in hiding along with his daughter Manja (Camilla Horn). Elsewhere, her fiancé, Wolgoff (Karl John), an officer from the once glorious Russian vessel *Sevastopol*, exclaims to his followers, "This is the fate that menaces all civilization! We must fight on!" The lovers eventually reunite and escape the marauding Bolsheviks on a warship seized in a counter-revolt. Goebbels noted the film "is quite moving in parts" and "has the right slant as well." The *New York Times* (July 31, 1937) wrote that the "German producers have mixed such a strong portion of *Bolshevist* horrors that it is likely to be an overdose for even the strongest stomachs."

Four years after its completion, *Salon Dora Green* (*The House of Dora Green*), which German expatriate Henrik Galeen had directed, also offered a warning about Russians. Premiering at the 86th Street Casino, it was in line with Nazi thinking regarding traitors and foreign spies. Anti–German plotters seek vital German ship designs. These enemies of the German state are apparently Russian-Jewish: one is named "Sucharow" (Leonard Stöckel) and the other is the non–Aryan "Ivan Keller" (Alfred Abel). The protagonist is the cabaret dancer Dora Green (Mady Christians), who falls in love with the spies' victim while saving his vital drawings from falling into enemy hands—engineer Frank Gebhard (Paul Hartmann). Mady Christians (1892–1951) was a German-American stage and screen performer.

R.A. Stemmle's *Der Raub der Sabinerinnen* (*The Rape of the Sabines*, 1935–1936) gave off a real whiff of anti–Semitism. Shown at the Casino Theatre in 1937, it was a Europa release of yet another German film that was not about what its title suggests. Rather than being a screen adaptation of the well-known episode in Roman history, the film turns out to be a comedy based on a decades-old popular European play by Franz von Schönthen. In 1900, in Oberlanningen, German professor Martin Gollwitz (Max Gülstorff) sees his classical tragedy, which he wrote in his madcap youth, turned into a farce by a shyster theatrical producer named "Emanuel Streise" (Bernhard Wildenhain). But the thing is a hit! Variations abounded along a theme like this that distracted filmgoers from the new reality, as it should have been called.

Entertainment and Nazi ethos blended happily, said a critic, in Hans Deppe's Ufa production *Das Schöne Fraülein Schragg* (*Pretty Miss Schragg*, 1936–1937), which was a Heimat film co-scripted by Fred Andreas from his novel. Historically, Prussian Junkers had opposed the plan of Frederick the Great to relocate veterans of the Seven Years' War and ex-convicts along the eastern frontier. In Nazi Germany, their well-off descendants were, ironically, wary of Hitler's intentions of doing something along similar lines: dividing their estates among landless peasants and unemployed city workers. For the Nazis, however, this meant emphasizing blood and soil. The theme played strongly in this film. The great Prussian king (Otto Gebühr) intervenes on behalf of the daughter (Hansi Knoteck) of a counselor of state determined to marry a young settler (Paul Klinger). Filmgoers might well have assumed that Der Führer—through the screen depiction of Frederick—would take similar action to solve Germany's agrarian problem. Frederick, however, doesn't ennoble the young Germans. Rather, he advises the young man and his well-bred wife to be model farmers and then raise lots of children.

Jumping from Berlin to the Mosel and the Rhine country, with views of rivers and mountains, of course, Carl Froelich's *Wenn wir alle Engel wären* (*We Can't All Be Angels*) was an unsubtitled CFE comedy, released in the U.S. in late 1937. A husband named Christian Kempenich (Heinz Rühmann), a bit tipsy, has spent his time at a "nitery" studying the "morality" of the girls. His wife Hedwig (Leni Marenbach), meanwhile, has her own tale to tell, because she has missed the last train home. When they meet up the next morning, mutual suspicions of infidelity are aroused. Since this comedy was produced in the year of the Berlin Olympics, its matrimonial misunderstandings and misadventures are all cleared up at the end—in court (in Nazi Germany, no less)! Goebbels designated the film "extremely valuable for the State and for Art," rating it the "best comedy for a long time," and said that he "laughed till I cried." In addition, he noted that Hitler was "also enthusiastic about the Froelich film."

Jürgen von Alten's first film to be shown the U.S. was the un-subtitled *Susanne im Bade* (*Susanna in the Bath*, 1937), produced by Minerva and released by CFE in late 1937. This tempest-in-a-teapot comedy revolves around the trouble art instructor Schrack (Hans Schlenck) gets himself into when he paints a female swimmer wearing nothing but a smile. Everyone finds out about it because of a jealous student named "Erika Knispel" (Erika von Thelmann), a presumed Jew. But the artist becomes famous, as does the subject of his work, Gussy Atkin (Manja Behrens, 1914–2003). Embarrassment and cover-up give way to truth-telling in the forest, where Schrack admits he loves Gussy.

Alten's Olympic-year film *Stärker als Paragraphen* (*Stronger than Regulations*, 1936), a tale based on Felix Helmer's play and produced by Minerva, is merely hypocritical. The film's theme is that in Nazi Germany, justice outweighs the law. It screened at the Casino Theatre in late 1937. Renate Hubrecht (Manja Behrens) discovers her uncle, the broker Theodor Hubrecht (Karl Hellmer), dead in his mansion. Renate, anxious about living alone in the mansion of a dead man, finds accommodations with the attorney, Birk (Paul Hartmnn). The police immediately arrest a man with a motive: Renate's lover, Robert Wendland (Karl Stepanek). He had had a terrible argument with Theodor Hubrecht on the night of his death. But Birk knows the killer's identity: a banker named Lörik, who had admitted that he was in Hubrecht's house on the night of the murder. Although the client-lawyer relationship bars him from coming forward, Birk defends Wendland without revealing anything about Lörik. Later, Lörik (Aribert Wäscher) is found guilty of murder and sentenced to ten years in jail.

Géza von Bolváry's *Das Schloss in Flandern* (*The Castle in Flanders*) begins with six English officers quartered in a Flemish castle, in Ypres, in 1918. Their only form of distraction is an old gramophone, and one record. They all fall in love with the voice they hear (Marta Eggerth's). One officer, named Fred Winsbury (Paul Hartmann), envisions meeting the singer, named Gloria Delamare. He is then reported killed. Five years later, Gloria spends a night at the castle in question, and meets what is apparently the officer's ghost. It turns out that the officer is alive, and that he's only been lying low, having honorably taken the blame for a forgery of bills committed by another man, named Bob Harrogate (Georg Alexander). Fred has returned from Australia to clear up matters about his reputation and that of the aristocratic Winsbury family. A production from the year of the Berlin Olympics, war, romance, mystery, and a tinge of the supernatural mixed with German music. "Her glorious lyric soprano voice in fine form," Eggerth—the undisputed first lady of German films—"sings and sings the tunes composed for her by Franz Grothe," wrote New York's *Daily News* (August 7, 1937). The key number was "Ein neus Laben fängt an"—"A New Life Begins." Paul Hartmann (1899–1977) served on one of Goebbels' arts committees. Shown at the Henka German Theatre in Passaic, N.J., in November 1937, the film was rumored to have caught the attention of Columbia Pictures, which wanted to produce an English-language version starring the singer Grace Moore.

Sacrifice and mother love are the themes of Bolváry's *Die Nacht der grossen Liebe* (*The Night of the Great Love*). The widow Thormaelen (Novotny) is a great diva who falls in love with a much-younger naval officer, Holger Rhon (Fröhlich). However, she weds an elderly diplomat (Fritz Odemar) for the sake of her daughter Ulla (Christine Grautoff). Ulla later falls in love with Rhon. The film starred Jarmila Novotny, discovered by Max Reinhardt, and Gustav Fröhlich and was scored by the anti–Nazi composer Robert Stolz. Deutsche Universal distributed the film in Germany and Europe in mid–1933. Four years later it was shown in the States, at New York's newest Yorkville-area theatre, called the Deutsche Lichtspiele. Bolváry's films from pre–Nazi Austria included *Mädchenpensionat* (*Girl's Dormitory*, 1936), with music by Frank Fux and produced by Styria, which asks, "Can a princess marry a man who is just an ordinary citizen?"—and answers, no. If the Nazis had produced it in 1936, they would have answered yes. In Bolváry's *Der Unwiderstehliche* (*The Irresistible Man*, 1937), produced by Terra, a wealthy woman seeks a man who loves her for herself alone. Incognito, she comes across the man of her dreams: a wealthy manufacturer posing as a salesman.

Rolf Hansen (1904–1990) was the unnamed director of *Liebe auf Umwegen* (*Love by Indirection*), in which two women of differing social classes—Gabriele, an heiress (Marianne Hoppe), and Fanny, a stewardess (Grete Weiser)—literally change dresses to see how the other half lives. Again, deception has its rewards. This film, which screened at the Casino Theatre late this year, was actually *Gabriele: eins, zwei, drei* (*Gabriele: One, Two, Three*, 1937). It didn't change opinions about the Nazis, even as the women marry down-to-earth Germans: the stewardess wins the heart of a local police chief and the heiress marries an engineer (Gustav Fröhlich).

Deception is also part of Lamac's Ufa-produced and star-studded musical *Der Postillon von Lonjumeau* (*The Postman from Lonjumeau*), which came to the 86th Street Garden Theatre as *King Smiles—Paris Laughs*. On his wedding night, the French mail-coach driver Chapelou (Willy Eichberger) is whisked off to Paris where Count Latour (Walter Slezak), an adversary of Louis XV (Walter Slezak), turns him into a great singer. At the same time the Marquise de Pompadour (Thekla Ahrens) is seeking another lover—and Chapelou is it. Eventually, the king and Chapelou's wife (Stradner) straighten things out. The Germans had produced this film in the year of the Berlin Olympics to commemorate the centenary of the Paris premiere of Adolphe Charles Adam's operetta *Postillon von Lonjumeau*. Costarring Rose Stradner, who left for Hollywood after the film's completion, the film rated a fair chance of success in the U.S. because of the "understandability and acceptability of the story," wrote *Variety* (November 24, 1937).

The keynote of a subsequent French period piece called *Fanny Elssler* (1937) is something more serious. An expensive Ufa production scripted by Paul Martin and Eva Leidmann, it starred Lilian Harvey, a Hollywood expatriate, and was directed by the man who often worked with her in Germany, Hungarian-born Paul Martin (1899–1967). Martin was a Hollywood expatriate who had directed *Orient Express* (1934) in America. Their first collaboration back in Germany had been one of Ufa's biggest German hits of 1935–36, *Schwarze Rosen* (*Black Roses*), in which Harvey played a Russian ballet dancer who sacrifices her life for that of a Finnish soldier-sculptor (Willi Fritsch) fighting for his nation's liberty against czarist Russia. Harvey depicts the famous nineteenth-century Austrian dancer Fanny Elssler as a patriotic and strong-willed opponent of Austrian Chancellor Metternich (Paul Hoffmann). The chancellor, a historical figure that Hitler loathed, opposes Napoleon's son, the duke of Reichstadt (the grandson of Austria's emperor), who claims the French throne. If the duke (Rolf Möbius,

Fanny Elssler (1937).

in his American debut) were to become France's king, he could scuttle Metternich's foreign policy regarding France. As it happens, when the Bourbon dynasty begins to totter, the young duke is ready but he won't act without the consent of the French! When it's clear that the duke and Elssler have fallen in love, Metternich, sensing he's lost control of events, throws the duke into jail and banishes Elssler. She flees to Paris. After the duke escapes to Paris, he receives news that Louis Philippe D'Orleans has become France's king. Returning to Vienna, the duke falls ill and dies. Elssler, grief stricken, finds solace in her art. Konstantin Irmen-Tschet (1902–1977) photographed the tearjerker, which screened at the 86th Street Garden Theatre in late 1937.

Erich Waschneck and the petite blonde Renate Müller (1906–37) collaborated one final time in *Eskapade*, produced by Tobis, a pro–Polish and pro–American spy tale set in prewar Paris and St. Petersburg. Müller plays a Polish agent trying to sneak into czarist Russia to help imprisoned friends. She meets an American (Georg Alexander) and asks for his help. He volunteers his services. She travels on his passport as his wife, but after they cross the border, the Russian-Jewish agent "Rakowsky" (Walter Franck) spots her. Complications follow but the young spy succeeds in her mission: she has an audience with, and receives the help of, the carefully guarded but supportive Grand Duke Ignatieff (Paul Otto). He promises clemency for her compatriots. She and the American return to Poland with the intention of making their fake marriage a real one. *Eskapade* had been made in 1936, when Germany hid its fangs. Also called *Seine offizielle Frau*, it was retitled and released in the U.S. by American Tobis Corp. under an apt Nazi title: *For Her Country's Sake*, in late 1937.

Who could object to a nationalistic film like that one? Or who could object to Waschneck's heartfelt, final film to screen in America? Ufa's mother-love tale *Streit um den Knaben*

Joe (*Strife Over the Boy Joe*, 1937), which screened at the 86th Street Garden near the end of the year, is about boys (Klaus Detlef Sierck and Eberhard Itzenplitz) who might have been exchanged at birth, in far off Cairo. When Jo and Erwin reach their thirteenth birthdays, they leave home in an effort to uncover their real German identities. The German mothers (Maria von Tasnady and Lil Dagover) panic. But the tale ends happily, for the boys turn out to be blood relations.

German blood is *the* element in the Heimat film *Das Schweigen im Walde* (*The Silence of the Forest*, 1937), directed by Hans Deppe, which makes reference to three German cultural works. As the title of a famous painting by the late nineteenth-century artist Arnold Böcklin, the film touched the sentimental nerve of filmgoers aware of the era, if not the artist's literary painting. Based on the novel of the same name by Ludwig Ganghofer, the sound film was a remake of the popular 1929 silent produced in Germany by Universal's Jewish-owned subsidiary Deutsche Universal and directed by the German-Jew Wilhelm Dieterle. In the Nazi rendition, which screened in the U.S. in late 1937, even an aristocrat has a place in the new Germany—if he's hiding his loathsome identity and willing to risk his life for German womanhood. In the silent forests of the Bavarian Alps a nobleman going incognito, Heinz von Ettingen (Paul Richter), saves the young Lo Petri (Hansi Knoteck) twice: once from a desperate forester, Toni Mezegger (Hermann Erhardt), and later, heroically, from a spectacular forest fire. Conversely, the young, strong forester Pepi Praxmaler (Gusti Stark-Gestettenbaur) is the prototypical German male in his courtship of an attractive country maiden, Burgl Brentlinger (played by the "dark beauty in the rough," Käthe Merk).

By contrast, a homeland film of a different people appeared on U.S. screens at the end of 1937. Joseph Green's Yiddish comedy *Der Purimspieler* (*The Purim Jester*, 1936), which had been produced in Warsaw, offers an endearing look at the joys and sorrows in a village in Polish Galicia, in pre–World War I. Its highlights are scenes of a Purim festival and wisecracks by the head shoemaker whose daughter is the heroine of the tale. "Many old-fashioned Ghetto types," wrote *Variety* (December 8, 1937), "give the film a different type of cast from that to which American audiences are accustomed. Bearded types of Jews, with their interesting faces in the supporting cast ... lend the picture charm."

The Nazis would later use footage from this film for diabolical purposes. Fritz Hippler incorporated scenes into his pseudo-documentary Hetzfilm—"smear film"—called *Der Ewige Jude* (1940).

1938

The Circle of German Stars

Early 1938 afforded American filmgoers a chance to become familiar with the newer stars in German films. They were the non-refugees: those who hadn't been removed, the performers who hadn't fled, and others who were doing their part to keep the German film industry afloat. The film to see was *Es leuchten die Sterne* (*The Circle of the Stars*, 1937–38), an American Tobis release at the 86th Street Garden Theatre with music by Leo Leux and directed by Hans H. Zerlett. The Nazi film was a remake of Tobis's Weimar production *Die Grosse Sehnsucht* (*The Great Yearning*, 1930), which had been directed by the Hungarian Jew Stefan Szekely. When Szekely's film had screened at New York's Vanderbilt Theatre, it was billed with Walter Ruttmann's *Melode der Welt* (*Melody of the World*, 1929), one of Germany's earliest sound films. An impression of the state of the world in 1929, examining similarities and differences in religion, customs, art and entertainment from around the world, Ruttmann's film was likened to a symphony. The *New York Times* (October 8, 1931) noted, "It is well calculated to show the essential oneness of humanity, despite the racial differences." In 1938, Zerlett's musical said the opposite.

Es leuchten die Sterne works around the tribulations of a movie-crazed young woman who leaves her job, family, and home to try to make it in Germany's movie colony. It highlights major performers in the German film firmament, along with entertainers from Scandinavia and elsewhere—and says something about the future. Containing a great deal of music and dancing, including the musical revues "Berlin," "The Magic of Films," "Sombrero," The Man of Iron," "Speak out, Grandmother," "Destiny," "Little Mama with Baby," Signs of the Zodiac," and "The Stars Shine," the film reaches its high point in the scenes depicting the march of historical German figures over a bridge connecting the present with eternity—a prediction that the Third Reich will last forever!

The film's cast included La Jana, Carla Rust, Paul Verhoeven, Max Schmeling, Paul Roschberg, Fritjof Mjoen, Vera Bergman, Rudi Godden, Ernst Fritz Fürbringer, Willi Forst, Luis Trenker, Georg Alexander, Lil Dagover, Karl Ludwig Diehl, Käthe Dorsch, Gustav Fröhlich, Heinrich George, Paul Hartmann, Käthe Hildebrand, Paul Hörbiger, Jupp Hussels, Jenny Jugo, Paul Kemp, Wolfgang Liebeneiner, Harry Liedtke, Theo Lingen, Albert Matterstock, Irene von Meyendorff, Hans Moser, Anny Ondra, Harald Paulsen, Hermann Pfeiffer, Johannes Riemann, Ralph Arthur Roberts, Sybille Schmitz, Hans Söhnker, Albrecht Schönhals, S.O. Schöning, Rudolf Schündler, Olga Tschechowa, Luise Ullrich, Grethe Weiser, Ida Wüst, Rudolf Caracciola, Manfred von Brauchitsch, Hermann Lang, Leo Leux, and Paul Linke.

No other Nazi film showcased more Aryan entertainers. Goebbels wrote in his diaries that the film is "good entertainment." It was also clear evidence of the changes that had taken place in German film and society since Germany mandated that Aryanism, rather than talent, led to employment. In the U.S. the reaction was along the lines of what the *New York Times* (May 21, 1938) wrote. "Strange to say," the leading parts are taken by "comparatively new players, while the old-timers have nothing to do but be recognized." After the war, one member of the circle of stars, the beautiful actress Sybille Schmitz, died under mysterious circumstances in 1955.

In 1938, boxing champion Max Schmeling, who was married to Anny Ondra, was an easily recognizable German star—on the screen and off. He had defeated Joe Louis in 1936 and expected to fight James J. Braddock for the World Heavyweight Championship in 1937. Instead, Louis fought Braddock and won. In June after *Es leuchten die Sterne* screened in New York, Schmeling was in Yankee Stadium to face Joe Louis for the title. Schmeling had made his film debut in *Liebe im Ring* (*Love in the Ring*, 1930), produced by the Jewish filmmaker Max Glass, after Schmeling had captured the European heavyweight title in June 1930. In 1938, Casino Film Exchange cashed in on Schmeling's name and the tremendous expectation surrounding the upcoming Schmeling-Louis rematch by releasing, un-subtitled, Carl Lamac's Bavaria production *Gross Reinemachen* (*General Housecleaning*, 1935), co-starring Ondra. She played the head of a squad of maids, capturing the heart of a rich young bachelor (Wolf Albach-Retty). In the film, Mrs. Schmeling was a winner. In the ring at Yankee Stadium that summer, Schmeling would lose to Louis in the first round.

Max Schmeling had access to the highest members of the Nazi regime, including Hitler, who had told Schmeling to call him if the champion needed anything while in America. Schmeling was perhaps the most well known German to travel regularly to America in the mid 1930s. The Nazi regime expected Schmeling to display German superiority. He was a great representative of the master race. In 1936, after Schmeling had defeated Joe Louis in their first match, the regime had made Schmeling a symbol of the new Germany when it circulated Hans H. Zerlett's film *Max Schmeling's Victory—Germany's Victory*. After Schmeling's shocking loss to the black American heavyweight, the Nazis did *not* make a film entitled *Max Schmeling's Defeat—Germany's Defeat*. Rather, the regime dropped Schmeling like a hot potato. No longer the personification of the master race or a moneymaking draw for Germany, Schmeling was ignored—boycotted, in effect—by the Nazis. The regime did what the Anti-Nazi League hadn't been able to do. Ignored, Schmeling (1905–2005) became a simple German soldier during the war.

Leni Riefenstahl's name recognition in America was second to Schmeling's. Director Riefenstahl, at Goebbels' behest, would come to America later in the year to try to improve Germany's image. A spirited, entertaining film from Germany's most famous director—*Olympia*—might do the trick. Before that, a German-language film starring Riefenstahl opened in America: Arnold Fanck's *Der Weisse Rausch* (*The White Intoxication*), released under the title *The Ski Chase*. Featuring ski champion Hannes Schneider opposite Riefenstahl, it was called "timely," by *Variety* (March 30, 1938), "falling in with ice and ski-minded America." Ignored were two important facts. One was that the film had been produced in Austria in 1931. The second was that co-star Schneider, who was Jewish, was arrested when the Nazis marched into Austria while *Der Weisse Rausch* was being shown in America. The score of *Der Weisse Rausch* had come from Jewish composer Paul Dessau, who had composed music for a Hebrew-language documentary about Jews rebuilding farms on barren land in Palestine called *Avodah* (*Work*, 1935). It had been produced in Hungary by refugees from Germany. By the time of Austria's union with Germany, Leni Riefenstahl, one of Fanck's protégés, was in the news for another reason. She had completed work on *Olympia* (1938), and would soon try to market it in America.

Missing from the list in Zerlett's film—aside from the refugees—were the regime's useful directors. They included Riefenstahl; Veit Harlan; Karl Ritter, whose dreadful films alone were said to have been seen by six million Germans between 1936 and 1939; Fritz Hippler; Erich Waschneck; Gustav Ucicky; Karl Hartl; Gustaf Gründgens; Paul Wegener; Carl Boese; Arnold Fanck; and Detlef Sierck. Also missing were the Aryan actors, technicians, and screenwriters who made the films that becalmed a German population aware of the regime's horrors. These film people helped to deflect attention from the slaughter then and later. Their moral relativism contributed to the Holocaust of six million. Some German filmmakers later argued that they "escaped" into film or the theatre, a so-called inner immigration that rightly separated them from the harsh realities of the outside world. But did they really do that? Hadn't they and the German nation become Hitler? Far too many Germans had read his mind, placed themselves in his shoes, and behaved as he did, or as he desired, or ordered. Hitler's actions, sensations, and emotions became theirs. By their actions, inaction, or apparent service to the state, the filmmakers abetted murder. It is kinder, of course, to say that German film people lacked courage. They wanted others to take up arms against Hitler and his henchmen. In effect, their excuse was that they expected the outside world to save them while they, on the inside, enjoyed a privileged existence: life and the chance to make entertaining films. Reams of "apologia" and guarded rationalizations can't cover up the Faustian bargains German filmmakers made in and with Hitler's regime.

One prominent filmmaker who made such a bargain was actor-director Gustaf Gründgens. In 1938, his *Liebe im Gleitflug* (*Love in Stunt Flying*, 1938) was released in the U.S. A tale inspired by the fate of the American Amelia Earhart, it ends happily when the protagonist gives up aviation and settles down. She comes to her senses, choosing hearth and home, like any good German woman. The director starred in the Terra production, along with his wife Marianne Hoppe (1909–2002).

Achieving domesticity is the heart of former German great Paul Wegener's Ufa production *Krach und Glück um Künnemann* (*Row and Joy About Künnemann*, 1936–37), a CFE release in 1938. Here, minor city employee Gustav Künnemann (Will Dohm), disgusted with his lazy and careless spouse (Maria Krahn), finds a 100-mark note. Künnemann lives it up one night with the girls. He has run-ins with all sorts of people, including a couple of crooks calling themselves Lady Elvira (Hilde von Stolz) and the Baron (Harald Paulsen). Having a hand in their capture, Künnemann earns a 500-mark reward. He becomes a hero. More important, his wife is inspired to reform her ways. If women had the will, they could find the way to harmony in Nazi Germany.

In early 1938, a production hailed in Germany as a true *Volksfilm*, a film for the people, opened in the States. Ufa's latest comedy, *Zwei lustige Abenteuer* (*Two Merry Adventurers*), which Karl Hartl directed, starred Hans Albers. Albers represented the epitome of Germanness. He had written to Goebbels in late 1935: "To fulfill my duty to the National Socialist state and in commitment to that state I have broken off my personal relationship with Frau Hansi Burg." His Jewish lover fled to England. In *Zwei lustige Abenteuer*, two so-called private detectives (Albers and Heinz Rühmann) are meeting with little success in their line of work. With little to lose, they decide to go incognito as nineteenth-century British sleuths. Morris Flint (Albers) enjoys posing as Sherlock Holmes; Flint's assistant, Macky McPherson (Rühmann), gets a charge out of being called Dr. Watson. During the 1936 World Exposition in Paris, "Holmes" and "Watson" come to the aid of the Berry sisters (Hansi Knoteck and Marie-Luise Claudius) in their efforts to retrieve rare stamps stolen by "Monsieur Lapin" (Siegfried Schurenberg), a presumed Jew. (The name "Lapin" was a common Jewish surname in northeast Poland and Belarus before the end of World War II.) However, Flint is arrested in the course of his work, on a charge of impersonation. However, a mysterious "laughing man" (Paul Bildt) gets him off the hook. At the climax of the tale, the mysterious stranger reappears. Conan Doyle is *his* name. He tells them, to their astonishment, that Sherlock Holmes never existed. At the same time, Doyle allows Flint to call himself "The Man Who Was Sherlock Holmes." That, it turns out, was the real name of this German film: *Der Mann, der Sherlock Holmes war* (1937).

In 1937, Hans Albers had also been a big hit in Gerhard Lamprecht's *Die Gelbe Flagge* (*The Yellow Flag*), a thriller based on the novel by Fred Andreas that is set aboard a quarantined ship called the *Elmtree*, which lies off the coast of South America, a favorite exotic locale in Nazi productions. The dashing Albers takes on a half-dozen thugs, proves himself a superb ladies' man—especially to Olga Tschechowa, playing an American journalist—and singlehandedly combats a whole raft of cannibals in the heart of the jungle. He lives to tell the tale—although the tale itself, which Americans reviewed in Europe, wasn't released in the States.

The director of *Zwei lustige Abenteuer* had impressed Hitler and Goebbels. In March 1938, Austria became part of the Greater Reich. Goebbels soon thereafter offered Austrian-born Hartl the job of artistic director of the newly created Wien Film. The year 1938 marked Hartl's twentieth year in the industry. He began as assistant director to Alexander Korda, a Jew, in Austria-Hungary. Austrian-born Gustav Ucicky's *Der Zerbrochene Krug* (*The Broken Jug*, 1937) had also impressed Hitler. Der Führer saw it often enough that Goebbels called the film, which Thea von Harbou scripted, Hitler's favorite. In early 1938, American Tobis released it in the States.

It's a comedy about nineteenth-century life, lovers, and bureaucracy in blue-eyed Holland. Based on the one-time classic play by Heinrich von Kleist, the film featured Emil Jannings as a villainous, lustful, and naïve judge who must decide a case about an antique jug whose destruction came at *his* hands. This leads to his ridiculous effort to deceive an investigating magistrate from Utrech. The story begins when the drunken "Adam" (Jannings) breaks into the bedroom of young Eve (Angela Sallöcker). Surprised by her lover, Ruprecht (Paul Dahlke), Adam is beaten, loses his wig, smashes an antique jug, and escapes. When Adam holds court the next day, the first case concerns the broken jug. Adam tries to pin the blame on the lover, but the visiting magistrate is suspicious. The climax comes with the arrival of an old woman bearing the telltale wig, found under Eve's window. Adam flees again—this time the whole village is after him—and he jumps into the river. In the film, Judge "Adam" (Jannings) is bald-headed, club-footed, lascivious, bibulous, and crafty—as unpleasant, and non–German an authority figure as the Nazis ever put on the screen. His subordinate is named "Licht" (Max Gülsdorf) while the honorable, visiting magistrate goes by the name Walter (Friedrich Keyssler).

Proving that even a genocidal butcher could cover his insanity

Emil Jannings under contract to Tobis (1930s).

with laughter, Hitler had another favorite in the popular comedian Weiss Ferdl. Ferdl starred in newly nationalized Tobis's first feature under the Nazi regime, Fred Sauer's pseudo-medical tale *Der Lachdoktor* (*The Laugh Doctor*, 1937). The plot centers on the exploitation of the sick by a quack. The man behind it is "Krämer Neidinger" (Josef Eichheim), who is identified as a crooked businessman. Dr. Magius (Paul Heidemann), the director of a Bavarian sanitarium, allows Neidinger to sell a cure-all to his patients. However, Dr. Kugler (Ferdl), a country doctor, is against it but his motives are questioned. His assistant, Dr. Lore Lenze (Carla Rust), helps Kugler derail the whole scheme. When they discover that Magius is not a physician and, therefore unable to make medical judgments, the game is up. Lore then marries Magius—who has seen the error of his ways.

Marriage between opposites is the theme in a film that scriptwriter Johannes Lippl directed for Ufa, called *Der Schimmelkrieg in der Holledau* (1935), which screened at the Garden Theatre this year. Here what's called a "merry" war has been going on between the villages of Hasselbach and Banzing for 30 years, since 1862. The cause of it all was the theft of a white horse from one of the villages by a man named Ziberl-Toni (Gustav Waldau). Burgomasters from the two sides have an idea: to restore peace, they suggest that a male from one side marry a female from the other side. At the end Anderl (Richard Haussler) sets off to work, while his new wife Anna (Heli Finkenzeller) heads home. This film reflected a 1933 Nazi decree. Married women could work only *inside* the home. Women were keepers of the near-sacred hearth, away from desks and decision-making. "Double earners" became a Nazi term of opprobrium.

In a similar thematic mode, Hans Deppe's *Gewitter im Mai* (*Storms in May*, 1938), also by Ufa, begins with an ocean storm and ends with the German ideal of a noble rescue during turbulent weather in the Bavarian mountains. When the hero's life is imperiled in scaling a peak to prove that he is still a mountaineer, it is his unselfish rival who comes to his aid. Between these natural outbursts come a few mental tempests by the jealous blacksmith Domini (Ludwig Schmid-Wildy), when he realizes his best friend, Poldi (Viktor Staal), has caught the eye of the village belle, Dorie (Hansi Knoteck). But, as in most Nazi films, honor and true loyalty among male competitors win out. "There are no real villains in this pictorially striking piece," wrote the *New York Times* (March 5, 1938) when the film screened at the Garden Theatre. Other films with the same professed values expressed dramatically within different storylines filled the era. But in 1938 in Germany and in Austria, there was no merriment for Jews. There were plenty of surprises, however. In March, Göring warned Jews to leave Austria: the Nuremberg Laws were soon to be applied there. In the "June action" (*Juniaktion*), Hitler ordered the destruction of Munich's Great Synagogue. That was followed by the destruction of synagogues in Nuremberg and Dortmund. In July, German Jews were issued special identity cards: most Jews could only fantasize about impersonation. In September Franz Stuckart, the man who had drafted the Nuremberg Laws, used the phrase "final solution" (Endlösung). That month, Jewish lawyers were forbidden to practice in Germany. In November, after the devastating economic and social upheavals of Kristallnacht, Göring announced that he favored Madagascar as a Jewish homeland. In December, France and Germany signed a friendship treaty, which included collaboration in film.

More to the point for hardcore German flag wavers than the previous entertaining German films was *Der Katzensteg* (*The Catwalk*, 1937), a feature film from Tobis. Its theme is of disgrace, of washing off with one's own blood the sins of the father against the blood and soil of his country. Based on Hermann Sudermann's story—Gerhard Lamprecht directed a rendition in Weimar Germany in 1927—*Der Katzensteg* was directed by Fritz Peter Buch. Screened at the Casino Theatre, it stresses patriotism, demonstrating that betrayal of one's country has consequences for more than just the betrayer. There are also consequences, says the film, for those who assist him, and for his descendents. During 1813 to 1815, when Prussia is under the thumb of Napoleon, a Prussian aristocrat, Werner (Hannes Stelzer), breaks with his pro–French father, Count Schranden (Fritz Reiff). At the fade-out, when Werner is riding at the head of Prussian forces heading to take on Napoleon at Waterloo, he still carries the stigma of his father's ignominious deed, which had led to the deaths of hundreds of Prussians. Prussians referred to him as the traitor's son because the old count had forced the village maid Regine (Brigitte Horney) to betray her German countrymen by guiding Napoleon's forces over the catwalk. It is *her* heroic death—not Werner's actions—that symbolizes sacrifice and ultimate triumph over the enemy. The film has true Nazi moments. One episode depicts Prussians forced to bury an old man who had sided with the French; another is the stoning of a pro–German maid for "treason and immorality"; and the third is the saber slashing of a Prussian soldier's face. The film also had the "usual good musical score," by Walter Gronostay, "slightly on the military side," wrote *Variety* (January 26, 1938), which "should please Teutonic ears." Goebbels considered this film, which he named winner of a National Film Prize, a harbinger of the future and a war education film along the lines of *Urlaub auf Ehrenwort* (1937) and *Ziel in den Wolken* (1938).

Tobis and Buch were also responsible for *Die Warschauer Zitadelle* (*The Warsaw Citadel*, 1937), a concocted tale of Poland's resistance against Russian domination in the nineteenth century. Russia's control of Warsaw and the old kingdom is symbolized by the czar's secret police official, "Colonel Korniloff" (Paul Hartmann), and by his adjutant, the Jewish-named "Botkin" (Peter Elsholtz). The oppressed Poles are led by Konrad Welgorski (Werner Hinz), a student, and by his girlfriend, Anna Losatzka (played by Vienna-born actress and scriptwriter Viktoria von Ballasko, 1909–1976). The drama depicts leftist Poles opposed by conservative Poles; a Polish student shot on a tower after he unfurls the Polish flag; and Polish prisoners sent to Siberia in cattle cars. The film also contains a rarity for a Nazi production that wasn't blatantly anti–Semitic—a brief depiction of a rabbi (Fritz Hube). This film screened un-subtitled at the Casino Theatre as, hypocritically, *Um Freiheit und Liebe* (*For Freedom and Love*). The Nazis again defended radicals and the oppressed of an earlier era. *Variety* (February 16, 1938), however, said the film "cannot be construed as Nazi propaganda although the theme is unfavorable to the steppe state." History didn't allow a completely happy ending for this tale. At the conclusion only a few Polish patriots head to liberty as a result of a far-fetched anti–Russian coup. Omitted from the tale is actual Polish independence, which didn't happen until 1919—thanks to Germany's defeat in the First World War.

Karl Ritter's name and Germany of the First World War were back in lights in New York when *Urlaub auf Ehrenwort* (*Furlough on Word of Honor*, 1937) was shown there in early 1938, only a few months after its successful Berlin premiere. The tale begins in August 1918. Seventy German soldiers led by a nineteen-year-old officer have a six-hour layover in Berlin before their transport from the eastern to the western front arrives. Since some of the men are from Berlin, they ask the officer for a few hours' leave. This is against orders, but their officer relents. He gives them a pass on a promise. "I have your word of honor," he says, "that you will return and fulfill your duty in this critical hour of the fatherland. The unit is counting on you—and so is Germany." The heart of the film deals with the temptations that assail the men and threaten the call to duty: family reunions, painful separations, scenes of distressed civilians, as well as socialists, and anti-war agitators who are called "little more than the scum of the earth." The officer, nervously biting his lips, awaits the soldiers' return. As the train is about to depart, all save one of his men are back. They include a young composer who prefers to die in battle for an already defeated Germany rather than live for the premiere of his symphony, success, and a career; a lonely soldier in love with a lonely young girl; and a left-wing intellectual who rejects the comradeship of fellow revolutionaries and his "red" girlfriend for the "real comradeship of fighting men." At the last second, the last soldier makes a mad dash for the train. He's

Ingeborg Theek and Fritz Kampers, in *Urlaub auf Ehrenwort.*

left his young wife to join the group. The situation is saved, and so is the new Germany, with men like these.

Urlaub auf Ehrenwort featured Käthe Haack (1892–1986), whose career began in 1915 and ended in the 1980s, and Ingeborg Theek (b. 1917), whose likeness to a young Greta Garbo set her film career in motion. Ritter's film, which was scored by Ernst Erich Buder, earned a "special recommendation" at the Venice Film Festival of 1938. The guiding force behind the film was Goebbels, implementing the screenplay from Charles Klein. The Nazis' themes of self-sacrifice beyond all bounds and the postponement or abandonment of personal happiness couldn't be stressed often enough, especially through the moral compass of World War I. Goebbels, Ufa, Klein, and Ritter had teamed to remind Germans and others of the main lessons from the First World War, as stated by a soldier in one of Ritter's war education films: "We soldiers are dying for our country while you drink, hold meetings, and make love." *Urlaub auf Ehrenwort* was shown in Philadelphia in April 1940 after bedroom scenes were excised.

Projecting in *Mein Kampf,* Hitler speculated about the meaning of the Great War: "For a thousand years to come nobody will dare to speak of heroism without recalling the German Army of the World War. And then from the dim past will emerge the immortal vision of those solid ranks of steel helmets that never flinched and never faltered. And as long as Germans live they will be proud to remember that these men were the sons of their forefathers."

Director Ritter, who had been a front-line officer in the First World War, loathed Weimar Germany because of what he called its Semitic parliament that was ruled by the "November criminals," who betrayed the fighting men of a glorious Germany. Ritter's ideas paralleled Hitler's. Ritter said, "My films deal with the unimportance of the individual—all that is personal must be given up for our cause." The theme of serving the fatherland was central to Ufa's *Unternehmen Michael*, yet another virulent film by Ritter, also designed by Walter Rohrig and with music by Herbert Windt, which opened in New York in early 1938. It had premiered in Berlin at the new year, commemorating the twentieth anniversary of a heroic German battle in the First World War. On March 21, 1918, German forces had launched their "Michael" offensive in France, hoping to break through the Allied lines before American reinforcements arrived. It was later remembered as the First Battle of the Somme. *Unternehmen Michael* presents a new kind of fighter: the German soldier of utter self-sacrifice to the cause. In the Nazi film, Heinrich George and Mathias Wieman are officers in this period of the German spring offensive. The military situation is dire, because the enemy—the British—holds an outpost in the village of Beaurevoir. Storm troopers are to be sent to wipe them out, but the night before the attack, their commanding officer is injured. An officer of the general staff, tired of sitting behind a desk and barking out orders, volunteers for command. He and his men capture the town, but soon find themselves surrounded. The question becomes, Should the Germans surrender? Some of the men propose vengeance and "heroic death" (*Heldentod*). In order to achieve victory, German officer Hegenau (Paul Otto) orders his artillery to shell the village just as the British enter it. The bombardment also kills their fellow Germans in what becomes known as Operation Michael. The dying officer's last words are, "We shall not be judged by the grandeur of our victory but by the depth of our sacrifice." In Berlin, at the film's premiere, it was rumored that the Wehrmacht's high-ranking officers were so shocked by the ending that it set off a heated controversy between the army and Goebbels. Ritter answered the army brass, saying, "I want to show the German youth that senseless, sacrificed death has its moral value."

Hitler had given *his* opinion in *Mein Kampf*. "In July 1917 we set foot for the second time on what we regarded as sacred soil. Were not our best comrades at rest here, some of them little more than boys—the soldiers who had rushed into death for their country's sake, their eyes glowing with enthusiastic love."

In the United States, the critical response to *Unternehmen Michael* was to downplay the call to death. The *New York Times* (May 14, 1938) wrote: "While the war is not prettified, its horrors are not emphasized." After World War II, Germany saw it differently: it banned the film from distribution.

In a frighteningly effective partnership, Ritter directed several other films for Goebbels. Director Ritter, wrote Goebbels in his diaries, "makes nationalistic points with a lack of inhibition that would make others blush." Ritter's ... *Über alles in der Welt* (*Above All Else in the World*), which Ufa produced and released in Berlin in March 1941, is a good example of what Goebbels meant. This is one of the most powerful of Goebbels' war education films. It's the only one financed by his ministry that depicts all the fronts involving German fighting forces in the first years of the First World War. The theme of "home is calling" in wartime is emphasized through a string of episodes that make up the tale. In the first episode, a German journalist in Paris at the outbreak of war is arrested and sent to a concentration camp. To mitigate his sentence, he agrees to broadcast anti–German propaganda for the so-called League of Human Rights as well as the British Secret Service. The league representative is depicted as a mean-spirited and cowardly Jew named Leo Samek (Oskar Sema). But during an air raid, the German escapes and reaches the German lines. At about the same time, a troupe of German singers, trapped in London, are arrested. Three members who agree to join the Free Austrian Forces are sent to France, but during the selfsame air raid they too escape to German lines. Another story involves the crew of a German tanker in Spanish waters that has been captured by the British cruiser *Arethusa*. When a U-boat sinks the British cruiser, Germans save Germans. Further episodes depict a Hinkel 111 plane that makes a forced landing behind Polish lines. A Dornier 17 under heavy fire then rescues its crew. When a German survey plane over France is hit, its crew bails out and then crosses the Alps to Italy. At the climax, German fighter planes take on 45 British Vickers-Wellington bombers. Germany's enemy loses all but eight planes, the victorious Germans displaying their military might for all to see. Although Goebbels named ... *Über alles in der Welt* winner of a National Film Prize, American critics in Germany managed to ignore this film.

Another Ritter-Goebbels film that American critics in Germany missed was *Kadetten* (*Cadets*, 1939–41), which was produced by Ufa, starring Mathias Wieman (1902–1969) and Klaus Detlef Sierck. It wasn't released in Germany until December 1941, when German troops were deep inside Soviet territory and the U.S. and Germany were declared enemies. But that's not to say that the film was unavailable for viewing by westerners in Berlin. This film hints at the possibility of Germany's defeat—and then uses that as a motive for propaganda, making a humiliated Germany the "moral victor." The film harkens back to 1760, when Frederick the Great battles the Austrians at Torgau. A Russian advance on Berlin forces three companies of the Kadettenkorps to retreat to Fort Spandou. A fourth company, made up of boys aged 9–12, however, has been left behind and is taken prisoner by Russians commanded by a Prussian, Captain von Tzülow. In the custody of Cossacks, the boys are treated inhumanly. Their suffering is depicted as beyond imagination, but they unite in a determined effort to demonstrate Prussian superiority to Slavic barbarians. The Russians, they believe, are only temporary conquerors. The captain is impressed with their bearing and pride. Calling them his Prussian blood brothers, he helps them slip away to an abandoned fort. The Russians, however, discover their location, and demand Captain von Tzülow's surrender. He gives himself up, but before he dies he manages to kill the Russian leader. Prussian hussars then arrive to fortify the fort and save the boys. The former renegade Prussian has become a true German hero.

A Latin-based German war film was also ignored in the Western press before the U.S. entered World War II. In 1938–39, photographers Allgeier, Benitz, and Hans Ertl accompanied director Arnold Fanck to Chile to shoot *Ein Robinson* (*A Robinson Crusoe*). In the 1914–18 war, the cruiser *Dresden* sinks near Juan Fernandez, off the coast of Chile. The crew makes it back to Germany, but one survivor, Carl Ohlsen (Herbert A. E. Böhme), is so disgusted with postwar Weimar conditions that he turns right back to what he calls "primitive" Chile. Anything is better than living in Jewish Weimar Germany. Ohlsen assumes a Robinson Crusoe existence for the next 11 years. On hearing of the Nazis' rise to power, however, and that the modernized cruiser *Dresden* is within reach, he knows what to do. He crosses the mountains of Patagonia and joins the new German Navy. The shores of Hitler's Germany are a welcome relief. This Bavaria production about one man's struggle to remain true to the cause of Germany's ideology—Nazism—premiered in Germany in April 1940.

Ufa's *Zu Neuen Ufern* (*To New Shores*, 1937), directed by Detlef Sierck, is an attack on another easy target: mid-nineteenth century British law. This film did screen in America. Zarah Leander, whom Germany touted as a "new Garbo," especially after her performance in Bolváry's *Premiere* (1936), played the protagonist Gloria Vane, of the London stage. She assumes the responsibility of having forged a check to save her lover, British officer Albert Finsbury (Willy Birgel), from a prison sentence. She gets seven years in Paramatta, a penal colony in Australia, where it so happens that her British lover becomes the aide-de-camp to the governor. Gloria meets Henry Hoyer (Viktor Staal), a farmer who falls in love with her. Although she sings, "I am standing in the rain and waiting for you," dedicated to her former lover, Gloria marries Henry, and is released from jail. And when Finsbury finds out that she had taken the rap for him back in London and that she no longer loves him, he takes his own life. The film contains a mock can-can at the Sydney Casino. The music is by Ralph Benatzky (1887–1957). Simulated scenes of Sydney, has mirrors galore, and packs in strong emotions all contribute to the all's-right-with-the-world ending.

Warner Bros. considered producing an English-language version of *Zu neuen Ufern*, especially after Sierck's German film was shown in New York in 1938 and in Los Angeles—thanks to Frank Ferenz of Continental Films—in January 1940. Nothing came of the idea nor did anything materialize after Sierk found a haven in America before the outbreak of World War II. By then he was Douglas Sirk, living freely in a nation he would come to reject. In Hollywood, Sirk reluctantly, as he recalled, turned to directing an independent film financed by German-Jewish émigrés Seymour Nebenzal and Emil Ludwig. After being stuck in Hollywood (as opposed to being stuck in Germany) as a director of B pictures, he accepted his first major film assignment in six years. Sirk re-shot some scenes for a film MGM had purchased from Producers Releasing Corp. The film's main character is a man Sirk had known: Reinhard Heidrich, the number two man in the SS. Released as *Hitler's Madman* (1943), that film was the first non–MGM film the studio distributed, because Louis B. Mayer liked it.

In 1959, Sirk returned to Germany, biting the hand that fed him and rejecting the nation that had given him sanctuary, declaring, "I had had enough. I had outgrown this kind of picture making which was typical of Hollywood in the fifties and of American society, too, which tolerated only the play that pleases, not the thing that disturbs the mind." In the 1930s, in Germany, Sierck couldn't bring himself to direct "the thing that disturbs the mind." Rather, his work had kept him on good terms with the Nazis. In Germany in the years 1963 to 1969, working as a theater director and as Detlef Sierck once again, he was free to tackle disturbing plays by Rostand, Ionesco, Shakespeare, Schiller, Molière, and Tennessee Williams.

Director Detlef Sierck had a son when he lived under Hitler. Klaus Detlef Sierck (1925–1944) was the child of Detlef Sierck and the theatrical performer Lydia Brincken. Their marriage lasted from 1924 to 1928. Klaus served the Reich in film and the army after his father fled Germany with a second wife, Hilda Jary, in the late 1930s. Klaus acted in a dozen films between 1937 and 1942. His major starring role was in Viktor de Kowa's Hitler Youth film *Kopf hoch, Johannes* (*Chin Up, Johannes*, 1941). Produced by Majestic Film on Goebbels' orders and costarring Dorothy Wieck, one of Hitler's favorite actresses, and Otto Gebühr, it was about a young German who grows up abroad but who comes to appreciate the discipline and comradeship that take hold in the Third Reich. Germany banned this production after the war. Klaus Sierck died on the Russian front. Dorothea Wieck (1908–1986), born in Switzerland, later starred opposite Heinrich George and Olga Tschechowa in Herbert Maisch's hysterical

Douglas Sirk (b. Sierck) in Hollywood, 1940s.

Andreas Schlüter (1941–1942). Rumors of her death during the war were premature. In 1973, German cinema awarded Wieck an honorary prize.

Detlef Sierck's star performer Zarah Leander had been introduced to German-language film through Bolváry's *Premiere* (1936)—an Austrian production not released in the U.S. It was a thriller about a murder during an opening night at a revue. *Premiere*'s choreography emulated Busby Berksley's Hollywood style, and featured an American, Floyd du Pont, as a dance choreographer. Leander's flirting and her sexy look in that production suited her more than did most of the roles that followed. Leander's most well-known German film is the Goebbels-backed musical *Die Grosse Liebe* (*The Great Love*, 1942), produced by Ufa, directed by Rolf Hansen, and costarring Viktor Staal (1909–1982), Paul Hörbiger, and Hans Schwarz Jr. It is set during the first years of World War II. The protagonists are an air force officer and his wife, a cabaret singer. Anxious about their relationship, the singer seeks a divorce when her husband suddenly vanishes. She then learns about Germany's attack on the Soviet Union, and that her husband, injured afterwards, had been in on the planning. She rushes to his side, realizing that a man's first duty is to the fatherland and that their happiness must wait. Leander sings the famous Nazi hits "Davon geht die Welt nicht unter" ("That Won't Be the End of the World") and "Es wird einmal ein Wunder geschehn" ("Some Time There'll Be a Miracle"). (This theme also resonates in Arthur Maria Rabenalt's *Fronttheater*, 1942, produced by Terra when Germany was at war with America. German women have supporting roles to play, as depicted by an actress who renounces her career while her husband is fighting and sacrificing for the Third Reich. Germany banned Rabenalt's film after the war.)

Before Detlef Sierck left Germany, he directed a pseudo-medical drama called *Die Heimat Ruft* (*Home Is Calling*), which the infamous Gerhard Menzel scripted and which has music by composer Lothar Brühne (1900–1958). What does the scriptwriter of *Morgenrot*, *Flüchtlinge*, and *Robert Koch* (1939) wish to tell us? He stresses the superiority, fighting spirit, and victory of the Nordic race and its principles; and the inferiority, corruption, and confusion of "demoplutocratic" Latin Americans. Zarah Leander played Astree Sternhjelm, a Swede who hears the famous number "La Habanera" while in Puerto Rico, and stays. She marries the powerful, handsome, and jealous bullfighter-landowner Don Pedro (Ferdinand Marian). After ten years, however, only one thing holds them together: their young son. Then Sven (Karl Martell), a former lover of hers, arrives on the island. He's depicted as a nosey Swedish physician seeking to solve the mystery of a deadly local fever—which has stumped even people from the Rockefeller Institute after eight years' effort. "Americans are so lax," say the islanders. Don Pedro knows that if rumors of the malady spread, panic will kill the market for the island's produce. It helps that Don Pedro has the island's governor and hospital officials under his thumb. The local prefect is depicted as easily corrupted, and tied up financially with the plutocratic class, which suppresses the wellbeing of the locals. Of course, the Nazis picture Latin Americans as savage, naïve, stupidly funny, uncontrolled in their emotions, and irresponsible. They are characterized as "not even Spanish, only dirty Caribbeans." Don Pedro, the chief representative of the country's plutocrats, is beside himself with anger when he learns that his wife plans to return to Sweden. The reason is that Astree longs for Nordic forests and snow. "I perish in this hell," she says of the island. In effect, Astree is nothing but a sweet snowflake from the far North who is melting away in the wretched heat and wicked politics of Latin America. She gets out through a stroke of luck: Don Perdo is stricken by the fever whose remedy he himself ordered destroyed. Blatantly racist, the film screened in the United States—although under the title *La Habanera* (1937). The *New York Times* (July 9, 1938) noted, "When *American* motion picture producers turn out films having to do with epidemics, graft and governmental inefficiency in foreign countries, they almost invariably locate the action in some imaginary country." Ufa and the truth-seeking film people of the Third Reich had no qualms about placing the action on a real American possession and expressing their attitudes about "greasy" Latins. It's not inconceivable that the Nazis hoped to stir up a bit of trouble on the democratic island, since they could have chosen other locations as appropriate settings for tropical adventure and savage glamour.

Other Nazi films set in Latin territory that screened in the States included Erich Waschneck's *Zwischen Hamburg und Haiti* (*Between Hamburg and Haiti*, 1939), Ufa's drama about German plantation owner Henry Brinkman (Gustav Knuth) who's in love with Anna Wittstock (Gisela Uhlen, 1919–2007), even though she's had a illegitimate child with unscrupulous "Melchior Schlömpp" (Walter Franck), alias "Larsen," and fled to Central America. Others were Robert Oelbermann's two-reel Ufa documentary *Im Lande der Inca, Maya, und Aztekan* (1934–35); Hans Helfrtiz's two-reel Ufa documentary *Guatemala* (1938–39); and Karl Anton's *Der Stern von Rio* (*The Star of Rio*, 1940), produced by Tobis.

In the Land of the Incas, Mayas, and Aztecs and *Guatemala* are travelogues written by Felix Lampe. Since the indigenous people depicted would not have been willing to brandish swastikas for the camera, the Nazis use a narrator in these films to get their points across. It's the commentator who has the task of twisting the visual in the desired direction. It's what he says and how he says it that has the dramatic effect. *In the Land of the Incas, Mayas, and Aztecs* begins in Peru. The Indians are described (by Theodor Mühlen) as having been suppressed by imperialistic forces since the early sixteenth century and as "living under rather modest conditions," with "the sun-maidens of the time of the Incas ... now converted into nuns." In the Yucatan, says the narrator, "after the domination by the Spanish the old Maya culture was forgotten; neglect and dissolution set in." And in Mexico, the Cathedral of Mexico City "stands on Aztec soil" while the "Aztecs have become tradesman, policeman, and ... bootblacks." *Guatemala* is set up as an expedition by auto and on horseback from the coastal lowlands to the mountains. The point is to make filmgoers believe that the local government can't care for the people or the land. Consequently, "something" should be changed and "somebody" should have the right to develop the culture and the people's wellbeing.

These pseudo-sympathetic propaganda films suggest that the Nazis had something bigger in mind: Nazi penetration into the region for the greater good. They address three audiences: Germans at home, Nazis abroad, and groups and individuals who are susceptible to Nazi thinking and influence. The same trio would soon be the target audience for the Nazis' hardcore cinematic depiction of Jews.

The fictionalized detective-thriller *Der Stern von Rio* makes similar points. Here the action, which involves a stolen diamond, shuttles between fabulous Rio de Janeiro and Amsterdam. La Jana stars as the hot-blooded but loving Aryan dancer Concha who can't wait to get her hands on a great diamond. She easily falls prey to seduction, since diamonds are a girl's best friend. A South American miner (who steals a diamond for La Jana) plans to give it to her, believing in the old superstition that giving a girl a diamond assures her fidelity. He and his people are depicted as harmless children, reacting to jewels like children and savages, thus not entirely responsible for their actions. The diamond, called the "Star of Rio," actually belongs to Concha's lover Don Felipe, who takes it to Amsterdam. There it disappears, and Concha is accused of stealing it. An investigating detective discovers that her guitarist Jacobo had made off with it.

The South American locale, in point of fact, serves as stock material in the depiction of materialism, exoticism, and colonialism. The real nationalistic emotion and the centerpiece of the tale are in La Jana's homeland. The Nazis' depiction of native peoples and Latin Americans, via fiction films and documentaries, can be seen as an effort by Hitler to make the world

Opposite: Scene from *Zwischen Hamburg und Haiti.*

a better place. Was anybody in the West surprised that the Nazis' open antipathy in film towards Jews was not far behind, if not already in the works? Shockingly, the answer is yes.

Dreiklang (*Triad*, 1938), which Hans Hinrich (1903–1974) directed and Ufa produced, is based on Sierck's screenplay. It screened un-subtitled at the Garden Theatre, which showed all of Sierck's films from Nazi Germany. It centers on Albert von Möller (Paul Hartmann) and his son Ulrich (Rolf Möbius). Both of them are in love with the same woman, Cornelia Contarini (Lil Dagover) who is spending time in a small German town. Albert is depicted as a vigorous, veteran German officer who plans to take her to South America. But in the climax he is killed in a duel with a man whom Cornelia had rejected: a jealous (Jewish) banker named "Henckelberg" (Carl Günther). Having pledged never to reveal what has happened to his father, Ulrich tells Cornelia that Albert decided to rejoin the army. She sails for South America, alone and away from the homeland. The son stays in the fatherland. Goebbels wrote that the patriotic melodrama, which takes place in 1910, was "decent in approach and outstanding in atmosphere."

Critical commentary noted that *Dreiklang* had not "succumbed to the Hollywood influence so apparent in many recent German productions," meaning that the tale doesn't end well, "although suggestions of the Prussian military machine creep into the film," wrote *Variety* (June 27, 1938). It called Möbius "one of best of the younger generation of Teuton movie actors." German star Lil Dagover (1897–1980), who was born Dutch, was discovered by Jewish director Robert Wiene. She appeared in his *The Cabinet of Dr. Caligari* (1919) and in prestigious silent films by Lang and Murnau. In 1931 Dagover made a film in Hollywood but rose to prominence during the Nazi years. A friend of Hitler, she received the War Merits Cross in 1944. Her career continued unabated in postwar West Germany.

Hinrich's followup film, which also screened at the Garden Theatre in 1938, was Ufa's *Zwischen den Eltern* (*Between the Parents*, 1937–1938), which Eva Leidmann scripted. Trouble starts when the seemingly happily married research physician Hans Ravenborg (Willy Fritsch) strays from his fireside and from the bed of his blonde wife Inge (Jutta Freybe). The other woman is brunette journalist (and former colleague) "Lisa Brinkmann" (Gustl Huber) who, although the film doesn't say so, *could* be Jewish. After Hans is gone for an entire night, Inge doesn't quite give up on her marriage. Depicted as the source of German character, she has sacrificed her medical studies on the altar of motherhood. "You should have stayed in our profession," a professor once remarked to her. The meaning of her question to him about the impact that would have on her son—"And my Peter?"—meshes with Nazi ideology. Thus, Inge rewrites her husband's research paper on an epidemic, hoping it will make him famous. But when the research guinea pigs upon which the paper is based suddenly die, Hans's reputation appears to be in tatters. Inge, however, stands by her man. Later it's discovered that Lisa, who had once "stayed in America," had killed the animals in order to get a scoop. At that point, Hans understands what his wife and her steadfast support mean to him and their family. Lisa, who made it clear earlier that she's not interested in children, says at the end, "Perhaps I have to change and become a real woman." The way the film's female protagonists are contrasted implied the Nazi female ideal: the blonde and excellent mother-housewife who is the source of German character as opposed to the other woman uninterested in family, hearth, and home.

George Jacoby's Ufa-produced *Gasparone* (1937) featured a real woman: Marika Rökk. Sleuthing and intrigue take center stage, so to speak, along with her typical dancing and singing. Released in the U.S. in 1938, only months after its Berlin premiere, *Gasparone* updated Nazi-favorite Karl Millöker's 1884 Austrian operetta. It starts with an apparent group of robbers in a woodland setting who turn out to be modern dancing girls, led by Ita (Rökk) singing "Ja, die Frauen sind gefährliche" ("Yes, women are dangerous"). Later, the musical revolves around the zany police pursuit of a (female) robber named Gasparone—the point being that there is no such person—so that the real culprit, Ita's uncle, Massaccio (Oskar Sima), can smuggle contraband coffee. At the conclusion, Ita can marry Sindolfo (Heinz Schorlemmer) while the handsome Erminio (Johannes Heesters), who's not the outlaw many took him for, carries off the Countess Carlotta (Edith Schollwer). Rökk (1913–2004) was on her way to becoming a major star in the Third Reich. Variety (January 1938), writing from Berlin, noted that Rökk was "stocked with the goods" in this film, which costarred Dutch-born, Nazi-favorite Heesters, just as German troops were being welcomed into Austria. Jacoby has "made a sure bet of a pic for the Fatherland," wrote *Variety*, "as well as surrounding countries where German is the official commercial language ... Germany has reached a high water mark with this picture." Hitler called Rökk "My little Hungarian," according to Goebbels.

Tragic love was the name of the game in Géza von Bolváry's *Zauber der Boheme* (*Charm of La Boheme*, 1937), an Austrian-German operetta scripted by Alfred Gerasch (1877–1955) and Ernst Marischka that played at New York's World Cinema and Chicago's World Playhouse. Based on Puccini's opera, with music by Robert Stolz, it starred Marta Eggerth as the modern woman who strives to get her lover (Jan Kiepura) a shot at opera stardom. Employing the wheel-within-a-wheel formula, the tale ends with the death of Denise (Eggerth) on stage. Frank S. Nugent of the *New York Times* (March 19, 1938) lamented that Vienna "has enough grief as it is without manufacturing it in its studios." But Mae Tinée of the *Chicago Tribune* (May 7, 1938) praised the film as "a picture that should have universal appeal. It plays on heartstrings from opening to closing curtain." The theme of a woman sacrificing for the greater good resurfaced in Viktor Janson's Austrian romance *Rendezvous in Wien* (1935–36), which screened at the 86th Street Garden Theatre in 1938. It pushes the idea of woman as helpmate when a mother and daughter launch the career of a young composer. Franz Lenhardt (Wolf Albach-Retty) is talented but impoverished. In love with true-blue Gusti (Magda Schneider), Franz would like to support her in the manner to which she is accustomed but he can't seem to make ends meet. Gusti and her aunt (Adele Sandrock) pull a few strings to ensure Franz's success. The film's distractions come from the character named "Marschner" (Leo Slezak), a presumed Jew, who is depicted as a self-important singer, and by "Percy Poole" (George Alexander), who is portrayed as a libidinous music publisher who finally prints Franz's work.

Eva, das Fabriksmädel (*Eva, the Factory Girl*) screened at the Garden Theatre three years after its completion, preaching responsibility, fairness, and fair play. A devil-may-care young heir, Georg von Hochheim (Hans Söhnker) takes on the project of putting a failing porcelain factory back on its feet. In order to get a bird's eye view of its operations, he poses as a lowly worker—and then he meets the lovely factory worker Eva (Magda Schneider). Status, the film says, is of little importance when it comes to matters of the heart. An Austrian production directed by Johannes Riemann and with music by Franz Lehar, the film was called a "younger generation picture" by the *New York Times* (January 8, 1938), meaning it apparently contained little propaganda. CFE's 1938 release of Georg Jacoby's *Husaren, heraus!* (*Hussar, Out!*, 1937) is a comedy of slapstick stunts, cavalry uniforms, pretty faces, and a hen-pecked husband. Called *Liebesregiment* in Austria, it featured Prussian soldiers and the music of composer Robert Stolz. CFE re-released it in summer 1941. Yet another German film that apparently helped ease alarm about the Nazis was Joe Stöckel's *Der Etappenhase* (*The Rabbit*, 1937), from Astra Film-Berlin. Conflict over which solders will get to enjoy a rabbit dinner concludes when some unlucky German soldiers unknowingly feast on a cat instead. This behind-the-lines look at the lives of fun-loving German soldiers in Belgium during the First World War came to the U.S. early in 1938.

In the Hunnia production *A Noszty Fiu Esete Toth Marival* (*Young Noszty and Mary Toth*, 1938), the lively and irresponsible young Hussar Feri Noszty (Pál Jávor) contracts debts, sings with gypsies, flings champagne glasses at café mirrors, and refuses to marry the heiress whose dowry would restore the family fortunes. But he has the good luck to marry her, nevertheless, having proved, by mistaking her for her maid, that he isn't after her money. She turns out to be a rich American, Mary Toth (Eva Szörényi). Directed by István Székely, a Jew born in Hungary, the film also depicts Hungarian military maneuvers as well as farm operations and harvesting. Its combination of romance and arms made it one of the few foreign films Goebbels allowed within Germany in 1938. The last of six films Hunnia co-produced with German studios in the period 1932–39, it screened at New York's Modern Playhouse in May 1938. The tale had a German counterpart: Hubert Marischka's *Ihr Liebhusar* (1938), which was not released in the U.S.

In early 1938, Reinhold Schünzel's *Amphitryon* quietly opened in New York's Garden Theatre under its working title: *Aus den Wolken kommt das Glück* (*Luck Comes from the Clouds*). It starred Willy Fritsch, Käthe Gold (b. 1907) and Adele Sandrock, with music by Franz Doelle (1883–1965). By then, Jewish-born director Reinhold Schünzel was in exile in Hollywood and *Amphitryon*'s producer, Günther Stapenhorst, was in England working for Alexander Korda. Stapenhorst (1888–1976) had worked on a score of films in Nazi Germany, beginning with *Morgenrot*. The *New York Times* (April 16, 1938) told filmgoers "who missed" *Amphitryon* in the "French edition at the Belmont a year ago" that they would find "compensation" this time around. The compensation included seeing Nazi actor Fritsch in a supernatural tale of heroes fighting for the fatherland, signaling that the film isn't merely a comedy. Returning soldiers are depicted worrying about the fidelity of their wives.

The Austrian romantic drama *Marie Bashkirtseff* (1935) was another production whose filmmakers—director Herman Kosterlitz, scriptwriter Felix Joachimson, and co-star Szöke Szakall—had found refuge in America by the time their film reached these shores. Their film is set in Paris in the 1880s, where Russian art student Maria (Lili Darvas) is under the tutelage of a respected teacher. One afternoon she is caught up in a street brawl, but a handsome young man saves her. He turns out to be Guy de Maupassant (Hans Jaray). She falls in love with him. Their lives revolve around art, dance palaces, and Montmartre cafés until Maria is taken ill with a lung ailment. Her death leaves him shattered. Gallic Films released this film in the U.S. in early 1938 under the more appealing title *Affairs of Maupassant*. In Hollywood the trio of Jewish filmmakers thrived. Their contributions were considerable. Between 1940 and 1951, Szakall, for instance, acted in nearly 40 films.

Germany in the early 1900s, city and country, was the setting for Frank Wysbar's next-to-last film from the Third Reich, called *Ball im Metropol* (1936–37), a Terra production that CFE distributed subtitled in the U.S. in 1938. Here a young woman, Margit Steitendorff (Hilde Weissner), goes to great lengths to protect a decent young nobleman, Eberhard von Waltzein (Heinz von Cleve), from the jealous rages of her husband (Franz Schafheitlin). Wysbar had garnered acclaim for his psychological drama *Die Unbekannte* (*The Unknown*, 1936), a Terra production not released in America, in which a young woman, Madeleine (Sybille Schmitz), is found floating in a river and delivered to the morgue with no trace of identity. But her beauty, even in death, compels the investigators to ask, Who is the woman? And why is she dead? She was a woman with a past and, wishes to protect her lover's reputation. He's the handsome explorer Thomas Bentick (Jean Galland). She commits suicide because she felt responsible for the loss of irreplaceable documents that he'd discovered in Egypt. The film's big concert scene has conductor Hermann Abenroth and the Berlin Philharmonic playing Beethoven's glorious Seventh and Schubert's B-Minor symphonies.

Marianne Hoppe starred in Wysbar's *Die Werft zum grauen Hecht* (*The Gray Pike's Wharf*, 1935), a CFE release, playing the love interest of a lowly mechanic (Hermann Speelmans) fleeing a former girlfriend (Fita Benkhoff). Produced by Terra and filmed along the shore of the

Havel region, the tale contained "no villains," said the *New York Times* (April 18, 1938), although a subplot involving a will, high finance, a property deal, and a jealous character carrying the German-Jewish surname "Ladewig" (Karl Stepanek) could have given one pause about the film's—and the reviewer's—sentiments. After Wysbar directed *Petermann ist dagegen* (*Petermann Is Against It*, 1938), a film in line with the new spirit within Germany, Wysbar fled to Hollywood. There he co-directed *The Mozart Story* (1948), which includes footage from Karl Hartl's Nazi-era hagiography about the Austrian composer, *Wen die Götter lieben* (*Whom the Gods Love*, 1942). With music by the Vienna Philharmonic, *The Mozart Story* starred the acclaimed German performers Hans Holt and Winnie Markus.

The "no villains" theme and the battle against big business are at the heart of Nazi-supporter Veit Harlan's *Kater Lampe*, the hero of which is a cat. In this Robert Neppach production from the year of the Berlin Olympics, released by Tobis and shown at the Casino Theatre in 1938, the action takes place in the Erzebirge Mountains of central Germany. The rustic comedy, with its conflicts and loves of the village folk, centers on a cat owned by struggling toy maker Fritz (Albert Lieven) that becomes the symbol of all that binds these true Germans. Suse Graf plays an American seeking to manufacture snowshoes in the region; she also helps Fritz win his battle against more powerful forces. By the mid–1930s, actor Albert Lievan (1906–1971) found himself at odds with the Nazi regime. Threatened with imprisonment, he fled to London.

Veit Harlan, one of the regime's rising talents, was in agreement with the regime. The Nazi filmmakers' high-mindedness and hypocrisy are reflected in his *Die Kreutzersonate* (*The Kreutzer Sonata*, 1937), an Ufa production based on Tolstoy's 1890 story. The Nazis used it to decry Russian society. It screened at the Garden Theatre in 1938. The story is a tale of a marriage—thus a culture—in ruin. Russian pianist Jelaina Posdnyschew (Lil Dagover) has given up her career to marry Andrej (Peter Petersen) and bear a son. However, during her birthday celebration, when she plays Beethoven's "Kreutzer Sonata" with the well-known violinist Gregor Tuchatschewsky (Albrecht Schönhals), Andrej's cousin, their passions are aroused. Gregor wants her; she resists. Andrej becomes jealous and throws Gregor out of his house. Later, ashamed and asking for forgiveness, Andrej offers his wife a trip to Germany. Traveling alone, she meets Gregor there. At the climax, when Gregor asks Andrej to give his wife a divorce, Andrej kills his wife in the presence of her would-be lover—just after she has decided to remain committed to her marriage.

Actor-director Wolfgang Liebeneiner's second of many films directed under Hitler was *Der Mustergatte* (*The Model Husband*, 1937), a comedy scripted by Jacob Geis (1890–1972) that reinforces the stereotypical formula for retaining a spouse's love: pretend to be a devil of a fellow. That will make your wife jealous and she will see the real you. Avery Hopwood's stage farce *Fair and Warmer* formed the basis for the story, which takes place in London and Venice. Fed up with faithless boyfriends, Margret (Leni Mahrenbach) impulsively accepts a marriage proposal from young British bank director Billy Bartlett (Heinz Rühmann). He proves to be a loyal and steadfast husband. Too loyal and steadfast for her. When his wife threatens divorce because of his lack of ardor, Bartlett is encouraged by his friend Jack Wheeler (Hans Söhnker) to play the field. That should make Billy's wife take notice. In fact, Billy winds up in a drunken orgy with Jack's wife, Doddy (Heli Finkenzeller), which establishes Billy's credibility. The star, Heinz Rühmann (1902–1994), was close to the Nazi regime. Goebbels called him a "nice, witty and charming chap." To remain true to Nazi ideals, Rühmann divorced his Jewish wife, Maria Bernheim, for actress-colleague Hertha Feiler.

Der Mustergatte, which was produced by Tobis and screened in early 1938 at the Garden Theatre in New York, later garnered a "special recommendation" award at the 1938 Venice Film Festival because of Rühmann's acting, even though Goebbels charged that there had been Jewish involvement in the making of the comedy. There *was* Jewish involvement in Liebeneiner's third film under the Nazis, called *Yvette* (1938), which was based on a story by de Maupassant. The film, which was not screened in the States, starred Ruth Hellberg, who was Jewish and married to Liebeneiner. Her career in German films ended when Liebeneiner divorced her for Hilde Krahl (1917–99), a Nazi Party member since 1936, who had a small part in *Yvette*. Produced by Tobis, *Yvette* is set in Paris in the gay '90s, where the illegitimately-born Yvette (Hellberg), the daughter of a courtesan raised in a convent, comes up against the city's libertine culture, represented by a wealthy banker (Johannes Riemann) with the Jewish-sounding name "Aristide de Saval." Only Jean Servigny (Albert Matterstock) recognizes Yvette's pure soul and, by falling in love with her, saves her from a fate worse than death.

Hans Steinhoff, another Nazi director worth noting, was responsible for *Eine Frau ohne Bedeutung* (*A Woman of No Importance*), a Majestic production based on Oscar Wilde's 1893 play of the same name. It was modernized to hypocritically satirize British plutocracy, which in Nazi terms meant the Jews. It focuses on Sylvia (Marianne Hoppe), a parson's daughter who is abandoned by her lover and rejected by his father, Lord Illingworth (Gustav Gründgens). Though she is pregnant, the old lord opposes the marriage because it's out of keeping with his son's social rank. Young Illingworth is suddenly ordered to India, where he devotes himself to work. He returns after two decades, having inherited his father's millions and castles. Matters come to a climax when Gerard, Sylvia's grownup son, notices young Illingworth paying a bit too much attention to Hester, who is Gerard's sweetheart. Gerard challenges him to a duel, but before the fateful event, Sylvia reveals the truth of their relationship. Clemens Schmalstich (1880–1960) scored the drama, which ran at the Europa Theatre in the Yorkville section of New York in 1938. Although it was produced in the year of the Berlin Olympics, the film did not fit the harmonious spirit of the games.

Satirizing British mannerisms and names, the Paul Martin–Lilian Harvey–Willy Fritsch musical *Sieben Ohrfeigen* (*Seven Boxes on the Ear*, 1937), scripted by Götz and produced by Ufa, was called the best Harvey vehicle in years, and Friedrich Schroeder's music was called eloquent. The film screened in the U.S. in mid-1938. Harvey played the English woman Daisy (Harvey *was* born in England) in love with a brash, apparently money-savvy Scotsman named William Tenson MacPhab (Fritsch) who, after losing a hefty amount of money (through ill-luck?) in the market, vows to slap the man he claims swindled him. He's going to do this each day for a week and let the press know about it. On the seventh day MacPhab finds out that the woman who loves him is the daughter of the nonchalant financial magnate he's been humiliating, Astor Terbanks (Alfred Abel). Other characters in the film were named Wennington Laskett (Oskar Sima), a reporter; the Earl of Wigglebottom (Erich Fiedler); and Mr. Strawman (Ernst Legal), the millionaire's assistant.

Napoleon ist an allem Schuld (*Napoleon Is All Debt*, 1938), directed by and starring Götz, is another example of German filmmakers making do without Jewish comedians. In the tale, the British aristocrat Cavershoot neglects his wife Josephine (Valerie von Martens) to pursue his real passion: Napoleon. But when he goes to Paris for a conference on Bonaparte, Cavershoot experiences his very own Waterloo. Captivated by a young dancer, he gets caught in risky entanglements, from which his wife Josephine emerges triumphant. Josephine embodies the Nazis' attitude toward Society. She compares it to a circus, which she calls "just the same." Society, she says, is composed of "illusionists thinking we don't see through their tricks." In an intimate moment with her husband, she asks, "Have you ever had one nice hour by that so-called society?" Hence, she states, "We shall know, at least, that the people who come in our house are our real friends." This production reached the States, as did both Götz, who carried Swiss citizenship, and his wife, Martens. They both fled to safety in Hollywood.

Ufa's *Das Mädchen von gestern Nacht* (*The Girl of Last Night*, 1938) also skewers British (and American) officialdom through their names, if not their actions. Superficially, it's a tale about confused actions, fighting, and making up, which involve upper-class gentleman—two British diplomats with the same first name of Stanley; and bankers, one of whom is named "Barrow" (Hans Liebelt). There's also a missing pearl necklace. In this production, which screened in 1938 at the 86th Street Garden Theatre, the rich young American Jean Miller (Gusti Huber), who is on a visit to London, does just about anything to prove to her father (Paul Westermeier), a financier, that she is an independent, modern woman. This includes jumping naked, at midnight, into the bed of another self-important official. But she finds it impossible to resist *his* charms. He's a handsome, wealthy bachelor who professes a belief in never putting a woman in a compromising position. His name is Lord Stanley Stalton (Willy Fritsch). When *he's* compromised, he finds love. In the film was newcomer Ingeborg von Kasserow playing Barrow's daughter, Evelyn, who falls for the other Stanley in the tale, Stanley Chestnut (Rudolf Platte). The director was Peter Paul Brauer (1900–1959), a Nazi Party activist. Goebbels appointed him production chief of Terra in 1939.

Brauer also directed Ufa's important-sounding production *Jugend von Heute* (*Youth of Today*), a tale in which all the girls love the art instructor, Professor Fromann (Hans Liebelt) whose theories of confidence building and mutual understanding on the surface, at least, clash with Nazi ideology regarding iron discipline. He, in turn, loves all the girls, helps them solve their little problems and joins them in their school activities. But it's just another subtle method of controlling the young. When one girl steals cash from a classmate, blame falls on another girl. Humiliated, the latter girl attempts to take her own life. After which all the students pitch in—at the suggestion of the professor—to find the real culprit. It turns out that Sibylle (Jutta Freybe) stole the money to pay off a couple of extortionists, one of whom is called "Leine Seiff" (Christine Grabe), a Jewish girl. Then all is forgiven, and everyone lives happily ever after in this comedy-drama about high school kids following a born leader. In Berlin this film had been titled *Was Tun, Sibylle?* (*What Now, Sibylle?*, 1938). It came to the Garden Theatre without subtitles but with, said *Variety* (November 9, 1938), "a hopeless jumble of words for any but those hep to the Nazi jive."

Géza von Bolváry's *Die Entführung* (*The Abduction*) is about deception on a minor scale, based on a play by Paul Armont and Marcel Gerbidon. In the film, eighteen-year-old Suzanne Merville (Marieluise Claudius) stages her own kidnapping—into a bathysphere. She does this to shame her un–German-like young mother Yvonne (Lola Chlud) into paying attention to her children and her middle-aged husband, George (Walter Jansson), rather than flirting with the phony would-be lover "Giverney Roger" (Theo Shall), a non–German. At the end, Yvonne and George realize they've both been self-absorbed and Suzanne finds love with the deep-sea scientist Gerard Frehel (Gustav Fröhlich). This mid–1938 CFE release was said by *Variety* (when it previewed the film in Berlin) to be "minus propaganda and turgidity common to German output." That was not totally surprising in light of the fact that it was released in April 1936, in the year of the Berlin Olympics.

The superficial reality, or normalcy within Germany, was obviously underscored with this film. Germany pushed this kind of film in a continual attempt to hide its real agenda in the darkness of intimidation, concentration camps, and torture. German films camouflaged the inhumanity of the Nazis—or emphasized it, depending on the audience. Much more real, perhaps, were Nazi films dealing with British colonialism, which was the political background to two Tobis-produced dramas by Richard Eichberg (1888–1953) that opened within two weeks of each other in New York, in April-May 1938.

Eichberg had directed one of Germany's earliest sound films, *Der Prinz die Tänzerin/Die Prinz und die Kokette* (1926). In the late 1920s Richard Eichberg worked at Deutsche Universal, which was Universal Studio's German subsidiary, and was witness to the mix of Germans and Jews in film in Weimar Germany. Charlotte Susa (1898–1976), who visited Hollywood in the early 1930s, was characterized as "fascinating" in Eichberg's *Königin der Underwelt* (*Queen of the Underworld*), which was shown in New York in 1932. Eichberg's *Es geht um mein Leben* (*My Life Is at Stake*, 1936), a Tobis production that screened in New York's Europe Theatre in early 1938, was called an old-fashioned whodunit. The plot revolves around the shooting of the singer-blackmailer ominously named Juan Navarro (Harry Hardt). He was the one-time fiancé of actress Christa Galeen (Kitty Jantzen), who's now married to a wealthy lawyer, Dr. "Lessner" (Karl Ludwig Diehl). Set in contemporary Germany, the tale has several false leads. Did Christa, her husband, or their friend Ernst Torsten (Walter Gross) do it? Then the identity of the mystery shooter is revealed: "Ilja Bogroff" (Robert Dorsay), a Jew.

Eichberg was the director of the action-packed production *Des Kurier der Zaren* (*The Czar's Courier*, 1936), a militarist drama of Russians battling Tartars, which was adapted from Jules Verne's novel. The czar (Hans Zesch-Ballot) must get a message from Moscow to his brother the archduke who is on the other side of Russia, in the city of Irkutsk. He calls upon his best courier, Capt. Michel Strogoff (Adolf Wohlbrück), to get the message across the Siberian frontier, which is threatened by Tartars, led by the emir of Bokhara (Bernhard Goetzke). The czar warns Michael about the treachery of a particular Russian assisting the invaders: "Ivan Ogareff" (Alexander Golling). During the journey, Strogoff meets Nadja (Maria Andergast), who is also traveling to Irkutsk to join her exiled father. Strogoff also meets British reporter Harry Blount (Theo Lingen) of *The Daily Telegraph*, who is covering the fighting, as well as the self-centered French journalist Jolivet (Kurt Vespermann). This pro–Russian film failed to be released in the States even after *Variety* (February 1936), reporting from Berlin, wrote that its "tension and speed, rare attributes of a German film, effectively lead up to the climax and breathtaking situations," during which Ogareff is taken prisoner and the Tatar hordes dispersed.

During the Nazis' rise to power and well into the 1930s, Eichberg forged a compromise with the regime: he worked abroad. In 1938, after making his India films, he moved to Switzerland and then the United States. In the 1940s he worked at Carnegie Hall. Eichberg was said to have an abundance of energy and vitality, which he imparted to his films.

Thea von Harbou's novel was the inspiration for Eichberg's action films set in exotic, British-controlled India. The first of his pair of India-based films was *Der Tiger von Eschnapur* (1938), released by American Tobis with music by Harald Böhmelt. At the start, a killer tiger is on the loose. The Maharaja Chandra (Frits van Dongen) manages to capture it; then a mysterious stranger, Sasha Demidoff (Gustav Diessl), shows up. A post-revolution Russian adventurer, he was a lover of Majarani Sitha from long ago, in Paris. Prince Ramigani (Alexander Golling, 1905–1989), who plots to overthrow the maharaja, is aware of the relationship. Demidoff passes his knowledge on to the jealous maharaja. The Indian ruler responds by throwing the Russian into an arena—against the tiger. But the Russian manages to kill the beast. Sitha (La Jana) then frees him from imprisonment and the two of them bolt India for Germany. The film ends with a huge conflagration in Berlin—that can only be blamed on Demidoff, the Russian. Costarring Eichberg's American wife Kitty Jantzen, the production was praised for its wealth of detail, location shooting outside of Nazi Germany, and a "background reminiscent of Hollywood in one of its exotic moods," wrote the *New York Times* (April 30, 1938). The film, which screened at the Casino Theatre, was hailed as an eye-opening spectacle—and a message to India (and Britain) from Germany. Germany is India's friend, implies the production, and an enemy of Britain. (The swastila had its origins in India.)

The second of Eichberg's exotic dramas is called *Das Indische Grabmal* (*The Indian Tomb*, 1938). It starts with the maharaja returning to India from friendly Germany empty-handed. Although he has failed to bring back his wife from Germany, the maharaja hasn't given up. In the lost city of Eschnapur, he plots revenge, ordering the super-efficient German architect Peter Fürbringer (Hans Stüwe) to construct an "Indian tomb." He intends it for his wife. Having returned to India and hidden in Bombay, Sitha is kidnapped by Ramigani and brought to the maharaja. She's imprisoned as German workers complete construction of the tomb. Demidoff, supported by the German construction workers, frees her and then exposes Ramigani's plot to unseat the maharaja. After doing away with the disloyal prince, Demidoff reconciles with the grateful Indian ruler. Sitha returns to her role as the loyal majarani.

Part two became one of the biggest moneymakers in Nazi-era movie-making. Schneeberger's exteriors, wrote *Variety* (February 1938) from Berlin, "vie with the artistic shade and light pattern of Ewald Daub's studio shots. Sound and editing as well as costumes do their share towards rounding out a two-serial spectacle thriller that fills a center spot in the German production which has long been vacant." The Russian family name Demidoff was well known when Eichberg shot his films. The family had acquired great wealth in the eighteenth century, largely through iron production and mining, and became patrons of the arts and sciences.

Viktor Tourjansky (1891–1976), born Vyacheslav Turzansky, was *the* prominent Russian filmmaker within the Third Reich. (Outside the Reich he was called Arnaldo Genoino, W. Tourjansky, V. Turzhansky, etc.) His career took him to Hollywood in the 1920s and France in the '30s, where his boy-loses-girl story *Les Yeux Noirs* (*Dark Eyes*, 1935), starring Simone Simon and Harry Baur, earned him praise for so-called sensitivity. Tourjansky and Hanns Schwarz co-directed *Le Mensonge de Nina Petrovna* (*The Lie of Nina Petrovna*, 1937), a tale of romantic intrigue along continental lines, when Schwarz, a German-Jewish director, was in exile in France. Schwarz headed to Hollywood, Tourjansky to Germany, where he made more than a dozen films under Hitler. When Himmler in early 1938 ordered the expulsion of Russian nationals who were Jewish—many of whom had been living in Germany since the Bolshevik Revolution—Russian-born Tourjansky (like Tschechowa and Tschet) made no move to leave the Third Reich along with his fellow Russians. Instead, Tourjansky became a busy director in the Third Reich. His films often starred the enigmatic, alluring Brigitte Horney. A few of their films were released in the States.

One of Tourjansky's first films to reach the States, in mid–1938, was the emotional *Verklungene Melodie* (*Dead Melody*, 1938), also known as *Mitternachtswalzer* (*Midnight Waltz*), an Ufa production that shifts from Africa to Germany to the U.S. The film was called *Der Weite Weg* (*The Wide Way*) in Austria. In this romance, Barbara Lorenz (Brigitte Horney) has waited long enough for her man, the Berlin businessman Thomas Gront (Willy Birgel), who is, however, incapable of appreciating the sincere love of this young German woman. They had met during a forced landing in the Sahara. An aspiring actress, she joined him in Berlin. His lack of interest causes her to move to New York. Years later he catches up with her on the docks of the American city, but she stays true to her new family, watching his ocean liner backing away from the quay. He's heard home calling.

Ufa liked to exploit stories that were exotically located. It backed the making of the German-French desert tale *S.O.S. Sahara* (1938), directed by Jacques de Baroncelli, about Arab attacks against foreign outposts and desperate men trying to forget their pasts. At a North African desert outpost the commander (Charles Vanel) of the French forces has real trouble when his wife (Marta Labarr) arrives. Her affair with a young officer (Jean-Pierre Aumont) arouses his anger but when the chips are down he puts duty above personal feelings to save the young officer's life.

Herbert Maisch's melodrama *Andalusische Nächte* (*Andalusian Nights*, 1938), highlights a non–German screen personality. The protagonist is Carmen, a catalyst for trouble, played by the Spanish actress Imperio Argentina (1906–2003). Ufa's production, which Phillip Lothar Mayring (1879–1948) and Fred Andreas scripted, contains a bit of Bizet and the bare-bones outline of Prosper Mérimée's story. Its chief concerns are bullfighting, smugglers, and pathos. In 1938, Florian Rey had featured Imperio Argentina, born Magdalena Nile del Río, in his Buenos Aires production *Noche Andaluz* (*Andalusian Nights*). The tone and theme echo the lament of the Argentine tango. It inspired *Andalusiche Nachte* and adaptations by Italian and French directors, in 1942 and 1943.

In *Andalusiche Nächte*, the heroine is the Seville gypsy and lover of both the soldier José (Friedrich Benfer) and the bullfighter Antonio (Karl Klüsner). Fortune-tellers say, "Whoever loves Carmen, the beautiful singer and dancer, shall die." She flirts, sings, dances, and finally mourns. In the end, Carmen stands by the side of José's coffin. Through his sacrificial death—the Nazi ideal—he had rehabilitated himself as a soldier. In New York's Spanish Harlem, Imperio Argentina's films became box-office poison because she openly sided with Franco's forces in the Spanish Civil War. Being proclaimed the "new star of the German film firmament" didn't help her screen image outside of Germany. Goebbels was said to have forced the film on Ufa but it was actually Hitler who gave the order to invite Imperio Argentina to work in Germany. The *New York Times* (September 24, 1938) wrote that her German film, which screened at the 86th Street Garden Theatre, along with Ufa's short *Briefe Fliegen über den Ozean* (*Brief Flight Over the Ocean*, 1935), "could almost induce a 100 percent Loyalist sympathizer to forget his principles."

Ufa also produced a Spanish version featuring Imperio Argentina called *Carmen de la Triana* (1938), which costarred Rafael Rivelles, Manuel Luna, and Margit Symo. This film was shown subtitled at New York's 48th St. Theatre in June 1940, when the Spanish Civil War was over. By then it was safe to release it in the States.

Un Mauvaise Garçon (*A Bad Lot*, 1936), directed by Jean Boyer and starring Danielle Darrieux, was also an Ufa production. The story is about a young lawyer (Darrieux) falling for her client (Henry Garat), who's charged with burglary. She later discovers that it's all a set-up by her father (Alerme) to have her marry him and give up her job. After making this film, Darrieux left Europe for Universal Studios in Hollywood. When *Un Mauvaise Garçon* screened at New York's Belmont Theatre under the title *Avocate d'amour* (*Counsel for Love*), the *New York Times* (September 8, 1938) proclaimed the "old doughboy proverb, 'The French, they are a funny race.'" In June 1940, however, the Non–Sectarian Anti–Nazi League exposed the Nazi connection. This film was the last A.C.E. production to screen in America before the U.S. entered World War II.

A.C.E.'s *Adrienne Lecouvreur* (1938), which Marcel L'Herbier directed, screened in Paris before the U.S. declared war on Germany, as did several other "French" productions, including *L'Entraineuse* (*Nightclub Hostess*, 1938–39) and *L'Héritier des Mondésir* (*The Mondesir Heir*, 1939). The latter two were directed by René Clair's protégé Albert Valentin (1908–1968). Ufa–A.C.E co-productions starred a range of French stars: Pierre Fresnay, Yvonne Printemps, Tramel, Fernandel, Jules Berry, Borel, etc. Foreign directors who worked for Ufa–A.C.E in Berlin included Marc Allégret, Jacques Becker, Georges Neveux, Pierre–Jean Ducis, René Pujol, George Lacombe, Roger Le Bon, Yves Mirande (director of *Baccara*, 1935), Jean Gremillon, and Maurice Gleize. Gremillon's drama *L'Etrange Monsieur Victor* (*The Odd Mr. Victor*, 1937–38) starred Raimu as a man living a double life. During the days he's an ordinary shopkeeper; at night he's a burglar. When the film premiered in Paris, *Variety* (May 1938) called it "one of the top French productions of the year." Gleize's drama *Le Récif de corail* (*Coral Reefs*, 1938), starred Jean Gabin as a gunrunner in Mexico. There he runs into Lillian White (Michele Morgan), who's on the run. *Variety* (May 3, 1939) wrote from Paris that the story "wanders half way around the earth," including Australia, but that the film "is destined for the home market only." Its "*French* ideas of a rough Australian town and Mexican rebels are far from reality." Nonetheless, the film had a screening in Mexico City, in June 1940.

Significantly, Jean Renoir's popular front, anti-war production *Grand Illusion* (1937) was well received abroad and shown in the U.S. in fall 1938, during the Munich crisis. Its "can't we just get along" message, however, played into the hands of the forces of terror and blackmail. Renoir's Germans of World War I were a far cry from the new Germans running and supporting the Third Reich—and threatening the world with devastating war. All one had to do was see Czech-born Karl Anton's *Mit versiegelter Order* (*Under Sealed Orders*, 1938), produced by Majestic, which takes place in a Near Eastern nation called "Karakat." A German company mines for copper, a badly needed raw material for the fatherland. In return the company is building the nation's waterworks. It awaits the German steamer *Patria*, which is carrying machine parts for the construction work. However, hidden enemies of Germany threaten the mutual arrangement. They're variously called foreign contractors, plutocrats, an international consortium, etc. Also against the agreement is a high-ranking police chief. A German asks, "Why not simply shoot those enemies around us?" When told "We better not," he responds, "Couldn't it happen just by accident?" Chief engineer Kessler (Paul Hartmann) is in despair, which causes the German ambassador, Dr. Reinhardt (Ernst Leudesdorff), to ask, "Are you really able to think only of yourself, of resigning and so depriving thousands of workers of their work and bread?" Matters reach a peak when Kessler is framed for murder. The ambassador, unable to save the engineer from the gallows, suggests a solution: suicide. However, Willi Reinhardt (Viktor de Kowa), the ambassador's nephew, knows that Germany needs engineers like Kessler. He takes the murder charge upon himself. He is helped in his decision by visions of billowing German cornfields and a beautiful German landscape. By sacrificing his life, Willi becomes a hero in Germany—and steals the glory from the men who only *live* for their country! Not surprisingly, the non–German proprietor named "Ibrahim Speere" (Hans Stiebner), who runs a resort that caters to foreigners, is depicted as greasy and despicable.

Reminders of Germany's losses in the First World War are the heart of Frank Wysbar's *Fährmann Maria* (*Ferryman Maria*), one of the rare, highly-regarded Nazi-era films in its day, and a production from the Olympic year. Produced by Terra, this tale of hope and love, which debuted in the U.S. late in the year, is the story of a woman (Sybille Shmitz) who operates a rope-ferry across a stream in old North Germany. She becomes enamored of a wounded German (Peter Voss), who had fought for his homeland in the First World War. She tries to prevent Death (Aribert Mog) from catching up to this German soldier, veteran, and patriot. He deserves to live forever.

The actor Aribert Mog (1904–1941) had his own moment in infamy. He was the narrator of Hanns Springer's documentary *Ewiger Wald* (*Eternal Forest*), a production from the year of the Olympics which Alfred Rosenberg, the Nazi Party's chief ideologue, had commissioned. Wolfgang Zeller scored and Sepp Allgeier and Guido Seeber photographed this work about the unity of people and forest. The film purports to portray the development of the German race in conjunction with the evolution of German woods and forests. It sketches the development of Germans from the Bronze Age to Hitler's Third Reich. By the end of the story, although many of Germany's forests have been cleared because of the nation's defeat in the previous world war, another kind of forest—swastika banners—has taken their place. Mog died on the Russian front.

While *Ewiger Wald* did not screen in America—and western critics missed it in Germany—mystical reverence for the connection between Germans and their forests is depicted in *Waldrausch* (1939), which did screen in the U.S.

The foreigners in Viktor Janson's spy drama *Sie und die Drei* (*She and the Three*), which played at the Casino Theatre four years after it played in Germany, were also up to no good. In this tale, which is set in Hamburg's Palast Hotel, a humble waiter, Rudolf Rostorff (Hans Söhnker), sees his duty and does it when he saves a German-American contractor, Dr. Bittner (Gustav Waldau), from being robbed of important papers, which will allow him to bid for a big industrial project in Romania. The waiter's reward is cash and the hand of the industrialist's stately blonde daughter, Lisa (Charlotte Susa). Hubert von Meyerink (1891–1971) played a foreign crook named André Nicol; Walter Steinbeck was "Alexander Bobinsky."

A new name appeared on American screens when Tobis's *Die Kleine und die grosse Liebe* (*The Minor and the Real Thing*, 1937–38) was released: that of Austrian-born director Josef von Baky (1902–1966). His breakthrough film under the Nazis had been Tobis's *Intermezzo* (1936), about a famous French singer (Tresi Rudolph) who, after skipping out of her wedding, flees to the gambling tables. There she literally loses her money and then her voice to a stranger. The man who wins her voice (Albrecht Schönhals) happens to be a composer. He makes the most of his prize, and all ends well. *Die Kleine und die grosse Liebe*, which Ulrich Bettac co-directed, is the story of the prince (Gustav Fröhlich) of an imaginary principality who gives up his title for the love of modern airline stewardess Erika Berghoff (Jenny Jugo). "The details of the story are unimportant," wrote the *New York Times* (July 23, 1938), even while the film, screening at the Casino Theatre, symbolically links the past—which must be forsaken—with contemporary Germany. Baky was also the director of Ufa's *Menschen vom Varieté/A variete csillagai* (*Stars of Variety*, 1939), an expensive German-Hungarian collaboration starring Hans Moser, La Jana, Christl Mardayn, Karin Hardt, and Attila Hörbiger. Scripted by Thea von Harbou, it's a backstage drama of the rivalry between a marksman and a magician over the latter's ex-wife, named "Silvia Castellani" (La Jana), a presumed Jew. Baky was praised for his depiction of the characters' emotional states but because of his film's more-than-average German heaviness, it was kept off American screens.

Instead, the impression that normality still reigned within Greater Reich came from other releases and other stars. One was E.W. Emo's and Karl Heinz Martin's Austrian comedy *Die Glücklichste Ehe der Welt* (*The Happiest Married Couple in the World*, 1937), which screened at the Garden Theatre in late summer 1938. Produced by Terra, the film has as its hero an Austrian-American millionaire (Leo Slezak) who is willing to pay a huge sum of money to the happiest couple in Vienna. The example of pure bliss, he is sure, will spur his daughter (Maria Andergast) to seek similar happiness in marriage. *Die Macht der Berge* (*The Power of the Mountains*), also shown at the Garden Theatre in late summer 1938, also stresses the bliss of marriage, motherhood, and righteousness. Directed by Austrian-born Gustav Ucicky, the film is set in the 1860s, leaving the Nazis plenty of time and room to show how liberal and concerned they were about people long dead. The story follows the travails of a widowed, Tyrolian proprietor (Franziska Kinz, 1887–1980), who stops the village scandal mongers by forthrightly announcing the engagement of her of daughter (Josefine Dora), who has just left the convent, to the man she loves (Gustav Fröhlich). This film, which co-starred Heidemarie Hatheyer as a waitress, was in fact *Frau Sixta* (1938), an Ufa production which presages Ucicky's hugely successful tale of mother love, called *Mutterliebe* (1939).

Admirers of sweet and sad romance flavored with waltzes set in Vienna could forget trouble—especially Austria's union with Germany in 1938—with *Unsterbliche Melodien* (*Immortal Melodies*, 1935), Ufa's production directed by Heinz Paul. An alleged episode in the life of the "waltz king," Johann Strauss Jr. appears in tune with Nazi ideology. At the age of 55, Strauss (Alfred Jürger) marries a young ballet student, Lilly Dietrich (Lizzi Holzschuh). But they divorce within a year. The composer, having gotten out of the way of the younger generation, then finds consolation in the affection of the operetta performer Maria Geistinger (Maria Paudler), who is his own age. She had left Germany for America because of her unrequited love for Strauss. But she returned home—the fatherland was calling—when she became aware that he was single again. The festive ballroom scenes "are the best," wrote *Variety* (April 27, 1938), "showing the pleasant customs and good European manners of another day." The actress

Maria Paudler (1900–1990), who was born in Czechoslovakia, was reported to have refused to make Nazi propaganda films. However, she had starred in Ufa's pro-war *Junges Blut* (*Young Blood*, 1936), a production that wasn't screened in America. Directed and produced by, and featuring Kurt Skalden (1895–?), the film, which co-starred Hans Scharlach and lay actors, is set in East Prussia at the historic Masurin Sea—where Hindenburg fought the Russians in 1914. The tale depicts Russian troops devastating the countryside before the German troops stem the tide. Then it's time for rest and relaxation in a village where sturdy German peasant life, a return to the soil, and love are played out.

The star of the nineteenth-century drama *Heimat* (*Home*, 1938) was Zarah Leander. The Nazis concocted this film from Hermann Sudermann's 1892 play *Die Heimat*, also called *Magda*, in which the protagonist, Magda Schwarze, leaves home because her father, Colonel Leopold Schwarze, disapproves of her match with Pastor Heffterdingk. Her father had said of modern ideas and free-thinking women:

> Oh, pshaw! I know them. But come into the quiet homes where are bred brave soldiers and virtuous wives. There you'll hear no talk about heredity, no arguments about individuality, no scandalous gossip. There modern ideas have no foothold, for it is there that the life and strength of the Fatherland abide. Look at this home! There is no luxury—hardly even what you call good taste—faded rugs, birchen chairs, old pictures; and yet when you see the beams of the western sun pour through the white curtains and lie with such a loving touch on the old room, does not something say to you, "Here dwells true happiness?"

In Berlin, Magda meets Councillor von Keller (Franz Schafheitlin), a bank director who seduces and abandons her. She gives birth to a girl. Magda then goes abroad, leaving her child with her sister. Eight years later, in 1885, she returns to her place of birth, Immendingen. She has comes back in triumph as Maddalena dall'Orto, a world-famous prima donna at the Met-

Heimat, starring Zarah Leander. Georg Alexander is at center (in white), and Franz Schafheitlin is at the far left.

ropolitan Opera. What matters most to her now is her music. But her rigid, hidebound father, Baron "Leopold von Schwarze" (Heinrich George), wants Magda to restore the family honor by marrying von Keller, who has settled in her hometown. If she doesn't, he threatens to kill her and himself. When she refuses, he is shocked. In the meantime, von Keller, exposed as an embezzler and blackmailer, kills himself. At the climax, Magda takes part in the performance of Bach's St. Matthew Passion. This act reconciles her with the townspeople and with her father. Magda also moves into his home with her grown-up daughter, Poldi.

This story worked to the Nazis' advantage in that the main characters could be taken as (Christianized) Jews. The Nazis depict families such as "von Schwarze," "von Keller," and "von Wendlowsky" as the middle-class representatives of loathsome prewar Germany. Produced by Ufa on the tenth anniversary of Sudermann's death, Goebbels wrote that this film "brilliantly captures the feel of the prewar period ... the mask is torn off a false and insincere morality of honor." Goebbels named *Heimat* winner of a National Film Prize. Carl Froelich was named best director at the 1938 Venice Film Festival for this Ufa hit, with music was by Theo Mackeben (1897–1953). The movie represented the peak of Leander's career in Germany. The film screened at the Garden Theatre in September 1938.

The popular German star Paul Hörbiger (1894–1981) played Heffterdingk, the organist in *Heimat*. The brother of Attila, Paul was one of the pillars of Austrian and German films. He helped the German film industry survive, if not thrive, in these terrible years. In 1945, the Gestapo arrested Hörbiger for espionage. The BBC reported his death, but his sister-in-law, acclaimed German actress Paula Wessely, used her connections with the Nazi regime to save him. He had a small part in *The Third Man* (1948), a film that equated complacency with the miracle of the cuckoo clock, after which his career continued unabated until his death. Hörbiger appeared in more than 100 films.

One of the biggest stars of the German film firmament in the 1930s was Brigitte Horney (1911–1988), the daughter of British psychologist Karen Horney. In Edward Waschnecht's *Anna Favetti* (1938), produced by Ufa and released in the U.S. in October under the title *Wintersturme* (*Winter Storms*), Horney played the daughter of a reclusive couple living in the mountains of St. Moritz. There they attend to her brother, a severely disabled veteran of the First World War. Her life is on hold—it has to be, says everyone around her—because of her brother's condition. She awakens to life's possibilities after the arrival of a young architect (Mathias Wieman) whose marriage is about to end. But only the death of her soldier-brother and her parents' consent free her to marry the architect.

One of new Germany's most prominent stars was Goebbels' lover, Lida Baarová. After turning down Hollywood offers in the 1930s, Baarová (1910–2000) said, "I could have been as famous as Marlene" Dietrich. She was featured in fall 1938 in Georg Jacoby's *Lt. Bobby, der Teufelskerl* (*Lt. Bobby, a Devil of a Fellow*, 1935), an Austrian production about well-heeled British society and its army, illustrating that life in Europe is a series of fancy balls, rough riding, flying stunts, and song. Baarová apparently thought otherwise. She fled Berlin for Prague in 1938 and went to Italy in 1941, where she made several films. After the war she was sentenced to 16 months in prison because of her ties to Goebbels and the Nazis. Baarová was back on the screen in Fellini's *I Vitelloni* (1953) and Fassbinder's *The Bitter Tears of Petra von Kant* (1970). Presumed dead, she was rediscovered in the 1990s through the documentary, *Lida Baarova's Bittersweet Memories* (1995), directed by Helene Trestikova.

George Jacoby's revue *Ein Nacht im Mai* (*A Night in May*, 1938), a late-1938 release in the U.S. that Goebbels called "amusing and well made," starred Marika Rökk. She played the temperamental Inge Fleming, who is out for a drive in the city even though her driver's license has expired. When she gets into an accident with the architect Waldemar Becker, she flees the scene. At a railway station, Fleming meets Willy Prinz (Victor Stahl), who persuades her to accompany him into the country for a costume ball. When Waldemar appears there as well, she flees again into a boat, this time with Willy, but the two soon become separated. Inge is unaware of the obvious: that Willy and Waldemar know each other. After the war, the Allies banned George Jacoby from filmmaking. The ban didn't last long. Resuming his career in 1950, Jacoby and his wife Marika Rökk made a final film together *Die Nacht vor der Premiere* (1959) of which Rökk said, "We flog the success craze to death."

In late 1938, as the Munich crisis made world headlines, Germany required an uplift in its image. The story of the 1936 Olympics would do the trick. Here was the vehicle for cleansing the German soul and shape shifting. In November 1938, Leni Riefenstahl sailed for America on the luxury liner *Europa*, hoping to sell her film *Olympia* (1938) to an American distributor. That would bolster her image as well as Germany's on the world stage. *Olympia*'s two parts had been released simultaneously in Germany on Hitler's birthday, April 20, 1938. The German press had been ecstatic. *Der Deutsche Film*, in May 1938, called *Olympia* "a result of National Socialism, which is penetrating the total life of the nation into its most detailed ramifications, with its idea-based directional force and which has accustomed us to see reality and idea together. Only in the ideological structure of National Socialism could this great documentary film have come into being.... Indeed it had never existed previously." Writing under the pseudonym "Frank Maraun," Erwin Goelz in 1940 had similar words of praise for *Der Ewige Jude*. The Allies indicted this Nazi journalist as a war criminal. He was acquitted. Riefenstahl's two-part film—*Fest der Voelker* (*Festival of the Nations*) and *Fest der Schönheit* (*Festival of Beauty*)—had been financed by Goebbels' Propaganda Ministry and Film-Kredit-Bank. Herbert Windt supplied its musical background. *Olympia* received acclaim as Riefenstahl presented it across Europe. To top it off, *Olympia* was named co-winner of the best film award at the 1938 Venice Film Festival.

Olympia, as much as its subject, promoted Germany's hoped-for new face. Goebbels, who said, "The sporting spectacle is a kind of civilian party rally," had also sent Riefenstahl to America to study Hollywood's techniques. Meanwhile, glass shattered across Germany and Jews died. Riefenstahl began her search for an American distributor while at sea. In her luggage she carried three prints of *Olympia* and copies of the book *Beauty in the Olympic Struggle—Schönheit im Olympischen Kampf*. That winter, the Boycott Council representing the American Jewish Congress and the Jewish Labor Committee asked American film distributors and exhibitors to reject Leni Riefenstahl's film. On the third day of Riefenstahl's visit to the United States, the Hollywood Anti–Nazi League, which was headed by screenwriters Donald Ogdan Steward and Dorothy Rothschild Parker, got into the act. It began a campaign against Germany, boosted perhaps by the events of, and by reactions to, Kristallnacht in early November. In Detroit, on November 18, 1938, doing her case no good, Riefenstahl met Henry Ford, an open admirer of Hitler. She then headed for California, via a stop in the Grand Canyon.

On Nov. 29, 1938, the Hollywood Anti–Nazi League ran an ad in *Daily Variety*, which said, "Today, Leni Riefenstahl, head of the Nazi film industry, has arrived in Hollywood. There is no room in Hollywood for Leni Riefenstahl. In this moment when hundreds of thousands of our brethren await certain death, close your doors to all Nazi agents.... Let the world know there is no room in Hollywood for a Nazi agent. Sign the petition for an economic embargo against Germany." Walt Disney was one Hollywood notable who publicly received her. On December 8 she took a three-hour tour of his studio. Disney, she said at the end, "has the German feeling." The Hollywood Anti–Nazi League, which had been founded in 1936, opposed the release of Riefenstahl's film on *generic* grounds, characterizing it as "part of the Nazi propaganda attack on American institutions and American democracy." The issue of Jews in Germany was subsumed by the emphasis on "democracy." The organization's support came from membership dues, contributions, motion picture producers, and donations from stage and screen stars. It claimed about 3,000 members and printed a newsletter under the name *Hollywood Now*.

Kristallnacht and Riefenstahl's notoriety killed any chances *Olympia* had in the States in late 1938—for a while anyway. Riefenstahl had come to embody Nazi films. America's boycott of her and her film was its strongest and most overt reaction against the release of Hitler's films in America. Riefenstahl's film, reported the *Los Angeles Times* in late December 1938, "is not to be released in America, according to present plans, because of anti–Nazi controversies." However, private screenings of the film were a different matter. The "record of the XI Olympiad" was quietly shown to Riefenstahl's Hollywood friends as the year came to a close. A year later, following the startling news of the Nazi–Soviet pact, the Hollywood Anti–Nazi League, which had communist ties, changed its name to the Hollywood League for Democratic Action. It also changed its tune towards Riefenstahl's film. In March 1940, with the Nazi–Soviet non-aggression pact in effect, leftist opposition to Rifenstahl and her film evaporated. Excelsior Pictures unabashedly distributed her two-part film under the title *Olympiad*. It was dubbed into English for American filmgoers.

Carl Junghans was one of the cinematographers of *Olympia*. Other cameramen who worked on *Olympia* were Wolf Hart (b. 1911), Walter Frentz (1908–2004), and Hans Ertl. Ertl (1908–2000) became infamous for documenting the Nazi war machine and photographing Hitler and the military campaigns of Rommel. The desert commander later awarded Ertl the Iron Cross. Ertl spent the second half of his life in Bolivia, where, he said, "I don't want to return to my country." That's because the Nazis were no longer in charge. However, Ertl maintained that working for Hitler's regime was vital to his work, and not a sign of his political beliefs: "I never shared the Nazi ideals and I never had anything against the Jews, particularly the Jewish women," he said. Near the end of his life he liked to wear a German army jacket.

Walter Frentz, a member of Hitler's inner circle, was responsible for the Nazi-commissioned film that glorifies workers, entitled *Hände am Werk* (*Hands at Work*, 1936). Frentz took photos of Hitler before the dictator's suicide and was imprisoned by the Allies after the war. He was the subject of the documentary *The Eye of the Third Reich* (1992). The 1936 Berlin Olympics had impressed British and American visitors, who were merely deceived, if one wants to be generous, by the apparent prosperity and well-being of most Germans. In addition to capturing the spirit of the games, Riefenstahl's production is preoccupied with German youth, health, and vigor. The Nazis' stress on health, vigor, and athletics in Riefenstahl's film was but a short step away from making illness a crime. Numerous German films continued to flow to America in the wake of the success and good health that Riefenstahl had tried to peddle in America in late 1938.

Georg Zoch's Bavaria production *Der Lachende Dritte* (*The Laughing Third Party*), shown in America in 1938, was produced in the year of the Olympics. The story about antagonists on German soil in a remote village in southern Bavaria, concerns an old, cunning farmer and the owner of a luxury hotel. The Bavarian farmer, Naz (Joseph Eichheim), has a pit of liquid manure on his property that raises quite a stink when the wind blows south. The more it blows in that direction, the more money the old man envisions coming from competing parties who will want to buy him out and rid the region of the stink. That's because there is a popular tourist house nearby, and when the wind blows in the wrong direction, well.... And the nearby luxury hotel operator (Oscar Sima) is not the only one who wants to see a change. Others get wind of the fact that the pit contains the mineral sulfur—making it valuable piece of real estate.

Erich Engels' *Die Graue Dame* (*The Gray Dame*), a Terra production set in Britain, has a famous sleuth (Hermann Speelmans) subverting the plans of a gang led by a man named "Baranoff" (Edwin Jürgenssen), a presumed Jew who is trying to steal the blueprints of an important invention for a foreign concern. Distributed by CFE in late 1938, the film was actually

Sherlock Holmes (1936–1937). It was the second German film on the fictional British detective to be shown in America this year.

Carl Boese was the director of the ABC production *Der Klapperstorchverband* (*The Stork Society*), about the need to increase the population of the Reich. It starred his favorite actress, Lucie Englisch. This film, another production from the year of the Berlin Olympics, was released in the U.S. in fall 1938. Boese—unnamed—was also the director behind the "Italian" film *Il Diamante Porta-Fortuna* (*The Lucky Diamond*), which was shown at the Broadway Cine Roma New York in fall 1938. However, this film was a German production, having been made by Itala Film in Germany as *Lisetta* (1933), with the ubiquitous Alberto Giacalone the producer. Scripted by Robert A. Stemmle, it's the story of a flower girl (Elsa Merlini) to whom a diamond brings luck, adventure, and love (via Vittorio De Sica).

Ironically, the German drama *Herzenlieb* (*Heart Thief*), which ran in New York in late summer 1938, *was* credited to director Carl Boese. In fact, Jewish filmmaker Max Neufeld had directed this production in Weimar in 1932, when it was called *Des Diamant des Zaren*. A complicating element involving an attempt to steal the famous Orloff diamond led to the film being known as *Der Orlow* as well. Austrian star Liane Haid played a Russian singer living in Germany who falls in love with a handsome countryman (Ivan Petrovich) working in an automobile factory. Naturally, he turns out to be a White Russian—a former grand duke—who found sanctuary in Germany. His identity is known only to a factory owner (Viktor de Kowa) whom he knew in Paris in pre–World War I days.

The sterling Italian star Antonio Gandusio was the star in *L'Antenato* (*The Ancestor*, 1936), an Astra Film-Munich production that screened at New York's Cine Roma in late 1938. Directed by Guido Brignone, the comedy concerns a baron who awakes after a spell that's lasted 300 years. Before he's kissed back to sleep, he manages to help a young descendant (Mauritzio D'Ancora) to do two important things: to marry and retain the family estate. His bride (Olivia Fried) is, of course, blonde.

Director Robert A. Stemmle's *Gleisdreieck* (*El-Track Triangle*, 1937), a Ufa production with music by Hans-Otto Borgmann, which screened at the Garden Theatre in 1938, features the subway as the setting for underworld intrigue and the venue for sketches of Berlin's lower class. The protagonist is the fine young stationmaster (Gustav Fröhlich) who falls in love with the depressed young woman Gerda Volkmann (Heli Finkenzeller). Her brother Max (Paul Hoffmann), however, is a petty criminal and the cause of her impulsive acts. The subway employee saves her life twice: each time he prevents her from leaping in front of a train. Max dies in a shootout with the police. The longtime supporting actor Oscar Sabo (1881–1969) played a taxi driver.

The film *Meine Freundin Barbara* (*My Friend Barbara*, 1937), another 86th Street Garden Theatre presentation in 1938 directed by Fritz Kirchhoff (1901–53), begins when an apartment manager—named simply "Lohmeyer" (P. Wilhelm Kreuger)—turns off the gas to the apartment of the Werners, who are always late with the rent. Nonetheless, the young Barbara Werner (Grethe Weiser, 1903–1970) displays nothing but common sense and a good heart. She saves the marriage between a neglected wife, Stefanie (Elisabeth Ried), and her husband Manfred Reinerz (Paul Hoffmann), a hard-working but distracted scientist; and then turns her own life around. Barbara does that by attracting the attention of Stefanie's new lover, the idle but rich Frank Andermann (Franz Zimmermann), and turning him into a responsible German. Nazi film ideology patronized women, who were depicted as often knowing what was best about matters involving marriage and the family. The music in *Meine Freundin Barbara* was by Willi Kollo (1905–1988). Kirchhoff's first Nazi film had been Ufa's *Wenn Frauen schweigen* (*When Women Keep Silent*, 1937), a comedy about love and gossip and keeping marriages intact that ran in the U.S. in mid-1937 without titles. His Ufa short about the danger of infidelity, *Papas Fehltritt* (*Daddy's Mistake*, 1936–37), based on the story by Ludwig Thoma, screened in Pennsylvania (in early 1939) after state censors cut what they considered objectionable lines of dialogue.

Kirchhoff's later *Anschlag auf Baku* (*Attack on Baku*, 1940–1941) was a major production in a different way. Financed by Goebbels and produced by Ufa when the Nazis' only European foe was England, *Anschlag auf Baku* is about intrigue, foreigners, and the expulsion, if not defeat, of Germany's enemies. Ufa slated this film for American release just as the U.S. entered World War II. The story takes place after Germany's defeat in the First World War. Ex-officer Hans Romberg (Willy Fritsch) is working in faraway Baku. He's in charge of security forces for the United Oil Company. Saboteurs and assassins are setting fire to and blowing up the Russian-controlled oilfields around Baku, and Romberg suspects who's behind it: the British. But Romberg can't persuade the local chief of police that the British are no friends of the Russians. After a Turkish security force, which had been sent in to restore order, massacres Christians and Moslems, the British, under pretense of restoring order, send in troops to occupy the oilfields. The shoe drops when the British appoint the next governor of Baku. The Russian chief of police needs no further proof that his German friend was right. He arms his men and, with Romberg's assistance, he ousts the British from the territory.

Werner Hochbaum was the director behind the Austrian-German production *Wir sind vom K. u. K. Infanterie-Regiment* (*We Are of the K. and K. Infantry Regiment*), a tale first filmed by Richard Oswald in 1926. The Styria film, which screened with English titles at the Garden Theatre, "is no mere tale of wine, women and song mixed with soldiering in the Austrian infantry before the World War," said the *New York Times* (November 18, 1938). Originally called *Vorstadtvariete* (*Suburban Variety*, 1934) when shown in Germany, Hochbaum's film (made before *Der Ewige Maske*) depicts the serious side of a romance between a promising Vienna cabaret singer (Luise Ullrich) and a jealous architect (Mathias Wieman) of peasant origin who opposes her career while he does his duty and joins the army. Hochbaum's film was said by later observers to have subverted the clichés of the Viennese operetta. Unlike like the play upon which it is based, the principals do not commit suicide, because Goebbels had insisted on a happy ending. Hochbaum's film, however, emphasizes militarism and the idea of duty above anything else, which were ideas in tune with Nazism and Germany's rearming in the mid-1930s. The music was by Anton Profes.

Erich Engel's *Der Maulkorb* (*The Muzzle*, 1938), a Tobis production, was also said to have been subversive. It starts when the exemplary, rural prosecuting attorney Herbert von Traskow (Ralph Arthur Roberts) gets drunk and puts his dog's muzzle on the statue of the reigning duke, who the locals refer to as the "beloved ruler." When the attorney sobers up, he has no recollection of what he's done. Duty requires that his office find the culprit behind this outrage. A reward is offered while every dog owner in the town is asked to account for himself and any muzzles in his possession. The only person who doesn't have an alibi—or a muzzle—turns out to be the attorney. But before he's interrogated, Wimm (Paul Henckels) and Baetes (Albert Schmitz) concoct a plan to get the reward. One plans to confess to the crime while the other turns him in. Their scheme unravels, however, and they're put on trial. Then the painter Rabenus (Will Quadflieg) comes forward to make a startling revelation. The statue of the duke is really that of someone else: Goethe. That means that no harm was done, and the case is dismissed as a harmless prank. Von Traskow is promoted. Two other schemers in the tale are called "Schibulski" (Adolf Fischer) and "Meyer" (Bernhard Gronau). The film, which screened at the Casino Theatre, is really another Nazi attack on the old order—and on a great German man of letters of the eighteenth century. In the cast were two young and promising stars in the new Germany, Charlotte Schellhorn and Will Quadflieg, along with popular performers Theodor Loos, Paul Henkels, Ludwig Schmitz, and Hilde Weissner. The *New York*

Sketch for *Anschlag auf Baku* produced by the studio.

Times (April 9, 1938) did point out that the film's muzzle "is not of the kind called to mind in connection with Nazi Germany." But the paper also said that the court scene is "tops."

Carl Boese's *Eine Nacht an der Donau* (*A Night on the Danube*) screened at the Casino Theatre three years after it ran in Germany. That's why it's about the talented young in the new Germany. A nobleman (Wolfgang Liebeneiner) who wants to be a classical musician finds his real talent lies elsewhere. When he meets a charming young blonde (Dorit Kreysler) and her female orchestra on a river steamer, he is inspired to write popular music. River scenes, rural views, and pleasing music present a charm world that is absent in late–1938 Germany. Ordinary, everyday working people made up Carl Boese's lovers' triangle called *Die Kleine Sünderin* (*The Little Sinner*). Shown at the Garden Theatre, it ran without German titles. In Germany it was called *Schwarzfahrt ins Glück* (1938). It takes place in and around a Berlin auto repair shop. When worldly Rudi (René Deltgen) learns that his friend and partner Hanni (Volker Collande) intends to marry the attractive waitress Erika (Ruth Hellberg), Rudi feels compelled to expose matters—up to a point. First he pleads with Erika to tell Hanni of their affair. When she refuses, he reveals to Hanni Erika's indiscretions—without mentioning his own relationship with Erika. Only after Hanni and Erika quarrel and Hanni calls the marriage off does Rudi reveal his affair with Erika. All of that ends their business and personal relationship until a crisis involving a mysterious villain (Paul Dahlke) proves Erika's lack of love for Hanni. Camaraderie between the two former friends is then restored. "Despite its comic accent, the story," wrote Dorothy Masters of the *Herald Tribune* (December 3, 1938),"is of sterner stuff than the sugared and spiced lunacies in vogue."

Two friends in a traveling show (Paul Hörbiger and Rudolf Karl), reduced to the status of tramps, seize on the chance to improve matters by masquerading as a famous composer and his musical colleague in Karl Lamac's *Die Landstreicher* (*The Hoboes*, 1937), a CFE release in late 1938. This German-Austrian production only hinted at the charms of an earlier musical classic along the storyline—*Zwei Herzen im 3/4 Takt* (1930)—co-starring Gretl Theimer (1910–72) and the ubiquitous Bavarian Lucie Englisch. *Die Landstreicher* also hinted at a later anti–Semitic production about hoboes masquerading as friends of Jews: *Robert und Bertram* (1939).

"Reviews" of *Die Kleine Sünderin*.

Robert Stolz provided the music for the un-subtitled Austrian-Czech-German romance *Liebe im Dreivierteltakt* (*Love in Three-quarter Time*, 1936), which Hubert Marischka directed. It centers on blonde Franzl Weinzierl (Lizzi Holzschuh), a working-class woman who disobeys her father Leopold (Leo Slezak) to marry the rich auto manufacturer Erich Lobmeyer (Hans Holt). CFE released the film as the Munich agreement was signed and Czechoslovakia capitulated to German-Italian-British demands that it surrender Sudetenland. Although the film aimed for lightheartedness, it failed as the sequel to *Zwei Herzen im dreiviertel Takt* (*Two Hearts in Three-quarter Time*, 1930), the classic which Géza von Bolváry had directed and which Robert Stolz scored. That musical ran for a year in New York after its release in October 1930. It ran for four months in Chicago, and had a special screening in Washington, D.C., in late 1933.

The musical *Nanon* (1938), shown in late 1938 in New York, presents another star of the Third Reich film firmament, Erna Sack (1897–1972), called the "German Nightingale." Directed by Herbert Maisch and produced by Ufa, the film concentrates on Mademoiselle Nanon Patin (Sack, a coloratura soprano) as a seventeenth-century woman in love with a nobleman (Johannes Heesters) in the court of Louis XIV whose life is saved by the influential Moliere (Otto Gebühr). The milieu of Louis XIV afforded the Nazi film world the opportunity of displaying the glamour of a long-ago court, although the producers had no ambition to hold the production to historical truth or to weigh their words. When at a cocktail party Nanon utters hostile comments about the upper classes, a Nazi moment, so to speak, her tactlessness passes quickly. At the end, the peasant girl is ennobled by the king into a countess and marquise. Composer Willy Schmidt-Gentner (1894–1964) handled the music. In Austria, Schmid-Gentner had worked with Jewish-born Walter Reisch, the author of *Two Hearts in Waltz Time* and *Masquerade in Vienna* and the director of the acclaimed comedy about postwar Vienna and the jazz hysteria of the era, *Episode* (1935), starring Paula Wessely. In America, Reisch scripted *Ninotchka* (1939), *That Uncertain Feeling* (1941), *Gaslight* (1944), and others.

Willy Schmidt-Gentner directed several films in the Nazi era, including the Austrian production *Der Weg des Herzens* (*The Way of Hearts*, 1936), which CFE released in the U.S. in late 1938 as *Wiener Prater*. This sketch of Vienna before Hitler came to power, screened in Germany in August 1937, depicts thieves, tricksters, skirt chasers, and suicide. Bavarian star Magda Schneider played a sideshow performer who flees to the Danube after a misunderstanding caused by the crooked gambler, cheater, and liar named "Baron Castelli" (Fred Hennings). Her excuse is heart disease. Taken in by Bohemian artists Fred Hochstedt (Willy Eichberger) and Niki (Hans Olden), she wins the heart and hand of the handsome painter Fred.

A white Christmas, was portrayed in Luis Trenker's and Werner Klingler's *Liebesbriefe aus dem Engadin* (*Love Letters from the Engadine*, 1938) produced by Tobis, which was shown in New York. The stalwart actor-director Trenker, who had been associated with Alpine films since the end of the First World War and whose films were last seen in the U.S. early in Hitler's regime, offered ski stunts and rigorous mountain climbing as the backdrop to romance at a Swiss hotel—but only after the preface and its huge display of a swastika. If nothing else, that public symbol marked a dubious way to stay on friendly terms with America. The plot hinges on a ruse by Toni Anewanter (Trenker). He lures young American Constance Farrington (Charlotte Daudert) to the slopes by sending her a pseudo-love letter supposedly written by a well-known European ski champion.

The last day of 1938 saw the arrival at the Casino Theatre of the comedy *Musketier Meier III* (*Rifleman Meier III*, 1938). Its release hinted at a new war to come in Europe. Joe Stöckel directed and Germania Film produced this drama, which emphasizes comradeship among front line soldiers on and off the battlefield. In December 1917, somewhere in Flanders, one German soldier is outwardly jovial and helpful, but a friend (a cook) notices that he never receives any mail. Suspecting that he's lonely, the cook has a female friend send him a parcel and a letter. When the two men are on leave in the cook's hometown, a different kind of comradeship is called for. Within this cruel new world, they encounter Jewish black marketers, war evaders, and corrupt politicians. It's up to the good German soldiers to clean up the town before heading back to the front. Reviews took no note of the anti-Semitism in this production, though Hitler had spewed forth his anti-Jewish wrath about wartime conditions in Germany in *Mein Kampf*.

Hitler had said:

> From the very beginning I had my own definite personal views. I intensely loathed the whole gang of miserable party politicians who had betrayed the people. I had long ago realized that the interests of the nation played only a very small part with this disreputable crew and that what counted with them was the possibility of filling their own empty pockets. My opinion was that those people thoroughly deserved to be hanged, because they were ready to sacrifice the peace and if necessary allow Germany to be defeated just to serve their own ends. To consider their wishes would mean to sacrifice the interests of the working classes for the benefit of a gang of thieves. To meet their wishes meant that one should agree to sacrifice Germany.

In German cinemas that worldview was a part of Bavaria's *Dreizehn Mann und eine Kanone* (*Thirteen Men and a Cannon*, 1938), directed by Johannes Meyer and co-scripted by Fred Andreas. It's set in the summer of 1916, when a Germany Army corps (starring Anton Pointner, 1890–1949; Erich Ponto; Otto Wernicke; Friedrich Kayssler; and Beppo Brem, 1906–90) on the Austro-Russian front finds itself outnumbered and out-gunned. Although there's little prospect for significant reinforcements, the unit does receive a battery with a long-distance 500-mm. gun, which is manned by 13 gunners. This battery had proven its worth on the western front. On the eastern front, this "ghost gun" ably shells the enemy's rear, disrupting lines of communication and halting a Russian attack. The company's success is short-lived. Soon the Russians are able to resume firing, shelling the long-range gun because signals from the German side at night pinpoint its whereabouts. When it's destroyed, one member of the German battery is killed. When the Germans suspect that there's traitor among the troops, Berlin sends an intelligence officer to investigate. Treachery is obvious when another soldier is found stabbed to death and a second is spotted trying to sneak out at night. Every member of the battery comes under suspicion. Worse still, they're told that they all face a firing squad unless the traitor is found. The traitor is discovered to be a German-speaking Russian who is shot on the spot. Released in late December, the film had been funded by Goebbels' ministry. It proved popular within the Third Reich, where it was called a "powerful war film and thriller." Although it was not shown in the U.S., British independent producers made an English version, also titled *Thirteen Men and a Gun* (1938), directed by Mario Zampi and starring Arthur Wontner.

Just as the transition from success and camaraderie to suspicion and the chance of sudden death before a firing squad appeared out of the normal for a German war film, fans of Nazi propaganda as well as ordinary filmgoers would find their expectations regarding the depiction of Russians in German films more confounding the next year.

PREWAR 1939
Hans Westmar *Signals German-Soviet Cordiality*

On February 20, 1939, the German-American Bund, publishers of a new weekly the *Free American*, held a rally to exhort "Americanization." The site was New York's Madison Square Garden; the date was George Washington's birthday. The crowd numbered 20,000. Witnesses claimed the Jew-baiting was the worst in American history. The assembled gathering vilified President Roosevelt and continuously yelled "Heil Hitler." The Bund characterized white Americans as the country's true patriots. Banners read, "Wake Up, America!" and "Smash Jewish Communism." Three feature-length anti–Semitic productions from the world of Nazi cinema were released in the United States in the wake of the rally.

A folk hero of sorts was at the center of the first, shown in New York in March 1939. It was called *Horst Wessel*. Hans Heinz Ewers's popular novel was the basis for the story about a Nazi fanatic actually named Horst Wessel, whose death in the late 1920s became Nazi lore and the subject of several German films. The earliest filmed rendition of his life is Johannes Häussler's documentary *Blutendes Deutschland* (*Bleeding Germany*, 1932), an excoriation of the Treaty of Versailles. Hans Bullerian (1885–1948) provided the score in that film. The Bruning regime in Weimar banned it, but after Hitler, one of the film's attractions, came to power, the Nazis released it for screenings at party functions. A second rendition was Franz Wenzler's short *Horst Wessel* (1932). The third rendition was Wenzler's feature-length *Hans Westmar* (1933). Ernst Hanfstängl, the enigmatic supporter-opponent of Hitler, and Guiseppe Becce composed the music. Wenzler (1893–1935?), whom colleagues remembered as odious and horrible, had begun his career at Deutsche Universal alongside its Jewish personnel. He had directed *Die Nacht ohne Pause* (*The Night without Pause*, 1931), starring Camilla Horn (1906–1996). (Hungarian-born Endre, or Andrew, Marton, who co-directed the film, had started his film career in Austria and Germany as an editor on films by Ernst Lubitsch and Kurt Bernhardt.)

Wenzler's feature-length *Horst Wessel* (the renamed *Hans Westmar*) was released in the U.S. in early 1939 when, compared to other Nazi rabble-rousing works shown in the U.S., it came across as almost harmless, harkening back to the rise of the brown-shirted Storm Troopers and their activities in the twilight of the Weimar era. The Night of the Long Knives in mid-1934, which signaled the end of the Brown Shirts, was a distant memory for filmgoers. Rather, the disintegration of Czechoslovakia was in the news. So who cared much about Nazi fanatic Hans Westmar (Emil Wilhelm Lohkamp), who takes to the streets in 1929 and becomes a martyr at the hands of Jews? One Jew in particular is an official who is an opponent of "Popish priests, socialist sheep, and that miserable pack of Brown Shirts financed by heavy industry." He warns the Nazi hooligans the streets belong to the communists. The communists shout, "Nazis, drop dead!"—a slogan that parallels the Nazis' own slogan, "Jews, drop dead!" The enemies in the film are "Frau Salm," "Klara," and "Kuprikoff."

The Nazis forced Jewish residents of Grenadierstrasse, in Berlin, to take part in the anti–Nazi crowd scenes. Otherwise, they would be "treated accordingly." Their actions and lines were simple. From the rooftops Jews had to yell, "Kill the Nazis!", "Death to Fascism!" and "Hail Moscow!" Two Jewish performers in the film were uncredited: Siegmund Nunberg in the role of a university professor advocating internationalism, and Hugo Döblin as a liberal member of the Reichstag. The star Lohkamp (b. 1902) made several films in Nazi Germany and appeared on German television in the 1960s. When Herthe Thiele (1908–1984) rejected a part in the production, Goebbels banned her from German film. Thiele fled to Switzerland, where she became a nurse.

In October 1935, the pro–Nazi organization calling itself the Friends of the New Germany (Die Freunde des Neuen Deutschland) had tried to screen Wenzler's feature under its original title *Hans Westmar*, in Paterson, N.J. But Police Chief John M. Murphy refused to issue a permit on the grounds that any showing would provoke riots. This was the group whose members pledged, "I do not belong to any secret organization of any kind [Freemasons, etc.]. I am of Aryan descent, free of Jewish or colored racial traces." The rejection, in a sense, worked to the Nazis' advantage four years later.

American critics liked *Horst Wessel*'s scenes of the funeral procession through the streets of Berlin, most notably as it passes Karl Liebnech House (Communist Party headquarters), which they characterized as convincing enough to give viewers the sense they were witnessing a national movement. At the conclusion of the film, Nazis and communists, however, are almost comrades. Was it conceivable that Germany and the Soviet Union were considering a rapprochement in 1939?

The second shocker from Nazi Germany in spring 1939 was R.A. Stemmle's *Ein Volk will Leben* (*A People Wants to Live*), which was shown at the Casino Theatre. The film had also been produced and released in Germany under another title: *Am seidenen Faden* (*On a Silk Thread*, 1938). This Ufa production, by Bruno Duday, is one of the key documents of Nazi ideology, conveying falsifications, anti–Semitism, and a loathing for the Weimar era. This film was one of the rare Nazi Zeitfilme ("films of the time") set in the Third Reich that screened in the States. The star, Willy Fritsch, was a Nazi Party member. Scored by Herbert Windt, *Am seidenen Faden* denounces "crooked Jewish capitalists" running an international trust in the postwar period in Germany. Weimar Germany is made to appear pauperized, its factories and plants sold pell-mell to international profiteers—all because of the unbearable weight of reparations. There is huge German unemployment because of the Treaty of Versailles, when, in fact, significant German unemployment only started in 1929.

The film begins in 1919. Germany has lost the war. Veteran Richard Hellwerth (Willy Fritsch) says, "I am not beaten.... Let me return home and you'll see what will happen." During those terrible years, when his parents had died, dubious people moved into his town and the family's chemical plant fell apart. With the help of the scientist Breuer (Bernhard Minetti), Hellwerth, having heard the call of the fatherland, opens up a factory that produces artificial silk. When the plant makes a profit, Hellwerth sells it to his future father-in-law, Wilhelm Eickhoff (Carl Kuhlmann). When the plant fails to flourish under new management, Hellwerth's wife Lissy (Käthy von Nagy) comes up with the idea of using the silk to make clothing. The plant is turned into a corporation and thrives. Soon after, when Hitler rules Germany, Eickhoff announces that he intends to sell the company to people who live abroad. The attorney "Theodor Kalbach" (Erich Ponto) and the banker "Brögelmann" (Paul Bildt) will handle the details. This idea spells trouble because the new owners intend to reduce clothing production within Germany. Hellwerth and the plant's employees are shocked. They barricade them-

Ufa's press hype for *Ein Volk will Leben.*

selves inside, halting all work. Eickhoff flees Germany. The manufacturing plant stays in the new Germany and under German control. Trade unions are banished.

The *New York Herald Tribune* (March 27, 1939) concluded the film was a "postwar screen romance about the birth of the artificial silk industry in Germany ... although the absence of English dialogue titles makes it difficult for persons whose knowledge of German is limited." The *New York World Telegram* (March 27, 1939) wrote, "It all has very little to do with a people at large, being a story of love and ambition."

In later years, Robert Adolf Stemmle, who had a hand in writing Luis Trenker's *Der Rebell*, directed dramas that stress duty and male bonds. His *Mann für Mann* (1939) was produced by Ufa after Goebbels ordered several changes to make it "politically good and artistically sound." The music was by Friedrich Schroeder. The story depicts four German workers helping the Nazi state construct its Reichsautobahnen. The first autobahn had opened in 1934. Hitler's strictly military highways were sometimes used as airstrips. Most evident in the tale are the sacrifices the men make and the lengths to which the four men of the day shift go to save fellow night-shift workers trapped during a disaster that's no fault of their own. An earthquake, the key change Goebbels demanded, causes a cave-in on the new road. Stemmle's tale was not released outside Germany, nor was Stemmle's film *Jungens* (*Boys*, 1941). Ufa produced and Goebbels backed *Jungens*, which Werner Egk (1901–1983) and Ludwig Preiss (1910–1996) scored. Young Germans are shown finding their way into society through life in German camps and the attendant regimentation. This way the young became fit for one thing: war. It's also a pseudotale of working class life in the new Germany. It shows how one member of a Hitler Youth group becomes a man—and a kind of rebel—by helping fishermen in a village along the Baltic Sea break free of autocratic rule by one man.

The third of the trio of Nazi shockers to premiere in America in early 1939 was called *Pour le Mérite* (*For Honor*, 1938). Its screening in the U.S. coincided with Hitler's fiftieth birthday. *Pour le Mérite*, produced by Ufa, was directed by Karl Ritter and photographed by Heinz von Jaworsky (b. 1912). Ritter and Fred Hildenbrandt (b. 1892) scripted it and Herbert Windt composed the score. This is as pure a Nazi piece of work as ever there was. When the film premiered in Berlin, Christmas week 1938, Hitler, party leaders, and the Wermacht's general staff were in the audience (at, naturally, the Ufa-Palast am Zoo). To the Nazis, this film buries the old, corrupt, Jewish-Bolshevized Weimar Republic.

In *Mein Kampf*, Hitler loved to attack what he labeled "Jewish Bolshevism." He also said of Jews, "They have not the slightest intention of building up a Jewish State in Palestine so as to live in it. What they really are aiming at is to establish a central organization for their international swindling and cheating. As a sovereign State, this cannot be controlled by any of the other States. Therefore it can serve as a refuge for swindlers who have been found out and at the same time a high school for the training of other swindlers."

Later speculation said that Germans would regret ever having produced this picture, which became a blunt admission of their crimes even though Germans claim they didn't see them as crimes. In retrospect, this film was the most outrageous Nazi production to have been shown in America in a decade of Nazi-era imported films. Germany banned the film after the war.

The film is a no-holds-barred, 40-episode-filled "history" of Germany since the First World War, filled with a cast of hundreds, including Paul Hartmann, Fritz Kampers, Wolfgang Staudte, Theo Shall, Paul Otto, and Jutta Freybe. *Pour le Mérite* follows the activities of a German fighter squadron and its heroic leader named Prank (Hartmann). We see details of the squadron's mess-hall life, its participation in military preparations, and the fighting in the last months of the great conflict, including action against French and American cavalry forces. One episode also involves the desertion of a German soldier named "Baumlang" (Walter Lieck). Then at the end of the war, Germany faces revolution. The kaiser abdicates, fleeing to Hol-

Pour le Mérite included the first air show in Nazi Germany. SS leaders are in the front.

land. The squadron stands firm: it will not surrender its planes to the new authorities. Instead, members fly them to Darmstadt, but two planes land at Mannheim, where communist rabble rousers destroy them. The pilots then take drastic action: they destroy the rest of their planes that by treaty had to be surrendered to the French forces. Ritter's film depicts how these soldiers fare in Weimar Germany, which is portrayed as a world full of misery and disgrace, with black marketers and war profiteers everywhere. The war is over, but not for these flyers. They have a new enemy: the so called November criminals who are pictured as a gang of bandits. In the spirit of "now it can be told," Ritter's film features a protagonist who, because he is unable to make a go of it in Weimar, has to try his hand at farming in southern Germany. There, in an old barn, he finds his old plane, which had been miraculously saved. However, communists appear out of nowhere and destroy it.

Things go from bad to worse for the one-time officer: he's imprisoned; his wife dies. When he's released he leaves Germany to work abroad as a commercial pilot. Then the glorious year of 1933 arrives—followed by Germany's rearming, conscription, and the introduction of the Luftwaffe. At a ceremony honoring the new German Air Force, Nazis are in the front rows. The pilot returns to the fatherland to take his rightful place in the new Reich. He and his fellow comrades sing to the new spirit of Germany, as signified by its highest commendation, the Ordre Pour le Mérite (also called the Blue Max), "while cheering masses gathered at memorial monuments" of the First World War. The soldiers are together again in the old regiment that bears the name "Richthofen."

Was anyone surprised, lulled into complacency by the Nazis' worldview? Nazi conspirators, saboteurs, organizers, and assassins are the heroes in the film; the Weimar Republic—and its democratic citizenry—is the enemy. Treachery, conspiracy, intrigue, and murder are lauded while hate is the only emotion extolled. Predictably, the former pilot, when talking of Jewish swindlers, sums up it all up by saying at his trial, "I hate democracy like the plague ... I will undermine and sabotage it whenever I can. We have to create a Germany that is in keeping with the ideas of a combat soldier."

With no sense of alarm, reviews in the U.S. were circumspect. "For non–Nazis, the first part, devoted to battles in the air and gay incidents when the aviators are not fighting, is the more interesting," wrote the *New York Times* (April 8, 1939). *Pour le Mérite* was Heinz Engelmann's first film. Ufa had signed Engelmann (1911–1996) to a contract because he represented the ideal-looking military man. His Germanic physique sent a clear message about the film's meaning. Quickly, Engelmann appeared in a succession of Ufa's most violent, prowar productions: *Drei Unteroffiziere* (1938–39), *D III 88* (1939), *Kongo-Express* (1939), and *U-Boote Westwärts* (1941).

At the Brink of War

In January 1939 the Third Reich forbade Jews from practicing as dentists, veterinarians, and chemists. That same month, a Nazi order erased the officer caste system, thus tying the army to the party. In March, Bohemia and Moravia became part of the Greater Reich. In April, Hitler turned fifty. With the world at the brink of conflagration, many of CFE's releases in 1939 were films that had been produced in the year of the Olympics. America's motion picture theaters continued to show German films glorifying the German fatherland, personifying the myth of peace in Germany, and denying the true course of events within the agenda of the Third Reich, which offered token camaraderie with other nations, at least in theory. Many films were also anti–Semitic, but no one said so.

The first CFE release of the year was from the soon-to-be infamous director Veit Harlan. He had stars galore at his disposal for *Alles für Veronika* (*All for Veronica*): Thekla Ahrens, Willy Eichberger, Walter Janssen, Gretl Theimer, Hans Moser, Theo Lingen, Grethe Weiser, Hubert Meyerinck, and Hilde Hildebrand. Scripted by Axel Eggebrecht, the film was a multi-production effort by German, Swiss, and Hungarian studios about young Veronika Sonntag (Ahrens), who borrows one of her store's expensive pieces of jewelry to impress her handsome boyfriend, Paul Schmidt (Eichberger), at a winter resort in the Alps. Her store's owner is named "Tutzinger" (Moser), a presumed Jew. Although she looks to be in trouble for walking away with something that isn't hers, her boss is in love with her. Whatever the German Veronika wants, the German Veronika can get from a Jew.

J.A. Hübler-Kahla's film *Das Veilchen vom Potsdamer Platz* (*The Violet of Potsdam Square*), produced by Stark-Film, is a *Stadtheimatfilm*, meaning that little had changed for the better within Germany. In the film, which screened in the U.S. in April 1939, "home" is a small part of Berlin: a cultural backwater that's a mixture of Prussian dreams and ideas about the picturesque life of the poor. The main character, besides the flower-seller Mariechen Bindedraht (Rotraut Richter), is an old horse named Gravelotte. The horse had been an honored German cavalry mount in the First World War. Now the horse is threatened by the slaughterer's knife, which would put cash in the hands of a few people. Two villains in the tale strive for a portion of the booty. One is the cheat named "Otto Schnöcker" (Fritz Kampers); the other is his sidekick "Max Seidewind" (Anton Pointner). Although neither is identified as Jewish, it's not hard to guess that they are. Thanks to the efforts of Mariechen, her grandfather, and all the other nice people of Berlin, Gravelotte is saved and awarded a medal. More important, the animal will spend the rest of his days as a "horse of honor" accorded special treatment in the army. This is his due, having served Germany.

A German's conception of his dream country is the hallmark of Karl Heinz Martin's Austrian-German *Konzert in Tirol* (1938), which exploits the endearing nature of the Vienna Boys Choir while subtly attacking Jews. The music is by Mozart and the villain in this film is the unscrupulous old village shopkeeper with the German-Jewish name "Wurzinger" (Fritz Kampers). In this folkloric romance, which screened at New York's Garden Theatre in early 1939, a health resort in the Austrian mountains is the backdrop for the drama about the farmer's daughter Leni Lahntaler (Heli Finkenzeller). She finds that her father (Ferdinand Maierhofer) opposes her marriage to the young schoolteacher Toni Kern (Hans Holt), whose pupils are the singing boys from Vienna. He'd rather she married a man with money: Wurzinger. Meanwhile, the alluring but dark-haired city visitor Sylvia von Hansen (Elfie Gerhart) has her eyes on Toni. Matters look bleak for Leni and her dreams after she's accused of setting fire to the barn in which the boys are rehearsing a Nativity play. The only one who stands by her side is Wurzinger. Everything falls neatly into place, however, after the real arsonist is identified— Wurzinger, of course. Leni and Toni are together when the boys hold their big concert in a new venue: a big hotel.

The wholesome air of the apparently carefree, happy-go-lucky days of Bavaria in the middle of the nineteenth century is depicted in a film that starred a youngster: eight-year-old Traudl Stark. She was the main attraction in the Austrian-produced *Prinzessin Sissy* (1938). Fritz Thiery (b. 1899) directed. Stark played the adventurous, favorite daughter of Duke Maximillian (Paul Hörbiger), destined to be Empress Elizabeth. Her father exemplifies Germanism: he loves to rove the forests with woodcutter friends, play the zither, and behave more like a peasant than a duke. In the film, a necklace the duke acquires as a gift for his young princess falls into the wrong hands. The hands are those of the circus director "Lindner" (Hans Olden), a presumed Jew. Lindner has also failed to bring his traveling circus to Munich even though he's already been paid. The views of the "courts, castles, countryside and the circus seem almost real," wrote the *New York Times* (January 14, 1939). Little else in *Prinzessin Sissy* has any connection to reality—except for its Jewish stereotyping and its hint at the possibility of another war in Europe. In fact, every good Viennese citizen knew the details of Sissy's later life. At 16, she became betrothed to Emperor Franz Joseph in the room where 61 years later he signed the declaration of war against Serbia.

With war fever in the air, Arthur M. Rabenalt's Austrian-German *Das Frauenparadies* (*Women's Paradise*, 1936)—another film from the year of the Olympics—came in the form of an operetta about one of those "hit-at-all-hazards concoctions," wrote the *New York Times* (June 24, 1939). When it screened at the Casino Theatre, its anti–Semitic stereotyping was overlooked. The film is set in Vienna. There the young employee Eva (Hortense Raky) strives to save the dress shop in which she works, which is heavily in debt. She turns to a wealthy man named "Mühldörfer" (Georg Alexander) for a loan. This is the same man she had once slapped for getting fresh. He obliges—but complications for her follow. In the end, she does three things well: she rids herself of Mühldörfer; she marries the shop's new boss, Gary Field (Ivan Petrovich); and she rescues the store from bankruptcy. The anti–Nazi Robert Stolz, who was called the first German-Austrian film composer, contributed a number of melodies to this pre–Anschluss production. By the time American Tobis released *Das Frauenparadies*, the actress Hortense Raky was safety in Britain, having refusing Goebbels' order to abandon her real-life non–Aryan lover.

The popular Heinz Rühmann appeared in Fritz Holl's *Nanu, Sie kennen Korff noch nicht?* (*So, You Don't Know Korff Yet?*, 1938), playing the amateur writer-detective Niels Korff. He recovers a painting stolen from Amsterdam art patron Vermeylen (Jacob Tiedke) by three bumbling, non-German crooks: "Dufour" (Viktor Janson), "Kelly" (Fritz Rasp), and "Morton" (Franz Schafheitlin). New York's Garden Theatre screened the film in spring 1939. During World War II, the Nazis turned art theft into an art.

The title of Carl Boese's *Dahinten in der Heide* (*Back to the Country*), which was shown at the Casino Theatre in early 1939, says it all again. This production from the year of the Berlin Olympics glorifies peasant folks and rural life, that is, Germany's blood and soil. Here, a supposedly dead man, Lüder Volkmann (Hans Stüwe), returns to the fatherland from America. He had no luck there. He's back just in time to keep the country lands in the family's hands and to make sure the heroine, Holde Roturmond (Hilde Weissner), weds the right man. Lüder must deal with the odious banker "von Dongern" (Helmut Weiss) and stop the jealous landowner, Baron "von Zollin" (Helmuth Rudolph), from trying to get him out of the way by framing him for a shooting.

Boese's comedy *Heimkehr ins Glück* (*Lucky Homecoming*), which the Yorkville Theatre screened in early 1939, six years after its production, was seen in the U.S. under a more emotional, earthy title: *O Schwarzwald, O Heimat* (*Oh Black Forest, Oh Home*). Its protagonist is wealthy shoe factory owner Gruber (Paul Hörbiger), who, sick and tired of the social climbing and flirtations of his wife Liane (Erika Falgar), runs off to the countryside, naturally, for a bit of peace and quiet. By chance he's mistaken for someone else—the actor/magician Amadori (Heinz Rühmann)—and then he accidentally runs into the saucy Liesl (Luise Ullrich), the daughter of an old shoemaker under whom he'd learned his trade. While Liane and *her* lover are trying to find him, Gruber falls in love with Liesl. After details emerge about his wife's private life during the village's annual celebration making divorce a foregone conclusion, Gruber is free to remarry.

Despite family value themes that were at odds with the political issues in Germany at the time, the theme of finding matrimonial harmony was a constant in Nazi filmmaking. This is at the center of a comedy that opened in New York early in 1939. Hans Deppe's Ufa-produced *2 x 2 im Himmelbett* (*Two by Two in a Four-Post Bed*, 1937), which screened un-subtitled at the Garden Theatre, involves two couples vacationing at the estate of a relative, who has promised to give them a summer home if they can all pass the time harmoniously. Imagine a lack of harmony in Germany! "The film featured popular actors such as Carola Höhn, Georg Alexander, Paul Henckels, Werner Stock, and Mady Rahl. "Through it all," wrote the *New York Times* (February 5, 1939), "there is the usual recent Teutonic emphasis on the outdoor life, the rugged feminine beauty, and stalwart males," although antics involving a nude statue eluded the censor's scissors.

Karl Ritter's *Die Hochzeitsreise* (*The Honeymoon Trip*, 1939), an Ufa production, told viewers that 1930s Germans never had it so good. A novel by nineteenth-century Belgian writer Charles de Coster formed the basis for the film, which CFE distributed. It's set in 1860s Flanders. French actress Francoise Rosay—speaking German in a film that had been produced in Nazi Germany—starred in a domestic drama as a self-centered, unhappy woman who nearly destroys her youthful daughter's marriage.

Russian-born Viktor Tourjansky's domestic drama *Der Blaufuchs* (*The Fox Fur Coat*, 1938), which Ufa produced, is based on the play that inspired Mauritz Stiller's highly-publicized Swedish *Erotikon* (1920). Tourjansky's film screened in the U.S. in early 1939. Swedish-born Zarah Leander played the beautiful Ilona, the wife of the distracted scientist Stephan Paulus (Paul Hörbiger). The trouble stars when he forgets their first wedding anniversary and the fur coat he promised his young wife. By being a bit flirtatious with an attractive flier, Tibor Vary (Willy Birgel), and the same with heartthrob tenor Trill (Karl Schönböck), Ilona changes everything. Her husband realizes he cares for Lisi (Jane Tilden), a woman more sympathetic to his work. At the end, Ilona falls into the arms of Tibor. But the film ends on an ambiguous note: the protagonist is neither punished by fate for her actions nor does she find her way back to the straight and narrow. After seeing it in New York in spring 1939, filmgoers may have been delighted (or incensed) by the tale, but they felt a keen interest in the movie. Was this production in some way subversive? Contributing to the film's popularity—as with nearly all Zarah Leander movies—were the star's musical numbers.

The fatherland is the setting for George Jacoby's musical *Herbstmanöver* (*Fall Manoeuvres*), shown in the States three years after its premiere in Germany. In the quiet town of Pölz, two neighbors (Leo Slezak is one) are in a spat over a new drainage ditch. They take the matter to court. Troops are also garrisoned in the town, and it happens that one of the soldiers gets involved with the daughter of one of the complainants. On the birthday of Colonel Leyden, the town's young people arrange a ball to restore *Ordnung* (order). The colonel comes up with a solution: he has his men dig the ditch, and all's well that ends well. Leo Slezak renders "Auf der Heide blühn die letzten Rosen," a number that became a folk classic within the Greater Reich.

An entertaining time in old-world Vienna is at the heart of *Fasching in Wien* (*Carnival in Vienna*). This film is actually *Konfetti*, a Gloria production (from Austria) that was directed by Hubert Marischka (1882–1959) in the year of the Berlin Olympics. It ran at the Garden Theatre in early 1939. Complications result when salesgirl Lisa (Friedl Czepa), wearing her store's finest gown to a crowded ball, tries every which way to locate the artist Martin (Richard Romanowsky), who's implicated in what is called a "misstep." The anti–Nazi Robert Stolz had scored the film before Austria became Germany's partner in real crime.

Vienna and its harmony of one hundred and fifty years earlier serves as the setting for Johannes Meyer's subtitled musical *Ihr Grösster Erfolg* (*Her Greatest Success*) an Allianz Vienna film taken out of mothballs five years after its completion and screened in early 1939 at the 86th St. Casino Theatre. It starred Marta Eggerth (as the famous early nineteenth-century stage performer Therese Krones) and her husband Jan Kiepura. The *New York Times* (February 12, 1939) wrote that if anyone doubted Eggerth's popularity, all one had to do was "drop in" at the theatre "some evening. When her charming shadow is being received by the audience there, she might concur that the film was her greatest success.... The music by Franz Grothe is pleasant, and the scenes of old Vienna are delightful."

The little-remembered Alwin Elling (d. 1973) had a stint in Nazi filmmaking. A number of his films came to the States in early 1939. Elling's *Kleines Bezirksgericht* (*Little Country Court*, 1938) starred Austrian actor Hans Moser as an overeager but order-conscious court clerk who makes a complicated fraud case still more complicated with his never-ending, duty-filled, investigative work. It requires more than his Viennese charm to come out with sound skin from the misunderstandings and entanglements. The film, which Astra Film-Berlin produced and which screened in New York in early 1939, co-starred Jewish actor Paul Otto. Just as light an atmosphere prevails in Elling's *Der Lustige Witwenball* (*The Merry Widow's Ball*, 1936). Slapstick and wisecracks attend the rivalry between the female owners of a beauty parlor and millinery shops in a small German city. Another Astra Film-Berlin production, it screened in the U.S. in spring 1939. Elling's comedy *Hummel-Hummel* (1939), a CFE release in March 1939, is set in Hamburg, "where there's life and laughter," according to the press release, as a prominent businessman's romantic youth comes back to embarrass him on the eve of his daughter's marriage. CFE re-released the film in early 1941.

Elling had directed Bavarian popular comedian Weiss Ferdl as a former army sergeant trying to make it as a civilian in *Befehl is Befehl* (*Orders Are Orders*). It screened in Germany and the U.S. in the year of the Olympics. Elling's first German film had been the Astra Film-Berlin production *Eine Seefahrt, die ist lustig* (*A Merry Sea Trip*, 1935), a tale about a middle-aged widow, Johanna Müller (Ida Wüst), accompanying her daughter Leni (Hilde Krüger) who is heading to a North Sea beach resort to a meet a prospective German mate. It had screened in the U.S. in late 1938. Elling and Miroslav Cikán had directed the Czech-German comedy about 1920s-style pirates who steal new dress ideas in harmonious Vienna, called *Kein Wort von Liebe/Poslícek lasky* (*Not a Word About Love*, 1937). It screened in the U.S. in fall 1938. Here, Steffie Leutner (Ellen Schwanneke) saves the professional secrets of Vienna clothing manufacturer Pavel Toman (Rolf Wanka) from the alluring but scheming "Stascha" (Margit Symo).

Director Carmine Gallone and producer Alberto Giacalone were responsible for a number of entertaining musicals released as Italian productions that were in German. Their Itala-Tobis musical *Dir gehört mein Herz* (*My Heart Belongs to Thee*, 1938) gave audiences the non–Jewish, smooth-voiced tenor Benjamino Gigli doing what he does best. His film screened at the Garden Theatre in early 1939. Hubert's brother Ernst Marischka (1893–1963) scripted the musical, which is about a foreign journalist (Carla Rüst) who imagines she has discovered a great tenor (Gigli) when she hears a peasant singing. Gigli, playing a famous American tenor, wants to spend a quiet vacation on a farm near Naples. We see him robustly singing in the fields of the Campania countryside in the opening scene. He spends time providing the singing voices for a local marionette operatic theater. The journalist devotes much of her time to launching the career of this "unknown talent," her "discovery." The tenor plays along with the charade and feigns ignorance during her musical tutoring and education. They have fallen in love, however, and only on the evening of the gala event does she realize who he is. The grand finale takes place in Naples, with Brahm's "Cradle Song" the highlight. Gallone also filmed the tale in Italian, a dubbed German version called *Marionette*, and it was one of the many co-productions that the Italian tenor Gigli (1890–1957) made during the 1930s and 1940s in Italy and Germany.

Alberto Giacalone was the producer of *Mutterlied* (*Mother Song*, 1937), directed by Carmine Gallone, which brought together the singing trio of Gigli, Maria Cebotari, and Michael Bohnen in a back-stage melodrama. Scripted by Thea von Harbou, this "old-time recipe ... can't miss," wrote *Variety* (January 1938) from Berlin, "within the Hitler-Mussolini confines." Star tenor Ettore Vanni (Gigli) is married to the singer Fiamma Appiani (Cebotari), who has a past. She has an illegitimate child. Her past catches up to her when the child's unsavory father, Cesare Doret (Bohnen), returns. But fortunately, Cesare's jealous wife, Ricarda (Hilde Hildebrand), murders him. While *Mutterlied* was not shown in the States, the less conspicuous Italian-language rendition called *Solo per Te* reached American filmgoers in late 1938, at the Broadway Cine Roma. Filmed in Berlin, Gallone's dubbed *Solo per Te* (*Only for Thee*, 1937–38) has glorious excerpts from *Andrea Chenier*, *Un ballo in Maschera* and Bizet's *Agnus Dei*, as well as the picture's title work.

Two of Gallone's fellow countrymen, Augusto Genina and Nunzio Malasomma, also had their hands, if not their hearts, in Nazi filmmaking. Genina directed the German-Austrian operatic tale *Blumen aus Nizza* (*Flowers from Nice*, 1936), produced by Tobis, which screened at the Garden Theatre in April 1939. A Paris working girl (Friedl Czepa) "makes a man" out of a gambler (Paul Schönboeck). He has faked a suicide for 40,000 francs as a publicity stunt for another woman (played by Erna Sack, the German coloratura soprano). Genina, however, was later responsible for the much more serious and pro-fascist *Sin Novedad en el Alcazar* (*Siege of the Alcazar*, 1940), an Italian-Spanish production relating the "legendary" 70-day defense of the city of Toledo by Franco's Falangists at the outbreak of the Spanish Civil War. Even though Franco's forces lost this battle, Goebbels called the tale "a modern heroic epic" and "deeply moving."

Malasomma was also no stranger to Deutschland, having directed dozens of Weimar silent films following the collapse of the Italian film industry in the mid–1920s. In the late 1930s,

Malasomma was back in Berlin's studios. There he directed Pola Negri and other well-known screen actresses, including Camilla Horn and Olga Tschechowa, "two of the Teuton screens' most capable and charming actresses," said the *New York Times* (April 15, 1939). They co-starred in Malasomma's *Rote Orchideen* (*Red Orchids*, 1938), an RFD production shown at New York's Casino Theatre. The action-filled tale is about industrial espionage. Draftsman Alexander Nica (Albrecht Schönhals), employed at the F.N. G. Company, is accused of selling state secrets to a foreign agent named "Professor Castro" (Herbert Hübner). Working for the professor is "Countess Ogolenska" (Horn). After fleeing for his life, Nica realizes what his duty is: he must save the life of fellow comrade and engineer Hendrik Laurenz (Fred Döberlein), also falsely accused of espionage, who faces the gallows. Camaraderie comes to the rescue once more.

Camaraderie in the *production* of German films was not something most people found objectionable in the 1930s. However, there was no reason to make it obvious that camaraderie was the norm between German filmmakers and filmmakers in other lands. One case in point was a film that opened in New York in early 1939. *Heart of Paris* was identified as a "Tri–National release" of an "André Daven production," starring the French greats Raimu and Michele Morgan. Veteran filmmaker Marc Allegret directed. Raimu was cast as the honorable bourgeois family man Camille Morestau, who while serving on a jury in a murder trial takes pity on the accused, the waiflike Natalie Rougin (Michele Morgan). Through a series of unlikely circumstances, Morestau invites Natalie to move in with his family for the duration of the trial. Morestau's son Claude (Gilbert Gil) takes an interest her, which causes trouble in the house-

The "French" film *Heart of Paris/Gribouille*, starring Raimu (center). Michelle Morgan is behind Raimu, and Gilbert Gil is at the far laft.

hold. Natalie decides to leave—but not before "borrowing" some valuables to finance her exit. *Heart of Paris* was actually *Gribouille* (1937), which had been produced by Ufa and its French affiliate A.C.E. in the heart of Germany: Berlin. No one raised an eyebrow when this German-French production, which appeared likely to be a moneymaker, screened in the U.S.

Allégret's colleague Raimu later starred in *Noix de coco* (*Coconut*, 1938), which Jean Boyer directed from a script by Marcel Achard. This film was the last joint effort by Ufa–A.C.E. After June 1940, Raimu portentously and proudly proclaimed he would never work in Vichy France. Of his work in Germany, the less said the better. Allégret had deep ties to German-backed productions. He was the director of *Sous les Yeux d'Occident* (*Under Western Eyes*, 1936), a Daven production for A.C.E. that had screened New York's Cameo Theater in March 1937 under the title *Razumov*. Set in revolutionary Russia, the tale concerns informer Razumov (Pierre Fresnay), who's taken for a hero because he unwittingly helped the assassin of a prime minister to escape. Allégret's venomous drama of a lovers' triangle, *Orage* (*Storm*, 1938), another Daven production for A.C.E., screened at New York's Waldorf Theatre at the end of 1938. It starred Charles Boyer and Michele Morgan. Allégret also directed *Entrée des Artists* (*Artists's Entrance*, 1938), which was a Films Sonores Tobis release in Paris. It screened at New York's 55th Street Playhouse in early 1939 under the title *Curtain Rises*, starring Louis Jouvet, Odette Joyeux, and Claude Dauphin as struggling artists at the Paris Conservatory, and Marcel Dalio as an examining judge. When the film's French producer, Regina, re-released the film in Paris in July 1944, the role played by Dalio had been excised. Dalio's name was also removed from the credits as well as the film's posters because he was Jewish. In that print of the film, although Dalio's scenes had been reshot with Fred Pasquili, Dalio's voice is retained on the soundtrack.

The unharmonious, emotion-filled Sudeten crisis—in films and in the news—serves as the background issue in two German-language Czech productions. German propaganda asserted Germany's rights to a portion, if not all, of Czechoslovakia. Perjury and its aftermath make up the plot of *Gottes mühlen mahlen Langsam* (*God's Mills Grind Slowly*, 1938), which showed up at New York's 86th Street Casino Theatre in late February 1939. Directed by Václav Wasserman and scripted by Josef Neuberg as *Bozi mlyny* (*God's Mills*), the tale was re-edited and credited to the non–Jew Josef Medeotti-Boháč, starring Karel Cerny and Jirina Stepnicková. Prag-Film had produced it, but the Continental Company received the credit. Wassermann and Stepkinová had collaborated on *Menschen in den Bergen* (*People in the Mountains*, 1937), the tale of an affair by a married German peasant (Willi Völker) that results in tragedy for him in the troubled region. Credited to Wolfram Film and released by AMROPA, it had screened at the 86th Street Casino in late 1938 under the more contemporary title *Fremd im Sudeten* (*Strangely in the Sudeten Country*).

Hungarian-born Viktor Gertler (1910–1968) directed a co-produced a war picture that opened in New York in early 1939. *Az Elcserelt Ember* (*The Man Who Was Exchanged*, 1938) was a Hunnia-Terra production (in Hungarian) about look-alikes who meet during the Great War. The one who is married is killed, and the other one, who is a kinder and gentler soul and is unmarried, is shell-shocked. Recovering—except for a case of amnesia—he returns to the home—and wife—of his dead friend, more or less resuming life where his dead friend left off. People change places, says the film, and sometimes they're better for it in somebody else's home.

Hungarian-born Roger von Norman (1908–2000), the film editor of the anti–Semitic *Togger*, tried his own hand at directing films for the Third Reich. He was responsible for Terra's comedy *Spiel in Sommerwind* (*Play in the Summer Breeze*, 1938). Percy (Rolf Moebius) is a young man who, after acknowledging the call to return to Germany after many years abroad, tries to avoid the marriage plans his mother has in store for him. The girl she's picked for him is named Aenne Osterkamp (Hannelore Schroth). Percy consults his sister, Edith (Lola Müthel) about this turn of events, but she is in on the plot, too. When Percy eventually falls in love with a baker's daughter named Amalie, he's in for a surprise. It's really Aenne. Sometimes a young German just has to go with the flow. "Persons wishing to see the historic beauty spots of Germany without putting much foreign exchange into the treasury of Hitler's Reich will find a pretty fair 'Ersatz' in this film," wrote the *New York Times* (April 1, 1939), when the film was featured at the Garden Theatre. Norman was also responsible for the Terra production *Himmelhunde* (*Sky Dogs*, 1941–42), a production that Goebbels' ministry financed, which asks Germany's disciplined and obedient young men to go with a different flow: to do their duty and join the Luftwaffe in Germany's battle against Britain.

Hübler-Kahla's *Ein Walzer um den Stefansturm* (*A Waltz around the Stefanstand*) is set in merry old Vienna. The comedy is of a widowed countess (Olga Tschechowa) in love with a handsome lawyer (Wolf Albach-Retty) who's been reduced to a taxi driver. At the same time, he is carrying on an affair with the woman's adopted daughter (Gusti Huber), now a chorus girl. The comedy results from the countess's chauffeur, played by the former Othello of the Metropolitan Opera Company, Leo Slezak, who is able to imitate radio broadcasts. Shown at the Garden Theatre in spring 1939 (on a double bill with Bolváry's musical *Zwei Herzen im dreiviertel Takt*, 1930), *Ein Walzer um den Stefansturm* had screened in the U.S. in February 1937 under the title *Freuhling im Wien* (*Springtime in Vienna*), although its actual Austrian-produced title was *Sylvia und ihr Chauffeur* (1935). The second time around *Ein Walzer um den Stefansturm* came with English titles so that filmgoers could enjoy its comedy, pleasing music, and scenes of Austria's capital.

Hübler-Kahla's burlesque of British life, called *Der Geheimnisvolle Mister X* (*The Mysterious Mister X*), played at the Casino Theatre, having first been shown in Germany in the year of the Berlin Olympics. The story begins when Nelly Taylor (Mady Rahl, b. 1915, in her film debut) writes to her boss, Lord Wilford (Ralph Arthur Roberts), who's traveling, that there's trouble at home. An inept sleuth named "Richard Murray" (Hermann Thimig) has been assigned to locate a stranger—a Mister X—purportedly hiding within Wilford's castle. His wife (Annemarie Steinieck), it turns out, concocted the story for a reason: she hopes this news will hasten her husband's return. Then, lo and behold, they discover a real crook (Curt Ackermann, 1905–1988). He turns out to be James, Wilford's nephew. Order is then restored within this confused British household.

Johannes Meyer's *Diskretion-Ehrensache* (*Discretion—Word of Honor*, 1938), which was released by Ufa, is a German effort at portraying the British. In this drama about mistaken identities, young inventor Peter Parker (Hans Holt) gets involved in the life of madcap heiress Mary Hopkins (Heli Finkenzeller) in the English countryside. That includes a scandal after she's discovered in a compromising position. Because her father had betrothed her to a Lord Benton (Theo Lingen), she winds up eloping with the inventor. Director Meyer, unlike his colleagues in their British-based Sherlock Holmes films, was unable to establish a believable British atmosphere. Meyer's conception of British nobility, however, fit the Nazi image of aristocratic England. The villain of the tale, which screened at the Garden Theatre in March 1939, turns out to be Benton, who's really an arch-criminal.

Exposing Britain's global reach is the backdrop of Austrian-born Eduard von Borsody's first film in America, Ufa's *Kautschuk* (1938). Documentary scenes of the Brazilian jungle and semi-historical nonsense are used to condemn the British for their exploitation of one of Brazil's natural resources—"kautschuk," the Indian word for rubber—in the nineteenth century. The Nazis once more present themselves as the ever-watchful protectors of peoples past. Called *The Green Hell* when it premiered in the U.S. in early 1939, *Kautschuk* starred Gustav Diessl, René Deltgen (1909–1979), and Roma Bahn (1896–1975), with a score by the prolific Werner Bochmann (1900–1993). Deltgen, who was Luxembourg's most famous collaborating actor in

Kautschuk.

the Third Reich, played the explorer Sir Henry Wickham, who in 1876 is on his way to Brazil on board the *Wellington*. His pretext is that he's looking for a rare Amazon butterfly. He meets and falls in love with Mary Waverley (Vera van Langen), fiancée to one of Brazil's biggest rubber plantation owners. Wickham's hairbreadth escapes enable him to smuggle hevea seeds of the forbidden tree out of the jungle. This "biopiracy" breaks Brazil's hold on rubber and leads to Britain's (unrightful) economic gain. Diessl played the ferocious, hot-tempered plantation owner Alonzo de Ribeira, who loses Mary to the British explorer. The tale's realism was said to have been due to graphic shots taken by members of producer-scriptwriter Franz Eichhorn's 1935–36 German expedition to the Amazon. In addition, Eichhorn's Weimar-era Amazon documentary *Die Grüne Hölle* (*The Green Hell*, 1931) had inspired the title.

Goebbels called Borsody's film a "hymn to British imperialism," "magnificently political and artistic." Ufa promoted the film in the States as a "super spectacle, abundant with thrills and stirring drama, outdoing anything Hollywood has ever achieved along similar lines." It also claimed that Borsody's film was the only German film to have "received four stars by American newspaper critics."

Director Borsody later directed Ufa's *Sensationsprozess Casilla* (*Sensational Casilla Trial*, 1939), which was a reminder of America's Lindbergh kidnapping case. In this tale, based on the novel by Hans Possendorff, a German named Peter Roland (Albert Hehn) is on trial in America in 1928 for the kidnapping of Sylvia Casilla, a child star. His lawyer is Vandegrift (Heinrich George), an American whom Roland had met on a flight in North Africa. Roland, in custody, had managed to land their plane after its pilots became ill. In gratitude, Vandergrift agreed to represent Roland at his trial. Roland admits he had a hand in the kidnapping. But he did it to save Sylvia—his daughter—from a worse fate. Her mother, residing in South

America, was injecting Sylvia with an anti-growth serum. Through this bit of pseudo-science, Sylvia remained young and a source of income for the girl's mother. Then, just as Sylvia is to appear at the trial as a witness, she is murdered. American critics in Europe missed this production. Liable to increase anti–German feelings in the States, *Sensationsprozess Casilla* was not shown in America.

The following year Borsody directed the hit of the season in Germany, the queasily uplifting *Der Wunschkonzert* (*Wish Concert*, 1940), which featured Hitler. In his only feature cameo, the German leader opens the 1936 Berlin Olympics. The tale's protagonists are young Germans who meet and fall in love at the games, parting company after three days because he (Carl Radditz) has to go to Spain to fight in the civil war. That's the last she (Ilse Werner) hears of him until September 1939. Then during a broadcast of a Wish Concert, his name comes up. At the end, they are a couple again.

When the film screened at the Apollo in Vienna in early 1941, *Film-Kurier* wrote: "Representatives of the Party, the State, the

Top and above: Das Wunschkonzert, with Ilse Werner.

Wehrmacht, and the city of Vienna attended the premiere. The German Weekly Newsreel and an Ufa cultural film *German Tanks*, which showed the development of this modern weapon, met with much applause. Then a Wehrmacht military band played marches.... Before the main feature there was a small applause. Over the loudspeaker the voice of the *Wish Concert* moderator, Heinz Goedecke, was heard from Berlin. He warmly greeted the Viennese audience and regretted that the ever-rising flood of requests from soldiers prevented his coming personally to Vienna. He wished the film all the best, and concluded with the words, "'Goodbye until Sunday, at the Wehrmacht Wish Concert.'" *Der Wunschkonzert*, which contains an actual Wish Concert by the Berlin Philharmonic, was slated for release in the States in late 1941, but December 7 ended its chances.

As the force and effects of German film propaganda increased, the messages became pervasive. No idea was left untouched. For example, did Hitler have a hero, perhaps a prototype? The local U.S. theater had the answer in early 1939. It was Johannes Meyer's *Fridericus* (1937), which was one of the more powerful of Germany's numerous films about Prussia's Frederick the Great. Goebbels referred to Frederick as "The great king, the only king" who spoke of Germany as often as he mentioned Prussia. With Hitler—Germany's twentieth-century Frederick—firmly in power, the film was bearing a clear message for the West. But first there was the calm before the storm.

The prologue sets the stage: "Prussia is in the ascendant after decades of fighting for the right to exist.... The whole world watches with astonishment and admiration as the Prussian king ... stands his ground ... Prussia's hour of destiny has come." During the Seven Years' War, the great Prussian king (Otto Gebühr) battles enemies within and without, including Madame Pompadour and Maria Theresa of Austria. The production, which Marc Roland scored, depicts the defeat of the Austrian General Laudon, after which the French send an army of 50,000 to deal with the patriotic Marquis de Brandenbourg. Although Frederick's army advances through the countryside, his position remains tenuous. Another of his enemies, Elizabeth of Russia, gives the order for her troops to march against Berlin as Frederick's forces are encircled. All appears lost until Frederick, who "loves war for glory," hears of the death of his beloved sister. Shocked, he is spurred on to attack, and with the help of Ziete's Husars, overwhelms his enemies. Frederick returns to Potsdam—victorious—ready to build the New Reich of which he has so long dreamed.

Kameraden auf See (*Comrades at Sea*, 1938), which Heinz Paul directed and Robert Küssel scored, offered Americans further opportunity to get a better feel for the expanding, contemporary German military machine. It is a rarity of sorts: a Nazi-era film that refers to the civil war in Spain, here presented as a communist plot against the legal, pro-fascist government of the country. The film came to the U.S. when the Spanish Civil War was over. The action is on the high seas. A young German lieutenant (Fred Döderlein), serving aboard a torpedo boat, is in love with a dark-haired young Spanish beauty (Carola Hoehn). But his commanding officer becomes her fiancé. The young man is in despair as his boat heads out to Spanish waters. The young woman, it turns out, happens to be on board a Spanish steamer captured by Russians. They kill its captain. Boldness on the lieutenant's part, in coordination with the German navy, saves the woman he wanted to wed. His daring earns the thanks of his commander, though the young officer does have to serve two days in the brig for disobeying orders. But the punishment is more than worth it to maintain camaraderie and honor among German military personnel.

"Dr. Goebbels' scenario writers had to weave out of whole cloth a none-too-dramatic episode involving a German torpedo boat and a 'Red' Spanish craft," wrote the *New York Times* (April 22, 1939). "This was quite unnecessary, because the technique is fine and the scenes around Kiel, on the Baltic during maneuvers and off the Spanish coast, or islands, are enough in themselves to make the film worth seeing." The critic called the mixing of the regulation naval salute with the Nazi salute "grotesque." Germany banned the film after the war.

At Ufa, Erich Engel directed *Hotel Sacher* (1939), which offers the air of reckless gaiety, intrigue, and the games of life and death that pervaded the capital and the famous hotel in Austria-Hungary on the eve of the First World War. For one man, honor comes before anything else. Containing English titles, *Hotel Sacher* reached New York's Garden Theatre—which called itself "Das Haus bester Deutscher Filmkunst"—in spring 1939. Willy Birgel plays the upright officer of Ruthenian origin and Sybille Schmitz is the "fellow Slav" trying to win him to the cause of Greater Russia. January 1, 1914, sees the end of New Year revelry and the start of tragedy, at least for Germans in the old empire.

In Vienna's famous Hotel Sacher, Austrian, French, and Russian aristocrats, diplomats, bank magnates, officers in splendid uniforms, and beautiful women celebrate New Year's Eve, 1914. At the Imperial Opera House everybody is in high spirits. The ballet dancers perform as never before. However, behind the scenes, many people of the Austrian Empire are full of unrest. Secret enemies are working to further the disintegration. The Russian Intelligence Service is busy in the Austrian province of Galicia, where members are assisting Poles against White Russians and Ruthenians. Najda Woroneff (Schmitz), working for Russia, tries to exploit her relationship with Austrian official Schefczuk (Birgel), who may be in love with her. Being a good and trustworthy Austrian, although born a Slav, he vows to turn her in to the secret police, thereby proving his loyalty to the nation. However, he has second thoughts. Perhaps Najda is right: Austria is really falling apart. Since he is in love with Najda and senses Austria's decline, there is only one solution for an honest German patriot who refuses to be branded a traitor: suicide. When Najda leaves the hotel, the police follow her. The game is up when in a secluded room of the hotel a shot rings out and a man lies dead on the floor. The first shot of the bloody year 1914 has claimed its first victim. Also in the cast was Karl Stepanek, who later earned Goebbels' displeasure and was designated *persona non grata* for having given a radio talk in London. Rosa Albach-Retty (1874–1980) and her son Wolf were in the cast as was Oskar Werner as a hotel page.

The film signaled war again. Goebbels called the film "wonderfully well made"—after making sure it was "politically watertight," although after the war, Engel's supporters argued that his film has pacifist overtones, if spectators use their imagination and what the director called "creative-cooperation."

Simultaneously, leftist-rumored Engel's *Hohe Schule* (*College*, 1934), a German-Austria production by Syndikat, was released in New York. It's the story of a mysterious artist working under the name Carlo Cavelli (Rudolf Forster) who always wears a black mask. A trick rider, he returns to Vienna after many years. He turns out to be a man with a secret: he was a former Austrian army officer dismissed from the military because he killed his best friend in a duel. The dead man's sister (Angela Sallocker) then falls in love with him while her father, a general, swears vengeance. But the disgraced officer had done his duty because his so-called friend had actually been spying for a foreign power and was sentenced to death in a courtmartial. Hans Moser as Cavelli's ever-faithful servant "controls the scenes," wrote *Reichsfilmblatt Berlin*, which in 1935 singled out the film for its "humanity." Future Hollywood actor Paul Heinreid costarred. A humane German film was certainly useful to the Nazis in the critical year 1939.

Engel also directed two other productions that were screened at the Casino Theatre before the U.S. declared war on Germany: *Gefährliches Spiel* (*A Dangerous Game*, 1936) and *Nanette* (1939). Both productions starred Jenny Jugo playing a resourceful, dynamic young German woman for whom nothing is impossible. In the former film, a drama produced by Klageman, Rosy (Jugo) saves her father, Baron Carl Erich von Wenden (Harry Liedke), from a jail sentence because he misappropriated 280,000 marks from his bank. After failing to convince her grandfather to bail out her father, Rosy falls in love with Dr. Helmut Boromäus (Karl Martell), who will cover the old man's indebtedness.

Jugo's Nanette, a "girl of the people" (according to Ufa's promotional material), is the fiery inspiration and muse for a playwright (Hans Söhnker) suffering from writer's block. Casino Film Exchange promoted *Nanette* as a "popular" film that "brings a sense of gladness and amusement into our hearts—there are hours of the very best" entertainment. In both films, there's a happy ending to life's tribulations.

In late May 1939, at the Garden Theatre, Wolfgang Liebeneiner's *Ziel in den Wolken* (*Target in the Clouds*, 1938), spelled out one of Germany's purported historical achievements: the nation's success at having built a fleet of modern military aircraft, in the early part of the twentieth century. The protagonist, who is depicted as a young Göring, lives by a simple motto: "Whoever takes off his uniform takes off his honor; who once in Prussia quits the army never is taken back," he says. "I am wearing the uniform also when I am in civilian clothes." Produced by Terra and shown the previous December in Berlin, the film, co-starring the alluring Brigitte Horney, begins in 1909, when Walter von Suhr (Albert Matterstock), a lieutenant in the 3rd Ulan Guards in Potsdam, is shocked at the state of German aircraft at a show in Johannisthal, in 1909. He proposes constructing new and efficient military machines. The old guard ridicules his suggestions, whereupon Suhr resigns his commission. At Lehmann's airfield, Suhr—a sort of young Göring—works on aeronautic designs with the likes of well-known scientists: Latham, Farman, Bleriot, Le Blanc, Krasselt, Kamphausen, and Menzel—all non-Jews. When Suhr finally demonstrates his new plane to the German Generstaff, they are impressed. Building the new German air force has become a reality. The film also contrasts two women. Leny Marenbach played the girl who sticks by Suhr, come what may, while Brigitte Horney played an actress determined to prevent her lover (Werner Futterer) from risking his life in the air. Released in New York, the film, scripted by Eberhard Frowein, depicts an older generation unable to foresee a Germany that "will be proud to have prepared for the time when planes will be the army of the future." Goebbels awarded the production a National Film Prize. American critics called the film "instructive and diverting."

Also that May, *Aufruhr in Damaskus* (*Tumult in Damascus*, 1939) let Americans know that the new Germany was a far cry from the Germany of the Weimar years. Screened here barely three months after its Berlin premiere, *Aufruhr in Damaskus* attacks the policies of pre–Hitler German military leaders in the Middle East. In 1918, on the Arabian-Syrian front, a certain Colonel Lawrence opposes German influence in the region. The British have surrounded a German garrison, led by Captain "Schulz" (Heinz Welzel), a presumed Jew. But the garrison's ammunition and food are running out. Schulz orders Lt. Hans Keller (Joachim Gottschalk) to head to Damascus for fresh supplies. With four others, Keller comes upon a caravan of mysterious Arabs from whom the five Germans rescue a kidnap victim: Vera Niemeyer (Brigitte Horney), who is German. But then, as Keller and his men are about to return, orders arrive from headquarters in Berlin for Schulz to *abandon* the German fort and for the troops to return home. Schulz dies trying to reach Damascus while Keller holds off the British as long as he can. Goebbels had a fondness for colonial themes, calling this film "well made," its "milieu, slant and attitude" superb. Gustav Ucicky, of *Morgenrot* infamy, directed the film, which Jacob Geis scripted. The *New York Times* (May 6, 1939) called *Aufruhr in Damaskus,* which screened at the Casino Theatre, "one of the best made and objective films based on the World War ever turned out by the Terra concern or any other German producer." The fact that "there can be no really 'happy ending' from the Teuton standpoint, as Damascus was occupied by British cavalry on Oct. 1 and twenty-nine days later Turkey sued for peace," wrote the *New York Times,* "is offset by the heroism of the German company in its battle with burning sands and human enemies."

Ad for *Hotel Sacher*.

Ufa contract to screen *Nanette*.

Retreat is exactly the kind of thing, the film implies, that the new rulers in the new Germany would never have done and will never do! The Nazis' pro-colonial theme reached a low with *Carl Peters* (1941), filmed in the year Gottschalk died. Goebbels had a hand in Gottschalk's death. Joachim Gottschalk had insisted that his wife accompany him to a meeting of the film industry's Artist's Association in Berlin. At their dinner the propaganda minister was charmed by Mrs. Gottschalk—until he discovered she was Jewish. Goebbels then ordered Gottschalk to divorce his wife if he wanted to continue his acting career. Unable to leave the country, 37-year-old Gottschalk, his wife, and their nine-year-old son gassed themselves to death in November 1941.

In May 1939, at the Casino Theatre, Anton Kutter's *Weisse Majestät* (*The White Majesty*, 1933–34) was taken out of storage and shown to Americans interested in an action-packed, Alpine German-Swiss-French production, featuring Austrian-born Gustav Diessl (1899–1948) and Hertha Thiele, in one of her last films from Hitler's Germany. It's a Heimat (home) melodrama about a young mountain guide named Jacob Burkhardt (Diessl) who is able to do feats of daring in the Alps. But he's illegitimately born, which makes him an outcast but at the same time a sort of hero (to the Nazis). He's accused of having killed Dr. Reymond (Carl de Vogt), a non–German federal high court judge. Local villagers shun him. Circumstances—a huge inheritance if he makes a particularly dangerous climb—and his love for young Monika Amatter (Thiele) bring him into the open.

A director of mountain films before the war, Kutter was responsible in wartime Nazi Germany for the production of military *kulturefilme* (short documentaries) that were screened before main features. Serge de Poligny and René Le Henaff directed a French-language version of *Weisse Majestät* titled *Un de la Montagne* (*Mountain Man*, 1934), which did not screen in the U.S. But the dubbed Italian version, called *Amore sulle Alpi*, premiered in October 1939 in New York. It starred Diessl and Simone Bourday.

Hammering home the message about the wonderful people of the great outdoors within the fatherland was Joe Stöckel's Panorama Film production *Stärker als die Liebe* (*Stronger Than Love*, 1938), which CFE released in May 1939. Here, the Nazis' blood-and-soil ethos is touched upon again. German foresters are soldiers, and so are their women. The heroine of the tale is Annemarie (Leny Marenbach), the daughter of chief forester Mierau (Paul Wegener). She finds herself torn between her love for handsome reprobate painter Rolf von Mansar (Ivan Petrovich) and her sense of duty to marry the widower assistant forester Carl Hoffmann (Paul Richter) who has a young son. When the painter is revealed as a long-wanted poacher, everything falls into place for the happy conclusion. Her sister Liesbeth (Karin Hardt) has an easier time of it and sets the right example. Early on she only has eyes for an honorable country youth. What turns out to be "stronger than love" are the heroine's sense of duty, and her feelings towards her father and the mythical German forest and its inhabitants. In contrast to the sturdy, virile East Prussians is the depiction of an Austrian named "Count Liebenow" (Georg Heinrich Schnell), a presumed Jew who is ridiculed but also comforted with the words, "In your country there is understanding for the more pleasant sides of life."

Duty and honor are the central conceits in Gustaf Gründgens's *Der Schritt vom Wege* (*Misstep*, 1938–39), produced by Terra, where a mother's marriage arrangement for her daughter leads to tragedy. But in this case, the tale takes place before the Hitler era. *Der Schritt vom Wege*—the fourth film the star actor Gründgens directed during the Hitler years—opens with Effi Briest's parents standing over Effi's grave. The story is then told in flashback. Effi Briest's mother (Käthe Haack) has news for her: Baron von Instetten (Karl Ludwig Diehl), the district manager in Kessin, in Meckenburg (remember *Morgenrot*), has asked for the girl's hand in marriage. Unsure but taken by her mother's excitement at the prospect of their climbing the social ladder, the seventeen-year-old Effi (Marianne Hoppe) accepts. Her marriage, however, is one of loneliness and boredom: the baron—this is not a surprise!—is more devoted to his career and to traditional living. Within this provincial society, Effi catches the attention of the charming Major Crampas (Paul Hartmann), and meets him at recitals, at dances, and at the theater. He's even there at the birth of her daughter. She ends the brief, innocent affair when her husband is offered a post in Berlin. Six years later, when Effi is visiting a spa, her

Ufa's press material for *Der Schritt vom Wege*.

life takes a tragic turn: her husband discovers incriminating letters from the captain, who has since retired to a farm. The baron challenges him to a duel, killing him. The baron's code of honor always allowed him to rationalize his actions in a "higher idea." "We are not alone and single in the world," he said. "We belong to a totality; if society disdains you, you will finally disdain yourself." Thus he could kill someone. The news shocks Effi. Her health quickly deteriorates. Estranged from her daughter, she dies of a broken heart in her parents' home. The baron gets the news of his wife's death—along with the news of a promotion.

Gründgens's film was one of the most highly rated of Germany's cultural films released in America. Based on German writer Theodor Fontane's most popular work, the 1895 novel *Effi Briest,* the film has been called one of Nazi Germany's centerpieces in attacking nineteenth-century attitudes and codes of honor with a hypocritical fervor. With music by composer Mark Lothar (1902–1985), the film's depiction of respectable, prewar upper-class life is in tune with Nazi loathing of the era, stressing the need to break with features of the past and create a new Germany. So as to make the message clear, the characters speak in modern German. The *Herald Tribune* (April 30, 1939) wrote that "wisely," the production company "enlisted a capable cast and able director to bring to German American audiences the tender drama" about the life and death of a child bride. Elisabeth Flickenschildt (1905–1977), a colleague of Gründgens, had a part in the film. "Denazified" after the war, she won German cinema's best actress award in 1963—the year Gründgens died.

Wolfgang Liebeneiner's *Der Florentiner Hut* (*The Leghorn Hat*, 1939), which Michael Jary scored, offered more opportunity for distraction. It is merely a film about an accident and its consequences. The hat in question turns out to be a problematic headcovering—not the one worn by Jews but one eaten by a horse—that threatens to derail the marriage plans of a bachelor in a hurry. On his way to the ceremony through the woods, Theo Farina (Heinz Rühmann) is caught unawares when his horse eats the hat of flirtatious Baroness Pamela von Sarabant (Christl Mardayn), who was spending a few moments with her lover. Farina has to find the very same rare headcovering to save her from humiliation. She can't go home without it because its absence would surely arouse the suspicions of her jealous husband (Paul Henckels). A new hat will also save the desperate Farina's upcoming marriage to Helene (Herti Kirchner). Terra's production was based Labiche and Michel's popular play *Un Chapeau de paille d'Italie,* which René Clair had successfully filmed in 1927. Certainly the Nazi rendition wasn't saying that the unintentional loss of property required owners to be compensated?

In June 1939, when Liebeneiner's film was shown in New York, the 26-year-old Kirchner was dead as a result of a car crash in Berlin. Liebeneiner himself had starred opposite Martha Eggerth in Viktor Janson's 1935 musical comedy *Blonde Carmen,* released four years later in the States. He played a librettist living in a small village, trying to complete an operetta entitled *Carmen the Blonde Woman.* A famous singer is vacationing in the same village, and he decides to get to know her, for inspiration both professionally and personally. Mix-ups all around were at the forefront of still another comedy from Nazi Germany. In Carl Boese's *Verliebte Herzen* (*Hearts of Love*, 1938), a June 1939 release in the States starring Karin Hardt and Paul Hörbiger, a doctor plans to "educate" a servant girl, that is, make her more German, before marrying her.

Arthur M. Rabenalt's circus tale of love and intrigue, *Männer müssen so sein* (*Men Are That Way*, 1938–1939), repeats the honor and saved-at-the-last-minute plot of *Truxa* (1937). A Terra production based on the novel by Heinrich Seiler and scored by Michael Jary that screened at the Casino Theatre in May 1939, it concerns young, alluring Beatrice Rasmussen (Hertha Feiler), who runs away from Hamburg to become a ringside dancer. The German animal trainer Ruda (Hans Söhnker) falls in love with her, then vanishes. Working at a second circus, she attracts the attention of the non–German marksman named Cameron (Hans Olden). Having already killed the wife of one circus performer, he plots to kill this dancer. Only Ruda's reappearance saves her from the jaws of this tiger.

In Atalanta-Film's circus drama *Die Gläserne Kugel* (*The Glass Ball*, 1937), which Hans Carste (1909–1971) scored and which CFE released in mid–1939, a man attempts to extricate himself from a disastrous love affair with a Jewish woman in Vienna. Peter Stanchina

(1899–1967) directed what Bavaria Film called a "silent cold mystery" about the consequences of the theft of 40,000 shillings. This was the only film he directed in the Third Reich, starring the longtime performer Albrecht Schönhals (1888–1978), who played Baron Axel von Schack, jailed for a crime his girlfriend Nina (Hilde von Stolz) had committed. She was the one who stole the money from her elderly, unlovable German-Jewish husband, the banker "Fritz Sylten" (Theodor Loos). Ten years later, when Nina's a widow, her former lover is living as the daredevil circus performer Fred Parker, whose stunt involves riding a glass ball. Nina threatens to expose his past—he's an escaped convict, after all—unless he gives up his circus sweetheart Nelly (Sabine Peters, 1913–1982). The film, which the *New York Times* (June 17, 1939) called "passable entertainment," co-starred Paul Henckels (1885–1967) as "Franz Sylten," the imperious banker's brother. He goes by the alias Trix, the inventor of the glass-ball stunt. German cinema awarded Schönhals an honorary prize for his life's work in 1965.

Viktor Janson's incongruously titled *Uber Alles die Treue* (*Honesty Is the Best Policy*) screened at the Casino Theatre in June 1939. The film, having been produced in the year of the Berlin Olympics, was actually *Mädchen in weiss* (*Girls in White*). Its German subtitle was, "I Am Here to Be Happy." *Mädchen in weiss* is a pre–World War I Russian tale starring the prominent Russian-born performers Ivan Petrovitch as the imperious Count "Feodor Iwanowitsch Schuwaloff" and Maria Cebotari (1910–1949) playing his fiancée, Daniela, one of the beautiful girls at St. Petersburg's Smolny Institute. Her mother had been a great opera diva and Daniela wishes to follow in her footsteps. But Schuwaloff opposes her plans. Then she meets Grand Duke Sergei Alexandrewitch (Georg Alexander), who falls in love with her. *His* girlfriend, Natalia (Hilde von Stolz), another student at the institute, becomes jealous, and concocts a story about Daniela stealing a valuable piece of jewelry from Schuwaloff. Cebotari, born in Bessarabia, was a well-known singer in the Third Reich who married German star Gustav Diessl.

In June 1939, Ufa's military-based production *Drei Unteroffiziere* (*Three Noncommissioned Officers*, 1939), which was directed by Werner Hochbaum, premiered in New York, barely 60 days after its Berlin release. German distributors were in a hurry to get the latest production to America, perhaps to suggest to Americans that war against Germany was a bad idea. Displaying up-to-date German implements of destruction, the film, hinting at war, relates the story of three warrant officers in the Wehrmacht, in spring 1939. Episodes of their service in peacetime instill a sense of calm and confidence, as do their feelings of German comradeship, since each man is always ready to help the other. Then there's trouble. The soldier Erich Rauscher (Albert Hehn) falls for the young actress Gerda Cyrus (Ruth Hellberg). He neglects his army duty. He even defies orders. The main portion of the tale deals with his comrades' efforts to save him from himself. Officers Fritz Kohlhammer (Fritz Genschow) and Struve (Wilhelm H. König) succeed masterfully. Now they're focused, ready for action, if and when called upon to do their duty for Hitler. In the cast was acclaimed opera singer Elisabeth Schwarzkopf (1915–2006), playing Carmen. This was the first of five films she made in Nazi Germany. Director Hochbaum purportedly made this film against his will. Reports had it that Goebbels then banned Hochbaum from film work within Germany. Or maybe Hochbaum saw the disastrous war ahead and quit before it was too late. Germany banned *Drei Unteroffiziere* after the war.

Luise and Jacob Fleck's Austrian comedy *Pfarrer von Kirchfeld* (*The Pastor from Kirchfeld*, 1937) starred the Jewish actor Hans Jaray as an emotional and understanding young problem-solving preacher dealing with a crazed mountaineer and an alluring, pretty maid (Hansi Storck). The film screened in the U.S. in spring 1939—a year after Germany's union with Austria—while Jewish director Jacob Fleck was interned in Dachau and Buchenwald. Freed after serving 16 months when Hollywood director William Dieterle bought his release, Jacob and Luise

Fleck made their way to China. Dieterle had starred in the Fleck's 1926 version of *Der Pfarrer von Kirchfeld*.

In summer 1939, *The Oppenheim Family* (1939), based on Lion Feuchtwanger's story "The Oppermanns," opened in New York, where it was said at the time that Hitler was a greater celebrity than Henny Youngman. A Mosfilm production which Grigori Roshal directed, it depicts a Jewish family's persecution in Berlin in the 1930s, leaving little to the imagination: the Nazis' racism, cruelty, and truncheons; the boots of the Storm Troopers; and the uniformed "mobocracy" in the window-smashing violence. *Variety* (June 1939) objected, accusing the filmmakers of falling into the "usual rut of choosing only outright villainous types for Nazi parts. It seems reasonable to suppose," it said, "that many of the Hitler storm troopers are merely misguided young Germans rather than deep-dyed stock-company heavies." The next German film to be released in the U.S. arrived after September 1, 1939.

September 1939–April 1940

....
"Where's the Enemy Hiding?"

In September, following Germany's invasion of Poland, six nations—Britain, France, Australia, New Zealand, South Africa, and Canada—declared war on Germany. Later that month, in Operation Saar, the French Army retreated from its "invasion" of five miles into Germany. In October, Hitler announced plans to "resolve" the "Jewish problem." In January 1940, the Nazi regime initiated gassings of Jews in an effort to purge Jews from Europe. In March 1940, Italy agreed to join Germany's war against Britain and France. As the world struggled to deal with German militarism, the first German-language film to open in the States after the start of World War II glorified military and autocratic rule. U.S. filmgoers who viewed Viktor Tourjansky's *Der Gouverneur* (1939), which was based on Otto Emmerich Groh's drama *The Flag*, were treated to Hitler's justification for Nazi rule in Germany. Its plot parallels the anti-parliamentarian views Hitler had espoused towards Weimar Germany.

In *Mein Kampf*, Hitler said, "Is it at all possible actually to call to account the leaders of a parliamentary government for any kind of action which originated in the wishes of the whole multitude of deputies and was carried out under their orders or sanction? Instead of developing constructive ideas and plans, does the business of a statesman consist in the art of making a whole pack of blockheads understand his projects? Is it his business to entreat and coach them so that they will grant him their generous consent?"

In the drama, which screened at the 86th Street Garden Theatre 90 days after its June 1939 Berlin premiere, Gen. Gregor Werkonen (Willy Birgel), a high-ranking officer in a European nation which appears to be a Scandinavian country, dissolves parliament—with the consent of the prince, of course—when civilian authorities are unable to handle tensions on the border. At the same time, the threat of a major civilian strike looms within the country. The general orders his army to assume control because of the "corruption of parliamentarianism" and a looming coup by radicals. The general names himself governor-general, head of government. While he's dealing with matters of state, his wife Maria (Brigitte Horney) begins to feel ignored. When radical party boss Dr. Sarko (Walter Franck) is murdered, evidence implicates Lieutenant Runeberg (played by the rising star Ernst von Klipstein). The young officer, to the governor-general's chagrin, serves in his regiment—a unit that has a 300-year tradition of honor to uphold. The young officer also has an airtight alibi for the night of the murder: he was with the governor-general's wife. The governor-general is faced with what seem to be irreconcilable choices: either to end his marriage or sentence to death an innocent man to

Publicity material for German films, 1938–41.

death. He makes a noble decision: he frees the young officer because, he says, the honor of the regiment ranks higher than his mere pride. If the army's reputation were besmirched, the people would lose faith in its nation's soldiers. They would equate its officers with the scoundrels who once ran the country. The general comes out ahead on two counts: he keeps his marriage intact and continues his one-man rule! Goebbels called Tourjansky's's film "delightful in attitude and slant," an assessment that *Variety* (June 14, 1939), reporting for the last time from Berlin, agreed with. It said that the film "has all the ingredients that keeps the Europe of today moving in circles—national honor, discipline, obedience, and the obligatory Führer faith."

The up-and-coming Hannelore Schroth (1922–1987), German star Käthe Haack's daughter, had a part in this film. It also signaled the start of a film career for von Klipstein (1908–1993): two-dozen productions under the Nazis over the next seven years, including Karl Ritter's *Stukas* (1941). Klipstein showed his mettle in Nazi films requiring heroes and vigorous patriotism. After the war, von Klipstein doubted he would be "denazified" for film work; he found refuge in the theatre. He didn't appear again on the screen until 1955.

Earlier in 1938, director Tourjansky and the actor in the title role of *Der Gouverneur*, Willy Birgel, had teamed up to make a similarly themed militarist and authoritarian tale, called *Geheimzeichen LB 17*, a Terra production, in which the government of an unnamed country finds itself threatened by anarchists, including army officers. A patriotic officer, however, foils the revolution by exposing the ringleader: the prefect of police. Americans didn't have a chance to see this one nor did westerners in Europe review it. Nor did Americans or western reviewers abroad manage to discover that Tourjansky made a film called *Feinde* (*Enemy*, 1940), a Bavaria production that inverts actual events that had transpired in Poland in 1939. Polish "atrocities" became the Nazis' justification for World War II. In *Feinde*, which Goebbels' ministry financed, the prologue gives the film away. "Humanity," it says, "will never forget the untold suffering of the German people in Poland, for whom the whole of the postwar period was a time of unceasing victimization." In 1939, "60,000 were slaughtered like cattle." The tale takes place in the days before September 1939, along the Polish-German border. Germans learn that Poles have attacked a neighboring German farm, killed the owner, plundered the farmhouse, and burnt the place to the ground. These kinds of attacks increase in the weeks ahead. Polish hooligans, secretly supported by local authorities, intensify their activities and daily threaten the Germans. The Germans realize that their time in Poland is up. Some try to depart but become trapped in a bog. Their leader (Ivan Petrovich, 1894–1961) returns to the village to try to find help. In an inn full of Poles, he meets a young girl (Brigitte Horney) who was born German. Knowing about the terrain, she leads her fellow Germans to the safety of the new Reich. Germany banned *Feinde* after the war.

Even as Americans were viewing foreboding German films in the late 1930s, they were unaware that they were witnessing the end of an era for Yiddish films. In the mid-1930s film critic Wolfe Kaufman had observed, "there isn't a language which is as international as Yiddish. In Russia or America, and even in darkest Africa, one finds Jews who stick to their language and use it constantly. In the world one finds Yiddish books of quality, Yiddish music with worth and Yiddish theatre which is real theatre, and which the world can recognize as art. But if any of these Jews want to see a film they must see it in English, or French, or Russian, or some other language."

New York's Continental Theatre had screened Alexander Ford's documentary *Children Must Laugh*, about a Jewish-run shelter in Warsaw, called the Vladimir Medem Sanitarium, which treated thousands of poverty-stricken Jewish children suffering from tuberculosis. This film, originally titled *Mir kumen an* (*I'm Marching On*, 1936), is one of the few surviving documentaries depicting prewar Jewish life in Poland and life at the Jewish Labor Bund's Medem Sanatorium, which existed from 1926–1942. "Out of the sorrows and shadows of the life of workers in Poland," wrote the *New York Times* (March 26, 1938), "a bright ray of hope has come." The film's narrator, speaking in Yiddish, declares, "Any child once here will work for a better world." That was impossible in anti-Semitic Poland in the late 1930s, which had also banned the film.

New York's Belmont Theatre hosted the last Yiddish film made in Poland, in September

1939: Joseph Green's *A Brivele der Mamen* (*A Little Letter to Mother*, 1939), a love story about a middle-aged Jewish-Ukranian storekeeper who loses a husband and two sons in the First World War. Through the efforts of New York's Hebrew Immigrant Aid Society (HIAS) the widow is reunited after the war with her youngest son, in America. The hope is that the rest of her life will be free of *tsuris* (trouble). Trouble is at the core of a second Yiddish feature about Jewish life that opened in New York at the start of World War II: George Rolland's *Liebe und Leidenschaft* (*Love and Sacrifice*, 1936), a Yiddish-language production (by the Jewish-owned Talking Picture Company) about a woman framed for murder. The film's director, George Rolland, had garnered attention in the early 1930s with his philo–Semitic *The Eternal Jew* (1933). A third Yiddish-language tale, *Tevya* (1939), lets the new world in on the old-world's racial prejudices "of another era," said the *New York Times* (December 22, 1939). Maurice Schwartz directed and starred in a story by Sholem Aleichem.

A last film of a different kind also showed up in the States, at New York's 55th Street Playhouse, in the closing months of 1939. French was the language of Henri Decoin's *Mademoiselle ma mère* (*My Mother is a Miss*, 1936), but the company that brought it into America was Tobis. This production had a certain distinction: it was the final production of two dozen films that the American Tobis Corp. released in the U.S. from 1935 to 1940. Tobis was Germany's largest film studio, after Ufa. American Tobis, which W.E. van Beverin headed in New York, was a branch of the International Corporation of Amsterdam, which had ties to Tobis Klangfilm, in Berlin, headed by Peter Henkel. American Tobis had indicated in summer 1936 that it was interested merely in "selling our product" and "rebuilding the market for foreign language pictures in the U.S." When Tobis threw in the towel, having failed to re-establish a place of eminence for German films in the States, Ufa released Tobis's subsequent productions in the U.S.

Adapted from Louis Verneuil's stage farce, *Mademoiselle ma mere* follows spoiled, rich girl Jacqueline (Danielle Darrieux) who vows to marry the seventh man who proposes to her. The lucky man is the widower Albert Letournel (Alerme), a man old enough to be her father. True to her word, she marries him, but only after he agrees to a sexless union. Jacqueline then falls in love with Albert's son Georges (Pierre Brasseur) who, however, balks at the notion of romancing his stepmother. Jacqueline's rich daddy (Michel Simon) watches the goings-on in silent confusion.

In their own way, Americans were watching the goings-on in German films in silent confusion. While Europe was under threat of continent-wide disaster in late 1939, Germany exported innocuous productions for the fall 1939 season in America. The impression these films left was little short of unreality. E.W. Emo's story of typical German relationships, *Familie Schimek* (1935) takes place in 1908 Berlin. There's no need to remind people of contemporary Germany. Ludwig Schigl (Hans Moser) is interested in the widow Schimek (Käthe Haack), who is raising three children. The best way to her heart, he imagines, is to get to know her pretty niece Hedwig (Hilde Schneider). But a friend, who maintains the widow's workshop, actually has his eye on Hedwig, which first leads to conflict and then a comfortable resolution for everybody.

Jürgen von Alten was responsible for bringing to the screen *Der Biberpelz* (*The Beaver Coat*, 1937), a CFE release of a turn-of-the-century play by Gerhart Hauptmann that ends with the line, "Honesty is the best policy." The Germans produced the film in honor of Nazi supporter Hauptmann's seventy-fifth birthday. At the start, in a German principality, pompous Baron von Wehrhahn (Heinrich George) boasts that he can eradicate a nest of poachers—favorite Nazi badboys—as well as the local petty crooks. Instead, he zeroes in on harmless people, imaging them to be free thinkers and revolutionaries. Real culprits like the thieving washerwoman Frau "Auguste Wolff" (Ida Wüst) and her husband "Julius" (Ewald Wenke), who poaches beavers, go about their business undisturbed. The oblivious baron even dismisses rumors of a plot to assassinate the prince. His efforts, however, come to fruition not through crime control or bluster but through something completely surprising. After the attempted suicide by Wolff's daughter "Leontine" (Sabine Peters), the dishonest inhabitants are shocked into abandoning their motto of "nobody ever got rich by being poor" for "honesty is the best policy." Fritz Odemar (1890–1955), who played Prince August Sigismund, was a prolific actor. He tried to remain "uncompromised," as he said, during the Nazi era, seeking harmless dramas, musicals or comedies. Yet Odemar was involved in several ignominious German productions: Jürgen von Alten's *Togger* (1936–37), Philipp Lothar Mayring's *Blutsbrüderschaft* (1940), and Herbert Selpin's *Carl Peters* (1941).

Jürgen von Alten's *Spätere Heirat nicht ausgeschlossen* (*Marriage Considered*, 1939) also preached honesty of a sort. Shown in the States, *Spätere Heirat nicht ausgeschlossen* is a two-reel, Ufa-produced semi-comedy about Miss Tremlin (Käthe Haack), who places an ad for an investor in her toyshop. Her ad suggests "marriage might be considered." Several men fall for the bait. She arranges to meet them one at a time. Captivated by her charms, they open up their wallets, having already lost their hearts. She then vanishes. The men know they've been duped but, swallowing their pride, they inform the Berlin police about a petty criminal on the loose. In German films of the era, it's that simple. By the late 1930s, Alten's film supported the impression that the bigger the crimes being committed by the Nazis in real life, the smaller the contemporary crimes on German screens. Jürgen von Alten survived the regime. He had a small part in Andrzej Wajda's *Eine Liebe in Deutschland* (1983).

Carl Boese's *Der Verkannte Lebemann* (*The Unrecognized Man of the World*), which was released at the Garden Theatre in September, was one more German film from the year of the Berlin Olympics. In it, author Ernst Schröder (Ralph Arthur Roberts), alias Fredo de Marana, bases his love stories on his own experiences. But when he falls for the charming country girl Lotte Bach (Trude Marlen), who despises his novels, he's in over his head. Of course, in this Bavaria comedy that contains a grand masquerade ball, these two opposites unite and live happily ever after.

Likewise in Erich Engel's *Ein Hoffnungsloser Fall* (*A Hopeless Case*, 1938–39), which played at the Casino the same week, Jenny Jugo (1905–2001)—often seen in Engel's films—played the headstrong, rich woman who manages to study medicine while ignoring the hard-boiled sales advice of surgeon-professor "Bruchsal" (Karl Ludwig Diehl), a presumed Jew: she should avoid emotional entanglements until she is well established in a career. Her career here is medicine. At the end, Jenny and fellow student Hans Faber (Hannes Stelzer) fall in love and sail for Argentina—which in 1939 was farther away from war fears but which many Germans called a home away from home.

Italian director Mario Camerini's *Ma non è una cosa seria* (*But It's Nothing Serious*, 1936) screened in the States in October 1939 and was based on Pirandello's story. Love and marriage are the last things on the protagonist's mind. Memmo Speranza (Vittorio de Sica) is a young man so afraid of getting married that he gives himself a sort of vaccination against the institution. That is, he marries Gasperina (Elisa Cegani), whom he's little interested in, then sets her up as half-housekeeper and half-proprietor of a suburban boarding house. He's now safely married, his wife is nowhere in sight, and he is secure against any other woman trying to lure him into a serious relationship. But the wife fools him. Soon, he discovers her—and finds her desirable. In the end, he's seriously married after all. Camerini's film *Ma non è una cosa seria*, which was produced by the ubiquitous Alberto Giacalone for Itala Film, had a German connection: *Der Mann, der nicht nein sagen kann* (*The Man Who Can't Say No*, 1937–38), which Camerini also directed.

The Italian rendition, which had been produced earlier, reached New York in October

1939. The German-language rendition, co-starring the comedian Werner Finck (1902–1978), reached the Casino Theatre in late 1940. *Der Mann, der nicht nein sagen kann* was one of Werner Finck's last Nazi films. Between 1933 and 1938, he appeared in nearly 50 productions. The Nazis had threatened to arrest him several times. On one occasion, Finck, while in the middle of saying something the Nazis found offensive, noticed a Gestapo officer taking notes. Finck confronted the man, asking, "Am I talking too fast? Do you want me to slow down so you can follow?" Finck's innocent facial expression belied his anti–Nazi sentiments.

In mid–October 1939, a new star in the German film firmament appeared on a screen in New York: Kristina Söderbaum (1912–2001). The Scandinavian-born actress was featured in Veit Harlan's mystery *Verwehte Spuren* (*Lost Traces*, 1938), which has a medical subtheme. Nazi supporter Thea von Harbou scripted this Majestic Film production, which the Casino Theatre hosted in October 1939. It screened with English titles. Söderbaum played Séraphine Lawrence, a young Canadian attending the World Exhibition in Paris in 1867, along with her mother Madeleine (Charlotte Schulz). Because accommodations are scarce, mother and daughter are forced to bed down for the night in different hotels. The following morning, Séraphine can't find her mother. Hotel officials, the police, the ship's crew, and a physician they met the day before, a Dr. Morot, deny knowledge of ever having seen the older woman. Having lost all traces of her, like sand in the wind, Séraphine feels herself going insane in a search for the truth. In the end, filmgoers learn that her mother suddenly died on the evening of her arrival in Paris. Dr. Morot (Frits van Dongen) had diagnosed the cause of death as the plague. To avoid panic during the great exhibition in the big city, the doctor, hotel owner Dompierre (Jacob Tiedke), and the city's prefect of police (Friedrich Kayssler) colluded to hide the old woman's body and then swear witnesses to secrecy. In the end, the police break their silence and the young doctor is there to comfort Séraphine in her grief.

Referring to Harlan's film, Hitler said, "I liked it very much." His regime would later make effective use of doctors in the camps in their slaughter of millions. We'd seen a hint of the good doctor in Detlef Sierck's *Schlussakkord*. There would be more from the Nazis along these lines, especially Hans Steinhoff's *Robert Koch* (1939) and Wolfgang Liebeneiner's *Ich Klage an* (*I Accuse*, 1941).

Harlan's and Söderbaum's careers were just taking off in the new Germany. The duo's second film—about another German man of science—quickly screened in the States. Harlan's biographical *Das Unsterbliche Herz* (*The Immortal Heart*), which Ufa produced, had premiered in Nuremberg in January 1939 under the patronage of none other than the city's *Gauleiter* (political leader), Julius Streicher. Based on a stage work by Harlan's father, Walter, it opened in Berlin in March as the Germans marched into what remained of Czechoslovakia. In April 1939, Veit Harlan married its star. Their second film together was released in late October in New York, which coincided with the birth of the Harlans' first child.

Kristina Söderbaum played Eve, the wife of sixteenth-century Nuremberg heretic Peter Henlein (Heinrich George), a locksmith obsessed with making an apparatus that can be used by German seamen to tell time. The loss of a German vessel on the Congo River is the catalyst for his work. However, Henlein faces a serious obstacle: he has a bullet lodged near his heart that threatens to kill him at any moment. Before *his* time runs out he will do all he can to serve his nation. Henlein's young wife is fighting a different battle: she has become attracted to Konrad Wundhalm (Raimund Schelcher), her husband's assistant. Nonetheless, she sticks by the side of her willful, single-minded husband, who works feverishly even after he is sentenced to death for being a friend of Martin Luther's. Henlein dies from the bullet wound just after creating his portable clock, which becomes known as the "Nuremberg egg." Henlein the heretic is then recognized for his contribution to science: he is pardoned by the emperor and carried to his grave with great pomp and circumstance.

Das Unsterbliche Herz.

Sections of the city of Nuremberg were cleared to reproduce the atmosphere of the romanticized tale produced by Tobis, most notably the market place and church locations. Germany's remaining talent took part in the production. Hermann Warm handled the design; Arno Richter the costumes; and Bruno Mondi the photography; and Wolfgang Schleif was assistant director. The Berlin Philharmonic played Bach, under Vienna-born musical director Alois Melichar (1896–1976), who served German filmmaking throughout the war. One thing stands out in this historical drama: the film's characters speak modern German. Harlan had indicated that his film would not be a great "costume show. Nor do we wish to show the style of Dürer or any old style to the public. The people will talk as they do today. It will be a film with a modern effective view of the world." In other words, the film presents Nazi ideology. Catholics are depicted as racist, superstitious, greedy, stupid, and opposed to science and progress; that is, Catholics are religious quacks. Martin Luther at one point says, "God's language is German and not Latin." The film, with music from Bach, contains numerous speeches in praise of the nobility of work. Henlein at one point says, "Accomplishment is superior to the fate of the individual. The deed is everything—man nothing." *Das Unsterbliche Herz* is banned in Germany, as is Harlan's *Jud Suss* (1940).

The huge success of Harlan's *Das Unsterbliche Herz*, winner of a National Film Prize, as well as that of Hans Steinhoff's *Robert Koch* (1939) inspired Goebbels to back more films about great Germans and charismatic artist-leaders in politics, science, art, and the military. Jews were not excluded from consideration if the subject matter depicted them in an unfavorable

light. The Nazis made the following biographies: *Die Rothschilds* (1940), *Friedrich Schiller* (1942, set in Württemberg, with plenty of Prussian barking of orders and Pan-German nationalism), *Friedemann Bach* (1940), *The Great King*, *Bismarck*, *The Dismissal*, *Ohm Krüger*, *Carl Peters*, *Wen die Götter lieben* (*Whom the Gods Love*, 1942, about Mozart), *Andreas Schluter*, *Diesel* (the pioneer of mechanical engineering), *Geheimakte WB 1* (*Secret Paper WB 1*, 1942, about Wilhelm Bauer, the inventor of the U-boat), *Rembrandt*, *Wien 1910* (about Mayor Karl Lüger, admired by Hitler), *Paracelsus* and *Der Unendliche Weg* (*The Endless Way*, 1943, about the mid-nineteenth-century economist-politician Friedrich List).

Martin Luther's Germanism received favorable treatment in yet another film from rising filmmaker Veit Harlan: *Jugend* (*Youth*, 1938). Produced by Tobis and distributed by Casino Film Exchange in the U.S. in late 1939, the tale is one of adolescent love in conflict with dictates

Top and above: Friedrich Schiller, **with Horst Caspar.**

of the church based on Max Halbe's controversial play of the 1890s and scripted by the Nazi writer Thea von Harbou. This tale takes place in southwest Prussia in 1890, near the Catholic Polish border. Minister Hoppe (Eugen Klöpfer), a strong peasant type, has taken the illegitimate child of his sister into his home and raised her. As a young woman, Annchen (Kristina Söderbaum) becomes friends with Chaplain Gregor von Schigorski (Werner Hinz), who wants her to enter a convent to atone for her mother's behavior. The chaplain stresses the sins of the father pass to the next generation. But when Annchen's eighteen-year-old cousin Hans (Hermann Braun) comes for a visit, they fall in love. The chaplain is also in love with her. Jealous, he drives her to distraction by reminding her that she and Hans are living in sin. Further, he tells she has forfeited her mother's and her own salvation.

The story of young lovers trying to following the dictates of nature leads to the inevitable end—Annchen's suicide—the result, says the film, of small-minded non–Germans and their religious dogma. Here again the Nazis hide one of the strands of their ideology—undermining the church—in the nineteenth century. In the film, the peasant minister is presented as a better leader than the chaplain who serves the church, which is denounced because it's a "taking" and not a "giving" institution. Goebbels praised the film; American critics said nothing about the film's anti-church depictions.

Ufa's comedy *Heimatland* (*Homeland*, 1939), directed by Ernst Martin, used rural views in winter and spring to re-remind filmgoers of the Nazis' back-to-the-soil movement. Here a farmer's daughter, Monika (Hansi Knoteck), falls for Berliner Günther Nordmann (Wolf Albach-Retty), a riding instructor on vacation. Günther is attracted to the unassuming young female from the Black Forest and its people, who enjoy *Kirschwasser* strictly for "medical purposes." Meanwhile she is attracted by his charm and worldliness. They get engaged, but then he heads back to work in the city. After no word from him for several weeks, Monika leaves the Black Forest to find him. In the metropolis of Berlin, she becomes lost, confused, and then shocked to discover that Günther is nothing but a lady's man. His values are not hers. So much for any man from the city!

Heimaland invited tourists to visit Germany and its great outdoors—even though the film was released in Berlin a precious few days before war started—and released at the Casino Theatre two months into the Second World War. The longtime theatrical actress Roma Bahn costarred. Bahn appeared in one of the first German films after the war, Carl Boese's *Beate* (1948). Simultaneously, the compilation *Why This War?* (1939), which Samuel Cummins produced, told American filmgoers that because a needless war was going on in Europe, the U.S. had to stay out of it. Its anti-war theme is in keeping with the theme from Cummins's *War Is a Racket* (1934): America's munitions manufacturers and others, if given the chance, will always push America into war. The production *Why This War?* suggests that "imperialists," war profiteers, warlords, and anybody else already involved in the European conflict will drag America into another war. Roosevelt is criticized for his so-called neutrality speech while a Gold Star mother fulminates against war, saying war is not the answer in October 1939.

The West and *its* values are the targets in Fritz Wendhausen's *Peer Gynt*, which screened at the Garden Theatre after World War II, had begun. A Bavaria production photographed by Carl Hoffmann, it starred Hans Albers as the jovial Norwegian. Initially, Peer Gynt sees life as play. When his mother, Aase (Lucie Höflich), dies, Gynt's attention turns to Solveig (Marieluise Claudius). But more than anything, he yearns to go to America. There is where he hopes to make his career and live in abundance. American women and power, he believes, will determine his course in life. In America, Peer Gynt, as the "Emperor of Africa," recalls that in France he learned the way of living, in England he learned how to work, in America he learned trade and business. "I dreamed of Italy ... but Germany taught me thinking." The Germans, he stresses, are a people of "poets and thinkers." Then one day Peer Gynt realizes something else. Away from the fatherland and rejecting the love of Baroness Agga (Olga Tschechowa), Gynt feels incomplete. "You Americans," he says, "helped me to see things clearly: the fight for power is worth nothing if one thing is missing: the great holy egoism. That's what I learned from you." Old and tired, he will return to his homeland, where salvation and the young Solveig wait for him. Heeding the call of his *Heimat* and seeking the security of blood and soil, Gynt will "be alone with my work."

Peer Gynt is that rare Ibsen play (1867) that doesn't deal with social problems. Ibsen had made his hero a kind of Faust in a fantastic world, but the Nazis turned him into a special kind of "leader." American critics ignored the film's glorification of Nazi ideas and remained silent about its criticism of the West. The *New York Times* (November 11, 1939) called the transformation from stage to screen "less fantastic and more credible" and Edward Grieg's music "delightful." The film, although it had been made in 1934, was a message from Germany about what it thought of the U.S in late 1939.

Norwegian novelist Knut Hamsun, who openly expressed admiration for Hitler, had his novel *Viktoria* adapted for the screen by the Nazis, in 1935. Carl Hoffman was the director. The drama starred Luise Ullrich as the protagonist in love with the sensitive writer Johannes (Mathias Wieman). When her rural family becomes impoverished, Viktoria is encouraged by her father (Alfred Abel) to marry her cousin Otto (Heinz von Cleve), who soon becomes rich. Johannes heads for the city where he composes poetry. When Viktoria arrives in the metropolis, the two meet and confess their love for one another. But a letter from Viktoria's father reminds her of her forthcoming wedding. Otto becomes aware of Viktoria's relationship with Johannes even as Johannes turns his attention to Camilla Seier (Erika Dannhoff). Viktoria celebrates her upcoming wedding by dancing until she breaks down. On a hunt the next day Otto falls on his rifle and is mortally wounded. Viktoria, revived, then seeks out Johannes, who rejects her because she had become engaged to another. Viktoria's father then perishes in a fire. Viktoria despairs and becomes ill. In her last hours she cries out for Johannes, and dies of a broken heart. In the city, Johannes receives an award for his work. In an acceptance speech he thanks Viktoria, whose love, he said, had made his achievement possible. The film did not screen in theatres in New York, Chicago, or Los Angeles. Instead, it screened in Pennsylvania in early 1939 under the title *The Love of a Lady*. The state's censors eliminated one scene: close-ups of the legs of can-can dancers.

No one objected to anything about two other productions when they screened in the U.S. The first one, called *Fünf Millionen suchen einen Erben* (*Five Million Seeks an Heir*, 1938), shifts between New York and Berlin. Two nephews, Peter and Patrick Pitt—a German and a Scotsman—are potential beneficiaries of a rich American uncle. To claim the money, the German has to prove he is happily married, while the Scotsman must remain single. Both "heirs" are played by Heinz Rühmann. An American gangster named "Blubberboom" (Oskara Sima) and his girlfriend Mabel (Leni Marenbach) try to sabotage the German's efforts so that they can get their hands on the fortune. A notary—a presumed Jew named "Gould" (Heinz Salfner)—helps them. Other millionaires in the tale are called "Bucklespring" (Albert Florath), "Kirkwood" (William Huch), and "Harris" (Valy Arnheim).

Carl Boese directed this Terra production, which screened at the Casino Theatre in late October 1939. The American High Commission in Germany banned it in 1950.

The second film that raised no eyebrows was Weiss Ferdl's last feature to make it to the States, screening at the Casino Theatre in late 1939. A rags-to-riches-tale called *Der Arme Millionär* (*The Poor Millionaire*, 1939), directed by Joe Stöckel, it features Ferdl as the master shoemaker Stangelmeier who, in his wildest dreams, never imagines he would actually inherit the fortune of a baron whose life he saved long ago. But the money makes Stangelmeier arrogant and vain. He abandons old friends and forbids his daughter Annerl (Trude Haefelin) from having anything to do with her boyfriend, the carpenter Xaverl (Ludwig Kerscher). Stangelmeier moves into the residence of the dead baron, seeking contact with the old aristocracy. He hires an assistant named Siebecke (Kurt Vespermann). But the man's real name is "Bobby Wallner," a presumed Jew. Stangelmeier meets purported aristocrats: "Countess Kolontay" (Ursula Grabley) and "Prince Walefsky" (George Alexander). When Walefsky expresses an interest in Stangelmeier's daughter, the old shoemaker is overjoyed: he's going to have a prince for a son-in-law! Naturally, the whole thing is a con game, in order for the pair to get at Stangelmeier's fortune. Only posing as aristocrats, they're really Jews, too, named "August Käsbur" and "Lotte Shulz." Although Wallner gets his hands on Stangelmeier's money, the police arrest him and the other poseurs. Annerl and Xavier unite in happiness.

But the critics loved the next one. Russia serves as the background for Ufa's musical-drama *Es war eine rauschende Ballnacht* (*It Was a Glittering Night at the Ball*, 1939), a surprising rendition of the life of Tchaikovsky. Commemorating the hundredth anniversary of the composer's birth, the film had premiered in Berlin in August 1939 just as the Nazi-Soviet Non–Aggression Pact was in the works. The musical screened subtitled at the Casino Theatre less than three months later. At Chicago's World Playhouse in September 1940 it screened as *The Life and Loves of Tchaikovsky*.

In Moscow, in 1865, the struggling 25-year-old composer Tchaikovsky (Hans Stüwe) has only two supporters: the dancer Nastassja (Marika Rökk) and his old teacher, named Hunsinger (Leo Slezak). The old music teacher is proud that, "Thank God, yes!", he's *German*. Hunsinger was the *first* one to notice the spark of genius in his Russian musician. Hunsinger tells Tchaikovsky, "Art is an inexorable mistress. Are you going to betray her?" He orders the composer to work. On that day, as Tchaikovsky the genius is born, he draws a curtain over his emotional life. The old German also introduces Tchaikovsky to the beautiful Katharina (Zarah Leander), who becomes his patron. The composer falls in love with her but says nothing because he wants to spare her the hardships of his life. Married to Michael Iwanowitsch Murakin (Aribert Wäscher), Katharina is able to finance Tchaikovsky until he achieves success. Years later, in 1893, when the composer gives a great concert, Katharina, who has separated from her husband, is in the audience. At the performance no one knows that he has contracted cholera, which is spreading throughout the city. The two lovers are doomed. The highlights of Carl Froelich's film—another in the arena of *Volksfilme*—were Leander's singing, Rökk's dancing, and Tchaikovsky's works played by the Berlin State Opera.

Werner Hochbaum's *Der Favorit der Kaiserin* (*The Favorite of the Empress*), an Itala period film by the ubiquitous producer Alberto Giacalone, opened in New York in late 1939 via CFE. Russian-born Olga Tschechowa played Elizabeth of Russia, the daughter of Peter the Great, who opposes an alliance with France. However, a plot is afoot to have her sign the treaty. Capt. Alexander Tomsky (Willy Eichberger) proves to the empress that such a thing would not be in Russia's interest. And by proving his worth to the empress, the captain is allowed a reward: the hand of Princess Irene (Trude Marlen). This film, which was produced in the year of the Berlin Olympics, had a political purpose in 1939–40. Full of action and sumptuous music (by Anton Profes), the film takes no bows to facts in its sympathetic view of the reign of a female Russian ruler and the case against a Russo-French alliance.

In late 1939, the Producers Releasing Corp. distributed Sam Newfeld's independently produced *Beasts of Berlin* to America's cinemas. The American production screamed that plenty of things were changing for the worse across the Atlantic. Based on Shephard Traube's story "Goose Step," it spotlights purported opposition to Hitler within Germany. Though it mixes fact and fiction, the one reality in the film is its depiction of violence inflicted on the innocent. The Pennsylvania Board of Censors, however, stopped the film in its tracks, labeling it "100 percent propaganda." They banned it from theaters in the state. Right on the heels of this

Robert Koch, with Emil Jannings and Elisabeth Flickenschild.

American production came a production that represented the first big Nazi bio-medical film to screen in America. *Robert Koch, der Bekämpfer des Todes* (*Robert Koch, the Battler Against Death*, 1939), which Hans Steinhoff directed, turned out to be quite a shock, an example that Nazi filmmaking had about as much to do with films as Nazi science had to do with science and Nazi doctors had to do with medicine. Rather, Nazi films had everything to do with lies and death. Steinhoff was said to know a bit about medicine, having studied it before becoming a theater actor and then a director in 1922, when he was 40. He had once directed a silent comedy about Jews. His *Famielientag im Hause Prellstein* (*Family Day in the Prellstein House*, 1927) is a story about German Jews bickering over an inheritance.

In *Robert Koch*, which the veteran writer Walter Wassermann (1893–1944) scripted and which co-starred veteran actress Lotte Neumann (1896–1977), Emil Jannings played the single-minded, nineteenth-century medical practitioner Dr. Heinrich Herman Robert Koch, a man merely trying to do his duty. All he wants is to save children from dying from a deadly lung disease. Every fourth child in the area is sick. Koch does his best research but is hampered by an unsupportive, if not indifferent wife (Hildegard Grethe), institutional bias, the jealousy of peers, superstitious locals, and one particular opponent. "Prof. Rudolf Virchow" (Werner Krauss), a medical scientist and liberal member of the Reichstag who has his own theories on illness, objects to Koch's work. This film makes clear Verchow is Jewish. Despite intrigue, slander, and his suspension from his job, Koch, about to turn 40, makes a breakthrough to prove his hypothesis: tuberculosis is caused by the tubercle bacillus. He has identified what he calls the enemy. Then the German Ministry of Health brings Koch to Berlin so that he can do further research. But just as quickly, Koch again faces opponents and intrigue.

At the end, Koch demands that "bacteria" must be eradicated from the German nation. "Where's the enemy hiding, what does he look like, what weapons do I need to fight him?" Koch demands. "When the torch falls from our hands," Koch predicts to an audience of young people, "you will pick it up again and carry it forward to a new and glorious day."

In 1905, in fact, Robert Koch (1843–1910) was recognized for his contributions to science. He was awarded the Nobel Prize in medicine and later called the "father of pathology," but the Nazis' film doesn't mention this fact. Rather, the Nazi film zeroes in on tried and true Nazi themes: the milieu of old reactionaries, faith in a great man's mission, martial terminology, and attacks on parliamentarianism and its supporters, the Jews. When Steinhoff's film premiered in Berlin's Ufa-Palast am Zoo, a statue of Robert Koch was onstage and the music of Beethoven wafted through the theater. Depicting a famous German doctor's battle against "bacteria," *Robert Koch*—as insidious a work as Liebeneiner's medical film *Ich Klage an* (1941)—is one of the most blatant anti–Semitic films the Nazis dared to export to America. Hans Steinhoff mixed his own brew of fact and fabrication this Tobis production, which had opened the August 1939 Venice Film Festival—to which a score of nations sent entrants. Capturing the top prize, *Robert Koch* was released in Berlin in September 1939, then released in the U.S. before the year was out. Goebbels called the prizewinner a "triumph for Germany." Hitler said, "I feel like Robert Koch in politics ... I discovered the Jews as the bacillus and ferment in social composition."

The *New York Times* (November 25, 1939) had written that although the producers of *Robert Koch* had "put over a bit of Nazi propaganda," the picture was nonetheless "serious and entertaining." In December, the National Board of Review of Motion Pictures named Hollywood's *Confessions of a Nazi Spy*, starring Francis Lederer, the year's best English-language film. The Nazis objected, letting the State Department know that the Warner Bros. production, which Jewish-born Anatole Litvak directed, was "poisoning" German-American relations (*Washington Post*, June 6, 1939). To make amends, the National Board selected *Robert Koch* as one of the best foreign-language films of the year. *Robert Koch* had screened briefly at New York's Casino Theatre. An effort to screen *Robert Koch* in early 1941 at the Pacific Electric Theatre in Los Angeles faced enough opposition that the screening was cancelled. This was a rare victory against the showing of Nazis film in America.

Another victory of sorts came from Warner Bros., which in the fall of 1939 produced a refutation of *Robert Koch* called *Dr. Ehrlich's Magic Bullet* (1939–1940). This film, directed by William Dieterle, is a rare example of an American film responding to a Nazi film. Screening in America in early 1940, *Dr. Ehrlich's Magic Bullet* depicts German hospital officials and state bureaucrats as bumbling and anti–Semitic. It portrays Robert Koch as pro–Jewish. The film's protagonist is the Jewish scientist-doctor Paul Ehrlich (Edward G. Robinson), who works as a hospital dermatologist. But his two passions are his family and his independent research into dyes and stains. When Ehrlich refuses to attend a lecture by none other than Robert Koch (Albert Bassermann), hospital officials have all the evidence they need to dismiss the annoying, independent-minded, Jewish doctor. But Koch is not offended. Rather, Koch asks Ehrlich to develop dyes to help him enhance the visibility of his newly discovered tubercle bacillus. Ehrlich's health is nearly broken by this intense research, but one success leads to another.

With Emil von Behring (Otto Krüger), Ehrlich makes his major contribution to medicine. He develops a serum that prevents diphtheria. Moved by the anxiety of desperate mothers, Ehrlich uses the serum on their children. His hospital superiors are furious, but the German state is grateful and Ehrlich is awarded his own institute. Ehrlich (1854–1915) then turns his attention to finding a magic bullet to treat syphilis, but his relationship with his German colleague von Behring becomes strained. He modifies arsenic derivatives until he achieves what he calls agent 606, in 1910. After a number of deaths in treated subjects, Ehrlich's enemies arrange a formal inquiry. Ehrlich, however, is exonerated and reconciles with his old German colleague, von Behring. Edward G. Robinson gave Ehrlich a saintly aura, culminating in the near-apotheosis of his deathbed scene, surrounded by scientific disciples.

This American film was a sharp refutation of the Nazis' *Robert Koch*. In the American film, Ehrlich's falling out with his German colleague, von Behring, is purely a disagreement over science. They differed between an immune view of disease prevention and Ehrlich's magic bullet view of killing germs. This film was not the only pro–Jewish film Dieterle directed in the 1930s. His *The Life of Emile Zola* (1937), starring the Jewish actor Paul Muni as the man who defends Alfred Dreyfus, implied that Jews again faced peril unless good men stood up to evil.

The scientist Paul Ehrlich was nowhere to be seen in Steinhoff's *Robert Koch*. The main Jew portrayed in the film was Rudolf Virchow (1821–1902), who as a founder of cellular pathology had been a progressive member of the Prussian lower house and later of the Reichstag (1880–93), and was a leader of the liberal party that opposed Bismarck, founder of the Second Reich. Virchow reappears in Wolfgang Liebeneiner's biography *Bismarck*, which Goebbels'

Bismarck.

ministry financed and which Tobis released in Berlin in December 1940. In February 1939, the Reich had launched the battleship *Bismarck*, which the British would sink in May 1941. Coincidentally, in spring 1941, the film *Bismarck* arrived in the U.S. Ufa Inc., the German studio's American affiliate, was about to distribute it when U.S. customs inspectors applied provisions of the Tariff Act and seized the film. The reason, the agency said, was Ufa's failure to "comply with certain customs formalities." *Bismarck* never screened in the U.S.

It should have, if only to make clear that the leader of the Third Reich saw himself as another Bismarck. In *Mein Kampf*, Hitler had concluded, "Bismarck's State was not founded on treason and assassination by deserters and shirkers but by the regiments that had fought at the front. This unique birth and *baptism of fire* [italics mine] sufficed of themselves to surround the Second Empire with an aureole of historical splendor such as few of the older States could lay claim to."

Bismarck begins in 1862, when it's clear that the division of Germany into 40 states is a disaster that endangers her existence. The House of Habsburg in Austria (which Hitler detested) and Wilhelm II of Prussia are both vying for control of Germany. Party politics is threatening Prussia's survival, and in desperation, Wilhelm (Friedrich Kayssler) appoints Otto von Bismarck (Paul Hartmann) head of state. Bismarck promptly dissolves parliament. His main opponent in that body is, of course, the pacifist Virchow (Karl Haubenreisser). Bismarck institutes press censorship and builds a modern army.

In spite of British intrigue, Bismarck unifies Germany and prevents Denmark from annexing Schleswig-Holstein. More important, an attempt on his life is thwarted: the assassin is identified as the "English Jew Cohen." Prussia defeats Austria at Königgätz and then unites with Austria against France in 1870. The film ends with Prussia's victory over France and the foundation of the Second Reich in 1871 with the Emperor-Proclamation in the Mirror Hall at Versailles. Bismarck at one point in the film promotes a non-aggression pact with Russia to strengthen the nation's eastern flank and on the other hand says, "The great questions of the present will not be solved by speeches and parliaments but by iron and blood." Rudolf von Virchow is again outflanked.

Bismarck, which Norbert Schultze (1911–2002) scored, was awarded a National Film Prize. But Goebbels and Tobis weren't done with Bismarck or his legacy. They produced a sequel called *Die Entlassung* (*The Dismissal*, 1942), also directed by Wolfgang Liebeneiner, photographed by Fritz Arno Wagner and scored by Herbert Windt. This film, which never reached America, is about the last years of Bismarck's rule—from 1885 until his dismissal—from the Nazis' point of view. It starred Emil Jannings. Virchow was no longer around to be pilloried, but the plot contains Nazi set pieces: shifty Jewish parliamentarians, intriguers in the bureaucracy, the cult of the dead, and the glorification of a great leader. Correcting Bismarck's pro–Russian treaty policy, Goebbels wrote that *Die Entlassung* "mustn't be arguing against our present war with the Soviet Union." He subsequently awarded it an honor above that for *Bismarck*, that of Film of the Nation.

A few weeks after the start of the Second World War, the Nazis released a film in Berlin that overtly stigmatizes Jews: *Leinen aus Irland* (*Irish Linen*, 1939). Produced by Wien Film, directed by Heinz Helbig, and scored by Anton Profes, *Leinen aus Irland* takes place in the era of the Habsburg Empire. Set in Austria in 1909, the plot is afoot when the ambitious "Dr. Egon Kühn" (Siegfried Breuer), who is Jewish, declares his desire to "acquire a decisive influence on the world market." As the manager of the textile company Libussa A.-G., he has the backing of his uncle "Sigi Pollack" (Fritz Imhoff) and company officers "Dr. Seligmann" (Ernst Arnold) and "Arnold Nagel" (Otto Schmoele), all Jews. And by gaining the support of Viennese officials such as "Count Horvath von Arpad-Falva" (Tibor von Halmay), "Kasimir von Kalinski" (Hans Olden), and Trade Minister "Meier" (Oskar Sima), Kühn plans to buy duty-free linen from Ireland rather than more expensive linen from local weavers in Nordböhmen. Kühn also has a personal stake in this idea. He's sure his business acumen will impress the blonde-haired Lilly (Irene von Meyendorff), daughter of the firm's trusting president, Kettner (Otto Tressler). On the surface, at least, most people would prefer cheaper (Irish) goods. While Kühn's approach makes good business and market sense, the local Germans are aghast: they characterize Kühn's idea as "un–German." Buying locally manufactured linen, they exclaim, supports local Germans. Kühn's plan will surely lead to a rise in unemployment in the region. The people protest to ministerial officials in Vienna. But most of those far-off officials do nothing: they're corrupt or bureaucratic, that is, Jewish. But Lilly falls in love with the one person who can see what Kühn's plan is all about: ministerial secretary Franz Goll (Rolf Wanka). They and Alois Hubermayer (Karl Skraup), a local owner of a linen firm, convince Ketter that what Kühn is doing is nothing short of sabotage and that the ministry is full of crooks. The linen will be purchased locally. "Germanic honesty and integrity," says the film, "triumph over the unscrupulousness of foreign elements." In addition, it's clear that blondes never fall in love with Jews.

Wien film coordinated its production with Nazi officials in Berlin, demonstrating its determination to conform to Nazi ideology and produce a work that, while looking at a serious economic issue, was plainly anti–Jewish. A number of well-known Austrians—Oskar Sima, George Alexander, Hans Olden and Karl Skraup—lent their talents. Oskar Werner (1922–1984) appeared here in one of his first films, as did the comedian Fritz Imhoff (1891–1961), who had been a close friend of Jewish tenor Richard Tauber in the 1920s. Goebbels noted that the film "has turned out very well," naming it winner of a National Film Prize. It did not screen in the U.S. nor did American critics in Germany seem to be aware of it. After 1945, allied military officials in Germany banned *Leinen aus Irland* from commercial screenings.

Helbig's Austrian comedy *Seine Tochter ist Peter* (*His Daughter is Peter*), another production from the year of the Olympics, had been shown in New York in March 1938 and later in Los Angeles. It is the old story concerning which parent gets custody of a child (Traudl Stark, Austria's Shirley Temple) after a divorce. The husband (Ludwig Diehl) gets her full-time by marrying a friend (Maria Andergast) of his wife (Olga Tschechowa), "the woman whom no man can understand." That's reason enough to be rid of her. In contrast in another film, Vienna (a Nazi city by late 1939) served as the background for the comedy, quarrels, loves, and music (by the Vienna Philharmonic) of the nineteenth-century Strauss family. Directed by E.W. Emo, produced by Tobis, and shown in the U.S. in late 1939, *Unsterblicher Walzer* (*Immortal Waltz*, 1939), a reminder of Harlan's *Immortal Heart*, presents many of the popular compositions of Johann Strauss Sr. (Paul Hörbiger) and his three sons, including "Donauwalser," "Trülingstinmen," and the "Radetsky March." Although there is plenty of competition among the brothers in their professional and personal lives, and the father is presented as a Bohemian, they reconcile thanks to an old music teacher—who reminds them of the importance of family tradition and unity. "I am always the second," Josef says at one point to Johan. But then he realizes that there is no first or second: he is proud just to be a Strauss! So here was another film that supported the Nazi ethos. "Each of us has to stand up for the other," says one of the Strauss brothers. Tribe and a family's tradition, and its honor and "common blood" are what matter.

Herbert Maisch's Ufa production *Frau Sylvelin* (1938), which was shown in America in December 1939 at the Garden Theatre, affirms the Nazi ethos of the obedient wife serving the husband-leader. Hungarian actress Maria von Tasnady starred opposite Nazi favorite Heinrich George (1893–1946), who played Manfred Block, an iron-willed company head treating his wife like a slave. One day she falls in love with a good-looking Austrian, Baron von Sollnau (Paul Richter), who is a business partner of the old man—and who is the object of the matrimonial intentions of her pretty young stepdaughter, Claire (Carla Rust). When the shares of her husband's company nosedive and he goes into a tirade, Sylvelin Block decides she can no longer bear the black moods of her uncouth, domineering spouse. She secretly joins the baron. But when her husband suffers a breakdown, Mrs. Block realizes that her husband's fate and the future of his work and that of thousands of his employees are in her hands. She does her German duty and returns. The company survives. Her husband realizes what Sylvelin means to him.

Hans Deppes *Das Ekel* (*The Grouch*, 1939), also shown at the Garden Theatre in December 1939, relates the tale of a petty tyrant, Karl Sträubler (Hans Moser), at home and in his immediate Austrian circle, who is brought to his senses another way: by a brief stay in jail. By the end of 1939, audiences in America should have been aware that German and Austrian films were a Nazi show. The Alpine-rich German nation was evil. Germany was a danger, despite its films' lovely sets (scenery), film scores (classical music), and themes of the fatherland, fidelity, and farm life. Beautiful views of Germany's mountainous regions did not mean that political conditions in Europe were being exaggerated. These were merely Aryan plotlines. The variations were apparently endless.

Géza von Bolváry's Austrian production *Ernte* (*Harvest*) contrasts urban depravity and rural purity—a favorite Nazi theme—in a story of an unhappy young woman who finds love. Also known as *Die Julika*, it takes place in early twentieth century Hungary. Former cavalry captain Karl von Tamassy (Attila Hörbiger) finds that when his father dies, he is a great deal less well-to-do than he imagined. The coachman's daughter, Julika Kutscher (Paula Wessely), persuades him not to abandon the 60 acres he owns. Together, they farm the land and expand it. When a society girl, Grit von Hellmers (Gina Falckenberg), crosses his path, he initially loses his heart to her but recovers in time, realizing that Julika is his true love. The atmospheric, nonviolent film was useful politically. By stressing realistic scenes of fields, countryside, planting, and harvesting, it reminded supporters and others of the Nazis' back-to-the-soil movement while depicting a grand but decadent ceremonial ball in the Vienna of Emperor Franz Josef. The Nazis resurrected this Bavaria production from the year of the Olympics and released it subtitled in the U.S. in December 1939.

One of the first German films released in the U.S. in 1940 was a film with a disturbing title. *Henker, Frauen, und Soldaten* (*Hangmen, Women, and Soldiers*). Released in Berlin in December 1935, it premiered in New York's Casino Theatre during the lull in the war in Europe. It turned out to be a mild anti–Soviet production by Johannes Meyer, no more implausible than the situation the world found itself in that January, especially after the Nazi-Soviet non-aggression pact of August 1939. Scripted by Max W. Kimmich and inspired by material from *Mein Kampf*, the film focuses on Capt. Michael von Prack (Hans Albers), a German World War I air ace held briefly by the British in the Middle East. He escapes and returns to Germany, which he finds in a near state of physical and moral collapse: anarchy and debauchery are the rule of the day. He wants none of it, so he heads east to Russia to fight Germany's enemy. He meets the Russian spy Vera Iwanowna—and they fall in love. Matters then take twists and unbelievable turns. The German aviator runs into a look-alike Russian cousin who just happens to be in command of Red Army troops fighting White Guard remnants of the czar and German adventurers (like Capt von Prack). After killing his double, von Prack impersonates the Russian general. However, the stately blonde Iwanowna (Charlotte Susa, born Charlotte Wegmuller in Russia) knows well her duty to her fatherland. She denounces him. The aviator eludes capture, but after successfully leading his German troops across a boggy moor and ambushing the communists, he is killed in action—along with the Russian spy. He has become a hero to his people while his Russian enemies are dead. Goebbels called it "exciting and enchanting," confirming the non-hostile ties between Germany and the Soviet Union.

A subsequent release of a German film in the States brought American filmgoers right up to date about German capabilities. Called *D III 88*, it was subtitled *The New German Air Force Attacks*. The story begins just before the start of World War II. During a training run, one of Germany's fighter planes, while dropping bombs into the ocean, experiences trouble. The crew bails out, except for a bomber who can't open his parachute. The only thing he can do is to try to land the crippled plane. The pilot, who had quickly bailed out, later feels humiliated. On their next exercise, over the Bavarian mountains in ice and fog, the bomber and the pilot crash land. Outraged, their commanding officer then bans them from further exercises. Bonicke (Otto Wernicke), the chief of ground operations, intercedes, urging the commanding officer to reconsider, reminding him that the two fighter pilots, named Paulsen (Heinz Welzel) and Eckhard (Hermann Braun), are veterans of the First World War. Flashbacks depict their earlier-era heroics with a plane named D III 88, which, coincidently, had also malfunctioned. The commander relents; the two veterans shake hands; and they then head out to attack the enemy (that is, British) naval forces at the start of the Second World War. When they fail to return from their mission, Bonicke sets out to find them in an old Fokker DR 1 triplane (registered D III 88). Locating the lost men, he guides a ship to their location, but on the way back Bonicke runs out of fuel. When his old D III 88 crashes, he dies. Bonicke's supreme sacrifice for comrades and the German nation will live in glory.

This Tobis production was scripted by Hans Bertram, photographed by Heinz von Jaworsky, and directed by Herbert Maisch. Having premiered in Berlin a month after World War II began, *D III 88* was the first German film in America to portray German action in World War II and to depict the new German Air Force in battle. Contemporary German pilots are presented as daring and resourceful as their heroic predecessors who fought for the fatherland in the First World War. However, "Americans are unlikely to be impressed" by *D III*, wrote the *New York Times* (February 17, 1940) when the movie screened at the Casino Theatre. Germans, however, "may well believe that Hitler can bomb his enemies to pieces whenever he feels like it."

The Jewish actor Paul Otto played a Nazi general in the film. Paul Otto survived in Nazi Germany and avoided the purge of Jews from German cinema by working under an assumed name. His real name was Paul Schlesinger. When his identity was uncovered, he and his wife committed suicide in 1943.

A sequel to *D III 88* (with the same characters and actors), called *Kampfgeschwader Lützow* (*Battle Squadron Lutzow*), continues the adventures of the crew, this time in Germany's attacks on Poland and France and against the British mainland. The co-stars are the military aircraft: Germany's D III, shown outside and in; the BF 109 Dora; the Czech B-534, and the French Curtiss H75. Even the Polish planes destroyed on the airfields were real. Tobis's production, which was photographed by Heinz von Jaworsky, and directed by Hans Bertram (1906–1993), was released in February 1941 in Berlin, but not screened in America. Goebbels named it a National Film Prize winner.

U.S. audiences also had the chance to see a production that tried to put a superhuman and sympathetic face to the ordinary people of Nazi Germany: Gustav Ucicky's German-Austrian *Mutterliebe* (*Motherly Love*, 1939). Its aim was to demonstrate that Germany's *Volksgenossinnen* ("female and national comrades") had critical roles to play in times of danger to the nation. They served and waited as wives and mothers during wartime, sacrificing for dear husbands in the battlefield and for Germany's children, who needed lots of love. Starring Käthe Dorsch (1890–1957), Wolf Albach-Retty, a young actor named Siegfried Breuer, and the new Czech actress Winnie Markus (1921–2002), the contemporary drama is about the tribulations of the mother of three boys and a girl (Traudl Stark) during wartime. Pilinger (Dorsch) is a middle-class woman who loses her husband in a work accident. Although in debt,

Kampfgeschwader Lützow.

she is unashamed about working as a laundress. She's driven to give her children the right education. When a well-situated man wants to marry her, she feels obliged to stick to her children who, however, are embarrassed by their mother. One of her boys, after getting into a fight, is in danger of losing his sight. His mother donates an eye to save him from going blind! She's also there to insure the wellbeing of her youngest son when he gets into difficulty. In the

Mutterliebe.

end her sacrifices for her family pay off: as the children grow up and marry, she becomes a beloved grandmother.

Goebbels praised *Mutterliebe*, which Wien Film produced and Gerhard Menzel scripted, for its "lifelike" line and as a "moving work of art." This tale of a German mother's *Leben, Kampf und Schiksal* ("life, struggle and fate"), as Ufa promoted it, was distributed by Casino Film Exchange in early 1940. Although it wasn't the first wife-and-mother film made by the Nazis, *Mutterliebe* led to a host of other films that continued to reassure the German nation in wartime. After the war, Ucicky never answered for his service to the Nazi regime, which spanned the years from *Morgenrot* to *Mutterliebe*. However, his reputation sank. Ucicky died during the shooting of *Das Letzte Kapital* (1961); his wartime colleague Wolfgang Liebeneiner, who also had much to answer for, completed the filming. Ucicky was married to German actress Betty Bird. Winnie Markus, one of the stars of *Mutterliebe*, made a score of films in the Reich, becoming one of Ufa's most important actors. German cinema awarded her its top prize in 1986.

Another German film that premiered at New York's Cinecitta Theatre in early 1940 offered both spectacle and violence. It was Austrian-born Luis Trenker's and Werner Klingler's Italian-German sixteenth-century drama *Giovanni de Medici, the Leader*, whose musical accompaniment was called very German and very martial. It was heard in the States in January 1940—when the guns were for the moment silent in Europe. But they blazed on the screen. Trenker played the protagonist, striving to unite a feudal Italy from the Alps to the sea. The legions of marching men rallying and charging around him looked a good deal like Fascist black shirts, saluted like Fascist black shirts, and talked a good deal like Fascist black shirts—

exalting discipline and duty. In Italy and Germany the film had been called *I Condottieri* (*The Knights*, 1936–1937). That was an apt title. Trenker's Giovanni was known as *Giovanni delle Bande Nere*—"Giovanni of the Black Bands"—a precursor to Italy's black-shirted thugs under Mussolini. Trenker managed to set facts aside in this lavish pageant that honors the overblown dictator Mussolini.

A few months earlier, in October 1939, Trenker's British-German production *The Challenge*, which Milton Rosmer co-directed, had made its rounds in America. This was the English-language version of Trenker's production *Der Berg Ruft* (*The Mountain Calls*, 1937). Trenker, who never could attract enough attention nor exhibit humility, played the Alpine guide named Jean-Antoine Carrel. Carrel, though competing against the British climber Edward Whymper (Robert Douglas) in a race to the summit of the Matterhorn in 1865, saves the British mountaineer from death. The villain of the tale, a man named "Favre" (Fred Groves), had tried to sow enmity between the two climbers. Albert Benitz, one of Germany's leading cameramen, and Georges Périnal shot the scenes of the great outdoors.

In 1940, Trenker and his production company, Luis Trenkerfilm, made use of his climbing skills to produce a one-reel army propaganda film for the Third Reich. Despite its brevity, the documentary represented Trenker's closest embrace of and service to the Nazi regime. Called *Unsere Gebirgspioniere* (*Our Mountain Pioneers*), it was an up-close look at the Wehrmacht, ready for action. Mock battles take place in rough terrain. Efficiency is the order of the day. Soldiers march out of the barracks at Mittenwald in Bavaria. Two attack forces separate; one climbs the Karwendel mountain range, crossing a ravine by constructing and then camouflaging a bridge. The other force strengthens its positions and digs trenches with pneumatic drills. It erects a suspension bridge and uses mules for transport. Tanks, coming down the mountain, attack. It is all very professional and well-rehearsed, after which the forces return to the barracks.

Trenker's co-director, Werner Kilingler, deepened *his* ties to the Nazi regime with a film he directed for Goebbels' ministry. It was not released in the States nor did American critics abroad seem to catch wind of it. Klingler's *Wetterleuchten um Barbara* (*Lightning Around Barbara*, 1941) is a *Heimat* drama that depicts Austria's *close* ties to Germany. It's set in Austria's Tyrol and Vorarlberg regions. In early 1938, members of the Austrian Heimwehr—the anti-Nazi home guard—raid a meeting of pro-Nazi Austrian peasants in the mountains. Barbara Stammer (Sybille Schmitz) and her husband Martin (Attila Hörbiger) escape and find refuge in Germany. They soon join other Austrian Nazis marching back into Austria with the conquering German troops that spring.

Luis Trenker's final Nazi effort involved a costarring role. It was Ufa's pseudo-medical drama *Germanin—Die Geschichte einer kolonialen Tat* (1943), directed by Max W. Kimmich. The story begins in 1914. Dr. Achenbach (Peter Peterson) is in German East Africa researching a serum called "Bayer 205," which he hopes will put an end to the scourge of sleeping sickness. The war intervenes, forcing his return to the fatherland, where Bayer scientists develop the serum. When the war ends—during which time Germany has been "robbed" of her African colonies—the good doctor wants to return to Africa to help its suffering natives. In 1923, the British agree, only if he can demonstrate that the new serum is harmless. His assistant (Trenker) takes the logical (German) step: he infects *himself* with sleeping sickness and is then cured by the serum. In Africa, Achenbach doesn't find it easy to do his important work: he is continually hampered by British acts of sabotage, including the destruction of his facilities. Then the British district commissioner develops sleeping sickness, as does the good doctor. But since there is only one vial of serum left, the German doctor, true to his medical ethics, gives it to the Englishman. The doctor dies but becomes a true German hero. Later, the life-saving serum is produced in large quantities, and it's called "Germanin." The Germans freely supply it to

I Condottieri, with Luis Trenker.

needy Africans, thereby remaining true to the spirit of the pioneers of German science. Who, then, could doubt which country was the more fit for colonial rule?

And is it conceivable that Leni Riefenstahl's later infatuation with Africa and its Nubians was actually a reflection and a continuation of Nazi Germany's colonial dramas and dreams? The actual 1921 German expedition aimed to eradicate sleeping sickness in coordination with British and Belgian doctors.

North Africa is the setting for Paul Martin's anti–British tale *Das Lied der Wüste* (*Desert Song*, 1939), with music by composer Nico Dostal (1895–1981), in which greed once more loses out to Nazi-depicted idealism. Scandinavian Zarah Leander played the stepdaughter of Sir Collins (Friedrich Domin), an international financier who works for the usual unnamed "foreign syndicate." He attempts to gain control of a copper mining operation in an international mandate territory. His foul methods include buying, that is, bribing, the local army. However, he is put to death in an Arab revolt led by a Swedish engineer, the idealist Nic Brenden (Gustav Knuth, 1901–1987). This northern European says of the Arabs, "I love them because they are oppressed." As the new administrator of the copper mining operation, he tries to ensure that the mine stays out of foreign hands. He also falls in love with the woman (Leander) who had saved his life during the Arabs' uprising. The *New York Times* (February 3, 1940) suggested that without Zarah Leander, *Das Lied der Wüste* "would be just another tale of an engineer ... determined to complete an irrigation dam." Postwar Germany had a different reaction. It banned *Das Lied der Wüste* from commercial release.

The Nazi production *Spiegel des Lebens* (*Life's Mirror*, 1938) starred another famous actress in the Nazi film firmament, Paula Wessely. The conflict between doctors and superstitious non-medical practitioners (*Kurpfuscherei*) comes to the fore when medical student Hanna (Wessely) faces a problem. She must choose which of two medical approaches to life is right for her. Her professor-lover Dr. Eberle (Attila Hörbiger) is certain of the value of medical science. Her father (Peter Petersen), a rich jeweler and amateur doctor, is dubious. He's convinced there's a subtler and more effective way to diagnose illnesses. He says he can do it by looking into a patient's eyes and deducing the proper course of healing. Authorities do not approve of his methods. This puts Hanna in a predicament, particularly when she administers an illicit drug prescribed by her father, and is caught in the act.

Although Wessely presents a reflection of a German woman's life that, ironically, comes across as schizophrenic, the subject was timely: medical ethics. The story supports rational medicine yet gives a nod to pseudo-science and mysticism. Taking place just before the outbreak of World War II, the film depicts Paula Wessely's character giving up medical school yet marrying the wise doctor who is a strong opponent of her father, and then having a baby. In this way she retains the love of both men. Her decision is the Nazi way of having a German woman subordinate herself to serve husband and father. In the death camps, Nazis would often quickly examine arriving inmates by looking into their eyes to try to gauge their age and well-being.

Shown in the U.S. in winter 1939–1940, *Spiegel des Lebens* was produced by Gloria Film of Vienna *after* the union of Germany and Austria. Hungarian-born Frank Fux (1908–1965) scored the film, which Géza von Bolváry directed. Paula Wessely (1907–2000) had made her film debut in Willi Forst's musical *Maskerade* (1934). Likeable, talented, and inspired, she was one of the highest paid actors in the Third Reich. Because she starred in Ucicky's bloodcurdling *Heimkehr* (1941)—yet another film American critics abroad overlooked at the time of its release—the Allies banned her from film. (Her husband, Attila Hörbiger, was also in that film, but he was overlooked.) The ban lasted barely three years. Wessely made her last film in 1986. Austrian-born Attila Hörbiger (1896–1987), brother of Paul, acted in films from 1922 until 1977, including numerous films during the Nazi era, and was awarded the *Bundesverdienstkreuz* from the Federal Republic of Germany in 1954.

On American screens this season was yet another German favorite, Kristina Söderbaum, "one of the foreigners helping keep the German film industry alive despite the loss of so much of its talent under the Nazi regime," wrote the *New York Times* (February 10, 1940). The paper couldn't bring itself to use the word Jewish regarding this "loss" of talent. The film in question was Veit Harlan's *Die Reise nach Tilsit* (*The Trip to Tilsit*, 1939), produced by Majestic. The film emphasizes the triumph of family, love, and motherhood, which had Goebbels singing its praises. Loosely based on a minor short story by Hermann Sudermann—"Litauische Geschichten," the source material for Murnau's *Sunrise* (1927)—it's the story of Endrik and his dealings with the "fascinating, sophisticated" Madlyn Sapierska (Anna Dammann), who comes from "Warsaw or some place like that." Working as their maid, she almost succeeds in taking Endrik (Frits von Dongen) from his wife Elske (Söderbaum). Set in a fishing village, the stifling, reactionary, and racist film climaxes on the bay of Tilsit during a trip in the couple's sailboat, when the husband is *tempted* to kill his wife because his father-in-law had insulted the maid. If Endrik can make the death look like an accident, he will avoid the shame of divorce and retain custody of his blond son. But just as quickly, he realizes the enormity of his plan. On the way back, fate takes revenge. Their boat capsizes, and his wife goes under. He then agonizes over what she went through. But the maid discovers his wife—miraculously saved from death—on the beach. She summons help. And to bring about the happy ending, the Polish lady disappears from the scene. This guarantees that an inconvenient obstacle gets out of the way of the German couple's reunion. The Allies also banned this film after the war.

In Boese's family drama *Drei Väter um Anna* (*Three Fathers for Anna*, 1939), a CFE release, the protagonist is the illegitimate daughter (Ilse Werner) of Donka (Roma Bahn), a Bavarian cabaret singer who, before her death, entrusts the care of the young woman to a country doctor, Anton Bruck (Hans Stuewe). But she doesn't reveal which of three World War I veterans is her father. The three are friends of the good doctor: Gsodmair (Georg Vogelsang), the village mayor and widower; Fenzl (Beppo Brem); and Ameiser (Theodor Danegger), the postman. Anna's and the doctor's relationship is cause for shock. The locals, including "Countess Weissenfels" (Anneliese von Eschstruth), are aghast that Anna lives with an unmarried man. Further, "Matschek" (Karl Stepanek) spreads malicious rumors because Bruck won't sell him a plot of his land. With friendships strained, resolution comes when the down-to-earth postman admits he's Anna's father. Anna then admits her love for Gsodmair's son, Martl (Tonio Riedl). The key thing American critics noted was that the "scenes of domestic life and community activities have an air of realism seldom encountered in the cinema," according to the *New York Times* (January 20, 1940).

Boese's *Das Glück auf dem Lande* (*Rural Happiness*), a Terra production shown at the Garden Theatre in February 1940, fit the general category of *Volksfilme* (popular films). *Das Glück auf dem Lande* had been produced in Germany as *Steputat & Co.* (1938) whereby the unpleasant but very rich shopkeeper Steputat (Erich Dunskus), living in an East Prussian village, causes trouble whenever he can. His favorite motto is: "From rich people one can learn, as one saves." Steputat wants to marry his young employee Hertha Mauroschat (Hildegard Barko), but she's in love with another employee, Ernst Masur (Hans Brausewetter). Steputat attempts to frame them for stealing winning lottery tickets—the same tickets he had rejected when he felt they were a waste of money. But the couple takes him to court. In that fair-minded arena, Steputat receives his just punishment. For once, the film's legal proceedings, as well as references to Hitler and the swastika, had American critics calling the story's atmosphere genuine.

While Europeans anxiously awaited Hitler's next moves, German themes centering on ordinary existence continued to abound on select American screens. Village-peasant life, man's struggle to control natural forces (raging rivers), and rural wisdom are the central preoccupations of two films by the director-producer Peter Ostermayr that were shown in the States in 1939–40. Both films were adapted from nineteenth-century works by the Nazis' favorite Heimat novelist, Ludwig Ganghofer, and were screened at the Garden Theatre. In *Edelweisskönig* (*King of the Edelweiss*, 1938), farmer Jörg (Victor Gehring) shelters his brother Ferdl (Paul Richter), a wood carver, from the police, who want him for the murder of a local official. Harmony is established when the carver is found innocent and unites with country maiden Veverl (Hansi Knoteck). In a subplot, mountain girl Hannerl (Ingeborg Wittmann) rejects the attention of a count and finds her soulmate in young forester Gidi (Gustl Stark-Gstettenbaur), who knows his edelweiss (a flower). The *New York Times* had written that there's no tragedy in the story, but there were tales of ghosts and shifty smugglers who had to be apprehended. One was named "Valtl" (Hermann Erhardt).

Ostermayr's second hero, as depicted in *Waldrausch* (*Forest Fever*, 1939), which is set in the period 1880–1890, is civil engineer Ambros Lutz (Paul Richer), who is charged with building a dam. He is up against not only the elements but something bigger: rural mysticism. His job is complicated by the fact that when the forest "murmurs" and the clouds of pollen fill the air, an intoxicating fever casts its spell over those who live in and wander the forest. The men then become restless, unruly, and unpredictable. Ambros's job, if not his life, is at risk. The film posits health through nature—a typical Nazi idea—via the extended scenes of a vigorous, experienced, and wise 100-year-old *Waldrauscher*, or forest dweller (Eduard Köck), curing a little girl by giving her a brew of special forest herbs

Arthur Maria Rabenalt's paganistic *Johannisfeuer* (*St. John's Fire*, 1939), produced by Terra and distributed by CFE in spring 1940, had enough heat to make American critics pay attention. Loosely based on a work by Hermann Sudermann, the film is a tale of the *other* woman, named Marikke (Anna Dammann). She is the daughter of a vagabond, the kind of societal outcast the Nazis always embrace in their films. During a night of revelry, festivities, and revelations as fires burn on German hills and restraints are cast aside, Marikke decides that the man for her is Georg Vogelreuter (Ernst von Klipstein), the son of a wealthy landowner. He has returned after five years in Africa to care for his aging father (Otto Wernicke) and marry his childhood sweetheart, Trude (Gertrude Meyen). But during St. John's Night, their concerns are thrown overboard.

A fiery gypsy femme fatale named Panna (Margit Symo), a ferocious poet-hobo named Silo (Attila Hörbiger), who is an accused murderer, and the married but neglected woman named Marie (Heidemarie Hatheyer, 1918–1990) who saves his life are the protagonists of Géza von Bolváry's *Zigeunerweisen* (*Gypsy-Wise*), which screened in the U.S. in early 1940. This *Heimat* tale makes use of the background of river and plains. This Third Reich film had been retitled from *Zwischen Strom und Steppe* (*Between River and Steppe*, 1939) to something more exciting. Bolváry also directed a Hungarian version, which Hunnia produced, called *Tiszavirag* (*Flower of the Tisza*, 1939), starring Arpad Lehotay and Klari Tolnay. It too was shown in the States, at the Modern Playhouse in New York's Yorkville section, although, said the *New York Times* (December 30, 1939), it lacks "most of the fiery love incidents usually associated with Magyar romance."

Bolváry's drama about revolution called *Maria Ilona* (1939) was fiery enough. The Terra production, which was released in the U.S. in spring 1940, is set during the 1848 Hungarian revolution, which was led by Louis Kossuth (a historical figure who favored Jewish emancipation). One man who opposes Kossuth and the Jews has the right attitude. That's Prince Karl Felix (Willy Birgil), head of the Austrian government, who, supported by Russian troops, aims to crush any uprising. Austrian Baroness Maria Ilona (Paula Wessely), who sympathizes with the Hungarians in their struggle but is in love with the prince, agrees to help bring Kossuth (Richard Häussler) around. The Austrian prince is portrayed as a man willing to give the Hungarians a fair shake until duty demands he use his iron fist. In other words, he's the kind of leader people need.

Maria Ilona depicts Austro-Hungarian historical events Hitler's way. In *Mein Kampf*, Hitler had concluded, "The European revolutionary movement of 1848 primarily took the form of a class conflict in almost every other country, but in Austria it took the form of a new racial struggle. In so far as the German-Austrians there forgot the origins of the movement, or perhaps had failed to recognize them at the start and consequently took part in the revolutionary uprising, they sealed their own fate. For they thus helped to awaken the spirit of Western Democracy which within a short while, shattered the foundations of their own existence."

Nineteenth-century Vienna and Mozart's music are the attractions in *Eine kleine Nachtmusik* (1940), which Tobis produced to commemorate the 150th anniversary of Mozart's death. Casino Film Exchange released it in spring 1940. Leopold Hainisch (1891–1979) directed Hannes Stelzer as the famous Austrian composer traveling from Vienna to Prague for the premiere of his *Don Giovanni*. (The Nazis considered that opera entirely German, and because of it Mozart beat the greatest Italian masters of the day on what had been exclusively their turf.) In the film, Mozart's wife (Christl Mardayn) is along for the ride, during which the great musician is inspired to compose the opera's finale. We also meet a countess (Heli Finkenzeller) who is in love with the famous Austrian musician and his works, especially his other purely German opera, *The Marriage of Figaro*. The Vienna Philharmonic, the Berlin Philharmonic, and the Vienna State Opera Ballet collaboratively presented Mozart's German compositions and ballet numbers. The Nazis called Mozart "God's musician." Goebbels had written, "The German soldier is also protecting Mozart's music." American critics united in praise of the film. Mozart's "spirit," said the *New York Times* (March 2, 1940), "could hardly have picked a better vehicle for its reincarnation." Who could object to a film like this or envision a devastating war when music like was coming from Germany?

Early in 1940, more music came from Benjamin Gigli, who was back at the Garden Theatre, in Karl Heinz Martin's Olympic-year production *Du bist mein Glück* (*You Are My Joy*). This Italian-German operetta has the famous tenor playing opposite blonde star Isa Miranda, with music by Guiseppe Becce. Munich, which was one of Hitler's favorite cities, provides the backdrop for the story of a music teacher (Josef Sieber) who loses his wife to his greatest pupil (Gigli). In revenge, the teacher does all he can to keep his former wife and daughter apart. A followup Martin-Gigli collaboration, *Die Stimme der Herzens* (*The Voice of the Heart*, 1937), a Bavaria production, faired poorly in Germany and Italy, and never made it to the States. However, a second Italian-German production starring Isa Miranda opened in New York in early 1940. That film, *Una Donna tra due Mondi* (*A Woman Between Two Worlds*, 1935), was directed by Goffredo Alessandrini. Undisclosed was the fact that Alessandrini's film was the Italian rendition of Arthur Rabenalt's *Die Liebe des Maharadscha* (1935), produced by Bavaria and Astra Film-Berlin, with music by Franz Grothe and starring Miranda and Gustav Diessl. In *Una Donna tra due Mondi*, Miranda is a pianist in a touring musical troupe. At a hotel along the coast in Italy, she meets an exotic maharaja from Bathaipore. He's attracted to her because she reminds him of a lost lover. Although she's in love with a cellist (Diessl) of the quartet and tries to resist the exotic maharaja, she eventually surrenders to him. Soon, however, she is convinced that the maharaja really pines for his dead lover. Miranda then returns to serene life with the cellist.

Astra Film-Berlin had been behind *Ho Perduto Mio Marito* (*I Have Lost My Husband*, 1937), which had screened at New York's Cinecitta Theatre. "Male visitors," wrote the *New York Times* (October 20, 1939), were likely to find the film "eminently satisfactory because of the charming shadow of one of the prettiest girls in the Italian film industry." That was young Vanna Vanni, playing second fiddle to the mature and glamorous Paola Borboni. The popular performer Nino Besozzi is the object of the matrimonial designs of Vanna's scheming mother (Vittorina Venvenuti) and of a distant cousin and former sweetheart. Director Enrico Guazzoni was said to have "made the most of many fine views, ranging from Florence to Naples, and of some slightly risqué situations."

In April 1940, at New York's Cine Roma, admirers of the so-called golden voice of Benjamin Gigli could hear it again in the Italian-German tragedy called *Legittima Difesa* (*Self-Defense*). Gigli played a tenor who slays "nasty" American impresario James Kennedy (Hans Olden) to save a ballet dancer (Christina Heiberg), whom he eventually later weds. "A. Giacolone" was listed as director. In fact, the film was *La Casa Lontana* (*The Far House*, 1939), directed by Johannes Meyer from a story by Max Kimmich. It co-starred a slew of German performers—Hans Holden (as the American named Kennedy), Hilde Korber, Elsa Wagner, Friedrich Keyssler, whose Italian is dubbed, and soprano Livia Caloni. In Germany the film was called *Der Singende Tor* (*The Singing Gate*).

Even more Germans were in Italian director Carmine Gallone's Bavaria production *Das Abenteuer geht weiter* (*Another Experience*, 1939), a comedy written by Ernst Marischka that screened at the Garden Theatre in early 1940. They included Theo Lingen, Victor Braun, Paul Kemp, Johannes Heesters, Richard Romanowsky, Jan Kiepura, Gusti Wolf, and Maria von Tasnady. A popular stage tenor (Heesters, b. 1903) can't stay away from his admirers (including Gusti Wolf) until his wife (Maria von Tasnady) threatens to divorce him. As in many other German, Italian, or Austrian productions, the misunderstandings, entanglements, and misdirections take second place to the music and singing in the mountains of Europe, but not to the message of home and hearth.

April 1940 brought Kurt Hoffmann's comedy *Paradies der Junggesellen* (*Bachelor's Paradise*, 1939) to a screen in New York. Produced by Terra, with music by the acclaimed composer Michael Jary, it starred the ubiquitous Nazi favorite Heinz Rühmann. Registrar of births, marriages, and deaths Hugo Bartels (Rühmann) is at loose ends: he's divorced for the second time. His landlady, however, has plans for them both: she's trying to lure him into a third marriage—with her. With the help of his wartime buddies, however, Hugo evades this danger by moving in with Dr. Balduin Hannemann (Hans Brausewetter), a pharmacist, and with Caesar Spreckelsen (Josef Sieber), a schoolteacher. Because they've all had bad luck with women, they vow to forsake the opposite sex so as to enjoy their bachelor's paradise. But Hugo falls for the landlady, Mrs. Platen, quickly breaking the promise. To get his two buddies to break their vows, he sets up a trap for them, helped by his ex-wives, Eva and Hermine. In the film, Brausewetter (1899–1945), an anti–Nazi who was briefly interned by the Gestapo, sings the number "Das kann doch einen seemann nicht erschüttern" ("That Cannot Shake a Sailor, Nevertheless"), which became one of his great popular successes in Germany.

Two comedies by Paul Verhoeven released in the U.S. in early 1940 also emphasize marriage. In *Der Tag nacht der Scheidung* (*The Day after the Divorce*, 1938), (Johannes Riemann) feels underappreciated in his marriage. Although his wife Bettina (Luise Ullrich) says she loves him, he leaves her for a cabaret singer (Hilde Hildebrand). Almost immediately, he regrets his decision. The abandoned wife then meets the young pilot Julian Bork (Hans Söhnker) when her car breaks down. Soon enough Bettina decides to go abroad with Bork. While retrieving her passport she runs into George, who admits he's had a change of heart: he does love her after all. When Bork goes to fetch Bettina, he discovers that the couple has reunited. The film, which screened at the Garden Theatre, contains the number "Du musst mir Deine Liebe erst beweisen" ("You Must Prove You Love Only Me").

Verhoeven's *Unsere kleine Frau* (*Our Little Wife*, 1938), a German-Italian production by Itala Film, starred Kathy von Nagy, Albert Matterstock, Grete Weisner, and Lucie Englisch in a bit of risqué business. It screened in the States in early 1940. A young woman becomes aware of her wandering husband and plots his comeuppance. This provokes a series of misunderstandings, which take place in London and Cairo, until the happy reunion of the pair. For those who were paying attention at the time, Verhoeven's Italian-language rendition of *Our Little Wife* had been shown a year earlier in New York's Cine Roma, under the title *Solo per Donne* (*For Women Only*), starring the same cast but "directed" by Alberto Giacolone. Dubbing allowed the German performers to speak the language of Dante in the film, which was titled *Mia Moglie si Diverte* (1938) in Italy.

The theatrical performer Verhoeven (1901–1975) had started his directing career with *Die Fledermaus* (*The Bat*, 1937), a Tobis production based on the operetta by Strauss that was supervised by the disreputable Hans H. Zerlett (1892–1949). It starred the Czech-born Lida Baarová (born Ludmila Babkova) but went unseen in the States. Verhoeven was also responsible for a disreputable film of his own: the anti–Weimar *Salonwagen E 417* (1939). It focuses on the inhabitants of a railroad car through the early decades of the twentieth century. In the years before World War I, the coach is home to a prince and his bride. During the war, Germany's enemies plunder the car. After the war, the coach lies in a siding, its inhabitants an unemployed German couple. It and they bear witness to the upheavals and corruption in the Weimar period from the perspective of the Nazis, including criminal activities by a so-called civil servant named "Max Lammer" (Otto Kronburger). The film was not released in America and overlooked by American critics in Germany.

In Germany, newcomer Helmut Käutner had scripted the story. Käutner also scripted *Die*

Stimme aus dem Äther (*The Voice from the Ether*, 1939), which Harald Paulsen (1895–1954) directed. Scored by Johannes Müller (d. 1969), it was a typical example of an everyday Nazi story that American critics abroad once again overlooked and that failed to reach the States. The setting is a broadcast studio. Brigitte von Gersdorf (Annelise Uhlig, 1905–1984) finds herself arguing with her father about her choice of work in radio. She moves in with a girlfriend and gets to know a broadcaster. He gets her on the air. She's a hit. When the station's director finds out, he allows her to stay on the air—but anonymously. Then a listener falls in love with the unidentified voice. The film had enough Nazi greetings, Nazi remarks and a prominent photo of Goebbels that the Allies banned it after the war.

German star Luise Ullrich (1911–1985) was back on American screens in spring 1940 in the Austrian-German production *Schatten der Vergangenheit* (*Shadows of the Past*), a psychological thriller that Werner Hochbaum had directed in the year of the Berlin Olympics. Here Ullrich played twin sisters. While Betty is the toast of Vienna, Helene is apparently the black sheep of the family, having served a four-year jail sentence for murder. District attorney Hans Hellwig (Gustav Diessl) is in love with Betty. After Betty accidentally drowns, circumstances permit Helene to masquerade as her sister. But before Helene can prove *her* innocence, she must deal with two criminals who know her secret identity and try to make the most of it. Their names are "Semmelweich" (Oscar Sima) and "Brillanten-Emil" (Anton Pointner). She also must overcome a dubious inspector named "Waraschitz" (Rudolf Carl).

Hochbaum's subsequent film *Man Spricht über Jacqueline* (*Talking About Jacqueline*, 1937), a Deka production scored by Anton Profes (1896–1976), also involves sisters. Jacqueline Topelius (Wera Engles) is married to Michael Thomas (Albrecht Schönhals), who is a diplomat, a cynic, and a woman-hater. Jacqueline uses her sister, June (Sabine Peters), to try to get out of her unsatisfying marriage. Hochbaum's drama, although American critics reviewed it in Berlin, never made it to the States. Wera Engels (1904–1988) worked in Hollywood in the early 1930s before returning to Germany to star in director Aleksandr Volkov's *Stjenka Rasin* (1936), a musical set in the 1920s.

Max W. Kimmich's *Der Fuchs von Glenarvon* (*The Fox of Glenarvon*, 1940), which Tobis produced, opened on Berlin screens during this period of the "phony war." For eight centuries—according to the Nazis—the Irish had been trying to free themselves from the British, who are portrayed as little more than rapists and murderers. In the early 1900s, revolt is in the air. One of England's "best" is a judge (Ferdinand Marian) whose wife is Irish. Returning with her to Ireland, he infiltrates the freedom-loving Irish Underground Movement. At the same time, another Irishman, an aristocrat, returns to Ireland, but he is no friend of the judge. The judge demonstrates his loyalty to the nation by calling the aristocrat an Irish traitor. At his trial, however, the aristocrat is found innocent. The judge—the hidden enemy—then reveals the whereabouts of the IUM to the British police. The Irish rebels, however, lure the British forces and the judge into a trap in a bog, where, in true Nazi fashion, they perish.

Goebbels wrote that the film, which was not released in America, "will come in very useful for our propaganda." He named Kimmich's film winner of a National Film Prize. It is one of several Nazi productions that depict Ireland as a sympathetic breeding ground for nationalism, revolt, and anti–British sentiment. Hans Bertram co-wrote the script, Fritz Arno Wagner served as photographer, and Otto Konradt supplied the music. The movie also featured Russian-born Olga Tschechowa, Lucie Höflich (1883–1956), Bernhard Goetzke, and a score of others. "State actress" Höflich agreed to make this film for the regime. Married to Emil Jannings, she was awarded German cinema's *Bundesverdienstkreuz* (Order of Merit) in 1955.

Interestingly, one of the overlooked figures in the history of German cinema is director Max ("Axel") W. Kimmich. Born the son of a university professor in Ulm in 1893, Kimmich attended a school for cadets. He studied medicine, but rejected it for work in the theater. The theater led to film and film led to the United States, where he worked as a scriptwriter for Universal—that Jewish studio—in the 1920s. He returned to Germany and worked for Deutsche Universal, hand-in-hand with Jewish writers, actors, and directors. Kimmich had produced the Eddie Polo comedy *Auf der Reeperbahn nachts um halb eins* (*In the Coney Island of Hamburg at 12:30*, 1929) directed by Fred Stranz. He scripted Deutsche Universal's World War I espionage thriller *Unter falscher Flagge* (*Under False Flag*, 1932), which Johannes Meyer directed. When the Nazis came to power, Kimmich found his place. In 1939, he married into power, wedding Goebbels' sister, Maria. With that, Kimmich had secured one of the many open spots in the Nazi film hierarchy.

In films, the Nazis were specialists in finding openings to attack their enemies. Their most vicious films, rather than skirting the subject, would take special aim at Jews. In spring 1940, "sports devotees and others disappointed at the postponement of the Olympic games in 1940" in Tokyo, wrote the *New York Times* (March 9, 1940), could take comfort in Leni Riefenstahl's youth-filled, inspirational documentary of the 1936 Berlin Olympics, called *Olympiad* (1938), the first part of which finally had a commercial screening in America, at New York's 86th Street Garden Theatre. Riefenstahl's name, however, appeared nowhere in connection with the film. With English narration, Riefenstahl's film raised no hackles in the U.S this year. The *New Yorker*'s Andy Mosher wrote: "There may seem to have been considerable commotion about a picture which has no propaganda value one way or another." American leftists agreed. None protested the release, which includes shots of Hitler, because Germany and the Soviet Union, after signing a non-aggression pact, were no longer open enemies. The film confirmed the opinions of those Americans who found little fault with Germany, or other Americans who imagined that Germany might yet return to its senses. The film's presentation of clean, wholesome sporting events and healthy Germans is not, however, the obverse of a film that the Nazi had in the works in late 1940, *Der Ewige Jude*. *Olympiad*, too, implies a deeply held anti–Semitism. Riefenstahl's film worked to the advantage of Nazi Germany in other ways. The film was both a form of

Olympiad: Erwin Huber.

misdirection and a statement of Germany's might. The people and nations in *Olympiad* had competed harmoniously against Germany on the field of sports. German athletes had won, so to speak. Lulled into complacency, afraid of Germany, or perhaps supportive of its policies, the people and nations in Riefenstahl's film were unwilling and unprepared to go against Germany and its allies on the field of battle.

MAY 1940–1942
Feldzug in Polen, Der Sieg im Westen, *and More*

In April and May 1940, the German Army invaded Denmark, Norway, the Netherlands, Belgium, and Luxembourg. By the end of June, those nations had surrendered to the Nazi regime, and France had agreed to an armistice. In September, the Nazis banned Free Masons, the Rotary Club, and the Red Cross; they deprived Jews of possessions and decreed that non–Jewish women could not work in Jewish homes. By the end of the year, German troops had occupied Romania and invaded Greece.

In February 1941, German planes attacked Iceland. In March, Rommel's Afrika Korps attacked British forces in Libya. In May, Germany invaded Crete, and a month later the U.S.S.R. Part of the invasion force came through "neutral" Sweden.

In August 1941, Marshal Phillipe Petain, chief of state of Vichy France, announced complete collaboration with Nazi Germany. While German films continued to be shown in America, Maurice Gleize's *Le Club de soupirants* (1941) was the first—and only—Vichy production released in the States during the war years. In September 1941 the German submarine U-652 fired at the U.S. destroyer *Greer* off the coast of Iceland. Germany ordered Jews in occupied countries to wear the Star of David. That same month, the Nazis murdered 33,000 Jews at Babi Yar, a ravine outside Kiev. In October 1941, when extermination in the East had already been practiced for several months, emigration from the Reich was forbidden. Late that month, in a meeting with Himmler and Heydrich, Hitler said, "It's not a bad idea by the way, that public rumor attributes to us a plan to exterminate the Jews." Within 90 days, in early 1942, SS leader Reinhard Heydrich led the infamous Wannsee conference, at which Nazi officials, including Adolf Eichmann, planned the elimination of Europe's Jews.

The period of the "phony war"—that is, the lull in the fighting in Western Europe after September 1939—was over. Was there a better time to stress Germany's military triumph and might—and its justification for continued war—and to intimidate Americans? In May 1940, Ufa released the sham documentary *Feldzug in Polen* (*Campaign in Poland*, 1939–40) in the U.S., beginning with a premiere in New York.

This full-length documentary depicts the destruction of Poland thanks to Nazi (and Soviet) aggression—and the West's indifference, if not cowardice, in the face of that aggression. The footage is extensive and divided into four parts:

1. Reasons for the war (as seen by Germany): the Danzig situation, effects of the Treaty of Versailles, the anti–German attitude of England and France, the annexation of Danzig, the advance of Germany troops into Poland.

2. Wehrmacht victory scenes, interrupted by pictures of Poland's destruction, the undam-

Josef Goebbels (first man from left) and Nazis at a screening of *Feldzug in Polen*.

aged condition of the Madonna of Czenstochau, welcoming scenes involving the German population, and arrests of Jews and Poles.

3. Scenes of the advance of German troops alternating with reports of German victories from the main battlefields, along with pictures of Polish prisoners of war and captured weapons and equipment.

4. The battle of Weichselbogen, the meeting of German and Russian forces in Brest-Litovsk, the capitulation of Warsaw, and Hitler's victory parade on October 5, 1939, in the Polish capital.

The heart of the production depicts the Germans readying themselves against the Poles on the coast of Danzig; Soviet Foreign Minister Ribbentrop signing the Nazi-Soviet Pact; Poles mobilizing; shots of fighting in the city of Danzig and then its union with East Prussia; German armies attacking Poland from the north and south; Jews fleeing and non-Jews welcoming the invaders; military maps and diagrams with details and shots of the progress of what the film calls the campaign; the Luftwaffe attacking vital points to assist the German advance; German naval attacks, the capture of Gdynia; Hitler and his officers visiting the fronts; the battles at Radom, Lemberg, and Kudno; and the Russians preparing to invade Poland from the east.

The film's screening at New York's pro–Nazi 96th Street Theatre alarmed the German-Jewish publication *Aufbau* (July 26, 1940). It noted something ominous but not surprising: the pro–German feeling among those in attendance. The "spirit of the fifth column," it said, "wafts through the auditorium." Russell Maloney of the *New Yorker* agreed. "It's quite an experience," he said, "to attend a showing of a German film in Yorkville." The "most instructive part of the exhibition was the reaction of the audience. They cheered and applauded every appearance of Hitler and the swastika flag."

The film's debut in the West meant something even more ominous: the continuation of the war *after* Poland. Its release in America coincided with Germany's attack on Western Europe. Directed by Fritz Hippler (1909–2002) and scored by Herbert Windt, the film had broken records in Berlin—a third of a million Germans saw it in the first three days, and by the end its first week, in mid-February 1940, the number had soared to three-quarters of a million. Goebbels called the reaction "extraordinarily favorable ... especially in view of a possible intensification of the war situation." Victory in the East implied that Germany was confident of victory in the West. At the conclusion of World War II, the Allies banned *Feldzug in Polen*.

The Germans had apparently learned a few lessons from their failures of earlier warfare, that is, from World War I. These lessons are the subjects of a second German war film to quickly reach the States. Tobis's *Die Hölle in Westen* was shown at the Casino just as the Nazis invaded France. This film recapitulates the First World War battles that took place around Fort Douaumont, a French stronghold that the Germans briefly captured during the Battle of Verdun. The "documentary" was really an updating of the Weimar-era *Douaumont/Die Hölle von Verdun*, which had been made with the cooperation of former German officers in 1931 and directed by Heinz Paul.

The re-titling of the film with the word *Westen*—West—implied that the Nazis foresaw a different outcome for German forces against the French in World War II. Re-created battle scenes, animated maps, spoken dialogue sequences, and original World War 1 footage depict German and French troops mobilizing, and German troops capturing, holding, and then losing the fort to their enemies, between February and October of 1916. *Die Hölle in Westen* stresses two things: military preparation and timing. Germany's defeat in the battle was due to its failure to attack as planned, in early February 1916. The delay had allowed the French to bring up reinforcements.

While the *New York Times* (June 28, 1940) called *Die Hölle in Westen* "just another war picture," one French filmmaker had his own response to German militarism. Alexandre Ryder directed the semi-documentary *Aprés Mein Kampf Mes Crimes* (1940) before France had signed an armistice with Germany. It tries, via newsreel footage and re-created action, to call Nazism to account. Despite the fact that American critics dismissed this 90-minute examination of the life of the German leader and his brutal regime as mediocre, the film, which was shown in New York in late summer 1940, was compelling enough to garner attention among Americans. And Germany's leading propagandist appreciated it for its propaganda value. When it fell into Goebbels' hands after France's capitulation, Goebbels' critical reaction was to call *Aprés Mein Kampf Mes Crimes* "subtle, effective and dangerous."

This example of fighting fire with fire on the screen was emulated by the American production *The Ramparts We Watch*. In late summer 1940, at Radio City Music Hall, Americans had the chance to see footage from Hans Bertram's *Feuertaufe* (*Baptism of Fire*, 1939–40)—but not as the Nazis had envisioned its release in the U.S. An evaluation of America's World War I experience and an argument for America to rearm, *Ramparts* warns against the consequences of a German victory. The film's director, Louis de Rochemont, incorporated scenes from *Feuertaufe*.

Feuertaufe presents Germany's invasion of Poland in September 1939 as a heroic triumph of the Luftwaffe. Germany is called the victim of Polish provocation and aggression. Newsreels and photographs depict Germany's response. Spectacular aerial images show Stukas bombing Warsaw and inflicting terrible damage, followed by scenes of Poland's capitulation and shots of Germany's preparations for war against Britain. Scored by Norbert Schultze, it contains Nazi commentary about one of the causes of the Second World War: Danzig in the 1930s. It goes like this: "The German fraction among the conglomerate of nationalities was ruthlessly persecuted," says the narrator. "German schools were closed, industrialists and landowners expropriated and large parts of the German populace were driven from the country. Numbers steadily growing, they tried to escape from Polish terror and seek protection on Reich territory. Hundreds of thousands of worn out, distressed and panic stricken people poured daily into German refugee camps."

The Nazis had released *Feuertaufe* in Western Europe before invading in May 1940. Göring called its effects "penetrating" as the Nazis penetrated Western Europe. Members of the U.S. Congress viewed *Feuertaufe* in July 1940 and it screened privately in Chicago, where it inspired Nazi supporters and boomeranged against those arguing that America had to prepare for war. "Fortunately," said the *Chicago Tribune* (January 16, 1941), "German equipment was designed for war under European conditions." America had no need to fear an invasion. America's isolationists declared such films as *Feuertaufe* pure propaganda. They attacked so-called warlords and warmongers as standing to profit from Congress's military appropriations.

In America, however, only the last twelve minutes from *Feuertaufe*, which had been seized by the British in Bermuda, were commercially available. These scenes were incorporated into the ending of the March of Time's *The Ramparts We Watch*, its first full-length feature, directed by Rochement and narrated by Westbrook van Voorhis.

The last minutes make up reels nine and ten of *Ramparts*. Reel nine shows German air strength and includes views of Hitler and Göring. In reel ten, German paratroopers and armor go into battle, Germans round up Polish prisoners, quislings identify anti–Nazi leaders, the Poles accept a surrender, and then the German narrator denigrates the U.S.

Variety (November 1940) noted that *Ramparts*' purpose was "to draw the inevitable comparison between world events of 25 years ago and the consequences of Hitler aggressions today. Then as now, the film declares, an apathetic America sought safety and security in neutrality." German embassy officials in Washington, D.C., called *Ramparts* "distorted and untrue" (*Washington Post*, October 30, 1940).

While these war "documentaries" were being released in the States, German features in late 1940 dealt with action of another kind than battle. Love triangles and plenty of movement are the key elements in Eduard von Borsody's second colonial drama of his career, *Kongo-Express* (1939), an Ufa production shown in the States as the "phony war" was ending, when apparently Austrian-financed films and their filmmakers were marketable in the States. In the story, Renate Brinkmann (Marianne Hoppe), a young Hamburg woman, heads to Africa to find out why her Belgian lover Gaston Thibault (René Deltgen) had broken their engagement. On the exotic Kongo-Express she meets gallant German adventurer Viktor Hartmann (Willy Birgel). He's survived on the continent for eight years. Later, two trains on the same line are heading towards each other, and Renate is aboard one of the speeding trains as it rounds sharp curves through the jungle. Gaston and Viktor are flying overhead, each in a separate plane, trying to avert what is certain to be a catastrophic train collision below.

Weeks later, we see an African liner steaming up the Elbe to Hamburg. Renate and Viktor are on the upper deck, enjoying each other's company. Gaston, in a miraculous bit of flying, had prevented the trains' collision but lost his life to save the two Germans. In the cast was Wilhelm Bendow (1884–1950). The setting is a favorite Nazi locale: Africa, in this case the Belgian Congo—why not German East Africa?—where whatever happens stays in the realm of adventure and could be dismissed as insignificant. At least that's the initial impression the film gives. On closer look, the film reveals something more. The German adventurer says of his time in Africa, "To live here means you have to be a real man.... Connections and protections don't exist; you have to conquer life every hour anew." The last reels sum up the

Nazi theme: death to non-Germans so that members of the master race might survive. There's no masking the truth here.

The Nazis made an indirect, unconscious, if not hypocritical, admission of a world already ablaze in Günther Rittau's *Brand im Ozean* (*Fire on the Ocean*, 1939). It was a Terra production with music by Lothar Brühne that was shown at the 86th St Casino Theatre in early October 1940. The film was one of many German films still in circulation in the U.S. after May 1940, nearly all of them ignored by American critics. Adventurers and speculators, including Tom Finberg (René Deltgen), are seeking oil off the Central American coast. As they push out into the ocean, they summon the best deep-sea diver in the business: Nick Dorland (Hans Söhnker). He's the one who strikes oil—and simultaneously discovers the wreckage of a boat, which is laden with gold. Oil and gold—what a lucky break for all concerned! McGowan (Michael Bohnen), chief of the Caribbean Oil Company, and his partner, Don Pedro de Alvarado (Rudolf Fernau), imagine a brighter future until fate, in the form of Juana (Winnie Marcus), Pedro's niece, arrives. Rivalry between two men for her hand, combined with their greed for the treasure, lead to an enormous oil fire on the ocean. But one man saves another, comradeship overcomes jealousy and hate, lovers are united, and the gold is forgotten. What matters is a handshake and the "warmth of a friendly heart," says the film, to make matters right in the world.

War was the last thing filmgoers confronted in concurrent features released from Germany. Rather, beautiful shots of picturesque landscapes in the peaceful Tyrol are at the heart of Joe Stöckel's *Das Recht auf Liebe* (*The Right to Love*, 1939), a CFE release. The gracious daughter Melonie (Anneliese Uhlig) of the rich landowner von Salurn (Paul Wegener) is about to marry the good-looking, educated Vinzenz Brunner (Viktor Stahl), who is the offspring of semi-prosperous German peasants. The lowly maid Vroni Mareiter (Magda Schneider) briefly comes between them. Her consolation prize is the estate foreman Martin Förchinger (Rolf Wanka). The young Klaus Detlef Sierck played Stefan, Melanie's illegitimate son.

Hans Schweikart's *Befreite Hände* (*Freed Hands*, 1939), produced by Bavaria, scripted by Erich Ebermayer, and scored by Lothar Brühne (from Beethoven) concerns the ideology of "healthy people" art, a theme found in *Mein Kampf.*

Hitler wrote about his efforts to reach artistic fulfillment: "Obstacles are placed across our path in life, not to be boggled at but to be surmounted. And I was fully determined to surmount these obstacles ... I had a better start, and the possibilities of struggling through were better. At that time my lot in life seemed to me a harsh one; but today I see in it the wise workings of Providence. The Goddess of Fate clutched me in her hands and often threatened to smash me; but the will grew stronger as the obstacles increased, and finally the will triumphed."

In *Befreite Hände*, which screened at the Casino Theatre, amateur sculptor Dürthen (Brigitte Horney), who works on a farm, has an illegitimate child by a farmhand but rejects his offer of marriage. Joachim (Carl Raddatz), who is the son of aristocrats, is the one she loves. But since she has a will and a mind of her own she leaves them both for work in Berlin, which, however, proves unsatisfying. Moving to Italy, she joins Joachim and accepts a job with Professor Wolfram (Ewald Balser), a sculptor who presents his philosophy of life and art to her: only through self-actualization can she become a true artist; only through struggle and creativity would she succeed. At the end, Dürthen remains in love with Joachim but is just as strongly devoted to her art. She remains unmarried. "Distinction," said the *New York Times* (May 24, 1940), "is given the film by some fine shots of rural life and the excellent rendering of parts of Beethoven's Fifth Symphony by the Hamburg Philharmonic Orchestra." After the war, the Allies felt differently about the film. They banned it because Nazi party member Carl Raddatz (1912–2004) had co-starred.

Kongo-Express starring Marianne Hoppe and Willy Birgel.

Director Schweikart (1895–1975) had been a member of Max Reinhardt's Berlin Theatre from 1918–1923, where he met his first wife, Käthe Nevill. She later fled Hitler's Germany for Palestine. In the 1920s, Schweikart had been a friend of Bertolt Brecht's. In 1943, Schweikart directed *Die Unendliche Weg* (*The Unending Road*, 1943), the story of nineteenth-century political scientist Friedrich List, who helps Germany become economically and politically united. Goebbels financed *Die Unendliche Weg* and awarded it a National Film Prize.

Hungarian-born Josef von Baky's *Ihr erstes Erlebnis* (*Her First Experience*, 1939), which came from Ufa's studios, reached the Casino Theatre in summer 1940. It's a young woman's story set in prewar Paris that offers art as its distraction. Scored by Georg Häntzschel, the film starred Ilse Werner as a talented country girl who thinks she is in love with her married, middle-aged art professor (Johannes Riemann). Of course, in Nazi ideology, she has to be shocked into realizing that her heart belongs to a young swain (Volker von Colande) and she belongs in the circle of friends her own age! The professor's wife rightfully manages to hold onto her husband despite the lure of the youthful rival.

Baky's subsequent and more insidious film also has a female as its protagonist. *Annelie* (1941), which Ufa produced thanks to Goebbels' finances, relates the story of a Berlin woman (Luise Ullrich) who grows up in the wake of Germany's military victory over France in 1870 and lives to see her grandchildren taking part in the military successes of the Third Reich. Goebbels named *Annelie* a winner of a National Film Prize but American critics in Germany apparently didn't know it existed. Baky also directed *Münchausen* (1943) and *Via Mala* (1944) and continued directing in the postwar years.

Bavaria's *Die Drei Um Christine* (*Those Three About Christine*) is yet another tale from the year of the Berlin Olympics, screening at the Casino Theatre in summer 1940. Hans Deppe directed this "darned good entertainment for simple folk," according to *Variety* (June 1936). When schoolteacher Christine Biehler (Maria Andergast) is sent to the remote Black Forest village of Tannach as a substitute instructor, she has no trouble mastering the unruly students. But she has no luck disciplining three men who fall in love with her: Bachmoser (Fritz Kampers), the widowed mayor; Balther (George Vogel), his troubled son; and Eggert (Hans Söhnker), a famous musician on vacation. Christine marries the wrong one, reported the *New York Times* (May 4, 1940). But in Nazi ideology she does the right thing. Her marriage to the mayor gets his son a mother.

The question of what makes a real mother is the conceit in Amleto Palermi's *Le Due Madri* (*The Two Mothers*, 1938), an Astra Film-Berlin production that screened un-subtitled at New York's Cinecitta Theatre. Amateur painter Salvatore (Vittoria de Sica) is conflicted. He can't decide between his foster, beloved "Mammarosa" (Bella Starace Sainati) and his wealthy, real mother Kiki (Lydia Johnson), a retired prima donna. "There is plenty of humor and a modicum of mental suffering in the picture," wrote the *New York Times* (May 17, 1940), "but it is disfigured by the gratuitous injection of a glorification of the Fascist invasion of Spain."

In summer 1940, Kurt Hoffmann's *Hurra! Ich bin Papa!* (*Hurrah! I'm a Papa!* 1939), which Goebbels wrote, "can be used for the war," screened in the U.S. It preaches male responsibility. Scripted by Thea von Harbau, *Hurra! Ich bin Papa!* presents Heinz Rühmann as the eternally jovial student Peter Ohlsen, whose dependence on his father knows no bounds. When, one day, Peter returns home drunk after celebrating with friends, he finds a three-year-old boy in his bed. His housekeeper brought the young, illegitimate lad home, along with a letter that identifies Peter as his father! The mother's identity is a mystery. Peter takes on the role of papa—and makes the decision to get a real job. He's become a father in the fatherland. That's only part of the plot that is set up by the boy's actual father and a young teacher, Kathrin Gebhardt (Carola Höhn), whom Peter meets and with whom he falls in love. The rest—marriage—will turn Peter into a full-fledged, upstanding and complete member of society, sacrificing for the greater good. New York's Board of censors approved the film's release only after "Jesus" was removed from the expletive "Jesus, Maria, and Josef."

E.W. Emo's comedy *Anton, der Letzte* (*Anton, the Last*, 1939), produced by Wien-Film, contrasts the old and the new, royalty and commoner, and the modern and the past—and declares modern the winner. This Nazi film uses Hans Moser, one of Austria's stars, as the bearer of a dose of propaganda. Valet Anton (Hans Moser, 1880–1964) serves the Earl of Erlenburg with all his heart, but he gets anxious when the principles of the old aristocracy come under siege. And there are many things to worry about. His master is about to marry a shady lady while young, unconventional Willy Erlenburg has fallen in love with the neighbor's daughter, the commoner Leni. When Willy defies his father and leaves for a hazardous expedition to Tehran, the now pregnant Leni begs Anton to help her. Thereafter, the faithful servant has a lot of work do, if there is to be a happy ending for everyone. He winds up supporting the young German couple against the objections of his master, even going so far as to threaten to quit if his boss doesn't relent.

Theo Lingen took a shot at directing when he made *Marguerite Drei* (*Marguerite Divided by Three*, 1939), a comedy scripted by an up-and-coming filmmaker named Helmut Käutner (1908–1980). It was based on a popular stage play about the young lovers Marguerite Kranz (Gusti Huber) and Jean (Richard Romanwosky), whose marriage is opposed by the young man's trio of dyed-in-the-wool, old-fashioned uncles named Findeisen: Ludwig (Franz Schaftheitin), Karl (Lingen), and Lorenz (Hermann Thimig). Soon enough, the older generation gets out of the way and the young people marry. This was the last feature *Variety* (June 1939) reviewed from Germany. It didn't screen in the U.S.

Arthur Maria Rabenalt's *Alle Stehen Kopf* (*General Confusion*), perhaps an apt title considering the world situation at the time, was released by CFE in late summer 1940. It involves snow, ice-skating, love, comedy in Vienna and Styria, and a message from the Nazis. Young German Michael Korff (Hans Stüwe) recognizes the right thing when it comes to marriage and love. He gives up the attractive Gloria Mills (Inge List), the daughter of the rich American Cyrus M. Mills (Alfred Abel), for the German girl. When the sports instructor Lex Wartenberg (Friedl Czepa), who is working in Bavaria, inherits a fortune after the death of an uncle, she drops her alias, revealing that she's actually "Alexandra Tressin," a Jew. This film was really *Millionenerbschaft* (*Million Inheritance*, 1937), produced by Franz Antel and scripted by Axel Eggebrecht (1899–1991).

Erich Engels's comedy *Peter, Paul und Nanette* is another example of a Nazi-era film reaching America six years after its completion—just as the Nazis were invading Western Europe. In the film, Peter Pellmann (Hermann Thimig) is a timid jewelry salesman in love with his boss's daughter, the charming blonde Nanette (Hilde Krüger). But there is trouble in the form of a notorious thief who resembles Peter. He carries the Jewish name "Paul Polter" (and is also played by Thimig). Screening at Garden Theatre, the film had the *New York Times* (May 24, 1940) calling it a "first-rate burlesque" of the "mystery-jewel-robbery-musical romance" popular with German filmmakers. What was also popular in Deutschland—but unmentioned by the critic—is that the film is anti–Semitic. Perhaps by this point, there was less of a reason for the Nazis to disguise their racism. No one in the U.S. had been counting how many films from Germany had denigrated Jews.

Summer 1940 saw the release at the Garden Theatre of a light-hearted production from pre–Nazi Vienna: Carl Lamac's *Walzerlange* (*Waltz Melodies*, 1938). Lamac's film centers on a theatrical revue, led by the director Josef Reinhold (Paul Hörbiger), that owes its success to a particular favorite, its star Marietta Duval (Marta Eggerth). When she marries and leaves the theater, the troupe's success goes out the door with her. A change of heart—marriage is not what it's cracked up to be—brings her back to the stage. She discovers that being a 100 percent housewife is unsatisfactory. Her husband, the landowner Hans von Waldenau (Dutch-born Frits van Dongen), reluctantly agrees that their professional lives do not have to be an obstacle for their marriage to succeed. The film co-starred three other ubiquitous screen personalities—Lucie Englisch, Hans Moser, and Theo Lingen. Also in the cast was Rudolf Carl, playing the presumed Jew "Alexander Korsakoff," alias "Harry Pressler." Also known as *Immer, wenn Ich glücklich bin...* (*I'm Lucky, Always...*), this production was the last film by Jewish-owned Projectograph-Film Oskar Glück before the Nazis settled themselves firmly into a welcoming Austria. When Germany went to war its message fit the new reality: German women are more than just housewives. *Walzerlange* was one of Lamac's last prewar German-language endeavors. He then began an odyssey throughout Europe, one step ahead of the Hitler gang. As with other Austrian films, the Nazis exploited Lamac's film to present an image of modernism in the affairs of man and woman. The liberalism did not apply to Jews.

In 1940, Germany was at war with Britain. To justify the conflict, the regime produced a film that blames the conflict on Jews. *Die Rothschilds* lays out a long history of conspiracy and intrigue at the highest circles of British politics—perpetrated by Jews, Germany's true enemy. The anti–Semitism comes into play when the Nazis attribute British actions to Jewish plots. The Nazis' target is the famous family that for more than two centuries had a financial and philanthropic dynasty without parallel in Jewish or general history. In the remotest *shtetl* of the Russian Pale of Settlement the name stood for unimagined wealth, a lifestyle of oriental splendor, and acquisition on a grand scale. To anti–Semites, the Rothschilds embod-

Die Rothschilds, with Herbert Wilke and Carl Kuhlmann (right).

ied Jewish power, international financiers, and manipulators of thrones, currencies, and the press. The Rothschilds had entered the center of British power, and the Nazis were coming after them.

In July 1940, Edward Warchneck's *Die Rothschilds*, produced by Ufa, made its Berlin premiere. American critics in Berlin were apparently oblivious to its existence. The film starred performers inside and outside Germany's circle of stars: Eric Ponto (Meyer Amschel Rothschild), Carl Kuhlmann (Nathan Rothschild), Michael Bohnen (Wilhelm IX), Herbert Hübner (Turner, the banker), Albert Florath (Bearing, the banker), Hans Liebelt (Louis XVIII), Theo Shall (Selfridge, the banker), Hilde Weissner (Sylvia Turner), and Gisela Uhlan (Phyliss Bearing). Robert Baberske was the cinematographer.

The film sets the stage for the Nazis' assault against Jews in Europe by assaulting on the screen the foremost and wealthiest Jewish family in the world. The Nazis' film attack on the Rothschilds (and all potential Rothschilds) starts during the Napoleonic wars. Prince Wilhelm IX, the son and heir of Langrave Frederick of Hesse-Cassel, the grandson of George II, has to flee ahead of Napoleon's troops. He heads the richest ruling house in Europe. In Frankfurt, he gives Mayer Amschel Rothschild 600,000 pounds sterling, which represents "blood money" for the German soldiers that Amschel had bought to fight alongside the English army. The film then depicts how the Rothschilds use this money to acquire power in Britain and create a Jewish-English plutocracy.

In fact, Mayer Amschel Rothschild (1744–1812) began his rise to fortune by selling old coins to well-born collectors and handling minor bank drafts and mortgages for Karl Buderus, one of the prince's financial advisors. He and his wife Gudele (1753–1849) had 20 children. Ten survived—five boys and five girls. "M.A. Rothschild und Sohne" was set up in Frankfurt, where the Rothschilds became Wilhelm's main debt-collectors. The modern Rothschild bank is the product of a storied empire: Mayer Amschel Rothschild's four sons set up sister banks in London, Paris, Vienna, and Naples. The London and Paris banks became the best known and most successful. The London bank made its name by smuggling gold coins across the English Channel to finance Wellington's campaign against Napoleon. From the early nineteenth century until World War I, the House of Rothschild was the biggest banking group in the world. It's not farfetched to believe that the Nazis dreamed of acquiring this wealth themselves.

Waschneck's film focuses on Nathan Mayer Rothschild (the third-oldest son), who, in 1803, becomes the London representative of the banking family. In the Nazis' view, he gains power and influence through devious (that is, Jewish) business deals and social contacts. Working with his younger brother James, who moves to Paris in 1812, Nathan acquires wealth by smuggling money from France into Spain to support the fight against Napoleon. After Napoleon's defeat, the brothers finance the reign of King Louis XVIII. When Napoleon escapes from Elba and advances with a new army, Nathan Rothschild sees his chance at making a real financial killing. He arranges a secret courier service from Waterloo to London. In 1815, he learns of Napoleon's defeat before anyone else, but then spreads a rumor of Napoleon's "victory" back home. In the ensuing panic on the London Stock Exchange, Nathan buys cheap securities and sells them after they skyrocket in value. Their fortune made, the Rothschilds consolidate their power everywhere: Solomon in Vienna (from 1816), Karl in Naples (from 1821), and Mayer Amschel in Frankfurt. The film presents myths associated with Nathan Rothschild: that he arranged his own transportation to the showdown between Napoleon and Wellington on the Belgian plain, viewed its outcome from a distance and then bribed a ship's captain to take him speedily back to London where he could profit on his knowledge of the battle's outcome. The more outlandish element of this series of myths has Nathan Rothschild *riding* alongside Wellington and then making a stormy crossing from Ostend to Dover. This feat allows him to make more than 135 million pounds on the London Stock Exchange.

If these myths were true, they showed real initiative on Rothschild's part. In fact, the Rothschilds had built a correspondence network of couriers and mailers that surpassed any in their day, connecting the brothers in the various cities, including Vienna. They routinely broke news of events of political importance. Their Judaism is beside the point.

That may explain why, ironically, the Nazi film was not a success in Germany, even after Goebbels named it winner of the National Film Prize. The final shots reveal the Nazis' anti–Semitism. One scene shows a background of the Star of David and a map of England going up in flames. Then the last managers of the House of Rothschild are shown fleeing Europe as refugees, escaping to their allies in England, "where the British plutocrats are carrying on." Ironically, in fact, the first branch of the family to dissolve was the German branch, in 1901. The Austrian branch dissolved during the Second World War. Waschneck's film was later retitled *Aktien auf Waterloo* (*Shares in Waterloo*), a title that reflects the Nazis' intense interest in money. Ufa, it seems, was ready to release the film in the States when it circulated promotional stills in late 1941. Germany banned the film after the war.

The story of a different Austrian subject took center stage in Géza von Bolváry's *Wiener G'schichten* (*Vienna Tales*, 1940), a CFE release in the U.S. in September 1940. This Vienna of lore and illusion (shot in Berlin) is easy-going and careless, a city of peace and quiet whose inhabitants are unconcerned with weightier questions of the day. The tale, set in 1905, concerns the widowed owner, Christine Lechner (Marte Harell), of the famous, lively Vienna establishment Café Fenstergucker. She is loved, without her knowing it, by headwaiter Ferdinand Reitmeier (Paul Hörbiger), who believes in progress, and is adored by the rest of the staff, especially by the waiter-factotum Josef Engler (Hans Moser), who's bound by tradition. Competition in the coffee business spells trouble for Christine and her employees. Another café is opening up across the street, owned by "Egon von Brelowsky" (Siegfried Breuer) and "Baroness

Neudegg" (Hedwig Bleibtreu), both presumably Jewish. But in the end the famous café and its beloved personnel survive. By presenting a bit of old Vienna, said the *New York Times* (September 28, 1940), *Wiener G'schichten* was likely to make former residents "pretty homesick," while those unfamiliar with the prewar capital "will get a better idea of what it was than they can from old guide books." If the reference was to the film's subtle anti–Semitism, it was negated because the paper called the production "delightful." It did, however, take the director to task for being "so sparing in the use of the music expected in a film of this type." Breuer and Bleibtreu (1868–1958) were featured in *The Third Man* (1948).

The Nazis got it right in one way: although this Vienna lived only in popular imagination, Austria and its capital were neither pro–Jewish nor opponents of the Third Reich. Along with Willi Forst's *Wiener Blut* (*Vienna Blood*, 1942), which premiered in the U.S. in 1951, and Bolváry's *Schrammeln* (1944), *Wiener G'schichten* was the Nazis' biggest international hit. Marte Harell (1907–1996) was a Vienna-born stage actress spotted by director Bolváry at Berlin's Deutsches Theater in the 1930s. Her successes included *Opernball* (1939) and *Rosen in Tirol* (1940). When her husband Karl Hartl became production manager of Wien-Film in 1938, thanks to Goebbels, Harell became a busy actress in the company, appearing in ten films until 1945. After the war, her film roles were scarcer, although her film career lasted until 1982.

The Nazi Security Service considered Marte's husband, director Karl Hartl, a sure-fire National Socialist, although it was rumored that Hartl had once omitted the Nazi salute. Hartl's final Nazi-era production was *Wen die Götter lieben* (*Whom the Gods Love*, 1942), a biography of Mozart in which Rosa Albach-Retty (Wolf's mother) played the composer's mother. Footage from Hartl's film was incorporated in Frank Wysbar's Hollywood production *The Mozart Story* (1948), which contains excerpts by the Vienna Philharmonic from *The Magic Flute, Don Giovanni, The Marriage of Figaro, The Abduction from the Seraglio* and the *Requiem*.

The release of mild-mannered productions in America in 1940–41 allowed the charade of normality in greater Germany to linger a while longer. The French-language film *Serenade* (1939), produced by Astra Film-Berlin and shown at New York's 55th St. Playhouse in September 1940, buttressed the notion of an innocent Austria. Directed by Jean Boyer, it starred Lilian Harvey as the British dancer Margaret Brenton, who falls in love with the dreamy, struggling composer Franz Schubert (Bernard Lancret). He is jealous of his great rival, Beethoven (Auguste Boverio). Out of their romance is born the Schubert's ballet *Rosamonde* and the illustrious *Serenade*.

Nazi films were on safe U.S. ground with the CFE release in fall 1940 of Bolváry's *Opernball* (*Opera Ball*, 1939), which affirms the principle that marriage is the only way a man and woman are permitted to live together. A musical comedy of matrimonial errors set in the oblivious Gay Nineties, the tale, produced by Terra, takes place when the automobile was new and bathing suits ungainly. So it is that at Vienna's famous masquerade ball more or less errant husbands and wives test each other's fidelity. The all-star Austrian cast included Paul Hörbiger, Hans Moser, Marte Harell, and Theo Lingen, as well as Heli Finkenzeller, Erika von Thellmann (1902–1988), and Fita Benkhoff.

Walter Janssen's *Leidenschaft* (*Passion*, 1939–1940) also has an all-star cast. Its debut in America, like other German films this year, made it appear that little out of the ordinary was happening across the Atlantic. Besides, the production co-starred Traudl Stark (b. 1930), known as Austria's Shirley Temple. But this production was young Stark's last. And the film carried an important message about Jews. In the film, which takes place in the countryside, Gerda (Olga Tschechowa), the mother of eight-year-old Angelika (Stark) from a previous marriage, is now the wife of the much-older Count "Hubert Stein" (Paul Otto). He hoards his money, and is aloof, old-fashioned, and a hunter. When the count is shot to death on his birthday, villagers suspect that Gerda did it. It was possibly crime of passion because she had been spending a lot of time with the young German forester Hans Strobel (Hans Stüwe). Gerda has no alibi; Hans does. However, the farmer's wife Leni Boddin (Hilde Körber) is no friend of Gerda's. In fact, she wants the forester for herself. She might have killed Stein in order to get Gerda out of the way. And then there are the oft-used Nazi bad boys identified as poachers, who go by the names "Basner" (G.H. Schnell) and "Peschke" (Paul Rehkopf). The count used to go after them. Perhaps they killed him. But things turn out well for Gerda and Hans. It was a case of revenge, but the killer was the farmer Boddin (Fritz Rasp). He had the means and the motive. The imperious count had shot Boddin's son while out hunting and had not been punished! The Nazi message was clear. Germans had to be passionate in their opposition to Jews, the wealthy, and the old-fashioned aristocracy. German peasants and farmers know how to mete out justice. "It seems strange," said the *New York Times* (September 24, 1940), "that the Terra concern could not have found something fresher for such a first-rate company."

In 1930, Olga Tschechowa had been signed by Universal to star in *Liebe auf Befehl* (*The Command to Love*), the German-language version of *Boudoir Diplomat* (1930), which was directed by Ernest Laemmle and Johannes Riemann. The film was Universal's only German production shot in Hollywood. The imported European cast, which included Hans Junkermann and Tala Birell, was featured in the risqué tale about a young attaché who becomes romantically linked to the wives of two ambassadors, one of whom is his boss. Deutsche Universal had distributed the film in Berlin in February 1931. *Film Daily* had assessed it as a sophisticated production. Tschechowa, who was related to Anton Chekhov, starred in a particularly mean-spirited Goebbels-backed production, *Menschen im Sturm* (*People in the Storm*, 1941). The story takes place on the Reich frontier with Yugoslavia. There sits the farm of a Slovenian, whose wife Vera (Tschechowa) is German. Billeted nearby is a Serbian officer organizing terror against *Volksdeutschen*. Vera can stand it no longer and begins see her duty clearly: to help Germans escape across the frontier to the fatherland. By her side is a German teacher in love with her daughter. Neither husband nor daughter is aware of Vera's activities, but they soon discover how great a patriot she is and what a great sacrifice she makes for the fatherland. After she is killed by Serbians, the truth comes out. The teacher, Vera's daughter, and the orphans make it back to the fatherland and safety. The film justifies Germany's assault on Yugoslavia in April 1941, when, the Nazis claimed, Serbians deserved to be slaughtered. Western critics abroad seem not to have taken notice of this production, which Fritz Peter Buch directed for Tobis.

Safety is at the core of a forgotten but serious Weimar production that premiered at New York's Thalia Theatre, in late 1940. This one is also set at the turn of the century, but the political climate within the film is radically different. International Road Shows—not Casino Film Exchange—released Richard Oswald's long-forgotten *Dreyfus* (1930), which had been scripted by Heinz Goldberg and Fritz Wendhausen, based on the novel by Bruno Weil. Two Jewish groups that opposed the showing of Nazi films in America, the Joint Boycott Council and the Non–Sectarian Anti-Nazi League, supported the release of this pre–Hitler German film. *Dreyfus* had been one of the most successful and impressive features in German theaters on the eve of the National Socialist seizure of power. Oswald worked with first-class actors on an early form of the historical docudrama. An engaging, objective, and sober chronicle of the Dreyfus affair, his film not only stresses the events with great historical accuracy but also explains their social background and relevancy to 1930s Germany. After 1933, the director and many of the actors faced a fate they had hoped to avoid through this film. Oswald's film was released under the title *The Dreyfus Case* at the Thalia in New York. It starred Fritz Kortner as the Jewish-French officer who in 1898 is found guilty of spying for Germany. Grete Mosheim played his wife Lucie, Albert Bassermann was Colonel Picquart, Oskar Homolka portrayed

Major Esterhazy, Paul Bildt played Clemenceau, and in a terrible irony, future Nazi adherent Heinrich George played the great Emile Zola.

Heinrich George, "despite his considerable bulk," was praised by the *New York Times*' Bosley Crowther (October 30, 1940) for the "impassioned plea, which Emile Zola makes for the preservation of truth and justice." The film also contains Picquart's exclamation, "Jew or gentile, there is one justice for all." Other members of the cast were Paul Henckels, Bernhard Goetzke, Fritz Kampers, and Fritz Rasp.

Goldberg and Wendhausen had also scripted Oswald's *1914, die letzten Tage vor dem Weltbrand* (*1914, the Last Days before the War*, 1931), starring Albert Bassermann, Reinhold Schünzel, Alfred Abel, and Oskar Homolka. Asking "Is Germany guilty?" of causing the First World War, Oswald's film *1914* places the blame on Russia's shoulders. Nonetheless, or perhaps because it would upset the Soviet Union, Oswald's World War I film was suppressed in Weimar Germany. It was shown at the Europa Theatre in New York in 1932.

Heinrich George, coincidentally, was starring in another German film across town at the Casino Theatre. The film was Gustav Ucicky's drama *Der Postmeister* (*The Postmaster*, 1939–40). Produced by Karl Hartl's Wien-Film, *Der Postmeister* had been the big winner (for film and director) at the 1940 Venice Film Festival. Based on the novel by Pushkin, *Der Postmeister* was scripted by the infamous Gerhard Menzel. Nazi politics in the glare of the non-aggression pact with the Soviet Union dictated the film's apparently passive stance regarding the Russians. Thus this is the story of a German postmaster (George) and his beautiful daughter Dunja (Hilde Krahl) who live in an out-of-the-way Russian village, where the only people they see are those changing horses. When dashing Captain Minsky (Siegfried Breuer) passes and spots Dunja, he promises her the world and pledges to marry her. With the postmaster's blessing, she departs with him for St. Petersberg, which accepts the innocent Dunja with open arms. She forgets the promises the Russian made to her father and her dreams of marriage. Instead, she becomes Minsky's mistress, her name the most notorious in the city. After she falls in love with young Lieutenant Mitja (Hans Holt), who knows nothing of her surroundings or friends, she vows to live a decent life. But when her father comes for a visit, she begs Minsky to go through with a mock wedding. The charade comes undone when the young lieutenant finds out he's been deceived. Exposed and ashamed, Dunja commits suicide, but not before getting Minsky to promise never to reveal the truth of their relationship to the old postmaster. Back home, the postmaster tells all who will listen of his daughter's wonderful marriage and of the Russian captain who never gave him an unhappy or shameful moment!

The not-so-subtle Nazi messages spoke of German ignorance and inaction in the face of outrage; but good riddance to the stultifying past, including those Russians. On the program at the Casino Theatre were two of Ufa's "educational" shorts: *Kinder aus aller Welt* (*Children of the World*, 1935) and *Sonne, Erde und Mond* (*Sun, Earth and Moon*, 1938). Nazi actor George, imprisoned by the Russians after the war, died in Sachsenhausen. *Der Postmeister* was not reviewed at the time of its release. Nor was the following film given much attention in the West when the Nazis produced and released it.

By November 1940, the Nazis moved a giant step closer to proving to themselves and others that the world could do without Jews. They produced a film that purports to be a realistic presentation of Jews: *Der Ewige Jude: Dokumentarfilm über das Weltjudentum* (*The Eternal Jew: A Documentary of World Judaism*). This film is the centerpiece of all Nazi *Hetzfilme*. The phrase "eternal Jew" had originated in 1821, when Ludwig Börne—born Loeb Baruch—published an essay called *Der Ewige Jude*. Calling Jews capitalists and capitalist society Jewish, Borne hammered home the idea that Judaism was at the root of evil in the modern world. This summation spread within Germany and France. Revolutionaries and reactionaries united in their belief in a new kind of certainty: sociological anti–Semitism and loathing of capitalism.

In November 1937, the Nazis mounted an exposition in Munich called "Der Ewige Jude." At its opening, Julius Streicher called Jews "children of the devil" and threatened to "bring an end to the reputation of eternal life possessed by the race of world criminals." The pamphlet from the exhibit, titled "The Eternal Jew," went on sale in New York City in May 1938. In late–1940, the Nazi production *Der Ewige Jude* premiered on German screens. The Reich Propaganda Office had commissioned it; Fritz Hippler had directed; and Franz R. Friedl (1892–1977) had scored the "documentary." It bolstered Nazis, supporters, and zealots within and outside the regime in the correctness of their worldview, and legitimatized actions against the Jews of Europe.

The film begins as a kind of expedition through the ghettoes of Poland, referred to as the "nesting place" of Jews. The scenes are from newsreel footage and photos taken after Poland's defeat in September 1939. "Hair, beard, skullcap, and caftan make the Eastern Jew recognizable to all," goes the narration. "It is an intrinsic trait of the Jew that he always tries to hide his origin when he is among non–Jews." "A bunch of Polish Jews," says the narrator, are "now wearing caftans—now ready to steal into Western civilization." Then, "similar to those Jewish wanderings throughout the world are wanderings of an equally restless animal, the rat," warns the film. Shots of Jews in Germany before the Nazis take power are compared to Eastern European Jews and "assimilated" Jews. There follow pictures of people identified as Jews influential in economics, culture, and politics. Those who "control" France (Leon Blum), Britain (Leslie Hore–Belisha) and America (Bernard Baruch), Jewish film personalities Max Ehrlich; Kurt Gerron; Paul Morgan, who was born Morgenstern, died in Buchenwald in 1938; Richard Oswald; Peter Lorre, born László Loewenstein; Ernst Lubitsch; Fritz Kortner; Max Reinhardt; and non–Jewish but British-born Charlie Chaplin. And dozens of others, from Walter Rathenau to Salomon Rothschild to Fiorello La Guardia to Albert Einstein.

Sham quotations from Jewish texts are used to discredit Jewish religious practices. Near the end come scenes of Jewish ritual slaughter meant to cause revulsion, followed by scenes of Hitler's speech to the Reichstag on January 30, 1939, during which he makes his infamous threat: "Europe cannot find peace before the Jewish question is resolved. Jews will just have to get used to the idea of performing some respectable, constructive activity, as other people do, or sooner or later they will face trouble they never dreamed of." The film closes with scenes of Nazi flags and banners and an excerpt from Leni Riefenstahl's *Triumph of the Will* (1934): "The eternal law of nature, to keep one's race pure, is the legacy which the National Socialist movement bequeaths to the German people forever."

"Whether in a newsreel or a German feature film," wrote the enthusiastic director Hippler, "[*Der Ewige Jude*] is a mirror in which the broad masses of the world see Germany." Hippler's film premiered at Berlin's Ufa Palast am Zoo twice on November 28, 1940. *Film Kurier* provided a summary of the action for attendees, Nazi Party officials and military leaders. Goebbels, however, was out of the country. The Nazi party monthly *Unser Wille und Weg* wrote: "One has a deep sense of salvation after seeing this film. We have broken their power over us. We are the initiators of the fight against Jewry, which now directs its hate, its brutal greed and destructive will toward us. We must win this battle for ourselves, for Europe, and the world. This film will be a valuable tool in that struggle."

Der Ewige Jude was shown throughout Germany and screened for Wehrmacht troops. It was released in France (as *Le Péril Juif*, produced by Pierre Ramelot), in April 1942, and later in the Netherlands (as *De Eeuwige Jood*). Two prominent Jews singled out in the film, Kurt Geron and Max Ehrlich, were in exile in the Netherlands at the time. The subtitled German version was also shown in Southern and Eastern Europe: Poland, Croatia, Romania, and Hungary, where, Goebbels said, "A dozen Jews were hanged because they had attempted to kill Germans." However, the film was not shown in the Northern European nations of Denmark,

Sweden, Norway, and Finland. Switzerland refused to screen it. In other words, where there were major deportations, there was *Der Ewige Jude*.

In the U.S., "prompt action," wrote the *Nation* (May 5, 1941), "forestalled its showing here—awaiting a 'favorable' turn of events. German releases received in advance describe it adequately." The German description was as follows: "Never before has there been shown a political movie with such success. *The Eternal Jew* is not a feature film but a documentary about world Jewry, which it pictures coolly and objectively in reportorial fashion. Most Germans know Jews only as civilized Western Europeans who move in all social circles. They are hardly acquainted with the original Jews of the Polish ghettos, whence came a steady stream of immigrants to the cultural West and especially to Germany."

The film screened in Buenos Aires in mid-1941. Clearly there were Americans in the U.S., Germany, and elsewhere who were aware of the film's existence, yet apparently believed, like the *New Yorker*, in "German releases" that "in advance describe it adequately." Only after the war did the film receive scrutiny. Postwar Germany banned its commercial screening. After the war, Fritz Hippler, who had joined the Nazi Party at the age of 18 in 1927 and was in Goebbels' Propaganda Ministry nine years later, faced war crimes charges. The German courts cleared him of charges. *Der Ewige Jude* has remained banned in Germany since the close of the war. One of the Jews in the film, however, managed a measure of revenge.

Humiliated and forced to leave Germany in 1933, Kurt Gerron, his wife, and parents fled to France, where Gerron produced two short comedies. Then he went to Austria. Rejecting an offer from Hollywood, even after he had helped Peter Lorre obtain passage to America, Gerron settled in Amsterdam where he made a detective film. In Rome he directed the Italian-Dutch drama *Drei Wenschen* (*Three Wishes*, 1937), which was a box-office failure. Trapped after May 1940 in Amsterdam, Gerron became director of the Jewish theatre Jood Schouwberg, whose other participants included Rudolf Nelson and Willi Rosen. In the middle of 1943, Gerron was incarcerated in Holland's infamous camp, Westerbork. Transported to Theresienstadt, Gerron, terrified of the Nazis and living under dispiriting conditions, performed his greatest act ever. Given the opportunity by the commandant of the camp in summer 1944, he accepted the job of directing a "documentary" on Jewish life in the camp and in the Czech city.

Shooting picture-perfect scenes of beautiful, non-blond Jewish children at play and at rest, athletic Jews playing soccer, and the many creative, talented, and still-lively Jews giving concerts, plays, and cabaret events, Gerron answered the horrid scenes of Jews that the Nazis had contrived four years earlier for *Der Ewige Jude*. He himself had been featured as a prime example of a Jew in that film, which had been screened in the Netherlands after the Nazi invasion. True, Gerron's documentary is also contrived—Theresienstadt's prisoners were not nearly as happy as they appear and many of them were on the verge of starvation—but Gerron's scenes beg the question, "Why are these people in a concentration camp?" They're unlike the Jews in that other Nazi film! In his own way, working under the noses of his captors, and keeping his motives to himself while fellow Jews accused him of collaboration, Gerron had answered—and gotten his revenge against—*Der Ewige Jude*. By making *his* anti-Nazi and philo-Semitic film Gerron had made a *subversive* Nazi film.

The Nazis titled it *Theresienstadt: Ein Dokumentarfilm aus dem jüdischen Siedlungsgebiet* (*A Documentary from the Jewish Settlement Area*, 1944). It is also known as *Der Führer schenkt den Juden Stadt* (*The Fuhrer Gives the Jews a City*). The Nazis intended to, but never screened, this "documentary" for their supporters in the neutral nations of Europe. In October 1944, Gerron was sent on the last transport from Theresienstadt to Auschwitz, and he died on the last day its ovens burned.

The year 1940 closed, ominously, perhaps presciently, when Jewish director Richard

"The Eternal Jew": 1937 Munich exhibit.

Oswald's film *The Living Dead* was released in America. This was actually Oswald's Grand Guignol tale *Unheimliche Geschichten* (*Gruesome Stories*, 1932), a Roto Film production produced by Gabriel Pascal from the last year of Weimar Germany. Scripted by Oswald's old colleague Heinz Goldberg, it had screened in Germany a few months before Hitler came to power. For shock value, Berlin critics had compared it to Robert Weine's *The Cabinet of Dr. Caligari* (1919). Adapted from works by Poe and Stevenson, the film follows a reporter (Harald Paulsen) in search of dangerous stories. He's in pursuit of a mad German scientist (Paul Wegener) who had strangled his wife and walled up her body in the basement. A black cat locates the corpse. The murderer finds refuge in a wax museum and then safety in an insane asylum among its inmates (Eugen Klöpfer, for one). Captured by the police, the murderer escapes. Six months later he's taken alive. Oswald's film is episodic, starting with an adaptation of Poe's "The Black Cat," followed by a wax museum scene, shifting to a rendition of Robert Louis Stevenson's "Doctor Tarr and Professor Fether," and concluding with Stevenson's "The Suicide Club." Atmospheric sets and *noir* camera work help to sustain the nightmarish mood.

This was one of director Oswald's and Goldberg's final films from their native Germany. After Hitler's rise to power, the two found safety in the Netherlands, where Goldberg worked with Kurt Gerron. Goldberg survived the war. Oswald worked in France, Britain, and Hollywood in the 1940s. In January 1941, Nazi films were still being released in the U.S.

Difficulty is what the patriot-hero faced in Luis Trenker's aptly titled Nazi production *Der Feuerteufel* (*The Fiery Devil*, 1939–40) — also aptly known as *Der Heldenkampf um Heimaterde* (*The Heroic Struggle for the Homeland Soil*). The action within this violent, militarist, and nationalistic nineteenth-century tale takes place in Austria. Napoleon's forces are conscripting Austrian peasants. But the mustachioed farmhand Valentin Sturmegger (Trenker) finds refuge in the mountains and collects a band of like-minded peasant-rebels to help him drive out the invaders. They make a series of raids against French forces, killing many of the enemy, but during one attack, Sturmegger is taken prisoner. He survives the mass execution of his compatriots and heads to Vienna. There he tries to assassinate Napoleon (Erich Ponto). He's captured but the emperor spares his life. Nonetheless, Sturmegger is unrepentant: he's obsessed with freeing his homeland. Leading a resistance group into battle once more, Sturmegger is double-crossed by a fellow countryman named "Rafael Kröss" (Walter Ladengast), a presumed Jew. Again Sturmegger flees into the mountains, pursued by the enemy and rejected by so-called friends. Trenker depicts the kind of pro–German Austrian that Hitler praised often in *Mein Kampf*. His film, scored by Guiseppe Becce, was not reviewed at the time of its release at the Garden in New York, apparently because it justifies Hitler's attack against France.

Goebbels' brother-in-law, director Max W. Kimmich, had his name back in New York when his anti–Semitic, pseudo-mystery-drama *Der Vierte kommt nicht* (*The Fourth Did Not Show Up*, 1938–39), produced by Tobis, showed up at the Casino Theatre in mid–January 1941. This film, however, was not reviewed at the time of its release in America. Charles Klein (1898–1981), the director of *Zigeunerblut* (*Gypsy Blood*, 1933–34), and *Wenn am Sonntagabend die Dorfmusik spielt* (*When the Village Band Plays Sunday Evening*, 1933), scripted the tale about four school buddies who have been getting together annually. This year, one of them, named Swenskhord, is absent. What has happened to their friend? A cursory investigation concludes he committed suicide. He worked as a cashier at a big Stockholm bank. Perhaps he was involved in shady dealings and was about to be exposed. His mother, however, insists it was something more sinister: murder. Dr. Irene Andersen (Dorothea Wieck) digs deeper and calls it a homicide. But who killed him and why? Well, the three amateur sleuths uncover the culprit. He turns out to be "Richard Kolman" (Ferdinand Marian), the director of Kolman Bank. This presumed Jew stole funds to support a lavish lifestyle, which edged his institution close to collapse. To cover up his tracks, he shot Swenskhord, pinning the embezzlement on him. Kolman tries to get away in a plane but, in the fashion the Nazis favored when dispatching their cinematic enemies, his demise must be horrible. It comes when his plane crashes into the sea. What this film is really about is weeding out those corrupt Jews in high places. Since 1933, Nazi films had depicted bankers, whether foreign or domestic, as Jewish bankers, and as Germany's enemies. The banker's name in this production, Kolman, is a variant of the Ashkenazi name Kalman or Kohlmann. Ferdinand Marian, who portrayed Kolman, would play the Jewish financier in *Jud Süss*.

The war in Europe had been going on for more than a year, yet the release in the States of German films remained unimpeded. The 86 *Strasse* Casino Theater, what it sometimes billed itself in promotional material in early 1941, premiered Carl Boese's *Hallo Janine* (*Hello Janine*, 1939), Ufa's "international" musical distraction, whose stars were from Holland (Johannes Heesters) and Hungary (Marika Rökk) rather than from Germany. Meaningless strivings for success and stardom—in light of the seriousness of the era—are the backdrop for the action in Paris, at a revue at the Montmarte-Bar. The dancer Janine hopes to become a *real* star, but she's got competition from the beautiful Yvette (Else Ester). To really get to the heights, Janine must impress several important men, including a composer. But first Janine wants to take revenge on Count René (Heesters), who stood up her best friend Charlotte. Janine wants him to fall in love with her—and then she'll drop him. At a masquerade ball at which Janine pretends to be a marquise, they have their first meeting, although neither is aware of it. Janine is disappointed in the "good gentleman" she encounters, unaware that he's also in disguise. The man at the ball whom she imagines is Count René is actually the composer-pianist Pierre (Rudi Godden) she'd been hoping to meet. Count René and Pierre had disguised and exchanged identities, which only adds to the confusion. René wants to use his new persona to make conquests, while Pierre hopes to meet the powerful music publisher Pamion (Erich Ponto). In spite of the goings-on, everybody gets what they want: Pierre has one of his works performed at the Montmarte-Bar and Janine succeeds in her dreams. Before a packed house yelling "Hello Janine," the curtain rises and Janine goes into her dance. René wins both fame and the beautiful Janine. Karl George Külb (1901–1980) scripted the convoluted tale. The film had premiered in Berlin just before the start of the Second World War. Despite the non–German cast, American critics ignored the film, perhaps embarrassed that German films were still being released in America.

Külb was also the director of Ufa's message-filled *Liebesschule* (*School for Love*, 1939–40), which screened, unreviewed, at the Casino Theatre in early 1941. In this one, Hanni Weber (Luise Ullrich) splits her time working as a secretary for writer Heinz Wölfing (Viktor Stahl) in the mornings, and for singer (and Casanova, naturally) Enrico Villanova (Johannes Heesters) in the afternoons. Of course, both men fall in love with her. After seven reels, Hanni goes for the more serious lover in the new Germany: the German author of the bestseller *Liebesschule* and writer of the soon-to-be published *Die Eheschule*, or *School for Marriage*.

In quick succession, the Casino Theatre hosted a series of German productions new to America. Perhaps the film theater's management, as well as reviewers, sensed the market for German films was evaporating. The American press ignored these releases. The comedy *Weisser Flieder* (*White Lilacs*, 1939–40), directed by Arthur M. Rabenalt for Terra, concerns playboy-businessman Hans Muth Jr. (Hans Holt), who owns a sock company. His calling card for any woman who catches his eye is a bouquet of white lilacs. He has a special habit. He alters the name of his motorboat whenever he makes a new conquest. Once it was nearly christened Charlotte, after Charlotte Rössler (Elga Brink), until her daughter Anni (Hannelore Schroth) found she was attracted to him. Scripted by Geza von Cziffra, with music by Michael Jary, the plot revolves around Anni protecting her willing mother from Hans, who's been less than honest about his intentions. If he can marry Charlotte, he'll secure an important business she owns: the Rössler Firm, which also manufactures socks. Muth's opponents are Rössler's director "Brennert" (Paul Henckels) and its top advertising man, "Max Mohr" (Rudolf Schündler), both presumably Jewish. In the end, Charlotte has to be content with being just a mother-in-law—but her business and that of her new son-in-law merge.

Werner Klingler's drama *Die Barmherzige Lüge* (*The Charitable Lie*, 1939), produced by Euphono and shown at the Casino Theatre in early 1941, raises the question of illegitimacy—a favorite Nazi theme. It also raises, yet again, the issue of posing as someone else in contemporary Germany. The Bremen explorer Clausen (Ernst von Klipstein) takes his wife Maria (Liselotte Klingler) on one of his expeditions, in Mongolia. Accompanying them is Anja Hoster (Hilde Krahl), his German mistress, who has been working in a bar somewhere in Mongolia. There's an accident, and Maria dies. Clausen vanishes while Anja, concerned about the future of her illegitimate child, heads to Germany and assumes the role of daughter-in-law. That's an easy thing to do because the explorer's parents had never met his actual *wife*. A series of complications, including blackmail by the Mongol Jean Goban (Paul Dahlke) and the murder of the kindly Dr. Henrici (Otto Gebühr), threaten to expose Anja's "charitable lie." Anja is tried on murder charges until Clausen shows up very much alive. Then he finds out he's a father. He and Anja marry and remain in Germany.

Erich Engel's *Unser Fräulein Doktor* (*Our Miss Doctor*, 1940), shown at the Casino Theatre in early 1941, produced by Klagemann-Film, is an effort that supports equality of the sexes, but we know it's all a patronizing act. The film's liberalism is undermined by the film's title. At a gymnasium, young males speak contemptuously about females' inferior learning. Then they meet Dr. Elizabeth Hansen (Jenny Jugo). She has been called in to substitute for Karl Klinger (Albert Matterstock), the school's mathematics and chemistry teacher. He has a broken a leg and can't make it to class. Hansen overcomes the boys' hostility through her competence, but it takes longer to bring the permanent teacher around. When Karl says "kleines Mädchen" to Elizabeth, she takes him to task for calling her a little girl. It's Karl who is told to "come down" from his high chair. At the end of the school year, however, when everyone goes on a traditional hike into the fine countryside, it comes as no surprise—a happy Nazi ending—that these two teachers, holding hands, have fallen in love.

Staying within the realm of the fanciful in early 1941, the Casino Theatre hosted a conflict-loaded drama by Johannes Riemann called *Spiel ums Glück* (*Playing Around with Luck*), which is actually the Itala production *Gauner im Frack* (*Black Legs in Full Dress*, 1937). The film is about the loss of home and hearth. The tale takes place in France, where the Parker brothers, Conny (Paul Klinger) and Fred (Karl Martell, 1906–1966), argue about selling their country house. A couple, the Moulins, drives by to see the estate. Mr. Moulin (Walter Steinbeck) is interested in buying the place, and is prepared to pay 50,000 francs. After much haggling Conny gets his way again, selling the family's beloved property for twice that. At the Riviera, where he's feeling lucky, Conny gambles—and loses everything. He then meets the mysterious Vera Dalmatoff (Camilla Horn), a refugee from Russia, and her partner, a presumed Jew named "Baroff "(Carl Günter), alias "Baron von Geldern." They're both chiselers. But Vera would like to put the past behind her after she takes an interest in Conny's fall from grace. She knows what it's like. Germany had hailed the film as a "triumphant victory of feeling." In America, the German press called it "exciting," "full of nature," and "unforgettable." The American press said nothing.

Rolf Hansen's *Sommer, Sonne, Erika* (*Summer, Sunshine, Erika*, 1939), which Bavaria produced, glorifies youth and summer. The active young people in a *Wandervögel*—German youth movement members—sing as they spend long periods in the water, hike, or take part in nature, their Nazi flags in full view. This film, too, quietly screened at the Casino Theatre. It featured

Sommer, Sonne, Erika, with Karin Hardt and Fritz Grenschow.

Fritz Genschow (1905–1977). This popular film, noted Goebbels, "will certainly make its way because it is so light-hearted, particularly in these difficult times."

At the close of January 1941, the infamous Karl Ritter had his name in lights once more on an American screen. He was the director of Ufa's *Münchner Faschingsball* (*Ball in Munich*, 1939), which is also known by the quaint French title *Bal paré* (*Masked Ball*). After directing a series of vitriolic films, including *Pour le Mérite,* which excoriates Hitler's enemies, democracy and its supporters, and Jews, Ritter seemed to be backtracking with this musical (via Theo Mackeben) that ran at the Casino Theatre. But the musical reflects Nazi ideology. It's the story of three nights in the life of Maxi Brunnhuber (Ilse Werner), a young and beautiful ballet dancer who anxiously attends her first masked ball, at the turn of the century in Munich. Hoping to become a prima ballerina, Maxi, on the night of the festivities, accepts the sponsorship of the industrialist Horst Heisterkamp (Paul Hartmann). He lavishes her with attention, taking a keen interest in her artistic abilities. He even puts her up at a private residence. On the second night, Maxi spends time with a different, exciting man: Heisterkamp's son, Hansjürgen (Hannes Stelzer). She laughs, dances, smokes, and kisses. On the third night, when Horst realizes why he's really interested in her—the love of an aging man for a young woman—he lets her go. But Maxi has experienced a new world of possibilities. At their own private ball, Maxi and Hansjürgen become engaged. Since the film gets the older, and old-fashioned, generation out of the way—signified when Hansjürgen heaves the jukebox of cranky "Uncle Florian" (Theodor Danneger) into the Isar River—a brighter future, in Germany, awaits the young lovers.

Ritter was up to his old self in his final film to reach the West before the Nazi regime was destroyed. That was *Stukas*, which Ufa produced and released in Berlin in spring 1941. As another of Goebbels' "war education" films and winner of a National Film Prize, the film deals with Luftwaffe pilots in the French campaign. In a rarity for the era, *Variety* (September 1,

1943) reviewed an insidious Nazi production. It said of *Stukas*: "In the 14 months since the Nazis first tried to smuggle this pic into Buenos Aires on the Portuguese vessel *Serpa Pinto*, only to have it nabbed by customs authorities, every Latin American country except Argentina ... has banned showings of German pictures." The review pointed out that in glorifying a Stuka squadron operating at the time of the fall of France, "every attempt is made to develop the idea that the squadron has an esprit de corps that can't be beaten." Interwoven is the story of a pilot who is shot down, recovering physically but not emotionally. Doctors come up with the perfect Nazi solution: to send him to the Bayreuth Wagner Festival where the sound of "Siegfried's Call" brings him back to life. "No one can come away from there without being deeply moved," says a German nurse. *Stukas* features the continual sound of engines and "Unter den Linden" language, Berlin slang and a rough way of talking that, it was said, could make one blush. Germany banned Ritter's film after the war.

Ritter was also responsible for one of the Nazis' last anti-communist films, which closed the books on the regime's anti–Bolshevik propaganda campaign and which they designated a National Film Prize winner. The film was *GPU* (1941–1942). Goebbels commissioned it; Ufa produced it. At the start, a White Russian survivor of the Bolshevik Terror joins the Soviet GPU in order to find the man who killed her parents. Twenty years later, in the summer of 1939 in Kovno, she finds him. An assassin and saboteur, he falls in love with her, but she denounces him to the Kremlin. He's executed. When she comes clean about why she joined the GPU, the Soviets execute her. Members of the Soviet secret police are presented as "Asiatic." One man who rises in the ranks is called neither "a Jew nor a proletarian." The film ends with scenes of the German Army marching into Holland, in May 1940. After the war, Ritter fled to Argentina, where he became head of Eros-Film Mendoza. He returned to Germany in the mid–1950s and formed Karl Ritter-Filmproduktion. He died in Buenos Aires.

In February 1941, one of the winners from the Venice Film Festival of August-September 1940 premiered at the Cine Roma, in New York. Esperia released a tragedy in which life imitates art, transposed from one Axis nation to another: from Japan to Italy. The drama's pro-

Above and opposite: Scenes from *Stukas*.

tagonist is the soprano Rosi Belloni (Maria Cebotari), who falls for the American pianist-conductor Harry Peters (Fosco Giachetti), who's playing in Bologna. When he announces that he's accepted an offer to work in New York, she stays behind. He leaves with a promise to return and make her his wife. He's unaware, however, that she's pregnant. She later gives birth to an illegitimate son. The American returns to Italy four years later, as a representative of the Metropolitan Opera Company. He's brought his American wife, Mary Peterson (Germana Paolieri), and his daughter. He hears Rosi sing magnificently in the premiere of *Madame Butterfly*. And then, like the character part she plays, she dies. The film co-starred the prolific German actress Lucie Englisch as Rosi's German friend and confessor, Anni Eigner. The music in the film, said the critics, is spectacular, featuring compositions from Puccini, Chopin, Lizst, Grieg, Donizetti, Schubert, and Johann Strauss. The film did well in communities having sizeable Italian populations. Called an Italian production, this film was co-produced by Germany under the title *Il Sogno di Butterfly* (*The Dream of Butterfly*, 1939). Carmine Gallone directed the drama from the script he wrote with Ernst Marischka (1893–1963).

In Terra's production *Frau nach Mass* (*The Tailored Lady*, 1939–40), which was based on Erich Kästner's work, the protagonist is another woman of the stage who is carrying the load alongside her mate. Annemarie (Leny Marenbach) is engaged to Christian Bauer (Hans Söhnker), the star and director of many a theatrical success. He decides that when they marry, Annemarie will stick to the kitchen and the children. He gets the shock of his life on learning that blonde-haired Annemarie has signed a contract to perform in his next show. Not only will she be a mate, she'll be a colleague. But when he orders her to abandon the notion, she breaks their engagement.

Still in love with Christian, however, Annemarie conceives of a ploy to get him back. She masquerades as her twin, the black-haired Rosemarie, a naïve country girl. Christian falls in love with Rosemarie, who carries all the female virtues he admires. They marry. Soon, however, Rosemarie's attributes begin to get on his nerves. He finds solace in the theatre, especially when he's offered a part in a play opposite Annemarie. He realizes he loves this blonde woman—and then discovers that he's been married to her all along.

One presumed Jewish character in the film is stereotyped. "Julius Campe" (Walter Steinbeck) is depicted as a high-strung, over-eager theatrical director. This film was directed and scripted by the up-and-coming filmmaker Helmut Käutner. He directed nine films in the Nazi years but only this one, his second effort under Hitler, was screened in the States, at the 86 *Strasse* Casino Theatre in New York, in spring 1941. But no American critic paid it any heed.

In Germany, which was still at peace with the United States, several singular films were having their first runs. American critics abroad paid them little or no heed also.

One production was Max W. Kimmich's *Mein Leben für Irland* (*My Life for Ireland*, 1941), which was released in Berlin in February, 1941. It was scripted by Toni Huppertz, photographed by Richard Angst, and co-starred Paul Wegener. The tale, which is set in the years 1903–21, is about Michael O'Brien (Werner Hinz), who's been educated at an English boarding school but has taken up arms in Ireland in support of Irish freedom. He is shot and dies in the arms of his wife, Maeve (Anna Dammann). Michael's classmate, the Irish-American Patrick O'Connor (Heinz Olsen), vows to continue the fight and sacrifice "my life for Ireland."

In essence, O'Brien represents another "SA-Mann Brand" or "Hitlerjunge Quex."

Goebbels noted that the "thickly applied pro–Irish approach" in Kimmich's second "rebel" film, which his ministry had financed, had perhaps backfired. The plot could be "reinterpreted by Poles and Czechs and applied to their own struggle for freedom against Germany," Goebbels wrote in his diaries, though that didn't stop him from awarding it a National Film Prize and having it shown in Italy as *La mia vita per L'Irlanda*. Ufa planned to release this film commercially in the States in late 1941—until Pearl Harbor and America's declaration of war against Germany ended its chances. But it was seen privately. Thomas Decker, in "Movies to Sell the Reich," which appeared in *The Nation* (July 5, 1941), pointed out that the German-American publication *Facts in Review* had praised the tone of *Mein Leben für Irland*. The pro–Nazi publication had referred to one Irish peasant as "one of the multitude who British Volunteers robbed and murdered," and it characterized three Irishmen as true "patriots" who, when in British custody, are described as walking "through the prison gates for the last time."

Herbert Selpin's *Carl Peters* (1941) is one of the most insidious Nazi colonial dramas released that season or any other in Germany. But you would have been hard-pressed to find any commentary about it by contemporary Western critics. Released in Berlin in March, 1941, the Bavaria-produced film, written by Walter Zerlett-Olfenius, designed by Fritz Maurischat (1893–1986), and scored by Franz Doelle, *Carl Peters* is the story of the man who relished the reputation "Hanging Peters." Here was a hero to the Nazis, openly presented to Germans as anti–Semitic and anti–British.

In 1941, German forces were in North Africa. Was there a better time to remind Germans and the world why Germany had a stake in Africa and who its enemies were? In the film, Peters (Hans Albers) is a man who loves only his mother. In reality, he was a womanizer, a racist, a sadist, and a killer who had others shot on his orders. The story begins in London, in 1882, when British intelligence is beginning to take notice of a young German who is promoting the idea of Germany acquiring African colonies. In Germany, however, members of the newly formed German Colonial Association are against Peters' idea. But Peters heads abroad, to Zanzibar, aiming to secure treaties with tribal leaders on East Africa's coast. A British attempt to assassinate him fails, while at home the colonial director in the German Foreign Office opposes his efforts, becoming his enemy. This is to be expected: the official, named "Leo Kayser" (Herbert Hübner), is a "baptized Jew." Zanzibar's rights to East Africa's coast fall into German hands and Peters is named administrator by the brutal German East Africa Company. Better yet, he has come to the attention of Bismarck (Friedrich Otto Fis-

Mein Leben für Irland, with Werner Hinz and Anna Dammann.

cher). "Territory," Peters exclaims, "is only won by men who are hard-headed and self-confident, men who don't wet their pants the moment an Englishman raises his eyebrows." But Peters' tenure lasts only until 1888. Opposition from the British in the region as well as from Social Democrat MP Count "Hohenlohe-Langenberg" (Friedrich Ulmer), another Jew, back home leads to Peters' downfall. When the official tells Peters that Germany is "the people," Peters says, "So, *you* are the people! I could never of course have suspected that." Jews rebuke

Peters for having used the hangman's noose to secure the African colony (which covered parts of present-day Tanzania, Rwanda, and Burundi). To which Peters answers, "True enough, *you* would never have done it. And *you* would never have won German East Africa." Although Peters is no longer in power, the colony continues to be administered by the German East Africa Company. Only later does history validate Peters' ideas, according to his diary. Germany, he wrote, "did not understand him." In 1891, the imperial government assumed control of the colony. Selpin's film was named a National Film Prize winner.

Hans Steinhoff's sprawling three-hour *Ohm Krüger* (*Uncle Krüger*, 1941), perhaps the biggest Nazi colonial drama of them all, was running in German theaters in spring 1941. Covering the years 1895–1938, *Ohm Krüger* begins when gold is discovered in the land of the Boers, the Transvaal, and the Orange Free State. The English under Cecil Rhodes (Ferdinand Marian) and minister for the colonies Joseph Chamberlain (Gründgens) covet it, so Boer peasant leader Ohm Krüger seeks a compromise with the English: he will allow them access to Boer land but wants guarantees of Boer independence. At home, however, Paul Krüger prepares for the worst. The British provoke war, and the Boers retaliate, lead by Commander de Wett (Hans Adalbert Schlettow). But London then changes tactics and appoints General Kitchener supreme commander. He makes war on the Boer civilians, burning farms, killing cattle, poisoning wells, arming Africans, and putting women and children in concentration camps. More than 25,000 Boers die of starvation and disease in the camps while "Uncle" Krüger is abroad, unsuccessfully seeking help. British diplomacy assures his failure while the Boers lose the fight back home and become part of the British Empire. Called before a tribunal of "world history," Krüger predicts "great and powerful nations will resist British tyranny, and then the way will be clear for a better world." Ohm Krüger finds sanctuary in Switzerland, and he issues a warning: "There can be no coming to terms with the British."

Goebbels financed this film for his patron Hitler, who in *Mein Kampf* recalled that in his youth, "the Boer War came, like a glow of lightning on the far horizon. Day after day I used to gaze intently at the newspapers and I almost 'devoured' the telegrams and communiqués, overjoyed to think that I could witness that heroic struggle, even though from so great a distance." Herbert Maisch and Karl Anton served as co-directors, Fritz Arno Wagner (1889–1958) photographed and Theo Mackeben wrote the film's score. At the film's Berlin premiere, Jannings said, "In the most difficult hours of his life Krüger clung always to the theory that no individual and no nation shall deviate from the path of duty by withdrawing from its mission of sacrificing itself for the future." After World War II, Jannings (1896–1950) declared that he had been "opposed to all tendentious and political films," but Goebbels wrote in his diaries that Jannings worked "on his Boer film like a man possessed ... Jannings excels himself. An anti-England film you wouldn't dream was possible." Goebbels named *Ohm Krüger* Nazi Germany's first Film of the Nation. Schlettow (1888–1945), a prolific actor, was a dyed-in-the-wool supporter of the regime, preferring hardcore Nazi films. He died defending Berlin against the Russians.

Ohm Krüger wasn't screened in the States but did receive American coverage. *Time* (April 28, 1941) reported from Berlin that "between bomb blasts, through the blackout, Berliners stumbled to their cinemas last week to get a Nazi-eye view of what the unspeakable British have been up to all these years. With noisy and immense satisfaction they saw beefy, aging Emil Jannings play Stephanus Johannes Paulus Krüger, South Africa's famed Boer statesman, in Tobis Film's production.... The Nazi rewrite of the Boer War for home consumption is pure propaganda." The *New Yorker* (September 19, 1942) blithely indicated *Ohm Krüger* was showing in Paris. The city was also host to "prewar French films," it said, but "only if there are no Jews in the cast." After the war, Germany banned *Ohm Krüger*.

Gustav Ucicky and scriptwriter-colleague Gerhard Menzel outdid *Morgenrot* when they collaborated on *Heimkehr* (*Homecoming*), which was financed by Goebbels' ministry and released in Berlin in March 1941. This was another *Hetzfilm* ("smear film"), produced by Karl Hartl's Wien Film, that American critics abroad missed. The setting is, ominously, Poland in early 1939. In the town of Luzk, Polish aggressiveness towards Germans has become a daily event— a la Tourjansky's earlier *Feinde* (1940), a production that Germany banned after the war. Within a few weeks the worst occurs. The subhuman Poles begin to murder Germans. In one scene, a woman is stoned to death after having a swastika necklace ripped off. On September 1, 1939, the town's Germans are huddled in a barn, listening to Hitler's speech about the upcoming war. Just then, Poles attack and throw the Germans into wagons, like cattle. Two hundred are about to be shot when suddenly there's an air-raid warning. The Poles scatter as German bombers fly overhead; then the first German tanks enter the town. Liberated, the Germans head towards a fatherland where, one German says, "When you go into a shop it won't be Yiddish or Polish you hear but German. And it won't only be the whole village that will be German, *everything* all around us will be German." The Ucicky-Menzel film earned the rare Nazi distinction of Film of the Nation.

A strong dose of pro–Japanese sentiment is what the Germans had in mind when *Port Arthur* screened at New York's Apollo Theatre in October 1941, when Hitler's forces were fighting Stalin's, and Japan's forces were fighting in the Far East. The film takes place during the Japanese siege of the Russian city of Port Arthur in 1904, an attack that caught the Russians napping. Footage of Japanese victories leaves the impression that, four decades after Japan defeated Russia, the Nazis would emulate the Japanese. Boris Ranewsky (Adolf Wohlbrück) is a captain in the Imperial Russian Navy. His wife's half-brother Ivamoura (Charles Vanel), however, works for the Japanese. Ivanoura forces his half-sister Youki (Danielle Darrieux) to reveal Russian military secrets. Charged with espionage, she claims that to save her husband from assassination she gave away state secrets about her beloved Russia. Her loyalty is there for all to see when she voluntarily dies alongside her husband on his ship, protecting the Russian flag from the conquering Japanese.

This production was made in the year of the Berlin Olympics, when it had carried a different meaning. In the mid–1930s, the film had been pro–Russian. That was not the case this time around. In March 1942, *Port Arthur* screened at the World Playhouse in Chicago under the title *I Give My Life*. FCL/Slavia was the maker of this German-Czech-French co-production, which Tobis had released in Europe. The AFE Corp. released the French-language version in the U.S., which was dubbed into English. Hungarian Nicolas Farkas (1890–1982) and Josef Gielen directed. Farkas, Henri Deçoin, and Arnold Lippschitz scripted the tale, based on the novel by Pierre Frondaie. Wohlbrück, Karin Hardt, and René Deltgen were featured in the German-language version, for which Kurt Heuser (1903–1975), a colleague of Detlef Sierck, and Hans Klaehr, a colleague of Richard Eichberg, wrote the dialogue.

In the light of the burgeoning horrors in Europe, the issue of Nazi films in America finally came to a head this year. Because Germany appeared unstoppable, independent theater owners in the New York area asked the American government to ban the importation of German and Italian films. The Independent Theater Owners Association, with 9,000 members, and the Allied Theatre Owners of New York, Inc., with 350 members, had since 1936 sided with the Non–Sectarian Anti–Nazi League in its efforts to suppress the release of German films in America. The organizations were reacting to "discrimination displayed by both Germany and Italy against American motion pictures." Banning German films, they said, would deprive Germany and Italy of money "used for the furtherance of propaganda inimical to the best interests" of America. Nazi strategists in America intended to circumvent any ban by showing their films in German halls and in non-theatrical settings, and, if need be, by operating the projection equipment themselves. The Nazi "documentary" *Der Sieg im Westen* (*Victory in the West*, 1940), which was produced by Germany's Army High Command, brought the subject of banning German films into the open. Svend Noldan (1893–1978), the film's director, had been one of the leading documentary directors in Weimar Germany. Fritz Hippler was credited as producer of this record of Nazi triumphs in Western Europe, which contained a musical score by Herbert Windt. Noland's film came in two parts.

In the first part, the Germans offer their version of the origins of the war in the West. They stress Germany's "victimization" in the 1930s and the need to defend the fatherland. It includes the German soldier's oath: "I solemnly swear before Almighty God, this sacred oath, that I will render unqualified obedience to the Führer of the German Reich and People, Adolf Hitler, Supreme Commander of the Armed Forces, and that I will always be ready, as a courageous soldier, to risk my life for this oath."

A series of animated maps illustrates the position in which Germany found itself in the 1930s, surrounded by enemies. Lots of commentary and footage of German victimization present a picture of a nation that had no choice but to go to war. "Along three great rivers—the Rhine, the Danube, and the Vistula—lies this beautiful land, for which, again and again we have had to fight," says a distraught narrator.

The second part of the film shows Germany's response to the danger it faced: its victorious military campaigns in Belgium, Holland, and France. Again, maps, xenophobic commentary, and documentary footage depict how the west was won. Dead English soldiers and burning French tanks are shown alongside smiling German soldiers, which completes the rationalization for war. Scenes of British soldiers retreating and captured at Dunkirk are accompanied by strains of "We'll hang Out the Washing on the Siegfrid Line." The musical score was noteworthy. Martial tunes and a deep-throated male chorus are heard when the Germans are advancing. The music turns squeaky, however, when French or English soldiers come into view.

When the film had premiered at the Ufa-Palast am Zoo Berlin in February 1941, *Film-Kurier* wrote: "Bright banners of the Reich War Flag and the replica of the Iron Cross above the entrance dominated the façade of the theatre. The interior was decked out in honor of the German Army.... Shortly before 4:30 P.M. the Supreme Commander of the Army, General Field Marshal von Brauchitsch, and Reichminister Dr. Goebbels entered the auditorium.... The curtains opened and a reinforced music corps of the Wehrmacht was on stage along with a flag detachment.... The marching song 'On the Roads of Victory' by Herbert Windt was performed."

Despite its glorification of the advance of German forces through France, the film had been approved for commercial release in America as a newsreel by the U.S. Department of State (*New York Daily News*, May 3, 1941). Irwin Edwards, the director of the department's motion picture division, thought the film would "tend to wake up Americans" to the Nazi menace "rather than intimidate them." *Der Sieg im Westen* opened in the U.S. in May 1941. It ran without English-language commentary. By stressing the Nazis' leadership brilliance, *Der Sieg in Westen* signaled to Americans that the war in Europe was about to take another turn. Germany, victorious in the West, was now able to turn its attention further east—against the Soviet Union. Like the release of *Feldzug in Polen* in America, which had signaled that the Nazis would attack to the West, the Nazis were giving their hand away with *Der Sieg im Westen*. It received a mixed reception in America.

"Instead of making Americans frightened of the terrible power of the Reich's Army," wrote *Variety* (May 14, 1941), the film "inflames them. It would probably make them anxious to take weapons in hand and teach these arrogant butchers pictured on the screen that no army

Opposite: Der Sieg im Westen, September 1941.

96th St. Theater

Dritte Avenue und 96. Strasse
Atwater 9-4015

Das Deutsche Theater Yorkville's

Held over 17th and 18th week
until THURSDAY, September 4th, 1941

Blitzkrieg 1939-40

:—:   **English Narration**   :—:

Continuous performances daily from 1 to 11 P. M.

Last complete show 8.30 P. M.

is invincible when it meets a foe determined to fight." But there was another side to this. "Because of the length and the Hitler-applauding crowds perpetually in line to see *Sieg* in Manhattan's 'Nazi Yorkville sector,'" continued *Variety*, the "house is showing no shorts or anything else. With *Feldzug in Polen* audiences got one of Paramount's 'Three Bears' cartoons.'"

When *Der Sieg im Westen* was screened to 2,000 Harvard students as a kind of psychology test by the school's Liberal Union organization, the *Nation* (July 3, 1941) reported that Prof. Gordon Willard identified the source of the film's power. "The theme of the film," he said, was "one of irresistible onrush shots taken from dive bombers and tanks, actual battle scenes, but never, never a dead body. One sees always German success, and the moral that resistance is hopeless. In the final scenes of the armistice, every ounce of melodramatic revenge is wrung from the scene. In a dictatorship, the whole man is not appealed to, only the excitable part."

John Mosher, in the *New Yorker* (May 1941), was unfazed. He called *Der Sieg im Westen* a "competent film, if somewhat monotonous at times." "As usual," he said, "there are no scenes of bloodshed, none of the dead and the wounded, and some caution is taken to indicate that works of art and historic importance have been guarded."

This was one of the few German productions *Variety* and other outlets had taken the time to cover after September 1939. The *New York Times* and other film periodicals had stopped reviewing German feature films in autumn 1940. Not that the reviews had mattered much. At best, American reviews had taken a neutral stance towards Nazi films; more to the point, they often had something positive to say. New York's papers often joined in a chorus of praise for Nazi productions, which Ufa used to its advantage. The German studio promoted its films in America via these reviews.

Der Sieg im Westen screened in New York from spring until fall 1941. The film attracted hordes of American filmgoers. The 96th Street Theatre, which was managed by Willie Mansbacher and Walter Bibi, sometimes faced picketers from the German-American Congress for Democracy and the Non-Sectarian Anti-Nazi League. Their placards read, according to the *New York Times* (May 8, 1941),"We Don't Favor Nazi, Fascist or Communist Dictatorships," "Down with All Dictators," and "Going to Nazi Theatres Helps to Undermine the American Defense Program." But the word "Jew" rarely appeared on any placard. Police guarded the theatre. The Anti-Nazi League tried to bolster its case for suppressing the Nazi film by charging that the film's producer, Ufa, had violated New York law when it declared *Sieg im Westen* a "newsreel."

It was a feature-length film, said the league, because *Der Sieg im Westen* did "not consist completely of news 'shots,'" several scenes were "posed," its music was "dubbed," there's a "connected narrative," and the production lasts two hours. Therefore, said the league, Ufa needed a *permit* from New York State to show the film. The league asked New York to find Ufa in violation of state law. New York's State Supreme Court denied the league's petition, and the film ran for months. In Boston, when the pro-Nazi group called Christian Front gathered to watch the film, the audience consisted of supporters of the rabidly anti-Semitic Father Coughlin. They heard one Francis P. Moran urge mothers to write their sons in the American army and "impress upon them the impossibility of any nation's defeating the German army."

In late 1941, while the pro-war productions *Der Sieg im Westen* and *Feldzug in Polen* were circulating in America, one filmgoer told the Anti-Nazi League that it was making a mistake trying to suppress Nazi war propaganda. The more *Der Sieg im Westen* is shown, he said, "the easier it will be to convince certain people how they have been misled by isolationists. It will wake up America to the perils which are in store for us." The U.S. Army was paying attention to Nazi documentaries for a different reason. It concluded that Nazi battlefield films could be of use to American forces. Col. M.E. Gillette, commander of the U.S. Signal Corps, said,

"Movies showing Panzers, dive bombers, and tanks in action, intended as fear propaganda, actually can give selectees and enlisted men a first-hand opportunity to analyze ... Nazi operations in the field."

In the months leading up to Pearl Harbor, the Roosevelt administration took steps to suppress German propaganda in America. It ordered the closing of German consulates nationwide; shut the doors of New York's German Library of Information, which promoted private screening of German films and distributed the free newsletter *Facts in Review* about the Third Reich; and put the Transocean News, which filed Nazi stories abroad, and other German propaganda agencies out of business. The administration did not shut down the German-American Bund or its pro–Nazi organ, *Deutscher Weckruf und Beobachter* (*German Wake-up and Observer*). In a summer 1940 issue, it had highlighted theaters in the U.S. that continued to screen Nazi films. After the United States entered World War II, the U.S. government outlawed the German-American Bund.

On November 29, 1941, the Vatican paper *Osservatore Romano* ran a piece about euthanasia. It called the practice "one of those social aberrations of false conception of humanitarian pietism with which one should, in the name of an alleged right, abbreviate the sufferings of an ailing person believed to be incurable." The paper then referred to the German film *Ich Klage an* (*I Accuse*, 1941), which had been shown the previous summer at the Venice Film Festival, as "a true invitation to homicide." Further elaboration was missing.

Ich Klage an (*I Accuse*, 1941) ia a Tobis production which Eberhard Frowein scripted from his popular 1936 novel called *Sendung und Gewissen* (*Mission and Conscience*). Directed by Wolfgang Liebeneiner, it invokes Emile Zola's famous cry against injustice. The "injustice" it refers to is that society does not consider medical killing a "form of love." Throughout his life Frowein (1881–1964) exhibited an interest in medicine and hygiene. In 1930 he had directed a medical tale called *Fruchtbarkeit* (*Fertility*) for Deutsche Universal. Under Hitler, German "medicine" became death.

The plot of *Ich Klage an* revolves around the young and beautiful Hanna (Heidemarie Hatheyer), who plays the piano beautifully. She suffers from multiple sclerosis. She tells her physician (Mathias Wieman), "I don't want to die away later with my body being reduced to a little more than a lump. Please, promise to help me before this moment comes." His response is, "I am a doctor, and as such I am a servant of life. Life must be preserved at any cost." Her husband (Paul Hartmann), newly appointed director of the Anatomical Institute at Munich University, searches desperately for a cure. Then when *he* slips his wife an overdose of sleeping pills after she expressed fears of becoming "somebody who is deaf, blind, and idiotic," he faces a murder charge (in the present German state!). During his trial, the family physician happens to pay a visit to the children's ward of a hospital. He's shocked to discover that every last child is incurable. In a dramatic change of heart, this doctor becomes the main witness for the defense. The defendant then portentously rises to say, "I accuse" those doctors and judges who, by adhering to "strict rules," fail to serve the people. "Try me," he continues. "Yes, I confess. I did kill my incurably ill wife." At that point, the film ends.

This so-called plea for a terminally ill patient's right to a "humane" death—and prelude to the Final Solution—was released in Germany on August 29, 1941, a week *after* Hitler had ordered a halt to the medical killing program, which may have ended the lives of two hundred thousand people. The medical killing had begun in late 1939, the ground having been prepared by Frowein's book and by the popular movies *Life Unworthy of Life* (1934–35), *Opfer der Vergangenheit* (*Victims of the Past*, 1937), and *Dasein ohne Leben* (*Existence without Life*, 1940–41). The organization that was in charge was called the Reich Committee for the Registering of Serious Hereditary and Congenital Illnesses. Doctors were ordered to report, for instance, all newborn children suffering from "idiocy," Down's syndrome, microcephaly, hydrocephaly, spastic paralysis, or missing limbs. Dozens of asylums with children's units (*Kinderfachabteilungen*) were involved in the selection and murder.

Ich klage an became required viewing in Nazi-controlled Europe. Produced by Ufa, photographed by Friedl Behn-Grund, and co-starring Bernhard Goetzke, the film is a rationalization after the fact for horrific Nazi crimes in the guise of German medicine and German science. The film was never commercially shown in America nor did Western critics review it abroad. After the war, Germany banned the film. The Allies banned Hatheyer from film. Her career resumed in 1949. In 1984 and 1988 Hatheyer (1919–1990) won German cinema's best actress award.

In 1964, Wolfgang Liebeneiner, who considered himself a citizen of good reputation, was put on trial for in Limburg for being an accessory to mass murder because *Ich Klage an* advocates medical killing. He justified his involvement on the grounds that the film was a "document of humanity in an inhuman time." The *New York Times* were inhuman, but what did he have to do with it? He made a fictional film about an ill woman who wants to end her life at a time when, in reality, millions of people were trying to *save* their own lives from German thugs. This monstrously hypocritical and pretentious focus on one life while innumerable others faced death against their wills is nothing sort of breathtaking. His film overlooked the reality outside Germany's movie theaters and offered a bit of solace to the human filmmakers. Nearly 40 years after making *Ich klage an*, Liebeneiner was able to direct a film called *Götz von Berlichingen mit der eisernen Faust* (*Götz with the Iron Fist*, 1979), which was based on a play by Goethe about a 16th-century German who lost a hand in battle. He made a prosthesis out of metal and became a hero. During World War II, a Panzer-Grenacher division was named for Götz. It was part of the Waffen SS.

Germany's largest studio, Ufa, had its own hands in Nazi medical filmmaking. It produced the one-reel educational documentary *Die Englische Krankheit* (*The English Illness*, 1941), directed by Kurt Stefan and scripted by Bettina Ewerbeck. A narrator emphasizes that rickets originated in England in the seventeenth century. The film claims—by presenting one article from a British newspaper—that the British intended to spread the illness to Germany during and after the First World War, the ultimate aim being to destroy the vitality of the German people. Diagrams outline the effects of rickets on children and adults, how the malady can be prevented, and how to treat it. The short film depicts Nazi efforts to prevent the affliction. In winter, the regime offers Germans artificial sunray treatment!

Before the U.S. entered the war, the Non–Sectarian Anti–Nazi League reported that pro–Axis propaganda was making its way to Latin America. Argentina headed the list of South American countries that welcomed German movies.

EPILOGUE
Bedeviled Gold

In September 1942, one of the first full-length motion pictures ever produced by the U.S. government came out. It was the hour-long documentary *The World at War*. Sam Spewack compiled the footage, which recapitulates the events of the decade leading up to Pearl Harbor. Some content came from two confiscated Nazi films: *Feldzug in Polen* and *Der Sieg im Westen*. These were perhaps the last scenes from Nazi films screened publicly in the States for the duration of the war. *The World at War* was offered free of charge to theaters across the country. MGM, Twentieth Century–Fox, Paramount, Warner Bros., and RKO Radio Pictures distributed *The World at War*. Yet the story of Nazi films in America wasn't quite over.

Photographer Günther Rittau (1893–1971) earned a measure of infamy when he directed one of the more loathsome films for Goebbels and for the Nazis: *U-Boote Westwärts* (*Submarines Heading Westward*, 1941), with music by Harald Böhmelt (1900–1982), which premiered in the West in pro–Nazi Buenos Aires in September 1942. It focuses on Germany's seamen who did the dirty but patriotic business of fighting for the fatherland. Cameraman Rittau (of *Metropolis* fame) directed Herbert Wilk, Joachim Brennecke (b. 1919), Josef Sieber, and Ilse Werner (1921–2005) in a tale of German heroism and British duplicity above and below the ocean line, and of the loved ones back in the fatherland who also sacrificed for the nation. The Germans are depicted as going out of their way to avoid conflict, while the British are depicted as double-crossers. All but one of the German seamen makes it home safely. The one missing man is posthumously decorated as a hero. Goebbels named Rittau's film a recipient of a National Film Prize.

Variety (September 30, 1942) reported that *U-Boote Westwärts* was "a lot more subtle and well rounded than some of the Nazi propaganda flickers to appear at the beginning of the war. Points emphasized in the film offer a pretty good idea of what sort of stuff German filmgoers are being offered." *Variety*'s review is evidence that Westerners had the opportunity to see Nazi films after the U.S. entered the war. But it was a rare examination of Nazi propaganda after December 1941.

"The racial question," Hitler had said in *Mein Kampf*, "gives the key not only to world history but to all human culture." In the "blood alone resides the strength as well as the weakness of man." And, "whoever knows the Jew, knows the devil"—"*Wer kennt den Jude, kennt der Teufel.*" In December 1942, at the San Martin Theatre in Buenos Aires, a certain film premiered. *Variety* wrote, "Opening stench-bomb in what appears to be a full-fledged anti–Semitic propaganda drive in Latin America ... a Klangfilm production distributed by Ufa, is as venom-spreading, hate-producing a job as ever turned out by Goebbels and his Wilhelmstrasse propagandists."

"It's a frightening example of the kind of nauseating poison being spread in the swastika occupied countries of Europe today, and its very release here, although protested by various organizations and dailies, is indicative of the depths to which Berlin is willing to go."

The film, said *Variety* (December 30, 1942):

> is based on historical events in the Duchy of Württemberg early in the eighteenth century ... [and] was specifically designed not only for German audiences but to produce, by appeal to lowest passions, hate against Jews in all occupied countries.
>
> Claiming to be based entirely on fact—introduction, inverting the usual prologue, insists everything is based on fact—seeks to lay at the feet of the Jews practically all the greed, avarice, treachery, cruelty and knavery conceivable.
>
> Purpose is also to seek to convince spectators of the fact that traits depicted are, and always have been, those of the Jewish race.... Behind direction can be seen the frothing-at-the-mouth violence of the Nazis, not simply to make a point, but to blast it home with a pile driver. Some scenes are so revolting that it's hard to see how they were even passed by local censors.

The film went by the title *El Demonio del Oro* (*Bedeviled Gold*). Implying unholy riches, the Nazi production was in fact *Jud Süss*.

Directed by Veit Harlan, co-directed by Alfred Braun and Wolfgang Schleif, scored by Wolfgang Zeller (1893–1967), and photographed by Bruno Mondi, *Jud Süss* starred Ferdinand Marian (Süss), Werner Krauss (in three roles: Rabbi Loew; Levy, Süss's secretary; and a "Jew"), Heinrich George, Kristina Söderbaum (Dorothea Stürm), Theodor Loos, Bernhard Goetzke, Jacob Tiedke, Wolfgang Staudte, and Erna Morena, and a score more actors from Germany's circle of stars.

Jud Süss centers on lies, death, and one other thing: sex. The protagonist, Oppenheimer, is presented as a man coveting the beautiful wife of a jailed official. He gains sexual favors in exchange for having her husband released from prison, after which she drowns herself. Her death leads to an anti–Jewish riot by the local Germans. After his benefactor dies, the 50-year-old Oppenheimer is arrested. He's tried, convicted, and hanged in 1738. Within a month all Jews are made to pay a price for Oppenheimer's crime. They are driven out of the region.

The actual historical events began with the fact that Joseph ben-Issachar Süsskind Oppenheimer was a German financier who became the best known of the "court Jews" employed by rulers of central European states from the sixteenth to the eighteenth centuries. Born in Heidelberg, he was a kinsman of financier Samuel Oppenheimer (1630–1703). In 1732, Süss Oppenheimer was appointed court factor to Karl Alexander, who became the duke of Württemberg the following year and made Oppenheimer responsible for the financial affairs of the duchy. Settled in a magnificent house in Stuttgart, Oppenheimer embarked on far-reaching financial plans to centralize power in the hands of the duke. Karl Alexander was despotic. He was also a Catholic ruler in a Protestant country. After the duke's death in 1737, Oppenheimer was accused of plotting to restore Catholicism to Württemberg—and was arrested. His trial was a scandal, for much of his interrogation consisted of probes into Oppenheimer's relationships with women. A number of them were arrested and forced into the witness box. Oppenheimer minimized his involvement in Jewish traditions and ignored co-religionists, yet the German-Jewish community attempted to buy his freedom. During imprisonment, Oppenheimer found sustenance in Judaism. Though the charge against him was never proven, he was condemned and his property confiscated. Oppenheimer was hanged in April 1738, and his body was strung up in an iron cage. He died uttering a Jewish prayer.

In Christian lore, Oppenheimer figured as an evil man—until Lion Feuchtwanger, a German Jew, set the record straight in his 1925 novel *Jud Süss*. In 1933, Goebbels called Feuchtwanger the German people's "worst enemy." Stripped of his German nationality and his doctorate, and with his Berlin house, property, and manuscripts confiscated, Feuchtwanger fled to France. Feuchtwanger lived long enough to know of Veit Harlan's desecration of his work.

Jud Süss had premiered at the Venice Film Festival on September 6, 1940, on the same program with *Il Sogno di Butterfly*. A young Venice critic wrote of *Jud Süss*, "We have no hesitation in saying if this is propaganda, then we welcome propaganda. It is a powerful, incisive, extremely effective film." The "critic" was Michelangelo Antonioni.

On September 24, *Jud Süss* premiered in Berlin. The film became a box-office hit, rationalizing the Nazis' treatment and deportations of Jews that had begun in February 1940. It was then distributed throughout the Reich. *Jud Süss* was shown in France (February 1941), where *Le Parisien* said it was "in keeping with historical facts that are more dramatic than any product of the imagination." Then the Germans released *Jud Süss* in Denmark (February 1941), the Netherlands, in St. Gregory on the Channel Islands, Portugal (May 1941), Finland (May 1941), and elsewhere.

The Italian newspaper through which the Vatican had expressed its rejection of *Ich klage an* had remained silent regarding *Jud Süss*. But Goebbels opined about the film. He wrote in his diaries that reports about *Jud Süss* were "quite magnificent. It caused demonstrations in the streets of Hungary. This film really is a new program." It was, he continued, "proof that films too can work and arouse enthusiasm that is entirely in line with our views." Goebbels awarded it a National Film Prize.

This film's release in the West in late 1942 was Germany's justification of the terrible events taking place in Europe. Today we are aware that incitement and hate language by those in power is a validated predictor of the intent to commit genocide. Germany banned *Jud Süss* after the war.

Feuchtwanger did not live long enough to see Harlan put on trial in 1950. The charges were crimes against humanity. *Jud Süss* was used as the main piece of evidence against him. Of particular interest to the German prosecutor was the role of the SS in recruiting Jewish extras for the film. Determined to depict German Jews as *Ostjude* (Eastern Jews) in a film justifying their expulsion from Germany, Harlan used extras from Lublin (in January 1940) and Prague (in March 1940). The Germans found Harlan innocent of the charges.

Jud Süss's star Ferdinand Marian was born Ferdinand Haschowec in 1902 in Vienna. He had made his name in 1930s German films as the mean but elegant rogue, outwardly attractive but inwardly cold, in *Madame Bovary* and *La Habanera*. Marian's unexpected death after the war sparked rumors that he committed suicide because of his association with *Jud Süss*.

Were *Jud Süss*, like *Die Rothschilds* (1940) and *Der Ewige Jude* (1940), ignored in the West for racist reasons? Western exposure of these films would almost certainly have affected the distribution of Nazi-produced or Nazi-owned films in the States. Outrage at their existence might have made clear the Nazis' aims for Europe's Jews. Governments might have been shamed into taking action, preventative and otherwise. After D-Day, Western critics were aware of what was being shown on German screens. "Most of the stars of the prewar German films are still around," said the *New Yorker* (August 19, 1944) in a piece called "German Movies." The stars included Jannings, Fritsch, Albers, Roekk, Wessely, Heinrich George, and Söderbaum. The publication noted some of the films that had played in Berlin in June 1944: Géza von Bolváry's *Lumpacivagabundus* (*Lumpaci the Vagabond*, 1936); Georg Jacoby's *Tanz mit dem Kaiser* (*The Emperor Waltz*, 1941); Herbet Maisch's *Die Zaubergeige* (*The Miracle Violin*, 1943); Herbert Frederdorf's *Der Täter is unter uns* (*The Culprit Is Among Us*, 1943); Veit Harlan's *Immensee* (1943); Stemmle's *Herr Sanders left gefärlich* (*Mr. Sanders Lives Dangerously*, 1943); Harald Braun's *Träumerei* (*Slumbering*, 1943–44); and Hans Deppe's *Majoratsherr* (1944). "Beethoven, Luther, Schiller and Goethe," said the magazine, "are being trotted out as subjects of film biographies. Vienna and the Tyrolese Alps are the favorite backgrounds."

To discover, the magazine said, "any of the old-line, fire-breathing, 100 percent Aryan jobs, you had to go back several years, to the days when Germans were taking their propaganda straight and without a chaser." The example the magazine gave was *Der Verlorene Sohn* (*The Prodigal Son*). That production had come out in 1934. Three infamous films from 1940—*Jud Süss*, *Die Rothschilds*, and *Der Ewige Jude*—had apparently been overlooked again.

The *New Yorker* came to several conclusions about German movies playing in the Third Reich in the summer of 1944. One was that the "present German film contains no propaganda." A second was that the German film industry, "which is apparently nobody's fool, has already written off this war as a total loss and is making harmless escapist films which it no doubt hopes will be acceptable for distribution after the armistice." By the time the Allies invaded Europe, German films had completed their tasks, which Hitler *had* made clear on paper much earlier in *Mein Kampf*: "In times of distress a wave of public anger has usually arisen against the Jew; the masses have taken the law into their own hands; they have seized Jewish property and ruined the Jew in their urge to protect themselves against what they consider to be a scourge of God. Having come to know the Jew intimately through the course of centuries, in times of distress they looked upon his presence among them as a public danger comparable only to the plague."

The film evidence for what the Nazis intended to do was on the screen. Hitler's major anti–Semitic films had included *SA-Mann Brand* (1933), *Hitlerjunge Quex* (1933), *Hans Westmar* (1933), *Flüchtlinge* (1933), *Konjunkturritter* (1934), *Das Alte Recht* (1934), *Ein Mann will nacht Deutschland* (1934), *Die Freundin eines grossen Mannes* (1934), *Um das Menschenrecht* (1934), *Verräter* (1936), *Weisse Sklaven* (1937), *Togger* (1937), *Patrioten* (1937), *Urlaub auf Ehrenwort* (1938), *Mit versiegelter Order* (1938), *Musketier Meier III* (1938), *Am seidenen Faden* (1938), *Pour le Mérite* (1938), *Der Vierte kommt nicht* (1938–39), *Der Gouverneur* (1939), *Robert und Bertram* (1939), *Robert Koch* (1939), *Leinen aus Irland* (1939), *Feldzug in Polen* (1939–40), *Der Ewige Quell* (1940), *Ein Robinson* (1940), *Die Rothschilds* (1940), *Jud Süss* (1940), *Der Ewige Jude* (1940), *Falschmünzer* (1940), *Bismarck* (1940), *Uber alles in der Welt* (1941), *Carl Peters* (1941), *Ohm Krüger* (1941), *... reitet für Deutschland* (1941), *Der Weg ins Freie* (1941), *Venus vor Gericht* (1941), *Ich klage an* (1941), *Heimkehr* (1941), *GPU* (1942), *Die Entlassung* (1942), *Münchausen* (1943), *Wien 1910* (1943), and *Titanic* (1943).

Der Ewige Quell, directed by Fritz Kirchhoff, is about gold fever and the resulting anarchy in a region in Bavaria, all blamed on Jews. Reischsführer SS Heinrich Himmler had once been police chief of Bavaria. The film was banned in Germany in 1950. In *Wien 1910*, directed by E.W. Emo, scripted by Gerhard Menzel and photographed by Hans Schneeberger, Vienna's early twentieth-century mayor Karl Lüger (Rudolf Forster), head of the Christian Social Party, fights for his city's financial health against the "speculative maneuvers" of "Vienna Jewry." Lüger was a rabble-rousing anti–Semite and demagogue whom Hitler admired—and said so in *Mein Kampf*. Lüger in Vienna represented the time and place of Hitler's earliest expressions of hatred toward Jews.

Nearly all the openly anti–Semitic films made by the Nazis before 1940 had been shown somewhere in the United States. There were plenty of lesser ones as well. Others, such as *Die Rothschilds*, *Bismarck* and *Riding For Germany* would have opened here but for America's entry into the war. All are offshoots of *Mein Kampf*. The Swedish production *Pettersson & Bendel* (1933) should not be overlooked. It served as a model for German anti–Semitic productions. Goebbels, in a rare gesture to a foreign production, screened it in Germany in 1935—just before the introduction of the Nuremberg Laws. It ran in the States in 1934.

A surprising number of German film people from the era—directors, actors, and technicians—lived normal or longer than expected life spans. Their service in 1930s and '40s Germany had energized their careers. After the war many Third Reich filmmakers were *paid* to make more movies!

The Nazis pretended that nothing had changed cinematically when they came to power. After the war, except for one or two cases, Germans pretended there hadn't been a war at all.

After the war, Hamburg's denazification committee acquitted director Veit Harlan. He could safely resume his film career. But then he was put on trial in July 1948 for having made the "inflammatory" *Jud Süss* (1940), starring Werner Krauss.

The charge against him was that his film "slandered Jewry and therefore provoked the pogrom." His defense was that the film presented the "Jewish question in artistic terms." Admitting to the "deplorable fact that in Germany a monstrous crime was perpetrated against Jewry," Harlan nonetheless bewailed the fact that after the war "Germans are therefore not entitled to talk about the all too human matter of the Jewish question." He didn't define the "Jewish question." Tried and condemned in public but freed by the court, Veit Harlan remained a free man.

Harlan's name was closely aligned to another name, that of Werner Krauss (1884–1959), an actor of wide repute. Krauss became a cultural icon of the Nazi regime, starring in *Robert Koch* (1939), *Jud Süss* (1940), *Die Entlassung* (1942), and *Paracelsus* (1943). Krauss had garnered a long list of Weimar-era screen credits, beginning with his breakthrough in *The Cabinet of Dr. Caligari* (1919). There followed the classics *Shattered* (1921), *Danton* (1921), *Othello* (1922), *Waxworks* (1923), *Streets of Sorrow* (1925), *Tartuffe* (1925), *Nana* (1925), *The Student from Prague* (1926), and *Yorck* (1931). In *Der Kaufmann von Venedig* (*The Merchant of Venice*, 1923), Krauss played Shylock. In the 1930s, Krauss remained in Germany. Goebbels appointed him vice president of the *Reichtheaterkammer* (Reich Theatre Chamber) and named him a *Preussischer Staatsrat*.

After the war Krauss embraced Austrian nationality and the stage. In 1947 Krauss lived in Stuttgart. There were several reasons for this. He sought denazification where the conditions were favorable, and Stuttgart fit the bill: the city had been pro–Nazi from the start. In Stuttgart, evidence against him was in short supply. Further, denazification approval by the four occupying powers was *not* required in that part of Germany. Travel to Stuttgart in postwar Germany "involves so many complications," wrote a reporter, "that it might as well be in another country." And finally, the real Jud Süss had lived and died in Stuttgart. Jews were scarce there, pro–Jewish sentiment absent.

Krauss's line of defense about his *three* Jew-baiting roles in *Jud Süss* was that he had sought to ameliorate really provocative interpretations. The Stuttgart court acquitted him. In late 1950, Krauss was in Berlin starring in Ibsen's *John Gabriel Borkman*. His presence caused a firestorm of protests and demonstrations from Jews. The performances were cancelled. Heinz Galinsky, head of the Jewish community in Berlin, had predicted that if Krauss were on stage he would be met with a reception that "no man has yet experienced" (Associated Press, December 12, 1950). In 1951 Krauss reacquired German citizenship and three years later was rehabilitated when German cinema awarded him its *Bundesverdienstkreuz* (Order of Merit). His film career a thing of the past, the theater was his salvation until his death.

It was a form of Holocaust denial to have allowed German filmmakers who had worked in the Third Reich to continue to work in films. It implied that they had done little or nothing wrong in helping a monstrous regime to survive for 12 years. In a real sense, the German filmmakers made the familiar excuse that they had no alternative: they had acted under orders. Could they not see that the loss of integrity and the complicity in the deaths of Jews, including colleagues to nearly all of them, was a far worse fate than not making films in brutal times?

Some of them were helped to get back on their feet. After Nazi Germany's defeat, the U.S. Army assumed control of film activities in the U.S. occupied zone of Germany. There were counterpart French and English administrators in the other zones; the three zones synchronized their film activities and regulations. One regulation in particular banned work permits to filmmakers identified with Hitler's regime. When distributor and author Arthur L. Mayer became administrator of U.S. film operations in Germany, he found himself at odds with the ban because, he said, "it had the effect of driving out talent." Moreover, "many filmmakers of merit, fled to the East ... and many became Communists. That is, they became Communists in name only, in the same way they were formerly Nazis in name only—in order to work." One filmmaker Mayer would have helped was Leni Riefenstahl. "Whether we like its possessor or not is of no consequence," he concluded. "We should use filmmaking talent to the greatest possible degree."

At the end of hostilities in Europe, U.S. officials in June 1945 asked for bids from Americans interested in licensing and distributing German films confiscated in America after December 1941. There were hundreds available for release. In order to decide which films were appropriate for viewing by Americans, the War Department and the Office of Strategic Affairs asked New York's Museum of Modern Art in 1942–43 to evaluate some of the confiscated productions. Those that were deemed objectionable or full of propaganda were locked away—for the time being. On the banned list was *Der Sieg im Westen*, which was classified as "unfit for American audiences." Among the offerings *for* release were Josef von Baky's operetta *Intermezzo* (1936), *Zigeunerbaron, Drei Vater um Anna, Johannisfeuer*, Erik Charell's Weimar classic *Congress Dances* (1931) and, shockingly, *Robert Koch*.

Postwar films downplayed genocide by focusing global attention on the future of Germany. Was this the need to return to normalcy or a denial? The same films, filmmakers and themes enjoyed new life in the postwar era. Josef von Baky and Gerhard Menzel's Austrian production *Dunja* (1955) was a remake of Ucicky and Menzel's Nazi-era *Der Postmeister* with a slight difference. At the end, the German postmaster, aware of what has happened, takes revenge on those (non–Aryans) who destroyed his daughter. This is depicted as justified under the circumstances. Ucicky and Menzel also collaborated on *Der Edelweisskönig* (1957), yet another remake of a Nazi-era film. Peter Ostermayr produced the 1938 version and its postwar double.

Ostermayr, in the 1950s, was responsible for producing a series of films that were little short of remakes of Nazi-era productions screened in the States: *Eherstreik, Der Klosterjäger, Schloss Hubertus, Das Schweigen im Walde*, and *Der Jäger von Fall*. In the same vein, Viktor Tourjansky filmed *Königswalzer* (1955), a remake of Herbert Maisch's 1935 musical, and Ernst Marischka directed *Opernball* (1956), starring Johannes Heesters, who had been one of Hitler's favorite actors. The latter postwar film was a remake of Bolváry's *Opernball* (1939), which Marischka had scripted. Doing his part to make the world forget his involvement as one of Hitler's filmmakers, Wolfgang Liebeneiner directed *Die Trapp-Familie* (1955), the basis of which later became *The Sound of Music*. Working in West Germany Liebeneiner also filmed *Urlaub auf Ehrenwort* (1955), a kinder rendition of Karl Ritter's Nazi-era tale of duty to Germany and comradeship among soldiers in the First World War.

Since long before the release of *Birth of a Nation*, before promotions proclaimed "Garbo Talks!" illusion and reality have played across the silver screen. No war has been left unfought in the movies, no romance kept secret, few acts of hate, evil, or kindness kept hidden. Anti-Semitism has been a cornerstone of German culture. Some say it *is* German culture. Feigned innocence is symptomatic of how Germans and Austrians have sold their role in Nazi history.

SELECTED BIBLIOGRAPHY

Unless otherwise noted, quotes from Joseph Goebbels come primarily from translations of his diaries, which in the original German constitute 15 volumes.

Cadars, Pierre. *Histoire du Cinéma Nazi*. Paris: E. Losfeld, 1972.
Garnett, Tay. *Light Your Torches and Pull Up Your Tights*. New Rochelle, N.Y.: Arlington House, 1973.
Haffner, Sebastian. *The Meaning of Hitler*. Cambridge, Mass.: Harvard University Press, 1979.
Hake, Sabine. *Popular Cinema of the Third Reich*. Austin: University of Texas Press, 2001.
Hitler, Adolf. *Mein Kampf*. Translated by James Vincent Murphy. London: Hurst and Blackett, 1937.
Hollywood Quarterly. Berkeley: University of California Press, 1945–1951.
Klaus, Ulrich J. *Deutsche Tonfilme*, vols. 1–15. Berlin: Klaus-Archiv, 1988–2006.
Kreimeier, Klaus. *The Ufa Story*. Berkeley: University of California Press, 1999.
Leiser, Erwin. *Nazi Cinema*. New York: Macmillan, 1974.
Mack, Max. *With a Sigh and a Smile*. London: Alliance Press, 1943.
Marton, Andrew, and Joanne D'Antonio. *Andrew Marton*. Metuchen, N.J.: Scarecrow Press, 1991.
Möller, Felix. *The Film Minister: Goebbels and the Cinema in the Third Reich*. Stuttgart: Axel Menges, 2000.
New York Times Directory of the Film. New York: Arno Press/Random House, 1971.
New York Times Film Reviews. New York: New York Times/Arno Press, 1970.
Non-Sectarian Anti-Nazi League to Champion Human Rights. *The Anti-Nazi Bulletin*, 1933–41. New York: Non-Sectarian Anti-Nazi League to Champion Human Rights.
Rentschler, Eric. *The Ministry of Illusion: Nazi Cinema and its Afterlife*. Cambridge, Mass.: Harvard University Press, 1996.
Sorge, Ernst. *With Plane, Boat, & Camera in Greenland; an Account of the Universal Dr. Fanck Greenland Expedition*. New York: D. Appleton-Century, 1936.
Variety Film Reviews. New York: R.R. Bowker, 1983.
Waldman, Harry. *Hollywood and the Foreign Touch: A Dictionary of Foreign Filmmakers and their Films from America, 1910–1995*. Lanham, Md.: Scarecrow Press, 1996.
Winkel, Roel V., and David Welch. *Cinema and the Swastika*. London: Palgrave, 2007.
Wottrich, Erika. *Deutsche Universal: transatlantische Verleih- und Produktionsstrategien eines Hollywood-Studios in den 20er und 30er Jahren*. Munich: Edition Text + Kritik, 2001.
Wright, Rochelle. *The Visible Wall: Jews and Other Ethnic Outsiders in Swedish Film*. Carbondale: Southern Illinois University Press, 1988.

INDEX

A Brivele der Mamen 221
A Noszty Fiu Esete Toth Marival 173
Abel, Alfred 35, 90, 97, 148, 151, 154, 176, 227, 255, 260
Abel mit der Mundharmonika 55, 126
Abenteuer geht weiter 243
Abenteuer im Engadine 117
Der Abenteurer von Paris 148
A.C.E. 36, 37, 47, 51, 53, 58, 60, 64, 70, 77, 79, 98, 101, 116, 119, 140, 145, 180, 204
Achtung! Feind hört mit! 89
Ackermann, Curt 205
Adieu les Beaux Jours 47
Der Adjutant seiner Hoheit 132
Adrienne Lecouvreur 180
L'Affairs of Maupassant 174
Ahrens, Thekla 156, 198
Albach-Retty, Wolf 45, 46, 135, 160, 173, 205, 235
Albers, Hans 34, 37, 42, 45, 48, 57, 60, 64, 80, 103, 161, 162, 226, 234, 270, 281
Alessandrini, Goffredo 243
Alexander, Georg 51, 103, 117, 135, 136, 155, 157, 159, 199, 216
Alien Property Custodian, Office of (APC) 68
All Quiet on the Western Front 23, 27, 29, 126
Alle Tage ist kein Sonntag 106
Allegret, Marc 203
Alles für Veronika 198
Alles um eine Frau 90
Allgeier, Sepp 19, 22, 92, 95, 132, 167, 181
L'Alliance Cinématographique Européenne *see* A.C.E.
Alpenkorps im Angriff 17
Alte Kameraden 105
Das Alte Recht 43, 282
Der Alte und der junge König 87
Alten, Jürgen von 124, 125, 155, 221, 222
Am seidenen Faden 194, 282
American Jewish Congress 78, 145
Amore sulle Alpi 213
Amphitryon 69, 145, 146, 174
Andalusische Nächte 180
Andergast, Maria 23, 86, 125, 142, 150, 178, 182, 233, 254
Der Angriff 17, 120
Angst, Richard 19, 22, 34, 55, 117, 270
Annette im Paradies 100
Anschlag auf Baku 16, 188, 189
Anton, Karl 154, 181
Antonioni, Michelangelo 281
Aprés Mein Kampf Mes Crimes 250
Argentina, Imperio 179, 180
Der Arme Millionär 227
Arno, Siegfried 26, 31, 54, 151
Aufbau 7, 249

Aufforderung zum Tanz 93
Aufruhr in Damaskus 210
August der Starke 118
Aus den Wolken kommt das Glück 174
Ave Maria 76, 140, 141
L'Avocate d'amour 180
Avodah 160
Az Elcserelt Ember 204

Baarová, Lida 98, 116, 126, 184, 244
Baky, Josef von 92, 182, 253, 284
Bal paré 267
Ball im Metropol 174
Ballo al Castello 142
Bánky, Vilma 22, 61
Barcarole 116
Die Barmherzige Lüge 266
Barsony, Rose 45, 46, 51, 60, 78
Bassermann, Albert 27, 36, 37, 41, 48, 69, 78, 230, 259, 260
Bavaria 9, 31, 32, 45, 46, 49, 67, 70, 77, 78, 84, 88, 97, 104, 105, 106, 107, 110, 118, 136, 147, 148, 152, 153, 160, 167, 186, 192, 199, 216, 220, 222, 226, 234, 238, 243, 252, 254, 255, 266, 270, 282
Beasts of Berlin 100, 228
Becce, Guiseppe 86, 139, 152, 193, 243, 264
Beck-Gaden, Hanns 72, 118, 151
Befehl is Befehl 201
Befreite Hände 252
Behn-Grund, Friedl 84, 153, 278
Die Beiden Seehunde 57
Benatzky, Ralph 168
Benitz, Albert 22, 167, 238
Der Berg Ruft 238
Berger, Ludwig 60, 61
Berlin Illustrieter 101
Berlin Olympics 4, 12, 95, 113, 114, 131, 140, 141, 145, 148, 155, 156, 175, 176, 177, 187, 201, 205, 207, 222, 228, 245, 246, 254, 273
Berliner, Trude 46, 48
Bernhardt, Kurt 22, 54, 64, 84, 193
Bertram, Hans 7, 16, 153, 235, 245, 250
Besuch am Abend 136
Der Bettelstudent 117
Der Biberpelz 221
Birgel, Willy 89, 90, 98, 108, 109, 116, 123, 144, 167, 179, 200, 209, 218, 220, 242, 251
Birth of a Nation 3, 284
Bismarck 51, 131, 225, 231, 232, 270, 282
Der Blaufuchs 200
Blinde Passagiere 105
Blonde Carmen 215
Die Blonde Christl 45

287

Index

Blumen aus Nizza 202
Blutendes Deutschland 193
Blutsbrüderschaft 139, 222
Boccaccio 147, 148
Boese, Carl 16, 27, 39, 46, 54, 57, 73, 74, 77, 80, 98, 118, 119, 142, 150, 151, 161, 187, 189, 190, 200, 215, 222, 226, 227, 241, 265
Bohnen, Michael 31, 102, 202, 252, 256
Bois, Curt 53
Bolváry, Géza von 16, 30, 48, 58, 60, 61, 92, 93, 101, 117, 155, 156, 167, 169, 173, 177, 191, 205, 234, 240, 242, 257, 258, 281, 284
Bomben auf Monte Carlo 32
Borgmann, Hans-Otto 187
Borsody, Eduard von 16, 205, 206, 207, 251
Boxoffice 132
Brand im Ozean 252
Der Brave Sünder 30
Brennendes Geheimnis 55
Breuer, Siegfried 86, 137, 153, 232, 235, 257, 260
Briefe Fliegen über den Ozean 180
Brink, Elga 49, 54, 97, 198, 265
Brooklyn Daily Eagle 133
Bryan, Julien 13
Bundesverdienstkreuz 240, 245, 283
Burian, Vlasta 132

Cabinet of Dr. Caligari 31, 57, 172, 264, 283
Camerini, Mario 222
Campo di Maggio 122
La Canzone del Sole 102
Carl Peters 7, 212, 222, 225, 270, 282
Carmen de la Triana 180
Casa Lontana 243
Casino Film Exchange *see* CFE
Casino Theatre 15, 32, 54, 67, 68, 70, 73, 74, 78, 91, 97, 101, 102, 105, 106, 107, 115, 118, 119, 120, 139, 142, 148, 152, 154, 155, 156, 163, 164, 175, 178, 181, 182, 188, 189, 191, 194, 199, 200, 201, 203, 204, 205, 209, 210, 213, 215, 216, 223, 226, 227, 228, 230, 234, 235, 252, 253, 254, 260, 264, 265, 266, 267, 270
Caspar, Horst 225
Casta Diva 135
Cavalerie légère 99
CFE 32, 67, 68, 69, 70, 71, 72, 74, 75, 76, 78, 82, 86, 91, 93, 96, 100, 101, 103, 104, 107, 112, 114, 116, 117, 118, 119, 121, 135, 136, 142, 145, 149, 150, 151, 155, 161, 173, 174, 177, 186, 190, 191, 198, 200, 201, 213, 215, 221, 228, 241, 242, 252, 255, 257, 258
Chalutzim 53
Le Chanson du souvenir 140
Chicago Tribune 1, 7, 8, 13, 60, 85, 88, 109, 140, 141, 148, 173, 251
Der Choral von Leuthen 79, 131
Christians, Mady 53
Cinecitta Theatre 237, 243, 254
Le Club de soupirants 248
Coup de feu a l'aube 47
Csardas 100
Die Czardasfürstin 76
Cziffra, Géza von 58, 59, 60, 265
Czinner Paul 36

D III 88, 198, 235
Dagover, Lil 7, 31, 34, 75, 99, 106, 108, 118, 158, 159, 172, 175
Dahinten in der Heide 200
Daily News 68, 155, 274
Daily Telegraph 178
Dammann, Anna 240, 242, 270

Deltgen, René 59, 98, 103, 190, 205, 251, 252, 273
El Demonio del Oro 280
Deppe, Hans 16, 46, 80, 81, 84, 101, 148, 151, 154, 158, 163, 200, 254, 281
Dessau, Paul 22, 31, 51, 160
Deutsche Allgemeine Zeitung 11
Der Deutsch Film 123
Deutsche Film 185
Deutsch Fox-Film 114
Deutsche Universal 4, 19, 20, 21, 22, 23, 25, 33, 43, 46, 55, 61, 69, 73, 75, 86, 88, 98, 103, 131, 151, 156, 158, 177, 193, 246, 259, 277, 285
Deutscher Weckruf und Beobachter 8, 277
Deyers, Lien 38, 75, 91, 97, 101, 117, 119, 149
Das Diamant des Zaren 187
Il Diamante Porta-Fortuna 187
Die—oder Keine 65
Die vom Niederrhein 70
Diehl, Carl Ludwig 30, 37, 61, 99, 115, 142, 152, 159, 178, 213, 222, 233
Diessl, Gustav 21, 57, 59, 90, 139, 178, 205, 206, 213, 216, 243, 245
Dieterle, William 88, 89, 104, 158, 216, 217, 230, 231
Les Dieux s'amusent 145, 147
Dir gehört mein Herz 202
Diskretion-Ehrensache 205
Dr. Ehrlich's Magic Bullet 230
Una Donna tra due Mondi 243
Donner, Blitz und Sonnenschein 139
Dorf im rotten Sturm 120
Doublepatte 105
Drei blau Jungs—ein blondes Mädel 119
Drei Kaiserjäger 72
Drei Mäderl im Schubert 142
Drei Tage Mittelarrest 77
Drei Unteroffiziere 198, 216
Drei Väter um Anna 241
Drei von der Kavallerie 74
Die Drei von der Tankstelle 119
Dreiklang 172
Dreizehn Mann und eine Kanone 192
The Dreyfus Case 259
Der Dschungel ruft 150
Le Due Madri 254

Eggerth, Marta 40, 48, 76, 104, 117, 133, 135, 140, 143, 155, 173, 201, 215, 255
Ehestreik 77
Ehrlich, Max 38, 46, 102, 151, 230, 231, 261
Eichberg, Richard 177, 178, 179, 273
Eichberger, Willy 49, 137, 156, 198, 228
86th Street Garden 12, 15, 32, 109, 120, 131, 132, 147, 149, 156, 157, 158, 159, 173, 177, 180, 187, 218, 246
Einmal eine grosse Dame sein 70
Einmal Möch' Ich keine Sorgen haben 53
Das Einmaleins der Lieb 142
Eisbrenner, Werner 84, 99
Das Ekel 234
Elling, Alwin 201, 202
Emo, E.W. 16, 39, 40, 74, 77, 78, 80, 142, 147, 149, 151, 182, 221, 233, 254, 282
Endstation 150
Engel, Erich 49, 66, 75, 100, 102, 131, 139, 188, 209, 222, 266
Engels, Erich 48, 54, 139, 148, 186, 245, 255
Englisch, Lucie 46, 55, 73, 74, 78, 101, 119, 150, 187, 190, 244, 255, 269
Englische Krankheit 278
Die Entführung 177
Entlassung 232, 282, 283

Episode 142, 191
Das Erbe in Pretoria 106
Ernte 234
Ertl, Hans 95, 167, 186
Es leuchten die Sterne 159, 160
Es war eine rauschende Ballnacht 228
Es war einmal ein Walzer 48
Es Waren zwei Junggesellen 107
Der Etappenhase 173
Eva, das Fabriksmädel 173
Der Ewige Jude 9, 45, 158, 246, 260, 261, 262, 281, 282
Der Ewige Maske 99, 144, 188
Ewige Quell 282
Ewiger Wald 181
Eye of the Third Reich 186

Fahrendes Volk 114
Fährmann Maria 181
Fahrt ins Grüne 101
Falkenstein, Julius 30, 35, 37, 40, 57
Ein Falscher Füffziger 119
Falschmünzer 124, 282
Falstaff in Wien 14, 16
Familienparade 149
Fanck, Arnold 19, 20, 21, 22, 25, 95, 117, 160, 161, 167, 285
Fanny Elssler 156, 157
Farkas, Nicolas 273
Fasching in Wien 201
Der Favorit der Kaiserin 228
Feinde 220, 273
Feldzug in Polen 13, 248, 249, 274, 276, 279, 282
Ferdl, Weiss 32, 45, 75, 105, 116, 150, 163, 201, 227, 241
Ferien vom Ich 80
Feuchtwanger, Lion 64, 217, 280, 281
Feuertaufe 7, 250, 251
Der Feuerteufel 264
Feyder, Jacques 113, 114, 152
55th Street Playhouse 47, 53, 60, 92, 98, 136, 147, 204
Film Daily 139, 143
Film Kurier 11, 19, 61, 153, 207, 261, 274
Filmwelt 124
Finanzen der Grossherzogs 84
Finck, Werner 223
Finkenzeller, Heli 99, 105, 136, 148, 163, 175, 187, 199, 205, 242, 258
Flickenschildt, Elisabeth 215
Fliegende Schatten 95
Der Florentiner Hut 215
Das Flötenkonzert von Sanssouci 29, 30
Flucht ins Dunkel 89
Flüchtling aus Chicago 104
Flüchtlinge 57, 58, 59, 60, 61, 169, 282
Forescu, Maria 46
Forever Yours 140
Forst, Willi 16, 30, 34, 66, 76, 93, 105, 136, 137, 138, 159, 240, 258
F.P. 1 antewortet nicht 42
Franco-American Film Corp 114
Das Frau des Anderen 149
Eine Frau, die weiss, was sie will 106
Frau nach Mass 269
Eine Frau ohne Bedeutung 176
Frau Sixta 182
Frau Sylvelin 233
Die Frau von der man Spricht 27
Eine Frau wie du 39
Die Frauen vom Tannhof 107
Das Frauenparadies 199
Fräulein—falsch Verbunden 77

Fraulein Frau 150
Fräulein Liselott 71
Der Frechdachs 46
Frederick the Great 9, 25, 27, 30, 79, 87, 154
Frentz, Walter 186
Freundin eines grossen Mannes 63, 282
Freut Euch des Lebens 51
Fridericus 208
Friederike 26
Friedrich Schiller 16, 225
Friesennot 120, 121
Frischer Wind aus Kanada 75, 126
Fritsch, Willy 14, 34, 45, 46, 51, 61, 132, 148, 150, 156, 172, 174, 176, 177, 188, 194, 281
Froelich, Carl 65, 79, 89, 96, 101, 102, 112, 131, 155, 184, 228
Fröhlich, Gustav 31, 48, 54, 79, 92, 97, 104, 116, 117, 125, 147, 156, 159, 177, 182, 187
Fronttheater 169
Fruchtbarkeit 277
Frühersparade 61
Frühlingsmärchen 89
Der Fuchs von Glenarvon 245
Fünf Millionen suchen einen Erben 227
Fürst Sepp'l 151
Fürst Woronzeff 51

Gaál, Franziska 46, 61, 98
Gabriele: eins, zwei, drei 156
Gallone, Carmine 133, 135, 202, 243, 269
Gandusio, Antonio 187
Ganghofer, Ludwig 45, 80, 81, 100, 148, 158, 241
Die Ganze Welt dreht sich um Liebe 114, 143
Ein Ganzer Kerl 118
Garden Theatre 115, 116, 117, 118, 125, 136, 141, 147, 148, 149, 152, 154, 163, 172, 173, 174, 175, 177, 182, 184, 187, 190, 199, 200, 202, 205, 209, 210, 222, 226, 233, 234, 241, 243, 244, 255
Garmisch-Partenkirchen 93
Garnett, Tay 20, 21, 22, 285
Gasparone 172
Gauner im Frack 266
Gebühr, Otto 30, 40, 79, 154, 168, 191, 208, 266
Gefahren der Liebe 27
Gefährliches Spiel 209
Geheimakte WB 1 84, 225
Das Geheimnis um Johann Orth 121
Der Geheimnisvolle Mister X 205
Gehetzte Menschen 57
Die Gelbe Flagge 162
General Film Corp. 27
Genina, Augusto 140, 202
Genschow, Fritz 148, 216, 267
George, Heinrich 50, 85, 91, 96, 101, 110, 140, 159, 166, 168, 184, 206, 221, 223, 260, 280, 281
Gerasch, Alfred 173
German-American Bund 8, 13, 193, 277
German East Africa 7, 82, 238, 251, 272
German Railroad Information Office 100
Gerron, Kurt 30, 45, 102, 119, 261, 262, 264
Gewehr Über 125
Gewisser Herr Gran 36
Gewitter im Mai 163
Giacolone, Alberto 243, 244
Gigli, Benjamin 140, 141, 142, 202, 243
Der Gipfelstürmer 151
Gleisdreieck 187
Das Glück auf dem Lande 241
Glückliche Reise 97
Glücklichste Ehe der Welt 182

Glückskinder 117, 150
Glückspilze 117
Der Glückszylinder 77
Godden, Rudi 153, 159, 265
Goebbels, Josef 1, 4, 5, 9, 10, 11, 12, 27, 28, 29, 34, 42, 43, 44, 50, 53, 55, 58, 64, 65, 67, 68, 69, 72, 79, 80, 82, 84, 86, 88, 89, 92, 95, 98, 99, 100, 102, 111, 118, 119, 123, 124, 125, 126, 127, 129, 137, 139, 140, 144, 145, 147, 150, 153, 154, 155, 156, 159, 160, 161, 162, 164, 165, 166, 167, 168, 172, 173, 174, 175, 177, 180, 184, 185, 188, 192, 194, 196, 199, 202, 205, 206, 208, 209, 210, 212, 213, 216, 219, 220, 224, 226, 230, 231, 232, 233, 234, 235, 237, 238, 240, 243, 245, 246, 249, 250, 253, 254, 257, 258, 259, 261, 262, 264, 267, 268, 270, 272, 273, 274, 279, 280, 281, 282, 283, 285
Goetzke, Bernard 43, 178, 245, 260, 278, 280
Gold 64
Der Gordian Tyrann 150
Gottes mühlen mahlen Langsam 204
Die Göttliche Jette 140
Gottschalk, Joachim 210, 212, 213
Götz, Curt 150
Der Gouverneur 218, 220, 282
GPU 268, 282
Graf, Suse 149, 175
Gräfin Mariza 69
Grand Illusion 181
Die Graue Dame 186
Green, Joseph 158
Grenzfeuer 118
Gretel zieht das grosse Los 74
Gribouille 203, 204
Gronostay, Walter 164
Gross Reinemachen 160
Grosse Attraktion 31
Der Grosse Bluff 151
Die Grosse Chance 70
Der Grosse König 79
Die Grosse Liebe 169
Grothe, Franz 77, 89, 155, 201, 243
Gründgens, Gustav 31, 73, 84, 85, 98, 106, 131, 132, 161, 176, 213, 215, 272
Die Grüne Hölle 206
Der Grüne Kaiser 59
G'schichten aus dem Wienerwald 135
Guatemala 170
Guazzoni, Enrico 243
La Guerre des Valses 60
Gülsdorff, Max 51

Haack, Käthe 86, 125, 165, 213, 220, 221, 222
Haas, Dolly 10, 30, 35, 36, 45, 73, 151
La Habanera 169, 281
Haid, Liane 39, 47, 57, 76, 101, 103, 136, 187
Hainisch, Leopold 16, 242
Hammenhög, Waldemar 44
Hände am Werk 186
Hans Westmar 193, 194, 282
Hansen, Max 35, 53, 66, 97, 100
Hansen, Rolf 169, 101, 156, 266
Häntzschel, Georg 139, 140, 253
Harbou, Thea von 70, 89, 127, 139, 140, 148, 162, 178, 182, 202, 223, 226
Hardt, Karin 70, 81, 91, 107, 126, 135, 138, 148, 149, 152, 178, 182, 213, 215, 267, 273
Harell, Marte 257, 258
Harlan, Veit 26, 58, 79, 86, 93, 116, 126, 137, 148, 161, 175, 198, 223, 225, 240, 280, 281, 283
Hartl, Karl 42, 64, 67, 77, 137, 144, 161, 258, 260, 273

Hartmann, Paul 73, 90, 106, 124, 154, 155, 159, 164, 172, 181, 196, 213, 232, 267, 277
Harvey, Lilian 10, 11, 34, 53, 119, 150, 156, 176, 258
Hässliche Mädchen 35
Hauptmann, Garhart 127, 221
Heesters, Johannes 118, 140, 173, 191, 243, 265, 284
Heideschulmeister Uwe Karsten 54
Heimaland 226
Heimat 183, 184,
Heimat am Rhein 55, 56
Heimkehr 7, 104, 200, 240, 273, 282
Heisses Blut 119
Helbig, Heinz 86, 232, 233
Heldentum und Todeskampf unserer Emden 65
Hellberg, Ruth 176, 190, 216
Helm, Brigitte 37, 47, 51, 52, 64, 133, 148, 151
Helyet az Öregeknek 78
Henaff, René Le 213
Henckels, Paul 83, 84, 105, 108, 131, 188, 200, 215, 216, 260, 266
Henker, Frauen, und Soldaten 234
Herald Tribune 76, 102, 137, 141, 190, 196, 215
Hermann und Dorothea 115
Hermine und die seiben Aufrechten 91
Der Herr auf bestellung 30
Herr Kobin geht auf Abenteuer 81, 126
Die Herren vom Maxim 142
Der Herrscher 126, 127, 129, 130
Herthas Erwachen 37
Herzenlieb 187
Hetzfilme 158, 260, 273
Heuberger, Edmund 107
Heute Nacht—eventüll 78
Hilde Peterssen, Postlagernd 149
Hille, Heinz 46, 93
Himmelhunde 205
Himmler 43, 49, 179, 248, 282
Hinrich, Hans 172
Hinz, Werner 88, 164, 226, 270
Hippler, Fritz 261, 262
Hitler, Adolf 1, 3, 4, 7, 8, 10, 11, 12, 13, 18, 19, 22, 26, 27, 28, 29, 30, 31, 32, 33, 34, 35, 36, 38, 39, 40, 43, 44, 46, 48, 49, 50, 51, 53, 54, 55, 57, 58, 59, 60, 63, 64, 65, 66, 67, 68, 69, 71, 72, 73, 76, 77, 78, 79, 80, 81, 82, 84, 85, 86, 87, 91, 92, 95, 96, 97, 98, 99, 100, 101, 104, 105, 107, 109, 110, 111, 114, 116, 119, 120, 123, 124, 126, 127, 129, 131, 132, 137, 139, 140, 142, 143, 144, 145, 147, 151, 154, 155, 156, 160, 161, 162, 163, 165, 166, 167, 168, 170, 172, 173, 175, 179, 180, 181, 185, 186, 191, 192, 193, 194, 196, 198, 202, 205, 207, 208, 210, 213, 216, 217, 218, 223, 225, 227, 228, 230, 232, 235, 241, 242, 243, 246, 248, 249, 250, 251, 252, 253, 255, 259, 261, 264, 267, 270, 272, 273, 274, 276, 277, 279, 282, 284, 285
Hitlerjunge Quex 43, 50, 51, 52, 270, 282
Hitler's Madman 168
Hitler's Reign of Terror 53
Ho Perduto Mio Marito 243
Hochbaum, Werner 66, 99, 144, 188, 216, 228, 245
Der Hochtourist 46
Hochzeit am Wolfgangsee 66
Hochzeitsnacht 16
Die Hochzeitsreise 200
Ein Hochzeitstraum 132
Hoffman, Carl 227
Hoffmann, Kurt 69, 244, 254
Hoffmann, Paul 156, 187
Ein Hoffnungsloser Fall 222
Das Hofkonzert 140, 141
Hohe Schule 209

Der Höhere Befehl 99
Hölle in Westen 250
The Hollywood Anti-Nazi League 185
The Hollywood Reporter 135, 147
Holt, Hans 175, 191, 199, 205, 260, 265
Holzapfel weiss Alles 78
Un homme de trop a bord 98
Hoppe, Marianne 54, 73, 97, 106, 126, 156, 161, 174, 176, 213, 226, 251
Hörbiger, Attila 135, 149, 182, 234, 238, 240, 242
Hörbiger, Paul 14, 30, 40, 42, 54, 60, 75, 76, 105, 135, 136, 142, 145, 147, 149, 159, 169, 184, 190, 199, 200, 215, 233, 255, 257, 258
Horn, Camilla 16, 33, 46, 54, 70, 114, 136, 154, 193, 203, 266
Horney, Brigitte 15, 49, 54, 61, 62, 69, 103, 164, 179, 184, 210, 218, 220, 252
Horst Wessel 193, 194
Hotel Sacher 209, 210
House of Rothschild 53, 257
Hummel-Hummel 201
Hundert Tage 122
Hunnia Studio 59, 78, 173, 174, 204, 242
Hurra! Ich bin Papa! 254
Husaren, heraus! 173
Husarenliebe 55

I Condottieri 238
Ich bei Tag, Du bei Nacht 61
Ich glaub' nie mehr an eine Frau 31
Ich kenn' Dicht nicht und liebe Dich 93
Ich Klage an 223, 230, 277, 278, 282
Ich sehne mich nach Dir 114
Ich sing' mich in dein Herz hinein 75
Ich und die Kaiserin 53
Ich will nicht wissen wer Du bist 30
Ein Idealer Gatte 148
Ihr erstes Erlebnis 253
Ihr Liebhusar 174
Ihre Majestät die Liebe 30
Im Banne des Eulenspiegels 91
Im Lande der Inca, Maya, und Aztekan 170
Imhoff, Fritz 232, 233
In Sachen Timpe 107
Das Indische Grabmal 178
Inge und die Millionen 49
Inkognito 147
Intermezzo 182, 284
Irmen-Tschet, Konstantin 69, 157
Ist mein Mann nicht fabelhaft? 117
Itala Film 40, 75, 77, 78, 102, 104, 125, 140, 141, 142, 151, 187, 202, 222, 228, 244, 266

Ja, treu ist die Soldatenliebe 78
Jacobson, Felix 143
Jacoby, Georg 41, 57, 76, 78, 80, 110, 117, 119, 135, 151, 172, 173, 184, 185, 201, 281
Der Jäger von Fall 148, 284
La Jana 152, 159, 170, 178, 182
Jana, das Mädchen aus dem Böhmerwald 106
Jannings, Emil 10, 11, 87, 88, 105, 111, 126, 127, 162, 229, 232, 245, 272, 281
Janson, Viktor 27, 47, 70, 73, 78, 106, 118, 149, 173, 181, 200, 215, 216
Janssen, Walter 64, 68, 91, 106, 198, 258
Jaray, Hans 98, 174, 216
Jary, Michael 84, 124, 139, 168, 215, 244, 265
Jaworsky, Heinz von 95, 196, 235
Jede Frau hat ein Geheimnis 149
Johannesnacht 75

Jud Süss 7, 9, 64, 137, 265, 280, 281, 282, 283
Judas von Tirol 72
Jugend 95, 96, 97, 225
Jugend von Heute 177
Jugo, Jenny 75, 84, 100, 114, 131, 137, 159, 182, 209, 210, 222, 266
Jülich, Herta 145
Der Junge Graf 117
Jungen Dessauers grosse Liebe 51
Jungens 196
Junges Blut 183
Jungfrau gegen Mönch 74
Junghans, Carl 95, 186
Junkermann, Hans 117, 259

Kadetten 41, 167
Der Kaiser von Kalifornien 143
Kálmán, Emmerich 76
Kameraden auf See 208
Kampers, Fritz 16, 40, 42, 46, 57, 72, 75, 77, 84, 86, 99, 116, 119, 196, 198, 199, 254, 260
Der Kampf mit dem Drachen 107
Kampfgeschwader Lützow 235, 236
Karl, Roger 37
Kater Lampe 175
Der Katzensteg 163
Der Kaufmann von Venedig 283
Käutner, Helmut 65, 244, 254, 270
Kautschuk 205, 206
Kein Wort, von Liebe 202
Keine Angst vor Liebe 101
Kemp, Paul 74, 76, 101, 159
La Kermesse Heroïque 113, 114
Keusche Geliebte 15, 16
Kiepura, Jan 133, 173, 201, 243
Kimmich, Max W. 16, 37, 75, 104, 138, 234, 238, 243, 245, 246, 264, 270
Kinderarzt Dr. Engel 144
Kinz, Franziska 50, 58, 133, 142, 182
Kirchhoff, Fritz 16, 139, 187, 188, 282
Kirschen in nachbars Garten 148
Der Klapperstorchverband 187
Klein, Charles 165, 264
Klein Dorrit 90
Klein-Rogge, Rudolf 140
Die Kleine Schwindlerin 151
Die Kleine Sünderin 190
Kleine und die grosse Liebe 182
Klingenberg, Heinz 27, 49, 70
Klinger, Paul 116, 155, 266
Klingler, Werner 132, 191, 237, 238, 266
Klipstein, Ernst von 218, 220, 242, 266
Klöpfer, Eugen 102, 226, 264
Der Klosterjäger 100, 284
Klügen Frauen 114
Knock-Out 97
Knopf, Erwin 21, 22, 25
Knoteck, Hansi 15, 51, 52, 77, 80, 81, 118, 147, 154, 158, 161, 163, 226, 241
Knuth, Gustav 170, 239
Kohner, Paul 20, 22, 24, 25, 117
Konfetti 201
Kongo-Express 198, 251, 253
Königin der Liebe 106
Königswalzer 105, 284
Konjunkturritter 75, 282
Konstantin, Leopoldine 35, 36, 47, 50, 69, 74, 157
Konzert in Tirol 199
Kopf hoch, Johannes 168
Kortner, Fritz 27, 30, 45, 97, 259, 261

Kosterlitz, Hermann 34, 35, 75, 91, 98, 100, 174
Kowa, Viktor de 77, 79, 84, 86, 89, 100, 101, 139, 168, 181, 187
Krach um Jolanthe 89
Krauss, Werner 33, 122, 137, 229, 280, 283
Kreutzer Sonata 175
Kreysler, Dorit 51, 74, 81, 126, 190
Kristallnacht 44, 163, 185, 186
Kuhlmann, Carl 194, 256
Külb, Karl George 265
Kulturfilme 16
Kurier der Zaren 178
Kutter, Anton 213

Lac aux Dames 114
Der Lachdoktor 163
Der Lachende Dritte 186
Lachende Erben 38
Laemmle, Carl 19, 20, 22, 88, 259
Lamac, Carl 30, 47, 90, 91, 97, 98, 102, 105, 106, 117, 156, 160, 190, 255
Lamprecht, Gerhard 36, 37, 70, 98, 116, 139, 151, 162, 163
The Land of Promise 93
Land ohne Frauen 133
Die Landstreicher 190
Lang, Fritz 28, 39, 84, 86, 104, 172
Lang, Hermann 159
Lantschner, uzzi 25, 117
Laufende Berg 15, 16
Leander, Zarah 167, 169, 183, 200, 201, 239
Le Bon, Roger 37, 79, 98, 180
Leichte Kavalerie 99
Leidenschaft 221, 258
Leinen aus Irland 232, 233, 282
Leman, Juda 93
Letzte Kompanie 64
Letzte Liebe 78
Letzte Rose 120
Der Letzte Walzer 135
Leux, Leo 152, 153, 159
Die Liebe des Maharadscha 243
Liebe dumme Mama 74
Liebe geht seltsame Wege 152
Liebe im Gleitflug 161
Liebe im Ring 160
Liebe in Uniform 57
Liebe muss 51
Liebe, Tod und Teufel 69
Liebe und die erste Eisenbahn 81
Liebe und Leidenschaft 221
Liebe und Trometenklang 104
Liebeneiner, Wolfgang 51, 89, 98, 106, 139, 140, 159, 175, 176, 189, 210, 215, 223, 230, 231, 232, 237, 277, 278, 284
Liebesbriefe aus dem Engadin 191
Liebesleute 115
Ein Liebesroman in Hause Habsburg 121
Liebesschule 265
Der Liebling von Wien 30
Das Lied der Sonne 102
Das Lied der Wüste 239
Ein Lied geht um die Welt 31, 116
Das Lied vom Glück 74
Liedke, Harry 30, 36, 57, 73, 83, 159, 209
Lievan, Albert 175
Lindbergh, Charles 13, 206
Lingen, Theo 75, 101, 114, 136, 142, 159, 178, 198, 205, 243, 254, 255, 258
Liselotte von der Pfalz 102

Litvak, Anatole 230
Lockvogel 79
Loos, Theodor 40, 148, 154, 188, 216, 280
Lorre 41, 42, 47, 48, 261, 262
Lubitsch, Ernst 30, 35, 55, 69, 100, 136, 193, 261
Ludwig der Zweite, König von Bayern 88
Lügen auf Rügen 47
Luise, Königin von Preussen 131
Der Lustige Witwenball 201
Die Lustigen Musikanten 57

Macht der Berge 182
Mack, Max 48, 285
Mackeben, Theo 184, 267, 272
Madame Blaubart 31
Madame Bovary 139, 281
Mädchen in Uniform 33, 96
Mädchen Johanna 85
Mädchen von gestern Nacht 176
Mädchenjahre einer Königin 131, 132
Mädchenpensionat 156
Ein Mädel der Strasse 30
Ein Mädel mit Tempo 151
Ein Mädel wirbelt durch die Welt 135
Mademoiselle ma mere 221
Madonna, wo bist du? 76
Maisch, Herbert 16, 105, 147, 168, 179, 191, 233, 235, 272, 281, 284
Malasomma, Nunzio 22, 131, 133, 139, 202, 203
Man Spricht über Jacqueline 245
Mann für Mann 196
Der Mann nicht nein sagen kann 222, 223
Der Mann Sherlock Holmes war 162
Ein Mann will nacht Deutschland 61, 63, 282
Marenbach, Leny 269
Maria Ilona 242
Die Maria Magd 148
Marian, Ferdinand 84, 139, 169, 245, 264, 265, 272, 281
Marie Bashkirtseff 174
Marion, das gehört sich nicht 40
Marionette 202
Marischka, Hubert 92, 173, 174, 191, 201, 202, 243, 269, 284
Markus, Winnie 237
Marlen, Trude 51, 54, 77, 137, 222, 228
Martin, Ernst 226
Martin, Karl Heinz 116, 148, 182, 199, 243
Martin, Paul 150, 156, 176, 239
Maskerade 136, 191, 240
Der Maulkorb 188
Maurischat, Fritz 270
Un Mauvaise Garçon 180
Max Schmeling's Sieg—ein deutcher Sieg 152
Max Schmeling's Victory—Germany's Victory 160
Die Mein Frau Hochstaplerin 45
Mein Herz ruft nacht Dir 133
Mein Kampf 3, 22, 26, 27, 71, 72, 73, 85, 92, 99, 124, 129, 132, 165, 166, 196, 218, 232, 234, 242, 250, 252, 264, 272, 279, 282, 285
Mein Leben für Irland 16, 270
Mein Leben für Maria Isabell 85
Die Meine Frau Schützenkönig 73
Meine Freundin Barbara 187
Meine Tochter lebt in Wien 16
Der Meisterdetektiv 45
Mendes, Philipp Lothar 139, 179, 22
Menschen im Sturm 259
Menschen vom Varieté 182
Menzel, Gerhard 28, 58, 85, 103, 116, 169, 210, 237, 260, 272, 273, 282, 284

Meyer, Johannes 47, 73, 103, 106, 114, 151, 192, 201, 205, 208, 234, 243, 246
Meyerink, Hubert von 104, 182
Millionenerbschaft 255
Mir kumen an 220
Miranda, Isa 243
Mit dir durch dick und dünn 46
Mit versiegelter Order 181, 282
Mitternachtswalzer 179
Morgan, Paul 261
Morgenrot 27, 28, 58, 72, 169, 174, 210, 213, 237, 272
Moritz Macht sein Glück 26
Moser, Hans 91, 132, 159, 198, 201, 209, 221, 234, 254, 255, 257, 258
Motion Picture Daily 102
Motion Picture Herald 1, 8
Der Müde Theodo 116
Müller, Renate 35, 38, 40, 60, 69, 102, 115, 125, 137
Münchausen 253, 282
Museum of Modern Art 50, 95, 144, 284
Musketier Meier III 191, 282
Mussolini 238
Das Mustergatte 175
Mutige Seefahrer 101
Mutter und Kind 51
Mutterliebe 75, 182, 235, 237
Mutterlied 202
Mysterium des Lebens 145

Eine Nacht an der Donau 189
Ein Nacht im Mai 184
Die Nacht mit dem Kaiser 131
Die Nacht ohne Pause 193
Nagy, Käthe von 30, 45, 58, 61, 63, 69, 70, 141, 194, 244
Nanette 209, 210, 212, 255
Nanon 191
Nanu, Sie kennen Korff noch nicht 199
Napoleon ist an allem Schuld 176
Nation 8, 79, 232, 262, 270, 272, 273, 276
National Board of Review 28, 144, 230
National Film 124, 164, 279
National Film Prize 58, 164, 279
Negri, Pola 137, 138, 139, 203
Neufeld, Max 53, 102, 142, 187
New Theatre 88
New York American 132
New York Times 1, 7, 8, 9, 12, 22, 28, 32, 33, 35, 36, 37, 40, 42, 44, 46, 48, 49, 51, 60, 69, 70, 72, 74, 75, 77, 80, 83, 85, 86, 91, 92, 93, 97, 98, 100, 101, 102, 105, 107, 108, 109, 112, 114, 115, 116, 118, 119, 121, 122, 123, 124, 125, 126, 131, 132, 133, 137, 142, 144, 154, 159, 163, 166, 169, 173, 174, 175, 178, 180, 182, 188, 198, 199, 201, 203, 205, 208, 210, 216, 220, 221, 227, 230, 235, 239, 240, 241, 243, 246, 250, 252, 254, 255, 258, 259, 260, 276, 278, 285
New York World-Telegram 102, 133, 136, 196
New Yorker 1, 7, 88, 117, 137, 139, 144, 147, 246, 249, 262, 272, 276, 281, 282
Niemandsland 29
Noche Andaluz 180
Noldan, Svend 274
Non-Sectarian Anti-Nazi League 78, 97, 180, 273, 276, 278
Nordpol Ahoi! 25, 55
Norman, Roger von 204
Nosseck, Max 53

Obal, Max 42, 57, 70, 80, 100, 101, 117, 149
Oberwachtmeister Schwenke 97
Ode, Erik 140

Odemar, Fritz 37, 46, 76, 125, 152, 156, 222
Ohm Kruger 7, 225, 272, 282
Olympia 25, 160, 185, 186
Ondra, Anny 30, 47, 91, 97, 106, 117, 159, 160
1A in Oberbayern 107
L'Opéra de quat' sous 66
Operette 137
Opernball 258, 284
Opernring 133
Opfer der Vergangenheit 23, 145, 277
Ophüls, Max 38
Oppenheim Family 217
Osten, Franz 72, 81, 107, 151
Ostermayr, Paul 80, 81, 151, 241, 284
Oswald, Richard 31, 33, 36, 69, 116, 188, 259, 260, 261, 264
Otto, Paul 57, 76, 78, 79, 98, 121, 157, 166, 196, 201, 235, 258
Our Flag Leads Us Forward 50

Pabst, G.W. 29, 33, 66, 71
La Paloma 116
Papas Fehltritt 188
Pappi 100
Paprika 46
Paracelsus 225, 283
Pasternak, Joseph 35, 61, 62, 151
Patachon 105
Patrioten 124, 125, 126, 282
Paulsen, Harald 48, 75, 112, 135, 141, 151, 159, 161, 235, 245, 264
Peer Gynt 80, 226, 227
Pension Mimosas 114
Peters, Sabine 7, 216, 222, 245
Pettersson & Bendel 43, 44, 282
Pfarrer von Kirchfeld 216
Pfeiffer, Harmann 124, 159
Piel, Harry 64, 150
Pointner, Anton 105, 192, 198, 245
Polenblut 91
Polgar, Alfred 30
Poligny, Serge de 47, 64, 140, 213
Ponto, Erich 192, 194, 256, 264, 265
Port Arthur 40, 273
Porten, Henny 51, 129, 131
Postillon von Lonjumeau 156
Potemkin 3
Pour le Mérite 28, 124, 196, 197, 198, 267, 282
Preis, Hasso 35, 81
Pressburger, Emeric 46
Eines Prinzen junge Liebe 51
Die Privatsekretärin Heiratet 35
Profes, Anton 245
Punks kommt aus Amerika 149
Der Purimspieler 158

Rabenalt, Arthur M. 16, 89, 90, 100, 114, 169, 199, 215, 241, 243, 255, 265
Raddatz, Carl 252
Rahl, Mady 200, 205
Raimu 180, 203, 204
Ralph, Louis 65
Ramparts We Watch 250, 251
Randolf, Rolf 40, 148
Rasp, Fritz 72, 79, 91, 118, 125, 200, 259, 260
Rätsel um Beate 7
Der Raub der Sabinerinnen 154
Der Rebell 22, 196
Das Recht auf Liebe 252
Le Récif de corail 180

Reichmann, Max 31, 32
Reifende Jugend 97
Reisch, Walter 31, 35, 41, 53, 142, 191
Reiter von Deutsch-Ostafrika 82
... reitet für Deutschland 89, 282
Rembrandt 225
Rendezvous in Wien 173
Richter, Paul 72, 74, 89, 100, 148, 149, 158, 233
Riefenstahl, Leni 19, 21, 22, 25, 55, 82, 96, 107, 160, 161, 185, 186, 239, 246, 247, 261, 284
Riemann, Johannes 41, 54, 114, 140, 145, 159, 173, 176, 244, 253, 259, 266
Ritt in die Freiheit 144
Rittau, Gunthar 144, 252, 279
Ritter, Karl 12, 16, 41, 75, 110, 123, 124, 125, 126, 161, 164, 165, 166, 167, 196, 197, 200, 220, 267, 268, 284
Robert Koch 9, 137, 169, 223, 224, 229, 230, 231, 282, 284
Robert und Bertram 44, 153, 190, 282
Roberts, Ralph Arthur 48, 54, 120, 150, 159, 188, 205, 222
Ein Robinson 167, 282
Robison, Arthur 51, 53
Rökk, Marika 99, 118, 119, 172, 173, 184, 185, 228, 265, 281
Roman einer Nacht 57
Romanowsky, Richard 93, 201, 243, 254
Rosen aus dem Süden 68, 69
Rote Orchideen 203
Die Rothschilds 9, 16, 17, 225, 255, 256, 257, 281, 282
Rühmann, Heinz 38, 45, 46, 103, 114, 119, 136, 137, 155, 161, 175, 199, 200, 215, 227, 244, 254
Rund um ein Million 53

SA-Mann Brand 27, 43, 49, 270, 282
Sabo, Oscar 30, 68, 187
Sandrock, Adele 27, 28, 77, 107, 114, 148, 173, 174
Sauer, Fred 30, 55, 92, 104, 150, 163
Savoy-Hotel 217, 103
Schabernac 149
Schatten der Vergangenheit 245
Scheinmann, Joseph 67
Der Schimmelkrieg in der Holledau 163
Der Schimmelreiter 80
Schlettow, Hans A. 73, 148, 272
Schloss Hubertus 80
Schloss im Süden 101
Das Schloss in Flandern 155
Schloss Vogelöd 101
Schlussakkord 4, 108, 109, 223
Schmeling, Max 97, 152, 159, 160
Schmid–Wildy, Ludwig 71, 163
Schmitz, Sybille 42, 64, 92, 97, 148, 159, 160, 174, 188, 209, 238
Schneeberger, Hans 19, 22, 86, 117, 140, 179, 282
Schneider, Magda 40, 45, 71, 77, 93, 97, 98, 133, 135, 147, 160, 173, 191, 221, 252
Schneider-Edenkoben, Richard 71, 147
Das Schöne Fraülein Schragg 154
Schönfelder, Erich 48
Schönhals, Albrecht 7, 51, 93, 98, 110, 138, 147, 159, 175, 182, 203, 216, 245
Schrammeln 258
Schritt vom Wege 213, 214
Schroeder, Friedrich 176, 196
Schüchterne Casanova 105
Der Schüchterne Felix 74
Schultze, Norbert 232, 250
Schulz, Fritz 76, 77, 78, 118, 150, 151
Schünzel, Reinhold 35, 69, 145, 174, 260

Schuss im Morgengrauen 47
Schwarze Rosen 156
Schwarze Walfisch 88
Schwarzer Jäger Johanna 73
Schwarzfahrt ins Glück 190
Schwarzkopf, Elizabeth 216
Schwarzwaldmädel 91
Die Schwebende Jungfrau 151
Das Schweigen im Walde 158, 284
Schweikart, Hans 66, 252, 253
Sechs Tage Heimaturlaug 125
Le Secret des Woronzeff 53
Seeber, Guido 42, 181
Eine Seefahrt, die ist lustig 201
Sein bester Freund 150
Seitz, Franz 32, 45, 46, 49, 70, 107
Die Selige Exzellenz 152
Selpin, Herbert 82, 83, 84, 148, 149, 222, 270, 272
Ein Seltsamer Gast 151
Sensationsprozess Casilla 206
79th Street Theater 8, 32, 40, 46, 47, 48, 51, 54, 57, 75, 77, 79, 80, 81, 83, 84, 85, 91, 97, 98, 99, 101, 106, 135
Shirer, William L. 8
Shmitz, Sybille 181
Sica, Vittorio de 102, 187, 222, 254
Sicherheitsdienst 123, 124
Sie und die Drei 181
Sieben Ohrfeigen 176
Sieg im Westen 248, 273, 274, 276, 279, 284
Sierck, Detlef 4, 66, 108, 109, 110, 140, 158, 161, 167, 168, 169, 172, 223, 252, 273
Sierck, Klaus Detlef 158, 167, 168, 252
Silver Shirts 8
Sima, Oscar 46, 47, 75, 79, 149, 173, 176, 186, 227, 232, 233, 245
Sin Novedad en el Alcazar 202
Singende Jugend 142
Singende Stadt 133
Der Singende Tor 243
Siodmak, Robert 33, 34, 40, 41
Slezak, Leo 51, 103, 135, 142, 143, 156, 173, 182, 191, 201, 205, 228
So ein Mädel vergisst man nicht 30
Söderbaum, Kristina 223, 226, 240, 280, 281
Il Sogno di Butterfly 269, 281
Der Sohn der weissen Berge 40
Söhnker, Hans 76, 101, 106, 117, 159, 173, 175, 181, 210, 215, 244, 252, 254, 269
Soldaten—Kameraden 120
Solo per Te 202
Sommer, Sonne, Erika 266, 267
Die Sonne geht Auf 75
Sonnemann, Emmy 92
Sonnenfeld, Sonja 79, 80
S.O.S. Eisberg 19, 20, 21, 25
S.O.S. Iceberg 21, 22, 25
S.O.S. Sahara 179
Spätere Heirat nicht ausgeschlossen 222
Speelmans, Hermann 42, 46, 80, 81, 118, 124, 152, 174, 186
Spewack 279
Spiegel des Lebens 239, 240
Spiel auf der Tenne 136
Spiel in Sommerwind 204
Spiel mit dem Feuer 54
Spiel ums Glück 266
Spione am Werk 37
Spione im Savoy-Hotel 35
Spira, Camilla 57, 72
Die Sporck'schen Jäger 148

Staal, Viktor 118, 163, 167, 169
Staatsauftragsfilme 5
Eine Stadt steht Kopf 84, 132
Stadtheimatfilm 198
Standschütze Bruggler 132, 135
Stärker als die Liebe 213
Stärker als Paragraphen 155
Staudte, Wolfgang 125, 196, 280
Steinbeck, Walter 270
Steinhoff, Hans 9, 30, 45, 50, 51, 79, 87, 101, 176, 223, 224, 229, 230, 231, 272
Stemmle, Robert 96, 97, 112, 117, 151, 154, 187, 194, 196, 281
Stepanek, Karl 60, 92, 155, 175, 209, 241
Der Stern von Rio 170
Der Stern von Valencia 47
Die Stimme aus dem Äther 245
Die Stimme der Herzens 243
Stöckel, Joe 49, 147, 153, 154, 173, 191, 213, 227, 252
Stolz, Robert 30, 60, 66, 111, 117, 156, 161, 173, 191, 199, 201, 216
Der Storch Streikt 151
Stosstrupp 1917 71
Stradivar 92
Stransky, Otto 40
Streicher, Julius 223, 261
Strich durch die Rechnung 46
Stukas 16, 131, 220, 250, 267, 268
Stützen der Gesellschaft 109, 110
Stüwe, Hans 27, 46, 75, 102, 179, 200, 228, 255, 259
Susa, Charlotte 40, 90, 106, 115, 178, 182, 234
Susanne im Bade 155
Svet Patrí Nám 132
Sylvia und ihr Chauffeur 205
Szakall, S.Z. 27, 30, 39, 40, 59, 78, 84, 151, 174

Tag der Freiheit—Unser Wehrmacht 96
Der Tag nacht der Scheidung 244
Tasnady, Maria 108, 158, 233, 243
Tauber 31, 78, 110, 233
Tausend für eine Nacht 48
Teilnehmer Antwortet nicht 84
Terra Studio 9, 73, 74, 78, 83, 84, 89, 91, 92, 100, 107, 116, 117, 124, 139, 148, 156, 161, 169, 174, 177, 181, 182, 186, 204, 205, 210, 213, 215, 220, 227, 241, 242, 244, 252, 258, 259, 265, 269
Testament of Dr. Mabuse 28
Theodor Körner 27
Theresienstadt: Ein Dokumentarfilm aus dem jüdischen Siedlungsgebiet 262
Thimig, Hermann 40, 69, 84, 91, 101, 103, 205, 254, 255
Thirteen Men and a Gun 192
Tiedke, Jakob 79, 97, 103, 200, 223, 280
Tiger von Eschnapur 178
Tinée, Mae 98, 141, 173
Titanic 75, 84, 282
Tobis Studio 4, 9, 11, 30, 32, 53, 59, 65, 66, 67, 78, 79, 93, 105, 112, 117, 120, 121, 125, 126, 131, 132, 133, 135, 136, 138, 142, 143, 144, 148, 149, 150, 152, 153, 154, 157, 159, 162, 163, 164, 170, 175, 176, 177, 178, 182, 188, 191, 199, 202, 204, 221, 224, 225, 230, 232, 233, 235, 242, 244, 245, 252, 255, 259, 264, 272, 273, 277
Die Tochter des Regiments 47
Tochter des Samurai 22
Tod über Schanghai 40
Togger 124, 125, 204, 222, 282
Tolle Bomberg 32
Ein Toller Einfall 45
Die Törichte Jungfrau 71

Tourjansky, Victor 16, 143, 179, 200, 218, 219, 220, 273, 284
Traum von Schönbrunn 104
Träumerei 281
Traummusik 16, 17
Traumulus 110, 111, 112
Trenker, Luis 19, 22, 23, 25, 40, 86, 143, 144, 159, 191, 196, 237, 238, 239, 264
Triumph of the Will 82, 261
Trivas, Victor 29
Truxa 152, 215
Tschechowa, Olga 37, 79, 89, 98, 104, 144, 152, 159, 162, 168, 179, 203, 205, 227, 228, 233, 245, 258, 259
Eine Tür geht auf 46
2 x 2 im Himmelbett 200

... Über alles in der Welt 166, 167, 282
U-Boote Westwärts 198, 279
Ucicky, Gustav 28, 29, 30, 32, 33, 58, 75, 85, 103, 161, 162, 182, 210, 235, 237, 240, 260, 272, 273, 284
Udet, Ernst 19, 25
Ufa 4, 6, 9, 11, 12, 14, 15, 16, 17, 22, 27, 28, 29, 32, 34, 35, 36, 37, 38, 41, 45, 46, 47, 48, 49, 50, 51, 53, 54, 55, 58, 59, 60, 61, 63, 64, 67, 68, 69, 70, 71, 75, 76, 77, 78, 79, 80, 81, 85, 89, 95, 98, 99, 100, 101, 103, 105, 106, 108, 109, 110, 112, 116, 117, 118, 119, 123, 124, 125, 126, 132, 135, 140, 141, 144, 145, 147, 148, 149, 150, 151, 154, 156, 157, 161, 163, 165, 166, 167, 169, 170, 172, 175, 176, 177, 179, 180, 182, 183, 184, 187, 188, 191, 194, 195, 196, 198, 200, 204, 205, 206, 208, 209, 210, 212, 214, 216, 221, 222, 223, 226, 228, 230, 232, 233, 237, 238, 248, 251, 253, 256, 257, 260, 261, 265, 267, 268, 270, 274, 276, 278, 279, 285
Uhlan, Gisela 256
Uhlig, Annelise 245
Ullrich, Luise 83, 98, 139, 142, 159, 188, 200, 227, 244, 245, 253, 265
Um das Menschenrecht 65, 282
Um Freiheit und Liebe 164
Umwege zur Heimat 99
Die Unbekannte 39, 174
... Und es Leuchtet die Puszta 46
... Und wer küsst mich? 77
The Unfinished Symphony 76
Der Ungetreue Eckehart 150
Die Unschuld vom Lande 74
Unsere Gebirgspioniere 238
Unsere kleine Frau 244
Das Unsterbliche Herz 223, 224
Untermyer, Samuel 78
Unternehmen Michael 124, 166
Unvollkommene Liebe 16
Der Unwiderstehliche 156
Urlaub auf Ehrenwort 164, 165, 282, 284

Valli, Alida 142
Der Vanderer Yid 38
Variety 1, 7, 8, 12, 25, 26, 27, 28, 31, 35, 37, 45, 47, 48, 50, 61, 76, 77, 78, 87, 88, 92, 96, 99, 102, 104, 109, 114, 116, 117, 120, 124, 126, 131, 133, 136, 137, 139, 140, 145, 149, 151, 156, 158, 160, 164, 172, 173, 177, 178, 179, 180, 182, 185, 188, 202, 217, 220, 251, 254, 255, 267, 274, 276, 279, 280, 285
Varkoni, Victor 22
Veidt, Conrad 42, 53, 64, 78, 92
Das Veilchen vom Potsdamer Plat 198
Venice Film Festival 113, 127, 133, 136, 141, 184, 268
Venus vor Gericht 154, 153, 282
Verebes, Ernö 26, 31, 69, 78, 102
Verhoeven, Paul 159, 244

Der Verkannte Lebemann 222
Verklungene Melodie 179
Verliebte, Herzen 215
Der Verlorene Sohn 23, 86, 282
Das Verlorene Tal 107
Verräter 12, 123, 124, 125, 282
Verwehte Spuren 223
Vetter aus Dingsda 97
Die Vier Musketiere 86
Der Vierte kommt nicht 264, 282
Viktor und Viktoria 69
La Voce del Sangue 32
Ein Volk will Leben 195
Volksfilme 110, 228, 241
Eine von Uns 151
Voskovec, George 132

Wagner, Fritz Arno 272
Waldrausch 45, 181, 241
Waldwinter 118
Wallburg, Otto 30, 35, 38, 40, 46, 47, 49, 76, 100, 151
Walther-Fein 36, 48
Ein Walzer für Dich 114
Ein Walzer um den Stefansturm 205
Walzerkrieg 60
Walzerlange 255
The Wandering Jew 78
War Propaganda and the United States (1940) 4
Warner Bros. 12, 13, 43, 66, 104, 168, 230, 279
Was bin ich ohne Dich? 89
Was Frauen träumen 48
Was Tun, Sibylle? 177
Was wissen den Männer 37
Waschneck, Erich 16, 17, 55, 85, 114, 115, 140, 157, 161, 170, 257
Washington Post 7, 8, 12, 114, 230, 251
Wasser für Canitoga 83
Der Weg des Herzens 191
Der Weg ins Freie 282
Wegener, Paul 20, 21, 49, 61, 63, 73, 79, 118, 138, 161, 213, 252, 264, 270
Weiberregiment 110
Weimar Republic 26, 29, 34, 49, 196, 198
Weiser, Grethe 159, 187, 198
Weisse, Hanni 19, 129, 131, 154, 160, 213, 282
Der Weisse Rausch 19, 160
Weisse Sklaven 154, 282
Weisser Flieder 265
Weissner, Hilde 79, 84, 112, 174, 188, 200, 256
Wen die Götter lieben 175, 225, 258
Wendhausen, Fritz 88, 149, 226, 259, 260
Wenn am Sonntagabend die Dorfmusik 264
Wenn der Hahn kräht 101
Wenn die Liebe mode Macht 38
Wenn die Musik nicht wär 135
Wenn Frauen schweigen 187
Wenn Herzen sich finden 54
Wenn wir alle Engel wären 155
Wenzler, Franz 38, 122, 151, 193

Wer nimmt die Liebe ernst? 100
Werich, Jan 132
Werner, Ilse 207, 241, 253, 267, 279
Werner, Oscar 209, 233
Wessely, Paula 136, 142, 184, 191, 234, 240, 242, 281
Why This War? 226
Wie sag' ich's Meinen Mann? 35
Wieck, Dorothea 69, 91, 168, 264
Wieman, Mathias 80, 91, 107, 125, 126, 144, 166, 167, 184, 188, 227, 277
Wien Film 162
Wien 1910 225, 282
Wiene, Conrad 31
Wiener Blut 31, 258
Wiener G'schichten 258
Wilder, Billy 30, 48
Wilhelm Tell: Das Freiheitsdrama eines Volkes 92
Windt, Herbert 28, 58, 82, 166, 185, 194, 196, 232, 250, 274
Winterstein, Eduard von 131
Wir sind vom K. u. K. Infanterie-Regiment 188
Wohlbrück, Adolf 60, 77, 101, 106, 136, 137, 178, 273
Wolff, Carl Heinz 54, 107
World at War 279
Wunder des Fliegens 86
Der Wunschkonzert 207, 208
Wüst, Ida 51, 58, 81, 159, 202, 221
Wysbar, Frank 91, 92, 174, 175, 181, 258

Yorck 33, 125, 283
Yorkville Theatre 8, 32, 34, 40, 45, 46, 49, 53, 55, 200
Yvette 151, 176, 265

Zapfenstreich am Rhein 26
Zauber der Boheme 173
Zeckendorff, Fritz 38
Zeisler, Alfred 46, 47
Zeller, Wolfgang 181, 280
Zelnik, Friedrich 35, 40
Der Zerbrochene Krug 162
Zerlett, Hans H. 47, 97, 152, 153, 159, 160, 244
Zerlett-Olfenius, Walter 84, 149, 270
Ziel in den Wolken 164, 210
Zigeunerbaron 77
Zigeunerblut 264
Zilzer, Wolfgang 99, 100
Zot Hi Ha'aretz 113
Zu Befehl, Herr Unteroffizer 48
Zu Neuen Ufern 167
Zu Strassburg auf der Schanz 107
Einer zuviel an Bord 98
Zwei gute Kameraden 42
Zwei Herzen im dreivertel Takt 30, 60, 190, 191, 205
Zwei im Sonnenschein 136
Zwischen den Eltern 172
Zwischen Hamburg und Haiti 170
Zwischen Himmel und Erde 70
Zwischen Strom und Steppe 242
Zwischen zwei Herzen 83

www.ingramcontent.com/pod-product-compliance
Lightning Source LLC
Chambersburg PA
CBHW060336010526
44117CB00017B/2852